The Sociology of Organizations

THE SOCIOLOGY OF ORGANIZATIONS

Classic, Contemporary, and Critical Readings

EDITOR

Michael J. Handel

University of Wisconsin, Madison

SAGE Publications
International Educational and Professional Publisher
Thousand Oaks ■ London ■ New Delhi

For information:

Sage Publications, Inc.
2455 Teller Road
Thousand Oaks, California 91320
E-mail: order@sagepub.com

Sage Publications Ltd.
6 Bonhill Street
London EC2A 4PU
United Kingdom

Sage Publications India Pvt. Ltd.
M-32 Market
Greater Kailash I
New Delhi 110 048 India

Printed in the United States of America

Library of Congress Cataloging-in-Publication Data

The sociology of organizations: Classic, contemporary, and critical
readings / [editor] Michael J. Handel.
    p. cm.
Includes bibliographical references (p.   ) and index.
 ISBN 0-7619-8766-5
 1. Organizational sociology. I. Handel, Michael J. (Michael Jeremy)
 HM786 .S63 2002
 302.3´5--dc21

          2002005208

04 10 9 8 7 6 5 4

Acquiring Editor:	Alison Mudditt
Editorial Assistant:	Mishelle Gold
Production Editor:	Diana E. Axelsen
Typesetter:	C&M Digitals (P) Ltd
Indexer:	Jeanne Busemeyer
Cover Designer:	Michelle Lee

CONTENTS

PREFACE

This work is intended to satisfy the need for a single volume of primary readings and overview essays that provides a relatively complete introduction to the sociology of organizations. The study of organizations is a central and dynamic subfield of sociology, and the field needed a new collection of the important works that have shaped it. Although the focus of this work is the sociology of organizations, it should also be useful for those in related fields, such as management, organizational behavior, and organizational psychology, as well as for those within political science and economics who are interested in how organizations function.

The selections contained in this volume represent a wide spectrum of theoretical schools, substantive topics, and intellectual perspectives. Most are either classics in the field or works that are widely known and cited. In a number of cases, I have included a critical work following a key reading, such as Harry Braverman's critique of Frederick W. Taylor, where a detailed treatment of contending perspectives seemed warranted; in some cases, such as Braverman, the critical work is a key text itself.

I have also written introductions to each section to give the reader a compact description of the context, related work, and debates engendered by the readings in that section. These overview essays function as a parallel text that defines terms, explains key themes and concepts, and summarizes established and recent thinking on the subjects raised by each section. Existing secondary work on organizations has tended to be relatively abstract. In the introductions, I have tried to make complex and sophisticated ideas come alive with a wide range of examples and accessible prose. I hope readers find these short overview essays useful.

These section introductions make the book a self-contained work that can be used as a stand-alone text, as well as to provide supplementary readings in a course using a textbook. The section introductions provide most of the additional detail and explanation that one finds in a textbook, presented in a briefer format. The readings themselves have been condensed for space purposes. Those wishing to explore a particular topic in greater detail should consult the original works and the other works cited in the relevant section introduction.

ACKNOWLEDGMENTS

I would like to thank a number of people for helping make this book possible. First and foremost, I thank the authors who consented to have their works reprinted in this volume. I hope this book brings their research to a wider and appreciative audience that is stimulated to explore their work further. I would also like to thank my colleague Mark Suchman and my parents, Gerald and Ruth Handel, for reading my section introductions and providing helpful comments and encouragement.

Finally, I would like to thank the editors and staff at Sage Publications who helped guide this book to completion. I'm grateful to Steve Rutter, my initial editor, who had the insight to recognize the value of such a work. Alison Mudditt, vice president and editorial director of Sage Publications, took subsequent responsibility for the project and with her assistant Mishelle Gold and permissions editor Veronica Oliva did all the heavy lifting required of publishers to turn an idea into reality. I thank them all for their patience, understanding, hard work, and support for this project.

INTRODUCTION

F ew aspects of modern life are untouched by formal organizations. Although both popular rhetoric and government policy praise markets and disparage bureaucracies, there is still much truth to the view that we live in an organizational society, as organizational sociologists often observe. Education, work, politics, government, religion, social services, charities, and frequently leisure activities take place within or through the involvement of organizations with greater or lesser degrees of structure and formalization.

But this is a relatively recent development. About 175 years ago, there were only a few examples of what we would recognize as organizations today, though many of them were powerful. They included traditional and modernizing government bureaucracies, churches, armies, universities, and voluntary associations such as charities and mutual assistance societies, guilds, clubs, and civic, cultural, and fraternal groups, such as the Free Masons (Skocpol, Ganz, and Munson 2000). In the United States, the national government was relatively small, and political parties were very basic organizations compared to today. Most people worked for themselves, and those who did work for others worked in small enterprises. Owners personally managed most farms, shops, and businesses. There were virtually no large private corporations and or professional managers running enterprises on behalf of their owners. By contrast, today about 85% of workers are employed by someone else, often a very large organization, and even many employees of small organizations are affected by the rules, standards, structure, and oversight of larger organizations, both private and governmental.

People are also involved in or affected by all kinds of organizations outside of work. Today when a group of like-minded people want to accomplish something, it is not unusual for them to think about forming an organization to help them achieve that goal, but this is a relatively modern impulse. Indeed, one school of thought within the sociology of organizations believes that the recent growth of formal organizations is a defining characteristic of modern society and that their efficiency as a tool for achieving goals accounts for that growth.

Precisely defining what is meant by the term *organization* is difficult. However, a common definition holds that organizations are

a. deliberately planned groups
b. with some specific apparent goal or goals,

    c. generally designed to outlive the participation of the particular individuals who participate at any one time,

    d. having a more or less well-developed set of formal rules and

    e. a relatively fixed structure of authority, roles, and responsibilities that is independent of the personal characteristics of those filling the roles at any particular time.

In this view, organizations are a means by which people working together can accomplish larger and more complicated tasks than they can as individuals acting separately. But this definition is not without problems.

Part of the problem in defining organizations is the very diversity of organizations themselves. They include schools and universities, large and small businesses, business associations such as the Chamber of Commerce, trade unions, professional associations such as the American Medical Association, government agencies, police departments, political parties, political advocacy groups such as those favoring or opposing abortion rights, churches, hospitals, museums, prisons, the military, Boy Scouts, neighborhood organizations, fraternities, and ethnic and social clubs. These organizations vary in the nature of their aims, size, formality, and governance. It would be hard for any definition to find the common ground shared by all them or to fit each case equally well.

But another part of the problem is a more basic disagreement over the nature of organizations themselves. To say that organizations are deliberately planned and crafted to achieve goals using formal rules, roles, and authority overlooks the fact that all organizations have an informal social life that develops spontaneously within them. This informal life as well as differences in power and perspectives among an organization's members often leads individuals and groups to pursue different and conflicting goals, some would argue to the point that it is misleading to think the organization itself is a real actor with goals of its own.

Or the organization may not be divided into different constituencies but may be unclear or contradictory as a whole about the goals to be pursued. Those who run prisons may not even know themselves whether or to what degree their mission is punishment, rehabilitation, or simply segregation of offenders from society, and their actions may reflect random fluctuations between these motives. Those running a state university may similarly be torn between imparting knowledge to students, providing them with a credential useful in the job market, supporting the faculty, promoting research, securing revenue through nonacademic pursuits such as college athletics, and providing service to the state that funds them.

Organizations may also develop goals that wander off track from their original mission, such as a focus on growth or continued survival for its own sake rather than for any larger purpose, known as *goal displacement* because the organization's well-being becomes an end in itself that displaces its original mission. For instance, many corporations in the 1960s-1980s pursued growth and merger policies that moved them far from their core competencies, often with ultimately negative consequences (Scherer 1988; Davis, Diekmann, and Tinsley 1994). The Tri-Borough Bridge Authority in New York City continued to collect tolls long after the costs of building the bridge were recovered so that the authority's chief, Robert Moses, an appointed civil servant, could have the freedom to fund a growing list of highway and other public works projects without effective oversight from or veto by elected officials. The Reform Party was originally formed in 1992 around the personality of

H. Ross Perot, a somewhat charismatic billionaire with a vaguely defined ideology who decided to run for president. Yet when Perot withdrew from presidential politics in the 2000 election, the party searched for a reason to remain active. The North Atlantic Treaty Organization (NATO) was formed to oppose the Warsaw Pact nations and prevent the expansion of communism in Europe, yet NATO remains intact more than a decade after the fall of communism, the dissolution of the Warsaw Pact, and incorporation of many of its members into NATO itself. The examples illustrate the fact that organizations generally do not dissolve themselves willingly and often grow if left to themselves, reflecting the general sentiments of members or the particular interests of the organization's leadership.

Finally, to say that organizations must have a formal system of authority would seem to imply that as a matter of principle they cannot be fully democratic and give equal decision rights to all members, which many would dispute (see Part XIII).

These difficulties in defining organizations as a social phenomenon reflect disagreements within the field over the basic nature of organizations themselves, many of which will become apparent in the different readings included in this volume. One of the most influential typologies of different approaches to studying organizations is Scott's (1998) division of approaches into *rational* (Parts I and II), *natural* (Parts III and IV), and *open systems* (Part VII) theories of organizations, which provides the structure for many of the early sections of this book.

Rational theories would approve of the initial definition of organizations offered above. Rational theories see organizations as instruments designed to attain specific goals using logical plans, impersonal rules, and a rational division of responsibilities among personnel. The size of the organization, the nature of its tasks, the tools or technology it uses, the environment it faces, and the quality of the information available to it may all affect an organization's structure and functioning, but there is no question that it seeks to achieve well-defined goals in the most logical and efficient manner within the constraints under which it operates.

Natural theories view organizations as more than simply rationally constructed tools to achieve specific goals, but also as social and human systems. There are diverse approaches within this group, but they share the view that there is more to organizations than their official rules, roles, and mission. Organizations are arenas in which people try to satisfy their needs for happiness, social recognition, prestige, money, self-interest, and power. Informal social relationships within the organization create a shadow structure that has a life of its own, which may have positive or negative consequences. People pursue their own interests distinct from those of the organization, creating an internal politics distinct from the formal rules or "official" procedures. Natural theories also embrace the symbolic or cultural dimensions of organizations, such as how some organizations promote an ideology or create atmospheres of community, paternalism, "family-feeling," entrepreneurialism, bureaucratic rigidity, interpersonal competitiveness, or sexism. The human or social dimensions of organizational life can support, undercut, or have little relation to the efficient accomplishment of an organization's goals, or may determine the specific ways in which those goals are defined and pursued, but clearly natural systems theories see organizations as a stage for many dramas more than simply a rationally chosen means to achieve clear ends.

Open systems theories shift attention from the internal structure and functioning of organizations to the organizations' external social environment. Unlike rational and natural theories, which have generally opposed views of organizations, open systems theories can take either a rational or natural systems approach, but they look at the relationship between organizations and their settings, such as the labor market, competitors, the community, government, and the wider culture and society. These features of the external environment may be critical sources of ideas, standards, opportunities, resources, and constraints for the organization, all of which would be overlooked if one focused on the individual organization by itself as if it were closed off from the outside world.

These different approaches to the study of organizations are well-represented in the readings in this volume, as well as the controversies they have produced. Many of these controversies relate to a further distinction among theories, between those that take a relatively benign view of organizations and those that are critical of their influence on society. The benign view often focuses on what makes organizations effective, takes a managerial point of view, and sees few fundamental conflicts between the organization's rulers and its members or between the organization and the wider society. Critical approaches tend to see deep conflicts of interest between managers and workers and between the power of large organizations and the general interest. The organization's power and actions are viewed within the context of the broader social, economic, and political structure. In this view, organizations are tools not for achieving some common group purpose but for pursuing the particular interests of an individual, subgroup, or class (Fischer and Sirianni 1984; Perrow 1986). These contrasts are also well-represented in the readings that follow.

But whatever one's perspective, the significance of the subject matter is clear. Organizations affect people's lives. Everyone spends a lot of their time in organizations. They are an important building block of society, a pervasive feature of social structure. They affect the distribution of money, power, and happiness in society by their impacts on both their members and those outside the organization. Organizations can be efficient and inefficient, rationally ordered and incoherent. They are sources of income and income inequality, satisfaction and alienation, social cohesion and division, taxes for the public good, political advocacy for diverse viewpoints, and political influence for narrow interests. They can reinforce harmful social tendencies, such as discrimination, or help ameliorate them. They provide valued goods and services but can erect obstacles to the satisfaction of needs through bureaucratic rigidity, the promotion of materialism for its own sake, and degradation of the environment.

Understanding organizations as a goal in itself is worthwhile, as is the desire to use this knowledge to improve their performance. But understanding organizations is also a step toward understanding how modern society functions and how we can live better with organizations and possibly make them serve our ends more effectively, or at least understand better the problems to be faced (Gouldner 1954, p. 244f.).

PART I

ORGANIZATIONS AS RATIONAL SYSTEMS I
Classic Theories of Bureaucracy and Administration

A. Early Definitions of Organization and Management

B. Scientific Management and the Treatment of Labor

A. EARLY DEFINITIONS OF ORGANIZATION AND MANAGEMENT

Max Weber

The sociology of organizations begins with the work of the German sociologist Max Weber (1864–1920), whose work on bureaucracy was first translated into English in the late 1940s (Reading 1). Weber's position as the intellectual founder of the field is interesting because, although he wrote from a historical perspective and was mainly concerned with changing patterns of political authority and governmental organization, most subsequent research focuses on business organizations and has little interest in the kinds of historical comparisons that motivated Weber. Yet Weber's ideas remain a central contribution rich with implications, though not unchallenged by later writers.

Weber was a rational systems theorist who believed that bureaucracy was the most efficient form of organization and a pillar of modern society. Americans today do not usually think of bureaucracy as efficient. Indeed, European writers and popular opinion scorned the rigidity, pettiness, and excessive influence of their government bureaucracies as early as the late eighteenth century (Albrow 1970). However, Weber's belief in bureaucracy's technical superiority makes more sense when it is compared to previous forms of state administration, and especially when seen in light of the spectacular success and discipline of the Prussian civil service and army, which turned Germany into a major European power after their reorganization in the nineteenth century in response to Prussia's defeat by Napoleon in 1806 (Albrow 1970).

Weber compared modern bureaucratic authority to two other kinds of authority, charismatic and traditional. Charismatic authority is based on the unique personal qualities of an exceptional individual, such as a religious prophet or magnetic

charismatic authority
traditional authority

political leader, rather than any established institutional position or office. The emergence of charismatic authority is unpredictable, and charismatics often oppose established rules and routines in favor of a leader's vision. Charismatic leaders can inspire their followers to impressive accomplishments, but because such people are rare and eventually pass from the scene, their achievements cannot be maintained in the long run unless their followers establish a more conventional, permanent organization and a stable mechanism for choosing a successor to leadership that does not depend on the unusual talent of a single individual. To outlast a charismatic leader, the group has to build an institution to replace the loose operations based on personal authority.

Authority in traditional political systems, such as monarchies, is based on long-standing and seldom questioned, often sacred, principles such as the hereditary superiority of nobles, religious position or status, or other reasons not necessarily related to one's ability to perform a role. Traditional authority has great stability—nearly all of human history has been lived under traditional authority systems—but also clear limitations, because it is not based on the technical qualifications or effectiveness of those in a position to make decisions.

In contrast to charismatic and traditional forms of authority, Weber described bureaucracy as a rational-legal form of authority. Bureaucracies are governed by a set of impersonal rules and procedures that are applied universally, without regard to the personal characteristics of particular individuals, and rationally designed to serve some broader purpose. Bureaucracies employ technically qualified, full-time experts assigned to unique areas of responsibility in a logical division of labor. There is a hierarchy of superiors and subordinates, and access to positions is based on knowledge and seniority. Subordinates obey superiors at work because they occupy an office with specific, defined, and limited rights, not because of any personal characteristics the office holder possesses. The office holder's personal property is clearly distinguished from that belonging to the organization, rather than intermingled with it, and there is extensive use of written documents and systematic record keeping. Today, such principles are usually taken for granted, but they represented real breakthroughs in the rational administration of organizations.

The efficiency of bureaucracy can be better understood if it is contrasted further with traditional forms of authority. In traditional systems, hierarchical position was not based on competence, but some combination of heredity, kinship, religious status, personal loyalty, or friendship connection. Office holders served at the whim of superiors. They were often "amateurs," who held their jobs on a part-time basis and had no particular training for their work. The division of labor among different functions was often haphazard, with overlaps and gaps in authority and responsibilities. Decisions were based on tradition or were arbitrary, depending on the individual making the decision rather than on a logical and consistent application of principles. Record-keeping systems were primitive. Office holders often had property rights over the resources provided to them by the organization, such as the right to sell their position or rights to a share of tax receipts in areas under their administration. This mixing of personal and official property often gave officials a motivation to overtax the ruler's subjects and the resources to operate independently of the ruler's purposes. This mixing also made rational accounting difficult, because it was hard to keep control over resources or distinguish what belonged to the organization and to the officials holding positions within it. In this context, it is easy to see why Weber would see rationality and efficiency as defining features of modern bureaucracy. A number of these contrasts also hold for the comparison of bureaucratic and charismatic authority, which has an even more personalistic, fluid, and unstable quality than traditional authority.

[margin note: rationality & efficiency. — the indicators of modern bureaucracy.]

For Weber, the use of expert specialists, impersonal norms, written documents, and the discipline of a command hierarchy give bureaucratic organizations a reliability, regularity, and precision in the execution of tasks that no other form of authority equals. In a bureaucracy, each member repeatedly executes a particular function according to prespecified standards in the service of a larger collective goal. It is not surprising that Weber famously described bureaucracy as a giant human machine, symbolizing not only its efficiency, but also its dehumanizing potential; and he also believed its further extension into all areas of social life was inevitable.

[margin note: ?]

Weber believed modernity meant rationality and the spread of a scientific approach to living, and he saw bureaucracy as the embodiment of these principles. By dividing tasks into logical pieces and parceling them out to full-time specialists, bureaucracies were ideally suited to accomplishing complex jobs of all sorts on a large scale. Modernity meant the spread of bureaucracy as the scale of tasks and the rationality with which they were approached increased. Not only the government civil service, but also churches, political parties, interest groups, armies, hospitals, charities, voluntary associations, business enterprises, indeed all large organizations become increasingly bureaucratic insofar as they require continuous administrative work by qualified professionals. Even intimate spheres such as the family are affected by government child welfare regulations, schools, and the social service bureaucracy. Weber predicted that socialist economies would be even more bureaucratic than capitalist systems, despite their utopian aspirations, because a planned economy requires collection of more technical knowledge than market economies and tries to exercise more conscious and directive control over the economy through government planning—a perceptive insight considering that Weber died before the Soviet system took shape.

[margin note: the more the technical knowledge the more bureaucratic a system shall be (socialistic even > capitalistic one]

Though developed as part of a comparative historical investigation, Weber's contrast between bureaucratic rationality and nonbureaucratic principles of organization applies to many contemporary situations. The separation of personal and organizational property would seem an obvious distinction today, but corporations and government agencies have had to develop increasingly strict rules regarding the value of gifts that purchasing managers and others with power to award contracts may accept from suppliers or potential contractors. If someone runs a very small business as an avocation and it grows, then at a certain point he or she will have to set up a business account separate from his or her personal finances to keep clear track of the business profits. The owner will also face the problem of how to choose a successor if the company is to continue to operate after current owner-manager retires or dies, just like a charismatic or other person-centered collectivity.

Succession is a problem for nonprofits as well. Media reports regularly describe exceptionally successful social service organizations that generate excitement and hope that their achievements can be replicated elsewhere, but that owe their success to an unusually energetic and charismatic leader rather than to a standard formula. Because the Reform Party did not solve the succession problem when its charismatic leader withdrew from active participation, the party fizzled into irrelevance just eight years after having received the largest share of votes of any third party in the twentieth century in 1992. Authoritarian governments run by strong leaders on a personalistic rather than a rational-legal basis face similar succession problems, but in their case the failure to plan for a successor can result in destabilizing coups and civil wars.

Both personalistic political organizations and family businesses may be tempted to fall back on traditional rather than technically rational principles to solve staffing problems by using kinship or nepotism rather than ability or merit to fill positions. These represent contemporary contrasts between charismatic or traditional authority and bureaucratic principles, which prescribe professional management and an impersonal system of rules, such as accounting and succession procedures.

Weber placed such a great emphasis on rationality, precision, and calculation in bureaucratic administration and modern life that the contemporary reader might find his assertions puzzlingly obvious. However, these principles also have relevance for both the recent past and present. Around the time that Weber wrote about the spread of bureaucracy, one of the largest U.S. corporations, General Motors, entered a crisis that would define its future. William Durant, the founder and then-president of GM, was a freewheeling, nineteenth-century style entrepreneur who had little inclination for standard rules or procedures and who ran the business with little more than his own intuition. In his memoirs, Alfred Sloan, another GM executive, described his impressions of his boss:

> I was of two minds about Mr. Durant. I admired his automotive genius, his imagination, his generous human qualities, and his integrity. . . . But I thought he was too casual in his ways for an administrator, and he overloaded himself. Important decisions had to wait until he was free, and were often made impulsively. (Sloan 1963, p. 25)

Sloan gave an example of Durant's style. Durant was planning a new office building in Detroit that was to be the largest in the world and named the Durant Building, though later it was renamed the General Motors Building. Both Sloan and Durant worked out of a New York City office at the time. Sloan wandered into a planning meeting one day and informally suggested a suitable site for the new building, giving a number of reasons:

> I mentioned these things to Mr. Durant, whereupon he said that the next time we went to Detroit we would all go up and take a look at [the site], which we did. . . . He started at the corner of Cass Avenue, paced a certain distance west. . . . Then he stopped, for no apparent reason, at some apartment houses. . . . He said that this was about the ground we wanted, and turned to me and said, "Alfred, will you go and buy these properties for us and Mr. Prentis [the GM Treasurer] will pay whatever you decide to pay for them." I wasn't in the real-estate business. I didn't even live in Detroit. (Sloan 1963, p. 26)

The events Sloan described occurred in 1919. Though this project was successful, by 1920, GM's creditors and investors forced Durant to resign as president of the company he had founded a dozen years earlier. A chaotic expansion plan had collided with a downturn in the economy, and Durant was discovered using his personal wealth and credit to try to prop up GM's stock price. This tied the organization's success to Durant's personal fortunes more than GM's backers found comfortable. Durant was successful at founding a very large corporation, but did not know how to organize or operate it on a logical basis. Rationality in business decision making was not always an obvious or standard matter in American corporations, even by 1920.

The problem is repeated today in many small- and medium-size businesses that grow larger. They often face difficulties when informal procedures and intuitive decision making by family members or other nonprofessionals are no longer adequate to solve new and larger problems. Leaders of the organization then face the need to formalize procedures, add more structure to their operations, and hire outside expertise they did not need when problems were simpler. The organization moves away from a family or informal basis and toward a more bureaucratic basis (see Reading 24).

Sloan, who became president of GM shortly after Durant's resignation, reorganized the company along lines that set the standard for the modern American corporation. Though many would come to see his creation as too rigidly bound to bureaucratic rules and procedures in a later, less stable era (see Reading 25), there is no doubt that the company could not have continued to operate in the personalistic and haphazard fashion of Durant.

Another key insight from Weber's work actually emerges from one of its flaws or ambiguities. Sometimes, Weber suggests that bureaucratic authority is based on position in the hierarchy of command, but other times he suggests it is based on expert knowledge; indeed, Weber considered them closely related so that those making most decisions had highly developed expertise. Weber did not clearly distinguish managers, who give directions, from professionals, who apply technical knowledge. In the modern corporation, this difference is reflected in the difference between "line" and "staff" departments. Line management forms a clear hierarchy of authority from the chief executive to division, department, or plant managers and first-line supervisors, and is responsible for the organization's core activities, such as production. Staff provides advice, support, and control in areas such as research and development, personnel, and accounting. Weber's failure to distinguish the two kinds of bureaucratic authority is notable, because the line-staff distinction originated in the Prussian army's use of a general staff to advise commanders on technical military matters (Wren 1987, p. 149).

More important, these two kinds of authority are often in tension with one another in modern organizations, as subsequent sections will show. Line management almost always has more formal and informal power in most organizations, whereas staff has more technical expertise and can control certain levers of power as a result, which can lead the two kinds of functions to conflict (see Reading 29). An exception to the generally inferior position of staff is organizations whose principal outputs are professional services, such as universities or hospitals, in which case there is a situation of plural authority, and a large part of the administrators' job is serving the professionals. Because internal relations among professionals are usually more egalitarian and collegial, some critics of bureaucratic organizations see professional organizations as an alternative model for organizations in general (Heckscher and Donellon 1994). Even though Weber tended to conflate hierarchical and expert authority, subsequent sociologists who recognized the distinction have used it as a fruitful basis for understanding a number of aspects of organizational life. Also, While Weber himself did not treat it in detail, he recognized that the more egalitarian *collegial* or *peer group* method of organization, such as one finds in parliaments, business or professional partnerships, and cooperatives, is another important form of legitimate authority distinct from charisma, tradition, and bureaucracy.

Another area in which Weber contributed to the sociology of organizations is in his view of the relationship between bureaucracy and democracy. Weber's colleague Robert Michels (see Reading 17) believed that democratic organizations, like trade unions or political parties, invariably develop into oligarchies as they grow larger and become more bureaucratic. The leadership and staff become more professional, the membership becomes less knowledgeable about how the organization is run, and the distance between leaders and rank-and-file members widens. By contrast, Weber believed bureaucracy and democracy were complementary, because democracy requires equality before the law and bureaucratic principles include the uniform application of rules and the use of meritocratic qualifications, rather than social status, to recruit office holders. The latter claim was a bit paradoxical, however, because aristocrats staffed the Prussian bureaucracy in Weber's time. Weber also recognized that professional civil servants could undermine the aims of democratically elected political leaders because of their insider knowledge and permanent status.

Nevertheless, one can see how bureaucracy and democracy support one another when one considers the recent expansion of rights and legal protections for disadvantaged groups. For example, occupational health and safety regulations, rules against sexual harassment, and government regulations to protect the well-being of human subjects participating in university research all require the expansion of formal rules or laws, some kind of enforcement agency to monitor and sanction violators, often some kind of certificate verifying compliance, and some kind of new function or department within the regulated organization to ensure compliance, all of which expands the scope of bureaucracy. Bureaucracy is a feature of most types of regulation, including the extension of social protections to historically underrepresented groups. However, as will be apparent in the Michels selection (Reading 17) and elsewhere, the expansion of bureaucracy can stifle democracy as well. Weber's insight was to show that in some respects the two are complementary.

Finally, though Weber saw bureaucracy as efficient, modern, and compatible with democracy, he did not view the growth of bureaucracy as an unmixed blessing. In the reading that follows, Weber speaks of bureaucracy in terms of the "dominance of a spirit of formalistic impersonality . . . without hatred or passion and hence without affection or enthusiasm." Elsewhere, Weber wrote that bureaucratic rationality "reduces every worker to a cog in this bureaucratic machine and, seeing himself in this light, he will merely ask how to transform himself into a slightly bigger cog. . . . The passion for bureaucratization drives us to despair" (Weber 1978, p. lix). Clearly, Weber was ambivalent about the consequences of bureaucracy.

Henri Fayol

Henri Fayol (1841–1925) is the second classic theorist of administration and, like Weber, a rational systems theorist. Also similar to Weber, Fayol's main work, published in 1916, was not translated into English until the late 1940s, though some of his American and English followers began promoting his ideas in the

1930s. Unlike Weber, Fayol was not an academic but a mining engineer who became chief of a large French coal-mining and steel company. Toward the end of his career, Fayol formulated general principles of management or "acknowledged truths" that he thought applicable to all large organizations, public and private. As a practitioner as well as a thinker, Fayol did not have the same kind of misgivings regarding bureaucracy as Weber had.

Fayol described the bureaucratic organization in terms similar to Weber's. A division of labor and specialization of function allows administrators to develop specialized knowledge and proficiency in their tasks. A chain of authority ensures coordination, discipline, and constancy of purpose. As one of Fayol's followers, Luther Gulick, reasoned, work, once divided, needs to be coordinated and knit back together according to a central design by a "single directing executive authority" (Gulick and Urwick 1977, p. 6). Individuals and departments need to subordinate their interests to those of the organization. Top management provides a unified sense of direction for the organization, but circumstances will dictate the degree to which discretion and decision-making must be centralized in the hands of superiors or decentralized to subordinates.

Above all, Fayol emphasized the need for order, discipline, and rationality, citing the military as a positive example. Fayol wrote that the function of management is to plan, organize, command, coordinate, and control. The language has a highly rationalistic tone, as do Fayol's definitions: "To prepare the operations is to *plan* and *organize*; to see that they are carried out is to *command* and *coordinate*; to watch the results is to *control*" (Fayol 1937, p. 103 emphasis in original). Like Weber, Fayol also spoke of each part of an organization as "only a cog in a big machine, all of whose parts must work in concert" (Fayol 1949: [1916]), but unlike Weber, he seemed less troubled by the possible human implications of this view.

Still, Fayol believed that management should encourage social harmony in the organization by being fair to workers, concerned for their welfare, and competent enough to elicit their "loyalty and obedience." Indeed, Fayol had reason to consider all these to be other aspects of organization, if only secondarily. He referred in the reading to the "great strikes of miners, railwaymen, and civil servants which, in these latter years, have jeopardized national life at home and elsewhere" (Fayol 1949 [1916]). In fact, strike activity in France had increased markedly after the turn of the century, around the time Fayol was writing (Shorter and Tilly 1974, pp. 361ff.).

Nor were problems restricted to employers and workers. Fayol looked favorably on the French army and believed it embodied his principles of organization (Fayol 1937, p. 110). However, in 1917, thousands of French soldiers mutinied when their commanders, safely removed from the battle lines, ordered their troops to make yet another in a series of suicidal and fruitless mass attack on German trench positions. Commanders regained control over their mutinous troops only after conceding to their demands and then executing some participants to serve as examples to the rest (Smith 1994). Here is an example, close to home, of leaders whose lack of ability and sensitivity did not inspire the confidence and loyalty of their subordinates, though they were able to recognize their mistakes and respond to dissent from below at some point. Not all countries were as lucky. Comparable, more rigidly enforced policies prompted similar mutinies by Russian soldiers that contributed to the revolution that brought the Bolsheviks to power. However, Fayol generally saw things from a managerial perspective,

[handwritten margin note: New from Weber]

and these specific examples of leadership failings did not find their way into his writings.

Nevertheless, Fayol contributed to the technical understanding of organizational structure in several ways. He recommended that no subordinate receive orders from more than one superior, as this will lead to confusion, disorder, and ill will when the directives of different supervisors conflict. Fayol made the first strong arguments for the use of organization charts to clarify lines of authority and communication and to demarcate areas of responsibility. Fayol introduced the distinction between line and staff into the study of organizations, recommending that staff perform the long-term research that operating management does not have time to conduct. He observed that the number of subordinates one could supervise effectively, known as *span of control,* depends on the complexity of the subordinates' work. His recommendation that managers supervise no more than six subordinates, whereas foremen can supervise 15–30, is still influential today. Unlike Weber, Fayol criticized excess use of paperwork. He suggested that managers focus on broad issues of goals and strategies rather than immersing themselves in detail. A related contemporary principle, derived from Frederick Taylor (see below), advises managers to delegate all regular business to subordinates and focus on deviations or exceptions to routine only (Wren 1987, p. 114).

As with Weber, many of Fayol's principles and those of his followers are taken for granted today, but some carry deeper implications than might be recognized at first sight. Specialization or division of labor may seem mundane and obvious at first glance, but is important to understanding social stratification, because once individuals do different things, they may be differently valued. This is recognized in Michels' work and the literature on alternatives to capitalist hierarchy (see Readings 17, 34, and 35).

Gulick made Fayol's connection between the division of labor, inequality, and hierarchy explicit. People differ in skills and aptitudes, and specialization leads to greater proficiency than if everyone performed the entire range of jobs in an office or factory; however, specialization leads to coordination problems and the possibility that the central purpose or overall task will fade from view as each person concentrates on his or her narrow function. For Gulick, the solution was management; that is, a specialist in planning, coordinating, and supervising who has the knowledge and authority to ensure that the different individuals and parts of the organization are working toward the common goal. From the need for a division of labor, Gulick deduces the necessity of hierarchy and a stratum of managerial specialists (Gulick and Urwick 1977 [1937]). By contrast, others outside the rational systems tradition believe that inequalities of income and power in bureaucratic organizations represent political forces, rather than efficiency concerns or technical necessities.

Both Weber and Fayol restricted their attention to the formal aspects of organization. Organizations are self-consciously designed tools used to attain specific goals, and the questions they address are the proper design of organizational structure and rules. A certain organizational blueprint meant increased efficiency.

Not long after the works of Weber and Fayol were translated into English, American sociologists began to offer an alternative view. Robert Merton (1957) was the first to challenge Weber's emphasis on the efficiency of bureaucracy. Reflecting the commonsense view that bureaucracies tend to be rigid, Merton tried to explain the reasons for this rigidity. In order to perform reliably, bureaucracies require their members to adhere strictly to rules, but this leads members to treat the rules as ends in themselves. Because conformity is clearly rewarded in the organization's rule book while departures from the rules put an official in uncharted waters, officials have a positive incentive to be cautious and refuse to make exceptions. Officials also derive their professional identity from consistent application of the established rules, irrational as that may be sometimes. However, another source of inflexibility is the norm of impersonality, which requires an official to treat individual cases according to an equal standard and which we might view as more justified.

Merton's work is only one of the first to engage the large question of the merits of the bureaucratic model, which is a central debate throughout history of organization studies.

B. Scientific Management and the Position of Labor

Weber and Fayol discussed organizational structure and functioning from the perspective of managers and civil servants. Another classic rational systems thinker, Frederick Winslow Taylor (1856–1915), is best known for his views on how to organize factory work and manage blue-collar workers. Taylor came from an affluent family in suburban Philadelphia and made the unusual decision to drop out of Harvard to become a machinist apprentice. Taking a job at Midvale Steel as a common laborer, Taylor rose to chief engineer within six years, earning a mechanical engineering degree along the way. In his different positions at Midvale, Taylor experimented with methods to improve output and developed a method and philosophy later called *scientific management*. Around the turn of the century, he became a business consultant and began publishing his ideas, which quickly found a wide audience. Until his death, Taylor promoted scientific management with missionary zeal, and he became the center of an efficiency movement, even craze, throughout United States and within international industry, teaching courses in scientific management during the early years of the Harvard Business School (1909–1914; Wren 1987). Although few businesses applied Taylor's principles exactly as he prescribed, his practical influence on organizations was enormous, but also controversial.

Large-scale factories first began to eclipse small-scale craft production in the nineteenth century, but management techniques did not always change as rapidly, as is clear from Durant's performance at GM as late as 1920. On the shop floor as well as in the office, knowledge, rules, and procedures were relatively unsystematic, but becoming more precise and methodical—a process Weber called *rationalization.*

Above all, Taylor wanted to transform the idiosyncratic work practices he first observed at Midvale into what he considered a rigorous science of work through observation and measurement. Taylor saw that management permitted each worker to perform his tasks differently, some of these variations reflecting previous craft practices and others merely the individual method of the worker. Neither management nor the worker knew which method was the best in terms of efficiency and minimizing strain on the human body.

Moreover, compared to management, workers had more intimate knowledge of the tools, methods, and materials with which they worked, and they used this knowledge to control their work pace. (Small work groups used peer pressure to enforce a moderate work pace on all their members, a practice known as *restriction of output.* They feared that if anyone worked too hard at any time, management would require all of them to work to that standard all the time, a *speed-up,* without any increase in pay. This practice was known as *rate cutting,* because those paid by the piece would now be paid a lower rate per unit produced. Issues of restriction of output and conflicts over appropriate effort levels were to arise repeatedly in both the history of American capitalism and the literature on organizations (see Readings 7, 8, 12, 15, and 30). Taylor recognized an important fact about all organizations: If one works alone, the problem of work discipline is only one of self-discipline; but in a cooperative or collective work process, there is a problem of control or how to ensure that other people will do what you want them to do, sometimes known as the *principal-agency problem* (see Reading 21).

Taylor was determined to eliminate restriction of output and break all worker resistance to management control of work methods and pace. Taylor saw his mission as recapturing knowledge and control of the production process from the workers for management by using the scientific method. He interviewed and observed workers, conducted controlled experiments to determine the most efficient techniques and maximum output levels, and devised detailed work rules and wage incentives to enforce those methods and production targets. In order to gather the necessary information, Taylor had workers perform their jobs using different methods, and he observed and timed their every movement in detail, a procedure known as *time and motion study.* In this fashion, Taylor determined what he thought was the one best way a job should be performed. Until this time, engineers had standardized only physical inputs; now they would standardize the human inputs.

Workers would work in rigid conformity to the prescribed method and would be expected to meet the output quotas that were determined to be feasible under this system. Taylor believed workers would not feel more tired, because the experiments were designed to find the procedure that imposed the least strain on the human body. To use a contemporary phrase, Taylor believed that people worked "smarter not harder" when they used the best methods devised by scientific management.

Taylor also believed that group life exerted a negative influence on workers' effort norms and that management should divide the work force and bargain with workers individually. Individuals would be paid an individual incentive wage based on their ability to meet or exceed output targets as a way to break the power of peer pressure to restrict output. Taylor believed that scientific management was in the best interests of both workers and management, because it eliminated disputes over the distribution of the economic pie by raising productivity and expanding the pie. He warned managers not to jeopardize reforms by cutting rates and confirming the fears that led workers to restrict their output. Even if workers were initially resistant to changing their accustomed behavior, he believed that they would embrace the new methods and work more diligently when they saw their incomes rise.

Weber, Fayol, and Gulick all wrote about the importance of the division of labor, but no one carried the principle further than Taylor. As a consequence of his techniques, workers who used to perform whole tasks, such as craft workers, found their jobs subdivided into narrow, simple tasks with a separate individual assigned to each. Perhaps the best illustration of this principle is the substitution of assembly lines and semi-skilled workers in the automobile industry for the previous hand-made methods of auto production involving predominantly craft workers (Womack, Jones, and Roos 1990).

The division of labor also dictated that all planning functions previously performed by craft or other workers be transferred to growing industrial engineering departments in the managerial bureaucracy, because Taylor believed workers lacked the time, expertise, and motivation required to conduct work experiments. Workers lost all discretion and now simply followed management's orders, and all planning was to come from above. If the organization were compared to a human body, management would be the brains and workers the hands. This philosophy continued to dominate U.S. manufacturing until the early 1980s, when managers began to rethink the idea that "workers should check their brains at the door."

Taylor and his followers also extended scientific management beyond the factory floor. Taylor developed methods of cost accounting that rationalized existing systems of record keeping, quite apart from labor management. One of his followers, Henry Gannt, also developed charts to track output and costs. William Leffingwell applied Taylor's principles to clerical work and office management. Certain kinds of routine white-collar work, such as insurance claims processing, were often organized along factory lines, and similar work today, such as data entry and telephone call centers, is often still organized along scientific management principles. Lillian Gilbreth applied scientific management to home economics and wrote such books as *Management in the Home: Happier Living Through Saving Time and Energy* (1955). Her husband Frank, a colleague of Taylor's, applied scientific management to his personal life, such as finding ways to reduce his shaving time by seventeen seconds by using two brushes to lather his face (Wren 1987). However, most of Taylor's influence in organization studies relates to his treatment of labor.

Taylor believed that workers would not mind the restructured jobs even if they were dull, repetitive, and stripped of all decision making, because the tasks would involve less physical strain and because workers could make more money than they would earn using the existing, less productive work methods. Having spent many years on the shop floor, Taylor considered himself to be a friend of the worker, though not of organized labor. He wrote during a time of labor agitation, high strike rates, and socialist politics, and he believed his methods would solve management-worker conflicts and inaugurate an era of industrial peace and cooperation.

The reality was quite a bit more complex. Speed-ups and rate cutting were common in manufacturing before scientific management and, although Taylor criticized the practices as fostering mistrust, employers found his method of time and motion study ideally suited for just this purpose of instituting speed-ups and cutting rates. After industrial engineers or efficiency experts schooled in Taylor's methods visited an employer, workers might find themselves working considerably harder for little or no extra pay. Workers' discontents with scientific management led to a number of well-publicized strikes and a congressional investigation during Taylor's lifetime. Many came to view Taylorism as a management ideology and a tool to control labor, output levels, and work pace.

Within social science, Harry Braverman is the sharpest critic of Taylor's influence on work and organizations (Reading 3). Braverman views Taylorism as a management device to wrest power from workers rather than merely as a neutral technique for enhancing efficiency. The philosophy of subdividing work into narrow tasks and rigidly separating planning from execution eliminates the need for scarce craft skills while turning meaningful work into alienating labor. Inequality also grows when managers substitute cheaper workers for better-paid skilled labor. The purpose of scientific management, in Braverman's view, is to lower labor costs, increase worker effort, limit workers' autonomy, and enhance management control. Braverman argues that the division of labor as currently practiced is not a technical requirement, as Gulick, Taylor, and managers would argue, but really an artificial means of denying workers a wider knowledge of the production process and guaranteeing a role for capitalists as integrators of the narrow jobs that they have consciously created by dividing unified craft work into small, unskilled pieces.

Braverman and others subscribing to de-skilling theory view Taylor's influence on capitalist management as pervasive and negative, not simply in the early twentieth-century factory but also in modern manufacturing, clerical, service, and professional work, in which there is a constant tendency to simplify tasks and replace skilled workers with less skilled workers (Braverman 1974; Garson 1988). However, others view this as a great exaggeration of Taylor's influence and do not believe that the trend in modern economies has been one of polarization between a small class of owners and managers, on the one hand, and a large class of de-skilled, poorly paid workers, on the other (Attewell 1987; Nelson 1995).

Taylor even has defenders who argue that his work benefited some workers. Modern industrial engineering considers Taylor to be the father of ergonomics, which is the science of arranging things people use so that the least strain is put on the human body. However, time and motion study for the purpose of setting output standards earned him few friends among workers, and even some of Taylor's defenders acknowledge that employer rate cutting and worker hostility were common in practice (Nelson 1995). Nevertheless, most organizational researchers would agree as a general principle that people within an organization, including managers, can gain power over others by hoarding knowledge rather than sharing it to make others dependent on them and create the sense that they are indispensable. The narrow and restrictive approach to structuring job tasks and their perceived dehumanizing character have also been recurring sources of discontent (see Readings 9–12, 15, 30, 34, and 35). Even Taylor wrote disparagingly of the level of intelligence required to perform the jobs he designed.

Like all rational systems theorists, Taylor believed that a correctly designed system could write many of the human and social dimensions of organizations out of the equation. With the proper management blueprint, organizations as artificial creations could run of themselves like well-oiled machines. For Taylor, an optimal work system required simply the correct physical layout of the work environment, determination of the workers' proper bodily motions, and the right monetary incentives to ensure employees would work to their physical potential. However, Taylor never really came to terms with the management bias embedded in his philosophy and how it affected the quality of the work lives of those who had to work under his system. Indeed, subsequent generations of managers would find the human element rarely proved so simple to control as Taylor supposed.

1

BUREAUCRACY AND LEGITIMATE AUTHORITY

MAX WEBER *almost after Taylor.*

III

THE TYPES OF LEGITIMATE DOMINATION

I. THE BASIS OF LEGITIMACY

2. The Three Pure Types of Authority

There are three pure types of legitimate domination. The validity of the claims to legitimacy may be based on:

1. Rational grounds—resting on a belief in the legality of enacted rules and the right of those elevated to authority under such rules to issue commands (legal authority).

2. Traditional grounds—resting on an established belief in the sanctity of immemorial traditions and the legitimacy of those exercising authority under them (traditional authority); or finally,

3. Charismatic grounds—resting on devotion to the exceptional sanctity, heroism or exemplary character of an individual person, and of the normative patterns or order revealed or ordained by him (charismatic authority).

In the case of legal authority, obedience is owed to the legally established impersonal order. It extends to the persons exercising the authority of office under it by virtue of the formal legality of their commands and only within the scope of authority of the office. In the case of traditional authority, obedience is owed to the *person* of the chief who occupies the traditionally sanctioned position of authority and who is (within its sphere) bound by tradition. But here the obligation of obedience is a matter of personal loyalty within the area of accustomed obligations. In the case of charismatic authority, it is the charismatically qualified leader as such who is obeyed by virtue of personal trust in his revelation, his heroism or his exemplary qualities so far as they fall within the scope of the individual's belief in his charisma.

[. . .]

II. LEGAL AUTHORITY WITH A BUREAUCRATIC ADMINISTRATIVE STAFF

3. Legal Authority: The Pure Type

[. . .] The following may thus be said to be the fundamental categories of rational legal authority:

(1) A continuous rule-bound conduct of official business.

(2) A specified sphere of competence (jurisdiction). This involves: (a) A sphere of obligations to perform functions which has been marked off as part of a systematic division of labor. (b) The provision of the incumbent with the necessary powers. (c) That the necessary means of compulsion are clearly defined and their use is subject to definite conditions. A unit exercising authority which is organized in this way will be called an "administrative organ" or "agency" (*Behörde*).

(3) The organization of offices follows the principle of hierarchy; that is, each lower office is under the control and supervision of a higher one. There is a right of appeal and of statement of grievances from the lower to the higher. Hierarchies differ in respect to whether and in what cases complaints can lead to a "correct" ruling from a higher authority itself, or whether the responsibility for such changes is left to the lower office, the conduct of which was the subject of the complaint.

(4) The rules which regulate the conduct of an office may be technical rules or norms.[1] In both cases, if their application is to be fully rational, specialized training is necessary. It is thus normally true that only a person who has demonstrated an adequate technical training is qualified to be a member of the administrative staff of such an organized group, and hence only such persons are eligible for appointment to official positions. The administrative staff of a rational organization thus typically consists of "officials," whether the organization be devoted to political, hierocratic, economic—in particular, capitalistic—or other ends.

(5) In the rational type it is a matter of principle that the members of the administrative staff should be completely separated from ownership of the means of production or administration. Officials, employees, and workers attached to the administrative staff do not themselves own the non-human means of production and administration. These are rather provided for their use, in kind or in money, and the official is obligated to render an accounting of their use. There exists, furthermore, in principle complete separation of the organization's property (respectively, capital), and the personal property (household) of the official. There is a corresponding separation of the place in which official functions are carried out—the "office" in the sense of premises—from the living quarters.

(6) In the rational type case, there is also a complete absence of appropriation of his official position by the incumbent. Where "rights" to an office exist, as in the case of judges, and recently of an increasing proportion of officials and even of workers, they do not normally serve the purpose of appropriation by the official, but of securing the purely objective and independent character of the conduct of the office so that it is oriented only to the relevant norms.

(7) Administrative acts, decisions, and rules are formulated and recorded in writing, even in cases where oral discussion is the rule or is even mandatory. This applies at least to preliminary discussions and proposals, to final decisions, and to all sorts of orders and rules. The combination of written documents and a continuous operation by officials constitutes the "office" (*Bureau*) which is the central focus of all types of modern organized action.

(8) Legal authority can be exercised in a wide variety of different forms which will be distinguished and discussed later. The following ideal-typical analysis will be deliberately confined for the time being to the administrative staff that is most unambiguously a structure of domination: "officialdom" or "bureaucracy."

[. . .]

4. Legal Authority: The Pure Type

The purest type of exercise of legal authority is that which employs a bureaucratic administrative staff. Only the supreme chief of the organization occupies his position of dominance . . . by virtue of appropriation, of election, or of having been designated for the succession. But even *his* authority consists in a sphere of legal "competence." The whole administrative staff under the supreme authority then consists, in the purest type, of individual officials (constituting a "monocracy" as opposed to the "collegial" type, which will be discussed below) who are appointed and function according to the following criteria:

(1) They are personally free and subject to authority only with respect to their impersonal official obligations.

(2) They are organized in a clearly defined hierarchy of offices.

(3) Each office has a clearly defined sphere of competence in the legal sense.

(4) The office is filled by a free contractual relationship. Thus, in principle, there is free selection.

(5) Candidates are selected on the basis of technical qualifications. In the most rational case, this is tested by examination or guaranteed by diplomas certifying technical training, or both. They are *appointed*, not elected.

(6) They are remunerated by fixed salaries in money, for the most part with a right to pensions. Only under certain circumstances does the employing authority, especially in private organizations, have a right to terminate the appointment, but the official is always free to resign. The salary scale is graded according to rank in the hierarchy; but in addition to this criterion, the responsibility of the position and the requirements of the incumbent's social status may be taken into account. *[. . .]*

(7) The office is treated as the sole, or at least the primary, occupation of the incumbent.

(8) It constitutes a career. There is a system of "promotion" according to seniority or to achievement, or both. Promotion is dependent on the judgment of superiors.

(9) The official works entirely separated from ownership of the means of administration and without appropriation of his position.

(10) He is subject to strict and systematic discipline and control in the conduct of the office.

This type of organization is in principle applicable with equal facility to a wide variety of different fields. It may be applied in profit-making business or in charitable organizations, or in any number of other types of private enterprises serving ideal or material ends. It is equally applicable to political and to hierocratic organizations. With the varying degrees of approximation to a pure type, its historical existence can be demonstrated in all these fields.

1. For example, bureaucracy is found in private clinics, as well as in endowed hospitals or the hospitals maintained by religious orders. Bureaucratic organization is well illustrated by the administrative role of the priesthood (*Kaplanokratie*) in the modern [Catholic] church, which has expropriated almost all of the old church benefices, which were in former days to a large extent subject to private appropriation. It is also illustrated by the notion of a [Papal] universal episcopate, which is thought of as formally constituting a universal legal competence in religious matters. Similarly, the doctrine of Papal infallibility is thought of as in fact involving a universal competence, but only one which functions "ex cathedra" in the sphere of the office, thus implying the typical distinction between the sphere of office and that of the private affairs of the incumbent. The same phenomena are found in the large-scale capitalistic enterprise; and the larger it is, the greater their role. And this is not less true of political

parties, which will be discussed separately. Finally, the modern army is essentially a bureaucratic organization administered by that peculiar type of military functionary, the "officer."

2. Bureaucratic authority is carried out in its purest form where it is most clearly dominated by the principle of appointment. There is no such thing as a hierarchical organization of elected officials. In the first place, it is impossible to attain a stringency of discipline even approaching that in the appointed type, since the subordinate official can stand on his own election and since his prospects are not dependent on the superior's judgement. [. . .]

3. Appointment by free contract, which makes free selection possible, is essential to modern bureaucracy. Where there is a hierarchical organization with impersonal spheres of competence, but occupied by unfree officials—like slaves or *ministeriales*, who, however, function in a formally bureaucratic manner—the term "patrimonial bureaucracy" will be used.

4. The role of technical qualifications in bureaucratic organizations is continually increasing. Even an official in a party or a trade-union organization is in need of specialized knowledge, though it is usually developed by experience rather than by formal training. In the modern state, the only "offices" for which no technical qualifications are required are those of ministers and presidents. This only goes to prove that they are "officials" only in a formal sense, and not substantively, just like the managing director or president of a large business corporation. There is no question, but that the "position" of the capitalistic entrepreneur is as definitely appropriated as is that of a monarch. Thus at the top of a bureaucratic organization, there is necessarily an element which is at least not purely bureaucratic. The category of bureaucracy is one applying only to the exercise of control by means of a particular kind of administrative staff.

[. . .]

5. Monocratic Bureaucracy

Experience tends universally to show that the purely bureaucratic type of administrative organization—that is, the monocratic variety of bureaucracy—is, from a purely technical point of view, capable of attaining the highest degree of efficiency and is in this sense formally the most rational known means of exercising authority over human beings. It is superior to any other form in precision, in stability, in the stringency of its discipline, and in its reliability. It thus makes possible a particularly high degree of calculability of results for the heads of the organization and for those acting in relation to it. It is finally superior both in intensive efficiency and in the scope of its operations, and is formally capable of application to all kinds of administrative tasks.

The development of modern forms of organization in all fields is nothing less than identical with the development and continual spread of bureaucratic administration. This is true of church and state, of armies, political parties, economic enterprises, interest groups, endowments, clubs, and many others. Its development is, to take the most striking case, at the root of the modern Western state. However many forms there may be which do not appear to fit this pattern, such as collegial representative bodies, parliamentary committees, soviets, honorary officers, lay judges, and what not, and however many people may complain about the "red tape," it would be sheer illusion to think for a moment that continuous administrative work can be carried out in any field except by means of officials working in offices. The whole pattern of everyday life is cut to fit this framework. If bureaucratic administration is, other things being equal, always the most rational type from a technical point of view, the needs of mass administration make it today completely indispensable. The choice is only that between bureaucracy and dilettantism in the field of administration.

The primary source of the superiority of bureaucratic administration lies in the role of technical knowledge which, through the development of modern technology and business methods in the production of goods, has become completely indispensable. In this respect, it makes no difference whether the economic system is organized on a capitalistic or a socialistic basis. Indeed, if in the latter case a comparable level of technical efficiency were to be achieved, it would mean a tremendous increase in the importance of professional bureaucrats.

[. . .]

knowledge ≠ rational.

Bureaucratic administration means fundamentally domination through knowledge. This is the feature of it which makes it specifically rational. This consists on the one hand in technical knowledge which, by itself, is sufficient to ensure it a position of extraordinary power. But in addition to this, bureaucratic organizations, or the holders of power who make use of them, have the tendency to increase their power still further by the knowledge growing out of experience in the service. For they acquire through the conduct of office a special knowledge of facts and have available a store of documentary material peculiar to themselves. While not peculiar to bureaucratic organizations, the concept of "official secrets" is certainly typical of them. It stands in relation to technical knowledge in somewhat the same position as commercial secrets do to technological training. It is a product of the striving for power.

Superior to bureaucracy in the knowledge of techniques and facts is only the capitalist entrepreneur, within his own sphere of interest. He is the only type who has been able to maintain at least relative immunity from subjection to the control of rational bureaucratic knowledge. In large-scale organizations, all others are inevitably subject to bureaucratic control, just as they have fallen under the dominance of precision machinery in the mass production of goods.

In general, bureaucratic domination has the following social consequences:

(1) The tendency to "levelling" in the interest of the broadest possible basis of recruitment in terms of technical competence.

(2) The tendency to plutocracy growing out of the interest in the greatest possible length of technical training. Today this often lasts up to the age of thirty.

(3) The dominance of a spirit of formalistic impersonality: *"Sine ira et studio,"* without hatred or passion, and hence without affection or enthusiasm. The dominant norms are concepts of straightforward duty without regard to personal considerations. Everyone is subject to formal equality of treatment; that is, everyone in the same empirical situation. This is the spirit in which the ideal official conducts his office.

The development of bureaucracy greatly favors the levelling of status, and this can be shown historically to be the normal tendency. Conversely, every process of social levelling creates a favorable situation for the development of bureaucracy by eliminating the office-holder who rules by virtue of status privileges and the appropriation of the means and powers of administration; in the interests of "equality," it also eliminates those who can hold office on an honorary basis or as an avocation by virtue of their wealth. Everywhere bureaucratization foreshadows mass democracy, which will be discussed in another connection.

[. . .]

XI

BUREAUCRACY

6. THE TECHNICAL SUPERIORITY OF BUREAUCRATIC ORGANIZATION OVER ADMINISTRATION BY NOTABLES

The decisive reason for the advance of bureaucratic organization has always been its purely *technical superiority* over any other form of organization. The fully developed bureaucratic apparatus compares with other organizations exactly as does the machine with the non-mechanical modes of production. Precision, speed, unambiguity, knowledge of the files, continuity, discretion, unity, strict subordination, reduction of friction and of material and personal costs—these are raised to the optimum point in the strictly bureaucratic administration, and especially in its monocratic form. As compared with all collegiate, honorific, and avocational forms of administration, trained bureaucracy is superior on all these points. And as far as complicated tasks are concerned, paid bureaucratic work is not only more precise but, in the last analysis, it is often cheaper than even formally unremunerated honorific service.

[. . .]

Today, it is primarily the capitalist market economy which demands that the official business of public administration be discharged precisely, unambiguously, continuously, and with as much speed as possible. Normally, the very large modern capitalist enterprises are themselves unequalled models of strict bureaucratic organization. Business management throughout rests on increasing precision, steadiness, and, above all, speed of operations. *[. . .]*

Bureaucratization offers above all the optimum possibility for carrying through the principle of specializing administrative functions according to purely objective considerations. Individual performances are allocated to functionaries who have specialized training and who by constant practice increase their expertise. "Objective" discharge of business primarily means a discharge of business according to *calculable rules* and "without regard for persons."

[. . .] The peculiarity of modern culture, and specifically of its technical and economic basis, demands this very "calculability" of results. When fully developed, bureaucracy also stands, in a specific sense, under the principle of *sine ira ac studio*. Bureaucracy develops the more perfectly, the more it is "dehumanized," the more completely it succeeds in eliminating from official business love, hatred, and all purely personal, irrational, and emotional elements which escape calculation. This is appraised as its special virtue by capitalism.

The more complicated and specialized modern culture becomes, the more its external supporting apparatus demands the personally detached and strictly objective *expert*, in lieu of the lord of older social structures who was moved by personal sympathy and favor, by grace and gratitude. *[. . .]*

8. THE LEVELING OF SOCIAL DIFFERENCES

Administrative Democratization

[. . .] Bureaucracy inevitably accompanies modern *mass democracy*, in contrast to the democratic self-government of small homogeneous units. This results from its characteristic principle: the abstract regularity of the exercise of authority, which is a result of the demand for "equality before the law" in the personal and functional sense—hence, of

the horror of "privilege," and the principled rejection of doing business "from case to case." Such regularity also follows from the social preconditions of its origin. Any non-bureaucratic administration of a large social structure rests in some way upon the fact that existing social, material, or honorific preferences and ranks are connected with administrative functions and duties. This usually means that an economic or a social exploitation of position, which every sort of administrative activity provides to its bearers, is the compensation for the assumption of administrative functions.

[. . .] Mass democracy which makes a clean sweep of the feudal, patrimonial, and—at least in intent—the plutocratic privileges in administration unavoidably has to put paid professional labor in place of the historically inherited "avocational" administration by notables.

[. . .]

We must expressly recall at this point that the political concept of democracy, deduced from the "equal rights" of the governed, includes these further postulates: (1) prevention of the development of a closed status group of officials in the interest of a universal accessibility of office, and (2) minimization of the authority of officialdom in the interest of expanding the sphere of influence of "public opinion" as far as practicable. Hence, wherever possible, political democracy strives to shorten the term of office through election and recall, and to be relieved from a limitation to candidates with special expert qualifications. Thereby democracy inevitably comes into conflict with the bureaucratic tendencies which have been produced by its very fight against the notables. The loose term "democratization" cannot be used here, in so far as it is understood to mean the minimization of the civil servants' power in favor of the greatest possible "direct" rule of the *demos [people]*, which in practice means the respective party leaders of the *demos*. The decisive aspect here—indeed it is rather exclusively so—is the *leveling of the governed* in face of the governing and bureaucratically articulated group, which in its turn may occupy a quite autocratic position, both in fact and in form.

[. . .]

NOTE

1. *[According to translator Talcott Parsons,]* Weber does not explain this distinction. By a "technical rule" he probably means a prescribed course of action which is dictated primarily on grounds touching efficiency of the performance of the immediate functions, while by "norms" he probably means rules which limit conduct on grounds other than those of efficiency. Of course, in one sense all rules are norms in that they are prescriptions for conduct, conformity with which is problematical.

2

THE PRINCIPLES OF SCIENTIFIC MANAGEMENT

FREDERICK WINSLOW TAYLOR

INTRODUCTION

[. . .] This paper has been written:

First. To point out, through a series of simple illustrations, the great loss which the whole country is suffering through inefficiency in almost all of our daily acts.

Second. To try to convince the reader that the remedy for this inefficiency lies in systematic management, rather than in searching for some unusual or extraordinary man.

Third. To prove that the best management is a true science, resting upon clearly defined laws, rules, and principles, as a foundation. And further to show that the fundamental principles of scientific management are applicable to all kinds of human activities, from our simplest individual acts to the work of our great corporations, which call for the most elaborate cooperation. And, briefly, through a series of illustrations, to convince the reader that

whenever these principles are correctly applied, results must follow which are truly astounding.

[. . .]

II

THE PRINCIPLES OF SCIENTIFIC MANAGEMENT

THE WRITER HAS FOUND THAT THERE ARE THREE QUESTIONS UPPERMOST IN THE MINDS OF MEN WHEN THEY BECOME INTERESTED IN SCIENTIFIC MANAGEMENT.

First. Wherein do the principles of scientific management differ essentially from those of ordinary management?

Reprinted from *The Principles of Scientific Management,* Frederick Winslow Taylor (1911/1967). New York: Harper and Brothers.

Second. Why are better results attained under scientific management than under the other types?

Third. Is not the most important problem that of getting the right man at the head of the company? And if you have the right man cannot the choice of the type of management be safely left to him?

One of the principal objects of the following pages will be to give a satisfactory answer to these questions.

THE FINEST TYPE OF ORDINARY MANAGEMENT

Before starting to illustrate the principles of scientific management, or "task management" as it is briefly called, it seems desirable to outline what the writer believes will be recognized as the best type of management which is in common use. This is done so that the great difference between the best of the ordinary management and scientific management may be fully appreciated.

In an industrial establishment which employs say from 500 to 1000 workmen, there will be found in many cases at least twenty to thirty different trades. The workmen in each of these trades have had their knowledge handed down to them by word of mouth, through the many years in which their trade has been developed from the primitive condition, in which our far-distant ancestors each one practised the rudiments of many different trades, to the present state of great and growing subdivision of labor, in which each man specializes upon some comparatively small class of work.

The ingenuity of each generation has developed quicker and better methods for doing every element of the work in every trade. Thus the methods which are now in use may in a broad sense be said to be an evolution representing the survival of the fittest and best of the ideas which have been developed since the starting of each trade. However, while this is true in a broad sense, only those who are intimately acquainted with each of these trades are fully aware of the fact that in hardly any element of any trade is there uniformity in the methods which are used. Instead of having only one way which is generally accepted as a standard, there are in daily use, say, fifty or a hundred different ways of doing each element of the work. And a little thought will make it clear that this must inevitably be the case, since our methods have been handed down from man to man by word of mouth, or have, in most cases, been almost unconsciously learned through personal observation. Practically in no instances have they been codified or systematically analyzed or described. The ingenuity and experience of each generation—of each decade, even, have without doubt handed over better methods to the next. This mass of rule-of-thumb or traditional knowledge may be said to be the principal asset or possession of every tradesman. Now, in the best of the ordinary types of management, the managers recognize frankly the fact that the 500 or 1,000 workmen, included in the twenty to thirty trades, who are under them, possess this mass of traditional knowledge, a large part of which is not in the possession of the management. The management, of course, includes foremen and superintendents, who themselves have been in most cases first-class workers at their trades. And yet these foremen and superintendents know, better than any one else, that their own knowledge and personal skill falls far short of the combined knowledge and dexterity of all the workmen under them. The most experienced managers therefore frankly place before their workmen the problem of doing the work in the best and most economical way. They recognize the task before them as that of inducing each workman to use his best endeavors, his hardest work, all his traditional knowledge, his skill, his ingenuity, and his goodwill—in a word, his "initiative," so as to yield the largest possible return to his employer. The problem before the management, then, may be briefly said to be that of obtaining the best *initiative* of every workman. And the writer uses the word "initiative" in its broadest sense, to cover all of the good qualities sought for from the men.

On the other hand, no intelligent manager would hope to obtain in any full measure the initiative of his workmen unless he felt that he was giving them something more than they usually receive from their employers. Only those among the readers of this paper who have been managers or who have worked themselves at a trade realize how far the average workman falls short of giving his employer his full initiative. It is well within the mark to state that in nineteen out of twenty industrial establishments the workmen believe it to be directly against their interests to give their employers their best initiative, and that instead of working hard to do the largest possible amount of work and the best quality of work for their employers, they deliberately work as slowly as they dare while they at the same time try to make those over them believe that they are working fast.

The writer repeats, therefore, that in order to have any hope of obtaining the initiative of his workmen the manager must give some *special incentive* to his men beyond that which is given to the average of the trade. This incentive can be given in several different ways, as, for example, the hope of rapid promotion or advancement; higher wages, either in the form of generous piecework prices or of a premium or bonus of some kind for good and rapid work; shorter hours of labor; better surroundings and working conditions than are ordinarily given, etc., and, above all, this special incentive should be accompanied by that personal consideration for, and friendly contact with, his workmen which comes only from a genuine and kindly interest in the welfare of those under him. It is only by giving a special inducement or "incentive" of this kind that the employer can hope even approximately to get the "initiative" of his workmen. Under the ordinary type of management the necessity for offering the workman a special inducement has come to be so generally recognized that a large proportion of those most interested in the subject look upon the adoption of some one of the modern schemes for paying men (such as piece work, the premium plan, or the bonus plan, for instance) as practically the whole system of management. Under scientific management, however, the particular pay system which is adopted is merely one of the subordinate elements.

Broadly speaking, then, the best type of management in ordinary use may be defined as management in which the workmen give their best *initiative* and in return receive some *special incentive* from their employers. This type of management will be referred to as the management of "*initiative and incentive*" in contradistinction to scientific management, or task management, with which it is to be compared.

The writer hopes that the management of "initiative and incentive" will be recognized as representing the best type in ordinary use, and in fact he believes that it will be hard to persuade the average manager that anything better exists in the whole field than this type. The task which the writer has before him, then, is the difficult one of trying to prove in a thoroughly convincing way that there is another type of management which is not only better but overwhelmingly better than the management of "initiative and incentive."

The universal prejudice in favor of the management of "initiative and incentive" is so strong that no mere theoretical advantages which can be pointed out will be likely to convince the average manager that any other system is better. It will be upon a series of practical illustrations of the actual working of the two systems that the writer will depend in his efforts to prove that scientific management is so greatly superior to other types. Certain elementary principles, a certain philosophy, will however be recognized as the essence of that which is being illustrated in all of the practical examples which will be given. And the broad principles in which the scientific system differs from the ordinary or "rule-of-thumb" system are so simple in their nature that it seems desirable to describe them before starting with the illustrations.

Under the old type of management success depends almost entirely upon getting the "initiative" of the workmen, and it is indeed a rare case in which this initiative is really attained. Under scientific management the "initiative" of the workmen (that is, their hard work, their good-will, and their ingenuity) is obtained with absolute uniformity and to a greater extent than is possible under the old system; and in addition to this improvement on the part of the men, the managers assume new burdens, new duties, and responsibilities never dreamed of in the past. The managers assume, for instance, the burden of gathering together all of the traditional knowledge which in the past has been possessed by the workmen and then of classifying, tabulating, and reducing this knowledge to rules, laws, and formulæ which are immensely helpful to the workmen in doing their daily work. In addition to developing a *science* in this way, the management take on three other types

— old system → via personal exp.
— scientific management : via rules, initiative/incentive system

of duties which involve new and heavy burdens for themselves.

These new duties are grouped under four heads:

First. They develop a science for each element of a man's work, which replaces the old rule-of-thumb method.

Second. They scientifically select and then train, teach, and develop the workman, whereas in the past he chose his own work and trained himself as best he could.

Third. They heartily cooperate with the men so as to insure all of the work being done in accordance with the principles of the science which has been developed.

Fourth. There is an almost equal division of the work and the responsibility between the management and the workmen. The management take over all work for which they are better fitted than the workmen, while in the past almost all of the work and the greater part of the responsibility were thrown upon the men.

It is this combination of the initiative of the workmen, coupled with the new types of work done by the management, that makes scientific management so much more efficient than the old plan.

Three of these elements exist in many cases, under the management of "initiative and incentive," in a small and rudimentary way, but they are, under this management, of minor importance, whereas under scientific management they form the very essence of the whole system.

The fourth of these elements, "an almost equal division of the responsibility between the management and the workmen," requires further explanation. The philosophy of the management of "initiative and incentive" makes it necessary for each workman to bear almost the entire responsibility for the general plan as well as for each detail of his work, and in many cases for his implements as well. In addition to this he must do all of the actual physical labor. The development of a science, on the other hand, involves the establishment of many rules, laws, and formulæ which replace the judgment of the individual workman and which can be effectively used only after having been systematically recorded, indexed, etc. The practical use of scientific data also calls for a room in which to keep the

books, records,[1] etc., and a desk for the planner to work at. Thus all of the planning which under the old system was done by the workman, as a result of his personal experience, must of necessity under the new system be done by the management in accordance with the laws of the science; because even if the workman was well suited to the development and use of scientific data, it would be physically impossible for him to work at his machine and at a desk at the same time. It is also clear that in most cases one type of man is needed to plan ahead and an entirely different type to execute the work.

The man in the planning room, whose specialty under scientific management is planning ahead, invariably finds that the work can be done better and more economically by a subdivision of the labor; each act of each mechanic, for example, should be preceded by various preparatory acts done by other men. And all of this involves, as we have said, "an almost equal division of the responsibility and the work between the management and the workman."

To summarize: Under the management of "initiative and incentive" practically the whole problem is "up to the workman," while under scientific management fully one-half of the problem is "up to the management."

Perhaps the most prominent single element in modern scientific management is the task idea. The work of every workman is fully planned out by the management at least one day in advance, and each man receives in most cases complete written instructions, describing in detail the task which he is to accomplish, as well as the means to be used in doing the work. And the work planned in advance in this way constitutes a task which is to be solved, as explained above, not by the workman alone, but in almost all cases by the joint effort of the workman and the management. This task specifies not only what is to be done but how it is to be done and the exact time allowed for doing it. And whenever the workman succeeds in doing his task right, and within the time limit specified, he receives an addition of from 30 per cent. to 100 per cent. to his ordinary wages. These tasks are carefully planned, so that both good and careful work are called for in their performance, but it should be distinctly understood that in no case is the workman called upon to work at a pace which would be injurious to his health. The task is always so regulated that the man who is well suited to his job will thrive while working at this rate during a long term of years and grow happier and more prosperous, instead of being overworked. Scientific management consists very largely in preparing for and carrying out these tasks.

The writer is fully aware that to perhaps most of the readers of this paper the four elements which differentiate the new management from the old will at first appear to be merely high-sounding phrases; and he would again repeat that he has no idea of convincing the reader of their value merely through announcing their existence. His hope of carrying conviction rests upon demonstrating the tremendous force and effect of these four elements through a series of practical illustrations. It will be shown, first, that they can be applied absolutely to all classes of work, from the most elementary to the most intricate; and second, that when they are applied, the results must of necessity be overwhelmingly greater than those which it is possible to attain under the management of initiative and incentive.

The first illustration is that of handling pig iron, and this work is chosen because it is typical of perhaps the crudest and most elementary form of labor which is performed by man. This work is done by men with no other implements than their hands. The pig-iron handler stoops down, picks up a pig weighing about 92 pounds, walks for a few feet or yards and then drops it on to the ground or upon a pile. This work is so crude and elementary in its nature that the writer firmly believes that it would be possible to train an intelligent gorilla so as to become a more efficient pig-iron handler than any man can be. Yet it will be shown that the science of handling pig iron is so great and amounts to so much that it is impossible for the man who is best suited to this type of work to understand the principles of this science, or even to work in accordance with these principles without the aid of a man better educated than he is. And the further illustrations to be given will make it clear that in almost all of the mechanic arts the science which underlies each workman's act is so great and amounts to so much that the workman who is best suited actually to do the work is incapable (either through lack of education or

through insufficient mental capacity) of understanding this science. This is announced as a general principle, the truth of which will become apparent as one illustration after another is given. After showing these four elements in the handling of pig iron, several illustrations will be given of their application to different kinds of work in the field of the mechanic arts, at intervals in a rising scale, beginning with the simplest and ending with the more intricate forms of labor.

One of the first pieces of work undertaken by us, when the writer started to introduce scientific management into the Bethlehem Steel Company, was to handle pig iron on task work. The opening of the Spanish War found some 80,000 tons of pig iron placed in small piles in an open field adjoining the works. Prices for pig iron had been so low that it could not be sold at a profit, and it therefore had been stored. With the opening of the Spanish War the price of pig iron rose, and this large accumulation of iron was sold. This gave us a good opportunity to show the workmen, as well as the owners and managers of the works, on a fairly large scale the advantages of task work over the old-fashioned day work and piece work, in doing a very elementary class of work.

The Bethlehem Steel Company had five blast furnaces, the product of which had been handled by a pig-iron gang for many years. This gang, at this time, consisted of about 75 men. They were good, average pig-iron handlers, were under an excellent foreman who himself had been a pig-iron handler, and the work was done, on the whole, about as fast and as cheaply as it was anywhere else at that time.

A railroad switch was run out into the field, right along the edge of the piles of pig iron. An inclined plank was placed against the side of a car, and each man picked up from his pile a pig of iron weighing about 92 pounds, walked up the inclined plank and dropped it on the end of the car.

We found that this gang were loading on the average about 12½ long tons per man per day. We were surprised to find, after studying the matter, that a first-class pig-iron handler ought to handle between 47 and 48 long tons per day, instead of 12½ tons. This task seemed to us so very large that we were obliged to go over our work several times before we were absolutely sure that we were right. Once we were sure, however, that 47 tons was a proper day's work for a first-class pig-iron handler, the task which faced us as managers under the modern scientific plan was clearly before us. It was our duty to see that the 80,000 tons of pig iron was loaded on to the cars at the rate of 47 tons per man per day, in place of 12½ tons, at which rate the work was then being done. And it was further our duty to see that this work was done without bringing on a strike among the men, without any quarrel with the men, and to see that the men were happier and better contented when loading at the new rate of 47 tons than they were when loading at the old rate of 12½ tons.

Our first step was the scientific selection of the workman. In dealing with workmen under this type of management, it is an inflexible rule to talk to and deal with only one man at a time, since each workman has his own special abilities and limitations, and since we are not dealing with men in masses, but are trying to develop each individual man to his highest state of efficiency and prosperity. Our first step was to find the proper workman to begin with. We therefore carefully watched and studied these 75 men for three or four days, at the end of which time we had picked out four men who appeared to be physically able to handle pig iron at the rate of 47 tons per day. A careful study was then made of each of these men. We looked up their history as far back as practicable and thorough inquiries were made as to the character, habits, and the ambition of each of them. Finally we selected one from among the four as the most likely man to start with. He was a little Pennsylvania Dutchman who had been observed to trot back home for a mile or so after his work in the evening about as fresh as he was when he came trotting down to work in the morning. We found that upon wages of $1.15 a day he had succeeded in buying a small plot of ground, and that he was engaged in putting up the walls of a little house for himself in the morning before starting to work and at night after leaving. He also had the reputation of being exceedingly "close," that is, of placing a very high value on a dollar. As one man whom we talked to about him said, "A penny looks about the size of a cart-wheel to him." This man we will call Schmidt.

The task before us, then, narrowed itself down to getting Schmidt to handle 47 tons of pig iron per day and making him glad to do it. This was done as follows. Schmidt was called out from among the gang of pig-iron handlers and talked to somewhat in this way:

"Schmidt, are you a high-priced man?"

"Vell, I don't know vat you mean."

"Oh yes, you do. What I want to know is whether you are a high-priced man or not."

"Vell, I don't know vat you mean."

"Oh, come now, you answer my questions. What I want to find out is whether you are a high-priced man or one of these cheap fellows here. What I want to find out is whether you want to earn $1.85 a day or whether you are satisfied with $1.15, just the same as all those cheap fellows are getting."

"Did I vant $1.85 a day? Vas dot a high-priced man? Vell, yes, I vas a high-priced man."

"Oh, you're aggravating me. Of course you want $1.85 a day—every one wants it! You know perfectly well that that has very little to do with your being a high-priced man. For goodness' sake answer my questions, and don't waste any more of my time. Now come over here. You see that pile of pig iron?"

"Yes."

"You see that car?"

"Yes."

"Well, if you are a high-priced man, you will load that pig iron on that car to-morrow for $1.85. Now do wake up and answer my question. Tell me whether you are a high-priced man or not."

"Vell—did I got $1.85 for loading dot pig iron on dot car to-morrow?"

"Yes, of course you do, and you get $1.85 for loading a pile like that every day right through the year. That is what a high-priced man does, and you know it just as well as I do."

"Vell, dot's all right. I could load dot pig iron on the car to-morrow for $1.85, and I get it every day, don't I?"

"Certainly you do—certainly you do."

"Vell, den, I vas a high-priced man."

"Now, hold on, hold on. You know just as well as I do that a high-priced man has to do exactly as he's told from morning till night. You have seen this man here before, haven't you?"

"No, I never saw him."

"Well, if you are a high-priced man, you will do exactly as this man tells you to-morrow, from morning till night. When he tells you to pick up a pig and walk, you pick it up and you walk, and when he tells you to sit down and rest, you sit down. You do that right straight through the day. And what's more, no back talk. Now a high-priced man does just what he's told to do, and no back talk. Do you understand that? When this man tells you to walk, you walk; when he tells you to sit down, you sit down, and you don't talk back at him. Now you come on to work here to-morrow morning and I'll know before night whether you are really a high-priced man or not."

This seems to be rather rough talk. And indeed it would be if applied to an educated mechanic, or even an intelligent laborer. With a man of the mentally sluggish type of Schmidt it is appropriate and not unkind, since it is effective in fixing his attention on the high wages which he wants and away from what, if it were called to his attention, he probably would consider impossibly hard work.

What would Schmidt's answer be if he were talked to in a manner which is usual under the management of "initiative and incentive"? say, as follows:

"Now, Schmidt, you are a first-class pig-iron handler and know your business well. You have been handling at the rate of 12½ tons per day. I have given considerable study to handling pig iron, and feel sure that you could do a much larger day's work than you have been doing. Now don't you think that if you really tried you could handle 47 tons of pig iron per day, instead of 12½ tons?"

What do you think Schmidt's answer would be to this?

Schmidt started to work, and all day long, and at regular intervals, was told by the man who stood over him with a watch, "Now pick up a pig and walk. Now sit down and rest. Now walk—now rest," etc. He worked when he was told to work, and rested when he was told to rest, and at half-past five in the afternoon had his 47½ tons loaded on the car. And he practically never failed to work at this pace and do the task that was set him during the three years that the writer was at Bethlehem. And throughout this time he averaged a little more than $1.85 per day, whereas before he had never received over $1.15 per day, which was the ruling rate of wages at that time in Bethlehem. That is, he received 60 per cent. higher wages than were paid to other men who were not working on task work. One man after another was picked out and trained to handle pig iron at the rate of 47½ tons per day until all of the pig iron was handled at this rate, and the men were receiving 60 per cent. more wages than other workmen around them.

The writer has given above a brief description of three of the four elements which constitute the essence of scientific management: first, the careful selection of the workman, and, second and third, the method of first inducing and then training and helping the workman to work according to the scientific method. Nothing has as yet been said about the science of handling pig iron. The writer trusts, however, that before leaving this illustration the reader will be thoroughly convinced that there is a science of handling pig iron, and further that this science amounts to so much that the man who is suited to handle pig iron cannot possibly understand it, nor even work in accordance with the laws of this science, without the help of those who are over him.

[. . .]

[After a series of experiments, Taylor's colleague Carl] Barth had discovered the law governing the tiring effect of heavy labor on a first-class man. *[. . .]*

The law is confined to that class of work in which the limit of a man's capacity is reached because he is tired out. It is the law of heavy laboring, corresponding to the work of the cart horse, rather than that of the trotter. Practically all such work consists of a heavy pull or a push on the man's arms, that is, the man's strength is exerted by either lifting or pushing something which he grasps in his hands. And the law is that for each given pull or push on the man's arms it is possible for the workman to be under load for only a definite percentage of the day. For example, when pig iron is being handled (each pig weighing 92 pounds), a first-class workman can only be under load 43 per cent. of the day. He must be entirely free from load during 57 per cent. of the day. And as the load becomes lighter, the percentage of the day under which the man can remain under load increases. So that, if the workman is handling a half-pig, weighing 46 pounds, he can then be under load 58 per cent. of the day, and only has to rest during 42 per cent. As the weight grows lighter the man can remain under load during a larger and larger percentage of the day, until finally a load is reached which he can carry in his hands all day long without being tired out. When that point has been arrived at this law ceases to be useful as a guide to a laborer's endurance, and some other law must be found which indicates the man's capacity for work.

[. . .] [I]n all work of this kind it is necessary for the arms of the workman to be completely free from load (that is, for the workman to rest) at frequent intervals. Throughout the time that the man is under a heavy load the tissues of his arm muscles are in process of degeneration, and frequent periods of rest are required in order that the blood may have a chance to restore these tissues to their normal condition.

To return now to our pig-iron handlers at the Bethlehem Steel Company. If Schmidt had been allowed to attack the pile of 47 tons of pig iron without the guidance or direction of a man who understood the art, or science, of handling pig iron, in his desire to earn his high wages he would probably have tired himself out by 11 or 12 o'clock in the day. He would have kept so steadily at work that his muscles would not have had the proper periods of rest absolutely needed for recuperation, and he would have been completely exhausted early in the day. By having a man, however, who understood this law, stand over him and direct his work, day after day, until he acquired the habit of resting at proper intervals, he was able to work at an even gait all day long without unduly tiring himself.

Now one of the very first requirements for a man who is fit to handle pig iron as a regular occupation is that he shall be so stupid and so phlegmatic that he more nearly resembles in his mental make-up the ox than any other type. The man who is mentally alert and intelligent is for this very reason entirely unsuited to what would, for him, be the grinding monotony of work of this character. Therefore the workman who is best suited to handling pig iron is unable to understand the real science of doing this class of work. He is so stupid that the word "percentage" has no meaning to him, and he must consequently be trained by a man more intelligent than himself into the habit of working in accordance with the laws of this science before he can be successful.

The writer trusts that it is now clear that even in the case of the most elementary form of labor that is known, there is a science, and that when the man best suited to this class of work has been carefully selected, when the science of doing the work has been developed, and when the carefully selected man has been trained to work in accordance with this science, the results obtained must of necessity be overwhelmingly greater than those which are possible under the plan of "initiative and incentive."

[. . .]

NOTE

1. For example, the records containing the data used under scientific management in an ordinary machine-shop fill thousands of pages.

3

THE DEGRADATION OF WORK IN THE TWENTIETH CENTURY

HARRY BRAVERMAN

4

SCIENTIFIC MANAGEMENT

The classical economists were the first to approach the problems of the organization of labor within capitalist relations of production from a theoretical point of view. They may thus be called the first management experts, and their work was continued in the latter part of the Industrial Revolution by such men as Andrew Ure and Charles Babbage. Between these men and the next step, the comprehensive formulation of management theory in the late nineteenth and early twentieth centuries, there lies a gap of more than half a century during which there was an enormous growth in the size of enterprises, the beginnings of the monopolistic organization of industry, and the purposive and systematic application of science to production. The scientific management movement initiated by Frederick Winslow Taylor in the last decades of the nineteenth century was brought into being by these forces. Logically, Taylorism belongs to the chain of development of management methods and the organization of labor, and not to the development of technology, in which its role was minor.[1]

Scientific management, so-called, is an attempt to apply the methods of science to the increasingly complex problems of the control of labor in rapidly growing capitalist enterprises. It lacks the characteristics of a true science because its assumptions reflect nothing more than the outlook of the capitalist with regard to the conditions of production. It starts, despite occasional protestations to the contrary, not from the human point of view but from the capitalist point of view, from the point of view of the management of a refractory work force in a setting of antagonistic social relations. It does not attempt to discover and confront the cause of this condition, but accepts it as an inexorable given, a "natural" condition. It investigates not labor in general, but the adaptation of labor to the needs of capital. It enters the workplace not as the representative of science, but as the representative of management masquerading in the trappings of science.

[...]

It is impossible to overestimate the importance of the scientific management movement in the shaping of the modern corporation and indeed all institutions of capitalist society which carry on labor processes. The popular notion that Taylorism has been "superseded" by later schools of industrial psychology or "human relations," that it "failed"—because of Taylor's amateurish and naive views of human motivation or because it brought about a storm of labor opposition or because Taylor and various successors antagonized workers and sometimes management as well—or that it is "outmoded" because certain Taylorian specifics like functional foremanship or his incentive-pay schemes have been discarded for more sophisticated methods: all these represent a woeful misreading of the actual dynamics of the development of management.

Taylor dealt with the fundamentals of the organization of the labor process and of control over it. *[...]* If Taylorism does not exist as a separate school today, that is because, apart from the bad odor of the name, it is no longer the property of a faction, since its fundamental teachings have become the bedrock of all work design.[2] *[...]*

[...] Control has been the essential feature of management throughout its history, but with Taylor it assumed unprecedented dimensions. The stages of management control over labor before Taylor had included, progressively: the gathering together of the workers in a workshop and the dictation of the length of the working day; the supervision of workers to ensure diligent, intense, or uninterrupted application; the enforcement of rules against distractions (talking, smoking, leaving the workplace, etc.) that were thought to interfere with application; the setting of production minimums; etc. A worker

is under management control when subjected to these rules, or to any of their extensions and variations. But Taylor raised the concept of control to an entirely new plane when he asserted as an *absolute necessity for adequate management the dictation to the worker of the precise manner in which work is to be performed.* That management had the right to "control" labor was generally assumed before Taylor, but in practice this right usually meant only the general setting of tasks, with little direct interference in the worker's mode of performing them. Taylor's contribution was to overturn this practice and replace it by its opposite. Management, he insisted, could be only a limited and frustrated undertaking so long as it left to the worker any decision about the work. His "system" was simply a means for management to achieve control of the actual mode of performance of every labor activity, from the simplest to the most complicated. To this end, he pioneered a far greater revolution in the division of labor than any that had gone before.

Taylor created a simple line of reasoning and advanced it with a logic and clarity, a naive openness, and an evangelical zeal which soon won him a strong following among capitalists and managers. His work began in the 1880s but it was not until the 1890s that he began to lecture, read papers, and publish results. His own engineering training was limited, but his grasp of shop practice was superior, since he had served a four-year combination apprenticeship in two trades, those of patternmaker and machinist. The spread of the Taylor approach was not limited to the United States and Britain; within a short time it became popular in all industrial countries. In France it was called, in the absence of a suitable word for management, "l'organisation scientifique du travail" (later changed, when the reaction against Taylorism set in, to "l'organisation rationnelle du travail"). In Germany it was known simply as *rationalization*; the German corporations were probably ahead of everyone else in the practice of this technique, even before World War I.[3]

[...]

The issue here turned on the work content of a day's labor power, which Taylor defines in the phrase "a fair day's work." To this term he gave a crude physiological interpretation: all the work a worker can do without injury to his health, at a pace that can be sustained throughout a working lifetime. (In practice, he tended to define this level of activity at an extreme limit, choosing a pace that only a few could maintain, and then only under strain.) Why a "fair day's work" should be defined as a physiological maximum is never made clear. In attempting to give concrete meaning to the abstraction "fairness," it would make just as much if not more sense to express a fair day's work as the amount of labor necessary to add to the product a value equal to the worker's pay; under such conditions, of course, profit would be impossible. The phrase "a fair day's work" must therefore be regarded as inherently meaningless, and filled with such content as the adversaries in the purchase-sale relationship try to give it.

Taylor set as his objective the maximum or "optimum" that can be obtained from a day's labor power. "On the part of the men," he said in his first book, "the greatest obstacle to the attainment of this standard is the slow pace which they adopt, or the loafing or 'soldiering,' marking time, as it is called." In each of his later expositions of his system, he begins with this same point, underscoring it heavily.[4] The causes of this soldiering he breaks into two parts: "This loafing or soldiering proceeds from two causes. First, from the natural instinct and tendency of men to take it easy, which may be called *natural soldiering*. Second, from more intricate second thought and reasoning caused by their relations with other men, which may be called *systematic soldiering*." The first of these he quickly puts aside, to concentrate on the second: "The natural laziness of men is serious, but by far the greatest evil from which both workmen and employers are suffering is the *systematic soldiering* which is almost universal under all the ordinary schemes of management and which results from a careful study on the part of the workmen of what they think will promote their best interests."

> The greater part of systematic soldiering is done by the men with the deliberate object of keeping their employers ignorant of how fast work can be done.
>
> So universal is soldiering for this purpose, that hardly a competent workman can be found in a large establishment, whether he works by the day or on piece work, contract work or under any of the ordinary

systems of compensating labor, who does not devote a considerable part of his time to studying just how slowly he can work and still convince his employer that he is going at a good pace.

> The causes for this are, briefly, that practically all employers determine upon a maximum sum which they feel it is right for each of their classes of employés to earn per day, whether their men work by the day or piece.[5]

That the pay of labor is a socially determined figure, relatively independent of productivity, among employers of similar types of labor power in any given period was thus known to Taylor. Workers who produce twice or three times as much as they did the day before do not thereby double or triple their pay, but may be given a small incremental advantage over their fellows, an advantage which disappears as their level of production becomes generalized. The contest over the size of the portion of the day's labor power to be embodied in each product is thus relatively independent of the level of pay, which responds chiefly to market, social, and historical factors. The worker learns this from repeated experiences, whether working under day or piece rates: "It is, however," says Taylor, "under piece work that the art of systematic soldiering is thoroughly developed. After a workman has had the price per piece of the work he is doing lowered two or three times as a result of his having worked harder and increased his output, he is likely to entirely lose sight of his employer's side of the case and to become imbued with a grim determination to have no more cuts if soldiering can prevent it."[6] To this it should be added that even where a piecework or "incentive" system allows the worker to increase his pay, the contest is not thereby ended but only exacerbated, because the output records now determine the setting and revision of pay rates.

Taylor always took the view that workers, by acting in this fashion, were behaving rationally and with an adequate view of their own best interests. He claimed, in another account of his Midvale battle, that he conceded as much even in the midst of the struggle: "His workman friends came to him [Taylor] continually and asked him, in a personal, friendly way, whether he would advise them, for their own best interest, to turn out more work. And, as a truthful man, he had to tell them that if he were in their place he would fight against turning out any more work, just as they were doing, because under the piece-work system they would be allowed to earn no more wages than they had been earning, and yet they would be made to work harder."[7]

The conclusions which Taylor drew from the baptism by fire he received in the Midvale struggle may be summarized as follows: Workers who are controlled only by general orders and discipline are not adequately controlled, because they retain their grip on the actual processes of labor. So long as they control the labor process itself, they will thwart efforts to realize to the full the potential inherent in their labor power. To change this situation, control over the labor process must pass into the hands of management, not only in a formal sense but by the control and dictation of each step of the process, including its mode of performance. In pursuit of this end, no pains are too great, no efforts excessive, because the results will repay all efforts and expenses lavished on this demanding and costly endeavor.

[. . .]

FIRST PRINCIPLE

"The managers assume . . . the burden of gathering together all of the traditional knowledge which in the past has been possessed by the workmen and then of classifying, tabulating, and reducing this knowledge to rules, laws, and formulae. . . ."[8] *[. . .]* This brings to an end the situation in which "Employers derive their knowledge of how much of a given class of work can be done in a day from either their own experience, which has frequently grown hazy with age, from casual and unsystematic observation of their men, or at best from records which are kept, showing the quickest time in which each job has been done."[9] It enables management to discover and enforce those speedier methods and shortcuts which workers themselves, in the practice of their trades or tasks, learn or improvise, and use at their own discretion only. Such an experimental approach also brings into being new methods such as can be devised only through the means of systematic study.

This first principle we may call the *dissociation of the labor process from the skills of the workers.* The labor process is to be rendered independent of craft, tradition, and the workers' knowledge. Henceforth it is to depend not at all upon the abilities of workers, but entirely upon the practices of management.

SECOND PRINCIPLE

"All possible brain work should be removed from the shop and centered in the planning or laying-out department. . . ."[10] Since this is the key to scientific management, as Taylor well understood, he was especially emphatic on this point and it is important to examine the principle thoroughly.

In the human, as we have seen, the essential feature that makes for a labor capacity superior to that of the animal is the combination of execution with a conception of the thing to be done. But as human labor becomes a social rather than an individual phenomenon, it is possible—unlike in the instance of animals where the motive force, instinct, is inseparable from action—to divorce conception from execution. This dehumanization of the labor process, in which workers are reduced almost to the level of labor in its animal form, while purposeless and unthinkable in the case of the self-organized and self-motivated social labor of a community of producers, becomes crucial for the management of purchased labor. For if the workers' execution is guided by their own conception, it is not possible, as we have seen, to enforce upon them either the methodological efficiency or the working pace desired by capital. *[. . .]*

This should be called the principle of the *separation of conception from execution*, rather than by its more common name of the separation of mental and manual labor (even though it is similar to the latter, and in practice often identical). This is because mental labor, labor done primarily in the brain, is also subjected to the same principle of separation of conception from execution: mental labor is first separated from manual labor and, as we shall see, is then itself subdivided rigorously according to the same rule.

The first implication of this principle is that Taylor's "science of work" is never to be developed by the worker, always by management. This notion, apparently so "natural" and undebatable today, was in fact vigorously discussed in Taylor's day, a fact which shows how far we have traveled along the road of transforming all ideas about the labor process in less than a century, and how completely Taylor's hotly contested assumptions have entered into the conventional outlook within a short space of time. Taylor confronted this question—why must work be studied by the management and not by the worker himself; why not *scientific workmanship* rather than *scientific management*?—repeatedly, and employed all his ingenuity in devising answers to it, though not always with his customary frankness.

[. . .]

Therefore, both in order to ensure management control and to cheapen the worker, conception and execution must be rendered separate spheres of work, and for this purpose the study of work processes must be reserved to management and kept from the workers, to whom its results are communicated only in the form of simplified job tasks governed by simplified instructions which it is thenceforth their duty to follow unthinkingly and without comprehension of the underlying technical reasoning or data.

THIRD PRINCIPLE

The essential idea of "the ordinary types of management," Taylor said, "is that each workman has become more skilled in his own trade than it is possible for any one in the management to be, and that, therefore, the details of how the work shall best be done must be left to him." But, by contrast: "Perhaps the most prominent single element in modern scientific management is the task idea. The work of every workman is fully planned out by the management at least one day in advance, and each man receives in most cases complete written instructions, describing in detail the task which he is to accomplish, as well as the means to be used in doing the work. . . . This task specifies not only what is to be done, but how it is to be done and the exact time allowed for doing it. . . . Scientific management consists very largely in preparing for and carrying out these tasks."[11]

In this principle it is not the written instruction card that is important. *[. . .]* Rather, the essential element is the systematic pre-planning and pre-calculation of all elements of the labor process, which now no longer exists as a process in the imagination of the worker but only as a process in the imagination of a special management staff. Thus, if the first principle is the gathering and development of knowledge of labor processes, and the second is the concentration of this knowledge as the exclusive province of management—together with its essential converse, the absence of such knowledge among the workers—then the third is the *use of this monopoly over knowledge to control each step of the labor process and its mode of execution.*

As capitalist industrial, office, and market practices developed in accordance with this principle, it eventually became part of accepted routine and custom, all the more so as the increasingly scientific character of most processes, which grew in complexity while the worker was not allowed to partake of this growth, made it ever more difficult for the workers to understand the processes in which they functioned. But in the beginning, as Taylor well understood, an abrupt psychological wrench was required.[12] We have seen in the simple Schmidt case the means employed, both in the selection of a single worker as a starting point and in the way in which he was reoriented to the new conditions of work. In the more complex conditions of the machine shop, Taylor gave this part of the responsibility to the foremen. It is essential, he said of the gang bosses, to "nerve and brace them up to the point of insisting that the workmen shall carry out the orders exactly as specified on the instruction cards. This is a difficult task at first, as the workmen have been accustomed for years to do the details of the work to suit themselves, and many of them are intimate friends of the bosses and believe they know quite as much about their business as the latter."[13]

Modern management came into being on the basis of these principles. It arose as theoretical construct and as systematic practice, moreover, in the very period during which the transformation of labor from processes based on skill to processes based upon science was attaining its most rapid tempo. Its role was to render conscious and systematic, the formerly unconscious tendency of capitalist production. It was to ensure that as craft declined, the worker would sink to the level of general and undifferentiated labor power, adaptable to a large range of simple tasks, while as science grew, it would be concentrated in the hands of management.

5

THE PRIMARY EFFECTS OF SCIENTIFIC MANAGEMENT

[. . .] A necessary consequence of the separation of conception and execution is that the labor process is now divided between separate sites and separate bodies of workers. In one location, the physical processes of production are executed. In another are concentrated the design, planning, calculation, and record-keeping. The preconception of the process before it is set in motion, the visualization of each worker's activities before they have actually begun, the definition of each function along with the manner of its performance and the time it will consume, the control and checking of the ongoing process once it is under way, and the assessment of results upon completion of each stage of the process—all of these aspects of production have been removed from the shop floor to the management office. The physical processes of production are now carried out more or less blindly, not only by the workers who perform them, but often by lower ranks of supervisory employees as well. The production units operate like a hand, watched, corrected, and controlled by a distant brain. The production units operate like a hand, watched, corrected, and controlled by a distant brain.

[. . .]

NOTES

1. It is important to grasp this point, because from it flows the universal application of Taylorism to work in its various forms and stages of development, regardless of the nature of the technology employed. Scientific management, says Peter F. Drucker, "was not concerned with technology. Indeed, it took tools and techniques largely as given" *[Peter F. Drucker, "Work and Tools," in Melvin Kranzberg and William H. Davenport, eds.,* Technology and Culture *(New York, 1972), pp. 192–93].*

2. "As a separate movement," says George Soule, "it virtually disappeared in the great depression of the 1930's, but by that time knowledge of it had become widespread in industry and its methods and philosophy were commonplaces in many schools of engineering and business management" *[George Soule,* Economic Forces in American History *(New York, 1952), p. 241].* In other words, Taylorism is "outmoded" or "superseded" only in the sense that a sect which has become generalized and broadly accepted disappears as a sect.

3. Lyndall Urwick, *The Meaning of Rationalisation* (London, 1929), pp. 13–16.

4. Frederick W. Taylor, *Shop Management,* in *Scientific Management,* p. 30. See also Taylor's *The Principles of Scientific Management* (New York, 1967), pp. 13–14; and *Taylor's Testimony* in *Scientific Management,* p. 8.

5. *Shop Management,* pp. 32–33.

6. Ibid., pp. 34–35.

7. *The Principles of Scientific Management,* p. 52.

8. Ibid, p. 36.

9. Ibid., p. 22.

10. *Shop Management,* pp. 98–99.

11. *The Principles of Scientific Management,* pp. 63, 39.

12. One must not suppose from this that such a psychological shift in relations between worker and manager is entirely a thing of the past. On the contrary, it is constantly being recapitulated in the evolution of new occupations as they are brought into being by the development of industry and trade, and are then routinized and subjugated to management control. As this tendency has attacked office, technical, and "educated" occupations, sociologists have spoken of it as "bureaucratization," an evasive and unfortunate use of Weberian terminology, a terminology which often reflects its users' view that this form of government over work is endemic to "large-scale" or "complex" enterprises, whereas it is better understood as the specific product of the capitalist organization of work, and reflects not primarily scale but social antagonisms.

13. *Shop Management,* p. 108.

PART II

ORGANIZATIONS AS RATIONAL SYSTEMS II
Contingency Theory and the Discovery of Organizational Variation

Weber and Fayol provided a single model of efficient organizations, the bureaucratic ideal-type composed of several elements that are consis tently found together as a package (e.g., hierarchy, division of labor, formal rules). But when modern social science studied the structure of actual organizations beginning in the late 1950s, they found a variety of organizational types in which the different elements might occur in varying combinations, rather than as a single, unified type. Yet these organizations seemed well-adapted to their particular circumstances. Researchers in what might loosely be called the *contingency theory* tradition sought to understand the reasons for this variation. In the process, they refined conceptions and measures of organizational structure. Although contingency theory is no longer actively pursued in its original form, this work remains the foundation for understanding organizational structure, and its insights have been incorporated into recent research on organizational structure (Baron, Hannan, and Burton 1999) and theories known alternately as post-bureaucratic, postindustrial, or post-Fordist (see Readings 25 and 26). Contingency theory is a rational systems perspective on organizations because it explains organizational structure and practice on the basis of an organization's efficient adaptation to its circumstances, but it departs from the classical tradition in recognizing that there is no one best way to organize under all circumstances.

Tom Burns and G. M. Stalker wrote one of the most important early studies of organizational variation in the early 1960s (Reading 4). They studied British firms in the textiles, heavy industry, and electronics industries, and found that firm structure varied depending on whether the firm operated in a stable or fast-changing environment. Firms in industries such as textiles produced a familiar product using well-established technology, and product characteristics and consumer demand were relatively stable. These organizations conformed to the traditional bureaucratic model, which Burns and Stalker called *mechanistic systems*. Burns and Stalker concluded that centralized decision making, specialization, sharply defined duties, formal rules, and hierarchical control were efficient ways to organize routine and repetitive activity in a predictable environment.

In contrast, the electronics industry was in its infancy, highly dynamic and innovative, and consumer tastes were changeable. The structure of firms in this industry was much looser. Job definitions and the boundaries between functions were more flexible, rules were less formalized, employees exercised more discretion, and hierarchy was less pronounced. Important communication moved laterally as well as vertically, and it contained a greater proportion of information and advice as opposed to directives and decisions. Rather than focusing narrowly on their own particular function, individuals worked more collaboratively and kept the organization's overall purpose in sight. Knowledge and commitment were solicited from all members of the organization, and expertise counted for more than formal position. These firms resembled professional organizations more than traditional bureaucracies; Burns and Stalker called them *organic systems*.

Burns and Stalker concluded that mechanistic bureaucracies were suitable for stable environments and routine tasks but that organic systems were better adapted to fast-changing, unpredictable environments. In this context, fixed rules are likely to become quickly out of date. Duties, tasks, and problems are so novel and in such flux that they cannot be broken down and assigned to stable roles, nor can authority be presumed to have all the answers. If a mechanistic system is used in an unstable environment, superiors will be overloaded by "exceptions" referred to them by subordinates, and the system will quickly break down. Burns and Stalker concluded that different conditions require different organizational structures for organizational effectiveness. Although they found organizations that did not have structures appropriate to their environments, these organizations were less effective and competitive than those with a better fit between their environment and structure.

They also provided an alternative model of organizing that many would find more attractive than traditional bureaucracy. Although their sympathies were clearly with the organic form, Burns and Stalker initially refrained from claiming more than that each form was appropriate to a particular set of circumstances. However, Burns later predicted that the tide of history would favor the organic form as rapid technological change and more rapidly changing, affluent consumer markets would increasingly require organizations to have greater flexibility, employee commitment, and knowledge intensity than traditional bureaucracies (Burns 1984 [1963]).

Burns and Stalker's ideas continue to be relevant. Their organic model and related ideas can be found in the writings of many current organization researchers, and their specific theories are the foundation of current theories of postbureaucratic and post-Fordist theories of emerging organizational forms (see Reading 25; Piore and Sabel 1984; Kanter 1991). The contrast between the highly successful and flexible organizations in California's Silicon Valley and the failed bureaucratic computer companies of Boston's Route 128, both operating in dynamic environments, would seem to be strong contemporary evidence for Burns and Stalker's ideas (cf. Saxenian 1994). However, it is possible that some of the organic characteristics of the Silicon Valley firms may wane as they grow larger and age (Baron, Hannan, Burton 1999), as other contingency theorists discussed below might argue. Small, flexible, science-based biotechnology firms might be another illustration of Burns and Stalker's ideas (Powell, Koput, and Smith-Doerr 1996).

Other research in the 1960s pursued a similar theme. Paul Lawrence and Jay Lorsch (1967) studied firms in the plastics, container, and packaged foods industries, which also varied in the stability and predictability of markets and technology. Lawrence and Lorsch's results were broadly consistent with Burns and Stalker's conclusions, but they also extended the principle to departments within organizations that faced different levels of change and uncertainty. Thus, departments such as research and development that face less predictable environments compared to manufacturing departments will also look less bureaucratic as a consequence. Lawrence and Lorsch coined the term *contingency theory* to describe the idea that the structure of successful firms is contingent on the kind of environmental or other conditions in which they function.

Joan Woodward (Reading 5) examined the effect of different production technologies on organizational structure among manufacturing establishments. She classified technologies on the basis of their complexity and level of sophistication, which also corresponded roughly to their historical age. Unit and small batch were characteristic of premodern craft production and are found today in such industries as tailoring, airplanes, and machine tools. Large batch and mass production, such as in auto manufacturing, are classic industrial age technologies. Continuous process production is the most modern and corresponds to a high level of automation in which materials flow continuously between operations with limited human intervention, rather than moving from one manned work station to the next. Chemicals, oil refining, and bottling are examples of this kind of production.

Woodward found that plants using mass production technology were more bureaucratized than those using small batch technology, and their production jobs were more Taylorized and less skilled. However, plants using continuous process technology tended to have a more organic structure, and their production jobs carried more responsibility and were more skilled. Woodward concluded that classical bureaucratic theorists had overgeneralized from their own historical experience and mistakenly assumed that the dominant form of organization in the early twentieth century was universally appropriate, rather than appropriate to one historical era and technology. Because continuous process technology represents the future, Woodward, like Burns, believed that historical trends favored a less rigid and alienating form of organization. Mechanistic bureaucracy turns out to be only a passing phase in this view, appropriate for industrial technology but not for postindustrial technology.

Robert Blauner (1964) examined four industries that used small batch craft technology (printing), mass production (textiles, autos), and continuous process technology (chemicals), and confirmed that alienation was greatest in mass production industries and lowest in industries using more traditional and more modern technologies. Case studies of highly automated and computerized production by Hirschhorn (1984) and Zuboff (1988) also conclude that more skilled jobs and organic forms of organization are more appropriate to workplaces using advanced technology.

However, not all researchers have found technology to be the critical contingency influencing organizational structure. Beginning in the late 1960s, Derek Pugh and his colleagues at Aston University in Birmingham, England, conducted organizational research using large sample surveys (Reading 8). The Aston group, as they came to be called, interviewed managers, asking vast numbers of questions about organizational characteristics that they combined into scales, some of which are reproduced in the reading by Pugh. The scales were operational measures of familiar Weberian concepts, such as the extent of role specialization, standardization of rules and procedures, centralization of decision making, and what they called configuration or organizational structure, which was composed of measures such as number of hierarchical levels, supervisory spans of control, and ratios of staff to line personnel.

The Aston group was a pioneering effort to develop statistically reliable measures of organizational structure and functioning. Rather than using binary measures that assume the different characteristics they measured are either present or absent in different organizations, they used continuous measures that allowed for the possibility that characteristics could be found in greater or lesser degrees. They also found that different organizations had different combinations of these characteristics and that the possible patterns were more varied than the mechanistic-organic dichotomy. Organizations can be bureaucratic in different degrees and in very different ways. However, the Aston group was still quite Weberian and viewed traditional bureaucratic characteristics as enhancing efficiency.

When the Aston group used their measures to develop a causal explanation of the patterns they observed, they concluded that the size of the organization (e.g., number of employees, value of assets) was the most important variable, not its technology. Larger organizations had greater role specialization and more formalized and standardized rules. Interestingly, larger organizations were also found to have more decentralized decision making, but this was mostly because when organizational tasks become too large for bosses to handle alone they must delegate. In fact, "decentralization" of decision making was often accompanied by such detailed rules and procedures that there was little scope for true discretion at lower levels. Control from above was maintained remotely through prescribed routines, so that superiors did not have to make all the decisions themselves or supervise personally or closely the subordinates who "made" the decision. As Pugh writes, under these conditions, "the organizational machine will run as it has been set to run," but this is very different from the more meaningful decentralization Burns and Stalker describe for organic systems.

According to the Aston group, larger organizations tended to be more structured in terms of specialization, formalization, and standardization. There was also some indication that as organizations age they become more structured, which is not surprising because a desire for stability and routine and success at establishing it are likely to grow over time. The Aston group's findings seem to imply that, insofar as organizations are becoming larger and aging, the trend is toward more mechanistic rather than organic forms of organization.

Also in the late 1960s, Peter Blau in the United States investigated the determinants of organizational structure. Like the Aston group, Blau found that size was a strong predictor of what he called structural complexity. Structural complexity had two dimensions, *differentiation*, or the number of organizational subunits with distinct functions, and *administrative intensity*, or the ratio of administrators to workers directly involved in producing the organization's goods or services, both measures of bureaucratization. Like the Aston group, Blau used continuous measures such as

1. Number of hierarchical levels (vertical differentiation)

2. Number of departments (horizontal differentiation)

3. Number of distinct occupations (specialization, division of labor)

4. Administrative structure (administrative intensity)
   a. Percentage of managers
   b. First-line supervisors' span of control
   c. Percentage of staff

Blau found that larger organizations were more differentiated than smaller ones because they permitted a more elaborated division of labor. However, larger organizations also had a smaller percentage of administrators, so in this respect they seemed to be less bureaucratic than smaller organizations, contrary to stereotype. Blau explained this unexpected finding by arguing that there were administrative economies of scale. All organizations need certain kinds of administrators independent of the volume of business they conduct, but the number of these administrators does not increase proportionately as the volume of work grows. However, the effects of size on both differentiation and administrative intensity are most pronounced when comparing relatively small organizations to somewhat larger ones. Comparing medium and large organizations, one finds much less difference in either differentiation or administrative intensity.

The negative effect of size on administrative intensity is also partly offset by the tendency for larger organizations to be more differentiated and for greater differentiation to be associated with greater administrative intensity. Increased heterogeneity within organizations increases the need for integration and coordination and raises the ratio of managers to other employees. Thus, the complexity of the managerial task partly offsets administrative economies of scale. Blau's model might be represented as follows, where plus and negative signs indicate positive and negative associations, respectively:

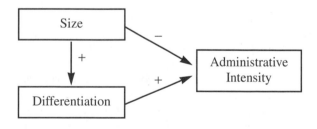

Figure II.1.

Henry Mintzberg's (1981) article gave a kind of final summary statement of the principles of contingency theory. In addition to integrating the variables environmental uncertainty, technological complexity, and organizational size and age into a single framework, Mintzberg also included the important concept of the degree to which an organization is subject to external control by higher-level corporate parents or the government, a dimension introduced by resource dependency theory (see Reading 18). To the extent that an organization is subject to external control, it is likely to be more centralized and formalized in order to cope with those demands, and therefore it will look more like a machine bureaucracy.

Mintzberg also describes alternatives to machine bureaucracy, such as the professional bureaucracy and an even looser kind of organic structure that he calls adhocracy. Mintzberg argues that though there is much enthusiasm for adhocracy, such organizations are better at innovating than at routine activities. Unless we are willing to pay the higher costs of handcrafted rather than mass-produced goods, Mintzberg believes traditional bureaucracy is here to stay. Age and growth will drive adhocracies toward more bureaucratic forms, Mintzberg believes.

Contingency theory was perhaps the most important stream of organizational research in the mid-1960s through mid-1970s. This work remains the foundation for understanding the internal structure of organizations (see, e.g., Morrill 1995, Chapter 2; Baron, Hannan, and Burton 1999). Contemporary theories of post-bureaucratic organizations—one focus of Part IX—often borrow more from this early work than they realize and could benefit from reexamining some of the empirical literature that argued for and against contingency theory to avoid reinventing the wheel and to understand the limitations of such propositions. Contingency theory provided some of the first rigorous definitions and operationalizations of key concepts, such as environmental turbulence, technological complexity, the division of labor, hierarchy, formalization, standardization, and centralization of decision making. All researchers now agree that there is no universally applicable bureaucratic model and that the appropriate structure is at least partly contingent on variables such as environmental uncertainty and complexity, technology, and size.

Still, a number of problems led to growing dissatisfaction with contingency theory by the late 1970s. Contingency theory always recognized that some organizations would be structured atypically relative to their circumstances, but argued that they would suffer from lower performance if their structure were inappropriate. However, some criticized the remaining determinism implicit in this view and argued that management had a wider range of discretion in choosing an organizational form that suited their preferences and managerial philosophy (Child 1997). The assumption that structure reflects efficiency has also been criticized as functionalist, in contrast to more recent institutionalist theories that view organizations as operating under myths of rationality that really reflect social norms and conventions regarding appropriate ways to organize (see Reading 19). Contingency theory neglected the role of power, choice, historical accident, fashion, ideology, norms, and values in the selection of organizational structure.

In addition, the methods of analysis used in these studies were often simple, faulty, or impressionistic, and the findings not always replicated (Pennings 1973; Starbuck 1981). Environmental uncertainty proved especially difficult to measure (Blau and Meyer 1987, pp. 110ff.), and many researchers claimed to find little or no evidence for Woodward's predictions regarding technology and organizational structure (Blau, Falbe, McKinley, and Tracy 1976; Gallie 1978; Dawson and Wedderburn 1980). Stronger support has been found for the effect of size on differentiation and administrative intensity (Marsden, Cook, and Kalleberg 1996), though often relationships found in cross-sectional samples disappeared when organizations were followed as they grew over time (Scott 1975).

4

The Management of Innovation

Tom Burns

G. M. Stalker

[. . .] When novelty and unfamiliarity in both market situation and technical information become the accepted order of things, a fundamentally different kind of management system becomes appropriate from that which applies to a relatively stable commercial and technical environment. *[. . .]*

If the form of management is properly to be seen as dependent on the situation the concern is trying to meet, it follows that there is no single set of principles for "good organization," an ideal type of management system which can serve as a model to which administrative practice should, or could in time, approximate. It follows also that there is an overriding management task in first interpreting correctly the market and technological situation, in terms of its instability or of the rate at which conditions are changing, and then designing the management system appropriate to the conditions, and making it work. *[. . .]*

MANAGEMENT STRUCTURE AND SYSTEMS

ORGANIZATION WITHIN A STABLE PROGRAMME

[. . .] The whole *[organization in a stable environment]* is visible as a pyramid of knowledge about the circumstances of the concern. As one descends through the hierarchy, one finds more limited information, technical and local, about these circumstances, and also more limited control over the

resources of the firm. One also finds each person's task more and more clearly defined by his superior, so that he is capable not only of knowing what to do in normal circumstances without consulting anyone else, but also knows just how far he may allow a situation to depart from the normal. Beyond a certain limit he has insufficient authority, insufficient information, and usually insufficient technical ability to be able to make decisions. He is informed, therefore, quite clearly when this limit occurs; beyond it, he has one course open—to report to his superior. Similarly, his part in the common purpose is defined and it is normally unnecessary for him to have to consider further how his task relates to the firm's commercial ends.

Although the specification and detachment of the individual member of the organization increases the lower down in the hierarchy he is, even the General Manager's task is carried out within the framework of a programme—indeed, of a very precisely defined programme, with uncertainties and expectations, so far as demand is concerned, ironed out for him beforehand.

The system of management within the factory was quite explicitly devised to keep production and production conditions stable. With this as the underlying principle, the system defined what information or instructions arrived at any one position in the hierarchy, what information or instructions might leave it, and their destination. Such definition was a matter of fixed, clear, and precise routine. Similarly, each working position in the hierarchy had its authority, information, and technical competence specified once for all. Moreover, since each position below the General Manager's in the hierarchy was specialized in all three features of authority, technique, and information, and nobody was empowered to act outside defined limits, all departures from stable conditions were swiftly reported upwards, and [. . .] the General Manager existed as the fountainhead of all information about commercial and other conditions affecting the affairs of the factory (as against technique). Such changes as did occur, therefore, were inaugurated at the top. There was, accordingly, a fairly stringent authoritarian character about the conduct of superiors to their subordinates. [. . .]

What we have been considering, in this example, is the structure of management in a concern for which technical and market conditions approximated very closely to stability. At all levels, decision-making occurred within the framework of familiar expectations and beliefs, many of which could be formulated numerically as a programme. Fluctuations in demand did occur, but these were treated as deviations from normality, and part of the task of management was to constrain the sales office in London to avoid such deviations. Production programmes, which in operational terms were planned for a week's run, were devised for monthly, three-monthly, and six-monthly periods so as to make it easier to run each weekly programme without alteration.

[. . .]

ORGANIZATION FOR A CONSTANT OR PREDICTABLE RATE OF NOVELTY

[. . .] All electronics firms encountered much higher rates of technical and other change. [. . .]

To take one of the successful radio firms, fortnightly meetings were held to consider "forward designs," and these were attended by the Works Director, Technical Director, Chief Engineer, Sales Manager, and Publicity Director. Another fortnightly series of meetings, alternating with the first series, dealt with current production modifications and the progress of the new models in production. But this formal system of meetings existed within a context of constant consultation between the directorate, consultation which involved their subordinates. Design engineers and planning engineers were equally specific about the way in which consultation about design and styling stemmed outwards from the managing director, through the top management group, to include them.

Of the forward designs meeting, one director said "We don't decide very much, but we help Mr. ___ (the Technical Director) to decide which kind of design to start. Sales have a lot to say about what they want, but nobody is dogmatic about it. I suppose the very fact that all this talk goes on with the Technical Director present helps him. You could say that all decisions are taken in the light of full knowledge of what other people think and of what they are doing. Similarly, they know about your decisions and what you are up to. This doesn't apply just to meetings."

At lower levels in management the same free and frequent contact between individuals was maintained as prevailed among the directors. "You go to the person who is most concerned with the problem in hand," whether foreman or director. "If you want authority to get something done, you go to the top of the tree—no, not my tree—theirs." Disputes with other departments could be referred to the directors, but these seldom arose, because "When enough people are brought into it, problems settle themselves. Practically every question is settled logically (*sic*), not on somebody's authority. . . . "

[. . .]

The consistent blurring of the definition given to individual positions in the management hierarchy becomes quite evident at this stage, especially as it begins to induce some insecurity. One manager, for example, said his "chief problem" was that "the limits of one's responsibilities and authority aren't defined." There was no organization chart. In all interviews, managers found difficulty in saying who were "at their own level" in the firm.

In the other major radio firm the "Monday morning meeting" was an even more important element in the management system *[. . .]*. It acted as a model for many other management meetings, many of which were also given executive powers. "We are" it was said, "always having meetings, because you don't bring about changes without meetings." And change, it was unnecessary to say, was the normal condition of things for this firm.

ORGANIZATION AND INNOVATIONS

Beyond this point, in the electronics industry proper, one begins to meet concerns in which organization is thought of primarily in terms of the communication system; there is often a deliberate attempt to avoid specifying individual tasks, and to forbid any dependence on the management hierarchy as a structure of defined functions and authority. The head of one concern, at the beginning of the first interview, attacked the idea of the organization chart as inapplicable in his concern and as a dangerous method of thinking about the working of industrial management. The first requirement of a management, according to him, was that it should make the fullest use of the capacities of its members; any individual's job should be as little defined as possible, so that it will "shape itself" to his special abilities and initiative.

In this concern insistence on the least possible specification for managerial positions was much more in evidence than any devices for ensuring adequate interaction within the system. This did occur, but as a consequence of a set of conditions rather than of prescription by top management. Some of these conditions were physical; a single-storeyed building housed the entire concern, two thousand strong, from laboratories to canteen. Access to anyone was, therefore, physically simple and direct; it was easier to walk across to the laboratories' door, the office door, or the factory door and look about for the person one wanted, than even to telephone. Written communication inside the factory was actively discouraged. Most important of all, however, was the need of each individual manager for interaction with others, in order to get his own tasks and functions defined, in the absence of specification from above. When the position of product engineer was created, for example, the first incumbents said they had to "find out" what they had to do, and what authority and resources they could command to do it.

In fact, this process of "finding-out" about one's job proved to be unending. Their roles were continually defined and redefined in connexion with specific tasks and as members of specific co-operative groups. This happened through a perpetual sequence of encounters with laboratory chiefs, with design engineers who had worked on the equipment the product engineers were responsible for getting made, with draughtsmen, with the works manager, with the foremen in charge of the production shops they had to use, with rate-fixers, buyers, and operatives. In every single case they, whose only commission was "to see the job through," had to determine their part and that of the others through complex, though often brief, negotiations in which the relevant information and technical knowledge possessed by them would have to be declared, and that possessed by others ascertained.

The sheer difficulty of contriving the correct social stance and the effective social manner for use in different negotiations, the embarrassment of having so to contrive, and the personal affront attached to failure to achieve one's ends by these means, induced in managers a nervous preoccupation with the hazards of social navigation in the structure and with the relative validity of their own claims to authority, information, and technical expertise.

"Normally," said a departmental manager, "management has a sort of family tree showing who is responsible for what, and what he is responsible for. It's a pity there's nothing like that here. It's rather difficult not knowing; there's a lot of trouble caused by this—you get an assistant to a manager who acts as though he were an assistant manager, a very different thing." Another man, a product engineer, said "'One of the troubles here is that nobody is very clear about his title or status or even his function." A foreman, explaining his relationship with senior managers, said of one, "It's generally gathered, from seeing T. standing about looking at the roof when something is being done to it and looking over machines, that he's in charge of plant and buildings." The same foreman, discussing his own job, said that when he had first been promoted he had been told nothing of his duties and functions. "Of course, nobody knows what his job is in here. When I was made foreman I was told to get on with the job—was just told 'You'll start in on Monday', so I came in and started in. That was really all that was said."

The disruptive effects of this preoccupation were countered by a general awareness of the common purpose of the concern's attitudes. While this awareness was sporadic and partial for many members of the firm, it was an essential factor in, for example, the ability of the "product engineers" to perform their tasks, dependent as they were on the co-operation of persons and groups who carried on the basic interpretative processes of the concern. Indeed, discussion of the common purposes of the organization featured largely in the conversation of cabals and extra-mural groups existing among managers.

[. . .]

MECHANISTIC AND ORGANIC SYSTEMS OF MEASUREMENT

MECHANISTIC AND ORGANIC SYSTEMS

We are now at the point at which we may set down the outline of the two management systems which represent for us [. . .] the two polar extremities of the forms which such systems can take when they are adapted to a specific rate of technical and commercial change. The case we have tried to establish from the literature, as from our research experience [. . .], is that the different forms assumed by a working organization do exist objectively and are not merely interpretations offered by observers of different schools.

Both types represent a "rational" form of organization, in that they may both, in our experience, be explicitly and deliberately created and maintained to exploit the human resources of a concern in the most efficient manner feasible in the circumstances of the concern. [. . .]

We have tried to argue that these are two formally contrasted forms of management system. These we shall call the mechanistic and organic forms.

A *mechanistic* management system is appropriate to stable conditions. It is characterized by:

(a) the specialized differentiation of functional tasks into which the problems and tasks facing the concern as a whole are broken down;

(b) the abstract nature of each individual task, which is pursued with techniques and purposes more or less distinct from those of the concern as a whole; i.e., the functionaries tend to pursue the technical improvement of means, rather than the accomplishment of the ends of the concern;

(c) the reconciliation, for each level in the hierarchy, of these distinct performances by the immediate superiors, who are also, in turn, responsible for seeing that each is relevant in his own special part of the main task.

(d) the precise definition of rights and obligations and technical methods attached to each functional role;

(*e*) the translation of rights and obligations and methods into the responsibilities of a functional position;

(*f*) hierarchic structure of control, authority and communication;

(*g*) a reinforcement of the hierarchic structure by the location of knowledge of actualities exclusively at the top of the hierarchy, where the final reconciliation of distinct tasks and assessment of relevance is made.

(*h*) a tendency for interaction between members of the concern to be vertical, i.e., between superior and subordinate;

(*i*) a tendency for operations and working behaviour to be governed by the instructions and decisions issued by superiors;

(*j*) insistence on loyalty to the concern and obedience to superiors as a condition of membership;

(*k*) a greater importance and prestige attaching to internal (local) than to general (cosmopolitan) knowledge, experience, and skill.

The *organic* form is appropriate to changing conditions, which give rise constantly to fresh problems and unforeseen requirements for action which cannot be broken down or distributed automatically arising from the functional roles defined within a hierarchic structure. It is characterized by:

(*a*) the contributive nature of special knowledge and experience to the common task of the concern;

(*b*) the "realistic" nature of the individual task, which is seen as set by the total situation of the concern;

(*c*) the adjustment and continual re-definition of individual tasks through interaction with others;

(*d*) the shedding of "responsibility" as a limited field of rights, obligations and methods. (Problems may not be posted upwards, downwards or sideways as being someone's else's responsibility);

(*e*) the spread of commitment to the concern beyond any technical definition;

(*f*) a network structure of control, authority, and communication. The sanctions which apply to the individual's conduct in his working role derive more from presumed community of interest with the rest of the working organization in the survival and growth of the firm, and less from a contractual relationship between himself and a non-personal corporation, represented for him by an immediate superior;

(*g*) omniscience no longer imputed to the head of the concern; knowledge about the technical or commercial nature of the here and now task may be located anywhere in the network; this location becoming the *ad hoc* centre of control authority and communication;

(*h*) a lateral rather than a vertical direction of communication through the organization, communication between people of different rank, also, resembling consultation rather than command;

(*i*) a content of communication which consists of information and advice rather than instructions and decisions;

(*j*) commitment to the concern's tasks and to the "technological ethos" of material progress and expansion is more highly valued than loyalty and obedience;

(*k*) importance and prestige attach to affiliations and expertise valid in the industrial and technical and commercial milieux external to the firm.

One important corollary to be attached to this account is that while organic systems are not hierarchic in the same sense as are mechanistic, they remain stratified. Positions are differentiated according to seniority—i.e., greater expertise. The lead in joint decisions is frequently taken seniors, but it is an essential presumption of the organic system that the lead, i.e. "authority," is taken by whoever shows himself most informed and capable, i.e., the "best authority." The location of authority is settled by consensus.

A second observation is that the area of commitment to the concern—the extent to which the individual yields himself as a resource to be used by the working organization—is far more extensive in organic than in mechanistic systems. Commitment, in fact, is expected to approach that of the professional scientist to his work, and frequently does. One further consequence of this is that it becomes far less feasible to distinguish "informal" from "formal" organization.

Thirdly, the emptying out of significance from the hierarchic command system, by which co-operation is ensured and which serves to monitor the working organization under a mechanistic system, is countered by the development of shared beliefs about the values and goals of the concern. The growth and accretion of institutionalized values, beliefs, and conduct, in the form of commitments, ideology, and manners, around an image of the concern in its industrial and commercial setting make good the loss of formal structure.

Finally, the two forms of system represent a polarity, not a dichotomy; there are [. . .] intermediate stages between the extremities empirically known to us. Also, the relation of one form to the other is elastic, so that a concern oscillating between relative stability and relative change may also oscillate between the two forms. A concern may (and frequently does) operate with a management system which includes both types.

The organic form, by departing from the familiar clarity and fixity of the hierarchic structure, is often experienced by the individual manager as an uneasy, embarrassed, or chronically anxious quest for knowledge about what he should be doing, or what is expected of him, and similar apprehensiveness about what others are doing. Indeed, as we shall see later, this kind of response is necessary if the organic form of organization is to work effectively. Understandably, such anxiety finds expression in resentment when the apparent confusion besetting him is not explained. In these situations, all managers some of the time, and many managers all the time, yearn for more definition and structure.

On the other hand, some managers recognize a rationale of non-definition, a reasoned basis for the practice of those successful firms in which designation of status, function, and line of responsibility and authority has been vague or even avoided.

The desire for more definition is often in effect a wish to have the limits of one's task more neatly defined—to know what and when one doesn't have

to bother about as much as to know what one does have to. It follows that the more definition is given, the more omniscient the management must be, so that no functions are left wholly or partly undischarged, no person is overburdened with undelegated responsibility, or left without the authority to do his job properly. To do this, to have all the separate functions attached to individual roles fitting together and comprehensively, to have communication between persons constantly maintained on a level adequate to the needs of each functional role, requires rules or traditions of behaviour proved over a long time and an equally fixed, stable task. The omniscience which may then be credited to the head of the concern is expressed throughout its body through the lines of command, extending in a clear, explicitly titled hierarchy of officers and subordinates.

The whole mechanistic form is instinct with this twofold principle of definition and dependence which acts as the frame within which action is conceived and carried out.

[. . .]

One other feature of mechanistic organization needs emphasis. It is a necessary condition of its operation that the individual "works on his own," functionally isolated; he "knows his job," he is "responsible for seeing it's done." He works at a job which is in a sense artificially abstracted from the realities of the situation the concern is dealing with, the accountant "dealing with the costs side," the works manager "pushing production," and so on. As this works out in practice, the rest of the organization becomes part of the problem situation the individual has to deal with in order to perform successfully; i.e., difficulties and problems arising from work or information which has been handed over the "responsibility barrier" between two jobs or departments are regarded as "really" the responsibility of the person from whom they were received. As a design engineer put in, "When you get designers handing over designs completely to production, it's 'their responsibility' now. [. . .] What happens is that you're constantly getting unsuspected faults arising from characteristics which you didn't think important in the design. If you get to hear of these through a sales person, or a production person, or somebody to whom the design was handed over to in the dim past, then, instead of being a design problem, it's an annoyance caused by that particular person, who can't do his own job—because you'd thought you were finished with that one, and you're on to something else now."

When the assumptions of the form of organization make for pre-occupation with specialized tasks, the chances of career success, or of greater influence, depend rather on the relative importance which may be attached to each special function by the superior whose task it is to reconcile and control a number of them. And, indeed, to press the claims of one's job or department for a bigger share of the firm's resources is in many cases regarded as a mark of initiative, of effectiveness, and even of "loyalty to the firm's interests." The state of affairs thus engendered squares with the role of the superior, the man who can see the wood instead of just the trees, and gives it the reinforcement of the aloof detachment belonging to a court of appeal. The ordinary relationship prevailing between individual managers "in charge of" different functions is one of rivalry, a rivalry which may be rendered innocuous to the persons involved by personal friendship or the norms of sociability, but which turns discussion about the situations which constitute the real problems of the concern—how to make products more cheaply, how to sell more, how to allocate resources, whether to curtail activity in one sector, whether to risk expansion in another, and so on-into an arena of conflicting interests.

The distinctive feature of the second, organic system is the pervasiveness of the working organization as an institution. In concrete terms, this makes itself felt in a preparedness to combine with others in serving the general aims of the concern. Proportionately to the rate and extent of change, the less can the omniscience appropriate to command organizations be ascribed to the head of the organization; for executives, and even operatives, in a changing firm it is always theirs to reason why. Furthermore, the less definition can be given to status, roles, and modes of communication, the more do the activities of each member of the organization become determined by the real tasks of the firm as he sees them than by instruction and routine. The individual's job ceases to be self-contained; the only way in which "his" job can be done is by his participating continually with others in the solution of problems which are real to the firm, and put in a language of requirements and activities meaningful to them all. Such methods of working put much heavier demands on the individual. *[. . .]*

We have endeavoured to stress the appropriateness of each system to its own specific set of conditions. Equally, we desire to avoid the suggestion that either system is superior under all circumstances to the other. In particular, nothing in our experience justifies the assumption that mechanistic systems should be superseded by organic in conditions of stability. The beginning of administrative wisdom is the awareness that there is no one optimum type of management system.

5

TECHNOLOGY AND ORGANIZATION

JOAN WOODWARD

3

ANALYSIS OF TECHNICAL VARIABLES

SYSTEMS OF PRODUCTION

[. . .] One interesting characteristic of classical management theory *[. . .]* is that it was developed in a technical setting but independently of technology. *[. . .]* It is true that several of the people concerned, including Taylor himself, were engineers with a technical background who had practised successfully in manufacturing industry. But they tended to generalize on the basis of their experience, and the expedients they found effective in practice were often given the status of fundamental truths or general laws by those attracted to their ideas. The result was that the assumption first put into words by Follett (1927)[1] that "whatever the purpose towards which human endeavour is directed, the principles of that direction are nevertheless the same" became an accepted part of management theory. There has been a tendency to develop ideas about the administrative process independently of technical considerations, and the technical backgrounds of the people who practised successfully as managers tend to have been overlooked or forgotten in the evaluation of their work.

Sociologists who turned their attention to problems of either administration or industrial behaviour, from Weber and Veblen onwards, took a different point of view in theory, assuming that the technological circumstances, either of a society in the wider sense or of a social system such as a factory was a major variable in the determination of its structure and behaviour. *[. . .]*

Dubin (1959)[2] went so far as to contend that technology is the most important single determinant of working behaviour. He also defined his use of the word technology by sub-dividing it into two major phases; first, the tools, instruments, machines, and technical formulas basic to the performance of the work, and secondly, the body of ideas which express the goals of the work, its functional importance, and the rationale of the methods employed. Indeed, a considerable part of the literature of industrial sociology in the last five years is concerned with the relationship between behaviour and technology at either the "tool" or the "control" level.

Having reached negative conclusions from the initial analysis of their material, the research workers turned almost automatically to their technological data. Was it possible to systematize this data in such a way as to show whether there was any relationship between organizational characteristics and technology? A difficulty immediately arose, for although the existence of a link between technology and behaviour is more or less taken for granted by social scientists, the technical variables on which the differences in structure and behaviour depend, have not yet been isolated. Except in relation to specific case studies the concept of a socio-technical system remains largely an abstraction and is therefore of little value as a predictive tool in the study of industrial behaviour.

What was needed by the research workers at this point in the analysis was a natural history of industry, something in the nature of a botanist's "Flora" that they could use to identify in technological terms the firms they had studied. Without a precise instrument of this kind all that could be done was to group together on a rough and ready basis all the firms in which manufacturing processes and methods appeared to be similar. The first point of interest to emerge from this grouping was that Dubin's two phases of technology are closely related. It soon became obvious that firms with similar goals and associated manufacturing policies had similar manufacturing processes—the range of tools, instruments, machines, and technical formulas was limited and controlled by manufacturing policy. For example, a firm restricting itself to the manufacture of bespoke suits was not able to use the same advanced techniques of production as a firm making mass-produced men's clothing.

Indeed, the first important breakdown of the firms studied was between those where production was of the "one off" kind, to meet customers' individual requirements, and those where production

was standardized. Firms making products on a "one off" basis were further sub-divided according to the nature of these products. Some were simple from a technical point of view (like the bespoke suits referred to above); others were more complex—for example prototypes of electronic equipment. The size of the unit product was important too; large equipments such as radio transmitting stations had to be fabricated in stages, the manufacturing methods differing considerably from those used in the production of smaller prototypes.

Firms making standardized products could also be sub-divided; in some, production went on continuously, in others it was interrupted at more or less frequent intervals. Furthermore, whereas in some firms there was considerable diversity of products, in others there was relatively little flexibility in production facilities.

Another possible way of dividing firms was to differentiate between those making integral products and those making dimensional products measured by weight, capacity, or volume. Firms making integral products are sometimes referred to collectively as manufacturing industry, and firms making dimensional products as process industry. Dimensional products are normally manufactured in chemical plants. Here again, in analysing the data a distinction could be drawn between the multi-purpose plant in which production was intermittent and the single-purpose plant in which production was continuous, stopping only in the event of a breakdown or for a complete overhaul.

It soon became obvious to the research workers that there were so many variations in manufacturing methods that every situation which they examined was to some extent unique. Nevertheless, if an attempt was to be made to assess the effect of technology upon organization, some system would have to be devised for dividing the firms studied into sections and for classifying firms with technical characteristics in common within each section. It was felt that the system of division normally used by production engineers into the three categories of jobbing, batch, and mass production was inadequate for this purpose, as each of these headings covered a very broad field. On the other hand it had to be borne in mind that the research data related to a hundred firms only. Thus too many categories would

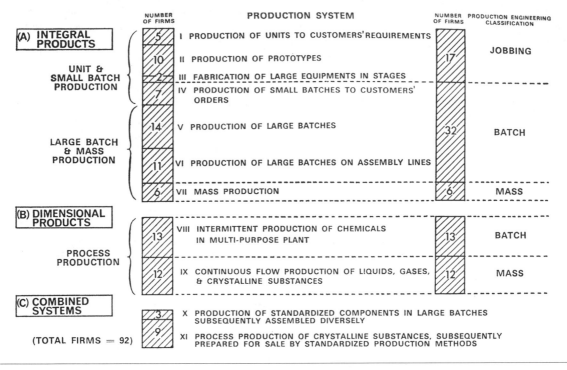

Figure 5.1. Production Systems in South Essex Industry

make the numbers in each too small to reveal trends or relationships.

In the final analysis, therefore, production systems were grouped into the eleven categories illustrated in Figure 5.1. It will be seen that in eighty firms a single system of production predominated, while in a further twelve, two systems were combined into one process of manufacture. These combinations were of two main kinds; one, agricultural engineering, for instance, consisted of the production of standard parts subsequently assembled into diverse products. The other, found in such industries as pharmaceutical chemical manufacture, combined the manufacture of a product in a plant with its subsequent preparation for sale by packaging. Dimensional products, measured by weight or volume, became integral products after further processing; a quantity of acetylsalicylic acid, for example, became a number of aspirin tablets.

Eight firms could not be fitted into any of the eleven categories: one was a Remploy factory operating under special conditions, another was concerned mainly with storage and servicing operations. In a further four production was extremely mixed, and the other two were in transition, radical technical changes bringing them out of one category into another.

PRODUCTION SYSTEMS AND SIZE

Having devised a system for classifying production systems, it was important to ensure that something more than merely reclassifying firms on a basis of size had been done; production systems were therefore related to size. As Figure 5.2 shows, however, there appeared to be no significant relationship; both large and small firms were found in each production category.

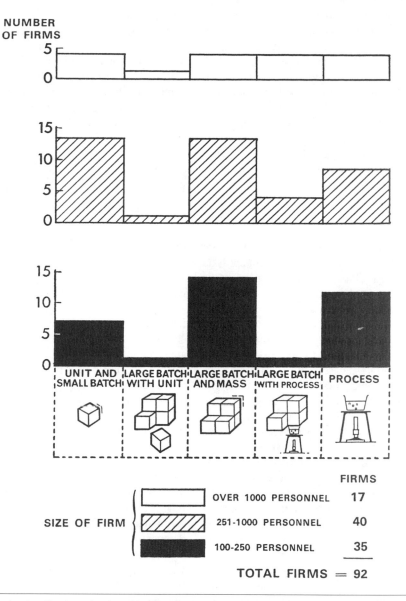

Figure 5.2.   Production Systems Analysed by Number Employed

Increasing Technical Complexity

It will be seen that the first nine systems of production given in Figure 5.1 form a scale; they are listed in order of chronological development, and technical complexity; the production of unit articles to customers' individual requirements being the oldest and simplest form of manufacture, and the continuous-flow production of dimensional products, the most advanced and most complicated. Moving along the scale from Systems I to IX, it becomes increasingly possible to exercise control over manufacturing operations, the physical limitations of production becoming better known and understood. Targets can be set and reached more effectively in continuous-flow production plants than they can in the most up-to-date and efficient batch production firms, and the factors likely to limit performance can be allowed for. [. . .] The difficulties of exercising effective control, particularly of prototype manufacture, are greatest in unit production. It is almost impossible to predict the results of development work either in terms of time or money.

In general it is also true to say that prediction and control are easier in the manufacture of dimensional production than in the manufacture of integral products.

[. . .] [T]he development of newer and more effective methods of manufacture does not necessarily mean that the older systems of production become outmoded. Each of the systems of production listed in Figure 5.1 has its own applications and limitations, and each is appropriate to the achievement of specific objectives. Continuous-flow production methods originally confined to the manufacture of liquids, gases, and crystalline substances are being increasingly introduced into the manufacture of solid shapes. Steel, paperboard, millboard, and some engineering parts are among the products concerned. But it is not easy to foresee their application to manufacture involving the assembly of large numbers of different components. Unit production, the simplest system, will continue as long as large items of equipment have to be fabricated and in industries where development proceeds at too rapid a rate to make standardization of products possible. Some firms also will probably continue to cater for individual idiosyncrasies.

Industrial administration theorists tend to be intolerant of individual idiosyncrasies. Urwick (1943)[3] says: "to allow the individual idiosyncrasies of a wide range of customers to drive administration away from the principles on which it can manufacture most economically is suicidal—the kind of good intention with which the road to hell or bankruptcy is proverbially paved." Standardization, specification, and simplification are the ideals on which modern manufacturing methods are based, and it is, of course, true that our increased standard of living depends upon standardized production. It is also true

that increases in the standard of living are likely to result in greater demands for goods manufactured to customers' individual requirements; more people will want and be able to afford such things as bespoke suits or gold-plated limousines. Thus the number of firms catering for individual idiosyncrasies is more likely to increase than decrease; unit production will probably be with us for many years to come.

4

TECHNOLOGY AND ORGANIZATION

ORGANIZATIONAL TRENDS

The next step in the survey was to relate the information about the way firms were organized and operated to the technical framework. This was done, and for the first time in the analysis patterns became discernible: firms with similar production systems appeared to have similar organizational structures. There were, of course, differences between some of the firms placed in the same production category, but the differences inside each category were not, on the whole, as marked as those between categories. The figures relating to the various organizational characteristics measured tended to cluster around medians, the medians varying from one category to another.

Therefore the main conclusion reached through this research project was that the existence of the link between technology and social structure first postulated by Thorstein Veblen (1904)[4] can be demonstrated empirically. It is not suggested that the research proved technology to be the only important variable in determining organizational structure, or that such factors as the history and background of a firm and the personalities of the people who built it up and subsequently managed it were unimportant. For example, the research workers soon became aware, going from firm to firm, that individual managers differed considerably in their willingness and ability to delegate responsibility for decision-making to their subordinates. Nevertheless, in spite of individual differences, there was more delegation and decentralization in process industry than in large batch and mass production industry.

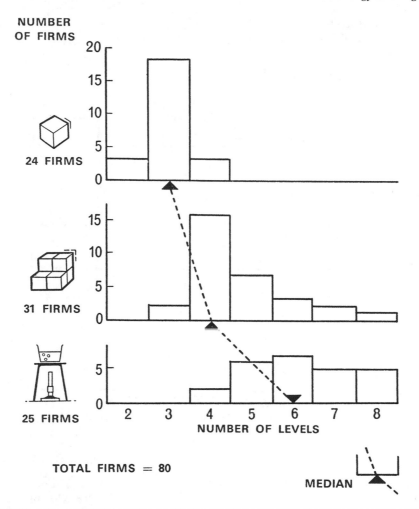

Figure 5.3. Levels of Management

Technology, although not the only variable affecting organization, was one that could be isolated for study without too much difficulty. The patterns which emerged in the analysis of the data indicated that there are prescribed and functional relationships between structure and technical demands. Trends in organization appeared to be associated with an increasing ability to predict results and to control the physical limitations of production. These trends were of two kinds, for whereas some organizational characteristics were directly and progressively related to the scale of technical advance formed by the first nine systems of production listed in Figure 5.1 others formed a different pattern; the production systems at each end of the scale resembled each other, while the greatest divergences were between the extremes and the middle ranges.

THE DIRECT RELATIONSHIP

Among the organizational characteristics showing a direct relationship with technical advance were: the

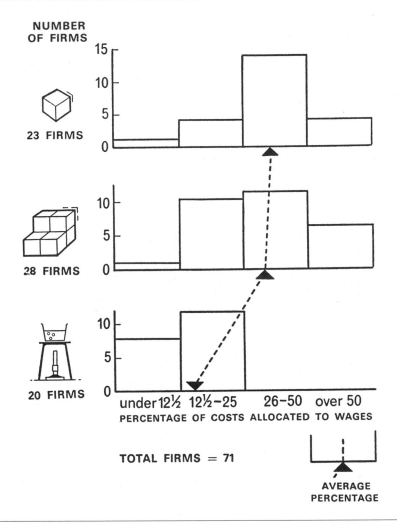

Figure 5.4.   Labour Costs

length of the line of command; [. . .] the percentage of total turnover allocated to the payment of wages and salaries, and the ratios of managers to total personnel, of clerical and administrative staff to manual workers, of direct to indirect labour, and of graduate to non-graduate supervision in production departments.

Figure 5.3 shows how the number of levels of management in direct production departments increased with technical advance, the longest lines being found in process industry. This diagram indicates clearly the way in which inside each production group statistics relating to organization tended to cluster around the median.

[. . .]

As already pointed out, the variations in the number of levels of management made it difficult to compare the size of the spans of control at the intermediate levels in detail. The figures that were obtained, however, suggested that these too varied with the degree of technical complexity. In direct contrast to the span of control of the chief executive, which grew larger with technical advance, spans of control at middle management levels grew smaller.

Table 5.1 Ratios of Managers and Supervisory Staff to Total Personnel in Selected Firms (analysed by technology)

Production system	Total number employed	Number of managerial and supervisory personnel	Number of non-supervisory personnel	Ratio
Unit and small batch				
Firm 1	455	20	435	1:22
" 2	948	25	923	1:37
" 3	4,550	175	4,325	1:25
Large batch and mass				
Firm 4	432	30	422	1:14
" 5	975	60	915	1:15
" 6	3,519	180	3,329	1:18
Process				
Firm 7	498	55	443	1:8
" 8	888	110	778	1:7
" 9	3,010	375	2,635	1:7

The small spans of control and the long lines of command characteristic of process industry meant that in this type of industry management structure could be represented by a long and narrowly based pyramid. In unit production the pyramid was short and broadly based.

As Figure 5.4 shows, the proportion of total turnover allocated to the payment of wages, salaries, and related expenditure was another characteristic varying with the type of production, the proportion becoming smaller with technical advance.

It can be seen from Figure 5.4 that the biggest difference in labour costs was between firms making integral products and firms making dimensional products. In firms making integral products, the decrease in labour costs associated with increasing technical complexity was relatively small. Labour costs in unit production firms tended to be largely development costs, whereas in large batch production they tended to be production costs. Moreover inside each production category the range was wide, the percentage distribution of costs being affected by a number of variables, the most important of which was the price of the raw materials used. The firms in the process production categories not only had very much lower labour costs, but were also more homogeneous as far as their cost structure was concerned. [. . .]

It was interesting to find that the ten firms in which labour costs were less than 12½ per cent of total turnover spent the greatest amount per head on employee welfare and services. There was also a tendency for firms in which labour costs were low to spend more money on the employment of specialists in the personnel management and human relations fields. Of the ten low labour cost firms, seven had high-status personnel departments covering all the accepted functions of personnel management, and a further two had welfare departments with more limited status and functions. Four of these nine firms employed fewer than 250 people. The obvious explanation was that firms in which labour costs were low and which were not so concerned with labour economies could afford the more highly paid specialists that function in the personnel management field. Industrial relations certainly seemed to be better in process industry than in large batch and mass production, but it is not safe to assume that the good relationships were due to the large number of specialist staff employed. As will be seen later, there were a number of contributory factors: less tension and pressure, smaller working groups, and smaller spans of control, for instance. In fact the firms that could afford these specialists may have needed them least.

There was also a link between a firm's technology and the relative size of its management group, the ratio of managers and supervisors to non-supervisory personnel increasing with technical advance. The [. . .] firms [. . .] having one

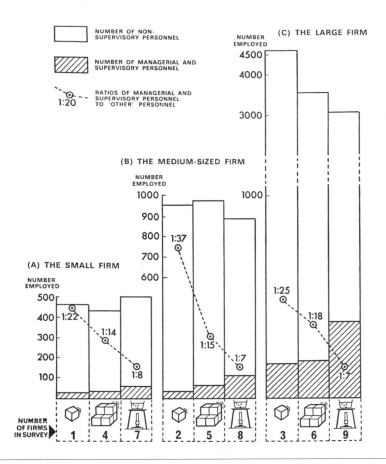

Figure 5.5. Ratio of Managers and Supervisory Staff to Total Personnel in Selected Firms (analysed by size)

supervisor to between five and nine non-supervisory personnel were all process production firms. On average in this type of industry the ratio was 1:8, whereas in large batch and mass production it was 1:16, and in unit and small batch production 1:23.

In Table 5.1 (see Figure 5.5) the numbers are given for three firms in each main production group, these firms having been selected as representative of small, medium, and large firms respectively.

Not only were there relatively more managers and supervisors in process industry but they were also better qualified; the degree of technical complexity being related to the number of graduates employed on production management. [. . .] [T]wenty process firms employed graduates on line

management, whereas only two unit production firms and one mass production firm did so.

Moreover, twelve of the fifteen firms operating regular and systematic management training courses were process firms; so were twenty of the thirty firms whose policy was to fill managerial posts almost exclusively by promotion from within. Most of the process production firms studied seemed to take in a group of graduate trainees each year and then promote from this group.

[. . .] [T]here were seven unit and small batch production firms and four mass and large batch production firms in which all the graduates employed were in staff departments. The majority were concerned with research and development or inspection functions, and their firms were those whose products themselves, rather than the methods of manufacturing, were technically complex.

[. . .] The clerical and administrative group, like the management and supervisory group, grows larger with technical advance. In the unit and small batch system of production, however, the range is wider than in the other systems. This is because the different types of unit production varied considerably; the firms making technically complex products, both prototypes or large equipments, had a higher ratio of clerical and administrative staff to hourly-paid than those making simple products to customers' individual requirements, either as unit articles or in small batches.

[. . .] [T]he ratio of indirect workers to direct workers gets larger with technical advance. It is process industry that employs a majority of indirect workers, many of whom are responsible for the maintenance of plant and machinery.

SIMILARITIES AT THE EXTREMES

Turning now to the figures that rose to a peak in the middle of the technical scale, the first discernible trend of this kind related to the size of the span of control of the first-line supervisors in production departments. Figure 5.6 shows the average number of hourly-paid workers controlled by first-line supervisors in the different systems of production, the highest averages being in the large batch and mass production firms. Figure 5.7 gives the averages for individual firms and shows clearly the similarity between the extremes of the technical scale.

The small spans of control in unit production and process production were an indication of the breakdown of the labour force into small primary working groups. As a result, the relationship between the group and its immediate superior was more intimate and informal in these types of production than in the large batch and mass production firms studied; this was probably a contributory factor to better industrial relations.

Another resemblance between unit production and process production was that it employed a large number of skilled workers in comparison with large batch and mass production; there were nineteen firms in which skilled workers outnumbered

semi-skilled workers, nine of them being unit production firms and ten process production firms. In all the large batch and mass production firms, the skilled workers were the smallest group. The skilled workers employed in unit production firms were concerned directly with production, the more mechanical parts of their job being delegated to semi-skilled workers, while unskilled workers serviced the craftsmen and fetched and carried for them. Occupational status was linked not only with numerical superiority and high pay, but also with a close identification with the immediate production objective. All the elements of skill, conceptual and perceptual, as well as the manual and motor, were brought together in the work of the craftsmen.

In the large batch and mass production firms studied, the semi-skilled workers not only outnumbered the craftsmen but were also the people actually responsible for production, the skilled men being in the main the indirect labour responsible for the maintenance of tools and plant. The unskilled workers did very much the same kind of job as they did in unit production, except that they were concerned more with the servicing of sections or departments than individuals. Standardized production and all that it implied had taken the perceptual and conceptual elements of skill out of the main production task, although much of the work still required a fair degree of motor skill and manual dexterity. In most of the large batch and mass production firms studied, the patterns of behaviour were no longer determined by the skilled men. Moreover, in the firms which ran incentive schemes, their earnings were hardly higher than those of the semi-skilled production workers.

[. . .]

In process production, although the organization of work was basically the same as in large batch and mass production, the skilled men were the indirect labour force responsible for the servicing and maintenance of plant. The maintenance function was of great importance, the maintenance department being the largest single department in most firms. Thus the skilled men were able to influence the situation more than their counterparts in mass production, and were in a more dominant position.

The main problem in this type of industry appeared to be establishing the occupational status

Technology and Organization

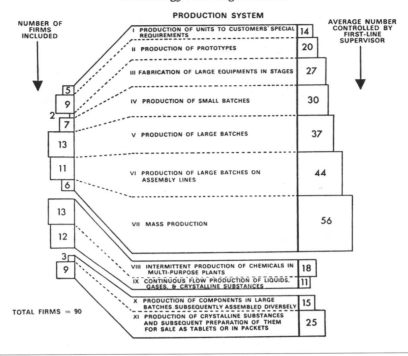

Figure 5.6.   Average Number Controlled by First-Line Supervisors in the Different Systems of Production

of the plant operators; these men, although often highly skilled, were not formally recognized as skilled outside their own firm. The traditional differentiation between the skilled and the semi-skilled worker does not allow for a situation in which the manual and motor elements of skill have been taken out of the main production task, while the conceptual and perceptual elements remain.

The skill of a plant operator is of the perceptual and conceptual kind in that over a period of time he has to learn to absorb a great deal of information and to act on it continuously. But, this skill not being recognized formally, the plant operator has to be recruited as a semi-skilled worker at a comparatively low rate of pay. Several firms felt that this created difficulties for them, as in the competitive labour situation of the area it was very difficult to find and keep men of sufficiently high calibre at this low figure. A job in which the emphasis is laid more on the intellectual elements of skill, and which calls for articulation in both speech

and writing, can attract only those with the minimum educational qualifications.

Firms at the top and bottom of the technical scale resembled each other in a number of ways, not so easy to illustrate by reference to figures. First, there was a tendency for organic management systems to predominate in the production categories at the extremes of the technical scale, while mechanistic systems predominated in the middle ranges. Clear-cut definition of duties and responsibilities was characteristic of firms in the middle ranges, while flexible organization with a high degree of delegation both of authority and of the responsibility for decision-making, and with permissive and participating management, was characteristic of firms at the extremes. There was less "organization consciousness" at the extremes; it was the firms in the middle ranges which found it easier to produce organization charts.

The second trend was for the line-staff type of organization to be more highly developed in the

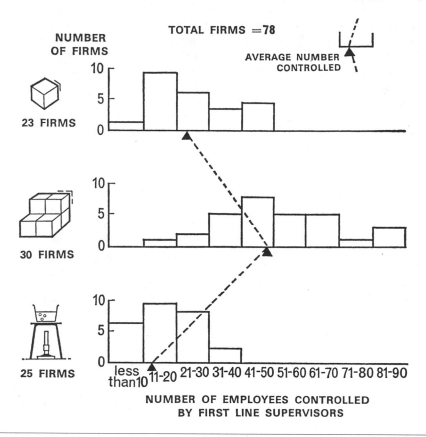

Figure 5.7.   Size of the Span of Control of First-Line Supervisors in Three Main Types of Production

middle ranges of the scale. The two firms in which there was functional organization and fifteen of the firms in which line organization predominated were process production firms. The other line organization firms were in the unit production categories.

In unit production firms, where relatively few specialists were employed inside production departments, the line supervisors themselves had to be technically competent. Their technical competence was, in most cases, of the kind acquired by long practical experience, and was based on "know-how" rather than professional training. It was interesting to find that in this type of production, supervisors and managers were on average about ten years older than their counterparts elsewhere.

In each of the three firms in which unit production had recently been superseded by standardized

production of parts and subsequent diverse assembly, the number of specialists employed had increased by about 25 per cent as a result of the reorganization.

Firms in the large batch production categories employed the largest number of specialists. In many cases the managerial and supervisory group broke down into two distinct sub-groups, general managers comprising one and specialists the other; these sub-groups had differing and sometimes conflicting objectives and ideologies. In these firms too there was the most rigid application of line-staff organization. On paper, at least, there was a clear-cut distinction between executive and advisory responsibility. On the organization charts some positions were linked with continuous lines and others with dotted lines, indicating line and staff roles respectively.

In process industry, it was extremely difficult to distinguish between executive and advisory responsibility. Not only was organization more flexible but in many cases it was also changing. The tendency seemed to be for firms to move away from the line-staff type of organization towards either functional or predominantly line organization. In some firms the line of command seemed to be disintegrating, executive responsibility being conferred on specialist staff. Eight of the twelve firms in which the status and prestige of the specialists were so high that it was impossible, in practice, to distinguish between advice, service, and control on the one hand, and executive responsibility on the other, were process production firms. In the other process production firms, specialist skills and knowledge were being increasingly incorporated in the line. In these firms, as in the unit production firms studied, stress was laid on the importance of the line managers being technically competent. Here, of course, the technical competence required was of a different kind; it was intellectual rather than intuitive and based on qualifications and knowledge rather than on long experience and "know-how." In comparison with the managers in unit production, those employed in process production were young. In one process production firm a hundred of the hundred and twenty managers and supervisors were under thirty-five.

It was interesting to find that two oil refineries, approximately equal in size and situated in the same area, were moving away from line-staff organization in opposite directions. In one, specialist skills were being incorporated into the line, line management being technically competent and of high status. In the other the line managers had limited status and were not professionally qualified, their functions being no more than the routine supervision of production operations. They worked alongside highly trained specialist staff who, although nominally advisory, did in effect make executive decisions.

Even in those process production firms with an organizational pattern of the line-staff type there was not the same dichotomy between general managers and specialists as in large batch and mass production firms. There were no clear-cut distinctions between the objectives and ideologies of the two kinds of management. The main reason for this seemed to be that in most of these firms line managers and specialists were interchangeable. Firms tended to recognize "specialisms" rather than specialists: the laboratory chemist of today could become the line manager of tomorrow. In some cases this interchangeability extended as far as the personnel management staff. A number of the personnel managers and officers in the process production firms included in the survey were scientists and engineers with general management experience, who expected to return to general management after a period in the personnel department.

Another distinction that was most clear-cut in the middle of the technical scale was that between production administration and the supervision of production operations. It was here too that production control procedures were most elaborate and sanctions most rigorously applied. At the bottom of the technical scale the difficulties of controlling production and predicting results appeared to be so great that few firms were prepared to attempt the task. On the other hand, the exercise of control in process production firms was such a relatively simple matter that conflict or stress was rarely associated with it; in many cases the mechanism for exercising control was built into the manufacturing processes themselves.

It would not be true to say that all the firms in the middle ranges of the scale had introduced equally elaborate production control procedures. Some of them still seemed to rely almost entirely on the clinical judgements of their line supervision. This meant that there was greater variation in the way in which production operations were planned and controlled between firms in the middle ranges of the scale than between firms at the extremes.

A similar pattern emerged in relation to communication methods. As might have been expected, the production control procedures in operation in the middle ranges of the scale gave rise to a considerable amount of paper work. Even allowing for this, however, it was interesting to find that in firms at the extremes of the scale communications between managers and departments tended to be verbal, while in the middle ranges they tended to be written. The amount of paper work—inter-departmental memoranda, operating instructions, and policy directives—increased as technology advanced, reaching a peak in assembly-line production firms.

As technology advanced beyond this point, however, the amount of paper work began to decrease, and in process production, communications were almost entirely verbal again.

The research workers got the impression that this tendency to communicate in writing in the middle ranges of the scale was linked with the pressures and stresses arising from batch production. The reduction in the area of discretion of line supervision, and the conflicts that arose between them and the specialist personnel encouraged them to safeguard themselves by communicating in writing. They felt it necessary to be able to produce copies of the memoranda they had sent to other managers so that they could clear themselves in the event of a dispute. Life in firms in the middle ranges of the technical scale was therefore less pleasant and easygoing than in firms at the extremes. The research workers themselves soon became aware of this, for they found that it was easier and less arduous to obtain information in unit production and process production firms than in large batch and mass production firms.

NOTES

1. Mary Parker Follett in Papers on Dynamic Administration, given at the annual conference of the American Bureau of Personnel Administration 1924–8. The majority of these reports are reproduced in a memorial volume entitled Dynamic Administration edited by Henry Metcalfe, and L. Urwick (Management Publication Trusts Ltd., West Willow and Harper Bros., New York).

2. Robert Dubin, "Working Union-Management Relations," The Sociology of Industrial Relations (Prentice Hall, Englewood Cliffs, N.J.).

3. L. Urwick, Elements of Administration (Pitman, London).

4. Thorstein Veblen, The Theory of Business Enterprise (Scribner).

6

THE MEASUREMENT OF ORGANIZATION STRUCTURES

D. S. PUGH

DOES CONTEXT DETERMINE FORM?

This article will give some answers, admittedly partial and preliminary, to the following questions: Are there any general principles of organization structure to which all organizations should adhere? Or does the context of the organization—its size, ownership, geographical location, technology of manufacture—determine what structure is appropriate? Last, how much leeway does the management of a company have to design the organization initially and tamper with it later on? Obviously, the questions are interdependent. If the context of the organization is crucial to determining the suitable structure, then management operates within fairly rigid constraints; it can either recognize the structure predetermined by the context and make its decisions accordingly or it can fail to recognize the structure

indicated by the context, make the wrong decisions, and impair the effectiveness or even the survival of the organization. This assumes, of course, that management retains the latitude to make the wrong decisions on structure.

Even more obviously, these questions are difficult to answer. Let's begin with the fact that systematic and reliable information on organizational structure is scarce. We have a plethora of formal organization charts that conceal as much as they reveal and a quantity of unsynthesized case material. What we need is a precise formulation of the characteristics of organization structure and the development of measuring scales with which to assess differences quantitatively.

We do know something about the decisions that top managers face on organizations. For example, should authority be centralized? Centralization may help maintain a consistent policy, but it may also inhibit initiative lower down the hierarchy. Again, should managerial tasks be highly specialized? The technical complexity of business life means that considerable advantages can accrue from allowing people to specialize in a limited field. On the other hand, these advantages maybe achieved at the expense of their commitment to the overall objectives of the company.

Should a company lay down a large number of standard rules and procedures for employees to follow? These may ensure a certain uniformity of performance, but they may also produce frustration—and a tendency to hide behind the rules. Should the organization structure be "tall" or "flat"? Flat structures—with relatively few hierarchical levels—allow communications to pass easily up and down, but managers may become overloaded with too many direct subordinates. Tall structures allow managers to devote more time to subordinates, but may well overextend lines of command, and distort communications.

All these choices involve benefits and costs. It also seems reasonable to suppose that the extent and importance of the costs and benefits will vary according to the situation of the company. All too often in the past these issues have been debated dogmatically in an "either/or" fashion, without reference to size, technology, product range, market conditions, or corporate objectives. Operationally, the important question is: In what *degree* should organizational characteristics such as those above be present in different types of companies? To answer this question there must obviously be accurate comparative measures of centralization of authority, specialization of task, standardization of procedure, and so on, to set beside measurements of size, technology, ownership, business environment, and level of performance. A program of research aimed at identifying just such measurements—of organization structure, operating context, and performance—was inaugurated in the Industrial Administration Research Unit of the University of Aston a number of years ago, and continues in the Organizational Behaviour Research Group at the London Business School and elsewhere. The object of the research is threefold:

(a) To discover in what ways an organization structures its activities,

(b) To see whether or not it is possible to create statistically valid and reliable methods of measuring structural differences between organizations,

(c) To examine what constraints the organization's context (i.e., its size, technology of manufacture, diffusion of ownership, etc.) imposes on the management structure.

Formal Analysis of Organization Structure

Measurement must begin with the ideas on what characteristics should be measured. In the field of organization structure the problem is not the absence of such ideas to distill from the academic discourse, but rather variables that can be clearly defined for scientific study.

From the literature we have selected six primary variables or dimensions of organization structure:

Specialization—the degree to which an organization's activities are divided into specialized roles.

Standardization—the degree to which an organization lays down standard rules and procedures.

Standardization of employment practices—the degree to which an organization has standardized employment practices.

Formalization—the degree to which instructions, procedures, etc., are written down.

Centralization—the degree to which the authority to make certain decisions is located at the top of the management hierarchy.

Configuration—the "shape" of the organization's role structure, e.g., whether the management chain of command is long or short, whether superiors have limited span of control—relatively few subordinates—or broad span of control—a relatively large number of subordinates, and whether there is a large or small percentage of specialized or support personnel. Configuration is a blanket term used to cover all three variables.

[. . .]

In our surveys, we have limited ourselves to work organizations employing more than 150 people—a work organization being analyzed as one that employs (that is, pays) its members. We constructed scales from data on a first sample of fifty-two such organizations, including firms making motor car bumpers and milk chocolate buttons, municipal organizations that repaired roads or taught arithmetic, large department stores, and small insurance companies, and so on. Several further samples duplicated the original investigation and increased the number of organizations to over two hundred.

Our problem was how to apply our six dimensions—how to go beyond individual experience and scholarship to the systematic study of existing organizations. We decided to use scales in measuring the six dimensions of any organizations—so that the positions of a particular organization on those scales form a profile of the organization.

Our approach to developing comparative scales also was guided by the need to demonstrate that the items forming a scale "hang together," that is, they are in some sense cumulative. We can represent an organization's comparative position on a characteristic by a numerical score, in the same way as an I.Q. score represents an individual's comparative intelligence. But just as an I.Q. is a sample of a person's intelligence taken for comparative purposes and does not detract from his uniqueness as a functioning individual, so our scales, being likewise comparative samples, do not detract from the uniqueness of each organization's functioning. They do, however, indicate limits within which the unique variations take place.

We began by interviewing at length the chief executive of the organization, who may be a works manager, an area superintendent, or a chairman. Then followed a series if interviews with department heads of varying status, as many as were necessary to obtain the information required. Interviews were conducted with standard schedules listing what has to be found out.

We were concerned with making sure that variables concerned both manufacturing and nonmanufacturing organizations. Therefore we asked each organization, for example, for which of a given list of

potentially standardized routines it had standardized procedure. (See Figure 6.1 for sample questions in the six dimensions.)

On the other hand, because this was descriptive data about structure, and was personal to the respondent, we made no attempt to standardize the interview procedures themselves. At the same time, we tried to obtain documentary evidence to substantiate the verbal descriptions.

Analysis of Six Structural Profiles

For purposes of discussion we have selected six organizations and have constructed the structural profiles for each one. Two are governmental organizations. The other four are in the private sector of the economy but the nature of the ownership varies drastically—one is family owned; another is owned jointly by a family and its employees; the third is a subsidiary of a large publicly owned company; the fourth is a medium-size publicly held company. The number of employees also varies widely from 16,500 in the municipal organization to only 1,700 in the manufacturing organization owned by the central government. We selected these six from the many available in order to demonstrate the sort of distinctive profiles we get for particular organizations and to underscore the way in which we can make useful comparisons about organizations on this basis.

With all this diversity, it is not too surprising that no two profiles look alike. What is surprising, and deserves further comment, are the similarities in several of the six dimensions between several of the six organizations (see Figure 6.2 below).

Organization A is a municipal department responsible for a public service. But it is far from being the classic form of bureaucracy described by Weber. By definition, such a bureaucracy would have an extremely high-score pattern on all our scales. That is, it would be highly specialized with many narrowly defined specialist "officers," highly standardized in its procedures, and highly formalized, with documents prescribing all activities and recording them in the files as precedents. If everything has to be referred upward for decision, then it would also score as highly centralized. In configuration it would have a high proportion of "supportive"

Specialization

1. Are the following activities performed by specialists—i.e., those exclusively engaged in the activities and not in the line chain of authority?

   a. activities to develop, legitimize, and symbolize the organizational purpose (e.g., public relations, advertising).
   b. activities to dispose of, distribute, and service the output (e.g., sales, service).
   c. activities to obtain and control materials and equipment (e.g., buying, stock control).
   d. activities to devise new outputs, equipment, processes (e.g., R&D, development).
   e. activities to develop and transform human resources (e.g., training, education).
   f. activities to acquire information on the operational field (e.g., market research).

2. What professional qualifications do these specialists hold?

Standardization

1. How closely defined is a typical operative's task (e.g., custom, apprenticeship, rate fixing, work study)?
2. Are there specific procedures to ensure the perpetuation of the organization (e.g., R&D programs, systematic market research)?
3. How detailed is the marketing policy (e.g., general aims only, specific policy worked out and adhered to)?
4. How detailed are the costing and stock control systems (e.g., stock taking: yearly, monthly, etc,; costing: historical job costing, budgeting, standard cost system)?

Standardization of Employment Practices

1. Is there a central recruiting and interviewing procedure?
2. Is there a standard selection procedure for foremen and managers?
3. Is there a standard discipline procedure with set offenses and penalties?

Formalization

1. Is there an employee handbook or rulebook?
2. Is there an organization chart?
3. Are there any written terms of reference or job descriptions? For which grades of employee?
4. Are there agenda and minutes for workflow (e.g., production) meetings?

Centralization

Which level in the hierarchy has the authority to
   a. decide which supplies of materials are to be used?
   b. decide the price of the output?
   c. alter the responsibilities or areas of work of departments?
   d. decide marketing territories to be covered?

Configuration

1. What is the chief executive's span of control?
2. What is the average number of direct workers per first-line supervisor?
3. What is the percentage of indirect personnel (i.e., employees with no direct or supervisory responsibility for work on the output)?
4. What is the percentage of employees in each functional specialism (e.g., sales and service, design and development, market research)?

Figure 6.1. Sample Questions in Six Dimensions

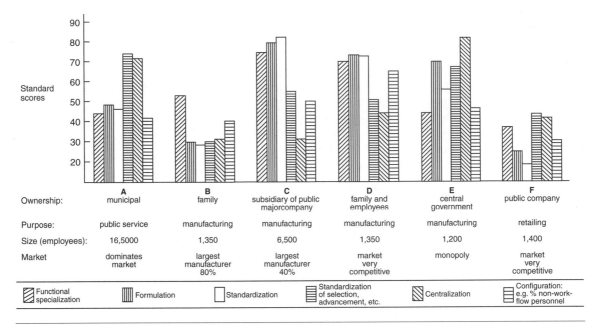

Figure 6.2. Structural Profiles of Six Organizations

or administrative or "non-workflow" personnel. But clearly this example does not fit this pattern completely; it is below standard in both specialization and configuration, which demonstrates the effectiveness of this method of determining empirically what profile actually exists in overcoming stereotyped thinking.

Organization B represents a relatively unstructured family firm, relying more on traditional ways of doing things. Although it has the specialities usual in manufacturing industry (and hence a comparatively high specialization score) it has minimized standardized procedure and formalized paperwork.

Organization C represents "big business." It is the subsidiary of a very large company, and its profile shows the effects of size: generally, very high scores on specialization, standardization, and formalization, but decentralized. The distinctively different relationship of centralization is typical. Centralization correlates *negatively* with almost all other structural scales. The more specialized, standardized, and formalized the organization, the *less* it

is centralized, or to put it the other way around, the more it is decentralized. Therefore these scales do not confirm the common assumption that a large organization and the routines that go with them "pass the buck" upward for decision with elaborate staff offices; in fact, such an organization is relatively decentralized.

But it is not only a question of size, as the profile of Organization D shows. It has the same number of employees as Organization B, yet its structure is in striking contrast and is more nearly that of a much larger firm. Clearly the policies and attitudes of the management of an organization may have a considerable effect on its structure, even though factors like size, technology, and form of ownership set the framework within which the management must function.

Organization E is an example of a manufacturing unit owned by the government and is characterized by a high centralization and a high formalization score. Comparison of the profiles of D and E brings home the fact that two organizations may be "bureaucratic" but in quite different ways.

Organization F is included as an example of the relatively low scores often found in retailing.

[. . .]

Analysis of Organizational Context

Once we have measured organization structure, the question arises, "Do organizations of different size have different kinds of structure?" Similarly, organizations can range from being technologically very advanced to being very simple, or from being owned and controlled by one man to being owned by many people and controlled (i.e., actually run) by none of them. Clearly we must employ as much vigor in measuring the non-structural or contextual aspects of organizations as we did in measuring the structural factors. To guide the measuring, we have identified the principal dimensions of context as follows:

Origin and History—whether an organization was privately founded, and the kinds or changes in ownership, location, etc. it has experienced.

Ownership and Control—the kind of ownership (e.g. private or public) and its concentration in a few hands or dispersion into many.

Size—number of employees, net assets, market position, etc.*Charter*—the nature and range of goods and services.

Technology—the degree of integration achieved in an organization's work process.

Location—the number of geographically dispersed operating sites.

Interdependence—the extent to which an organization depends on customers, suppliers, trade unions, any owning groups, etc. Figure 6.3 lists some examples of the information that was obtained.

Exploring Structure and Context

Now it has become possible to explore in a wide range of diverse work organizations the relationship between structural and contextual characteristics. How far, for example, is specialization a function of size? Note that the question is not "Is specialization a result of large size or is it not?" Now we are in a position to rephrase the question: *To what extent* is

size associated with specialization? The correlation between size and overall role specialization in the first sample was 0.75—thus size is the most important single element. But what part do other factors play? The correlation of "Workflow Integration"—a scale that has been developed for measuring comparative technology (see Figure 6.3)—and overall specialization was 0.38. This is not very large in itself, but since there is no relationship between size and technology (correlation of 0.08), we should expect an analysis using both dimensions to produce a higher relationship than size alone. This is in fact what happens, and the multiple correlation of size with technology and specialization is 0.81. Thus knowing an organization's score on our scales of size *and* technology, we can predict to within relatively close limits what its specialization score will be. Likewise, knowing an organization's dependence on other organizations and its geographical dispersion over sites tells a great deal about the likely centralization of authority in its structure (multiple correlation of 0.75).

These relationships of context and structure we have found to be reasonably stable in surveys of different samples. Where differences in the relationships have been found they have been easily related to the varying characteristics of the samples studied. In general, the framework has been adequate for thinking about the degree of constraint that contextual factors place on the design of organizational structures. The degree of constraint appears to be substantial (about 50 percent of the variability between structures may be directly related to contextual features such as size, technology, interdependence, etc.) but it allows considerable opportunities for choice and variation in particular organizations based on the attitudes and views of the top management.

In other words, context is a determining factor—perhaps overall the determining factor—designing, shaping, and modifying the structure of any organization. But within these contextual limits, top management has plenty of leeway left to make its influence felt—50 percent is a major margin of freedom. With this approach, we can discuss a number of basic issues of organizational design, such as those indicated at the beginning of this article. And

Workflow integration

A highly workflow-integrated technology is signified by:

1. Automatic repeat-cycle equipment, self-adjusting.
2. Single-purpose equipment.
3. Fixed "line" or sequence of operations.
4. Single input point at commencement of "line."
5. No waiting time between operations.
6. No "buffer stocks" between operations.
7. Breakdown anywhere stops workflow immediately.
8. Outputs of workflow (production) segments/departments become inputs of others, i.e., flow from department to department throughout.
9. Operations evaluated by measurement techniques against precise specifications.

A technology low in workflow integration is at the opposite extremes on these items.

Vertical integration (components scale of dependence)

1. Integration with suppliers: ownership and tied supply/long contracts/single orders.
2. Sensitivity of outputs volume to customer influence: outputs for schedule and call off/order/stock.
3. Integration with customers: ownership and tied market/long-term contracts/regular contracts/single orders.
4. Dependence of organization on its largest customer: sole/major/medium/minor outlet.
5. Dependence of largest customer on organization: sole/major/medium/minor supplier.

Dependence

1. Status of organizational unit: branch/head branch/legal subsidiary/principal unit.
2. Unit size as a percentage of parent-group size.
3. Representation on policy-making boards.
4. Number of specialist services contracted out.
5. Vertical integration.

Figure 6.3.   Some Contextual Scales

we can conduct the discussion on the basis of a number of comparative empirical findings—which inevitably underline the range of variation possible—rather than merely on individual views and experiences—which inevitably tend to dogmatic overgeneralization.

The Effects of Technology on Organizations

Does technology determine organization? Is the form of organization in a chemical plant, for instance, dictated by the fact that it is a chemical plant—that is, by its highly automated equipment and continuous flow process? And is the organization of a batch production engineering factory shaped by the way its work is done—that is, by its rows of machine tools and its varying batches?

This is a contentious question. It also asks how far the number of levels of management, the centralization of major decisions, the proliferation of standard procedures, the development of specialist "service" sections, and the many other features of the structure of an organization depend on its technology.

In a study that has had considerable impact both on management and behavioral science writers, Joan Woodward in *Management and Technology* maintains that "It was possible to trace a cause and effect relationship between a system of production and its associated organizational pattern and, as a result, to predict what the organizational requirements of a firm are likely to be, given its production system."

Woodward took this view as a result of comparing as many as 80 firms on a unit and small batch, large batch and mass, and flow process classification. She found, for example, that the line of command from the chief executive of each firm was shortest in unit and small batch firms, lengthened in large batch and mass, and was longest in process firms. Another example of this relationship was the ratio of managers to total personnel, which also increased from unit up to process technology.

In contrast, it appeared that the spans of control of the first-line production supervisors were widest in large batch and mass production (average 46), but dropped away in unit and small batch on the one side (to average 22) and in process industries to an average of 14. Other suggested examples of this pattern were clear definition of duties and amount of paperwork, which were also greatest in large batch/mass technology.

Woodward's study immediately raised the question of whether it was possible to develop general management principles of organization, as advocated by such writers as Fayol, Urwick, Gulick, and Brown. Woodward maintained that this was now no longer possible. The principles that they had advocated—such as the necessity of clear lines of authority and responsibility (one man, one boss, etc.) and limited spans of control for effective supervision—might well apply in large batch and mass production forms, for they rested primarily on the experience of managers and consultants in this range of technology. But outside this range, in unit/jobbing and process technologies, different principles probably would be required.

The studies that we have carried out include replications of the Woodward work, since technology is one of a range of contextual factors that we examined. Equipped with a much more comprehensive analysis of organization structure than Woodward we can explore much more systematically what the *relative* effects of technology are on organization structure.

In addition to using Woodward's categories, the present research program also developed a measure of technology based on the items in Figure 6.3 and labeled "Workflow Integration." This discriminates among organizations on the basis of the rigidity or flexibility of the sequence of operations carried out by the equipment on the work. This has affinities with the Woodward classification but is not equivalent to it. Thus it was possible to examine the relationships of these two measures with the dimensions of organization structure.

Did the organizations with the most process-oriented technologies have the largest scores on specialization of management roles, standardization of procedures, etc.? In the first study, taking manufacturing organizations only, a correlation of 0.52 was found between Woodward technology and standardization. This would suggest considerable support for the proposition that the technology of manufacture has considerable bearing on the management structure. But the advantage of a survey that takes a range of factors into account becomes immediately apparent when we consider the relationship of other factors. The correlation of size with specialization is 0.83, and with standardization it is 0.65, both of which are considerably higher than the technology relationships. When we recall that size and technology are correlated among manufacturing organizations, and the effects of size are discounted by the technique known as partial correlation, then the remaining relationships of technology to structure are slight indeed (0.26 with specialization, 0.07 with standardization). In general, our studies have confirmed that the relationship of technology to the main structural dimensions in manufacturing organizations are always very small and play a secondary role relative to other contextual features such as size and interdependence with other organizations (such as owning group, customers, suppliers, etc.).

Where technology is shown to be related to manufacturing organization structures is in a number of highly specific jobs ratios that we consider under the heading of "configuration" (see Figure 6.1).

The ratio of subordinates to first-line supervisors is the only point at which the Woodward results and the present results agree exactly. Supervisors have most subordinates in large batch/mass production. This is where each foreman often has forty or fifty workers turning out large quantities of standard items, whereas in jobbing or in process plants he has a smaller group.

Hence the proportion of employees in inspection work and in maintenance work is also greatest at the large batch stage, and lower in both unit production and processing.

The proportions in production control are highest from unit or jobbing to the mass stage, dropping away in process technologies where production control is built into the processes themselves and does not require the clerical and progress-chasing effort imposed by complex assemblies.

The detailed examination of these features is interesting, but it is of much less consequence than their implications taken as a whole. What is distinctive about them, as against the range of organizational characteristics not related to technology?

The first-mentioned characteristic, ratio of subordinates to first-line supervisors, is an element of organization at the level of the operative and his immediate boss. Obviously, the number of men a supervisor requires to run a row of lathes differs from the number he requires to run the more continuous integrated workflow of an automatic transfer machine. Thus, subordinate/supervisor ratio is an aspect of organization that reflects activities directly bound up with the technology itself. Also, it is the variety of equipment and products in batch production that demands larger numbers of inspectors and of maintenance personnel; unit and process technologies are less demanding in this respect. It is the complexity of technology both in variety of equipment and in sequences of operations that requires relatively large numbers of production control personnel outside the more automatic process-type technologies.

The point is made more clearly by the contrast with, say, activities such as accounting or market research that are not directly implicated in the work technology itself—where research results show no connection with the technological factors.

[...]

So among the extensive range of organizational features studied, only those directly centered on the production workflow itself show any connection with technology; these are all "job-counts" of employees on production-linked activities. Away from the shop floor, technology appears to have little influence on organization structure.

Further Developments

Our on-going research program is exploring new areas. For example, what changes in organization structure take place over time? In one small study that we have already undertaken, 14 organizations were restudied after a period of four to five years. The organizations were all manufacturing firms. [...] There was an overall decrease in size of 5 to 10 percent, as measured by number of employees, but the other contextual features remained constant. In spite of this stability there was a clear tendency for structuring scores to increase (more specialization, standardization, formalization), but with a decrease in centralization. If within certain limits—imposed by the organization's context—top management may be able to accentuate one of two broad strategies of control, *either* to retain most decision making at the top and put up with wider spans of control *or* to delegate decisions to lower-level specialists and rely on procedures and forms to maintain control, then on this evidence they are consistently choosing the second alternative, at least in manufacturing.

Clearly, more evidence is required before the significance of this trend can be evaluated. And evidence is also required on the *processes* by which organization structures get changed. What are the interdepartmental power struggles, the interpersonal conflicts, the pressures for and resistance to proposed changes that make up the evolving structure as it responds to changes in the organization's context? Studies have already been carried out that show a clear relationship of structure to organizational climate and morale. One study, for example, has shown that greater structuring of activities is accompanied by more formal interpersonal relationships, and greater centralization of authority leads to a greater degree of "social distance" between the levels in an organization—social distance being the degree to which a manager regards his supervisor as boss only and not as a colleague as well. These important concomitants of structure need to be more fully investigated.

Implications of the Research

It has long been realized that an organization's context is important in the development of its structure. What is surprising is the magnitude of the relationships outlined above. People often speak as if the personalities of the founder and directors of a business had been the most important influence in creating the present organization. Other people point to historical crises or to the vagaries of government policy as being the stimuli that caused the business to develop in a particular way. Though we would certainly expect personality, events, and policies to play their part, the fact that information relating solely to an organization's context enables us to make such good predictions indicates that context is more important than is generally realized.

[. . .]

SELECTED BIBLIOGRAPHY

The full details of the research described in this paper are given in a series of papers in *Administrative Science Quarterly*.

The details of the way in which the dimensions of structure are developed and the organizational profiles built up is given in D.S. Pugh et al., "Dimensions of Organizational Structure," A.S.Q. 1968, No. 18, pages 65–105. The relation of structure to the organizations' context is given in D. S. Pugh et al., "The Context of Organizational Structure," A.S.Q. 1969, Vol. 14, pages 47–61. The classification of organizations is discussed more fully in D. S. Pugh et al., "An Empirical Taxonomy of Structures of Work Organizations," A.S.Q. 1969, Vol. 14, pages 115–126. The particular relationships between the operating technology and the organization structure are detailed in D. J. Hickson, D. S. Pugh, and D. C. Pheysey, "Operations Technology and Organization Structure: an Empirical Reappraisal," A.S.Q. 1969, Vol. 14, pp. 378–397.

PART III

ORGANIZATIONS AS HUMAN AND SOCIAL SYSTEMS I
The Impulse to Reform Work

A. The Early Human Relations Movement

B. Humanistic Management and Contemporary Employee Involvement

As should be clear by now, the history of organization studies often meant wrestling with the classical model articulated by Weber, Fayol, and Taylor. Merton, Braverman, and contingency theorists who detected a trend toward organic systems were critical of the classical bureaucratic model, whereas other contingency theorists such as Blau and the Aston group mostly built on this early foundation. However, the first criticism of the classical rational model of organizations historically came from the Human Relations school, which was the first to argue that organizations should be seen as human and social systems, a view that is also called a natural systems approach to organizations. The Human Relations school's analysis of the experiments at Western Electric's Hawthorne plant in the late 1920s through early 1930s remains the most famous work in organization studies, a staple of all management textbooks, and one of the most influential works of social science.

Like Taylorism, Human Relations spawned an industry of management consultants to spread its gospel during the 1930s–1950s. The original Human Relations studies generated an immense literature of praise, interpretation, and criticism. Human Relations continues to influence both organization theory and the practice of management, in part through its successors, such as the humanistic management school, among others.

AT&T's Western Electric division supplied telephone equipment to its corporate parent. The initial work experiments at Western Electric's Hawthorne plant outside Chicago were fairly standard industrial engineering efforts to understand the effects of varying physical conditions, in this case lighting, on workers' output. Later experiments manipulated other physical conditions thought to affect human performance, such as rest breaks and length of the workday, and experimented with incentive pay plans. Since Taylor's work, industrial engineers operated under the belief that the main determinants of output were the physical ease or difficulty of workers' labor and the material incentives offered to workers.

However, workers' behavior at Hawthorne did not seem to conform to the industrial engineers' expectations. Output rose when the physical working conditions were improved, but it also rose or failed to fall when conditions were returned to their previous level or made worse, the so-called Hawthorne effect. Two Harvard Business School researchers, Elton Mayo (1880–1949) and Fritz J. Roethlisberger (1898–1974), and a Western Electric personnel executive, William J. Dickson, explained the unexpected results sociologically.

They pointed out that the various small experimental groups were separated from the main part of the factory, supervised less strictly, and given special attention by higher management. The workers in these special situations became a tightly knit group of friends, which, along with the greater freedom from supervision they enjoyed, made work more fun, met their emotional needs for social belonging, and reduced the usual anxiety and pressure they felt at work. Workers felt important because of their special situation and felt appreciated because upper management paid unusual and often personal attention to them. Management seemed to encourage workers' participation in decisions about how to organize their work, asking their opinion and suggestions, allowing them to vote on proposals, and sometimes following their advice. This met workers' emotional needs for social recognition and generated norms of cooperation with management goals within the group. At various times workers received free physical exams, lunch, and ice cream and cake as refreshments, which motivated workers to return the consideration and work hard for the company, what some economists today call *gift exchange* (Akerlof 1982). Higher output also reflected effective leadership in the work group, as hard-working, well-respected workers emerged as informal leaders, setting the pace for others and providing a sense of common purpose. The example showed that group loyalties could be enlisted in the service of the organization's goals, contrary to Taylor's view.

One work group did not respond to changes in experimental conditions. Members continued to restrict output and used peer pressure to punish fellow workers who exceeded effort norms ("rate busters") in exactly the manner Taylor described. The group had a notion of what constituted a fair day's work, and anyone who worked more or less than that lost the respect of coworkers and was ostracized from the group. The group also had experienced many disruptive technological changes recently without their prior notification or participation in the process. The Hawthorne researchers explained that this group's desire to protect itself from further external interference resulted in a "blind resistance" to change. Although the workers claimed they feared a rate cut or job losses if they worked harder—indeed the experiment was conducted during the Great Depression—the Hawthorne researchers argued the fear was irrational, because none had experienced a rate cut previously, though the company was laying off workers by now. The Human Relations researchers concluded that lack of communication from above generated a negative solidarity among workers and resulted in restriction of output.

Human Relations theory represented a significant departure from current ideas. In contrast to scientific management, Human Relations researchers argued that higher output does not depend on technical conditions, such as the physical features of the work environment, human physical capacities, or economic incentives, but on social conditions and organizational climate. The workplace was a social system. Workers needed to be part of an organized social group with opportunities for social interaction and connection to others. Supervision needed to be more democratic, and effective leaders needed to appreciate workers' need for participation and social recognition to elicit their cooperation. A cold, formal organization that tried to satisfy workers' economic needs but not their human and social needs would cause unhappiness, uncooperative attitudes, and lower output. Output depended on group norms and job satisfaction, which reflect the degree of social integration among peers and between workers and management.

Human Relations theory was not completely unprecedented. Previous management reforms had tried to increase worker loyalty, raise productivity, and dampen union sentiment. Most notable was the system of fringe benefits, grievance mechanisms, joint worker-management committees and suggestion schemes, and company-sponsored unions known as *welfare capitalism* adopted in the 1920s (Edwards 1979; Jacoby 1997). But the Hawthorne experiments, which seemed to have all the rigor of scientific management experiments, were the first to give scientific credibility to the idea that high productivity depended on worker motivation, morale, and job satisfaction, though the validity of this proposition has been debated ever since (Kanter and Brinkerhoff 1981, p. 333; Perrow 1986, pp. 84ff.). The Human Relations school was also explicitly sociological in the importance it gave to the operation of small, informal groups, in contrast to the formal organization chart. The distinction would be central to later research in the sociology of organizations (see Readings 13-15).

Still, Human Relations quickly attracted criticism for a number of reasons, many of which are discussed by Dana Bramel and Ronald Friend (Reading 8). Critics questioned whether the experiments were conducted as rigorously as claimed and whether a Hawthorne effect was genuinely observed at all (Wren 1987, pp. 321ff.). The Human Relations researchers exaggerated worker happiness in the experimental groups and minimized the conflicts between management and labor. At times, supervisory pressures and threats, rather than a "family" atmosphere, seem to have been used to maintain output.

Though the Human Relations school claimed that it wanted to reform work in ways that improved worker satisfaction, the larger goal of raising output and effort levels also led to accusations of pro-management bias. Human Relations assumed that workers and managers had a natural identity of interests and that any worker opposition to management goals reflected nonlogical, irrational sentiments. Workers' material dissatisfactions were reinterpreted as signs of unmet psychological and emotional needs that the employer needed to address in symbolic terms, rather than a real clash of economic interests (Wren 1987, p. 241). The emphasis on workers' "sentiments" and nonmonetary motives suggested workers were less rational than managers and easily placated with inexpensive symbols of recognition rather than wage increases.

In practice, Human Relations consultants' recommendations often amounted to little more than a pretense of worker participation in decision making. Groups of workers discussed issues that were either minor, such as when to schedule breaks, or questions that management had already decided. A facilitator might direct the discussion to make it appear to workers that they were arriving at the predetermined conclusions themselves as a way to gain their consent. Critics charged that Human Relations was a manipulative technique to secure greater worker commitment and management control (Etzioni 1964; Wren 1987, p. 318).

Human Relations also did not recommend any changes in how work was performed, despite its many criticisms of scientific management assumptions. To the extent that workers' discontents did reflect unmet psychological needs, Human Relations researchers seemed unaware that it may have been the deadening nature of Taylorized jobs that required reform. Mayo believed that technology, industrial society, and the decline of community were responsible for many of workers' emotional problems. He thought that cooperation in the workplace could ameliorate these problems, but he never considered reforming the alienating quality of work tasks themselves (Pugh and Hickson 1989). This led Braverman to argue that Human Relations consultants really taught personnel departments how to be the "maintenance crew" for the industrial engineers, psychologically patching up workers damaged by an alienating work system and sending them back to the jobs that were the source of their problems (Braverman 1974). Although Human Relations encouraged employers to take an enlightened approach to management, it acquired a reputation as a social engineering technique that sought to adjust workers to the existing factory system rather than change work tasks to better reflect human needs.

By the late 1950s, a new philosophy of work reform, humanistic management, displaced classical Human Relations theory. The new approach built on psychologist Abraham Maslow's (1908–1970) work on motivation (1992 [1943]). Maslow offered an alternative to the behaviorist orthodoxy within psychology, which had a philosophic kinship with scientific management. Behaviorism was an aggressively scientific and measurement-oriented psychology that explained all human action on the basis of pleasure seeking and pain avoidance, in which pleasure and pain were ultimately defined as satisfying physical needs of the organism, like those of pigeons or rats, rather than specifically human wants or desires.

Against this mechanistic view, Maslow proposed a humanistic psychology that recognized a hierarchy of human needs. The most basic human needs are physiological and safety needs. If these lower-order needs are not met, then people do not pursue higher-order goals. However, these needs are largely satisfied in modern society and cease to motivate behavior. People are motivated now by needs such as those for love, social affiliation, and social esteem or prestige. The few people who have fulfilled these needs are motivated by the highest human need, which Maslow called the need for self-actualization or self-fulfillment. This was a need to realize one's full potential and was found among those engaged in creative pursuits such as poetry, music, the search for knowledge, and above all the search for meaning in the cosmos.

Maslow's work became extremely popular during the late 1960s as part of the reaction against authority and bureaucratic institutions, because it emphasized the creative impulse and human self-fulfillment. Maslow did not apply his ideas to the study of organizations, but Douglas McGregor, a management professor at the Massachusetts Institute of Technology, used it as the basis for a theory of humanistic management in the early 1960s (Reading 9).

McGregor argued that if organizations understood human motivation using Maslow's ideas, "unimagined resources of human creativity could become available." The problem was that the dominant managerial philosophy assumed, like Taylor, that workers were naturally lazy and resistant to the organization's goals, requiring management to exercise tight control through close supervision, material incentives, and discipline. But the relatively high wages, benefits, and safer working conditions in postwar industry satisfied workers' physiological and safety needs, and consequently ceased to motivate behavior anymore. Scientific management frustrated workers' emerging needs for self-esteem, status, and self-actualization in the workplace. The result is that scientific management provoked the very antagonism and resistance among workers that it assumed to be the unfortunate but natural way things were, in a kind of self-fulfilling prophecy. In these circumstances, workers will demand more money because it is the only means to available to satisfy their needs and offers an outlet to express their frustration.

McGregor argued that this coercive and adversarial system should be replaced by a recognition that all employees are motivated by challenges, take pride in their work, seek to exercise their imagination and creativity, and have the potential to bear responsibility and contribute toward the organization's goals. Employees' need for self-actualization meant that all workers want a job that is intrinsically meaningful and interesting, rather than merely a means to a comfortable income or extrinsic reward.

By this logic, McGregor came to challenge the dominant scientific management philosophy of fragmented tasks, as well as its authoritarian management style. Organizations have to redesign jobs at the bottom of the hierarchy so they involve more variety, known as *job enlargement*, and more skill and discretion, known as *job enrichment*. Fragmented work should be reconstituted into meaningful wholes that reunite thinking and doing. Organizations have to decentralize decision making, delegate more tasks, reduce levels of hierarchy, and widen spans of control so managers are not able to control everyone in the traditional fashion. Workers should genuinely participate in decision making and lower-level goal setting. By unleashing workers' potential, management can rely less on less external control of workers' behavior and more on workers' internal commitment, self-control, and self-direction. In short, McGregor advocated something very close to an organic system for all organizations, regardless of their size, environment, or technology. In an implicit criticism of Human Relations practice, McGregor also warned that problems will arise when participation is just a "device for kidding people into thinking they are important."

Humanistic management quickly replaced Human Relations as the dominant critique of traditional management philosophy. About the same time as McGregor, Chris Argyris argued that scientific management and classical organization theory were at odds with human nature because they did not treat employees as mature individuals who have the need and capacity for initiative, independence, and diverse competencies. Frustration of self-actualization needs resulted in such dysfunctions and inefficiencies as competition and rivalries at work, high turnover, apathy, resistance, output restriction, and upward striving to gain power and autonomy. In response, management increases controls, including "pseudohuman relations programs," that only further increase the distance and mistrust between workers and management (Argyris 1984 [1960]). Argyris even suggests that self-actualization may be crucial to organizational survival.

Other authors, such as Frederick Herzberg, Rensis Likert, and Eric Trist, made similar arguments regarding the importance of satisfying higher-order needs and boosting internal work motivation through more interesting jobs and more participative organizations.

Humanistic management differed from Human Relations in at least two ways. Unlike Human Relations, humanistic management put the blame for low output and poor organizational climate squarely on management. In this view, it was not workers who were irrational, but managers and the dominant organizational philosophy that contradicted basic human needs. Consequently, humanistic management sought to reverse Taylor's philosophy of job design, and the recommendation for a more collaborative management style was taken to the point of recommending an organic structure, which was beyond anything Human Relations advocated. Humanistic management also criticized insincere human relations efforts and placed relatively more emphasis on satisfying employees' needs rather than raising productivity.

Humanistic management shared with Human Relations the view that job satisfaction was critical to productivity and that a softer management style was necessary. Like Human Relations, humanistic management also produced a new wave of consultants to spread these ideas.

Richard Walton, a Harvard Business School professor, was one of the most important of these consultants (Reading 10). The reading from Walton describes in more concrete fashion how Quality of Work Life (QWL) programs, as they came to be called in the 1970s, actually worked in practice, at least when they were successfully implemented.

The assumptions of humanistic management seemed to be confirmed after General Motors opened a highly automated assembly line in Lordstown, Ohio, in the early 1970s. GM hired mostly young workers for the new plant, many fresh from service in Vietnam, and was confronted with a level of alienation, industrial sabotage, and bitter labor conflict that received extensive national media coverage. Commentators began to refer to the "blue-collar blues," and the U.S. Secretary of Health, Education, and Welfare issued a cabinet-level report called *Work in America* that largely endorsed the view that affluence and higher levels of education among workers meant that demands for more meaningful work would only grow (United States, Department of Health, Education, and Welfare 1973).

Still, few plants implemented QWL programs in the 1970s, and even these frequently discontinued the programs after a few years due to management resistance to a redefinition of their roles. One of the most publicized successes was in Sweden, where Volvo radically restructured and democratized its factories, eliminating supervisors and the traditional assembly line in favor of self-directed teams of workers building whole automobiles.

By the early 1980s, the mood began to change. American manufacturing was rocked by waves of foreign imports, particularly from Japan, in areas such as steel, autos, computers, and consumer electronics. Japanese goods were not only less expensive than their American counterparts, but also significantly higher in quality. In the early 1980s, numerous manufacturing plants across the country closed in response to this competition, and the United States entered the deepest recession since the Great Depression.

Japan was known for its highly committed, well-trained workers who participated in quality control problem-solving groups, as well as for worker-friendly policies, such as reduced status differences between management and labor, high benefits, and no-layoff guarantees. Japanese companies claimed they treated their blue-collar workers like "whole people," rather than merely a set of hands, in many ways similar to their treatment of white-collar workers. However, the Japanese work system was still more hierarchical, Tayloristic, and regimented than the Volvo plants (Appelbaum and Batt 1994).

The Japanese competitive threat seemed to give new credibility to humanistic management, and business interest began to grow in earnest. However, in recognition of the new competitive pressures, advocates no longer described the programs as a way to improve the quality of working life or raise worker satisfaction, but as ways to improve productivity and quality through "high performance work teams."

Still, humanistic management in its various forms always had its critics. Like Human Relations, it sees few inherent conflicts of interest between management and workers, argues that workers want self-fulfillment from work more than higher pay, and seeks to promote industrial harmony ultimately in the interest of management goals. For all the criticism of management practices that a change agent, such as a paid consultant or a business professor, may make, he or she was still working at the invitation of management. Any QWL program they implemented was invariably something that management found acceptable and often part of a union-avoidance strategy (Kochan, Katz, and McKersie 1989, p. 150). Even Maslow wondered whether McGregor's work represented a legitimate application of his theory (Wren 1987, p. 376). Braverman argued that the proposed changes in job content were mainly symbolic and did little to genuinely reverse Taylorism or increase the skill content of work (1974, pp. 35ff.). The Japanese model has come under particular criticism relative to the Swedish system for its retention and even intensification of Tayloristic principles (Berggren 1994). Even American advocates of Japanese practices acknowledge their similarity to scientific management in several respects (Adler 1993; Adler and Cole 1993). Indeed, Japanese quality control techniques are partly based in American scientific management methods, as well as in humanistic management (Wren 1987, pp. 405ff.; Guillen 1994, p. 83).

In an article written especially for this volume, Saul Rubinstein describes GM's Saturn plant as an example of Richard Walton's high-commitment system, which perhaps drew inspiration from the Swedish case (Reading 11). Previously, GM had entered a joint venture with Toyota to operate a California plant known as the New United Motor Manufacturing Incorporated (NUMMI). NUMMI embodied more of the structured, Japanese approach (Adler 1993; Adler and Cole 1993). As Rubinstein explains, Saturn encourages greater union participation in the actual governance of plants and provides less rigid jobs, though there is a real question as to how much Saturn's innovations can diffuse to other parts of GM.

Laurie Graham's article (Reading 12) provides a contrasting account of a Japanese-owned auto plant in the United States that uses Japanese management techniques to exercise a more oppressive form of control over workers.

Clearly, Human Relations, humanistic management, and humanistic management's current applications have been the subject of controversy. Researchers debate whether the reforms are genuine and meaningful, or whether they aim to manipulate and control on some deeper level than previous management practice. Some see historical cycles of "hard-headed," rationalistic management ideologies alternating with "softer," more human-focused methods (Barley and Kunda 1992), but the case studies in this section suggest that current methods of participation and quality control represent a peculiar combination of rational and natural approaches whose implications for workers and organizations have not yet fully played out (Guillen 1994).

7

THE HAWTHORNE EXPERIMENTS

GEORGE C. HOMANS

IV

THE WESTERN ELECTRIC RESEARCHES

Perhaps the most important program of research studied by [*the Committee on Work in Industry*] is that which has been carried on at the Hawthorne (Chicago) Works of the Western Electric Company. This program was described by H. A. Wright and M. L. Putnam of the Western Electric Company and by F. J. Roethlisberger, Associate Professor of Industrial Research, Graduate School of Business Administration, Harvard University, particularly at a meeting of the Committee held on March 9, 1938. These men, together with Elton Mayo and G. A. Pennock, both members of the Committee, had been intimately associated with the research.[1]

A word about the Western Electric Company is a necessary introduction to what follows. This company is engaged in manufacturing equipment for the telephone industry. Besides doing this part of its work, it has always shown concern for the welfare of its employees. In the matter of wages and hours, it has maintained a high standard. It has provided good physical conditions for its employees; and it has tried to make use of every established method of vocational guidance in the effort to suit the worker to his work. The efforts of the company have been rewarded in good industrial relations: there has been no strike or other severe symptom of discontent for over twenty years. In short, there is no reason to doubt that while these researches were being carried out the morale of the company was high and that the employees, as a body, had confidence in the abilities and motives of the company management. These facts had an important bearing on the results achieved.

The program of research which will be described grew out of a study conducted at Hawthorne by the Western Electric Company in collaboration with the National Research Council, the aim of which was to determine the relation between intensity of illumination and efficiency of workers, measured in output. One of the experiments made was the following: Two groups of employees doing similar work under similar conditions were chosen, and records of output were kept for each group. The intensity of the light under which one group worked was varied, while that under which the other group worked was held constant. By this method the investigators hoped to isolate from the effect of other variables the effect of changes in the intensity of illumination on the rate of output.

In this hope they were disappointed. The experiment failed to show any simple relation between experimental changes in the intensity of illumination and observed changes in the rate of output. The investigators concluded that this result was obtained, not because such a relation did not exist, but because it was in fact impossible to isolate it from the other variables entering into any determination of productive efficiency. This kind of difficulty, of course, has been encountered in experimental work in many fields. Furthermore, the investigators were in agreement as to the character of some of these other variables. They were convinced that one of the major factors which prevented their securing a satisfactory result was psychological. The employees being tested were reacting to changes in light intensity in the way in which they assumed that they were expected to react. That is, when light intensity was increased they were expected to produce more; when it was decreased they were expected to produce less. A further experiment was devised to demonstrate this point. The light bulbs were changed, as they had been changed before, and the workers were allowed to assume that as a result there would be more light. They commented favorably on the increased illumination. As a matter of fact, the bulbs had been replaced with others of just the same power. Other experiments of the sort were made, and in each case the results could be explained as a "psychological" reaction rather than as a "physiological" one.

This discovery seemed to be important. It suggested that the relations between other physical conditions and the efficiency of workers might be obscured by similar psychological reactions. Nevertheless the investigators were determined to continue in their course. They recognized the existence of the psychological factors, but they thought of them only as disturbing influences. They were not yet ready to turn their attention to the psychological factors themselves. Instead, they were concerned with devising a better way of eliminating them from the experiments, and the experiments they wanted to try by no means ended with illumination. For instance, there was the question of what was called "fatigue." Little information existed about the effect on efficiency of changes in the hours of work and the introduction of rest pauses. The investigators finally came to the conclusion that if a small group of workers was isolated in a separate room and asked to co-operate, the psychological reaction would in time disappear, and they would work exactly as they felt. That is, changes in their rate of output would be the direct result of changes in their physical conditions of work and nothing else.

The decision to organize such a group was in fact taken. A small number of workers was to be selected and placed in a separate room, where experiments were to be made with different kinds of working conditions in order to see if more exact information could be secured. Six questions were asked by those setting up the experiment. They were the following:

1. Do employees actually get tired out?

2. Are rest pauses desirable?

3. Is a shorter working day desirable?

4. What is the attitude of employees toward their work and toward the company?

5. What is the effect of changing the type of working equipment?

6. Why does production fall off in the afternoon?

It is obvious that several of these questions could be answered only indirectly by the proposed experiment, and several of them touched upon the "psychological" rather than the "physiological" factors involved. Nevertheless, all of them arose out of the bewilderment of men of experience faced with the problem of dealing with fellow human beings in a large industrial organization. In fact, one of the executives of the company saw the purpose of the experiment in even simpler and more general terms. He said that the experiment grew out of a desire on the part of the management to "know more about our workers." In this way began the experiment which is referred to as the Relay Assembly Test Room. With this experiment and the others that followed, members of the Department of Industrial Research of the Graduate School of Business Administration, Harvard University, came to be closely associated.

In April 1927, six girls were selected from a large shop department of the Hawthorne works. They were chosen as average workers, neither inexperienced nor expert, and their work consisted of the assembling of telephone relays. A coil, armature, contact springs, and insulators were put together on a fixture and secured in position by means of four machine screws. The operation at that time was being completed at the rate of about five relays in six minutes. This particular operation was chosen for the experiment because the relays were being assembled often enough so that even slight changes in output rate would show themselves at once on the output record. Five of the girls were to do the actual assembly work; the duty of the sixth was to keep the others supplied with parts.

The test room itself was an area divided from the main department by a wooden partition eight feet high. The girls sat in a row on one side of a long workbench. The bench and assembly equipment were identical with those used in the regular department, except in one respect. At the right of each girl's place was a hole in the bench, and into this hole she dropped completed relays. It was the entrance to a chute, in which there was a flapper gate opened by the relay in its passage downward. The opening of the gate closed an electrical circuit which controlled a perforating device, and this in turn recorded the completion of the relay by punching a hole in a tape. The tape moved at the rate of one-quarter of an inch a minute and had space for a separate row of holes for each operator. When punched, it thus constituted a complete output record for each girl for each instant of the day. Such records were kept for five years.

In this experiment, then, as in the earlier illumination experiments, great emphasis was laid on the rate of output. A word of caution is needed here. The Western Electric Company was not immediately interested in increasing output. The experiments were not designed for that purpose. On the other hand, output is easily measured, *i.e.*, it yields precise quantitative data, and experience suggested that it was sensitive to at least some of the conditions under which the employees worked. Output was treated as an index. In short, the nature of the experimental conditions made the emphasis on output inevitable.

From their experience in the illumination experiments, the investigators were well aware that factors other than those experimentally varied might affect the output rate. Therefore arrangements were made that a number of other records should be kept. Unsuitable parts supplied by the firm were noted down, as were assemblies rejected for any reason upon inspection. In this way the type of defect could be known and related to the time of day at which it occurred. Records were kept of weather conditions in general and of temperature and humidity in the test room. Every six weeks each operator was given a medical examination by the company doctor. Every day she was asked to tell how many hours she had spent in bed the night before and, during a part of the experiment, what food she had eaten. Besides all these records, which concerned the physical condition of the operators, a log was kept in which were recorded the principal events in the test room hour by hour, including among the entries snatches of conversation between the workers. At first these entries related largely to the physical condition of the operators: how they felt as they worked. Later the ground they covered somewhat widened, and the log ultimately became one of the most important of the test room records. Finally, when the so-called Interviewing Program was instituted at Hawthorne, each of the operators was interviewed several times by an experienced interviewer.

The girls had no supervisor in the ordinary sense, such as they would have had in a regular shop department, but a "test room observer" was placed in the room, whose duty it was to maintain the records, arrange the work, and secure a co-operative spirit on the part of the girls. Later, when the complexity of his work increased, several assistants were assigned to help him.

When the arrangements had been made for the test room, the operators who had been chosen to take part were called in for an interview in the office of the superintendent of the Inspection Branch, who was in general charge of the experiment and of the researches which grew out of it. The superintendent described this interview as follows: "The nature of the test was carefully explained to these girls and they readily consented to take part in it, although they were very shy at the first conference. An invitation to six shop girls to come up to a superintendent's office was naturally rather startling. They were assured that the object of the test was to determine the effect of certain changes in working conditions, such as rest periods, midmorning lunches, and shorter working hours. They were expressly cautioned to work at a comfortable pace, and under no circumstances to try and make a race out of the test." This conference was only the first of many. Whenever any experimental change was planned, the girls were called in, the purpose of the change was explained to them, and their comments were requested. Certain suggested changes which did not meet with their approval were abandoned. They were repeatedly asked, as they were asked in the first interview, not to strain but to work "as they felt."

The experiment was now ready to begin. Put in its simplest terms, the idea of those directing the experiment was that if an output curve was studied for a long enough time under various changes in working conditions, it would be possible to determine which conditions were the most satisfactory. Accordingly, a number of so-called "experimental periods" were arranged. For two weeks before the operators were placed in the test room, a record was kept of the production of each one without her knowledge. In this way the investigators secured a measure of her productive ability while working in the regular department under the usual conditions. This constituted the first experimental period. And for five weeks after the girls entered the test room no change was made in working conditions. Hours remained what they had been before. The investigators felt that this period would be long enough to reveal any changes in output incidental merely to the transfer. This constituted the second experimental period.

The third period involved a change in the method of payment. In the regular department, the girls had been paid according to a scheme of group piece-work, the group consisting of a hundred or more employees. Under these circumstances, variations in an individual's total output would not be immediately reflected in her pay, since such variations tended to cancel one another in such a large group. In the test room, the six operators were made a group by themselves. In this way each girl received an amount more nearly in proportion to her individual effort, and her interests became more closely centered on the experiment. Eight weeks later, the directly experimental changes began. An outline will reveal their general character: Period IV: two rest pauses, each five minutes in length, were established, one occurring in midmorning and the other in the early afternoon. Period V: these rest pauses were lengthened to ten minutes each. Period VI: six five-minute rests were established. Period VII: the company provided each member of the group with a light lunch in the midmorning and another in the midafternoon, accompanied by rest pauses. This arrangement became standard for subsequent Periods VIII through XI. Period VIII: work stopped a half-hour earlier every day—at 4:30 P.M. Period IX: work stopped at 4 P.M. Period X: conditions returned to what they were in Period VII. Period XI: a five-day work week was established. Each of these experimental periods lasted several weeks.

Period XI ran through the summer of 1928, a year after the beginning of the experiment. Already the results were not what had been expected. The output curve, which had risen on the whole slowly and steadily throughout the year, was obviously reflecting something other than the responses of the group to the imposed experimental conditions. Even when the total weekly output had fallen off, as it could hardly fail to do in such a period as Period XI, when the group was working only five days a week, daily output continued to rise. Therefore, in accordance with a sound experimental procedure, as a control on what had been done, it was agreed with the consent of the operators that in experimental Period XII a return should be made to the original conditions of work, with no rest pauses, no special lunches, and a full-length working week. This period lasted for twelve weeks. Both daily and weekly output rose to a higher point than ever before: the working day and the working week were both longer. The hourly output rate declined somewhat but it did not approach the level of Period III, when similar conditions were in effect.

The conclusions reached after Period XII may be expressed in terms of another observation. Identical conditions of work were repeated in three different experimental periods: Periods VII, X, and XIII. If the assumptions on which the study was based had been correct, that is to say, if the output rate were directly related to the physical conditions of work, the expectation would be that in these three experimental periods there would be some similarity in output. Such was not the case. The only apparent uniformity was that in each experimental period output was higher than in the preceding one. In the Relay Assembly Test Room, as in the previous illumination experiments, something was happening which could not be explained by the experimentally controlled conditions of work.

There is no need here to go into the later history of the test room experiment, which came to an end in 1933. It is enough to say that the output of the group continued to rise until it established itself on a high plateau from which there was no descent until the time of discouragement and deepening economic depression which preceded the end of the test. The rough conclusions reached at the end of experimental Period XII were confirmed and sharpened by later research. T. N. Whitehead, Associate Professor of Business in the Graduate School of Business Administration, Harvard University, has made a careful statistical analysis of the output records. He shows that the changes which took place in the output of the group have no simple correlation with the experimental changes in working conditions. Nor can they be correlated with changes in other physical conditions of which records were kept, such as temperature, humidity, hours of rest, and changes of relay type. Even when the girls themselves complained of mugginess or heat, these conditions were not apparently affecting their output. This statement, of course, does not mean that there is never any relation between output rate and these physical conditions. There is such a thing as heat prostration. It means only that, within the limits in which these conditions were varying in the test room, they apparently did not affect the rate of work.

The question remains: With what facts, if any, can the changes in the output rate of the operators in the test room be correlated? Here the statements of the girls themselves are of the first importance. Each girl knew that she was producing more in the test room than she ever had in the regular department, and each said that the increase had come about without any conscious effort on her part. It seemed easier to produce at the faster rate in the test room than at the slower rate in the regular department. When questioned further, each girl stated her reasons in slightly different words, but there was uniformity in the answers in two respects. First, the girls liked to work in the test room; "it was fun." Secondly, the new supervisory relation or, as they put it, the absence of the old supervisory control, made it possible for them to work freely without anxiety. *survelliance*

For instance, there was the matter of conversation. In the regular department, conversation was in principle not allowed. In practice it was tolerated if it was carried on in a low tone and did not interfere with work. In the test room an effort was made in the beginning to discourage conversation, though it was soon abandoned. The observer in charge of the experiment was afraid of losing the co-operation of the girls if he insisted too strongly on this point. Talk became common and was often loud and general. Indeed, the conversation of the operators came to occupy an important place in the log. T. N. Whitehead has pointed out that the girls in the test room were far more thoroughly supervised than they ever had been in the regular department. They were watched by an observer of their own, an interested management, and outside experts. The point is that the character and purpose of the supervision were different and were felt to be so.

The operators knew that they were taking part in what was considered an important and interesting experiment. They knew that their work was expected to produce results—they were not sure what results—which would lead to the improvement of the working conditions of their fellow employees. They knew that the eyes of the company were upon them. Whitehead has further pointed out that although the experimental changes might turn out to have no physical significance, their social significance was always favorable. They showed that the management of the company was still interested, that the girls were still part of a valuable piece of research. In the regular department, the girls, like the other employees, were in the position of responding to changes the source and purpose of which were beyond their knowledge. In the test room, they had frequent interviews with the superintendent, a high officer of the company. The reasons for the contemplated experimental changes were explained to them. Their views were consulted and in some instances they were allowed to veto what had been proposed. Professor Mayo has argued that it is idle to speak of an experimental period like Period XII as being in any sense what it purported to be—a return to the original conditions of work. In the meantime, the entire industrial situation of the girls had been reconstructed.

Another factor in what occurred can only be spoken of as the social development of the group itself. When the girls went for the first time to be given a physical examination by the company doctor, someone suggested as a joke that ice cream and cake ought to be served. The company provided them at the next examination, and the custom was kept up for the duration of the experiment. When one of the girls had a birthday, each of the others would bring her a present, and she would respond by offering the group a box of chocolates. Often one of the girls would have some good reason for feeling tired. Then the others would "carry" her. That is, they would agree to work especially fast to make up for the low output expected from her. It is doubtful whether this "carrying" did have any effect, but the important point is the existence of the practice, not its effectiveness. The girls made friends in the test room and went together socially after hours. One of the interesting facts which has appeared from Whitehead's analysis of the output records is that there were times when variations in the output rates of two friends were correlated to a high degree. Their rates varied simultaneously and in the same direction—something, of course, which the girls were not aware of and could not have planned. Also, these correlations were destroyed by such apparently trivial events as a change in the order in which the girls sat at the work-bench.

Finally, the group developed leadership and a common purpose. The leader, self-appointed, was an ambitious young Italian girl who entered the test room as a replacement after two of the original members had left. She saw in the experiment a chance for personal distinction and advancement. The common purpose was an increase in the output rate. The girls had been told in the beginning and repeatedly thereafter that they were to work without straining, without trying to make a race of the test, and all the evidence shows that they kept this rule. In fact, they felt that they were working under less pressure than in the regular department. Nevertheless, they knew that the output record was considered the most important of the records of the experiment and was always closely scrutinized. Before long they had committed themselves to a continuous increase in production. In the long run, of course, this ideal was an impossible one, and when the girls found out that it was, the realization was an important element of the change of tone which was noticeable in the second half of the experiment. But for a time they felt that they could achieve the impossible. In brief, the increase in the output rate of the girls in the Relay Assembly Test Room could not be related to any changes in their physical conditions of work, whether experimentally induced or not. It could, however, be related to what can only be spoken of as the development of an organized social group in a peculiar and effective relation with its supervisors.

Many of these conclusions were not worked out in detail until long after the investigators at Hawthorne had lost interest in the Relay Assembly Test Room, but the general meaning of the experiment was clear at least as early as Period XII. A continuous increase in productivity had taken place irrespective of changing physical conditions of work. In the words of a company report made in January, 1931, on all the research which had been done up to that date: "Upon analysis, only one thing seemed to show a continuous relationship with this improved output. This was the mental attitude of the operators. From their conversations with each other and their comments to the test observers, it was not only clear that their attitudes were improving but it was evident that this area of employee reactions and feelings was a fruitful field for industrial research."

[. . .]

In order to study this kind of problem further, to make a more detailed investigation of social relations in a working group, and to supplement interview material with direct observation of the behavior of employees, the Division of Industrial Research decided to set up a new test room. But the investigators remembered what happened in the former test room and tried to devise an experiment which would not be radically altered by the process of experimentation itself. They chose a group of men—nine wiremen, three soldermen, and two inspectors—engaged in the assembly of terminal banks for use in telephone exchanges, took them out of their regular department and placed them in a special room. Otherwise no change was made in their conditions of work, except that an investigator was installed in the room, whose duty was simply to observe the behavior of the men. In the Relay Assembly Test Room a log had been kept of the principal events of the test. At the beginning it consisted largely of comments made by the workers in answer to questions about their physical condition. Later it came to include a much wider range of entries, which were found to be extremely useful in interpreting the changes in the output rate of the different workers. The work of the observer in the new test room was in effect an expansion of the work of keeping the log in the old one. Finally, an interviewer was assigned to the test room; he was not, however, one of the population of the room but remained outside and interviewed the employees from time to time in the usual manner. No effort was made to get output records other than the ones ordinarily kept in the department from which the group came, since the investigators felt that such a procedure would introduce too large a change from a regular shop situation. In this way the experiment was set up which is referred to as the Bank Wiring Observation Room. It was in existence seven months, from November, 1931, to May, 1932.

The method of payment is the first aspect of this group which must be described. It was a complicated form of group piecework. The department of which the workers in the observation room were a part was credited with a fixed sum for every unit of equipment it assembled. The amount thus earned on paper by the department every week made up the sum out of which the wages of all the men in the department were paid. Each individual was then assigned an hourly rate of pay, and he was guaranteed this amount in case he did not make at least as much on a piecework basis. The rate was based on a number of factors, including the nature of the job a worker was doing, his efficiency, and his length of service with the company. Records of the output of every worker were kept, and every six months there was a rate revision, the purpose of which was to make the hourly rates of the different workers correspond to their relative efficiency.

The hourly rate of a given employee, multiplied by the number of hours worked by him during the week, was spoken of as the daywork value of the work done by the employee. The daywork values of the work done by all the employees in the department were then added together, and the total thus obtained was subtracted from the total earnings credited to the department for the number of units of equipment assembled. The surplus, divided by the total daywork value, was expressed as a percentage. Each individual's hourly rate was then increased by this percentage, and the resulting hourly earnings figure, multiplied by the number of hours worked, constituted that person's weekly earnings.

Another feature of the system should be mentioned here. Sometimes a stoppage which was beyond the control of the workers took place in the work. For such stoppages the workers were entitled to claim time out, being paid at their regular hourly rates for this time. This was called the "daywork allowance claim." The reason why the employees were paid their hourly rate for such time and not their average hourly wages was a simple one. The system was supposed to prevent stalling. The employees could earn more by working than they could by taking time out. As a matter of fact, there was no good definition of what constituted a stoppage which was beyond the control of the workers. All stoppages were more or less within their control. But this circumstance was supposed to make no difference in the working of the system, since the assumption was that in any case the workers, pursuing their economic interests, would be anxious to keep stoppages at a minimum.

This system of payment was a complicated one, but it is obvious that there was a good logical reason for every one of its features. An individual's earnings would be affected by changes in his rate or in his output and by changes in the output of the group as a whole. The only way in which the group as a whole could increase its earnings was by increasing its total output. It is obvious also that the experts who designed the system made certain implicit assumptions about the behavior of human beings, or at least the behavior of workers in a large American factory. They assumed that every employee would pursue his economic interest by trying to increase not only his own output but the output of every other person in the group. The group as a whole would act to prevent slacking by any of its members. One possibility, for instance, was that by a few weeks' hard work an employee could establish a high rate for himself. Then he could slack up and be paid out of all proportion with the amount he actually contributed to the wages of the group. Under these circumstances, the other employees were expected to bring pressure to bear to make him work harder.

peer pressure

Such was the way in which the wage incentive scheme ought to have worked. The next question is how it actually did work. At first the workers were naturally suspicious of the observer, but when they got used to him and found that nothing out of the ordinary happened as a result of his presence in the room, they came to take him for granted. The best evidence that the employees were not distrustful of the observer is that they were willing to talk freely to him about what they were doing, even when what they were doing was not strictly in accord with what the company expected. Conversation would die down when the group chief entered the room, and when the foreman or the assistant foreman entered everyone became serious. But no embarrassment was felt at the presence of the observer. To avoid misunderstanding, it is important to point out that the observer was in no sense a spy. The employees were deliberately and obviously separated from their regular department. The observer did not, and could not, pass himself off as one of them. And if only from the fact that a special interviewer was assigned to them, the members of the group knew they were under investigation.

The findings reached by the observer were more detailed but in general character the same as those which had emerged from the early interviews of other groups. Among the employees in the observation room there was a notion of a proper day's work. They felt that if they had wired two equipments a day they had done about the right amount. Most of the work was done in the morning. As soon as the employees felt sure of being able to finish what they considered enough for the day, they slacked off. This slacking off was naturally more marked among the faster than among the slower workmen.

As a result, the output graph from week to week tended to be a straight line. The employees resorted to two further practices in order to make sure that it should remain so. They reported more or less output than they performed and they claimed more day-work allowances than they were entitled to. At the end of the day, the observer would make an actual count of the number of connections wired—something which was not done by the supervisors—and he found that the men would report to the group chief sometimes more and sometimes less work than they actually had accomplished. At the end of the period of observation, two men had completed more than they ever had reported, but on the whole the error was in the opposite direction. The theory of the employees was that excess work produced on one day should be saved and applied to a deficiency on another day. The other way of keeping the output steady was to claim excessive daywork allowance. The employees saw that the more daywork they were allowed, the less output they would have to maintain in order to keep the average hourly output rate steady. The claims for daywork allowance were reported by the men to their group chief, and he, as will be seen, was in no position to make any check. These practices had two results. In the first place, the departmental efficiency records did not represent true efficiency, and therefore decisions as to grading were subject to errors of considerable importance. In the second place, the group chief was placed in a distinctly awkward position.

The findings of the observer were confirmed by tests which were made as a part of the investigation. Tests of intelligence, finger dexterity, and other skills were given to the workers in the room, and the results of the tests were studied in order to discover whether there was any correlation between output on the one hand and earnings, intelligence, or finger dexterity on the other. The studies showed that there was not. The output was apparently not reflecting the native intelligence or dexterity of the members of the group.

Obviously the wage incentive scheme was not working in the way it was expected to work. The next question is why it was not working. In this connection, the observer reported that the group had developed an informal social organization, such as had been revealed by earlier investigations. The foreman who selected the employees taking part in the Bank Wiring Observation Room was co-operative and had worked with the investigators before. They asked him to produce a normal group. The men he chose all came out of the same regular shop department, but they had not been closely associated in their work there. Nevertheless, as soon as they were thrown together in the observation room, friendships sprang up and soon two well-defined cliques were formed. The division into cliques showed itself in a number of ways: in mutual exclusiveness, in differences in the games played during off-hours, and so forth.

What is important here is not what divided the men in the observation room but what they had in common. They shared a common body of sentiments. A person should not turn out too much work. If he did, he was a "rate-buster." The theory was that if an excessive amount of work was turned out, the management would lower the piecework rate so that the employees would be in the position of doing more work for approximately the same pay. On the other hand, a person should not turn out too little work. If he did, he was a "chiseler"; that is, he was getting paid for work he did not do. A person should say nothing which would injure a fellow member of the group. If he did, he was a "squealer." Finally, no member of the group should act officiously.

The working group had also developed methods of enforcing respect for its attitudes. The experts who devised the wage incentive scheme assumed that the group would bring pressure to bear upon the slower workers to make them work faster and so increase the earnings of the group. In point of fact, something like the opposite occurred. The employees brought pressure to bear not upon the slower workers but upon the faster ones, the very ones who contributed most to the earnings of the group. The

pressure was brought to bear in various ways. One of them was "binging." If one of the employees did something which was not considered quite proper, one of his fellow workers had the right to "bing" him. Binging consisted of hitting him a stiff blow on the upper arm. The person who was struck usually took the blow without protest and did not strike back. Obviously the virtue of binging as punishment did not lie in the physical hurt given to the worker but in the mental hurt that came from knowing that the group disapproved of what he had done. Other practices which naturally served the same end were sarcasm and the use of invectives. If a person turned out too much work, he was called names, such as "Speed King" or "The Slave."

It is worth while pointing out that the output of the group was not considered low. If it had been, some action might have been taken, but in point of fact it was perfectly satisfactory to the management. It was simply not so high as it would have been if fatigue and skill had been the only limiting factors.

In the matter of wage incentives, the actual situation was quite different from the assumptions made by the experts. Other activities were out of line in the same way. The wiremen and the soldermen did not stick to their jobs; they frequently traded them. This was forbidden, on the theory that each employee ought to do his own work because he was more skilled in that work. There was also much informal helping of one man by others. In fact, the observation of this practice was one means of determining the cliques into which the group was divided. A great many things, in short, were going on in the observation room which ought not to have been going on. For this reason it was important that no one should "squeal" on the men.

A group chief was in immediate charge of the employees. He had to see that they were supplied with parts and that they conformed to the rules and standards of the work. He could reprimand them for misbehavior or poor performance. He transmitted orders to the men and brought their requests before the proper authorities. He was also responsible for reporting to the foreman all facts which ought to come to his attention. The behavior of the employees put him in an awkward position. He was perfectly well aware of the devices by which they maintained their production at a constant level. But he was able to do very little to bring about a change. For instance, there was the matter of claims for daywork allowance. Such claims were supposed to be based on stoppages beyond the control of the workers, but there was no good definition of what constituted such stoppages. The men had a number of possible excuses for claiming daywork allowance: defective materials, poor and slow work on the part of other employees, and so forth. If the group chief checked up on one type of claim, the workers could shift to another. In order to decide whether or not a particular claim was justified, he would have to stand over the group all day with a stop watch. He did not have time to do that, and in any case refusal to honor the employees' claims would imply doubt of their integrity and would arouse their hostility. The group chief was a representative of management and was supposed to look after its interests. He ought to have put a stop to these practices and reported them to the foreman. But if he did so, he would, to use the words of a short account of the observation room by Roethlisberger and Dickson, "lose sympathetic control of his men, and his duties as supervisor would become much more difficult."[2] He had to associate with the employees from day to day and from hour to hour. His task would become impossible if he had to fight a running fight with them. Placed in this situation, he chose to side with the men and report unchanged their claims for daywork. In fact there was very little else he could do, even if he wished. Moreover he was in a position to protect himself in case of trouble. The employees always had to give him a reason for any daywork claims they might make, and he entered the claims in a private record book. If anyone ever asked why so much daywork was being claimed, he could throw the blame wherever he wished. He could assert that materials had been defective or he could blame the inspectors, who were members of an outside organization. In still another respect, then, the Bank Wiring Observation Room group was not behaving as the logic of management assumed that it would behave.

Restriction of output is a common phenomenon of industrial plants. It is usually explained as a highly logical reaction of the workers. They have increased their output, whereupon their wage rates for piecework have been reduced. They are doing more work for the same pay. They restrict their output in order to avoid a repetition of this experience. Perhaps this explanation holds good in some cases, but the findings of the Bank Wiring Observation Room suggest that it is too simple. The workers in the room were obsessed with the idea that they ought to hold their production level "even" from week to week, but they were vague as to what would happen if they did not. They said that "someone" would "get them." If they turned out an unusually high output one week, that record would be taken thereafter as an example of what they could do if they tried, and they would be "bawled out" if they did not keep up to it. As a matter of fact, none of the men in the room had ever experienced a reduction of wage rates. What is more, as Roethlisberger and Dickson point out, "changes in piece rates occur most frequently where there is a change in manufacturing process, and changes in manufacturing process are made by engineers whose chief function is to reduce unit cost wherever the saving will justify the change. In some instances, changes occur irrespective of direct labor cost. Moreover, where labor is a substantial element, reduction of output tends to increase unit costs and instead of warding off a change in the piece rate may actually induce one."

What happened in the observation room could not be described as a logical reaction of the employees to the experience of rate reduction. They had in fact had no such experience. On the other hand, the investigators found that it could be described as a conflict between the technical organization of the plant and its social organization. By technical organization the investigators meant the plan, written or unwritten, according to which the Hawthorne plant was supposed to operate, and the agencies which gave effect to that plan. The plan included explicit rules as to how the men were to be paid, how they were to do their work, what their relations with their supervisors ought to be. It included also implicit assumptions on which the rules were based, one of the assumptions being that men working in the plant would on the whole act so as to further their economic interests. It is worth while pointing out that this assumption was in fact implicit, that the experts who devised the technical organization acted upon the assumption without ever stating it in so many words.

There existed also an actual social situation within the plant: groups of men, who were associated with one another, held common sentiments and had certain relations with other groups and other men. To some extent this social organization was identical with the technical plan and to some extent it was not. For instance, the employees were paid according to group payment plans, but the groups concerned did not behave as the planners expected them to behave.

The investigators considered the relations between the technical organization and the social. A certain type of behavior is expected of the higher levels of management. Their success is dependent on their being able to devise and institute rapid changes. Roethlisberger and Dickson describe what happens in the following terms: "Management is constantly making mechanical improvements and instituting changes designed to reduce costs or improve the quality of the product. It is constantly seeking new ways and new combinations for increasing efficiency, whether in designing a new machine, instituting a new method of control, or logically organizing itself in a new way." The assumption has often been made that these changes are designed to force the employee to do more work for less money. As a matter of fact, many of them have just the opposite purpose: to improve the conditions of work and enable the employee to earn higher wages. The important point here, however, is not the purpose of the changes but the way in which they are carried out and accepted.

Once the responsible officer has decided that a certain change ought to be made, he gives an order, and this order is transmitted "down the line," appropriate action being taken at every level. The question in which the investigators were interested was this: What happens when the order reaches the men who are actually doing the manual work? Roethlisberger and Dickson make the following observations: "The worker occupies a unique position in the social organization. He is at the bottom of a highly stratified organization. He is always in the position of having to accommodate himself to changes which he does not originate. Although he participates least in the technical organization, he bears the brunt of most of its activities." It is he, more than anyone, who is affected by the decisions of management, yet in the nature of things he is unable to share management's preoccupations, and management does little to convince him that what he considers important is being treated as important at the top—a fact which is not surprising, since there is no adequate way of transmitting to management an understanding of the considerations which seem important at the work level. There is something like a failure of communication in both directions—upward and downward.

The worker is not only "asked to accommodate himself to changes which he does not initiate, but also many of the changes deprive him of those very things which give meaning and significance to his work." The modern industrial worker is not the handicraftsman of the medieval guild. Nevertheless, the two have much in common. The industrial worker develops his own ways of doing his job, his own traditions of skill, his own satisfactions in living up to his standards. The spirit in which he adopts his own innovations is quite different from that in which he adopts those of management. Furthermore, he does not do his work as an isolated human being, but always as a member of a group, united either through actual co-operation on the job or through association in friendship. One of the most important general findings of the Western Electric researches is the fact that such groups are continually being formed among industrial workers, and that the groups develop codes and loyalties which govern the relations of the members to one another. Though these codes can be quickly destroyed, they are not formed in a moment. They are the product of continued, routine interaction between men. "Constant interference with such codes is bound to lead to feelings of frustration, to an irrational exasperation with technical change in any form, and ultimately to the formation of a type of employee organization such as we have described—a system of practices and beliefs in opposition to the technical organization."

The Bank Wiring Observation Room seemed to show that action taken in accordance with the technical organization tended to break up, through continual change, the routines and human associations which gave work its value. The behavior of the employees could be described as an effort to protect themselves against such changes, to give management the least possible opportunity of interfering with them. When they said that if they increased their output, "something" was likely to happen, a process of this sort was going on in their minds. But the process was not a conscious one. It is important to point out that the protective function of informal organization was not a product of deliberate planning. It was more in the nature of an automatic response. The curious thing is that, as Professor Mayo pointed out to the Committee, these informal organizations much resembled formally organized labor unions, although the employees would not have recognized the fact.

Roethlisberger and Dickson summarize as follows the results of the intensive study of small groups of employees: "According to our analysis the uniformity of behavior manifested by these groups was the outcome of a disparity in the rates of change possible in the technical organization, on the one hand, and in the social organization, on the other. The social sentiments and customs of work of the employees were unable to accommodate themselves to the rapid technical innovations introduced. The result was to incite a blind resistance to all innovations and to provoke the formation of a social organization at a lower level in opposition to the technical organization."

It is curious how, at all points, the Relay Assembly Test Room and the Bank Wiring Observation Room form a contrast. In the former, the girls said that they felt free from the pressure of supervision, although as a matter of fact they were far more thoroughly supervised than they ever had been in their regular department. In the latter, the men were afraid of supervision and acted so as to nullify it. The Bank Wiremen were in the position of having to respond to technical changes which they did not originate. The Relay Assemblers had periodic conferences with the superintendent. They were told what experimental changes were contemplated; their views were canvassed, and in some instances they were allowed to veto what had been proposed. They were part of an experiment which they felt was interesting and important. Both groups developed an informal social organization, but while the Bank Wiremen were organized in opposition to management, the Relay Assemblers were organized in co-operation with management in the pursuit of a common purpose. Finally, the responses of the two groups to their industrial situation were, on the one hand, restriction of output and, on the other, steady and welcome increase of output. These contrasts carry their own lesson.

[. . .]

NOTES

1. This research has been described in detail in a number of papers and in at least three books. The books are:

E. Mayo, "The Human Problems of an Industrial Civilization," The Macmillan Company, New York, 1933.

T. N. Whitehead, "The Industrial Worker," (2 vols.), Harvard University Press, Cambridge, 1938.

F. J. Roethlisberger and W. J. Dickson, "Management and the Worker," Harvard University Press, Cambridge, 1939.

2. F. J. Roethlisberger and W. J. Dickson, "Management and the Worker," Harvard Business School: Division of Research, Business Research Studies, No. 9 (a monograph). (All quotations relating to the Western Electric researches are from this study as well as from the book of the same title by the same authors.)

8

HAWTHORNE, THE MYTH OF THE DOCILE WORKER, AND CLASS BIAS IN PSYCHOLOGY

DANA BRAMEL
RONALD FRIEND

One of the creation myths of social and industrial psychologists, and of industrial sociologists as well (Miller & Form, 1951), revolves around the famous Hawthorne experiments at the Chicago Western Electric plant (1924–1933), out of which were born the "Hawthorne effect" and the "human relations movement" in industry. The importance of this work for the fields of psychology and sociology in the ensuing 50 years scarcely requires documentation (Dunnette, 1976; Haire, 1954; Sills, 1968; Vroom, 1969).

Two Harvard University psychologists associated with the research, Elton Mayo (e.g., 1933, 1945) and Fritz Roethlisberger (e.g., 1941), were important in calling attention at an early date to what they saw as the major implications of this research for changing the relationship between management and workers. We intend to show that the distortions introduced in large part by these two pioneers were probably important in preserving a view of workers as irrational and unintelligent and of the capitalist factory as nonexploitative and free of class conflict. This view, which is clearly identified with defense of the capitalist mode of production, persists to the present time in discussions of the psychology of industry and particularly in reference to the Hawthorne research.

Mayo had excellent credentials for assuming the role of humanizer of American business. And business in the Depression era of the 1930s certainly needed an improved image (Carey, 1977; Mills, 1948). He was an integrator of social science fields (psychiatry, social psychology, social anthropology, political science), had research experience in industry (but was not compromised by being an owner or manager), knew how to socialize with working people, had a faith in the basic health and rationality of the capitalist system, yet knew that the industrial elite would have to find new techniques of human control (other than assembly lines, Pinkertons, the National Guard, beating up labor organizers, etc.)[1] if it was to maintain its position of dominance (Baritz, 1960; Mulherin, 1980; Smith, 1975). As a close associate of John D. Rockefeller, Jr., and much respected by important people at the Laura Spelman Rockefeller Memorial (later merged with the Rockefeller Foundation), Mayo became the choice in 1926 to play a central role in the Rockefeller-financed Department of Industrial Research at Harvard's Graduate School of Business Administration (Mulherin, 1980). Mayo and Roethlisberger (his protegé at Harvard) did not design or conduct the crucial Hawthorne experiments, but they were closely involved with various stages of the research and certainly with the popularization of certain conclusions from them, especially in business circles.

Mayo argued with passion that social and clinical psychological approaches could be incorporated into an enlightened management in such a way that the social-emotional needs of workers would be met, thus ending various kinds of irrational hostility in the factory and the "need" for workers to unite in opposition to management (i.e., via unionization). This is in direct contradiction, as Mayo was quite aware, to the Marxist view, which posits an irreconcilable conflict of interest between workers and owner-managers. Marxists believe that capitalist relations of production are exploitative and necessarily produce resistance and self-organization among workers. This individual and collective resistance may or may not be expressed at any given time as class consciousness and a political threat to the firm or to the system as a whole, but it is always present in one form or another.[2]

It is by suppressing the fact of this resistance, by trying to explain it away psychologically, and finally, by developing human relations techniques designed to prevent workers' development of class consciousness that the Mayo group contributed to the attempt to save the capitalist system from the fate Marxists said lay in waiting for it. We believe that psychologists and others have been insufficiently critical of these anti-working-class ideas and practices that came wrapped in the prestige of Harvard University and seemed to open up endless vistas for employment in the application of social science. The renewed pressures now, in another period of economic crisis, for psychologists to join hands with management make it urgent that we look at what we are doing in a more clear-headed fashion.

Interpretations of the Hawthorne research provide a significant case study of how psychologists may have allowed promanagement or procapitalist commitments and ideologies to distort their understanding of the world of industrial work. The Mayo group's dream of "wholehearted cooperation" between workers and bosses, which they claimed was supported by the results of the Hawthorne experiments, came under sharp criticism from many industrial sociologists in the 1940s and 1950s (cf. Gilson, 1940; Lynd, 1937; Mills, 1948; and the summaries in Landsberger, 1958, and Smith, 1975). Members of Mayo's group were accused of a lack of realism about unions, of being blinded by promanagement commitments, of being psychological reductionists, and so forth. "Human relations" was described as a technique for fighting unionization. Wilensky and Wilensky (1951) argued that it had been effective in this at Western Electric. Much of this criticism was probably justified, and the human relations movement that Mayo symbolized lost much of its glamor in the 1950s and 1960s.

Our focus here is somewhat different. We wish to show not simply that Mayo's conclusions were unrealistic and politically reactionary but also that they did not follow from the public data about Hawthorne, with which he and Roethlisberger were quite familiar. That is, we wish to show bias at the level of interpretation of the available data. Our second intention is to show that psychologists have subsequently been much too uncritical in accepting the accounts of the original researchers and popularizers.

In presenting this case it might seem most reasonable to pose the question, What *really* happened at Hawthorne? and to proceed to show the kinds of error of interpretation made by the original researchers and subsequent commentators, systematically comparing the "facts" with the alleged errors of analysis. However, the facts about an investigation carried out more than 50 years ago are difficult to establish. A number of investigators (e.g., Franke, 1979; Franke & Kaul, 1978; Parsons, 1974; Wrege, 1976) have begun a thorough reanalysis of the original documents, including output records and interview protocols, but the complexity of insufficiently controlled research designs, possible selectivity in recording of workers' comments (not to mention the likelihood that many such comments would have been intentionally misleading), and possible failure to report significant events and data make it unlikely that any definitive conclusions will ever be forthcoming.

We propose a somewhat different approach, in some ways a more conservative test of the Marxist hypothesis that class bias exists in regard to Hawthorne. We have examined a good proportion of the major published accounts of the research, including Roethlisberger and Dickson's (1939) *Management and the Worker*, Whitehead's (1938) *The Industrial Worker*, Mayo's (1933) *Human Problems of an Industrial Civilization*, Mayo's (1945) *Social Problems of an Industrial Civilization*, and Roethlisberger's (1941) *Management and Morale*. We show, limiting ourselves largely to the empirical material presented by these authors themselves, that the conclusions drawn from the research, especially by Mayo and Roethlisberger, are systematically biased. Unlike Franke and Kaul (1978), we are not primarily concerned with proving that "human relations" does not work and did not work at Hawthorne. We wish to show that one reason it does not work very well, and did not work at Hawthorne, is that it assumes workers are easily fooled.

OVERVIEW OF THE HAWTHORNE RESEARCH

It is convenient to divide the Hawthorne research into three categories. First were the illumination experiments (1924–1927) organized by engineers under the direction of an industry-supported research group, the Committee on Industrial Lighting. Output of workers was related to variations in conditions of illumination of a room, and it turned out to be very difficult to find any systematic relation between the two variables. It was noted, for example, that production sometimes went up when illumination was made less adequate. Some of the researchers became aware of the possibility that supervision and "test psychology" factors might have something to do with output changes.

The second set of experiments included the first Relay Assembly Test Room (RATR; April 1927–February 1933), the Second Relay Assembly Group (August 1928–March 1929), and the Mica Splitting Test Room (October 1928–September 1930). These three experiments, whether singly (especially the RATR) or in combination, constituted the research basis for the Hawthorne effect and a good part of the human relations movement (Roethlisberger & Dickson, 1966, chap. 2). The most famous is the first one, RATR, in which five women whose job was to put together electrical relays for telephones were separated from the others in a special room where the researchers could make all sorts of experimental changes in the conditions of their work (cf. Roethlisberger & Dickson, 1939; Whitehead, 1938). The conclusions drawn by the Harvard group (which became involved beginning with Mayo's visit to Hawthorne in April 1928) was that productivity increased markedly over time primarily as a function of the changed supervision of the workers in RATR (and also somewhat in the Mica Splitting Test Room); physical changes (rest pauses, free lunches, shortened hours) and small-group-incentive payment plans (in RATR and the Second Relay Assembly Group) were considered relatively less important as influences. The summing up in Roethlisberger and Dickson (1939, pp. 154–157) is certainly more balanced and complex than that found in the more popular treatments (Mayo, 1933, 1945; Roethlisberger, 1941), which tend to focus heavily on the major changes in the way workers in RATR were supervised, ignoring some of the complications introduced by results from the other two experiments.

It appears that the purpose of the relaxation of managerial discipline, the more free-and-easy, friendly style in the RATR, was primarily to make the workers sufficiently relaxed and communicative that the effects of rest pauses and shorter working hours could be assessed. The experimenters felt that it was necessary to get the "complete cooperation" of the workers, including full discussion in advance and approval from them of the experimental changes to be introduced. In this way the physical factors could be studied without contamination from possible negative psychological influences. The Hawthorne effect is, of course, the name now ordinarily given to the observation that the output of the workers seemed to be responding to the transformed interpersonal relationship to the "boss" (or experimenters)—supposedly a constant and inert setting for the experiment—rather than to the explicitly introduced variations in physical conditions of work (Roethlisberger & Dickson, 1966).

The third category of research at Hawthorne was nonexperimental. It included the famous Bank Wiring Observation Room Study (November 1931–May 1932), in which informal social relations and work restriction norms in a group of men were studied. We would also include here the massive interviewing program (September 1928–early 1931) in which new nondirective techniques were introduced to find out what workers were thinking and, at the same time, to help them blow off steam and get their personal problems off their chests.

THE RESULTS AS PRESENTED BY MAYO AND ROETHLISBERGER

Here is how Mayo describes the social-psychological interpretation of the development of a "self-governing team," a team that "gave itself whole-heartedly and spontaneously to cooperation in the experiment" (Mayo, 1945, p. 64):

> Undoubtedly, there had been a remarkable change of mental attitude in the group. This showed in their recurrent conferences with high executive authorities. At first shy and uneasy, silent and perhaps somewhat suspicious of the company's intention, later their attitude is marked by confidence and candor. Before every change of program, the group is consulted. Their comments are listened to and discussed; sometimes their objections are allowed to negative a suggestion. The group unquestionably develops a sense of participation in the critical determinations and becomes something of a social unit. This developing social unity is illustrated by the entertainment of each other in their respective homes, especially operatives one, two, three, and four. (Mayo, 1933, p. 69)

The picture Mayo presents here and elsewhere is one of smooth and rather rapid development of a very positive attitude toward management on the part of the five workers. Only rarely, as in the above quotation, does he refer to hostility or resistance to company policy. When he does so, it is described as an irrational attitude quickly dispelled. In describing the results as a whole, he continually marvels at the "steadily increasing output" (Mayo, 1945, p. 63).

The general picture presented of the RATR study by Mayo and Roethlisberger is one of steadily increasing output attributed to "revolutionized supervision," which rather quickly produced "wholehearted cooperation with management." They make it sound easy to transform workers into an enthusiastic team eagerly pushing its production ever higher, regardless of the particular physical or economic conditions in the factory. This version of human relations and the Hawthorne effect has been widely adopted, as we show below. What is disturbing is that even a cursory look at the more detailed published reports shows major discrepancies from the image of easily manipulated workers presented by almost all descriptions of what happened at Hawthorne. We are not the first to have noticed this (cf. especially Argyle, 1953; Carey, 1967; Sykes, 1965), but we intend to look at it and its implications more closely than has heretofore been done. Earlier critiques have clearly not been sufficient to dispel this most persistent myth.

EVIDENCE OF WORKER RESISTANCE

We begin with information contained in abundance in Roethlisberger and Dickson (1939). Reading these authors, one realizes that supervision was not always as "revolutionized," friendly, and permissive as some reports imply. When the workers were diligent and not spending too much time talking and goofing off, the supervisor was "free and easy," but when things started getting out of hand (and productivity fell off), supervisory style often shifted back to reprimands, sending workers up to the front office, and threats to end the "experiment" or extend the disliked experimental conditions. In Period 3 (about three months after the start of the experiment), talking among the workers got to the point where the experimenters felt it jeopardized the experiment. Things got so bad that it was found necessary to bring four of the five workers before the foreman for reprimands in early August 1927. Log notes from the observer record that on the second of these reprimands, the foreman told the workers that they "would be taken back to the regular department, and in the most offending cases laid off (dismissed from the company), if improvement was not made" (Franke, 1979, p. 863). Two of these workers in particular (Operators 1A and 2A) failed to display "that 'wholehearted cooperation' desired by the investigators" (Roethlisberger & Dickson, 1939, p. 53). Six months into the experiment, with productivity thought to be static or falling, these two women were being continually reprimanded and threatened with disciplinary action. Finally, after eight months (in Period 8), Operators 1A and 2A were dismissed from the experiment for "gross insubordination" and low output (Roethlisberger & Dickson, 1939; Whitehead, 1938, Vol. 1, p. 118).

Interestingly, Mayo told the story rather differently, saying that 1A and 2A had "dropped out" (1933, p. 56), were "permitted to withdraw" (1933, p. 110), or had "retired" (1945, p. 62). He also said, "At no time in the five-year period did the girls feel that they were working under pressure" (Mayo, 1933, p. 69). Homans (1940/1958), who worked on related research at Hawthorne during this period, said blandly, "Two of the original members had left" (p. 587).

As Argyle pointed out in 1953, and as has been more systematically shown in a quantitative analysis by Franke and Kaul (1978), this relatively little-known (or forgotten) incident in the Hawthorne experiment was probably by itself a major factor in the increased production viewed over time. One of the two workers brought in to replace Operators 1A and 2A, Operator 2, became the informal leader of the group and pushed the others to produce more (Whitehead, 1938, chaps. 16 and 17). Further, since both replacements immediately produced at a higher rate than had any of the original five when they started the experiment, and at a much higher rate than had Operators 1A and 2A during the entire eight-month period up to then, there are significant grounds for questioning whether there would have been any Hawthorne effect in the absence of this bit of methodological unorthodoxy.

Our purpose in bringing up this incident, however, is not to criticize the research methodology. That has been done in rather convincing fashion by others (especially Argyle, 1953; Baritz, 1960; Carey, 1967; Franke, 1979). It is not the replacement of Workers 1A and 2A in such a difficult field experiment situation that is so disturbing. What does require comment is that Mayo and Roethlisberger suppressed the underlying resistance by workers to management that this incident and others reveal. Apparently, the Hawthorne effect did not arise as simply and spontaneously from the "revolutionized supervision" as we have been led to believe.

What is the evidence for our claim that there was a significant amount of hostility, conflict, and active resistance to "cooperation" among the workers in this research? Take the case of Operator 2A as described by Mayo. We have seen that she was not simply "permitted to withdraw." She was thrown out of the experiment (Roethlisberger & Dickson, 1939, p. 182; Whitehead, 1938, Vol. 1, p. 118). This occurred on January 25, 1928. Three months later, in a letter written to his benefactor at the Laura Spelman Rockefeller Memorial, executive Beardsley Ruml, Mayo said of this worker, "One girl, formerly in the test group, was reported to have 'gone Bolshevik' and had been dropped" (cited in Mulherin, 1980, ch. 3, p. 54). Here, in a personal letter, Mayo seemed to show awareness of conflict of a class and even political nature in the experiment itself, but he quickly explained it away by claiming that Operator 2A had been anemic at the time of the incident (Mayo, 1933, p. 110). In the same letter, he wrote, "This was interesting as relating together pessimistic or paranoid preoccupations, fatigue and organic disability" (cited in Mulherin, 1980 ch. 3, p. 54). After treatment for the anemic condition, "she rapidly recovered in respect of both cell count and hemoglobin percentage and in subsequent discussion disavowed her former criticisms of the company" (Mayo, 1933, p. 110). This illustrates a constant theme in Mayo's industrial work: Conflict between workers and management is always due to something other than a basic antagonism of interests in the exploitative capitalist relations of production. In this case, it is due to a medical condition that produces "paranoid preoccupations." In other cases, it represents a misunderstanding, a lack of communication. As Mayo said repeatedly, the "complaint only rarely, if ever, gave any logical clue to the grievance in which it had origin" (1945, p. 82).

One gets some clue of the nature of Operator 2A's "paranoia" and misunderstanding from the report Roethlisberger and Dickson (1939) gave of interviews with her four months after she was replaced:

> She also said that she had heard comments from girls in the regular department to the effect that what the company really was after in the test room was maximum output, and that the test room was not being run, as the investigators said, to determine the best working conditions. (p. 170)

Roethlisberger and Dickson, of course, rejected this explanation, since they knew that the experiment was benevolent, in the workers' best interests.[3] (And Dickson was an officer of the Western Electric Company.)

Let us compare Operator 2A's paranoia with what the observer's notes recorded during Period 5, before her replacement for lack of cooperation. On September 17, 1927, the supervisor (who was rather high level; see Roethlisberger & Dickson, 1939, p. 340) told the operators that "the earnings as shown by the test room records are too high and that they would only be paid 60 percent," although the test room records indicated that they should earn 71%. On September 26, with test room earnings at 75% the supervisor returned and "questioned them as to why it was that they could make 75 percent in the test room and much less working in the regular department" (Wrege, Note 1). Coming from an individual of the supervisor's status, this interrogation constituted an explicit threat to cut the piece rate—certainly for the test room workers and possibly for others as well—whether actually carried out or not. How, then, can one argue seriously that worker suspicion and self-defense strategies are only symptoms of mental unbalance?

[. . .]

Another example of worker distrust of and antagonism to management can be found in the Mica Splitting Test Room experiment, which attempted to test for the effects of rest pauses independently of changes in the wage incentive plan. The researchers

had a hard time finding enough workers willing to participate in this experiment (Roethlisberger & Dickson, 1939, p. 136). Operator M, asked why she had agreed to participate, said about the attitude of the workers in the regular department, "The girls all tried to say they were just going to get us in there and time us and then cut the rates, but I thought the other girls who were going were all nice and then, too, it would be quiet in there" (Roethlisberger & Dickson, 1939, pp. 143–144). It is interesting that she reportedly said that her co-workers "all" felt suspicious of company intentions and that only a minority were apparently willing to take part.

Returning to the RATR experiment for the moment, we simply note that a significant surge in productivity was achieved in early 1928 by replacing a worker "reported to have 'gone Bolshevik'" with another (Operator 2) who developed an exceptionally close relationship with all levels of management and who "forced the group into a partial adoption of her enthusiasms; she constituted herself the keeper of its conscience; she admonished this one, encouraged that one, and built up an entire system of control based on social favors and prestige" (Whitehead, 1938, Vol. 1, p. 158). One solution to the (suppressed) problem of worker resistance to management is therefore to get rid of troublemakers and replace them with more ambitious—and hence more cooperative—workers!

Whether Operator 2A's distrust of and opposition to management was due to anemia or not, she was not the only one who maintained this kind of attitude well into the experiment. Let us look at what took place during the famous Period 12, 16 months after the start of the experiment and 7 months after the departure of Operator 2A. Had the Hawthorne effect fully taken hold such that a harmonious group of workers caught up in the enthusiasm of spontaneous cooperation with a humanized management would respond with increased output at every new change in the work conditions, regardless of whether these changes were in themselves desirable? Despite efforts by Mayo and Roethlisberger to present this view, it does not tally with the published reports.

The first place to look, perhaps, is the output record itself. Did output in fact go up in Period 12, despite the long hours and the absence of rest pauses and free lunches? We begin here partly because Mayo (1945) himself took output as an "index of well-being" (p. 62) or an "index of improved conditions" (p. 63). We may thus ask whether this "index" suggests improved morale in the work group.

It seems reasonable, if output is taken for the moment to be an index of morale, to look at average *hourly* output as an indicator of how efficiently work is being done. This would seem to respond most closely to the mental attitude of the workers. An alternative would be to look at total weekly output, but it is contaminated by the variation from period to period in the number of hours worked per week. Roethlisberger and Dickson (1939) refer to this problem of indices when, after presenting the "hourly rate" for Period 12, they go on to introduce the "total weekly output" in the following terms; "Inasmuch as the industrial manager is interested not only in the rate of output but also in the total output, the total weekly outputs for each operator . . . arc shown" (p. 77). However, writing a few years later, Roethlisberger (1941) seems to have forgotten about the hourly rate (which dropped sharply in Period 12!) and says, referring to the total weekly output, "Output, instead of taking the expected nose dive, maintained its high level" (p. 13). True, the weekly rate did not fall; it actually went up (cf. Franke & Kaul, 1978, p. 639; Roethlisberger & Dickson, 1939, Figure 7, p. 78). Mayo (1933, 1945) refers only to daily and weekly output when he says that "output rose to a point higher than at any other time" (1933, p. 63).

Mayo seems, however, to have been slightly uneasy about this grand conclusion concerning Period 12. After all, Roethlisberger and Dickson (1939) said quite candidly,

> In one case only (Period XII) does the hourly rate behave in the way it might have been expected to. But although the hourly rate for all operators starts to decline when the operators return to a full 48-hour week with no rests, it never reaches the level of Period III, when similar working conditions were in effect. (p. 77)

How does one demonstrate an increase in morale and cooperation when the hourly rate shows that the workers have *slowed down*? Emphasis remained on the increase in *weekly* output (the week being six hours longer than during the preceding period), which fit the human relations theory more neatly.

But the stubborn fact remains that the hourly output dropped for four of the five workers in Period 12 and then increased dramatically for all five in Period 13 with the return of rest pauses (Roethlisberger & Dickson, 1939, p. 76). Why the slowdown in Period 12? Roethlisberger and Dickson (1939) said that the workers were afraid "that, should their previous performance be maintained or improved in this period, rest pauses might never again be reinstated" (p. 180). And yet, we are told, in extensive prior discussions the workers had been given reassurance concerning what was to be a strictly temporary (12-week) period. Despite this guarantee, apparently, they were still ready to believe that management was really interested in how to squeeze the most out of them, rather than in making their working conditions better for *them*. Roethlisberger and Dickson (1939), again, were rather frank about recognizing this:

> The girls came into the test with a somewhat suspicious and apprehensive attitude. . . . When the introduction of these rests was accompanied by an immediate and definite rise in output, they began to worry about whether or not they would receive the increased earnings resulting from this rise. In other words, *they were never sure that they were not going to be victimized in some fashion or other by the experimenters or by management.* By Period XIII, however, this apprehension of authority was almost entirely dissipated. (p. 85, italics added)

The published record shows, indeed, that the response of the workers to the much-disliked Period 12 was far from what one would want to call "spontaneous cooperation." Operator 3 said, "Give me back the rests and see how my output goes up" (Roethlisberger & Dickson, 1939, p. 72). Whitehead (1938) reported the following comment by one of the workers in Period 12: "We must not be higher now than we were when we had rest periods, because we want our rest periods" (p. 127). The struggle that went on between workers and management is more concretely evoked perhaps by a few excerpts from the record kept by the test room observer. On November 6, 1928 (Period 12), it is recorded that Operator 2 said, "I'll take my own rest period like I did this morning at 9:30." On the next day, with discipline apparently at a new low, the observer reported:

> Operators were laughing and talking extremely loud during the middle part of the afternoon. . . . They were told then that if the present period did not prove satisfactory at the conclusion of the twelfth week, it might become necessary to run without rests and lunches for a month or two more. (Wrege, Note 1)

The evidence shows that four of the five workers actually slowed down, and it is apparent that this slowdown was intentional, not a mechanical effect of the worsened working conditions. The workers were quite consciously adopting a strategy intended to induce the experiments to return quickly to the preferred conditions. If the workers had in fact had the kind of trust in management's good intentions that Mayo claims, would they have found it necessary to resist the experimenters so actively in this period? The picture we get, instead, is of a group of rather wary workers engaged in a continuing skirmish with management and determined not to be taken advantage of. Rather than become a part of the company "team," they became a team of their own, rather coolly looking out for their own economic interests in an adversary relationship with management, regardless of how much they may have personally liked certain members of the research team.

OTHER INDICATIONS OF WORKER RESISTANCE AT HAWTHORNE AND HOW IT WAS EXPLAINED AWAY

As part of our argument that worker resistance to management was commonplace at Hawthorne (despite absence of a union), yet tended to be covered up in the popular writings of Mayo and Roethlisberger, it is instructive to look briefly at descriptions of the Bank Wiring Observation Room study, even though it is not the basis for what is known as the Hawthorne effect. [. . .]

This nonexperimental observation study owes its reknown to its elaborate description of a work restriction norm within a group of men putting together telephone equipment (see, e.g., Homans, 1950). It offers a striking contrast, on first sight, to the group of women in the Relay Assembly Test Room study, since the existence of a cohesive group in bank wiring was associated with stable rather than with increasing production. Mayo was much impressed with this apparent contrast. One could say that much of his persistent advocacy of "human relations in industry" found its rationale in the problem of how to manipulate workers in such a way as to harness the power of the cohesive group in the "good" direction (relay assembly) rather than have that power turned against management (bank wiring).

[. . .]

As one has seen, Mayo and Roethlisberger were able to hide the actual resistance of the relay assembly women behind the magic of an allegedly smoothly rising curve of productivity. This was not possible with the men in bank wiring. The existence of restrictive practices directed against management control of work pace (cf. Noble, 1977; Whyte, 1955) hit the observer in the face. Rather than deny it or hide it away, it was necessary to deal with it more openly, which could be accomplished in essentially two ways. First, and most important, management (and their researchers, of course) would have to find out how to stop that sort of thing. Second, if the image of the factory as a big happy family in which there is no conflict of interest was to be preserved, this kind of worker resistance would have to be explained away as irrational, emotional, based on misunderstanding, and so on. Otherwise, the Marxists and other critics of business would surely exploit the results of the bank wiring study as indicating workers' consciousness of a fundamental contradiction in capitalist society.

On why restriction must by done away with—the technical problem—Roethlisberger (1960) said,

> Restriction of output among workers, for instance, although functional for the solidarity of the group and the emotional security of its members, is disfunctional (sic) for the group's identification with the economic objectives of the enterprise. (p. xiii)

On proving the irrationality—the ideological problem—of workers engaged in restriction, consider the following comments about the reasons the bank wiring men gave to interviewers for their actions:

It follows that this group of operators could not be said to be acting in accordance with their economic interests even if we assume that the reasons they gave for their actions were supportable by experimental evidence, which, of course, was not the case. (Roethlisberger & Dickson, 1939, p. 533)

[. . .]

Their behavior, in other words, was not based upon their own concrete experience with the company. *[. . .]* (pp. 532–533)

First, there was nothing in the behavior of this group that even faintly resembled conscious, planned opposition to management. . . . Of course, their endeavor to preserve their internal organization did result in a certain amount of opposition to management. This opposition came about indirectly and quite inevitably; there was no conscious intent. (pp. 535–536)

Mayo (1945) eradicated any lingering traces of "opposition" in the following bland description:

The final experiment, reported under the title of the Bank Wiring Observation Room, was set up to extend and confirm these observations [about workers' conception of a "fair day's work"]. Simultaneously it was realized that these facts did not in any way imply low working morale as suggested by such phrases as "restriction of output." On the contrary, the failure of free communication between management and workers in modern large-scale industry leads inevitably to the exercise of caution by the working group until such time as it knows clearly the range and meaning of changes imposed from above. (pp. 70–71)

Contrast this with what Operator W3 was reported as saying: "Well, you see if they start turning out around 7,300 [terminals wired] a day over a period of weeks and if three of them do it, then they can lay one of the men off, because three men working at that speed can do as much as four men working at the present rate" (Roethlisberger & Dickson, 1939, p. 417). When a smart-aleck interviewer then asked Operator W8, "Why do you work at all?" he replied simply that work "should be spread around more" (p. 419). Note that workers expressed concern not only for their own individual security but also for consequences to others doing the same work (pp. 531–532).

There is not space here to detail fully the ill-disguised contempt for workers' intelligence and

rationality expressed by these writers. The interested reader should examine Roethlisberger and Dickson's (1939) analysis of worker complaints (e.g., pp. 256–268), where unsanitary washrooms are blamed on "the carelessness of some employees," grievances about piece rates are explained away as showing simply, for example, that "B's present earnings, due to his wife's illness, are insufficient to meet his current financial obligations," and so on. Roethlisberger (1941) wrote, "Many times they found that people did not really want anything done about the things of which they were complaining" (p. 19). Employee complaints and arguments were seen as based on a "logic of sentiment," symptoms of other problems of which the workers seemed unaware: "Examples of what is meant here are the arguments employees give which center around the 'right to work,' 'seniority,' 'fairness,' 'the living wage'" (Roethlisberger & Dickson, 1939, p. 564).

Nevertheless, despite the alleged distortion in employees' comments to interviewers, Mayo seemed to feel that valuable information could be gained for management's use.

[. . .]

It is clear that he *was* aware of industrial conflict. He wanted to get close to it in order to understand it and develop techniques (human relations, counseling) to combat the development of class consciousness but *at the same time* publicly claim that the conflict was somehow unreal, irrational, and unnatural.

Some might claim that the view of workers presented by Mayo and by Roethlisberger, even though far from fully accurate, nevertheless constituted a distinct advance over the views current in the 1920s and 1930s. Indeed, Frederick Taylor's decorticated worker (cf. Braverman's, 1974, critique), the engineer's worker as extension of a machine, or even the worker who is nothing but a bundle of skills waiting to be matched to the right job—relative to these, Mayo's flesh and blood worker with feelings, with a need for esteem and comradeship, and even possessed of an unconscious (albeit sexless and not very aggressive), appears closer to reality and more worthy of respect. In fact, it is clear that Mayo was a persistent advocate of a less dehumanized image of the worker (Mulherin, 1980). We are willing, grudgingly, to give Mayo that credit. What disturbs us, however, is the way in which he used a combination of psychoanalysis and Pareto to suppress an important part of the truth about what it means to be a human being in an exploitative economic system. He refused to admit that resistance to exploitation could be rational in 20th-century America.

It is ironic that the Hawthorne effect, which is considered to have given scientific recognition to the psychological, subjective point of view of the factory worker, should be based upon a research project which in its generally accepted conclusions suppressed a major part of that subjectivity: collective resistance to exploitation.

[. . .]

NOTES

1. As late as 1936, however, Western Electric was still hiring the union-busting Corporations Auxiliary Company, according to Gilson (1940).

2 One does not have to be a Marxist to see conflict, but it helps—especially in the case of *class* conflict. Most sociologists who criticized Mayo in the 1940s and 1950s (e.g., Bendix & Fisher, 1949; Blumer, 1947; Kerr & Fisher, 1957; see also Coser, 1956, who makes a similar critique of Lewin) for his unwillingness to deal *openly* with the question of unions noted that he generally avoided talking about real conflicts of interest. But these authors, however much influenced by Marxism, did not ordinarily see conflict as involving fundamentally antagonistic classes. Their objection to Mayo was not, as with us, his attempts to destroy class consciousness. Rather, they considered his defense of capitalism to be based on a lack of realism about the kinds of methods that would be necessary to integrate workers into a "pluralist" capitalist system. *[. . .]*

3 Much worker suspicion of management intentions at Hawthorne centered on fear that increased output would result in changes in piece rate, so that pay gains would soon be lost while work rate was increased. Was it necessarily "paranoid" to feel uneasy in the RATR, when the man selected to be supervisor-observer "had had considerable experience in setting piece rates," as pointed out by Roethlisberger and Dickson (1939, p. 22)? Mayo's psychiatric approach was later outgrown by some of his students. Whyte (1955), for example, assembled a large amount of evidence on the clever strategies by which workers try to outwit the perennial enemy, the time-study person.

REFERENCE NOTE

Wrege, C. D. Personal communications, 1979.

REFERENCES

Argyle, M. The Relay Assembly Test Room in retrospect. *Occupational Psychology*, 1953, *27*, 98–103.

Baritz, L. *The servants of power: A history of the use of social science in American industry*. Middletown, Conn.: Wesleyan University Press, 1960.

Bendix, R. & Fisher, L. H. The perspectives of Elton Mayo. *Review of Economics and Statistics*, 1949, *31*, 312–319.

Blumer, H. Sociological theory in industrial relations. *American Sociological Review,* 1947, *12*, 271–278.

Braverman, H. *Labor and monopoly capital*. New York: Monthly Review Press, 1974.

Carey, A. The Hawthorne studies. A radical criticism. *American Sociological Review,* 1967, *32*, 403–416.

Carey, A. The Lysenko syndrome in Western social science. *Australian Psychologist*, 1977, *12*, 27–38.

Coser, L. *The functions of social conflict*. New York: Free Press of Glencoe, 1956.

Dunnette, M. D. (Ed.). *Handbook of industrial and organizational psychology*. Chicago: Rand McNally, 1976.

Franke, R. H. The Hawthorne experiments: Re-view: *American Sociological Review*, 1979, *44*, 861–867.

Franke, R. H. & Kaul, J. D. The Hawthorne experiments: First statistical interpretation. *American Sociological Review*, 1978, *43*, 623–643.

Gilson, M. B. Review of *Management and the worker. American Journal of Sociology.* 1940, *46*, 98–101.

Haire, M. Industrial social psychology. In G. Lindzey (Ed)., *Handbook of social psychology* (Vol. 2). Reading, Mass.: Addison-Wesley, 1954.

Homans, G. C. *The human group*. New York: Harcourt, Brace, 1950.

Homans, G. C. Group factors in worker productivity. In E. E. Maccoby, T. M. Newcomb, & E. L. Hartley (Eds.), *Readings in social psychology* (3rd ed.). New York: Holt, Rinehart & Winston, 1958. (Originally published, 1940.)

Kerr, C., & Fisher, L. H. Plant sociology: The elite and the aborigines. In M. Komarovsky (Ed.), *Common frontiers of the social sciences*. New York: Free Press of Glencoe, 1957.

Landsberger, H. A. *Hawthorne revisited*. Ithaca, N.Y.: Cornell University Press, 1958.

Lynd, R. S. Review of Whitehead's *Leadership in a free society. Political Science Quarterly,* 1937, *52,* 590–592.

Mayo, E. *The human problems of an industrial civilization.* Cambridge, Mass.: Harvard University Press. 1933.

Mayo, E. *The social problems of an industrial civilization.* Cambridge, Mass.: Harvard University, Graduate School of Business Administration, 1945.

Miller, D. C. & Form, W. H. *Industrial sociology.* New York: Harper, 1951.

Mills, C. W. The contribution of sociology to studies of industrial relations. *Proceedings of the Industrial Relations Research Association,* 1948. *1,* 199–222.

Mulherin, J. *The sociology of work and organizations: Historical context and pattern of development.* Unpublished doctoral dissertation, University of California, Berkeley, 1980.

Noble, D. F. *America by design—Science, technology, and the rise of corporate capitalism.* New York: Knopf, 1977.

Parsons, H. M. What happened at Hawthorne? *Science,* 1974, *183,* 922–932.

Roethlisberger, F. J. *Management and morale.* Cambridge, Mass.: Harvard University Press, 1941.

Roethlisberger, F. J. Introduction. In E. Mayo, *The human problems of an industrial civilization* (2nd ed.). New York: Viking Press, 1960.

Roethlisberger, F. J., & Dickson, W. J. *Management and the worker,* New York: Wiley, 1939.

Roethlisberger, F. J., & Dickson, W. J. *Counseling in an organization: A sequel to the Hawthorne researches.* Cambridge, Mass: Harvard University, Graduate School of Business Administration, 1966.

Sills, D. L. (Ed.). *International encyclopedia of the social sciences.* New York: Macmillan, 1968.

Smith, J. H. Foreward. In E. Mayo, *The social problems of an industrial civilization.* London: Routledge & Kegan Paul, 1975.

Sykes, A. J. M. Economic interest and the Hawthorne researches. *Human Relations,* 1965, *18,* 253–263.

Vroom, V. H. Industrial social psychology. In G. Lindzey E. Aronson (Eds.), *Handbook of Social psychology* (Vol. 5, 2nd ed.). Reading, Mass.: Addison-Wesley, 1969.

Whitehead, T. N. *The industrial worker* (2 vols.). Cambridge, Mass.: Harvard University Press, 1938.

Whyte, W. F. *Money and motivation.* New York: Harper & Row, 1955.

Wilensky, J. L., & Wilensky, H. L. Personnel counseling: The Hawthorne case. *American Journal of Sociology,* 1951, *57,* 265–280.

Wrege, C. D. Solving Mayo's mystery: The first complete account of the origin of the Hawthorne studies— The forgotten contributions of C. E. Snow and H. Hibarger. *Academy of Management Proceedings,* 1976, 12–16.

9

THE HUMAN SIDE OF ENTERPRISE

DOUGLAS McGREGOR

It has become trite to say that the most significant developments of the next quarter century will take place not in the physical but in the social sciences, that industry—the economic organ of society—has the fundamental know-how to utilize physical science and technology for the material benefit of mankind, and that we must now learn how to utilize the social sciences to make our human organizations truly effective.

[. . .]

I

[. . .] We know that past conceptions of the nature of man are inadequate and in many ways incorrect. We are becoming quite certain that, under proper conditions, unimagined resources of creative human energy could become available within the organizational setting.

[. . .]

Management's Task: Conventional View

The conventional conception of management's task in harnessing human energy to organizational requirements can be stated broadly in terms of three propositions. In order to avoid the complications introduced by a label, I shall call this set of propositions "Theory X":

1. Management is responsible for organizing the elements of productive enterprise—money, materials, equipment, people—in the interest of economic ends.

2. With respect to people, this is a process of directing their efforts, motivating them, controlling their actions, modifying their behavior to fit the needs of the organization.

3. Without this active intervention by management, people would be passive—even resistant—to organizational needs. They must therefore be persuaded,

rewarded, punished, controlled—their activities must be directed. This is management's task—in managing subordinate managers or workers. We often sum it up by saying that management consists of getting things done through other people.

Behind this conventional theory there are several additional beliefs—less explicit, but widespread:

4. The average man is by nature indolent—he works as little as possible.

5. He lacks ambition, dislikes responsibility, prefers to be led.

6. He is inherently self-centered, indifferent to organizational needs.

7. He is by nature resistant to change.

8. He is gullible, not very bright, the ready dupe of the charlatan and the demagogue.

The human side of economic enterprise today is fashioned from propositions and beliefs such as these. Conventional organization structures, managerial policies, practices, and programs reflect these assumptions.

In accomplishing its task—with these assumptions as guides—management has conceived of a range of possibilities between two extremes.

The Hard or the Soft Approach?

At one extreme, management can be "hard" or "strong." The methods for directing behavior involve coercion and threat (usually disguised), close supervision, tight controls over behavior. At the other extreme, management can be "soft" or "weak." The methods for directing behavior involve being permissive, satisfying people's demands, achieving harmony. Then they will be tractable, accept direction.

This range has been fairly completely explored during the past half century, and management has learned some things from the exploration. There are difficulties in the "hard" approach. Force breeds counterforces: restriction of output, antagonism, militant unionism, subtle but effective sabotage of management objectives. This approach is especially difficult during times of full employment.

There are also difficulties in the "soft" approach. It leads frequently to the abdication of management—to harmony, perhaps, but to indifferent performance. People take advantage of the soft approach. They continually expect more, but they give less and less.

Currently, the popular theme is "firm but fair." This is an attempt to gain the advantages of both the hard and the soft approaches. It is reminiscent of Teddy Roosevelt's "speak softly and carry a big stick."

Is the Conventional View Correct?

The findings which are beginning to emerge from the social sciences challenge this whole set of beliefs about man and human nature and about the task of management. The evidence is far from conclusive, certainly, but it is suggestive. It comes from the laboratory, the clinic, the schoolroom, the home, and even to a limited extent from industry itself.

The social scientist does not deny that human behavior in industrial organization today is approximately what management perceives it to be. He has, in fact, observed it and studied it fairly extensively. But he is pretty sure that this behavior is *not* a consequence of man's inherent nature. It is a consequence rather of the nature of industrial organizations, of management philosophy, policy, and practice. The conventional approach of Theory X is based on mistaken notions of what is cause and what is effect.

[. . .]

II

Perhaps the best way to indicate why the conventional approach of management is inadequate is to consider the subject of motivation. In discussing this subject I will draw heavily on the work of my colleague, Abraham Maslow of Brandeis University. *[. . .]*

Physiological and Safety Needs

Man is a wanting animal—as soon as one of his needs is satisfied, another appears in its place. This process is unending. It continues from birth to death.

Man's needs are organized in a series of levels—a hierarchy of importance. At the lowest level, but preeminent in importance when they are thwarted, are his physiological needs. Man lives by bread alone, when there is no bread. Unless the circumstances are unusual, his needs for love, for status, for recognition are inoperative when his stomach has been empty for a while. But when he eats regularly and adequately, hunger ceases to be an important need. [. . .] The same is true of the other physiological needs of man—for rest, exercise, shelter, protection from the elements.

A satisfied need is not a motivator of behavior! This is a fact of profound significance. It is a fact that is regularly ignored in the conventional approach to the management of people. [. . .] Consider your own need for air. Except as you are deprived of it, it has no appreciable motivating effect upon your behavior.

When the physiological needs are reasonably satisfied, needs at the next higher level begin to dominate man's behavior—to motivate him. These are called safety needs. They are needs for protection against danger, threat, deprivation. Some people mistakenly refer to these as needs for security. However, unless man is in a dependent relationship where he fears arbitrary deprivation, he does not demand security. The need is for the "fairest possible break." When he is confident of this, he is more than willing to take risks. But when he feels threatened or dependent, his greatest need is for guarantees, for protection, for security.

The fact needs little emphasis that, since every industrial employee is in a dependent relationship, safety needs may assume considerable importance. Arbitrary management actions, behavior that arouses uncertainty with respect to continued employment or which reflects favoritism or discrimination, unpredictable administration of policy—these can be powerful motivators of the safety needs in the employment relationship *at every level* from worker to vice president.

Social Needs

When man's physiological needs are satisfied and he is no longer fearful about his physical welfare, his social needs become important motivators of his behavior—for belonging, for association, for acceptance by his fellows, for giving and receiving friendship and love.

Management knows today of the existence of these needs, but it often assumes quite wrongly that they represent a threat to the organization. Many studies have demonstrated that the tightly knit, cohesive work group may, under proper conditions, be far more effective than an equal number of separate individuals in achieving organizational goals.

Yet management, fearing group hostility to its own objectives, often goes to considerable lengths to control and direct human efforts in ways that are inimical to the natural "groupiness" of human beings. When man's social needs—and perhaps his safety needs, too—are thus thwarted, he behaves in ways which tend to defeat organizational objectives. He becomes resistant, antagonistic, uncooperative. But this behavior is a consequence, not a cause.

Ego Needs

Above the social needs—in the sense that they do not become motivators until lower needs are reasonably satisfied—are the needs of greatest significance to management and to man himself. They are the egoistic needs, and they are of two kinds:

1. Those needs that relate to one's self-esteem—needs for self-confidence, for independence, for achievement, for competence, for knowledge.

2. Those needs that relate to one's reputation—needs for status, for recognition, for appreciation, for the deserved respect of one's fellows.

Unlike the lower needs, these are rarely satisfied; man seeks indefinitely for more satisfaction of these needs once they have become important to him. But they do not appear in any significant way until physiological, safety, and social needs are all reasonably satisfied.

The typical industrial organization offers few opportunities for the satisfaction of these egoistic needs to people at lower levels in the hierarchy. The conventional methods of organizing work, particularly in mass-production industries, give little heed to these aspects of human motivation. If the practices of scientific management were deliberately calculated to thwart these needs—which, of course, they are not—they could hardly accomplish this purpose better than they do.

Self-Fulfillment Needs

Finally—a capstone, as it were, on the hierarchy of man's needs—there are what we may call the needs for self-fulfillment. These are the needs for realizing one's own potentialities, for continued self-development, for being creative in the broadest sense of that term.

It is clear that the conditions of modern life give only limited opportunity for these relatively weak needs to obtain expression. The deprivation most people experience with respect to other lower-level needs diverts their energies into the struggle to satisfy *those* needs, and the needs for self-fulfillment remain dormant.

III

[. . .] We recognize readily enough that a man suffering from a severe dietary deficiency is sick. The deprivation of physiological needs has behavioral consequences. The same is true—although less well recognized—of deprivation of higher-level needs. The man whose needs for safety, association, independence, or status are thwarted is sick just as surely as is he who has rickets. And his sickness will have behavioral consequences. We will be mistaken if we attribute his resultant passivity, his hostility, his refusal to accept responsibility to his inherent "human nature." These forms of behavior are *symptoms* of illness—of deprivation of his social and egoistic needs.

The man whose lower-level needs are satisfied is not motivated to satisfy those needs any longer. For practical purposes they exist no longer. [. . .] Management often asks, "Why aren't people more productive? We pay good wages, provide good working conditions, have excellent fringe benefits and steady employment. Yet people do not seem to be willing to put forth more than minimum effort."

The fact that management has provided for these physiological and safety needs has shifted the motivational emphasis to the social and perhaps to the egoistic needs. Unless there are opportunities *at work* to satisfy these higher-level needs, people will be deprived; and their behavior will reflect this deprivation. Under such conditions, if management continues to focus its attention on physiological needs, its efforts are bound to be ineffective.

People *will* make insistent demands for more money under these conditions. It becomes more important than ever to buy the material goods and services that can provide limited satisfaction of the thwarted needs. Although money has only limited value in satisfying many higher-level needs, it can become the focus of interest if it is the *only* means available.

The Carrot and Stick Approach

The carrot and stick theory of motivation [. . .] works reasonably well under certain circumstances. The *means* for satisfying man's physiological and (within limits) his safety needs can be provided or withheld by management. Employment itself is such a means, and so are wages, working conditions, and benefits. By these means the individual can be controlled so long as he is struggling for subsistence. Man lives for bread alone when there is no bread.

But the carrot and stick theory does not work at all once man has reached an adequate subsistence level and is motivated primarily by higher needs. Management cannot provide a man with self-respect, or with the respect of his fellows, or with the satisfaction of needs for self-fulfillment. It can create conditions such that he is encouraged and enabled to seek such satisfactions *for himself*, or it can thwart him by failing to create those conditions.

But this creation of conditions is not "control." It is not a good device for directing behavior. And so management finds itself in an odd position. The high standard of living created by our modern technological know-how provides quite adequately for the satisfaction of physiological and safety needs. The only significant exception is where management practices have not created confidence in a "fair break"—and thus where safety needs are thwarted. But by making possible the satisfaction of low-level needs, management has deprived itself of the ability to use as motivators the devices on which conventional theory has taught it to rely—rewards, promises, incentives, or threats and other coercive devices.

Neither Hard nor Soft

The philosophy of management by direction and control—*regardless of whether it is hard or soft*—is inadequate to motivate, because the human needs on which this approach relies are today unimportant motivators of behavior. Direction and control are essentially useless in motivating people whose important needs are social and egoistic. Both the hard and the soft approach fail today because they are simply irrelevant to the situation.

People deprived of opportunities to satisfy at work the needs that are now important to them behave exactly as we might predict—with indolence, passivity, resistance to change, lack of responsibility, willingness to follow the demagogue, unreasonable demands for economic benefits. It would seem that we are caught in a web of our own weaving.

[. . .]

IV

For these and many other reasons, we require a different theory of the task of managing people based on more adequate assumptions about human nature and human motivation. I am going to be so bold as to suggest the broad dimensions of such a theory. Call it "Theory Y," if you will.

1. Management is responsible for organizing the elements of productive enterprise—money, materials, equipment, people—in the interest of economic ends.

2. People are *not* by nature passive or resistant to organizational needs. They have become so as a result of experience in organizations.

3. The motivation, the potential for development, the capacity for assuming responsibility, the readiness to direct behavior toward organizational goals are all present in people. Management does not put them there. It is a responsibility of management to make it possible for people to recognize and develop these human characteristics for themselves.

4. The essential task of management is to arrange organizational conditions and methods of operation so that people can achieve their own goals *best* by directing *their own* efforts toward organizational objectives.

This is a process primarily of creating opportunities, releasing potential, removing obstacles, encouraging growth, providing guidance. *[. . .]*

And I hasten to add that it does *not* involve the abdication of management, the absence of leadership, the lowering of standards, or the other characteristics usually associated with the "soft" approach under Theory X. *[. . .]*

Some Difficulties

The conditions imposed by conventional organization theory and by the approach of scientific management for the past half century have tied men to limited jobs which do not utilize their capabilities, have discouraged the acceptance of responsibility, have encouraged passivity, have eliminated meaning from work. *[. . .]*

People today are accustomed to being directed, manipulated, controlled in industrial organizations and to finding satisfaction for their social, egoistic, and self-fulfillment needs away from the job. This is true of much of management as well as of workers. Genuine "industrial citizenship" *[. . .]* is a remote and unrealistic idea, the meaning of which has not even been considered by most members of industrial organizations.

Another way of saying this is that Theory X places exclusive reliance upon external control of human behavior, whereas Theory Y relies heavily on self-control and self-direction. It is worth noting that this difference is the difference between treating people as children and treating them as mature adults. After generations of the former, we cannot expect to shift to the latter overnight.

V

[. . .] Consider with me a few innovative ideas which are entirely consistent with Theory Y and which are today being applied with some success.

Decentralization and Delegation

These are ways of freeing people from the too-close control of conventional organization, giving them a degree of freedom to direct their own activities, to assume responsibility, and, importantly, to satisfy their egoistic needs. In this connection, the flat organization of Sears, Roebuck and Company provides an interesting example. It forces "management by objectives" since it enlarges the number of people reporting to a manager until he cannot direct and control them in the conventional manner.

Job Enlargement

This concept, pioneered by I.B.M. and Detroit Edison, is quite consistent with Theory Y. It encourages the acceptance of responsibility at the bottom of the organization; it provides opportunities for satisfying social and egoistic needs. In fact, the reorganization of work at the factory level offers one of the more challenging opportunities for innovation consistent with Theory Y. [. . .]

Participation and Consultative Management

Under proper conditions these results provide encouragement to people to direct their creative energies toward organizational objectives, give them some voice in decisions that affect them, provide significant opportunities for the satisfaction of social and egoistic needs. [. . .]

The not infrequent failure of such ideas as these to work as well as expected is often attributable to

the fact that a management has "bought the idea" but applied it within the framework of Theory X and its assumptions.

Delegation is not an effective way of exercising management by control. Participation becomes a farce when it is applied as a sales gimmick or a device for kidding people into thinking they are important. Only the management that has confidence in human capacities and is itself directed toward organizational objectives rather than toward the preservation of personal power can grasp the implications of this emerging theory.

[. . .]

VI

[. . .] The ingenuity and the perseverance of industrial management in the pursuit of economic ends have changed many scientific and technological dreams into commonplace realities. It is now becoming clear that the application of these same talents to the human side of enterprise will not only enhance substantially these materialistic achievements but will bring us one step closer to "the good society." Shall we get on with the job?

Whenever physical needs' are met, social need, egotistic need, etc. appear and the org ought to encourage or help employees discover these; otherwise, they will be supressed, eliminated, and feel deprived.

10

FROM CONTROL TO COMMITMENT IN THE WORKPLACE

RICHARD E. WALTON

The larger shape of institutional change is always difficult to recognize when one stands right in the middle of it. Today, throughout American industry, a significant change is under way in long-established approaches to the organization and management of work. Although this shift in attitude and practice takes a wide variety of company-specific forms, its larger shape—its overall pattern—is already visible if one knows where and how to look.

Consider, for example, the marked differences between two plants in the chemical products division of a major U.S. corporation. They make similar products and employ similar technologies, but that is virtually all they have in common.

The first, organized by businesses with an identifiable product or product line, divides its employees into self-supervising 10- to 15-person work teams that are collectively responsible for a set of related tasks. Each team member has the training to perform many or all of the tasks for which the team is accountable, and pay reflects the level of mastery of required skills. These teams have received assurances that management will go to extra lengths to provide continued employment in any economic downturn. The teams have also been thoroughly briefed on such issues as market share, product costs, and their implications for the business.

Not surprisingly, this plant is a top performer economically and rates well on all measures of employee satisfaction, absenteeism, turnover, and safety. With its employees actively engaged in identifying and solving problems, it operates with fewer levels of management and fewer specialized departments than do its sister plants. It is also one of the principal suppliers of management talent for these other plants and for the division manufacturing staff.

In the second plant, each employee is responsible for a fixed job and is required to perform up to the minimum standard defined for that job. Peer pressure keeps new employees from exceeding the minimum standards and from taking other initiatives that go beyond basic job requirements. Supervisors, who manage daily assignments and monitor performance, have long since given up hope for anything more than compliance with standards, finding sufficient difficulty in getting their people to perform adequately most of the time. In fact, they and their workers try to prevent the industrial engineering department, which is under pressure from top plant management to improve operations, from using changes in methods to "jack up" standards.

A recent management campaign to document an "airtight case" against employees who have excessive absenteeism or sub-par performance mirrors employees' low morale and high distrust of management. A constant stream of formal grievances, violations of plant rules, harassment of supervisors, wildcat walkouts, and even sabotage has prevented the plant from reaching its productivity and quality goals and has absorbed a disproportionate amount of division staff time. Dealings with the union are characterized by contract negotiations on economic matters and skirmishes over issues of management control.

No responsible manager, of course, would ever wish to encourage the kind of situation at this second plant, yet the determination to understand its deeper causes and to attack them at their root does not come easily. Established modes of doing things have an inertia all their own. Such an effort is, however, in process all across the industrial landscape. And with that effort comes the possibility of a revolution in industrial relations every bit as great as that occasioned by the rise of mass production the better part of a century ago. The challenge is clear to those managers willing to see it—and the potential benefits, enormous.

APPROACHES TO WORK-FORCE MANAGEMENT

What explains the extraordinary differences between the plants just described? Is it that the first

is new (built in 1976) and the other old? Yes and no. Not all new plants enjoy so fruitful an approach to work organization; not all older plants have such intractable problems. Is it that one plant is unionized and the other not? Again, yes and no. The presence of a union may institutionalize conflict and lackluster performance, but it seldom causes them.

At issue here is not so much age or unionization but two radically different strategies for managing a company's or a factory's work force, two incompatible views of what managers can reasonably expect of workers and of the kind of partnership they can share with them. For simplicity, I will speak of these profound differences as reflecting the choice between a strategy based on imposing *control* and a strategy based on eliciting *commitment*.

The "Control" Strategy

The traditional—or control-oriented—approach to work-force management took shape during the early part of this century in response to the division of work into small, fixed jobs for which individuals could be held accountable. The actual definition of jobs, as of acceptable standards of performance, rested on "lowest common denominator" assumptions about workers' skill and motivation. To monitor and control effort of this assumed caliber, management organized its own responsibilities into a hierarchy of specialized roles buttressed by a top-down allocation of authority and by status symbols attached to positions in the hierarchy.

For workers, compensation followed the rubric of "a fair day's pay for a fair day's work" because precise evaluations were possible when individual job requirements were so carefully prescribed. Most managers had little doubt that labor was best thought of as a variable cost, although some exceptional companies guaranteed job security to head off unionization attempts.

In the traditional approach, there was generally little policy definition with regard to employee voice unless the work force was unionized, in which case damage control strategies predominated. With no union, management relied on an open-door policy, attitude surveys, and similar devices to learn about employees' concerns. If the work force was unionized, then management bargained terms of employment and established an appeal mechanism. These activities fell to labor relations specialists, who operated independently from line management and whose very existence assumed the inevitability and even the appropriateness of an adversarial relationship between workers and managers. Indeed, to those who saw management's exclusive obligation to be to a company's shareowners and the ownership of property to be the ultimate source of both obligation and prerogative, the claims of employees were constraints, nothing more.

At the heart of this traditional model is the wish to establish order, exercise control, and achieve efficiency in the application of the work force. Although it has distant antecedents in the bureaucracies of both church and military, the model's real father is Frederick W. Taylor, the turn-of-the-century "father of scientific management," whose views about the proper organization of work have long influenced management practice as well as the reactive policies of the U.S. labor movement.

Recently, however, changing expectations among workers have prompted a growing disillusionment with the apparatus of control. At the same time, of course, an intensified challenge from abroad has made the competitive obsolescence of this strategy clear. A model that assumes low employee commitment and that is designed to produce reliable if not outstanding performance simply cannot match the standards of excellence set by world-class competitors. Especially in a high-wage country like the United States, market success depends on a superior level of performance, a level that, in turn, requires the deep commitment, not merely the obedience—if you could obtain it—of workers. And as painful experience shows, this commitment cannot flourish in a workplace dominated by the familiar model of control.

THE "COMMITMENT" STRATEGY

Since the early 1970s, companies have experimented at the plant level with a radically different work-force strategy. The more visible pioneers—among them, General Foods at Topeka, Kansas; General Motors at Brookhaven, Mississippi; Cummins Engine at Jamestown, New York; and Procter & Gamble at Lima, Ohio—have begun to show how great and productive the contribution of a truly committed work force can be. For a time, all new plants of this sort were nonunion, but by 1980 the success of efforts undertaken jointly with unions—GM's cooperation with the UAW at the Cadillac plant in Livonia, Michigan, for example—was impressive enough to encourage managers of both new and existing facilities to rethink their approach to the work force.

Stimulated in part by the dramatic turnaround at GM's Tarrytown assembly plant in the mid-1970s, local managers and union officials are increasingly talking about common interests, working to develop mutual trust, and agreeing to sponsor quality-of-work-life (QWL) or employee involvement (EI) activities. Although most of these ventures have been initiated at the local level, major exceptions include the joint effort between the Communication Workers of America and AT&T to promote QWL throughout the Bell System and the UAW-Ford EI program centrally directed by Donald Ephlin of the UAW and Peter Pestillo of Ford. In the nonunion sphere, the spirit of these new initiatives is evident in the decision by workers of Delta Airlines to show their commitment to the company by collecting money to buy a new plane.

More recently, a growing number of manufacturing companies has begun to remove levels of plant hierarchy, increase managers' spans of control, integrate quality and production activities at lower organizational levels, combine production and maintenance operations, and open up new career possibilities for workers. Some corporations have even begun to chart organizational renewal for the entire company. Cummins Engine, for example, has ambitiously committed itself to inform employees about the business, to encourage participation by everyone, and to create jobs that involve greater responsibility and more flexibility.

In this new commitment-based approach to the work force, jobs are designed to be broader than before, to combine planning and implementation, and to include efforts to upgrade operations, not just maintain them. Individual responsibilities are expected to change as conditions change, and teams, not individuals, often are the organizational units accountable for performance. With management *[handwritten annotations in top margin: "→ use the power of peer pressure (have everyone become a manager) — sharing goals / objectives."]*

hierarchies relatively flat and differences in status minimized, control and lateral coordination depend on shared goals, and expertise rather than formal position determines influence.

People Express, to cite one example, started up with its management hierarchy limited to three levels, organized its work force into three- or four-person groups, and created positions with exceptionally broad scope. Every full-time employee is a "manager": flight managers are pilots who also perform dispatching and safety checks; maintenance managers are technicians with other staff responsibilities; customer service managers take care of ticketing, security clearance, passenger boarding, and in-flight service. Everyone, including the officers, is expected to rotate among functions to boost all workers' understanding of the business and to promote personal development.

Under the commitment strategy, performance expectations are high and serve not to define minimum standards but to provide "stretch objectives," emphasize continuous improvement, and reflect the requirements of the marketplace. Accordingly, compensation policies reflect less the old formulas of job evaluation than the heightened importance of group achievement, the expanded scope of individual contribution, and the growing concern for such questions of "equity" as gain sharing, stock ownership, and profit sharing. This principle of economic sharing is not new. It has long played a role in Dana Corporation, which has many unionized plants, and is a fundamental part of the strategy of People Express, which has no union. Today, Ford sees it as an important part of the company's transition to a commitment strategy.

Equally important to the commitment strategy is the challenge of giving employees some assurance of security, perhaps by offering them priority in training and retraining as old jobs are eliminated and new ones created. Guaranteeing employees access to due process and providing them the means to be heard on such issues as production methods, problem solving, and human resource policies and practices is also a challenge. In unionized settings, the additional tasks include making relations less adversarial, broadening the agenda for joint problem solving and planning, and facilitating employee consultation.

Underlying all these policies is a management philosophy, often embodied in a published statement, that acknowledges the legitimate claims of a company's multiple stakeholders—owners, employees, customers, and the public. At the center of this philosophy is a belief that eliciting employee commitment will lead to enhanced performance. The evidence shows this belief to be well grounded. In the absence of genuine commitment, however, new management policies designed for a committed work force may well leave a company distinctly more vulnerable than would older policies based on the control approach. The advantages—and risks—are considerable.

THE COSTS OF COMMITMENT

Because the potential leverage of a commitment-oriented strategy on performance is so great, the natural temptation is to assume the universal applicability of that strategy. Some environments, however, especially those requiring intricate teamwork, problem solving, organizational learning, and self-monitoring, are better suited than others to the commitment model. Indeed, the pioneers of the deep commitment strategy—a fertilizer plant in Norway, a refinery in the United Kingdom, a paper mill in Pennsylvania, a pet-food processing plant in Kansas—were all based on continuous process technologies and were all capital- and raw-material-intensive. All provided high economic leverage to improvements in workers' skills and attitudes, and all could offer considerable job challenge.

Is the converse true? Is the control strategy appropriate whenever—as with convicts breaking rocks with sledgehammers in a prison yard—work can be completely prescribed, remains static, and calls for individual, not group, effort? In practice, managers have long answered yes. Mass production, epitomized by the assembly line, has for years been thought suitable for old-fashioned control.

But not any longer. Many mass producers, not least the automakers, have recently been trying to reconceive the structure of work and to give employees a significant role in solving problems and improving methods. Why? For many reasons, including to boost in-plant quality, lower warranty costs, cut waste, raise machine utilization and total capacity with the same plant and equipment, reduce operating and support personnel, reduce turnover and absenteeism, and speed up implementation of change. In addition, some managers place direct value on the fact that the commitment policies promote the development of human skills and individual self-esteem.

The benefits, economic and human, of worker commitment extend not only to continuous-process industries but to traditional manufacturing industries as well. What, though, are the costs? To achieve these gains, managers have had to invest extra effort, develop new skills and relationships, cope with higher levels of ambiguity and uncertainty, and experience the pain and discomfort associated with changing habits and attitudes. Some of their skills have become obsolete, and some of their careers have been casualties of change. Union officials, too, have had to face the dislocation and discomfort that inevitably follow any upheaval in attitudes and skills. For their part, workers have inherited more responsibility and, along with it, greater uncertainty and a more open-ended possibility of failure.

Part of the difficulty in assessing these costs is the fact that so many of the following problems inherent to the commitment strategy remain to be solved.

Employment Assurances

As managers in heavy industry confront economic realities that make such assurances less feasible and as their counterparts in fiercely competitive high-technology areas are forced to rethink early guarantees of employment security, pointed questions await.

Will managers give lifetime assurances to the few, those who reach, say, 15 years' seniority, or will they adopt a general no-layoff policy? Will they demonstrate by policies and practices that employment security, though by no means absolute, is a higher priority item than it was under the control approach? Will they accept greater responsibility for outplacement?

Compensation

In one sense, the more productive employees under the commitment approach deserve to receive better pay for their better efforts, but how can managers balance this claim on resources with the harsh reality that domestic pay rates have risen to levels that render many of our industries uncompetitive internationally? Already, in such industries as trucking and airlines, new domestic competitors have placed companies that maintain prevailing wage rates at a significant disadvantage. Experience shows, however, that wage freezes and concession bargaining create obstacles to commitment, and new approaches to compensation are difficult to develop at a time when management cannot raise the overall level of pay.

Which approach is really suitable to the commitment model is unclear. Traditional job classifications place limits on the discretion of supervisors and encourage workers' sense of job ownership. Can pay systems based on employees' skill levels, which have long been used in engineering and skilled crafts, prove widely effective? Can these systems make up in greater mastery, positive motivation, and work-force flexibility what they give away in higher average wages?

In capital-intensive businesses, where total payroll accounts for a small percentage of costs, economics favor the move toward pay progression based on deeper and broader mastery. Still, conceptual problems remain with measuring skills, achieving consistency in pay decisions, allocating opportunities for learning new skills, trading off breadth and flexibility against depth, and handling the effects of "topping out" in a system that rewards and encourages personal growth.

There are also practical difficulties. Existing plants cannot, for example, convert to a skill-based structure overnight because of the vested interests of employees in the higher classifications. Similarly, formal profit- or gain-sharing plans like the Scanlon Plan (which shares gains in productivity as measured by improvements in the ratio of payroll to the sales value of production) cannot always operate. At the plant level, formulas that are responsive to what employees can influence, that are not unduly influenced by factors beyond their control, and that are readily understood, are not easy to devise. Small stand-alone businesses with a mature technology and stable markets tend to find the task least troublesome, but they are not the only ones trying to implement the commitment approach.

Yet another problem, very much at issue in the Hyatt-Clark bearing plant, which employees purchased from General Motors in 1981, is the relationship between compensation decisions affecting salaried managers and professionals, on the one hand, and hourly workers, on the other. When they formed the company, workers took a 25% pay cut to make their bearings competitive, but the managers maintained and, in certain instances increased, their own salaries in order to help the company attract and retain critical talent. A manager's ability to elicit and preserve commitment, however, is sensitive to issues of equity, as became evident once again when GM and Ford announced huge executive bonuses in the spring of 1984 while keeping hourly wages capped.

Technology

Computer-based technology can reinforce the control model or facilitate movement to the commitment model. Applications can narrow the scope of jobs or broaden them, emphasize the individual nature of tasks or promote the work of groups, centralize or decentralize the making of decisions, and create performance measures that emphasize learning or hierarchical control.

To date, the effects of this technology on control and commitment have been largely unintentional and unexpected. Even in organizations otherwise pursuing a commitment strategy, managers have rarely appreciated that the side effects of technology are not somehow "given" in the nature of things or that they can be actively managed. In fact, computer-based technology may be the least deterministic, most flexible technology to enter the workplace since the industrial revolution. As it becomes less hardware-dependent and more software-intensive and as the cost of computer power declines, the variety of ways to meet business requirements expands, each with a different set of human implications. Management has yet to identify the potential role of technology policy in the commitment strategy, and it has yet to invent concepts and methods to realize that potential.

Supervisors

The commitment model requires first-line supervisors to facilitate rather than direct the work force, to impart rather than merely practice their technical and administrative expertise, and to help workers develop the ability to manage themselves. In practice, supervisors are to delegate away most of their traditional functions—often without having received adequate training and support for their new team-building tasks or having their own needs for voice, dignity, and fulfillment recognized.

These dilemmas are even visible in the new titles many supervisors carry—"team advisers" or "team consultants," for example—most of which imply that supervisors are not in the chain of command, although they are expected to be directive if necessary and assume functions delegated to the work force if they are not being performed. Part of the confusion here is the failure to distinguish the behavioral style required of supervisors from the basic responsibilities assigned them. Their ideal style may be advisory, but their responsibilities are to achieve certain human and economic outcomes. With experience, however, as first-line managers become more comfortable with the notion of delegating what subordinates are ready and able to perform, the problem will diminish.

Other difficulties are less tractable. The new breed of supervisors must have a level of interpersonal skill and conceptual ability often lacking in the present supervisory work force. Some companies have tried to address this lack by using the position as an entry point to management for college graduates. This approach may succeed where the work force has already acquired the necessary technical expertise, but it blocks a route of advancement for workers and sharpens the dividing line between management and other employees. Moreover, unless the company intends to open up higher level positions for these college-educated supervisors, they may well grow impatient with the shift work of first-line supervision.

Even when new supervisory roles are filled—and filled successfully—from the ranks, dilemmas remain. With teams developed and functions delegated, to what new challenges do they turn to utilize fully their own capabilities? Do those capabilities match the demands of the other managerial work they might take on? If fewer and fewer supervisors are required as their individual span of control extends to a second and a third work team, what promotional opportunities exist for the rest? Where do they go?

Union-Management Relations

Some companies, as they move from control to commitment, seek to decertify their unions and, at the same time, strengthen their employees' bond to the company. Others—like GM, Ford, Jones & Laughlin, and AT&T—pursue cooperation with their unions, believing that they need their active support. Management's interest in cooperation intensified in the late 1970s, as improved work-force effectiveness could not by itself close the competitive gap in many industries and wage concessions became necessary. Based on their own analysis of competitive conditions, unions sometimes agreed to these concessions but expanded their influence over matters previously subject to management control.

These developments open up new questions. Where companies are trying to preserve the non-union status of some plants and yet promote collaborative union relations in others, will unions increasingly force the company to choose? After General Motors saw the potential of its joint QWL program with the UAW, it signed a neutrality clause (in 1976) and then an understanding about automatic recognition in new plants (in 1979). If forced to choose, what will other managements do? Further, where union and management have collaborated in promoting QWL, how can the union prevent management from using the program to appeal directly to the workers about issues, such as wage concessions, that are subject to collective bargaining?

And if, in the spirit of mutuality, both sides agree to expand their joint agenda, what new risks will they face? Do union officials have the expertise to deal effectively with new agenda items like investment, pricing, and technology? To support QWL activities, they already have had to expand their skills and commit substantial resources at a time when shrinking employment has reduced their membership and thus their finances.

THE TRANSITIONAL STAGE

Although some organizations have adopted a comprehensive version of the commitment approach, most initially take on a more limited set of changes, which I refer to as a "transitional" stage or approach. The challenge here is to modify expectations, to make credible the leaders' stated intentions for further movement, and to support the initial changes in behavior. These transitional efforts can achieve a temporary equilibrium, provided they are viewed as part of a movement toward a comprehensive commitment strategy.

The cornerstone of the transitional stage is the voluntary participation of employees in problem-solving groups like quality circles. In unionized organizations, union-management dialogue leading to a jointly sponsored program is a condition for this type of employee involvement, which must then be supported by additional training and communication and by a shift in management style. Managers must also seek ways to consult employees about changes that affect them and to assure them that management will make every effort to avoid, defer, or minimize layoffs from higher productivity. When volume-related layoffs or concessions on pay are unavoidable, the principle of "equality of sacrifice" must apply to all employee groups, not just the hourly work force.

As a rule, during the early stages of transformation, few immediate changes can occur in the basic design of jobs, the compensation system, or the management system itself. It is easy, of course, to attempt to change too much too soon. A more common error, especially in established organizations, is to make only "token" changes that never reach a critical mass. All too often managers try a succession of technique-oriented changes one by one: job enrichment, sensitivity training, management by objectives, group brainstorming, quality circles, and so on. Whatever the benefits of these techniques, their value to the organization will rapidly decay if the management philosophy—and practice—does not shift accordingly.

A different type of error—"overreaching"—may occur in newly established organizations based on commitment principles. In one new plant, managers allowed too much peer influence in pay decisions; in another, they underplayed the role of first-line supervisors as a link in the chain of command; in a third, they overemphasized learning of new skills and flexibility at the expense of mastery in critical operations. These design errors by themselves are not fatal, but the organization must be able to make mid-course corrections.

EXHIBIT 10.1   Work-force Strategies

	Control	*Transitional*	*Commitment*
Job design principles	Individual attention limited to performing individual jobs	Scope of individual responsibility extended to upgrading system performance, via participative problem-solving groups in QWL, EI, and quality circle programs.	Individual responsibility extend to upgrading system performance.
	Job design deskills and fragments work and separates doing and thinking.	No change in traditional job design or accountability.	Job design enhances content of work, emphasizes whole task, and combines doing and thinking.
	Accountability focused individual.		Frequent use of teams as basic accountable unit.
	Fixed job definition.		Flexible definition of duties, contingent on changing conditions.
Performance expectations	Measured standards define minimum performance. Stability seen as desirable		Emphasis placed on higher, "stretch objectives," which tend to be dynamic and oriented to the marketplace.
Management organization: structure systems, and style	Structure tends to be layered, with top-down controls	No basic changes in approaches to structure, control, or authority.	Flat organization structure, with mutual influence systems.
	Coordination and control rely on rule and procedures.		Coordination and control based more on shared goals, values, and traditions.
	More emphasis on prerogatives and positional authority.		Management emphasis on problem solving and relevant information and expertise.
	Status symbols distributed to reinforce hierarchy.	A few visible symbols change.	Minimum status differentials to deemphasize inherent hierarchy.
Compensation policies	Variable pay where feasible to provide individual incentive.	Typically no basic changes in compenation concepts.	Variable rewards to create equity and to reinforce group achievements: gain sharing, profit sharing.
	Individual pay geared to job evaluation.		Individual pay linked to skills and mastery.
	In downturn, cuts concentrated on hourly payroll.	Equality of sacrifice among employee groups.	Equality of sacrifice.
Employment assurances	Employees regarded as variable costs.	Assurances that participation will not in loss of job.	Assurances that participation will not result in loss of job.
		Extra effort to avoid layoffs.	High commitment to avoid or assist in reemployment.
			Priority for training and retaining existing work force.

(Continued)

EXHIBIT 10.1 (Continued)

	Control	*Transitional*	*Commitment*
Employee voice policies	Employee input allowed on relatively narrow agenda. Attendant risks emphasized. Methods include open-door policy, attitude surveys, grievance procedures, and collective bargaining in some organizations.	Addition of limited, ad hoc consultation mechanisms. No change in corporate governance.	Employee participation encouraged on wide range of issues. Attendant benefits emphasized. New concepts of corporate governance.
	Business information distributed on strictly defined "need to know" basis.	Additional sharing of information.	Business data shared widely.
Labor-management relations	Adversarial labor relations; emphasis on interest conflict.	Thawing of adversarial attitudes; Joint Sponsorship of QWL or EI; emphasis on common fate.	Mutuality in labor relations; joint planning and problem solving on expanded agenda.
			Unions, management, and workers redefine their respective roles.

RATE OF TRANSFORMATION

How rapidly is the transformation in work-force strategy, summarized in Exhibit 10.1, occurring? Hard data are difficult to come by, but certain trends are clear. In 1970, only a few plants in the United States were systematically revising their approach to the work force. By 1975, hundreds of plants were involved. Today, I estimate that at least a thousand plants are in the process of making a comprehensive change and that many times that number are somewhere in the transitional stage.

In the early 1970s, plant managers tended to sponsor what efforts there were. Today, company presidents are formulating the plans. Not long ago, the initiatives were experimental; now they are policy. Early change focused on the blue-collar work force and on those clerical operations that most closely resemble the factory. Although clerical changes has lagged somewhat—because the control model has not produced such overt employee disaffection, and because management has been slow to recognize the importance of quality and productivity improvement—there are signs of a quickened pace of change in clerical operations.

Only a small fraction of U.S. workplaces today can boast of a comprehensive commitment strategy, but the rate of transformation continues to accelerate, and the move toward commitment via some explicit transitional stage extends to a still larger number of plants and offices. This transformation may be fueled by economic necessity, but other factors are shaping and pacing it—individual leadership in management and labor, philosophical choices, organizational competence in manag-ing change, and cumulative learning from change itself.

11

A DIFFERENT KIND OF COMPANY

From Control to Commitment in Practice

SAUL A. RUBINSTEIN

INTRODUCTION AND OVERVIEW

Intense global competition in the automotive industry during the 1970s and 1980s put enormous pressure on General Motors (GM) and other U.S. producers. GM invested more than $50 billion dollars during the 1970s in an effort to automate its way to greater productivity and quality. Unfortunately, this effort did not solve GM's competitive problems. By the early 1980s, GM was importing most of its small cars from Japan as it faced an estimated $2,000 per vehicle cost disadvantage and had concluded that it could not produce these vehicles under its existing industrial relations and manufacturing systems.[1] During this time, GM began to explore solutions that went beyond technology and addressed both labor-management relations and work organization.

One experiment was the New United Motor Manufacturing, Inc. (NUMMI), a joint venture between GM and Toyota that converted an older GM plant with poor productivity and quality to a Japanese-style management system using original employees belonging to the United Auto Workers union (UAW), but operating under Toyota management using a team-based production system. NUMMI became a highly productive factory that also demonstrated that U.S. workers could produce world-class quality automobiles. However, NUMMI also represented a departure from both the labor relations and work organization of the rest of GM.[2]

At the same time, GM began developing another alternative for small car production that later became known as Saturn. Management approached the UAW with a proposal jointly to investigate the possibilities for developing a new form of manufacturing organization with innovative systems, structures, and labor-management relations. The organization for Saturn was the result of a joint union-management committee that benchmarked best practices worldwide. In 1985, the committee's recommendations for the new Saturn organization were codified in a 28-page Memorandum of Agreement between GM and the UAW. This agreement served as the contract between the company and the union replacing the more than 400-page national GM-UAW agreement. Instead of an elaborate set of job classifications and work rules, the memorandum set out a set of organizing principles (see Figure 11.1) and a structure for work teams and joint union-management governance (Figure 11.2).

The Saturn Partnership agreement negotiated in 1985 between GM and the UAW contained four key provisions: (1) The workforce would be organized into self-directed work teams; (2) decisions would be made through a consensus process; (3) the union would be a full partner in all business decisions; and (4) the organization would be governed by joint labor-management committees at all levels—corporate, manufacturing, business unit/plant and department/module. With its unique organization and attention to quality and customer service, Saturn's slogan described itself as "a different kind of company."

Saturn was originally constructed in the late 1980s as a greenfield operation in Spring Hill, Tennessee, with a $3 billion investment. The facility included an engine and transmission plant, a body plant, and an assembly plant with 7,800 employees, and is the largest integrated automotive operation build in the United States since Henry Ford constructed his Rouge plant in Detroit, Michigan. In a controversial move, GM recognized the UAW in the new facility before any workers were hired. This arrangement was challenged by the National Right to Work Committee on the grounds that it violated the National Labor Relations Act. The case was dismissed by the National Labor Relations Board, and Saturn has been operating as a union plant since it opened in Tennessee, a right-to-work state.

THE WORLD OF THE WORKER

Like NUMMI, Saturn built its manufacturing system on self-directed teams rather than on the Taylorist system used traditionally by GM that employs an extensive system of individual job classifications requiring coordination and control by supervision over the division of labor. Instead of the hundreds of job classifications typical at GM plants, Saturn had only one production job classification and six for the skilled trades. Saturn's 700 teams typically have between 6 and 15 members, and they elect their own leaders who remain working members of the team. Team members rotate through all of the jobs for which their team is responsible (see Figure 2), including many that are supervisory in other GM plants.

Saturn's emphasis on training and skill development is another critical component of its culture and work system. New Saturn employees were given between 350 and 700 hours of training before they were allowed to build cars. Training topics included problem solving, decision making, conflict resolution, and work team organization in addition to skills typically reserved for supervision, such as budgeting, business planning, scheduling, cost analysis, ergonomics, industrial engineering, manufacturing methods, job design, accounting, quality control, and data analysis. These latter topics are necessary because the teams have taken over many of the tasks typically handled by supervision. The union proposed linking training to the compensation plan, because it recognized the need for a work force that continued to upgrade its high skill levels.

Compensation is based on a unique "risk and reward" plan in which wages are paid as salary and are pegged to a percentage of the UAW-GM nationally negotiated rate. An additional amount bringing wages to the GM level is put at risk and tied to a training goal of 5% of hours worked, or 92 hours of training for every employee. An additional reward, or bonus, is contingent on achieving mutually negotiated performance goals, such as quality, cost, productivity, production schedule, profitability, and volume.

Job security is also guaranteed for a minimum of 80% of the workforce with the most seniority. Even when the small car market softened in the late 1990s, Saturn upheld this commitment, which severely affected is productivity as the plant produced well below capacity with many workers engaged in training, problem solving, and planning activities rather than the direct production of automobiles.

Treat people as a fixed asset. Provide opportunities for them to maximize their contributions and value to the organization. Provide extensive training and skill development to all employees.

The Saturn organization will be based on groups that will attempt to identify and work collaboratively toward common goals.

Saturn will openly share all information including financial data.

Decision making will be based on consensus through a series of formal joint labor-management committees, or Decision Rings. As a stakeholder in the operation of Saturn, the UAW will participate in business decisions as a full Partner, including site selection and construction, process and product design, choice of technologies, supplier selection, make-buy decisions, retail dealer selection, pricing, business planning, training, business systems development, budgeting, quality systems, productivity improvement, job design, new product development, recruitment and hiring, maintenance, and engineering. However, GM would retain discretion over investment and new product decisions.

Self-managed teams or Work Units will be the basic building blocks of the organization.

Decision-making authority will be located at the level of the organization where the necessary knowledge resides, and where implementation takes place. Emphasis will be placed on the work unit.

There will be a minimum of job classifications.

Saturn will have a jointly developed and administered recruitment and selection process, and work units will hire their own team members. Seniority will not be the basis for selection, and the primary recruiting pool will consist of active and laid-off GM/UAW employees.

The technical and social work organization will be integrated.

There will be fewer full-time elected UAW Officials and fewer Labor Relations personnel responsible for contract administration.

Saturn's reward system will be designed to encourage everyone's efforts toward the common goals of quality, cost, timing and value to the customer.

Figure 11.1. Saturn's Organizing Principles.[3]

The vast majority of Saturn employees were former GM employees, relocating from 136 GM facilities in 34 states. The first wave of hires from 1986 to 1991 voluntarily left jobs in other GM facilities to come to Saturn. Due to GM's downsizing in the late 1980s and 1990s, those hired from 1992 to 1996 consisted mainly of younger workers who were laid off with no recall rights or senior workers in plants subject to closure. As might be expected, there was a difference in attitude toward the Saturn partnership arrangement between people who came to Saturn voluntarily in the early years and those who came because they had been laid off or their plants were closing.

Saturn's recruitment and selection process was jointly developed and resulted in an extensive week-long process of testing and interviews, including a significant amount of assessment by team members themselves who would interview potential candidates and determine who would get job offers. In order to

Work units are organized into teams of 6 to 15 members, electing their own leaders who remain working members of the unit. They are self-directed and empowered with the authority, responsibility, and resources necessary to meet their day-to-day assignments and goals, including producing to budget, quality, housekeeping, safety and health, maintenance, material and inventory control, training, job assignments, repairs, scrap control, vacation approvals, absenteeism, supplies, record keeping, personnel selection and hiring, work planning, and work scheduling.

Saturn has no supervisors in the traditional sense. Teams interrelated by geography, product, or technology are organized into modules. Modules have a common **Advisor**.

Modules are integrated into three **Business Units**: Body Systems (stamping, body fabrication, injection molding, and paint); Powertrain (lost foam casting, machining and assembly of engines and transmissions), and Vehicle Systems (vehicle interior, chassis, hardware, trim, exterior panels and assembly).

Joint Labor-Management **Decision Rings** meet weekly:

* At the corporate level the **Strategic Action Council** (SAC) concerns itself with company-wide long range planning, and relations with dealers, suppliers, stockholders, and the community. Participating in the SAC for the union is the local president, and on occasion a UAW national representative.
* The **Manufacturing Action Council** (MAC) covers the Spring Hill manufacturing and assembly complex. On the MAC representing the local is the union president and the four vice presidents who also serve as the UAW bargaining committee.
* Each **Business Unit** has a joint labor-management **Decision Ring** at the plant level. The Local President appoints an elected executive board member who is joined by UAW module advisors and crew coordinators in representing the union.
* **Decision Rings** are also organized at the **Module** level. Module advisors and the elected work unit counselors (team leaders) participate in the module decision rings.

Figure 11.2. Saturn Partnership Structure.[4]

be hired by Saturn, an applicant would have to be recommended by the team in which he or she would ultimately work. Skills and abilities, as opposed to GM seniority, were the main criteria for selection.

Saturn team members are responsible for determining the tasks needed for their team's portion of the production process. Task cycles vary from one minute—the standard in the industry whereby each worker performs a small set of tasks on every vehicle—up to six minutes, in which each worker on a team finishes a more complete set of tasks, skips five cars and then starts a new cycle.

ORGANIZATIONAL GOVERNANCE

The use of production teams and an intensive selection and training procedures is not unique to Saturn or NUMMI. However, where Saturn departs from NUMMI and other team-based organizations is through the system of co-management and joint governance it developed. The Memorandum of Agreement called for the union to be a "full partner" in business decisions (except for investment and new product decisions) and for "consensus" to be the preferred method of decision making. The agreement also called for the organization to be governed by joint labor-management committees at all levels—corporate (Strategic Action Council), manufacturing (Manufacturing Action Council), business unit for the engine, body and assembly plants, and department. These committees meet to discuss the strategic and operational issues facing the company and each unit. Through this joint governance structure, the union is able to represent the collective interests of its members in the creation of firm policies. The organization was designed in ways that would utilize the skills and knowledge of employees while they shared in the resulting risks and rewards. Saturn's governance structures also reflect a stakeholder model of the firm by providing employees and other stakeholders a direct voice in key decisions.

CO-MANAGEMENT

Although representation in decision making takes place through these joint governance committees, this occurs off-line through weekly meetings apart from the daily operations. However, the most unique aspect of the Saturn organization is the formal role that has been created for union members on-line through daily managerial decision making. Typically, five to seven teams make up a department or module of approximately 100 members. Each module is co-managed jointly by an average of two module advisors who work together to provide leadership, expertise, training, and advice to the teams. Half of the module advisors are represented by the UAW, the other are GM managers. Represented and nonrepresented module advisors are "partnered" with each other, and work together to lead each module. Thus, at the core of this partnership arrangement has evolved a system of co-management that gives hundreds of jointly selected union members the responsibilities of operations and staff management, filling jobs which in any other GM facility would not be open to bargaining unit members. As a result, the union is regularly represented in daily operating decisions. These union and nonrepresented partners share offices and participate equally in decision making through the use of a consensus process outlined in the Memorandum of Agreement.

Formal one-on-one partnerships between nonrepresented managers and union representatives have taken place within the line and staff organizations in which these partners share managerial responsibility. Over 400 UAW members have taken on these co-management roles in operations management; engineering, sales, service and marketing; finance; industrial engineering; quality assurance; health and safety; training; organizational development;

corporate communications; maintenance; and process and product development. This co-management arrangement is one of the key differences between Saturn and most other manufacturers, including NUMMI. In order to fulfill the language in the agreement calling for "full participation," union leaders at Saturn pushed for these on-line co-management arrangements because they wanted more direct involvement in operational decision making than they could obtain from the off-line labor-management committee structure. As a result, union participation has been extended beyond that envisioned in the original agreement, as management is seen as task rather than a class of employees. Through co-management at Saturn, the union has created a dense network among its leaders that facilitates both horizontal and vertical communication and coordination and has had a significant impact on quality performance.[5]

This co-management arrangement, however, has not raised the indirect staffing headcount when compared to traditional plants. For example, in the production areas, the ratio of workers to co-managers is 50:1 compared to the average worker to supervisor ratio in the rest of GM of 25:1[6] or 18:1 at NUMMI.[7] This is possible in part because of the supervisory responsibilities teams have assumed and the unique co-management arrangements.

In developing this unique system of co-management and joint governance in which so many union members are filling staff and line management positions, Saturn has challenged not only the Taylorist tradition of a horizontal division of labor represented by extensive job classifications, but also the vertical separation of managerial "thinking" work from the "doing" work of labor. In doing so, the Saturn model also breaks from the separation of labor and management roles assumed under current U.S. labor law. Union co-managers and union officers at Saturn are performing managerial work, and therefore the partnership arrangement and co-management are clearly inconsistent with the doctrine that there be a clear line of demarcation between bargaining unit members and supervisors. Supreme Court decisions suggest that such employees could lose the protection provided by the National Labor Relations Act.

EMPLOYEE ATTITUDES TOWARDS SATURN

Saturn employees were interviewed to assess their attitudes towards this different kind of company, work system, and union.[8] Representative excerpts from these interviews reveal both the successes of this unique organization and some of the challenges.

Most Saturn employees see value in the way in which the local union is able to represent the collective interests of its membership in business decision making, and they approved of the union's performance in this arena. The following quotations are from individual team members:

I believe we're seeing a lot of input. One thing we said early on is as UAW members, we have a heck of a lot of power around here. We can change some decisions and make decisions.

We're quite proud of the fact that the whole shop was put together from ground up and organized by UAW, and runs today, with UAW people only. We do not have any input from any management folks on daily affairs.

However, complaints have surfaced regarding inadequate representation to ensure equity and due process. Team members also reported frustration that they could not file grievances against decisions the union itself participated in making:

As far as the old world [of G.M.], I'd never had to have someone represent me. But it was nice to know that there was somebody there to hear if you were ever in trouble. . . .

Last week I went to the union office and I said I wanted to write a grievance. I was told that I couldn't write a grievance because the decisions made were not solely management . . . they were union and management.

Members also described the challenge of taking over supervisory responsibility:

Without having supervisors here, you're left to . . . deal with your own conflict. To manage [our]selves and watch over and make sure everybody does right. . . . [For the] most part people here fare pretty good. But . . . it's really hard for people to deal with certain types of team issue. . . . But it's been my experience that a lot of teams would rather have somebody else deal with that in the way that the supervisor used to.

Though serious questions regarding the forms of representation have surfaced, the majority of Saturn employees strongly preferred the partnership arrangement to the work system of GM:

The structure here is good. In implementing the structure there are rough roads. I would [say] that 85 percent of it I prefer. There are possibly areas that we need to improve on, and I imagine that will be an ongoing thing. We're never going to get it perfect. I prefer this structure.

Other team members appreciated the increased level of responsibility they could take on through the partnership arrangement, particularly around the issue of manufacturing quality:

I'd have to say that I prefer the way things are now. I feel like we run our own little business in our team. I think the more responsibility we show, the more that you're kind of left on your own to do what you need to do.

This particular process, the partnership, the team concept, it requires more of the worker than old GM work [system]. When I say more I didn't say stress, but I mean overall work and looking at your quality. Old GM world, you went in, found your machine, and you watched your schedule. People say stress. I have not experienced the stress, what I was referring to was responsibility. No you don't work harder. More responsibility [is] delegated to you.

Finally, some team members, while acknowledging the problems still to be worked out at Saturn, felt that it represented a step forward that has brought them a greater sense of dignity:

[Even with] the conflict and everything we have down here, [it] is still a heck of a place to work. I wish I got here twenty years ago, really, because I can afford a little conflict once in a while.

All in all, this is probably the best place I ever worked. I'd rather work here than to go back to GM.

So, union has brought a dignity to the work force, and without that dignity the work force wouldn't be able to produce its quality products if they wanted to.

Overall, employees interviewed showed strong support for the Saturn partnership. These interview findings are consistent with a 1993 survey of the entire membership by the union in which 84% responded very positively about Saturn and its direction, while only 10% expressed negative views. As another indication, the Saturn rate of absenteeism is less than half of that found in the rest of GM.[9]

ORGANIZATIONAL PERFORMANCE

The performance of Saturn's partnership model has been mixed. Saturn has achieved remarkable results on quality. J. D. Power and Associates' customer satisfaction index has shown that in 1992, after only two years of production, and every year since Saturn has led domestic car lines in consumer ratings based on vehicle quality, reliability, and satisfaction after one year of ownership. Saturn's rating has also exceeded all brands worldwide, with the exception of Lexus and Infiniti (Acura and Mercedes in 1997 only), which are much costlier luxury lines.[10] Compensation has been tied to performance through the risk and reward bonus plan. Wages above the GM level are paid based on achieving mutually agreed goals for quality, cost, schedule, profitability, and volume. From 1992 through 1999, the Saturn bonus averaged more than $5,400, whereas GM employees averaged $500 in a profit-sharing bonus. In part, these bonuses reflected Saturn's extraordinary performance in launching new vehicles in 1996, 1997, 1998, and 1999. Changing over from one model to another has typically taken GM 60 to 300 days to get back to normal production levels. Using a team-based approach to de-bug the production process before changing over to the new model, Saturn has been able to launch new models without any loss in production or quality levels, setting new benchmarks for GM and for other automakers as well.[11]

Productivity and profitability have proved to be more variable. Profitability is difficult to judge, because there is no consensus on what portion of the up-front costs should be charged against the Saturn division or the overall corporation. Furthermore, though the original business plan called for Saturn in Spring Hill to have capacity for 500,000 vehicles a year, it currently only has 60% of that capacity, and there is ongoing debate as to what level of profitability can be expected at that level. Saturn actually produced operating profits in 1993, two years ahead of

the original plan, and company documents showed that Saturn produced higher profits per vehicle in 1995 and 1996 than any other unit in GM's small car division. However, when the small car market declined from 1997 to 1999, so did Saturn's profits. Saturn's productivity in 1994 and 1995 ranked either first or second among all GM plants. However, by 1997–1998, its productivity had fallen in labor hours per vehicle and relative to other GM plants.[12] As described earlier, both productivity and profitability performance were due in part to Saturn's employment security commitment because it did not use layoffs to deal with a decline in the small car market. Instead, it absorbed production workers into other work, training, or community service activities.

Saturn's original mission, governance structure, and internal processes fit the characteristics of a stakeholder firm in which employees establish themselves as influential, definitive stakeholders by using their knowledge to improve organizational performance. The local union likewise contributes to firm performance by organizing workers into a dense social network that contributes to problem solving, conflict resolution, and quality improvement. In turn, the company has increased its commitment to employees through employment security and training. Saturn was clearly established to exceed the productivity and quality levels in traditional GM-UAW facilities, and operating at full capacity it appeared to do so. However, Saturn's productivity may be held to different standards than other companies internationally because by design it seeks to balance multiple objectives for all stakeholders with regard to productivity, costs, quality, customer satisfaction, and job security.

THE FUTURE OF THE SATURN MODEL

Beyond productivity and profitability, another concern for Saturn's future comes from uncertainty regarding its relationship to the rest of the GM organization. Some of Saturn's autonomy has been lost in recent years as it has been integrated into GM's Small Car Group. As part of this integration, GM has begun to further limit Saturn's independence by planning to converge it with other models into a "common" platform while centralizing decisions on suppliers, new model development, and capacity expansion. Furthermore, in 1996, GM announced that its Wilmington, Delaware, Assembly plant would become the second Saturn assembly facility adding an additional 2,600 employees. The Wilmington plant produces the larger sedans and wagons, the "L" series, and although it uses teams, it operates under the national UAW-GM contract, a significant difference from the separate partnership arrangement developed by the parties in Tennessee.

These moves to limit Saturn's autonomy, centralize decision making within GM, and produce Saturn-branded vehicles in plants that do not operate under a joint governance and co-management arrangement threaten the future of the Saturn model in Spring Hill, and minimize the chances that the model will diffuse to other parts of GM.

As the most controversial experiment in labor-management relations and organizational governance in America today, the first decade of the Saturn partnership challenges deeply ingrained ideological principles, traditions of both management and labor, and legal doctrines. It serves as a symbol for a "different kind of company" with both advantages and risks attendant to such a position. Yet, despite its success producing high-quality products while increasing employee influence and expanding collective representation, this type of organizational form will not be widely adopted or sustained unless there are significant changes in labor law as well as considerable shifts in power and ideology in society, inside corporations, and in labor organizations.

Notes

1. See Thomas A. Kochan and Saul A. Rubinstein, "Toward a Stakeholder Theory of the Firm: The Saturn Partnership," *Organization Science*, Volume 11, No. 4, July–August 2000, pp. 367–386.

2. NUMMI has been well studied by academic researchers. See, for example, Paul Adler, "The Learning Bureaucracy: The New United Motors Manufacturing Inc.," in Larry L. Cummings and Barry M. Staw (eds.) *Research in Organizational Behavior*, vol 15, Greenwich, CT: JAI Press, 1992, pp. 180–205. Welford Wilms, *Restoring Prosperity: How Workers and Managers are Forging a New Culture of Cooperation*, New York: Times Business, 1996, or David I. Levine, *Reinventing the Workplace*. Washington, D.C.: The Brookings Institution, 1995.

3. Memorandum of Agreement, Saturn Corporation, 1985.

4. Saul Rubinstein, Michael Bennett and Thomas Kochan, "The Saturn Partnership: Co-Management and the Reinvention of the Local Union," in Bruce Kaufman and Morris Kleiner (eds.) *Employee Representation: Alternatives and Future Directions*, Madison, Wisconsin: Industrial Relations Research Association, 1993, pp. 339–370.

5. The full quantitative analysis of the impact of co-management on quality can be found in Saul A. Rubinstein, "The Impact of Co-Management on Quality Performance: The Case of the Saturn Corporation," *Industrial and Labor Relations Review*, Volume 53, No. 2, January 2000, pp. 197–218.

6. Interviews with GM Human Resources Management from the Saginaw and Inland Fisher Guide Divisions, December 1992.

7. Interview with Buzz Wilms, UCLA, December 11, 1992.

8. Ten one-hour focus group interviews were conducted with a stratified (by business unit and shift) random sample of assembly line and maintenance workers and module advisors in May and June, 1994. The interviews were audiotaped and then transcribed, and the dialogue was coded to reflect both the common themes that emerged and the differences in points of view expressed. See Saul A. Rubinstein, "A Different Kind of Union: Balancing Co-Management and Representation." *Industrial Relations*, Volume 40, No. 2, April 2001, pp. 163–203.

9. Saul A. Rubinstein and Thomas A. Kochan, *Learning From Saturn: Possibilities for Corporate Governance and Employee Relations*, Cornell University Press, Ithaca, 2001, p. 81.

10. J. D. Power & Associates. 1992, 1993, 1994, 1995, 1996, 1997, 1998. Customer Satisfaction Index. Agoura Hills, Calif.

11. Saul A. Rubinstein and Thomas A. Kochan, p. 42–43.

12. The Harbour Report. Harbour and Associates, Detroit, 1995, 1999.

12

INSIDE A JAPANESE TRANSPLANT

A Critical Perspective

LAURIE GRAHAM

Since the 1970s, researchers have suggested that modern Japanese management provides a new cooperative, managerial model based on work force participation (Cole, 1979; Dore, 1973). Theorists argue that participation programs are potentially a winning situation for both parties (Piore & Sabel, 1984; Zwerdling, 1980), that "they engage workers' minds with the managerial aspects of their jobs" (Safizadeh, 1991, p. 61), and that they provide greater employee involvement in decision making thus improving worker satisfaction (Brown & Reich, 1989).

A different approach to the theme of participation suggests that it has the potential to expand worker control at the expense of management. It assumes that participation schemes give workers a level of control over their work, which will increase their expectations and cause them to seek even greater control (Derber & Schwartz, 1988; Edwards, 1979; Kornbluh, 1984). Both approaches share a common assumption that participation schemes potentially increase workers' control on the shop floor, one from a technical perspective, the other from a political perspective.

The automobile industry has become a focus of the debate about the transferability of participative schemes based on the Japanese approach (Brown & Reich, 1989). Research by Florida and Kenney (1991) concerning Japanese transplants suggests that management has been successful in transferring the Japanese model to the United States. However, their analysis measures success by the mere existence of structures. Worker response to those structures was not assessed.

Distinctive features of Japanese management are the extraordinary commitment, identification, and loyalty employees exhibit toward their firms (Lincoln & Kalleberg, 1985, p. 738). Theorists argue that participation schemes and, more specifically, the "Japanese experience rejects the assumption that technological advance occurs only at the expense of employees . . . [instead] Japanese managers have succeeded in blending technological improvements with good human relations" (Hull & Azumi, 1988, p. 427). The assumption behind this body of work is a belief in the fundamental compatibility of the interests of workers and management (Blauner, 1964).

Research has challenged this compatibility and the assumption that participatory methods lead to greater worker control (Fantasia, Clawson, & Graham, 1988; Graham, 1985). Participation is viewed as a conscious attempt to undermine current union organization (Parker, 1985; Parker & Slaughter, 1988; Slaughter, 1983) and to defeat future organizational drives (Grenier, 1988).

Two general questions emerge from these findings. The first is whether worker control is enhanced by the Japanese model; the second is if the intraorganizational components of Japanese management can be successfully transferred without a high level of cooperation and commitment from its employees.

The present research, involving a direct participant/observation in a Japanese automobile transplant, challenges the assumption that worker control is enhanced by this participatory scheme. In fact, these findings suggest the opposite. Ironically, *kaizening*[1] and decision making by consensus served to reinforce the unequal power relation between workers and management. During kaizening, management tightly controlled the topics that could be raised for consideration and decision making by consensus was simply a mirage. A legitimate consensus between management and workers, who are vulnerable to discipline or job loss, was simply impossible. Management controlled which decisions were reached because of the unequal relationship. Concerning the assumption that worker autonomy is increased through decentralized management structures, in the present case study, decentralized authority created a situation where workers had virtually no autonomy.

In addition to challenging the promises of enhanced worker control, the present findings challenge the successfulness of management's ability to transfer a Japanese intraorganizational environment to the United States. Emergent patterns of shop floor behavior indicate that Japanese management practices can result in a range of individual and collective resistance among U.S. workers. These findings provide additional insight concerning the nature and effectiveness of worker resistance. Workers participated in both spontaneous and planned resistance. Whether spontaneous or planned, only collective resistance produced the strength necessary to effectively challenge management's control on the shop floor. Two methods of resistance effectively upset the balance of power: collective, sustained resistance and collective, spontaneous resistance.

[. . .]

RESEARCH SETTING AND DATA

The research focuses on the work experience within a single Japanese automobile transplant. From July 1989 through January 1990, I worked as a hidden participant/observer at Subaru-Isuzu Automotive (SIA) located near Lafayette, Indiana.[2] Both management and workers were unaware that they were under observation.

The intent of this research is to identify patterns of behavior that reflect the relationship among workers and between workers and management in their day-to-day work experience. The analysis is based on extensive field notes involving informal discussions with numerous co-workers and team members,[3] on day-to-day observations of co-worker and worker/management interactions, and on formal documents distributed by the company.

The analysis has many limitations, the greatest of which is that evidence concerning the nature and effectiveness of management's control strategies are deduced from the position of a worker. There is no way of knowing management's intentions; they can only be inferred from observations and documents. Another limitation concerns the time period of the study. It is unique because it is during the company's initial months of production. People working in the plant today are experiencing a faster assembly line, a second shift now exists, and temporary workers work side by side with regular employees. Another unique aspect of the start-up period is that a certain amount of excitement over beginning production existed among many workers; this excitement may dissipate as the newness wears off. On the other hand, the start-up also provides an ideal setting for management to take advantage of workers' optimism and to attempt to induce a spirit of cooperation and "pulling together" to beat the competition. Therefore, patterns that emerge contrary to this goal will serve as evidence of management's inability to gain control through cooperation and effectively transfer its intraorganizational environment.

[. . .]

The setting for the bulk of the observations is the trim and final department of the plant. Trim and final is the most labor-intensive area of the plant, where Subaru cars and Isuzu trucks are assembled. The car and truck bodies entered our department as empty shells and were driven off the line ready to be sold.

I worked on Team 1 in car assembly. There were 12 team members plus a team leader. Team 1 was part of a group of four teams under one group leader. The group leader was the lowest-level salaried employee. A total of about 14 teams assembled the cars. Each worker was responsible for one station that, at that time, involved about 5 minutes of work on every car. We worked at a constant pace as the cars moved along the line, repeating the same set of tasks every 5 minutes.

[. . .]

On the line, each station (or person) had control of the car for a predetermined distance. Workers walked next to the moving car, installing parts as it moved through their area. Although the distance did not vary, the speed of the line could be changed so that the amount of time the team had to work on the car was increased or decreased. The tact time[4] was not supposed to vary from station to station; however, many of the processes did not work as smoothly as anticipated by the Team 1 trainer, so some stations took more time than others. In addition, most people simply did not work at exactly the same speed, so some workers just barely kept up. Also, after the start of production, the team was plagued by hand and wrist injuries (at one point, 7 out of the 12 team members had hand or wrist problems), which forced a change in the way certain parts were installed, usually involving more time. Finally, due to injuries, many workers were forced

to work in wrist splints, which also slowed team members down.

When designing the Team 1 stations, the Japanese trainer used standardized times based on how long it took workers in Japan to install each part. The times were recorded to the tenth of a second, and the timing for the installation of each part was broken down step by step. From this, he calculated the number of stations necessary for installing all of the parts designated for our area within a tact time of 3 minutes and 40 seconds (the goal time for full production). He jokingly told team members, "We could each have an armchair at our station for resting between cars." The 5-minute tact time was a hectic pace for some and a reasonable pace for others.

[. . .]

In addition to the duties directly related to working on the line, each worker was responsible for keeping the stations neat and clean, recording the level of the "oilers" and pressure gauges on the air lines located above the stations, recording each car number, and keeping tools in good condition. *[. . .]* Whenever possible, each person tried to work ahead by beginning his or her station before the car actually crossed the line to enter his or her area. This gave the team an edge against breakdowns and parts shortages—the things that brought great emotional and physical stress because they caused the team to fall behind. Once behind, the team had to work intensely to catch up. Once the line speed began to increase toward goal tact time, the opportunity to work ahead steadily decreased and the Team 1 trainer ordered us to stop working ahead. Eventually, it became a moot point; there was no extra time. If someone on the team could see that another worker needed help, he or she would help if possible. It was, however, clearly a matter of pride to keep one's station under control and operating at the goal time.

[. . .]

In trim and final, a typical day began at 6:25 a.m. (5 minutes before the scheduled start of work) when music was played over the loudspeaker signaling morning exercises. After 5 minutes of exercises, the team members would stand in a circle for a meeting. When the paint department worked out its problems, and the line was moving throughout the day, the team meeting lasted no longer than 5 minutes, because the line started moving at 6:35 a.m. At the end of the meeting, the team performed a daily ritual. Each person extended his or her left arm into the center of the circle, with the hand clenched into a fist. The team leader then called on one of the members to deliver an inspirational message to the team. The usual message was, "Let's have a safe and productive day." A few of the team members sometimes told a good-natured joke, making light of the ritual. After the message, all of the team members brought their right arms around into the circle with everyone's hands meeting in the center in clenched fists. While doing this, the members shouted "Yosh!" (a long "o" sound) and then broke up and went to work.[5]

At exactly 6:35 a.m. a buzzer sounded, and the assembly line began to move. At 8:30 a.m. it stopped for a 10-minute break. At 10:30 a.m. the line stopped for a half-hour, unpaid lunch. At 1:00 p.m. it stopped for another 10-minute break and at 3:00 p.m. the work day was over.

The type of work each team member performed varied as to its physical demands, its potential for injury, the speed in which it could be performed, and whether or not he or she was able to speak to other team members. For the most part, however, working on the line required a worker's undivided attention. During plant start-up, workers had time for conversation between each car and even while working the stations. As line speed increased, time for interactions between workers and periods of rest continually decreased. Increased line speed was also accompanied by the emergence of injuries. Once the speedup began, the workers experienced constant pressure from the assembly line. Everyone was forced to work at a continuous, rapid pace.

FINDINGS

Of primary significance in the Japanese management scheme is its multidimensional structure. This multidimensional approach is most consistent with Burawoy's (1979) concept of hegemonic control, providing the qualification that Burawoy misses the resistance that is present in workers' adaptations in production (Thompson, 1989). Its goal is to gain

workers' total cooperation in the company's competitive struggle.

Each component in this system of control does not seem very powerful when examined separately. When combined, however, they form a formidable obstacle to the individual worker. When workers failed to resist collectively, practices such as speedup and working off the clock were common. Some workers could be seen working during their breaks to get caught up, and others came in early to set up their stations. At the same time, however, this system of control gave rise to resistance by many workers. In general, it was only through collective action that workers were able to effect any balance in control on the shop floor.

To describe the full range of worker response and the dynamic nature of worker reaction to this system, the findings are divided into two sections: compliance and resistance. The first section connects examples of worker compliance to each component in the management's scheme. For this analysis, the management scheme at SIA is separated into seven components. Five components focused on controlling the social aspects of production:

1. Preemployment selection process

2. Orientation and training for new workers

3. The team concept

4. A philosophy of kaizen

5. Attempts at shaping shop floor culture

Two components comprised the technical aspects of control:

6. The computerized assembly line

7. Just-in-time production.

The second section analyzes the range and effectiveness of resistance to this management scheme.

Compliance to Management's Scheme

Selection Process

The first component in SIA's system of control began before a worker was hired with a preemployment selection process. All applicants underwent a battery of tests and observed exercises. I began my attempt to gain employment at the company in February 1989, and 6 months later I was finally hired.

The selection process focused on eliminating potential workers. Applicants were evaluated after each step of the process and, if successful, were invited to participate in the next level of testing. The first step involved a 4-hour General Aptitude Test (GAT). Anyone who scored a certain percentile (when I applied it was above 85%) was invited to participate in Phase 1, a 4-hour exercise involving 20 applicants.

During Phase 1, the participants were divided into groups of five and each group participated in team scenarios involving problem-solving exercises. If an applicant passed the Phase 1 evaluation, then he or she would be invited to participate in Phase 2. Phase 2 involved approximately 8 hours of written attitude tests and timed exercise assembling parts. Following Phase 2, the successful applicants were scheduled for a physical examination and drug screening at a local clinic. The final step in the hiring process was an interview with three team leaders at the plant. Even though team leaders were hourly workers, they made the ultimate decision on hiring.

After I was hired, I discussed the selection process with other workers. The more cynical view was that most people had succeeded in being selected because they were smart and had figured out the process, not because they were team players. There was a general sentiment that SIA used the selection process to get rid of anyone the company considered undesirable. One person thought the process was an effort to screen out anyone who was not willing to be cooperative. Another said that the GAT was given to cut out anyone who was not fairly intelligent. One worker was pretty certain the whole selection process was aimed at exposing any union supporters.

[. . .]

Based on their statements, it appears that many workers complied with the perceived terms and conditions of employment at SIA by involving themselves in a kind of charade. Even those who expressed apprehension about working in a team setting said that they had made an effort to appear cooperative and enthusiastic when interacting with other applicants during team scenarios. When questioned, several people stated that they really were not team players, that they would rather work alone if given the choice. Other workers stated that, right from the start, they knew what type of behavior the company was looking for. There were many sources from which potential employees could deduce the requisite qualities of the successful SIA worker. A booklet explaining the company's team philosophy was made available when applicants first filled out applications. Area newspapers ran several articles focusing on the company's "new style" of management based on a team concept that stressed cooperation and quality.

[. . .]

Orientation and Training

Management's second mechanism aimed at social control on the shop floor emerged through the company's orientation and training program. Every worker underwent 1 week of orientation and a minimum of 2 weeks of classroom training. The instruction fell into three general areas. The first area included "nuts and bolts" information concerning such items as benefits, pay schedules, work rules, uniform fittings, and tours of the plant. Within this area were basic lessons in reading blueprints, using statistical process control, and structuring time studies. The second area involved lessons on the company's history and philosophy including testimonials from instructors and management. Also within this category were instructions in the concept of kaizening (a philosophy of continuous improvement) and lectures designed to demonstrate SIA's egalitarian nature. The third area of instruction involved an attempt to socialize workers as to their expected behavior at SIA. This took place through formal, video-driven behavior training sessions and also through facilitating informal interactions with other classmates. Generally, the nuts-and-bolt area of instruction involved practical training, whereas the second and third components worked toward shaping attitudes and values.

[. . .] Out of 127.5 hours of orientation and training, approximately 56 hours were actually

spent in practical training. The remaining 71.5 hours were concentrated on attitude and behavior.

[...]

The bond of friendship that formed between classmates was a useful tool in the company's overall attempt at shaping a cooperative work force. First, it laid the groundwork for a smooth transition into the plant. As a new worker in a factory environment, I experienced less alienation and fear than I had when beginning work in previous factory jobs. A primary reason for this was that I had already formed connections with other workers; the training experience was often the first topic of conversation when a new worker joined the team.

Team Concept

Perhaps the most powerful aspects of SIA's scheme was located in the team concept and its reorganization of work. Organizing work around the team could control workers in three ways. First, a form of self-discipline emerged from the responsibilities of team membership. Workers often pushed themselves to the limit in order to keep up their "end of the bargain." Second, peer pressure "clicked in" if self-discipline failed. For example, when a worker fell behind or made mistakes, others on the team suffered because they were forced to correct those errors before the vehicle left the area. It was highly likely that, if the team member did not solve the problem, he or she would experience resentment from the others. For example, a worker from another team told me that he was training one of his team members on a station and that the team member was very slow. In reference to that worker's speed he said, "You know, it kind of makes me mad." A third level of direct control was exerted through the team leader and the Japanese trainers.

Self-discipline emerged as a part of the team structure. I found that I quickly internalized the responsibilities of team membership. I went to extreme measures to "hold up my end of the bargain." An example of this occurred during a period of time when management began altering my station. Each change increased the time it took to complete my series of tasks, forcing me to change other areas of the station in order to keep up. At one point, it simply became impossible to do the amount

of work required, and I kept falling behind. Even though I knew the team leader had set unrealistic goals for my station, I felt guilty and feared the other team members would resent me for falling behind.

The following example illustrates the type of peer pressure that could be exerted by team mates. One member of our team, "Joe," regularly made mistakes and fell behind. We were understaffed, and each of us was working at least two and sometimes three stations. Joe was covering two stations. Because he was having problems, the rest of us observed him and found that he was not following any prescribed order when doing his stations. One simply could not predict which part he would pick up first. In turn, this meant that we never knew which part or parts he might forget. Because our responsibilities included checking the work already completed and correcting any mistakes, Joe's unpredictability increased the level of stress for the team members that followed him. The team leader and team members tried to get Joe to use a system, but he refused.

The team leader decided that Joe was simply pretending to be slow and confused in order to get out of working those particular stations. Finally, the team leader devised a scheme to correct the situation. The team leader informed the rest of the team of the plan. None of the team members told Joe of the potentially humiliating plan. Team members cooperated with the team leader in an attempt to put pressure on another team member concerning his job performance.

Direct control was exerted through the team concept by the team leader. There was a team leader for about every seven workers, so a worker's behavior was constantly monitored. Workers actions were under close scrutiny, and if inappropriate behavior occurred, workers were pressured to change. At times this meant a "friendly" visit from the group leader. At other times, the attention of a department manager was engaged.

[...]

Another aspect of the team structure was that it gave the company technical control over job assignments. Team members were cross-trained to perform one another's jobs, so management was able to move workers around freely within the team or between similar teams. This not only increased flexibility, it allowed the company to hire fewer workers, because covering for absent or injured workers was handled by other team members.

Philosophy of Kaizen

The fourth element of SIA's system of control was epitomized in the phrase, "Always searching for a better way." This was how one vice president described the philosophy of kaizen during orientation and training. What it meant was that everyone was expected to continually make his or her job more efficient, striving to work to maximum capacity. Kaizening could be directly enforced through periodically decreasing the tact time by speeding up the line. This forced workers to find ways of shaving additional seconds from work tasks. Indirectly, it had a "domino effect" on the work force. Making one person's job more efficient often meant shifting part of that process to another worker or team, thereby intensifying someone else's job.

A large part of kaizening involved time study. During training, workers were taught to perform time studies on each other and to check against the established standard for each task. This practice continued on the shop floor and was used to speed up each person's work process. If any time was left after the completion of a process, other tasks or sub-assemblies could be added, intensifying the job. [. . .] The goal was for workers to be working every second of every minute.[6]

Although the Japanese system is most consistent with the concept of hegemonic control, not every aspect of Burawoy's theory is applicable. "Making out"—the idea that workers play games to create spare time and still make quotas, and by doing so, develop a consensual relationship within production—took on a different form in the present case. Instead of a consensual relationship developing through workers' games, kaizening attempted to block workers from making out in two ways. First, it threatened a worker with constant disruption by suddenly introducing changes in the workstation, directly interfering with the making out process. Just when a worker had a station under control, with a few seconds to spare, he or she ran the risk of having it kaizened—intensifying the job. Second, through the kaizen philosophy of continual improvement,

management attempts to gain control over workers' creative knowledge and to use it to its own advantage. Kaizening is not only designed to capture a worker's secrets for gaining spare time; once management appropriates that knowledge, it controls when, where, and how those ideas are implemented. Kaizening, therefore, is an extremely effective procedure. It essentially convolutes the making out process, which under other management systems benefits the worker, into a process that puts continuous stress on the worker and forces workers' compliance.

Shop Floor Culture

The fifth element, cultural control, was two-tiered. First, at the level of the shop floor, there was an attempt to shape workers' culture through the team structure. Organizing work around the team circumvented the natural formation of small informal work groups, a traditional mechanism of worker solidarity and support (Roy, 1983). By formalizing work groups, management created a structure in which team members worked together to meet company goals. If the company could successfully appropriate workers' solidarity and support, then they would identify their interests with the company's. Daily quotas and speedup placed increased demands on workers and created resentment toward management. The culture of the team was one mechanism of dissipating resistance to those demands. Quite simply, when helping other team members keep up, workers supported the speedup.

The second level of cultural control was the organizational level. There was an active campaign to create a companywide team culture at SIA, premised on the concept of egalitarianism. This was an attempt to elevate the responsibilities of team membership and identification to the level of the company.

Attempts to create an egalitarian culture occurred through specialized symbols, ideology, language, and rituals. For example, everyone from the company president on down wore the same uniforms, parked in the same parking lot, and used the same cafeteria. Workers were never referred to as employees or workers. Instead everyone, including management, was an associate. In addition, the company president and vice presidents were often seen on the shop floor.

The team metaphor was used at all levels of the company. Company documents compared team leaders to basketball captains and group leaders to coaches (*Subaru-Isuzu Automotive, Inc.—Facts and Information*, 1989, p. 2). The team metaphor was further extended to embrace the company's struggle in the market place. When defining its corporate character in the *Associate Handbook*, the second principle was, "Together, we must beat the competition." The company song was "Team Up for Tomorrow." At one department meeting right before the start of official production (when we began building cars that would be sold in this country), the trim and final manager gave a speech that was reminiscent of a coach's "go get 'em" right before the big game. In a very solemn tone he told the workers that "we are finally entering into the competition. The company has done everything to prepare us for this moment. Now it is up to us to beat the competition."

Company rituals included morning exercises, team meetings, department meetings, and company celebrations. These rituals brought workers in contact with management in a relaxed and casual atmosphere. At department meetings the teams sat together in the cafeteria, smoking and drinking pop while the trim and final manager delivered a "pep talk."

Company celebrations not only included workers but workers were often the focus of the celebration. At the ceremony commemorating the official start of production, state dignitaries, community leaders, and top management from Fuji Heavy and Isuzu were present. The ceremony was laden with images of nationalism, the marching band from the local university played, and baton twirlers performed. The climax of the celebration occurred when all of the employees from the plant marched across the stage through a haze of smoke as the company song "Team Up for Tomorrow" played over the speaker system. An associate from Team 2 said, "It seems kind of like graduation." One might argue that it is odd for a Japanese company to appropriate all of these American symbols, however, if the company's goal is control through enlisting workers' cooperation as team members, then appropriating American symbols seems quite natural.

Computerized Assembly Line

The most direct form of control at SIA was the computerized assembly line. It not only set the pace of work; the mainframe computer system had the ability to focus everyone's attention on any team that fell behind. For example, when a worker fell behind, he or she pulled a yellow cord located above the line. At that instant, the team's music (each team was assigned a few bars of music) would be heard throughout the area occupied by the 14 teams that assembled the cars in trim and final via the loudspeaker system. The computerized music was played repeatedly until the cord was pulled again by the team leader, signaling that things were under control. If the line actually stopped, the music continued until the line began moving again. This had the effect of focusing departmentwide attention on the team with the problem.

In addition to playing music, the computer system kept track of the number of times each team pulled the cord and how long the line was stopped. Such a system of "bookkeeping" allowed management to put tremendous pressure on specific team and group leaders. This pressure was passed on to team members. For example, at the morning team meetings, in addition to receiving a defect report, other teams' problems were often topics of discussion. Problems arising within the team were a definite focus of conversation. During start-up, our group leader attended one morning meeting to inform us that we were "the only team in trim and final that was still having trouble making tact time."

Just-in-Time Production

The final mechanism of control that had the effect of directly intensifying and speeding up our work was just-in-time production. This is a method of inventory control in which the company keeps parts stocked on the line for only a few hours of work. This put severe time constraints on the material handlers who stocked the line and on the workers assembling the cars and trucks. Because the line was only stopped when absolutely necessary, the vehicles often continued moving, even when parts were missing. This meant that when the missing part arrived, the team had to work down the line installing that part after other parts had been attached, a difficult and time-consuming job. Even if the missing part arrived only a few seconds late, it was often enough to put that worker behind. Once behind, a worker often could not catch up and, therefore, the rest of his or her day was affected. No one wanted to fall behind and experience this pressure, thus workers often made extreme efforts to see that their parts were stocked. Sometimes workers left the moving line and, literally, ran down the aisle in search of a material handler to warn him or her that the line was becoming dangerously low on a part. Such actions could also put workers behind and increased the intensity of the jobs.

Summary: The points outlined above indicate that the combination of these components of control was quite powerful in controlling the individual worker. Only through collective action were workers able to effect any balance of power on the shop floor. The next section analyzes the nature and success of worker resistance.

The Nature of Resistance

Evidence of worker resistance to SIA's system of management emerged in various collective and individual forms. Collective resistance emerged as sabotage when workers surreptitiously stopped the assembly line. Collective resistance emerged when workers collectively protested and refused to participate in company rituals. Collective resistance emerged in the form of direct confrontation when workers refused management requests, and in the form of organized agitation at team and department meetings. Individual resistance was expressed through silent protest when workers, on an individual basis, refused to participate in company rituals and in the form of complaints through anonymous letters written to the company as part of the company's program of rumor control.

Collective Resistance

Sabotage occurred when workers on one of the trim and final teams discovered how to stop the assembly line without management tracing their location. Whenever one of their team members fell behind and the "coast was clear," they stopped the line. This not only allowed people on their team to catch up, it gave everyone time away from the line.

In addition, it provided entertainment as workers watched management scramble around trying to find the source of the line stoppage. At one morning team meeting, our team leader reported that the line had stopped for a total of 20 minutes the day before, and the company was unable to account for the time. Clearly, that team was taking a chance, however, the workers who were aware of the sabotage never told management. Whether the reason for the complicity was selfish, because of the appreciated breaks, or was loyalty to other workers, their silence was a direct act of resistance and evidence of a lack of commitment to the company.

Collective resistance also emerged in the form of protest. For example, in response to what they considered an unfair action by the company, Team 1 refused to participate in company rituals such as exercises and team meetings. This occurred in response to the company unilaterally taking away a 5-minute cleanup period at the end of the day.

Collective resistance emerged in the form of direct confrontation with management. When the cleanup period was no longer allowed, workers refused management's request to work "after the buzzer" (the end of the shift) in order to clean up and put away tools. For example, even when management directly requested workers' assistance in this matter, they were met with direct resistance at meetings and on the line. The group leader for our area called a special meeting of Team 1 and Team 2 to enlist help in cleaning up after the buzzer. At the meeting, several workers from both teams directly confronted the group leader. A worker from Team 1 said, "This is the kind of b___ s___ that brings in a union." A second remarked, "This place is getting too Japanese around here, pretty soon you will be asking us to donate our Saturdays." A worker from Team 2 assured the group leader that he was "not a volunteer." As a group, they were adamant that they would not work after the buzzer. On the following day, the line continued moving until the buzzer sounded, and as it happened, I was so far behind that when the line stopped, I did not realize the buzzer had sounded and I kept working. As two teammates walked by, they called to me, "Laurie, don't do it!" I put down my tools. As I was leaving, I overheard our team leader ask another team member a question concerning work. He replied, "Look, it's after 3:00.

I don't know" and he walked on by. From that day on, whenever the line ran up to quitting time, everyone on the team dropped whatever they were doing and immediately walked out, leaving the team leader to lock up the tools and clean the area. At a team meeting, the team leader complained that she had stayed almost an hour after work cleaning up and putting away our tools. One team member said, "She was crazy to do it, and we weren't going to."

Another form of collective resistance that emerged was jokes. Workers made light of company rituals and the philosophy of kaizen. For example, as mentioned above, some workers told jokes at the team meeting when called on for an inspirational message during the "yosh" ritual. They were making light of what was presented to us as a fairly solemn ritual. Another example of making light of rituals occurred at morning exercises when workers would jump around and act silly. Kaizening, the company's philosophy of continuous improvement, was also the brunt of workers' jokes. When the line stopped, someone would say, "Let's kaizen that chair," or if something really went wrong, they would say, "I guess they kaizened that."

Several examples of resistance emerged in response to management's unilateral scheduling and unscheduling of overtime. Resistance to overtime became resistance to the company's philosophy of cooperation.

[. . .]

Two days before December vacation, the car manager decided to work the team overtime without sufficient notice. Our team leader asked us individually whether or not we were willing to stay over. I declined and so did another woman on my team. Previously, the company had handed down a policy concerning overtime that stated that "scheduled" and "emergency" overtime were mandatory, but "unscheduled" was not. Scheduled was defined as having been announced by the end of the shift on the previous day. Therefore, in this case, the overtime was unscheduled, and we had the right to refuse.

That afternoon, the group leader approached me and asked why I was not willing to work. I, of course, had not expected to work and had a medical appointment I wanted to keep. Shortly after that, our team leader informed us that, "According to human

resources, if we left at 3:00, it would be an unexcused absence." The company was instituting this policy on the spot. This caused a third woman on our team to also refuse the overtime. She said that it was obvious to her that the company was simply fabricating the policy to force us to work. On principle, she decided to leave with us to protest the company's method of assigning unexcused absences. Now three team members were leaving. When the group leader learned this, he informed the car manager that there would not be enough people to keep the line moving. At this point, the car manager approached me with the group leader by his side. He said, "Look, here at SIA we are trying to be different. If this was any other place, I wouldn't bother to talk to you. I'd just tell the group leader to tell you to work or else. I don't want to get into a position where I am talking discipline with an employee, because I know you are a good worker. I've seen you work." I replied, "This wasn't scheduled over time and he himself had said it wasn't an emergency, so how could he discipline me?" He said, "Anyone who leaves the line while it is moving is in jeopardy of being fired."

At this juncture, our team leader made a surprising announcement, she told the car manager that she was also leaving. He put immediate pressure on her, in front of the team, informing her that she was putting her job in jeopardy if she left. Finally, when faced with the intended departure of 4 team members, and the fact that this would shut the line down, management backed down. I suggested to the manager that if he agreed that no one would get an unexcused absence for leaving, both the team leader and the other protester would agree to stay. They accepted those terms; the other worker who needed to leave and I left. The next day, our teammates informed us that only three cars were built after we left. They described the demands made on us as a "power play by management."

Finally, collective resistance emerged through organized agitation at team and department meetings. This occurred as workers attempted to stop the company from instituting a policy of shift rotation. Management announced the policy and stated that it was "not up for discussion." All workers would have to rotate when the second shift was added. This infuriated many workers. Several people stated that it was typical of the kinds of decisions workers were not allowed to participate in. Many things that had a direct effect on workers' lives, such as overtime, line speed, and shift rotation were not up for discussion. The essence of the participation workers were granted involved at best, improving quality, at worst, and more commonly, speeding up the job. Workers informally passed the word around the plant to "keep the pressure on by bringing it up at meetings." After that, the issue of shift rotation was brought up almost daily at the morning team meetings. Department meetings were regularly disrupted when various workers would state how "unfair" it was that we had no input into the shift rotation decision. The issue continued to surface. Eventually, management changed its ruling, and an announcement was made that there would be no shift rotation.

Individual Resistance

Silent protest was a common form of individual resistance and an easy target was morning exercises. For example, workers arrived late for work in order to avoid morning exercises or else they remained sitting while others participated. The exercises were a relatively safe target of protest because they occurred before the start of the shift. Legally, workers had the right to refuse. A second form of individual resistance emerged in anonymous letters to the company.

The anonymous letter was a weak form of resistance because it involved little risk to the individual and it used a formal procedure instituted by the company. As part of their "fair treatment policy," the company distributed prestamped, self-addressed envelopes for people to write in anonymously with questions or comments. The comments were posted throughout the plant on special bulletin boards with both the worker's comment and the company's reply. Between October 26, when the first batch was posted, and January 5, 150 comments, questions, and complaints were aired. At first they were optimistic, containing questions concerning the future. For example, people asked if there would be a credit union, a car purchase program, daycare facility, or a fitness gym. Later it became a sounding board for

complaints and dissatisfaction. Concerns emerged over scheduling overtime without notification. Parents complained that scheduling meetings after work and long hours of overtime conflicted with their children's hours at the day-care center. Workers also expressed concern that favoritism existed in parking, lunch hours, bonus plans, scheduling of overtime, and the loaning out of company cars. Repeated complaints emerged that group leaders and team leaders were being chosen without any job postings. Trim and final associates wanted to know why maintenance associates were paid $2 more per hour. There were repeated concerns that quality was being sacrificed in order to meet daily quotas. Workers questioned why seniority was used for some things such as enrollment in the pension plan but not for transfers and promotions. One worker wanted to know why security checks were unequally applied as people with lunch boxes were searched when leaving through the front door, whereas those with briefcases were not checked. Another worker quoted state law concerning overtime pay, stressing that it was illegal for the company to require workers to clean their areas and put their tools away after the shift had ended. There were also the more predictable complaints concerning the food and long lines in the cafeteria, uniforms, gloves, and plant temperature. Many complaints revealed that the company was not totally successful in instituting a spirit of cooperation and a culture of egalitarianism.

[. . .]

CONCLUSION

Data collected from this case study do not support the contention that the participation scheme found in modern Japanese management increases worker control. This was true technically and politically.

First, although deskilling and task fragmentation are traditional means of gaining greater technical control, they do not address the case at hand. Job enrichment or enlargement more accurately described the assignment of tasks. The number of tasks tended to be expanded rather than narrowed, as expected in a deskilling process. However, even though workers performed a wider range of tasks, they were not "reskilled." Jobs were fragmented and rationalized to the tenth of a second. Additionally, even though workers were trained to perform others' stations, this cross-training did not increase worker control over the technical aspects of work. The opposite was true. Flexibility increased management's control by making workers more vulnerable to job intensification and speedup. When a worker was absent or fell behind, the others were forced to pick up the extra load.

Second, these findings do not support the contention that participation schemes engage workers' minds in managerial aspects of their jobs. The kaizen process had the opposite effect. Management controlled the parameters of what was within the realm of consideration and also how, when, and where a job was altered. Kaizening provided a mechanism for keeping decisions under the tight control of management. Workers were seldom allowed to make even the most inconsequential decision on their own. Additionally, the company's use of consensus in decision making strengthened management's control over the outcomes. The unequal relationship between worker and management made it nearly impossible to reach a consensus involving little more than token input from workers.

Finally, at SIA control was decentralized through the team leader and the management structure was flat, not the hierarchical structure found in bureaucratic control. The lack of a burdensome bureaucracy may, on the surface, seem to be a reason for arguing that the team structure is a winning situation for both parties. However, decentralized authority within the plant created a situation where workers had very little autonomy. On the average, every seven workers were under the direct supervision and close scrutiny of the team leader. The concept of team participation in a decentralized structure hid the capitalist-worker relationship through an ideology of egalitarianism. This calls into question Edwards's (1979) contention that bureaucratic structures are required to mask the capitalist-worker relationship. Although bureaucratic structures can do what Edwards says, so can other structures.

Concerning the issue of transference, the resistance by workers at SIA provides additional evidence that intraorganizational transference of Japanese management practices may not be as successful as research has indicated. This is particularly the case when including a political dimension of analysis, shop floor control. This research, with its emphasis on patterns of worker behavior, suggests that successful transference at one level of measurement is not synonymous with successful adaptation of worker behavior on the shop floor. This raises the question of whether the existence of formal structures is a reliable measure for determining the successfulness of intraorganizational transference, particularly when a distinctive feature of that organization is employee commitment, identification, and loyalty.

NOTES

1. *Kaizening* is a philosophy of continuous improvement. It is instituted by asking workers to continually find faster or more efficient ways of performing their jobs.

2. Gaining employment and working in the plant as a hidden participant/observer is the method of choice for this particular study for several reasons. First, entry could not be gained with management's knowledge. Second, it has been used by other researchers when attempting to understand shop floor culture and experience (Cavendish, 1982; Kamata, 1982; Linhart, 1981; Pfeffer, 1979). Third, entering the plant without the knowledge of management or worker speeds up the process of gaining acceptance and is least disruptive to the natural course of events—as people may attempt to modify their behavior if aware that they are under observation. Finally, this type of methodology allows questions to be asked and observations to be made as events occur (Bollens & Marshall, 1973).

3. Through the course of the preemployment selection process and the 6 months working at SIA. I talked with 150 employees; 46 were women, 3 were Black.

4. Tact time is the amount of time a worker is given to complete a station; it was the same throughout the entire plant.

5. It was our understanding that "Yosh!" was a cheer, meaning something similar to "Let's go!" Every team in trim and final performed this daily ritual.

6. In a typical American auto plant, workers maintain a 40- to 50-second-a-minute work pace whereas Japanese auto plants tend to run close to 60 seconds a minute (Fucini & Fucini, 1990, p. 37).

REFERENCES

Blauner, R. (1964). *Alienation and freedom: The factory worker and his industry.* Chicago: University of Chicago Press.

Bollens, J., & Marshall, D. (1973). *Guide to participation.* Englewood Cliffs, NJ: Prentice-Hall.

Brown, C., & Reich, M. (1989). When does union-management cooperation work? A look at NUMMI and GM-Van Nuys. *California Management Review*, Summer, pp. 26–44.

Burawoy, M. (1979). *Manufacturing consent: Changes in the labour process under monopoly capitalism.* Chicago: University of Chicago Press.

Cavendish, R. (1982). *Women on the line.* London: Routledge and Kegan Paul.

Cole, R. (1979). *Work, mobility, and participation: A comparative study of American and Japanese industry.* Berkeley: University of California Press.

Derber, C., & Schwartz, W. (1988). Toward a theory of worker participation. In F. Hearn & R. Belmont (Eds.), *The transformation of industrial organization.* Belmont, CA: Wadsworth.

Dore, R. (1973). *Japanese factory, British factory.* Berkeley: University of California Press.

Edwards, R. (1979). *Contested terrain.* New York: Basic Books.

Fantasia, R., Clawson, D., & Graham, G. (1988). A critical view of worker participation in American industry. *Work and Occupations, 15*, 468–488.

Florida, R., & Kenney, M. (1991). Transplanted organizations: The transfer of Japanese industrial organization to the U.S. *American Sociological Review, 56*, 381–398.

Fucini, J., & Fucini, S. (1990). *Working for the Japanese: Inside Mazda's American auto plant* New York: Free Press, Macmillan.

Graham, G. (1985). Bureaucratic capitalism and the potential for democratic control. *Humanity and Society, 9*, 443–457.

Grenier, G. (1988). *Inhumane relations: Quality circles and anti-unionism in American industry.* Philadelphia: Temple University Press.

Hull, F., & Azumi, K. (1988). Technology and participation in Japanese factories: The consequences for morale and productivity. *Work and Occupations, 15*, 423–448.

Kamata, S. (1982). *Japan in the passing lane.* New York: Pantheon.

Kornbluh, H. (1984). Work place democracy and quality of work life: Problems and prospects *Annals of the American Academy of Political and Social Sciences, 473*, 88–95.

Lincoln, J., & Kalleberg, A. (1985). Work organizations and work force commitment: A study of plants and employment in the U.S. and Japan. *American Sociological Review, 30*, 738–760

Linhart, R. (1981). *The assembly line.* Amherst: University of Massachusetts Press.

Parker, M. (1985). *Inside the circle: A union guide to QWL.* Boston: South End.

Parker, M., & Slaughter, J. (1988). *Choosing sides: Unions and the team concept.* Boston: South End.

Pfeffer, R. (1979). *Working for capitalism.* New York: Columbia University Press.

Piore, M. J., & Sabel, C. F. (1984). *The second industrial divide.* New York: Basic Books.

Roy, D. F. (1983). "Banana time": Job satisfaction and informal interaction. In J. Hackman E. Lawler, & L. Porter (Eds.), *Perspectives on behavior in organizations* (pp. 329–335). New York: McGraw-Hill.

Safizadeh, M. H. (1991). The case of workgroups in manufacturing operations. *California Management Review*, Summer, pp. 61–82.

Slaughter, J. (1983). *Concessions and how to beat them.* Detroit: Labor Education and Research Project.

Subaru-Isuzu Automotive, Inc.—Facts and information. (1989), Produced in cooperation with Indiana Department of Employment and Training Services.

Thompson, P. (1989). *The nature of work: An introduction to debates on the labour process* (2nd ed.). Atlantic Highlands, NJ: Humanities Press International.

Zwerdling, D. (1980). *Workplace democracy.* New York: Harper Colophon.

PART IV

ORGANIZATIONS AS HUMAN AND SOCIAL SYSTEMS II
Informal Organization as Shadow Structure

Human Relations and humanistic management studied the human and social dimensions of organizational life as part of an effort to reform work and organizations. However, Human Relations also established a precedent for studying small groups, informal relations, and operative norms for their own sake. Sociologists studying organizations in the 1950s, shortly after Weber's work appeared in English, found that the informal organization was as important to understanding how things worked as the formal rules and organization chart, both among managers and workers. Weber depicted organizations as artificial, rational constructions governed by their official policies, but sociologists found an informal social life that develops spontaneously within them, establishes its own patterns and rules, and complicates any effort to run an organization according to a preestablished blueprint.

Alvin Gouldner's (1954) study of a factory found that the formal rules operated in ways that could not be well understood using Weber's ideas. Formal rules functioned to relieve the supervisor of appearing to exercise personal authority over workers, which workers resented. Supervisors enforcing discipline could point to the rules as requiring them to take certain actions. As one supervisor said, "I can't help laying them off if they're absent. *It's not my idea.* I've got to go along with the rules *like everyone else.* What *I* want has nothing to do with it" (Gouldner 1954, p. 165, emphasis original). The formal rules act as "an impersonal crutch" for supervisory authority that helps obscure power disparities within the organization (*ibid.*).

However, rules could also be enforced irregularly as a way of maintaining positive workplace relations. A supervisor who is technically obligated to enforce certain rules but chooses to look the other way when workers violate them wins loyalty and cooperation from those working under him or her. But if conflicts developed between the two groups, supervisors engaged in a "fever of enforcement" of rules previously dormant (Gouldner 1954, p. 173). The rules became a bargaining chip between supervisors and workers. If one took a rational systems perspective, one would expect that a rule performs some useful function at face value, but here the rules are subject to selective enforcement for ulterior reasons having nothing to do with the matters covered by the rules themselves.

But the informal aspect of formal rules was a double-edged sword. Workers also frequently agree to violate the letter of the rules to help supervisors who needed to make a tough schedule or other consideration. But in conflict situations, workers could point to the rules as a basis for performing only the minimum work required, a practice known as *work to rule*. In actual practice, no set of rules can specify exactly how everyone should behave in all circumstances. All work systems rely on some informal understandings and cooperation among participants if they are to function effectively. By acting according to the letter of the rules, workers had an official excuse to withhold that kind of informal cooperation and undercut the supervisor's efforts. Gouldner makes the additional point that the extreme elaboration of rules likely reflects a lack of trust in subordinates that can encourage only minimally cooperative behavior on their part, which leads the organization to further expand the set of rules.

Clearly, this view of formal rules goes far beyond their "official" character. Rules do not function simply to enhance technical efficiency; they are also a political device to legitimate supervisory authority and a tool used by contending groups to pursue their opposing interests.

Melville Dalton studied relations among managers at about the same time as Gouldner studied relations between management and workers (Reading 13). Like Gouldner, Dalton studied the actual way organizational life and behavior worked rather than simply the ideal. In the reading for this section, Dalton examined tensions between staff and line management departments.

Officially, the staff provided expert advice to help line management improve production operations. Informally, intergroup conflict was intense. Each had responsibilities, resources, interests, and status that put them at odds, but neither department was officially subordinate to the other, ensuring persistent tension. Some of this tension could be relieved by the kind of mutual back scratching and rule breaking described by Gouldner, though often this meant the staff had to compromise their professional standards in practice. Staff members were willing to do this in part because line positions had more authority, prestige, and income, and staff often tried to transfer into them with help from friends they cultivated in line management.

This case illustrates the limits of bureaucratic impersonality in practice, the role of informal cooperative and conflictual relations that are not represented in official organizational blueprints, and the relatively weak position of experts compared to those with command authority. This represents a natural or social systems approach to organizations, in contrast to the view of organizations as artificial, rational constructions.

Organizational politics is not only interdepartmental. Robert Jackall described the rampant politics between supervisors and subordinates within the management of a large corporation in the 1980s (Reading 18). The reality of hierarchy dominates how managers think about the world. Authority relationships are highly personalized. Bosses demand deference and devotion from their subordinates and reward protégés with preferential treatment and promotions in an exchange of loyalty for favors. Jackall uses Weber's term *patrimonial* to describe this situation, a word that Weber used for premodern bureaucracies that operated under a monarch in which the officials are servants of the king rather than independent professionals. Individuals move ahead in the corporation by struggling to impress their boss and by forming cliques and alliances with peers. Arbitrary decisions and shuffling of personnel are common and anxiety is pervasive.

Weber saw bureaucracy as a stable hierarchy with an impersonal application of legalistic rules, predictability, and a separation of offices and persons. However, life in large corporations as Jackall describes it involves personal loyalty, currying favor with the powerful, preferential treatment, and continual uncertainty.

A contemporary of Melville Dalton, Donald Roy, studied informal relations among factory workers in the 1940s and 1950s, including the group dynamics surrounding restriction of output. Michael Burawoy also studied output norms in the 1970s, and discovered, quite coincidentally, that he was restudying Roy's plant thirty years later (Reading 15). Burawoy worked as a machine operator in an engine plant in which workers were paid by the piece and were expected to produce at least a certain quota.

Taking the perspective common at the time, Roy asked why workers did not produce more, and concluded that harsh supervision led to output restriction, which could be remedied with human relations initiatives. Burawoy wondered why workers worked as hard as they did. He found workers made a game out of the work process as a way to pass time and make the work more interesting. Workers built up buffer supplies of pieces to compensate for times when it was difficult to make quota, always making sure they never exceeded the quota by too much to avoid possible rate cuts. Supervisors colluded with workers in this process to keep things running smoothly, even though higher management would be opposed if they were to find out.

This informal arrangement was mutually advantageous, but it also served to channel workers' discontents in a relatively harmless direction. It allowed workers some satisfaction, but within the terms of capitalist work relations, and it diverted attention from alternative ways of organizing production. As Burawoy said, "The very activity of playing a game generates consent with respect to its rules." Ultimately, the game is played within limits set by management and is a way of manufacturing consent.

Recently, some have questioned whether Burawoy's explanation of the consent generated by piecework in manufacturing can be applied easily to work in service industries, which have a different character and account for a far greater share of employment. Likewise, critics believe that the exclusion of race and gender issues in the workplace in favor of a strict focus on labor-management relations ignores an important element in how consent to capitalist work relations is secured among the white male working class (Leidner 2001).

One historical footnote is in order here: Burawoy conducted his research in the 1970s at the end of the longest boom in American history. When Roy conducted his research immediately after World War II, the plant was independently owned, management was coercive, and output quotas were relatively difficult to meet. When Burawoy studied the plant, it had been acquired by a large multinational, management arbitrariness was constrained by a set of worker protections and rules, and production quotas were easier to meet, reflecting the postwar accommodation between American management and labor, which was underwritten substantially by the U.S. dominance of the postwar international economy and rapidly rising living standards (Burawoy 1979, pp. 60, 71ff.). In Burawoy's terms, a coercive system was replaced with a more consensual system.

However, some of those improvements have been rolled back since then in certain respects. The economic slowdown and the competitiveness crisis of the late 1970s and 1980s depressed U.S. corporate profits, and companies searched for ways to lower costs. Workers' efforts to control their own work pace through banking parts and what management viewed as restriction of output were precisely the practices the Japanese *kaizen* and just-in-time methods, described by Laurie Graham, and Taylor's scientific management sought to eliminate (see Reading 12). In the 1980s and 1990s, American corporations implemented such programs on a wide scale to wring as much slack from the system as possible. If the plant Burawoy studied is still functioning and if Burawoy were to visit it today, he might well find that the workers have even less scope for the kind of small satisfactions he observed.

13

CONFLICTS BETWEEN STAFF AND LINE MANAGERIAL OFFICERS

MELVILLE DALTON

[. . .] The present paper is the result of an attempt to study processes among industrial managers. It is specifically a report on the functioning interaction between the two major vertical groupings of industrial management: (1) the *staff* organization, the functions of which are research and advisory; and (2) the *line* organization, which has exclusive authority over production processes.

Industrial staff organizations are relatively new. Their appearance is a response to many complex interrelated forces, such as economic competition, scientific advance, industrial expansion, growth of the labor movement, and so on. During the last four or five decades these rapid changes and resulting unstable conditions have caused top industrial officials more and more to call in "specialists" to aid them toward the goal of greater production and efficiency. These specialists are of many kinds including chemists, statisticians, public and industrial relations officers, personnel officers, accountants, and a great variety of engineers, such as mechanical, draughting, electrical, chemical, fuel, lubricating, and industrial engineers. In industry these individuals are usually known as "staff people." Their functions, again, for the most part are to increase and apply their specialized knowledge in problem areas, and to advise those officers who make up the "line" organization and have authority[1] over production processes.

This theoretically satisfying industrial structure of specialized experts advising busy administrators has in a number of significant cases failed to function as expected. The assumptions that (a) the staff specialists would be reasonably content to function without a measure of formal authority[2] over production, and that (b) their suggestions regarding improvement of processes and techniques for control over personnel and production would be welcomed by line officers and be applied, require closer examination. In practice there is often much conflict between industrial staff and line organizations and in varying degrees the members of these organizations oppose each other.[3]

The aim of this paper is, therefore, to present and analyze data dealing with staff-line tensions.

Data were drawn from three industrial plants[4] in which the writer had been either a participating member of one or both of the groups or was intimate with reliable informants among the officers who were.

Approached sociologically, relations among members of management in the plants could be viewed as a general conflict system caused and perpetuated chiefly by (1) power struggles in the organization stemming in the main from competition among departments to maintain low operating costs; (2) drives by numerous members to increase their status in the hierarchy; (3) conflict between union and management; and (4) the staff-line friction which is the subject of this paper.[5] This milieu of tensions was not only unaccounted for by the blue-print organizations of the plants, but was often contradictory to, and even destructive of, the organizations' formal aims. All members of management, especially in the middle and lower ranks,[6] were caught up in this conflict system. Even though they might wish to escape, the obligation of at least appearing to carry out formal functions compelled individuals to take sides in order to protect themselves against the aggressions of others. And the intensity of the conflict was aggravated by the fact that it was formally unacceptable and had to be hidden.

For analytical convenience, staff-line friction may be examined apart from the reciprocal effects of the general conflict system. Regarded in this way, the data indicated that three conditions were basic to staff-line struggles: (1) the conspicuous ambition and "individualistic" behavior among staff officers; (2) the complication arising from staff efforts to justify its existence and get acceptance of its contributions; and, related to point two, (3) the fact that incumbency of the higher staff offices was dependent on line approval. The significance of these conditions will be discussed in order.

MOBILE BEHAVIOR OF STAFF PERSONNEL

As a group, staff personnel in the three plants were markedly ambitious, restless, and individualistic. There was much concern to win rapid promotion, to make the "right impressions," and to receive individual recognition. Data showed that the desire among staff members for personal distinctions often over-rode their sentiments of group consciousness and caused intra-staff tensions.[7]

The relatively high turnover of staff personnel quite possibly reflected the dissatisfactions and frustrations of members over inability to achieve the distinction and status they hoped for. Several factors appeared to be of importance in this restlessness of staff personnel. Among these were age and social differences between line and staff officers, structural differences in the hierarchy of the two groups, and the staff group's lack of authority over production.

With respect to age, the staff officers were significantly younger than line officers. This would account to some extent for their restlessness. Being presumably less well-established in life in terms of material accumulations, occupational status, and security, while having greater expectations (see below), and more energy, as well as more life ahead in which to make new starts elsewhere if necessary, the staff groups were understandably more dynamic and driving.[8]

Age-conflict was also significant in staff-line antagonisms. The incident just noted of the young staff officer seeking to get direct acceptance by the line of his contribution failed in part—judging from the strong sentiments later expressed by the line superintendent—because of an age antipathy. The older line officers disliked receiving what they regarded as instruction from men so much younger than themselves, and staff personnel clearly were conscious of this attitude among line officers.[9] In staff-line meetings staff officers frequently had their ideas slighted or even treated with amusement by line incumbents. Whether such treatment was warranted or not, the effects were disillusioning to the younger, less experienced staff officers. Often selected by the organization because of their outstanding academic records, they had entered industry with the belief that they had much to contribute, and that their efforts would win early recognition and rapid advancement. Certainly they had no thought that their contributions would be in any degree unwelcome. This naiveté was apparently due to lack of earlier first-hand experience in industry (or acquaintance with those who had such experience), and to omission of realistic instruction in the social sciences from their academic training. The unsophisticated staff officer's initial contacts with the shifting, covert, expedient arrangements between members of staff and line usually gave him a severe shock. He had entered industry prepared to engage in logical, well-formulated relations with members of the managerial hierarchy, and to carry out precise, methodical functions for which his training had equipped him. Now he learned that (1) his freedom to function was snared in a web of informal commitments; (2) his academic specialty (on which he leaned for support in his new position) was often not relevant[10] for carrying out his formal assignments; and that (3) the important thing to do was to learn who the informally powerful line officers were and what ideas they would welcome which at the same time would be acceptable to his superiors.

Usually the staff officer's reaction to these conditions is to look elsewhere for a job or make an accommodation in the direction of protecting himself and finding a niche where he can make his existence in the plant tolerable and safe. If he chooses the latter course, he is likely to be less concerned with creative effort for his employer than with attempts to develop reliable social relations that will aid his personal advancement. The staff officer's recourse to this behavior and his use of other status-increasing devices will be discussed below in another connection.

The formal structure, or hierarchy of statuses, of the two larger plants from which data were drawn, offered a frustration to the ambitious staff officer. That is, in these plants the strata, or levels of authority, in the staff organizations ranged from three to five as against from five to ten in the line organization. Consequently there were fewer possible positions for exercise of authority into which staff personnel could move. This condition may have been an irritant to expansion among the staff groups. Unable to move vertically to the degree possible in the line organization, the ambitious staff officer

could enlarge his area of authority in a given position only by lateral expansion—by increasing his personnel. Whether or not aspiring staff incumbents revolted against the relatively low hierarchy through which they could move, the fact remains that (1) they appeared eager to increase the number of personnel under their authority,[11] (2) the personnel of staff groups *did* increase disproportionately to those of the line,[12] and (3) there was a trend of personnel movement from staff to line,[13] rather than the reverse, presumably (reflecting the drive and ambition of staff members) because there were more positions of authority, as well as more authority to be exercised, more prestige, and usually more income in the line.

Behavior in the plants indicated that line and staff personnel belonged to different social status groups and that line and staff antipathies were at least in part related to these social distinctions. For example, with respect to the item of formal education, the staff group stood on a higher level than members of the line. In the plant from which the age data were taken, the 36 staff officers had a mean of 14.6 years of schooling as compared with 13.1 years for 35 line superintendents, 11.2 years for 60 general foremen, and 10.5 years for 93 first-line foremen. The difference between the mean education of the staff group and that of the highest line group (14.6–13.1) was statistically significant at better than the one per cent level. The 270 non-supervisory staff personnel had a mean of 13.1 years—the same as that of the line superintendents. Consciousness of this difference probably contributed to a feeling of superiority among staff members, while the sentiment of line officers toward staff personnel was reflected in the name-calling noted earlier.

Staff members were also much concerned about their dress, a daily shave, and a weekly hair-cut. On the other hand line officers, especially below the level of departmental superintendent, were relatively indifferent to such matters. Usually they were in such intimate contact with production processes that dirt and grime prevented the concern with meticulous dress shown by staff members. The latter also used better English in speaking and in writing reports, and were more suave and poised in social intercourse. These factors, and the recreational preferences of staff officers for night clubs and "hot parties," assisted in raising a barrier between them and most line officers.

The social antipathies of the two groups and the status concern of staff officers were indicated by the behavior of each toward the established practice of dining together in the cafeterias reserved for management in the two larger plants. Theoretically, all managerial officers upward from the level of general foremen in the line, and general supervisors in the staff, were eligible to eat in these cafeterias. However, in practice the mere taking of one of these offices did not automatically assure the incumbent the privilege of eating in the cafeteria. One had first to be invited to "join the association." Staff officers were very eager to "get in" and did considerable fantasying on the impressions, with respect to dress and behavior, that were believed essential for an invitation. One such staff officer, a cost supervisor, dropped the following remarks:

> There seems to be a committee that passes on you. I've had my application in for three years, but no soap. Harry [his superior] had his in for over three years before he made it. You have to have something, because if a man who's in moves up to another position the man who replaces him doesn't get it because of the position—and he might not get it at all. I think I'm about due.

Many line officers who were officially members of the association avoided the cafeteria, however, and had to be *ordered* by the assistant plant manager to attend. One of these officers made the following statement, which expressed more pointedly the many similar spontaneous utterances of resentment and dislike made by other line officers:

> There's a lot of good discussion in the cafeteria. I'd like to get in on more of it but I don't like to go there— sometimes I have to go. Most of the white collar people [staff officers] that eat there are stuck-up. I've been introduced three times to Svendsen [engineer], yet when I meet him he pretends to not even know me. When he meets me on the street he always manages to be looking someplace else. G__ d___ such people as that! They don't go in the cafeteria to eat and relax while they talk over their problems. They go in there to look around and see how somebody is dressed or to

talk over the hot party they had last night. Well, that kind of damn stuff don't go with me. I haven't any time to put on airs and make out I'm something that I'm not.

COMPLICATIONS OF STAFF NEED TO PROVE ITS WORTH

To the thinking of many line officers, the staff functioned as an agent on trial rather than as a managerial division that might be of equal importance with the line organization in achieving production goals. Staff members were very conscious of this sentiment toward them and of their need to prove themselves. They strained to develop new techniques and to get them accepted by the line. But in doing this they frequently became impatient, and gave already suspicious line officers the impression of reaching for authority over production.

Since the line officer regards his authority over production as something sacred, and resents the implication that after many years in the line he needs the guidance of a new-comer who lacks such experience, an obstacle to staff-line cooperation develops the moment this sore spot is touched. On the other hand, the staff officer's ideology of his function leads him to precipitate a power struggle with the line organization. By and large he considers himself as an agent of top management. He feels bound to contribute something significant in the form of research or ideas helpful to management. By virtue of his greater education and intimacy with the latest theories of production, he regards himself as a managerial consultant and an expert, and feels that he must be, or appear to be, almost infallible once he has committed himself to top management on some point. With this orientation, he is usually disposed to approach middle and lower line with an attitude of condescension that often reveals itself in the heat of discussion. Consequently, many staff officers involve themselves in trouble and report their failures as due to "ignorance" and "bull-headedness" among these line officers.

On this point, relations between staff and line in all three of the plants were further irritated by a rift inside the line organization. First-line foremen were inclined to feel that top management had brought in the production planning, industrial relations, and industrial engineering staffs as clubs with which to control the lower line. Hence they frequently regarded the projects of staff personnel as manipulative devices, and reacted by cooperating with production workers and/or general foremen (whichever course was the more expedient) in order to defeat insistent and uncompromising members of the staff. Also, on occasion (see below), the lower line could cooperate evasively with lower staff personnel who were in trouble with staff superiors.

EFFECT OF LINE AUTHORITY OVER STAFF PROMOTION

The fact that entry to the higher staff offices in the three plants was dependent on approval of top line officers had a profound effect on the behavior of staff personnel. Every member of the staff knew that if he aspired to higher office he must make a record for himself, a good part of which would be a reputation among upper line officers of ability to "understand" their informal problems without being told. This knowledge worked in varying degrees to pervert the theory of staff-line relations. Ideally the two organizations cooperate to improve existing methods of output, to introduce new methods, to plan the work, and to solve problems of production and the scheduling of orders that might arise. But when the line offers resistance to the findings and recommendations of the staff, the latter is reduced to evasive practices of getting some degree of acceptance of its programs, and at the same time of convincing top management that "good relations" exist with officers down the line. This necessity becomes even more acute when the staff officer aspires (for some of the reasons given above) to move over to the line organization, for then he must convince powerful line officers that he is worthy. In building a convincing record, however, he may compromise with line demands and bring charges from his staff colleagues that he is "selling out," so that after moving into the line organization he will then have to live with enemies he made in the staff. In any case, the need among staff incumbents of pleasing line officers in order to perfect their careers called for accommodation in three major areas: (1) the observance of staff rules, (2) the introduction of new techniques,

and (3) the use of appropriations for staff research and experiment.

With respect to point one, staff personnel, particularly in the middle and lower levels, carried on expedient relations with the line that daily evaded formal rules. Even those officers most devoted to rules found that, in order not to arouse enmity in the line on a scale sufficient to be communicated *up* the line, compromising devices were frequently helpful and sometimes almost unavoidable both for organizational and career aims. The usual practice was to tolerate minor breaking of staff rules by line personnel, or even to cooperate with the line in evading rules,[14] and in exchange lay a claim on the line for cooperation on critical issues. In some cases line aid was enlisted to conceal lower staff blunders from the upper staff and the upper line.[15]

Concerning point two, while the staff organizations gave much time to developing new techniques, they were simultaneously thinking about how their plans would be received by the line. They knew from experience that middle and lower line officers could always give a "black eye" to staff contributions by deliberate mal-practices *[sic]*. Repeatedly top management had approved, and incorporated, staff proposals that had been verbally accepted down the line. Often the latter officers had privately opposed the changes, but had feared that saying so would incur the resentment of powerful superiors who could informally hurt them. Later they would seek to discredit the change by deliberate malpractice *[sic]* and hope to bring a return to the former arrangement. For this reason there was a tendency for staff members to withhold improved production schemes or other plans when they knew that an attempt to introduce them might fail or even bring personal disrepute.

Line officers fear staff innovations for a number of reasons. In view of their longer experience, presumably intimate knowledge of the work, and their greater remuneration, they fear[16] being "shown up" before their line superiors for not having thought of the processual refinements themselves. They fear that changes in methods may bring personnel changes which will threaten the break-up of cliques and existing informal arrangements and quite possibly reduce their area of authority. Finally, changes in techniques may expose forbidden practices and departmental inefficiency. In some cases these fears have stimulated line officers to compromise staff men to the point where the latter will agree to postpone the initiation of new practices for specific periods.

In one such case an assistant staff head agreed with a line superintendent to delay the application of a bonus plan for nearly three months so that the superintendent could live up to the expedient agreement he had made earlier with his grievance committeeman to avoid a "wildcat" strike by a group of production workmen. The lower engineers who had devised the plan were suspicious of the formal reasons given to them for withholding it, so the assistant staff head prevented them (by means of "busy work") from attending staff-line meetings lest they inadvertently reveal to top management that the plan was ready.

The third area of staff-line accommodations growing out of authority relations revolved around staff use of funds granted it by top management. Middle and lower line charged that staff research and experimentation was little more than "money wasted on blunders," and that various departments of the line could have "accomplished much more with less money." According to staff officers, those of their plans that failed usually did so because line personnel "sabotaged" them and refused to "cooperate." Specific costs of "crack-pot experimentation" in certain staff groups were pointed to by line officers. Whatever the truth of the charges and countercharges, evidence indicated (confidants in both groups supported this) that pressures from the line organization (below the top level) forced some of the staff groups to "kick over" parts of the funds appropriated for staff use[17] by top management. These compromises were of course hidden from top management, but the relations described were carried on to such an extent that by means of them— and line pressures for manipulation of accounts in the presumably impersonal auditing departments— certain line officers were able to show impressively low operating costs and thus win favor with top management that would relieve pressures and be useful in personal advancement. In their turn the staff officers involved would receive more "cooperation" from the line and/or recommendation for transfer to the line. The data indicated that in a few such cases men from accounting and auditing staffs were given general foremanships (without previous line experience) as a reward for their understanding behavior.

SUMMARY

Research in three industrial plants showed conflict between the managerial staff and line groups that hindered the attainment of organizational goals. Privately expressed attitudes among some of the higher line executives revealed their hope that greater control of staff groups could be achieved, or that the groups might be eliminated and their functions taken over in great part by carefully selected and highly remunerated lower-line officers. On their side, staff members wanted more recognition and a greater voice in control of the plants.

All of the various functioning groups of the plants were caught up in a general conflict system; but apart from the effects of involvement in this complex, the struggles between line and staff organizations were attributable mainly to (1) functional differences between the two groups; (2) differentials in the ages, formal education, potential occupational ceilings, and status group affiliations of members of the two groups (the staff officers being younger, having more education but lower occupational potential, and forming a prestige-oriented group with distinctive dress and recreational tastes); (3) need of the staff groups to justify their existence; (4) fear in the line that staff bodies by their expansion, and well-financed research activities, would undermine line authority; and (5) the fact that aspirants to higher staff offices could gain promotion only through approval of influential line executives.

NOTES

1. *Inside* their particular staff organization, staff officers also may have authority over their subordinates, but not over production personnel.

2. To the extent that staff officers influence line policy they do, of course, have a certain *informal authority*.

3. *[. . .]* A high line officer in a large corporation denounced staff organizations to the writer on the ground of their "costing more than they're worth," and that "They stir up too much trouble and are too theoretical." He felt that their function (excepting that of accountants, chemists, and "a few mechanical engineers") could be better carried out by replacing them with "highly-select front-line foremen [the lowest placed line officers] who are really the backbone of management, and pay them ten or twelve thousand dollars a year."

4. These plants were in related industries and ranged in size from 4,500 to 20,000 employees, with the managerial groups numbering from 200 to nearly 1,000. Details concerning the plants and their location are confidential.

5. Because these conflict areas were interrelated and continually shifting and reorganizing, discussion of any one of them separately—as in the case of staff-line relations—will, of course, be unrealistic to some extent.

6. From bottom to top, the line hierarchy consisted of the following strata of officers: (1) first-line foremen, who were directly in charge of production workmen; (2) general foremen; (3) departmental superintendents; (4) divisional superintendents; (5) assistant plant manager; (6) plant manager. In the preceding strata there were often "assistants," such as "assistant general foreman," "assistant superintendent," etc., in which case the total strata of the line hierarchy could be almost double that indicated here.

In the staff organizations the order from bottom to top was: (1) supervisor (equivalent to the first-line foreman); (2) general supervisor (equivalent to the general foreman); (3) staff head—sometimes "superintendent" (equivalent to departmental superintendent in the line organization). Occasionally there were strata of assistant supervisors and assistant staff heads.

7. In a typical case in one of the plants, a young staff officer developed a plan for increasing the life of certain equipment in the plant. He carried the plan directly to the superintendent of the department in which he hoped to introduce it, but was rebuffed by the superintendent who privately acknowledged the merit of the scheme but resented the staff officer's "trying to lord it over" him. The staff organization condemned the behavior of its member and felt that he should have allowed the plan to appear as a contribution of the staff group rather than as one of its members. The officer himself declared that "By G__ it's my idea and I want credit. There's not a damn one of you guys [the staff group] that wouldn't make the same squawk if you were in my place!"

8. One might also hypothesize that the drive of staff officers was reflected in the fact that the staff heads and specialists gained their positions (those held when the data

were collected) in less time than did members of the line groups. E.g., the 36 staff officers discussed above had spent a median of 10 years attaining their positions, as against a median of 11 years for the first-line foremen, 17 years for the general foremen, and 19 years for the superintendents. But one must consider that some of the staff groups were relatively new (13–15 years old) and had grown rapidly, which probably accelerated their rate of promotions as compared with that of the older line organization.

9. Explaining the relatively few cases in which his staff had succeeded in "selling ideas" to the line, an assistant staff head remarked: "We're always in hot water with these old guys on the line. You can't tell them a damn thing. They're bull-headed as hell! Most of the time we offer a suggestion it's either laughed at or not considered at all. The same idea in the mouth of some old codger on the line'd get a round of applause. They treat us like kids."

Line officers in these plants often referred to staff personnel (especially members of the auditing, production planning, industrial engineering, and industrial relations staffs) as "college punks," "slide-rules," "crackpots," "pretty boys," and "chair-warmers."

10. Among the staff heads and assistants referred to earlier, only 50 per cent of those with college training (32 of the 36 officers) were occupied with duties related to their specialized training. E.g., the head of the industrial relations staff had a B.S. degree in aeronautical engineering; his assistant had a similar degree in chemical engineering. Considering that staff officers are assumed to be specialists trained to aid and advise management in a particular function, the condition presented here raises a question as to what the criteria of selection were. (As will be shown in a separate paper, the answer appeared to be that personal—as well as impersonal—criteria were used.) Among the college-trained of 190 line officers in the same plant, the gap between training and function was still greater, with 61 per cent in positions not related to the specialized part of their college work.

11. This was suggested by unnecessary references among some staff officers to "the number of men under me," and by their somewhat fanciful excuses for increase of personnel. These excuses included statements of needing more personnel to (1) carry on research, (2) control new processes, (3) keep records and reports up-to-date. These statements often did not square with (1) the excessive concern among staff people about their "privileges" (such as arriving on the job late, leaving early, leaving the plant for long periods during working hours, having a radio in the office during the World Series, etc.); (2) the great amount of time (relative to that of line officers) spent by lower staff personnel in social activities on the job, and

(3) the constantly recurring (but not always provoked) claims among staff personnel of their functional importance for production. The duties of middle and lower staff personnel allowed them sufficient time to argue a great deal over their respective functions (as well as many irrelevant topics) and to challenge the relative merit of one another's contributions or "ideas." In some of the staffs these discussions could go on intermittently for hours and develop into highly theoretical jousts and wit battles. Where staff people regarded such behavior as a privilege of their status, line officers considered it as a threat to themselves. This lax control (in terms of line discipline) was in part a tacit reward from staff heads to their subordinates. The reward was expected because staff superiors (especially in the industrial relations, industrial engineering, and planning staffs) often overlooked and/or perverted the work of subordinates (which was resented) in response to pressures from the line. This behavior will be noted later.

12. In one of the larger plants, where exact data were available, the total staff personnel had by 1945 exceeded that of the line. At that time the staff included 400 members as against 317 line personnel composed of managerial officers and their clerical workers, but not production workers. By 1948 the staff had increased to 517 as compared with 387 for the line (during this period *total* plant personnel declined over 400.). The staff had grown from 20.8 per cent larger than the line in 1945 to 33.6 per cent larger in 1948, and had itself increased by 29.3 per cent during the three years as against a growth in the line of 22.1 per cent. Assuming the conditions essential for use of probability theory, the increase in staff personnel could have resulted from chance about 1.5 times in a hundred. Possibly post-war and other factors of social change were also at work but, if so, their force was not readily assessable.

13. This movement from staff to line can disorganize the formal managerial structure, especially when (1) the transferring staff personnel have had little or no supervisory experience in the staff but have an academic background which causes them to regard human beings as mechanisms that will respond as expected; (2) older, experienced line officers have hoped—for years in some cases—to occupy the newly vacated (or created) positions.

14. In a processing department in one of the plants the chemical solution in a series of vats was supposed to have a specific strength and temperature, and a fixed rate of inflow and outflow. Chemists (members of the chemical staff) twice daily checked these properties of the solution and submitted reports showing that all points met the laboratory ideal. Actually, the solution was usually nearly triple the standard strength, the temperature was about 10 degrees Centigrade higher than standard, and the rate of flow was in excess of double the standard. There are, of course, varying discrepancies between laboratory theory and plant practice, but the condition described here resulted from production pressures that forced line foremen into behavior upsetting the conditions expected by chemical theory. The chemists were sympathetic with the hard-pressed foremen, who compensated by (1) notifying the chemists (rather than their superior, the chief chemist) if anything "went wrong" for which the laboratory was responsible and thus sparing them criticism; and by (2) cooperating with the chemists to reduce the number of analyses which the chemists would ordinarily have to make.

15. Failure of middle and lower staff personnel to "cooperate" with line officers might cause the latter to "stand pat" in observance of line rules at a time when the pressures of a dynamic situation would make the former eager to welcome line cooperation in rule-breaking. For example, a staff officer was confronted with the combined effect of (1) a delay in production on the line that was due to an indefensible staff error; (2) pressure on the line superintendent—with whom he was working—to hurry a special order; and (3) the presence in his force of new inexperienced staff personnel who were (a) irritating to line officers, and (b) by their inexperience constituted an invitation to line aggression. Without aid from the line superintendent (which could have been withheld by observance of formal rules) in covering up the staff error and in controlling line personnel, the staff officer might have put himself in permanent disfavor with all his superiors.

16. Though there was little evidence that top management expected line officers to refine production techniques, the fear of such an expectation existed nevertheless. As noted earlier, however, some of the top executives *were* thinking that development of a "higher type" of first-line foreman might enable most of the staff groups to be eliminated.

17. In two of the plants a somewhat similar relation, rising from different causes, existed *inside* the line organization with the *operating* branch of the line successfully applying pressures for a share in funds assigned to the *maintenance* division of the line.

14

THE WORLD OF CORPORATE MANAGERS

ROBERT JACKALL

2

THE SOCIAL STRUCTURE OF MANAGERIAL WORK

I

The hierarchical authority structure that is the linchpin of bureaucracy dominates the way managers think about their world and about themselves. Managers do not see or experience authority in any abstract way; instead, authority is embodied in their personal relationships with their immediate bosses and in their perceptions of similar links between other managers up and down the hierarchy. When managers describe their work to an outsider, they almost always first say: "I work for [Bill James]" or "I report to [Harry Mills]" or "I'm in [Joe Bell's] group,"[1] and only then proceed to describe their actual work functions. Such a personalized statement of authority relationships seems to contradict classical notions of how bureaucracies function but it exactly reflects the way authority is structured, exercised, and experienced in corporate hierarchies.

American businesses typically both centralize and decentralize authority. Power is concentrated at the top in the person of the chief executive officer (CEO) and is simultaneously decentralized; that is, responsibility for decisions and profits is pushed as far down the organizational line as possible. For example, Alchemy Inc., as already noted, is one of several operating companies of Covenant Corporation.[2] When I began my research, Alchemy employed 11,000 people; Covenant had over 50,000 employees and now has over 100,000. Like the other operating companies, Alchemy has its own president, executive vice-presidents, vice-presidents, other executive officers, business area managers, staff divisions, and more than eighty manufacturing plants scattered throughout the country and indeed the world producing a wide range of specialty and commodity chemicals. Each operating company is, at least theoretically, an autonomous, self-sufficient organization, though they are all monitored and coordinated by a central corporate staff, and each president reports directly to the corporate CEO. Weft Corporation has its corporate headquarters and manufacturing facilities in the South; its marketing and sales offices, along with some key executive personnel, are in New York City. Weft employs 20,000 people, concentrated in the firm's three textile divisions that have always been and remain its core business. The Apparel Division produces seven million yards a week of raw, unfinished cloth in several greige (colloquially gray) mills, mostly for sale to garment manufacturers; the Consumer Division produces some cloth of its own in several greige mills and also finishes—that is, bleaches, dyes, prints, and sews—twelve million yards of raw cloth a month into purchasable items like sheets, pillowcases, and tablecloths for department stores and chain stores; and the Retail Division operates an import-export business, specializing in the quick turnaround of the fast-moving cloths desired by Seventh Avenue designers. Each division has a president who reports to one of several executive vice-presidents, who in turn report to the corporate CEO. The divisional structure is typically less elaborate in its hierarchical ladder than the framework of independent operating companies; it is also somewhat more dependent on corporate staff for essential services. However, the basic principle of simultaneous centralization and decentralization prevails and both Covenant and Weft consider their companies or divisions, as the case may be, "profit centers." Even Images Inc., while much smaller than the industrial concerns and organized like most service businesses according to shifting groupings of client accounts supervised by senior vice-presidents, uses the notion of profit centers.[3]

The key interlocking mechanism of this structure is its reporting system. Each manager gathers up the profit targets or other objectives of his or her subordinates and, with these, formulates his commitments to his boss; this boss takes these commitments and those of his other subordinates, and in turn makes a commitment to his boss.[4] At the top of the line, the president of each company or division, or, at Images Inc., the senior vice-president for a group of accounts, makes his commitment to the CEO. This may be done directly, or sometimes, as at Weft Corporation, through a corporate executive vice-president. In any event, the commitments made to top management depend on the pyramid of stated objectives given to superiors up the line. At each level of the structure, there is typically "topside" pressure to achieve higher goals and, of course, the CEO frames and paces the whole process by applying pressure for attainment of his own objectives. Meanwhile, bosses and subordinates down the line engage in a series of intricate negotiations—managers often call these "conspiracies"—to keep their commitments respectable but achievable.

This "management-by-objective" system, as it is usually called, creates a chain of commitments from the CEO down to the lowliest product manager or account executive. In practice, it also shapes a patrimonial authority arrangement that is crucial to defining both the immediate experiences and the long-run career chances of individual managers.[5] In this world, a subordinate owes fealty principally to his immediate boss. This means that a subordinate must not overcommit his boss, lest his boss "get on the hook" for promises that cannot be kept. He must keep his boss from making mistakes, particularly public ones; he must keep his boss informed, lest his boss get "blindsided." If one has a mistake-prone boss, there is, of course, always the temptation to let him make a fool of himself, but the wise subordinate knows that this carries two dangers—he himself may get done in by his boss's errors, and, perhaps more important, other managers will view with the gravest suspicion a subordinate who withholds crucial information from his boss even if they think the boss is a nincompoop. A subordinate must also not circumvent his boss nor ever give the appearance of doing so. He must never contradict his boss's judgment in public. To violate the last admonition is thought to constitute a kind of death wish in business, and one who does so should practice what one executive calls "flexibility drills," an exercise "where you put your head between your legs and kiss your ass goodbye." On a social level, even though an easy, breezy, first-name informality is the prevalent style of American business, a concession perhaps to our democratic heritage and egalitarian rhetoric, the subordinate must extend to the boss a certain ritual deference. For instance, he must follow the boss's lead in conversation, must not speak out of turn at meetings, must laugh at his boss's jokes while not making jokes of his own that upstage his boss, must not rib the boss for his foibles. The shrewd subordinate learns to efface himself, so that his boss's face might shine more clearly.

In short, the subordinate must symbolically reinforce at every turn his own subordination and his willing acceptance of the obligations of fealty. In return, he can hope for those perquisites that are in his boss's gift—the better, more attractive secretaries, or the nudging of a movable panel to enlarge his office, and perhaps a couch to fill the added space, one of the real distinctions in corporate bureaucracies. He can hope to be elevated when and if the boss is elevated, though other important criteria intervene here. He can also expect protection for mistakes made, up to a point. However, that point is never exactly defined and depends on the complicated politics of each situation. The general rule is that bosses are expected to protect those in their bailiwicks. Not to do so, or to be unable to do so, is taken as a sign of untrustworthiness or weakness. If, however, subordinates make mistakes that are thought to be dumb, or especially if they violate fealty obligations—for example, going around their boss—then abandonment of them to the vagaries of organizational forces is quite acceptable.

Overlaying and intertwined with this formal monocratic system of authority, with its patrimonial resonance, are patron-client relationships. Patrons are usually powerful figures in the higher echelons of management. The patron might be a manager's direct boss, or his boss's boss, or someone several levels higher in the chain of command. In either case, the manager is still bound by the immediate, formal authority and fealty patterns of his position but he also acquires new, though more ambiguous, fealty relationships with his highest ranking patron. Patrons play a crucial role in advancement, a point that I shall discuss later.

It is characteristic of this authority system that details are pushed down and credit is pulled up. Superiors do not like to give detailed instructions to subordinates. The official reason for this is to maximize subordinates' autonomy. The underlying reason is, first, to get rid of tedious details. Most hierarchically organized occupations follow this pattern; one of the privileges of authority is the divestment of humdrum intricacies. This also insulates higher bosses from the peculiar pressures that accompany managerial work at the middle levels and below: the lack of economy over one's time because of continual interruption from one's subordinates, telephone calls from customers and clients, and necessary meetings with colleagues; the piecemeal fragmentation of issues both because of the discontinuity of events and because of the way subordinates filter news; and the difficulty of minding the store while sorting out sometimes unpleasant personnel issues. Perhaps more important, pushing details down protects the privilege of authority to declare that a mistake has been made. A high-level executive in Alchemy Inc. explains:

> If I tell someone what to do—like do A, B, or C—the inference and implication is that he will succeed in accomplishing the objective. Now, if he doesn't succeed, that means that I have invested part of myself in his work and I lose any right I have to chew his ass out if he doesn't succeed. If I tell you what to do, I can't bawl you out if things don't work. And this is why a lot of bosses don't give explicit directions. They just give a statement of objectives, and then they can criticize subordinates who fail to make their goals.

Moreover, pushing down details relieves superiors of the burden of too much knowledge, particularly guilty knowledge. A superior will say to a subordinate, for instance: "Give me your best thinking on the problem with [X]." When the subordinate makes his report, he is often told: "I think you can do better than that," until the subordinate has worked out all the details of the boss's predetermined solution, without the boss being specifically aware of "all the eggs that have to be broken." It is also not at all uncommon for very bald and extremely general edicts to emerge from on high. For example, "Sell the plant in [St. Louis]; let me know when you've struck a deal," or "We need to get higher prices for [fabric X]; see what you can work out," or "Tom, I want you to go down there and meet with those guys and make a deal and I don't want you to come back until you've got one." This pushing down of details has important consequences.

First, because they are unfamiliar with—indeed deliberately distance themselves from—entangling details, corporate higher echelons tend to expect successful results without messy complications. This is central to top executives' well-known aversion to bad news and to the resulting tendency to kill the messenger who bears the news.

Second, the pushing down of details creates great pressure on middle managers not only to transmit good news but, precisely because they know the details, to act to protect their corporations, their bosses, and themselves in the process. They become the "point men" of a given strategy and the potential "fall guys" when things go wrong. From an organizational standpoint, overly conscientious managers are particularly useful at the middle levels of the structure. [. . .]

Credit flows up in this structure and is usually appropriated by the highest ranking officer involved in a successful decision or resolution of a problem. There is, for instance, a tremendous competition for ideas in the corporate world; authority provides a license to steal ideas, even in front of those who originated them. Chairmen routinely appropriate the useful suggestions made by members of their committees or task forces; research directors build their reputations for scientific wizardry on the bricks laid down by junior researchers and directors of departments. Presidents of whole divisions as well are always on the lookout for "fresh ideas" and "creative approaches" that they can claim as their own in order to put themselves "out in front" of their peers. A subordinate whose ideas are appropriated is expected to be a good sport about the matter; not to balk at so being used is one attribute of the good team player. The person who appropriates credit redistributes it as he chooses, bound essentially and only by a sensitivity to public perceptions of his fairness. One gives credit, therefore, not necessarily where it is due, although one always invokes this old saw, but where prudence dictates. Customarily, people who had nothing to do with the success of a project can be allocated credit for their exemplary efforts. At the middle levels, therefore, credit for a particular idea or success is always a type of refracted social honor; one cannot claim credit even if it is earned. Credit has to be given, and acceptance of the gift implicitly involves a reaffirmation and

strengthening of fealty. A superior may share some credit with subordinates in order to deepen fealty relationships and induce greater efforts on his behalf. Of course, a different system obtains in the allocation of blame.

Because of the interlocking character of the commitment system, a CEO carries enormous influence in his corporation. If, for a moment, one thinks of the presidents of operating companies or divisions as barons, then the CEO of the corporation is the king. His word is law; even the CEO's wishes and whims are taken as commands by close subordinates on the corporate staff, who turn them into policies and directives. A typical example occurred in Weft Corporation a few years ago when the CEO, new at the time, expressed mild concern about the rising operating costs of the company's fleet of rented cars. The following day, a stringent system for monitoring mileage replaced the previous casual practice. Managers have a myriad of aphorisms that refer to how the power of CEOs, magnified through the zealous efforts of subordinates, affects them. These range from the trite "When he sneezes, we all catch colds" to the more colorful "When he says 'Go to the bathroom,' we all get the shits."

Great efforts are made to please the CEO. For example, when the CEO of Covenant Corporation visits a plant, the most significant order of business for local management is a fresh paint job, even when, as in several cases, the cost of paint alone exceeds $100,000. If a paint job has already been scheduled at a plant, it is deferred along with all other cosmetic maintenance until just before the CEO arrives; keeping up appearances without recognition for one's efforts is pointless. [. . .]

The second order of business for the plant management is to produce a book fully describing the plant and its operations, replete with photographs and illustrations, for presentation to the CEO; such a book costs about $10,000 for the single copy. By any standards of budgetary stringency, such expenditures are irrational. But by the social standards of the corporation, they make perfect sense. It is far more important to please the king today than to worry about the future economic state of one's fief, since, if one does not please the king, there may not be a fief to worry about or indeed vassals to do the worrying.

By the same token, all of this leads to an intense interest in everything the CEO does and says. In all the companies that I studied, the most common topic of conversation among managers up and down the line is speculation about their respective CEO's plans, intentions, strategies, actions, style, public image, and ideological leanings of the moment. Even the metaphorical temper of a CEO's language finds its way down the hierarchy to the lower reaches of an organization. In the early stages of my fieldwork at Covenant Corporation, for example, I was puzzled by the inordinately widespread usage of nautical terminology, especially in a corporation located in a landlocked site. As it happens, the CEO is devoted to sailboats and prefers that his aides call him "Skipper." Moreover, in every corporation that I studied, stories and rumors circulate constantly about the social world of the CEO and his immediate subordinates—who, for instance, seems to have the CEO's ear at the moment; whose style seems to have gained approbation; who, in short, seems to be in the CEO's grace and who seems to have fallen out of favor. In the smaller and more intimate setting of Images Inc., the circulation of favor takes an interesting, if unusual, tack. There, the CEO is known for attaching younger people to himself as confidants. He solicits their advice, tells them secrets, gets their assessments of developments further down in the hierarchy, gleans the rumors and gossip making the rounds about himself. For the younger people selected for such attention, this is a rare, if fleeting, opportunity to have a place in the sun and to share the illusion if not the substance of power. In time, of course, the CEO tires of or becomes disappointed with particular individuals and turns his attention to others. "Being discarded," however, is not an obstacle to regaining favor. In larger organizations, impermeable structural barriers between top circles and junior people prevent this kind of intimate interchange and circulation of authoritative regard. Within a CEO's circle, however, the same currying and granting of favor prevails, always amidst conjectures from below about who has edged close to the throne.

[. . .]

Within the general ambiance established by a CEO, presidents of individual operating companies or of divisions carry similar, though correspondingly reduced, influence within their own baronies. Adroit and well-placed subordinates can, for instance, borrow a president's prestige and power to exert great leverage. Even chance encounters or the occasional meeting or lunch with the president can, if advertised casually and subtly, cause notice and the respect among other managers that comes from uncertainty. Knowledge of more clearly established relationships, of course, always sways behavior. A middle manager in one company, widely known to be a very close personal friend of the president, flagged her copious memoranda to other managers with large green paperclips, ensuring prompt attention to her requests. More generally, each major division of the core textile group in Weft Corporation is widely thought to reflect the personality of its leader—one hard-driving, intense, and openly competitive; one cool, precise, urbane, and proper; and one gregarious, talkative, and self-promotional. Actually, market exigencies play a large role in shaping each division's tone and tempo. Still, the popular conception of the dominance of presidential personalities *[. . .]* underlines the general tendency to personalize authority in corporate bureaucracies.

Managers draw elaborate cognitive maps to guide them through the thickets of their organizations. Because they see and experience authority in such personal terms, the singular feature of these maps is their biographical emphasis. Managers carry around in their heads thumbnail sketches of the occupational history of virtually every other manager of their own rank or higher in their particular organization. These maps begin with a knowledge of others' occupational expertise and specific work experience, but focus especially on previous and present reporting relationships, patronage relationships, and alliances. Cognitive maps incorporate memories of social slights, of public embarrassments, of battles won and lost, and of people's behavior under pressure. They include as well general estimates of the abilities and career trajectories of their colleagues. I should mention that these latter estimates are not necessarily accurate or fair; they are, in fact, often based on the flimsiest of evidence. For instance, a general manager at Alchemy Inc. describes the ephemeral nature of such opinions:

It's a feeling about the guy's perceived ability to run a business—like he's not a good people man, or he's not a good numbers man. This is not a quantitative thing. It's a gut feeling that a guy can't be put in one spot, but he might be put in another spot. These kinds of informal opinions about others are the lifeblood of an organization's advancement system. Oh, for the record, we've got the formal evaluations; but the real opinions—the ones that really count in determining people's fates—are those which are traded back and forth in meetings, private conferences, chance encounters, and so on.

[. . .] This is one reason why it is crucial for the aspiring young manager to project the right image to the right people who can influence others' sketches of him. [. . .] Biographical detail [. . .] constitutes crucial knowledge because managers know that, in the rough-and-tumble politics of the corporate world, individual fates are made and broken not necessarily by one's accomplishments but by other people.

One must appreciate the simultaneously monocratic and patrimonial character of business bureaucracies in order to grasp the personal and organizational significance of political struggles in managerial work. As it happens, political struggles are a constant and recurring feature in business, shaping managers' experience and outlooks in fundamental ways. Of course, such conflicts are usually cloaked by typically elaborate organizational rhetorics of harmony and teamwork. However, one can observe the multiple dimensions of these conflicts during periods of organizational upheaval, a regular feature of American business where mergers, buyouts, divestitures, and especially "organizational restructuring" have become commonplace occurrences. As Karl Mannheim, among others, has pointed out, it is precisely when a social order begins to fall apart that one can discern what has held it together in the first place. A series of shake-ups that occurred in Covenant Corporation, all within a period of a few years, present a focused case study of political processes basic to all big corporations.

II

In 1979, a new CEO took power in Covenant Corporation. The first action of most new CEOs is some form of organizational change. On the one hand, this prevents the inheritance of blame for past mistakes; on the other, it projects an image of bare-knuckled aggressiveness much appreciated on Wall Street. Perhaps most important, a shake-up rearranges the fealty structure of the corporation, placing in power those barons whose style and public image mesh closely with that of the new CEO and whose principal loyalties belong to him. Shortly after the new CEO of Covenant was named, he reorganized the whole business, after a major management consulting firm had "exhaustively considered all the options," and personally selected new presidents to head each of the five newly formed companies of the corporation—Alchemy, Energy, Metals, Electronics, and Instruments. He ordered the presidents to carry out a thorough reorganization of their separate companies complete with extensive "census reduction," or firing as many people as possible. The presidents were given, it was said, a free hand in their efforts, although in retrospect it seems that the CEO insisted on certain high-level appointments.

The new president of Alchemy Inc.—let's call him Smith[6]—had risen from a marketing background in a small but important specialty chemicals division in the former company. Specialty chemicals are produced in relatively small batches and command high prices, showing generous profit margins; they depend on customer loyalty and therefore on the adroit cultivation of buyers through professional marketing. Upon promotion to president, Smith reached back into his former division, indeed back to his own past work in a particular product line, and systematically elevated many of his former colleagues, friends, clients, and allies. Powerful managers in other divisions, particularly in a rival process chemicals division, whose commodity products, produced in huge quantities, were sold only by price and who exemplified an old-time "blood, guts, and courage" management style were: forced to take big demotions in the new power structure; put on "special assignment"—the corporate euphemism for Siberia, sent to a distant corner office where one looks for a new job (the saying is: "No one ever comes back from special assignment"); fired; or given "early retirement," a graceful way of doing the same thing. What happened in Alchemy Inc. was typical of the pattern in the other companies of the conglomerate. Hundreds of people throughout the whole corporation lost their jobs in what became known as "Bloody Thursday," the "October Revolution," or in some circles, the "Octoberfest." I shall refer back to this event as the "big purge."

Up and down the chemical company, former associates of Smith were placed in virtually every important position. Managers in the company saw all of this as an inevitable fact of life. In their view, Smith simply picked those managers with whom he was comfortable. The whole reorganization could easily have gone in a completely different direction had another CEO been named, or had the one selected picked someone besides Smith, or had Smith come from a different work group in the old organization. Fealty is the mortar of the corporate hierarchy, but the removal of one well-placed stone loosens the mortar throughout the pyramid. And no one is ever quite sure, until after the fact, just how the pyramid will be put back together.

The year after the "big purge," Alchemy prospered and met its financial commitments to the CEO, the crucial coin of the realm to purchase continued autonomy. Smith consolidated his power and, through the circle of the mostly like-minded and like-mannered men and women with whom he surrounded himself, further weeded out or undercut managers with whom he felt uncomfortable. At the end of the year, the mood in the company was buoyant not only because of high profits but because of the expectation of massive deregulation and boom times for business following President Reagan's first election. On the day after the election, by the way, managers, in an unusual break with normal decorum, actually danced in the corridors.

What follows might be read as a cautionary tale on the perils of triumph in a probationary world where victory must follow victory. Elated by his success in 1980, and eager to make a continued mark with the CEO vis-à-vis the presidents of the other four companies, all of whom were vying for the open presidency of Covenant Corporation, Smith became the victim of his own upbeat marketing optimism. He overcommitted himself and the chemical company financially for the coming year just as the whole economy began to slide into recession. By mid-1981, profit targets had to be readjusted down and considerable anxiety pervaded Smith's circle and the upper-middle levels of management, whose job it became both to extract more profits from below and to maintain a public facade of cheerful equanimity. A top executive at Alchemy Inc. describes this anxiety:

> See, the problem with any change of CEO is that any credibility you have built up with the previous guy all goes by the board and you have to begin from scratch. This CEO thinks that everybody associated with the company before him is a dummy. And so you have to prove yourself over and over again. You can't just win some and lose some. You have to keep your winning record at least at 75 percent if not better. You're expected to take risks. At least the CEO says that, but the reality is that people are afraid to make mistakes.

Toward the end of the year, it became clear that the chemical company would reach only 60 percent of its profit target and that only by remarkable legerdemain with the books. Publicly, of course, managers continued to evince a "cautious optimism" that things would turn around; privately, however, a deepening sense of gloom and incipient panic pervaded the organization. Stories began to circulate about the CEO's unhappiness with the company's shortfall. To take but one example, managers in chemical fertilizers were told by the CEO never again to offer weather conditions or widespread farmer bankruptcy as excuses for lagging sales. Rumors of every sort began to flourish, and a few of these are worth recounting.

Smith was on his way out, it was feared, and would take the whole structure of Alchemy Inc. with him. *[. . .]*

Smith would survive, it was said, but would be forced to sacrifice all of his top people, alter his organization's structure, and buckle under to the increasingly vigorous demands of the CEO.

The CEO, it was argued, was about to put the whole chemical company on the block; in fact, the real purpose of creating supposedly self-contained companies in the first place might have been to package them for sale. At the least, the CEO would sell large portions of Alchemy Inc., wreaking havoc with its support groups at corporate headquarters.

There were disturbing rumors too about the growth of personal tension and animosity between

Smith and the CEO. The CEO was well-known for his propensity for lording it over his subordinates, a behavioral pattern that often emerges in top authority figures after years of continual suppression of impulses. He was now said to have targeted Smith for this kind of attention. Managers up and down the line knew instinctively that, if the personal relationship between Smith and the CEO were eroding, the inevitable period of blame and retribution for the bad financial year might engulf everyone, and not just well-targeted individuals. Managers began to mobilize their subordinates to arrange defenses, tried to cement crucial alliances, and waited. In the meantime, they joked that they were updating their résumés and responding graciously to the regular phone calls of headhunters.

[. . .]

As the economy continued to flounder *[. . .]*, Alchemy's earnings dipped even further, and the CEO's demands on Smith became relentless. By this point, the watchword in the corporation had become "manage for cash" and the CEO wanted some businesses sold, others cut back, still others milked, and costs slashed. Particular attention began to be focused on the chemical company's environmental protection staff, a target of hostility not only from the CEO's people but from line managers within Alchemy itself. In response to an environmental catastrophe in the late 1970s, and to the public outrage about chemical pollution in general, Smith had erected, upon his ascendancy to the presidency, an elaborate and relatively free-roaming environmental staff. Though costly, Smith felt that this apparatus was the best defense against another severely embarrassing and even more expensive environmental debacle. The company had, in fact, won an industrial award and wide public recognition for its program; the CEO himself, of course, had been a principal beneficiary of all this public praise and he basked in that attention. But, as the political atmosphere in the country changed with the conservative legislative, budgetary, and regulatory triumphs after President Reagan's election, line managers in Alchemy began chafing under staff intrusions. They blamed the environmental staff for creating extra work and needless costs during a period of economic crisis. The CEO agreed with these sentiments, and his opinion helped deepen the splits in the chemical company. In the early fall, faced with unremitting pressure because of the company's declining fortunes, internal warring factions, and, worse, the prospect of public capitulation to the CEO on the structure of his supposedly autonomous company, Smith chose to resign to "pursue other interests," pulling the cord on his "golden parachute" (a fail-safe plan ensuring comfortable financial landing) as he left.

[. . .]

Alchemy Inc. went into a state of shock and paralysis at Smith's resignation, and the rumor mills churned out names of possible replacements, each tied to a scenario of the future. Once again, the mortar of fealty loosened throughout the pyramid even as it bound managers to their pasts. Managers know that others' cognitive maps afford little escape from old loyalties, alliances, and associations. At the same time, they realize that they must be poised to make new alliances in a hurry if their areas get targeted for "restructuring."

As things turned out, a great many managers found themselves in exactly that position. *[During Alchemy's crisis, Smith reorganized the management and transferred an unpopular Alchemy vice-president named Brown to another company owned by Covenant, to the great satisfaction of those remaining. But the CEO of Covenant rescued Brown by making him boss of another company in the conglomerate, albeit less profitable and prestigious.— Ed.]* To almost everyone's astonishment, and to the trepidation of many, the CEO [of Alchemy's parent Covenant] brought Brown back and made him the new president of Alchemy. *[. . .]* He became known as the "CEO's boy" and everyone recognized that he had a mandate to wield a "meat axe" and to wreak whatever mayhem was necessary to cut expenditures. At every level of the company, managers began furiously to scramble—writing position papers, holding rushed meetings, making deals—to try to secure their domains against the coming assault. Within a short time, Brown had fired 150 people, mostly at the managerial level, focusing particular attention on "streamlining" the environmental staff, slashing it by 75 percent. The survivors from the environmental staff were "moved close to the action," that is, subordinated to the business units, each of which was made more "free-standing," and thus the staff was effectively neutralized. The official rationale was as follows. The company had gone through an extraordinary learning experience on environmental issues and had benefited greatly from the expertise of the environmental staff. It had, however, by this point fully integrated and institutionalized that knowledge into its normal operations. Moreover, since there were no longer any environmental problems facing the company, a modest reduction in this area made good business sense. Privately, of course, the assessments were different. Brown himself said at a managerial meeting that good staff simply create work to justify their own existence. Many line managers echoed this opinion. More to the point, the feeling was that work on environmental issues had lost any urgency in the Reagan era. The Environmental Protection Agency (EPA) was dead. Moreover, the only real threat to corporations on environmental issues was in the courts, which, however, judge past actions, not present practices. By the time the courts get to cases generated by contemporary practices, typically in fifteen years, those executives presently in charge will have moved on, leaving any problems their policies might create to others. Managers noted, some ruefully, some with detached bemusement, the irony of organizational reform. The public outcry against Covenant after the environmental disaster of the late 1970s produced thoroughgoing internal reform designed to ward off such incidents in the future. But the reforms also unintentionally laid down the bases of resentment among managers who did not benefit from the staff increase. During a crisis, these managers grasped the chance to clamor for dismantling the safeguards that might prevent future catastrophes.

Brown's "housecleaning" created extreme anxiety throughout Alchemy. Even managers who agreed with Brown's attack on the staff and his wholesale pruning of other areas expressed astonishment and sometimes outrage that mostly persons of managerial rank had been fired. This seemed an ominous violation of the managerial code.

[. . .]

III

This sequence of events is remarkable only for its compactness. One need only regularly read *The Wall Street Journal*, the business section of *The New York Times*, any of the leading business magazines, let alone more academic publications, to see that these sorts of upheavals and political struggles are commonplace in American business. In Weft Corporation, one could observe exactly similar patterns, though played out over a much longer period of time. For instance, more than a decade ago, a new CEO was brought into the company to modernize and professionalize what had been up to that point a closely held family business. His first act was to make a rule that no executives over sixty years old could hold posts above a certain high-ranking management grade. In one stroke, he got rid of a whole cohort of executives who had ruled the company for a generation. He then staffed all key posts of each division, as well as his own inner circle, either with people who had served under him in the Army during World War II, or with whom he had worked in another corporation, or with former consultants who had advised him on how to proceed with the reorganization, or with people from the old organization with whom he felt comfortable. All of these managers in turn brought in their own recruits and protégés. They established a corporate order notable for its stability for many years. As the CEO and his subordinates grew older, of course, he eliminated the rule governing age. Eventually, however, retirement time did come. The new CEO was handpicked by the outgoing boss from the high reaches of another corporation where he had been vice-chairman and thus effectively dead-ended. He graciously bided his time until the old CEO had entirely left the scene and then moved decisively to shape the organization to his liking. The most important move in this regard was the rapid elevation of a man who had been a mere vice-president of personnel, normally the wasteland of the corporate world. Within a year of the new CEO's ascendancy, this manager was given control over all other staff functions. He then moved into an executive vice-president post as the closest aide and confidant of the CEO on the Central Management Committee, with decisive say-so over financial issues and thus over operations. Tough, seasoned managers in the operating divisions—men and women of great drive and ambition—began to see their own chances for future ascendancy possibly blocked. Many began to depart the corporation.

The posts of those who left were filled by men and women whose loyalties and futures lay with the new regime. Thus, the compressed sequence of events at Covenant Corporation simply allows one to be particularly attentive to ongoing, and usually taken for granted, structural and psychological patterns of corporate life.

Here I want to highlight a few of these basic structures and experiences of managerial work, those that seem to form its essential framework. First of all, at the psychological level, managers have an acute sense of organizational contingency. Because of the interlocking ties between people, they know that a shake-up at or near the top of a hierarchy can trigger a widespread upheaval, bringing in its wake startling reversals of fortune, good and bad, throughout the structure. Managers' cryptic aphorism, "Well, you never know . . . ," repeated often and regularly, captures the sense of uncertainty created by the constant potential for social reversal. Managers know too, and take for granted, that the personnel changes brought about by upheavals are to a great extent arbitrary and depend more than anything else on one's social relationships with key individuals and with groups of managers. Periods of organizational quiescence and stability still managers' wariness in this regard, but the foreboding sense of contingency never entirely disappears. Managers' awareness of the complex levels of conflict in their world, built into the very structure of bureaucratic organizations, constantly reminds them that things can very quickly fall apart.

The political struggles at Covenant Corporation, for instance, suggest some immediately observable levels of conflict and tension.

First, occupational groups emerging from the segmented structure of bureaucratic work, each with different expertise and emphasis, constantly vie with one another for ascendancy of their ideas, of their products or services, and of themselves. It is, for instance, an axiom of corporate life that the greatest satisfaction of production people is to see products go out the door; of salesmen, to make a deal regardless of price; of marketers, to control salesmen and squeeze profits out of their deals; and of financial specialists, to make sure that everybody meets budget. Despite the larger interdependence of such work, the necessarily fragmented functions performed day-to-day by managers in one area often put them at cross purposes with managers in another. Nor do competitiveness and conflict result only from the broad segmentation of functions. Sustained work in a product or service area not only shapes crucial social affiliations but also symbolic identifications, say, with particular products or technical services, that mark managers in their corporate arenas. Such symbolic markings make it imperative for managers to push their particular products or services as part of their overall self-promotion. This fuels the constant scramble for authoritative enthusiasm for one product or service rather than another and the subsequent allocation or re-allocation of organizational resources.

Second, line and staff managers, each group with different responsibilities, different pressures, and different bailiwicks to protect, fight over organizational resources and over the rules that govern work. The very definition of staff depends entirely on one's vantage point in the organization. As one manager points out: "From the perspective of the guy who actually pushes the button to make the machine go, everyone else is staff." However, the working definition that managers use is that anyone whose decisions directly affect profit and loss is in the line; all others in an advisory capacity of some sort are staff. As a general rule, line managers' attitudes toward staff vary directly with the independence granted staff by higher management. The more freedom staff have to intervene in the line, as with the environmental staff at Alchemy or Covenant's corporate staff, the more they are feared and resented by line management. For line managers, independent staff represent either the intrusion of an unwelcome "rules and procedures mentality" into situations where line managers feel that they have to be alert to the exigencies of the market or, alternatively, as power threats to vested interests backed by some authority. In the "decentralized" organizations prevalent today in the corporate world, however, most staff are entirely dependent on the line and must market their technical, legal, or organizational skills to line managers exactly as an outside firm must do. The continual necessity for staff to sell their technical expertise helps keep them in check since line managers, pleading budgetary stringency or any number of other acceptable rationales, can thwart or ignore proffered assistance. Staff's dependent position often produces jealous respect for line management tinged with the resentment that talented people relegated to do "pine time" (sit on the bench) feel for those in the center of action.

[. . .]

This kind of ambivalent resentment sometimes becomes vindictiveness when a top boss uses staff as a hammer.

[. . .]

Third, powerful managers in Alchemy Inc., each controlling considerable resources and the organizational fates of many men and women, battle fiercely with one another to position themselves, their products, and their allies favorably in the eyes of their president and of the CEO. At the same time, high-ranking executives "go to the mat" with one another striving for the CEO's approval and a coveted shot at the top. Bureaucratic hierarchies, simply by offering ascertainable rewards for certain behavior, fuel the ambition of those men and women ready to subject themselves to the discipline of external exigencies and of their organization's institutional logic, the socially constructed, shared understanding of how their world works. However, since rewards are always scarce, bureaucracies necessarily pit people against each other and inevitably thwart the ambitions of some. The rules of such combat vary from organization to organization and depend largely on what top management countenances either openly or tacitly.

[. . .]

At the same time, all of these struggles take place within the peculiar tempo and framework each CEO establishes for an organization. Under an ideology of thorough decentralization—the gift of authority with responsibility—the CEO at Covenant actually centralizes his power enormously because fear of derailing personal ambitions prevents managers below him from acting without his approval.

[. . .]

In effect, the CEO of Covenant, who seems to enjoy constant turmoil, pits himself and his ego against the whole corporation even while he holds it in vassalage. Other CEOs establish different frameworks and different tempos, depending on self-image and temperament. The only firm rule seems to be that articulated by a middle-level Covenant manager: "Every big organization is set up for the benefit of those who control it; the boss gets what he wants."

Except during times of upheaval, the ongoing conflicts that I have described are usually hidden behind the comfortable and benign social ambiance that most American corporations fashion for their white-collar personnel. Plush carpets, potted trees, burnished oak wall paneling, fine reproductions and sometimes originals of great art, mahogany desks, polished glass tables and ornaments, rich leather upholstery, perfectly coiffured, attractive and poised receptionists, and private, subsidized cafeterias are only a few of the pleasant features that grace the corporate headquarters of any major company. In addition, the corporations that I studied provide their employees with an amazing range and variety of services, information, and social contacts. Covenant Corporation, for instance, through its daily newsletter and a variety of other internal media, offers information about domestic and international vacation packages; free travelers' checks; discounted tickets for the ballet, tennis matches, or art exhibits; home remedies for the common cold, traveling clinics for diagnosing high blood pressure, and advice on how to save one's sight; simple tests for gauging automotive driving habits; tips on home vegetable gardening; advice on baby-sitters; descriptions of business courses at a local college; warning articles on open fireplaces and home security; and directions for income tax filing. The newsletter also offers an internal market for the sale, rental, or exchange of a myriad of items ranging from a Jamaican villa, to a set of barbells, to back issues of *Fantasy* magazine. Covenant offers as well intracompany trapshooting contests, round-robin tennis and golf tournaments, running clinics, and executive fitness programs. Weft Corporation's bulletin is even more elaborate, with photographic features on the "Great Faces" of Weft employees; regular reports on the company's 25- and 50-year clubs; personal notes on all retirees from the company; stories about the company's sponsorship of art exhibits; human-interest stories about employees and their families—from a child struggling against liver cancer to the heroics of a Weft employee in foiling a plane hijackers; and, of course, a steady drumbeat of corporate ideology about the necessity for textile import quotas and the desirability of "buying American."

My point here is that corporations are not presented nor are they seen simply as places to work for a living. Rather the men and women in them come to fashion an entire social ambiance that overlays the antagonisms created by company politics; this makes the nuances of corporate conflict difficult to discern. A few managers, in fact, mistake the first-name informality, the social congeniality, and the plush exterior appointments for the entire reality of their collective life and are surprised when hard structural jolts turn their world upside down. Even battle-scarred veterans evince, at times, an ambivalent half-belief in the litany of rhetorics of unity and cohesive legitimating appeals. The latter are sometimes accompanied by gala events to underline the appeal. For instance, not long after the "big purge" at Covenant Corporation when 600 people were fired, the CEO spent $1 million for a "Family Day" to "bring everyone together." The massive party was attended by over 14,000 people and featured clowns, sports idols, and booths complete with bean bag and ring tosses, foot and bus races, computer games, dice rolls, and, perhaps appropriately, mazes. In his letter to his "Fellow Employees" following the event, the CEO said:

> I think Family Day made a very strong statement about the [Covenant] "family" of employees at [Corporate Headquarters]. And that is that we can accomplish whatever we set out to do if we work together; if we share the effort, we will share the rewards. The "New World of [Covenant]" has no boundaries only frontiers, and each and everyone can play a role, for we need what *you* have to contribute.

The very necessity for active involvement in such rituals often prompts semicredulity. But wise and ambitious managers resist the lulling platitudes of unity, though they invoke them with fervor, and look for the inevitable clash of interests beneath the bouncy, cheerful surface of corporate life. They understand implicitly that the suppression of open conflict simply puts a premium on the mastery of the socially accepted modes of waging combat.

The continuous uncertainty and ambiguity of managerial hierarchies, exacerbated over time by masked conflict, causes managers to turn toward each other for cues for behavior. They try to learn from each other and to master the shared assumptions, the complex rules, the normative codes, the underlying institutional logic that governs their world. They thus try to control the construction of their everyday reality. Normally, of course, one learns to master the managerial code in the course of repeated, long-term social interaction with other managers, particularly in the course of shaping the multiple and complex alliances essential to organizational survival and success.

Alliances are ties of quasiprimal loyalty shaped especially by common work, by common experiences with the same problems, the same friends, or the same enemies, and by favors traded over time. Although alliances are rooted in fealty and patronage relationships, they are not limited by such relationships since fealty shifts with changing work assignments or with organizational upheavals.

Making an alliance may mean, for instance, joining or, more exactly, being included in one or several of the many networks of managerial associates that crisscross an organization. [. . .] One becomes known, for instance, as a trusted friend of a friend; thought of as a person to whom one can safely refer a thorny problem; considered a "sensible" or "reasonable" or, especially, a "flexible" person, not a "renegade" or a "loose cannon rolling around the lawn"; known to be a discreet person attuned to the nuances of corporate etiquette, one who can keep one's mouth shut or who can look away and pretend to notice nothing; or considered a person with sharp ideas that break deadlocks but who does not object to the ideas being appropriated by superiors.

[. . .] It therefore becomes important to choose one's social colleagues with some care and, of course, know how to drop them should they fall out of organizational favor.

Alliances are also made wholly on the basis of specific self-interests. [. . .] Managers in a power clique map out desired organizational tacks and trade off the resources in their control. They assess the strengths and weaknesses of their opponents; they plan coups and rehearse the appropriate rationales to legitimate them. And, on the other hand, they erect requisite barriers to squelch attempted usurpations of their power. Cliques also introduce managers to new, somewhat more exclusive networks and coteries. Especially at the top of a pyramid, these social ties extend over the boundaries of one's own corporation and mesh one's work and life with those of top managers in other organizations.

[. . .] At bottom, all of the social contexts of the managerial world seek to discover if one "can feel comfortable" with another manager, if he is some- one who "can be trusted," if he is "our kind of guy," or, in short, if he is "one of the gang." *[. . .]* In any event, just as managers must continually please their boss, their boss's boss, their patrons, their president, and their CEO, so must they prove themselves again and again to each other. Work becomes an endless round of what might be called probationary cru- cibles. Together with the uncertainty and sense of contingency that mark managerial work, this con- stant state of probation produces a profound anxiety in managers, perhaps the key experience of manage- rial work. It also breeds, selects, or elicits certain traits in ambitious managers that are crucial to getting ahead.

NOTES

1. Brackets within quotations represent words or phrases changed or added by the author, either to protect identity or to provide grammatical fluency.

2. Alchemy is a chemical company *[Ed.]*.

3. Images Inc. is a public relations firms *[Ed.]*.

4. Henceforth, I *[Jackall]* shall generally use only "he" or "his" to allow for easier reading.

5. "Patrimonial bureaucracy" is a term Weber used to describe the organization of officials who served under traditional monarchs, in which personal loyalty and obe- dience to one's superior and dependence on his favor, rather than impersonal rules and duties, governed behav- ior (Jackall 1988, p. 11) *[Ed.]*.

6. All personal names in the field data throughout the book are pseudonyms.

15

MANUFACTURING CONSENT

Changes in the Labor Process Under Monopoly Capitalism

MICHAEL BURAWOY

4

THIRTY YEARS OF MAKING OUT

THE PIECE-RATE SYSTEM

[. . .] In a machine shop, operators are defined by the machine they "run" and are remunerated according to an individual piece-rate incentive scheme. While machine operators comprise the majority of workers on the shop floor, there are also auxiliary workers, whose function it is to provide facilities and equipment as well as assistance for the "production" workers (operators). For each production operation the methods department establishes a level of effort, expressed in so many pieces per hour, which represents the "100 percent" benchmark. Below this benchmark, operators receive a base rate for the job, irrespective of the actual number of pieces they produce. Above this standard, workers receive not only the base rate for the job but, in addition, a bonus or incentive, corresponding to the number of pieces in excess of "100 percent." Thus, output at a rate of 125 percent is defined as the "anticipated rate," which—according to the contract—is the amount "a normal experienced operator working at incentive gait" is expected to produce and represents 25 percent more pieces than the base rate. Producing at "125 percent," an operator will earn himself or herself an incentive bonus that adds around 15 percent to the amount earned when producing at 100 percent or less. Earned income per hour is computed as follows:

Base earnings (determined by job's labor grade)

+ Base earnings × (% Rate – 100%) (if rate is greater than 100%)

+ Override (determined by job's labor grade)

+ Shift differential (25 cents for second and third shifts)

+ Cost-of-living allowance

In 1945 the computation of earnings was simpler. The system of remuneration was a straight piece-rate system with a guaranteed minimum. There were no extra benefits. Each operation had a *price* rather than a *rate*. Earnings were calculated by simply multiplying the number of pieces produced in an hour by the price. If the result was less than the guaranteed minimum, the operator received that guaranteed minimum, known as the day rate. If output was greater than that corresponding to the day rate, an increase of 25 percent in the number of pieces led to a 25 percent increase in earnings. How the day rate was determined was not always clear. It reflected not only the job but also the operator's skill. Thus Roy received a day rate of 85 cents per hour, but Al McCann, also working on a radial drill on second shift but a more experienced operator, received a day rate of $1.10. The day rate on first shift was 5 cents lower than on second shift, so that, to make 85 cents an hour, Joe Mucha, Roy's day man, had to work harder than Roy. The price for a given operation, however, was the same for all operators.[1]

The two systems thus encourage different strategies for achieving increased earnings. In 1945 Geer operators might fight for higher day rates by bargaining individually with management, but this did not guarantee them increased earnings if they were regularly turning out more pieces than corresponded to the day rate. Furthermore, the very operators who might be eligible for higher day rates would also be the ones for whom a guaranteed minimum was not so important. So the way to drive up income was to increase prices, and this could be accomplished either by fighting for across-the-board-increases on all prices or by fighting with the time-study man for improved prices on particular jobs. Operators did in fact spend a great deal of time haggling with time-study men over prices. These ways of increasing earnings are now relatively insignificant compared

to two alternative methods. The first is via increases in the base earnings for the job and the fringes that go along with each labor grade. These are all negotiated at three-year intervals between management and union. Under the present system, the methods department is not necessarily involved in changes in the *price* of an operation, since this varies with base earnings. Increases in fringes, such as override, are also independent of the piece-rate system. The second method is to transfer to another job with higher base earnings—that is, of higher labor grade—or with easier rates. Frequently, the higher the labor grade, the easier the rates; for to encourage workers to remain on the more skilled jobs, of the higher labor grades, and thereby avoid the cost of training new workers, the rates on those jobs tend to be looser. In 1945, when earnings were closely tied to experience and less associated with particular types of jobs, transfer to another job was frequently used as a disciplinary measure, since it was likely to lead to reduced earnings.[2]

The implications are not hard to foresee. Whereas in 1945 bargaining between management and worker over the distribution of the rewards of labor took place on the shop floor, in 1975 such bargaining had been largely transferred out of the shop and into the conference room and worker-management conflict on the shop floor had found a safety valve in the organization of job transfers on a plant-wide basis. As a consequence of changes in the system of remuneration, management-worker conflict has abated and individualism has increased.

MAKING OUT—A GAME WORKERS PLAY

In this section I propose to treat the activities on the shop floor as a series of games in which operators attempt to achieve levels of production that earn incentive pay, in other words, anything over 100 percent. The precise target that each operator aims at is established on an individual basis, varying with job, machine, experience, and so on. Some are satisfied with 125 percent, while others are in a foul mood unless they achieve 140 percent—the ceiling imposed and recognized by all participants. This game of making out provides a framework for evaluating the productive activities and the social relations that arise out of the organization of work. We can look upon making out, therefore, as comprising a sequence of stages—of encounters between machine operators and the social or nonsocial objects that regulate the conditions of work. The rules of the game are experienced as a set of externally imposed relationships. The art of making out is to manipulate those relationships with the purpose of advancing as quickly as possible from one stage to the next.

[. . .]

After receiving their first task, operators have to find the blueprint and tooling for the operation. These are usually in the crib, although they may be already out on the floor. The crib attendant is therefore a strategic person whose cooperation an operator must secure. If the crib attendant chooses to be uncooperative in dispensing towels, blueprints, fixtures, etc., and, particularly, in the grinding of tools, operators can be held up for considerable lengths of time. Occasionally, operators who have managed to gain the confidence of the crib attendant will enter the crib themselves and expedite the process. Since, unlike the scheduling man, the crib attendant has no real interest in whether the operator makes out, his cooperation has to be elicited by other means. For the first five months of my employment my relations with the crib attendant on second shift were very poor, but at Christmas things changed dramatically. Every year the local union distributes a Christmas ham to all its members. I told Harry that I couldn't be bothered picking mine up from the union hall and that he could have it for himself. He was delighted, and after that I received good service in the crib.

[. . .]

While I was able to secure the cooperation of the crib attendant, I was not so fortunate with the truck drivers. When I was being broken in on the miscellaneous job, I was told repeatedly that the first thing I must do was to befriend the truck driver. He or she was responsible for bringing the stock from the aisles, where it was kept in tubs, to the machine. Particularly at the beginning of the shift, when everyone is seeking their assistance, truck drivers can hold you up for a considerable period. While some treated everyone alike, others discriminated among operators, frustrating those without power, assisting those who were powerful. Working on the

miscellaneous job meant that I was continually requiring the truck driver's services, and, when Morris was in the seat, he used to delight in frustrating me by making me wait. There was nothing I could do about it unless I was on a hot job; then the foreman or scheduling man might intervene. To complain to the foreman on any other occasion would only have brought me more travail, since Morris could easily retaliate later on. It was better just to sit tight and wait. Like the crib attendants, truckers have no stake in the operator's making out, and they are, at the same time, acutely conscious of their power in the shop. All they want is for you to get off their backs so that they can rest, light up, chat with their friends, or have a cup of coffee—in other words, enjoy the marginal freedoms of the machine operator. As one of the graffiti in the men's toilet put it, "Fuck the company, fuck the union, but most of all fuck the truckers because they fuck us all." Operators who become impatient may, if they know how, hop into an idle truck and move their own stock. But this may have unfortunate consequences, for other operators may ask them to get their stock too.

While it is difficult to generalize, it does appear that under Geer the service of the truck drivers—or stock chasers, as they were called—was more efficient. For one thing, there were two truckers in 1945 but only one in 1975 to serve roughly the same number of operators. For another, as the setup man told me from his own experience,

"In the old days everyone knew everyone else. It was a big family, and so truck drivers would always try and help, bringing up stock early and so on. In those days operators might not even have to tell the truck driver to get the next load. Now everyone moves around from job to job. People don't get to know each other so well, and so there's less cooperation."

As they wait for the stock to arrive, each operator sets up his machine, if it is not already set up. This can take anything from a few minutes to two shifts, but normally it takes less than an hour. Since every setup has a standard time for completion, operators try to make out here, too. When a setup is unusually rapid, an operator may even be able to make time so that, when he punches in on production, he has already turned out a few pieces. A setup man is available for assistance. Particularly for the inexperienced, his help is crucial, but, as with the other auxiliary personnel, his cooperation must be sought and possibly bargained for. He, too, has no obvious stake in your making out, though the quicker he is through with you, the freer he is. Once the machine is set up and the stock has arrived, the operator can begin the first piece, and the setup man is no longer required unless the setup turns out to be unsatisfactory.

[. . .]

The assigned task may be to drill a set of holes in a plate, pipe, casting, or whatever; to mill the surface of some elbow; to turn an internal diameter on a lathe; to shave the teeth on a gear; and so on. The first piece completed has to be checked by the inspector against the blueprint. Between inspector and operator there is an irrevocable conflict of interest because the former is concerned with quality while the operator is concerned with quantity. Time spent when an operation just won't come right—when piece after piece fails, according to the inspector, to meet the specifications of the blueprint—represents lost time to the operator. Yet the inspector wants to OK the piece as quickly as possible and doesn't want to be bothered with checking further pieces until the required tolerances are met.

When a piece is on the margin, some inspectors will let it go, but others will enforce the specifications of the blueprint to the *n*th degree. In any event, inspectors are in practice, if not in theory, held partly responsible if an operator runs scrap. Though formally accountable only for the first piece that is tagged as OK, an inspector will be bawled out if subsequent pieces fall outside the tolerance limits. Thus, inspectors are to some extent at the mercy of the operators, who, after successfully getting the first piece OK'd, may turn up the speed of their machine and turn out scrap. An operator who does this can always blame the inspector by shifting the tag from the first piece to one that is scrap. Of course, an inspector has ample opportunity to take revenge on an operator who tries to shaft him.

[. . .]

When an inspector holds up an operator who is working on an important job but is unable to satisfy the specifications on the blueprint, a foreman may intervene to persuade the inspector to OK the piece.

[. . .]

After the first piece has been OK'd, the operator engages in a battle with the clock and the machine. Unless the task is a familiar one—in which case the answer is known, within limits—the question is: Can I make out? It may be necessary to figure some angles, some short cuts, to speed up the machine, make a special tool, etc. In these undertakings there is always an element of risk—for example, the possibility of turning out scrap or of breaking tools. If it becomes apparent that making out is impossible or quite unlikely, operators slacken off and take it easy. Since they are guaranteed their base earnings, there is little point in wearing themselves out unless they can make more than the base earnings—that is, more than 100 percent. That is what Roy refers to as goldbricking. The other form of "output restriction" to which he refers—quota restriction—entails putting a ceiling on how much an operator may turn in—that is, on how much he may record on the production card. In 1945 the ceiling was $10.00 a day or $1.25 an hour, though this did vary somewhat between machines. In 1975 the ceiling was defined as 140 percent for all operations on all machines. It was presumed that turning in more than 140 percent led to "price cuts" (rate increases), and *[. . .]* this was indeed the case.

In 1975 quota restriction was not necessarily a form of restriction of *output*, because operators *regularly turned out* more than 140 percent, but turned *in* only 140 percent, keeping the remainder as a "kitty" for those operations on which they could not make out. Indeed, operators would "bust their ass" for entire shifts, when they had a gravy job, so as to build up a kitty for the following day(s). Experienced operators on the more sophisticated machines could easily build up a kitty of a week's work. There was always some discrepancy, therefore, between what was registered in the books as completed and what was actually completed on the shop floor. Shop management was more concerned with the latter and let the books take care of themselves. Both the 140 percent ceiling and the practice of banking (keeping a kitty) were recognized and accepted by everyone on the shop floor, even if they didn't meet with the approval of higher management.

Management outside the shop also regarded the practice of "chiseling" as illicit, while management within the shop either assisted or connived in it. Chiseling (Roy's expression, which did not have currency on the shop floor in 1975) involves redistributing time from one operation to another so that operators can maximize the period turned in as over 100 percent. Either the time clerk cooperates by punching the cards in and out at the appropriate time or the operators are allowed to punch their own cards. In part, because of the diversity of jobs, some of them very short, I managed to avoid punching any of my cards. At the end of the shift I would sit down with an account of the pieces completed in each job and fiddle around with the eight hours available, so as to maximize my earnings. I would pencil in the calculated times of starting and finishing each operation. No one ever complained, but it is unlikely that such consistent juggling would have been allowed on first shift.

How does the present situation compare with Geer? As Roy describes it, the transfer of time from one operation or job to another was possible only if they were consecutive or else were part of the same job though separated in time. Thus Roy could finish one job and begin another without punching out on the first. When he did punch out on the first and in on the second, he would already have made a start toward making out. Second, if Roy saved up some pieces from one shift, he could turn those pieces in during his next shift only if the job had not been finished by his day man. Accordingly, it was important, when Roy had accumulated some kitty on a particular job, that he inform Joe Mucha. If Mucha could, he would try to avoid finishing the job before Roy came to work. Shifting time between consecutive jobs on a single shift was frequently fixed up by the foreman, who would pencil in the appropriate changes. Nonetheless, stealing time from a gravy job was in fact formally illicit in 1945.

[. . .]

[T]hese examples do suggest that, while chiseling went on, it was regarded as illegitimate at some levels of management.

What can we say about overall changes in rates over the past thirty years? Old-timers were forever telling me how "easy we've got it now," though that in itself would hardly constitute evidence of change. To be sure, machines, tooling, etc., have improved, and this makes production less subject to arbitrary holdups, but the rates could nonetheless be tighter. However, an interesting change in the shop vernacular does suggest easier rates. Roy describes two types of jobs, "gravy" and "stinkers," the former having particularly loose and the latter particularly tight rates. While I worked in the small-parts department, I frequently heard the word "gravy" but never the word "stinker." Its dropping out of fashion probably reflects the declining number of jobs with very tight rates and the availability of kitties to compensate for low levels of output. *[. . .]*

What is the foreman's role in all these operations? He is seen by everyone but senior plant management as expediting and refereeing the game of making out. As long as operators are making out and auxiliary workers are not obstructing their progress, neither group is likely to invite authoritarian interventions from the foreman. For their part, foremen defend themselves from their own bosses' complaints that certain tasks have not been completed by pointing out that the operators concerned have been working hard and have successfully made out. We therefore find foremen actively assisting operators to make out by showing them tricks they had learned when they were operators, pointing out more efficient setups, helping them make special tools, persuading the inspector to OK a piece that did not exactly meet the requirements of the blueprint, and so on. Foremen, like everyone else on the shop floor, recognize the two forms of output restriction as integral parts of making out. When operators have made out for the night and decide to take it easy for the last two or three hours, a foreman may urge more work by saying, "Don't you want to build up a kitty?" However, foremen do not act in collusion with the methods department and use the information they have about the various jobs and their rates against the operators, because rate increases would excite animosity, encourage goldbricking, increase turnover, and generally make the foreman's job more difficult.

However, the operator's defense, "What more do you want? I'm making out," does have its problems, particularly when there is a hot job on the agenda. Under such circumstances, operators are expected to drop what they are doing and punch in on the new job, "throwing everything they've got" into it and, above all, ignoring production ceilings—though of course they are not expected to turn *in* more than 140 percent. On occasions like this, unless the foreman can bring some sanctions to bear, he is at the mercy of the operator who may decide to take it easy. For this reason, foremen may try to establish an exchange relationship with each individual operator: "You look after me, I'll look after you." Operators may agree to cooperate with their foreman, but in return they may expect him to dispense favors, such as the granting of casual days, permission to attend union meetings during working hours, permission to go home early on a special occasion, etc. One of the most important resources at the disposal of the foreman is the "double red card," which covers time lost by operators through no fault of their own at a rate of 125 percent. Red cards may be awarded for excessive time lost while waiting for materials because a machine is down or some other adventitious event occurs that prevents an operator from making out. Bargaining usually precedes the signing of a red card; the operator has to persuade the foreman that he has made an earnest attempt to make out and therefore deserves compensation. Finally, one may note, as Roy did, that rules promulgated by high levels of plant management are circumvented, ignored, or subverted on the shop floor, with the tacit and sometimes active support of the foreman, in the interests of making out.

In 1945 foremen and superintendent played a similar role in facilitating making out, although they seemed to view many of these activities as illicit. The ambivalence of Steve, Roy's superintendent on second shift, is revealed in the following conversation.

> I told Steve privately that I was made out for the evening with $10.00.
> "That's all I'm allowed to make isn't it?" I asked.
> Steve hesitated at answering that one. "You can make more," he said, lowering his eyes.
> "But I'd better not," I insisted.
> "Well, you don't want to spoil it for yourself," he answered.[3]

Shop management frequently sided with operators in their hostility to the methods department when rates were tight and making out was impossible. Yet operators were always on the lookout and suspicious of foremen as potential collaborators with the methods department. The primary criterion by

which foremen were evaluated was their relationship with time-study men.

Another possible change revolves around the attitude of the foreman to goldbricking. Certainly, in 1945, foremen were not well disposed toward operators' taking it easy when rates were impossible, whereas in 1975 they tended to accept this as a legitimate practice. In general, Allied operators appeared to be less hostile and suspicious of shop supervision and exhibited greater independence in the face of authoritative foremen. [. . .] In all these respects my account of changes are similar to those described by Reinhard Bendix, Frederick Taylor, Richard Edwards, and others, namely, the diminution of the authority of the foreman and the parceling-out of his functions to more specialized personnel.[4]

THE ORGANIZATION OF A SHOP-FLOOR CULTURE

So far we have considered the stages through which any operation must go for its completion and the roles of different employees in advancing the operation from stage to stage. In practice the stages themselves are subject to considerable manipulation, and there were occasions when I would complete an operation without ever having been given it by the scheduling man, without having a blueprint, or without having it checked by the inspector. It is not necessary to discuss these manipulations further, since by now it must be apparent that relations emanating directly from the organization of work are understood and attain meaning primarily in terms of making out. Even social interaction not occasioned by the structure of work is dominated by and couched in the idiom of making out. When someone comes over to talk, his first question is, "Are you making out?" followed by "What's the rate?" If you are not making out, your conversation is likely to consist of explanations of why you are not: "The rate's impossible," "I had to wait an hour for the inspector to check the first piece," "These mother-fucking drills keep on burning up." When you are sweating it out on the machine, "knocking the pieces out," a passerby may call out "Gravy!"—suggesting that the job is not as difficult as you are making it appear.

Or, when you are "goofing off"—visiting other workers or gossiping at the coffee machine—as likely as not someone will yell out, "You've got it made, man!" When faced with an operation that is obviously impossible, some comedian may bawl out, "Best job in the house!" Calling out to a passerby, "You got nothing to do?" will frequently elicit a protest of the nature, "I'm making out. What more do you want?" At lunchtime, operators of similar machines tend to sit together, and each undertakes a postmortem of the first half of the shift. Why they failed to make out, who "screwed them up," what they expect to accomplish in the second half of the shift, can they make up lost time, advice for others who are having some difficulty, and so on—such topics tend to dominate lunchtime conversations. As regards the domination of shop-floor interaction by the culture of making out, I can detect no changes over the thirty years. Some of the details of making out may have changed, but the idiom, status, tempo, etc., of interaction at work continue to be governed by and to rise out of the relations in production that constitute the rules of making out.

In summary, we have seen how the shop-floor culture revolves around making out. Each worker sooner or later is sucked into this distinctive set of activities and language, which then proceed to take on a meaning of their own. Like Roy, when I first entered the shop I was somewhat contemptuous of this game of making out, which appeared to advance Allied's profit margins more than the operators' interests. But I experienced the same shift of opinion that Roy reported:

> [. . .] attitudes changed from mere indifference to the piecework incentive to a determination not to be forced to respond, when failure to get a price increase on one of the lowest paying operations of his job repertoire convinced him that the company was unfair. Light scorn for the incentive scheme turned to bitterness. Several months later, however, after fellow operator McCann had instructed him in the "angles on making out," the writer was finding values in the piecework system other than economic ones. He struggled to attain quota "for the hell of it," because it was a "little game" and "keeps me from being bored."[5]

Such a pattern of insertion and seduction is common. In my own case, it took me some time to understand the shop language, let alone the intricacies of making out. It was a matter of three or four months before I began to make out by using a number of angles and by transferring time from one operation to another. Once I knew I had a chance to make out, the rewards of participating in a game in which the outcomes were uncertain absorbed my attention, and I found myself spontaneously cooperating with management in the production of greater surplus value. Moreover, it was only in this way that I could establish relationships with others on the shop floor. Until I was able to strut around the floor like an experienced operator, as if I had all the time in the world and could still make out, few but the greenest would condescend to engage me in conversation. Thus, it was in terms of the culture of making out that individuals evaluated one another and themselves. It provided the basis of status hierarchies on the shop floor, and it was reinforced by the fact that the more sophisticated machines requiring greater skill also had the easier rates. Auxiliary personnel developed characters in accordance with their willingness to cooperate in making out: Morris was a lousy guy because he'd always delay in bringing stock; Harry was basically a decent crib attendant (after he took my ham), tried to help the guys, but was overworked; Charley was an OK scheduling man because he'd try to give me the gravy jobs; Bill, my day man, was "all right" because he'd show me the angles on making out, give me some kitty if I needed it, and sometimes cover up for me when I made a mess of things. In the next chapter I will consider the implications of being bound into such a coercive cultural system and of constituting the labor process as a game.

THE DISPERSION OF CONFLICT

I have shown how the organization of a piecework machine shop gives rise to making out and how this in turn becomes the basis of shop-floor culture. Making out also shapes distinctive patterns of conflict. Workers are inserted into the labor process as individuals who directly dictate the speed, feed, depth, etc., of their machines. The piece wage, as Marx observed, "tends to develop on the one hand that individuality, and with it the sense of liberty, independence, and self-control of the labourers, on the other, their competition one with another."[6] At the same time, the labor process of a machine shop embodies an opposed principle, the operator's dependence on auxiliary workers—themselves operating with a certain individual autonomy. [. . .]

I have already suggested that pressures to make out frequently result in conflict between production and auxiliary workers when the latter are unable to provide some service promptly. The reason for this is only rarely found in the deliberate obstructionism of the crib attendant, inspector, trucker, and so on. More often it is the consequence of a managerial allocation of resources. Thus, during the period I worked on the shop floor, the number of operators on second shift expanded to almost the number on first shift, yet there was only one truck driver instead of two; there were, for most of the time, only two inspectors instead of four; there were only two foremen instead of four; and there was only one crib attendant instead of two or three. This merely accentuated a lateral conflict that was endemic to the organization of work. The only way such lateral conflict could be reduced was to allow second-shift operators to provide their own services by jumping into an idle truck, by entering the crib to get their own fixtures, by filling out their own cards, by looking through the books for rates or to see whether an order had been finished, and so on. However, these activities were all regarded as illegitimate by management outside the shop. When middle management clamped down on operators by enforcing rules, there was chaos.

In the eyes of senior management, auxiliary workers are regarded as overhead, and so there are continual attempts to reduce their numbers. Thus, [. . .] the objective of the quality-control manager was to reduce the number of inspectors. [. . .] But, so long as every operation had to have its first piece checked, the decline in the number of inspectors merely led to greater frustration on the shop floor.

A single example will illustrate the type of conflict that is common. Tom, an inspector, was suspended for three days for absenteeism. This meant that there was only one inspector for the entire department, and work was piling up outside the window of Larry (another inspector). I had to wait two hours before my piece was inspected and I could get

on with the task. It was sufficiently annoying to find only one inspector around, but my fury was compounded by the ostentatious manner in which Larry himself was slowing down. When I mentioned this to him, jokingly, he burst forth with "Why should I work my ass off? Tom's got his three days off, and the company thinks they are punishing him, but it's me who's got to break my back." In this instance, conflict between Tom and the company was transmuted into a resentment between Tom and Larry, which in turn provoked a hostile exchange between Larry and me. "Going slow," aimed at the company, redounds to the disadvantage of fellow workers. The redistribution of conflict in such ways was a constant feature of social relations on the shop floor. It was particularly pronounced on second shift because of the shortage of auxiliary workers and the fact that the more inexperienced operators, and therefore the ones most needing assistance, were also on that shift.

Common sense might lead one to believe that conflict between workers and managers would lead to cohesiveness among workers, but such an inference misses the fact that all conflict is mediated on an ideological terrain, in this case the terrain of making out. Thus, management-worker conflict is turned into competitiveness and intragroup struggles as a result of the organization of work. The translation of hierarchical domination into lateral antagonisms is in fact a common phenomenon throughout industry, as was shown in a study conducted on a sample of 3,604 blue-collar workers from 172 production departments in six plants scattered across the United States:

[. . .] work pressure in general is negatively correlated to social-supportive behavior, which we have called cohesive behavior, and positively related to competitive and intra-group conflict behavior. Cohesive behavior is generally untenable under high pressure conditions because the reward structure imposed by management directs employees to work as fast as they can individually.[7]

The dominant pattern of conflict dispersion in a piecework machine shop is undoubtedly the reconstitution of hierarchical conflict as lateral conflict and competition. [. . .]

Indeed, over the past thirty years conflict between management and worker has diminished, while that among workers has increased. This was how Donald Roy reacted to my observations at Allied:

> [. . .][I]n my time the main line of cleavage was the worker management one . . . operator relations were mainly cooperative, and most of the auxiliaries (stock chasers, tool crib men, etc.) were helpful. There were employees in the Jack Shop then who recalled the "whistle and whip" days before the local union was organized.[8]

There are a number of suggestions in his dissertation as to why there should have been greater antagonism between management and worker and less competition and conflict among workers. First, because of wartime conditions, there were more auxiliary workers for the same number of operators. Second, there was a generalized hostility to the company as being cheap, unconcerned about its labor force, penny-pinching, and so on,[9] whereas the attitudes of workers at the engine division of Allied were much more favorable to the company. This was exemplified by the large number of father-son pairs working in the plant. If your son had to work in a factory, many felt that Allied was not a bad place. Third, Allied treated its employees more fairly than Geer. Part of this may be attributed to the greater effectiveness of the union grievance machinery in 1975 than in 1945. Furthermore, as part of Allied, a large corporation, the engine division was less vulnerable to the kinds of market exigencies that had plagued Geer Company. It could therefore afford to treat its employees more fairly. Also, Allied did not appear to be out to cut rates with the militant enthusiasm that Roy had encountered. Fourth, as Roy himself notes above, the period of CIO [union] organizing was still close at hand, and many Geer employees remembered the days of sweatshops and arbitrary discipline. Among the workers I talked to, only the older ones could recall the days of the "whistle and whip," and, when they did, it was mainly in reference to the tribulations of their fathers.

[. . .]

These changes do not seem to support theories of intensification of the labor process or increase of managerial control through separation of conception and execution. What we have observed is the expansion of the area of the "self-organization" of workers as they pursue their daily activities.

5

THE LABOR PROCESS AS A GAME

[. . .] In their assessment of such supposedly autonomous responses of workers to the demands of capitalist work, sociologists express a deep ambivalence. On the one hand, they recognize that these relative satisfactions contribute to the psychological and social health of the laborer, but on the other hand they see these satisfactions as undermining management objectives. [. . .] Games create opposition of interests where before there was only harmony. In their classic [Hawthorne] study, F. J. Roethlisberger and William Dickson argued that "employees had their own rules and their own 'logic' which, more frequently than not, were opposed to those which were imposed on them."[10] [. . .] The view that the workers at the Hawthorne Plant evolved their own autonomous principles of work reaches its apotheosis in the writings of Elton Mayo, who speaks of the formation of a "social code at a lower level in opposition to the economic logic [of management]."[11] [. . .]

All these treatments share the view that workers autonomously erect their own cultural and production systems in opposition to management. Ironically, the very sociologists for whom a class analysis would be anathema are also the ones who offer the greatest support for such an approach. Unfortunately, their empirical evidence is as weak as their theoretical framework is inadequate. There is ample evidence in *Management and the Worker* that the group chief, section chief, assistant foreman, and foreman either connived or actively assisted in playing a game that was supposed to undermine management interests.[12] [. . .] Stanley Mathewson offers numerous examples of management organizing the forms of output restriction that Elton Mayo attributes to the workers' instinctual and nonlogical opposition to management.[13] On the other hand, when games (such as doubling-up on assembly lines) really do threaten managerial objectives, that is, jeopardize profit margins, management does indeed come in with a stick.[14] *[. . .]* In short, where games do take place, they are usually neither independent of nor in opposition to management.

These conclusions are confirmed by my observations of shop management's role in the making-out game at Allied and by Roy's observations at Geer.

[. . .]

The significance of creating a game out of the labor process, however, extends beyond the particularities of making out. The very activity of playing a game generates consent with respect to its rules.

[. . .]

As long as workers are engaged in a game involving their relations to a machine, their subordination to the process of production becomes an object of acquiescence.

[. . .]

As always, Roy puts it graphically:

Could "making out" be considered an "end in itself"? *[. . .]* "Making out" called for the exercise of skill and stamina; it offered opportunities for "self expression." The element of uncertainty of outcome provided by ever-present possibilities of "bad breaks" made "quota" attainment an "exciting game" played against the clock on the wall, a "game" in which the elements of control provided by the application of knowledge, skill, ingenuity, speed and stamina heightened interest and lent to the exhilaration of "winning" feelings of "accomplishment." Although operators constantly shared their piecework experience as a chief item of conversation, and always in terms of "making money," they were, in reality, communicating "game scores" or "race results," not financial success or disappointments. It is doubtful if any operator ever thought that he had been "making money." It is likely that had anyone been able to communicate accurately such a conviction, he would have been laughed out of the shop.[15]

In other words, making out cannot be understood simply in terms of the externally derived goal of achieving greater earnings. Rather, its dominance in the shop-floor culture emerges out of and is embodied in a specific set of relations in production that in turn reflect management's interest in generating profit. The rewards of making out are defined in terms of factors immediately related to the labor process—reduction of fatigue, passing time, relieving boredom,

and so on—and factors that emerge from the labor process—the social and psychological rewards of making out on a tough job as well as the social stigma and psychological frustration attached to failing on a gravy job.

It is not so much the monetary incentive that concretely coordinates the interests of management and worker but rather the play of the game itself, which generates a common interest in the outcome and in the game's continuity. *[. . .]* When the labor process is organized into some form of game involving the active participation of both management and worker, the interests of both are concretely coordinated.

[. . .]

CONCLUSION

In this chapter I have tried to show how the constitution of the labor process as a game contributes to the obscuring and securing of surplus labor. *[. . .]*

[. . .] [J]ust as playing a game generates consent to its rules, so participating in the choices capitalism forces us to make also generates consent to its rules, its norms. It is by constituting our lives as a series of games, a set of limited choices, that capitalist relations not only become objects of consent but are taken as given and immutable. *[. . .]* Alternatives are eliminated or cast as utopian.

[. . .]

Thus, the differences between the organization of work at Geer and Allied suggest ever greater "quantitative" choice within ever narrower limits. In identifying the separation of conception and execution, the expropriation of skill, or the narrowing of the scope of discretion as the broad tendency in the development of the capitalist labor process, Harry Braverman missed the equally important parallel tendency toward the expansion of choices within those ever narrower limits. It is the latter tendency that constitutes a basis of consent and allows the degradation of work to pursue its course without continuing crisis. Thus, we have seen that more reliable machines, easier rates, the possibility of chiseling, and so forth, all increase the options open to the operator in making out. The tendency is also expressed more generally in schemes of job enrichment and job rotation. *[. . .]*

NOTES

1. By coincidence, sociologist Donald Roy studied the same plant as Burawoy in 1944–1945, when it was a smaller, independent company he called Geer Company. In 1953 it was acquired and became a division of the much industrial giant Burawoy called Allied Company (Burawoy 1979, pp. 33ff.). *[Ed.]*

2. Donald Roy, "Restriction of Output in a Piecework Machine Shop," (Ph.D. diss., University of Chicago, 1952), p. 76.

3. Roy, "Restriction of Output," p. 102.

4. Reinhard Bendix, *Work and Authority in Industry: Ideologies of Management in the Course of Industrialization* (New York: John Wiley, 1956); Frederick Taylor, *Shop Management*; Richard Edwards, "The Social Relations of Production in the Firm and Labor Market Structure," *Politics and Society* 5 (1975): 83–108.

5. Donald Roy, "Work Satisfaction and Social Reward in Quota Achievement," *American Journal of Sociology* 57 (1953): 509–10.

6. Karl Marx, *Capital*, 3 vols. (New York: International Publishers, 1967), vol. 1, p. 555.

7. Stuart Klein, *Workers under Stress: The Impact of Work Pressure on Group Cohesion* (Lexington, Ky.: University of Kentucky Press, 1971), p. 100.

8. Personal communication, July 1975.

9. Roy, "Restriction of Output," chap. 11.

10. F. J. Roethlisberger and William Dickson, *Management and the Worker* (Cambridge: Harvard University Press, 1939), p. 457.

11. Elton Mayo, *The Human Problems of an Industrial Civilization* (New York: Macmillan, 1933), pp. 119–20.

12. Roethlisberger and Dickson, *Management and the Worker*, chap. 19.

13. Stanley Mathewson, *Restriction of Output among Unorganized Workers* (New York: Viking Press, 1931), chap. 2.

14. Stanley Aronowitz, *False Promises: The Shaping of American Working Class Consciousness* (New York: McGraw-Hill, 1973), p. 38; Emma Rothschild, *Paradise Lost: The Decline of the Auto-Industrial Age* (New York: Vintage Books, 1974), chap. 4.

15. Roy, "Restriction of Output," p. 511.

PART V

RATIONALITY AND NON-RATIONALITY IN ORGANIZATIONAL DECISION MAKING

Decision making in organizations or by organizations has been the subject of much debate between rational and natural systems perspectives. The most intuitive way to think about decision making is that actors have a clear sense of their goals, consider all available information and possible options, and select the solution that will best help them achieve their goals. Although appealing, this simple view is often not very realistic as a description of decision making by either individuals or organizations. Researchers views of organizational decision making have moved from models of perfect rationality, to imperfect or intended rationality, and finally to models that incorporate politics, disorder, and irrationality.

James March and Herbert Simon (1958), who pioneered the study of decision making in organizations, begin by noting that individuals are not omniscient, the world contains much complexity and uncertainty, and devoting time and attention to gathering information and problem solving are costly. This means actors are only capable of limited or *bounded rationality*, which creates strong pressure on actors to choose the first satisfactory option they come across rather than the best possible one, which March and Simon called *satisficing*. In their memorable phrase, people search a haystack not for the sharpest needle, but for one that is sharp enough to sew with. Lacking perfect information and cognitive ability, people and organizations find that mental effort, search time, and attention are all costs that need to be minimized.

Individuals and organizations try to simplify problems. When problems are familiar, they will develop a fixed routine to use as a stock response, which March and Simon call *programmed behavior* or *standard operating procedures*, and which involves little search, deliberation, active problem solving, or conscious choice. Most of the time, people do not bother really making decisions at all; they simply follow existing routines, draw on a stock of preestablished options, or follow the role expectations embedded in their position.

When new circumstances require some novel response, the first impulse of individuals and organizations is not to construct an entirely new solution or routine, but to recombine elements of existing routines and to stop searching when they find one that is adequate. As Merton noted, organizations will continue to use existing rules and standard procedures even when changed circumstances mean they are no longer rational or appropriate. Individuals and organizations do not challenge their preexisting assumptions or rationally reevaluate them each time unless they are compelled to do so. The result, according to this view, is a decision making process that is a somewhat disjointed, incremental process of trial and error, which Charles Lindblom (1959) called *muddling through*, that produces sloppy decisions that make a general sense.

Close empirical research on managerial decision making lends much support to March and Simon's view. Henry Mintzberg (1985) shadowed managers at work and reviewed other studies for information on what managers actually do on a daily basis. Whereas Fayol and other rational organizational theorists described managers in rationalistic terms as planning, organizing, and controlling, Mintzberg found most managers are strongly action oriented and shun reflection and systematic planning (see also Kanter 1977, pp. 40ff.). The work pace is unrelenting, and managers are forced to jump from issue to issue to respond to needs of the moment in bursts of brief and discontinuous activity. Managers prefer verbal communication and soft information like hearsay, speculation, and anecdote over hard data generated by management information systems. After seeing the first piece of hard information he received all week, a standard cost report, one chief executive put it aside, saying, "I never look at this" (Mintzberg 1985, p. 300). Managers have all kinds of communication, leadership, motivational, and conflict-resolution roles and ceremonial duties as heads of their organizational unit that make claims on their time but are not amenable to the methods of management "science." The manager's job still involves a great deal of intuition and judgment, despite advances in management techniques and computer data-processing capabilities.

This view of management decision making still assumes that action is goal oriented and intendedly rational, even if usually falling far short of the simple ideal of perfect rationality. The research on decision making in the 1950s through the early 1970s viewed its ultimate mission as helping individuals and organizations to push back the frontiers of bounded rationality in order to help organizations improve decision making.

This perspective also led to a more rationalistic view of organizations as information processors whose structure and division of labor reflect the need to subdivide problems and distribute tasks among functions. The organization is seen as a brain in which higher levels make decisions with respect to goals and lower levels decide on means (Morgan 1997). One danger is that each subunit will see its function too narrowly and ignore the wider mission and interests of the organization as a whole.

But other research moved much further away from rationalist assumptions. Even March and Simon's early work recognized that different subunits within an organization may have conflicting goals, so that an organization's actions are the result of a more complex internal negotiation process than decision making within individuals. It is incorrect to think of an organization as some kind of superperson with a single will and intent. Organizations are *coalitions* of individuals and groups, not unitary actors. The final outcome of a decision process may be something that no individual or organizational subunit individually desired or predicted. Decisions and actions can be a complex outcome of the interaction and negotiation of different constituencies.

However, March's later work argued that individuals and departments may not even be clear about their own goals or may hold contradictory goals without recognizing the inconsistency. In March's *garbage-can* model of decision making, problems, solutions, and decision makers come together because of a coincidence of timing, like items mixed up in a garbage can. Individuals with an interest in a certain kind of action walk around considering a "solution" in search of problems to which it could be applied. Decision makers wander in and out of decision-making processes, fighting for the right to participate and then losing interest as shifting demands divert their attention. Key actors may be left out of the process. Crucial information may be ignored. One observer of the U.S. Department of Energy commented, "Analyses are being produced, but it is not clear for what or for whom" (Martin 1992, p. 142). Great contention over policy formation can be followed by indifference over implementation.

Meetings and other decision-making processes may be more rituals than rational and disinterested problem-solving sessions. They may be occasions for interpreting recent events and justifying actions ("defining virtue and truth"), socializing members, distributing glory and blame, expressing or discovering self- and group interests, displaying friendship, exhibiting antagonistic and power/status relations, or simply for "having a good time" (March and Olsen 1981, pp. 249ff.). As March and Olsen write,

> Decisions are the stage for many dramas.... [The] formal decision-making process sometimes is directly connected to the maintenance or change of the organization as a social unit as well as to the accomplishment of making collective decisions and producing substantive results (March and Olsen 1981, pp. 250, 254).

March believes there is a pervasive disorder in organizational decision making and many organizations function more like *organized anarchies*. The facts of bounded rationality and imperfect information support these nonrational aspects of decision making, because they would not be possible if problems and their solutions were obvious and transparent. March concludes that there is a "fundamental mismatch between conceptions of intelligent choice and the behavior of complex organizations" (March and Shapira 1992, p. 286).

In fact, sometimes "decisions" are only after-the-fact rationalizations of actions taken for completely unrelated reasons. Mintzberg and Waters argue that the concept of a decision is "an artificial construct" that imputes prior commitment to action, when in fact any commitment may have been vague and hazily understood when an action was first initiated (Mintzberg and Waters 1990). A company with a strongly egalitarian culture has an open office layout with cubicles and partitions that managers retrospectively imply was chosen because it promotes informal communication and minimizes status differentials, but the layout may really reflect a decision to save on the cost of office space at the time (Martin 1992, pp. 31,145). Sometimes, it is hard to know who decided something and when. Informal group opinion coalesces and becomes official policy or certain courses of action simply develop their own momentum.

Some researchers have objected that current thinking is too strong a reaction against rational models (Butler 1990). Clearly, the extent of bounded rationality, situational novelty, goal clarity, organizational unity, and a decision's complexity, importance, and political sensitivity are variable. These variables will affect the amount of attention a decision receives, the extent to which solutions are preprogrammed or involve reflection and judgment, the degree of compromise between subunits needed, and which level of the hierarchy addresses the issue (Butler 1990). The locus of decision making can be diffuse rather than centralized, especially when high levels of uncertainty, complexity, or ambiguity involves more specialists and subunits in the process, but decision making is often more orderly and rational, rather than random, than March and similar analysts grant, according to this view.

It should also be noted that organizations vary in their approach to similar situations. When faced with difficult decisions, some are defensive or reactive, others follow leader organizations, and others are bolder and more proactive in seeking new solutions.

Despite these qualifications, there is much evidence of political and other influences on organizational decision making that contradict the rational model. Computer forecast models appear to be objective and scientific tools of management science, but the numbers are often manipulated to reflect political needs. Managers pressure forecasting professionals to rig their earnings predictions in a more favorable direction so they can receive a greater share of internal organizational resources, easier access to bank loans, and inflated stock prices (Galbraith and Merrill 1996). Likewise, corporate consultants and government panels of experts are regularly used to provide intellectual credibility for decisions that have already been made by those in authority.

Investigating the role of emotions in decision making, Barry Staw and Jerry Ross (1989) note that once organizations make a decision, they can be reluctant to reverse direction and may even escalate their commitment to a losing course of action after becoming deeply committed, despite evidence of their mistake. They cite the prolonged American military involvement in the Vietnam War as an example. Individuals and organizations continue to hope that just somewhat more time and money will resolve things, and they bend information or their perception of the facts to conform to their hopes. Actors do not always make dispassionate decisions, but feel a need to save face and justify past actions, especially when they played a leading and visible role in making the initial commitment.

Economics teaches that a rational actor makes future investments only on the basis of their expected return, not on the basis of how much may have been lost in this effort in the past, the so-called sunk cost fallacy. But many actors behave more like gamblers on a losing streak who bet even more than otherwise to recoup losses even though the extent of their losses does nothing to alter the odds or the wisdom of gambling further. Sunk costs clearly influence subsequent investment decisions in real situations.

However, it is not only the perception of losing that motivates organizations to continue their commitment to losing courses of action. Inertia, breakdowns in communication, and overreliance on standard operating procedures can also lead to resource allocations that do not make sense from an outside or "rational" point of view (Staw and Ross 1989).

Though Graham Allison's analysis of the Cuban Missile Crisis (Reading 16) does not include these later perspectives on emotions in organizations, his article is a classic statement of how the same event can be viewed differently with contrasting models of decision making.

16

CONCEPTUAL MODELS AND THE CUBAN MISSILE CRISIS

The Cuban missile crisis is a seminal event. For thirteen days of October 1962, there was a higher probability that more human lives would end suddenly than ever before in history. Had the worst occurred, the death of 100 million Americans, over 100 million Russians, and millions of Europeans as well would make previous natural calamities and inhumanities appear insignificant. Given the probability of disaster—which President *[John F.]* Kennedy estimated as "between 1 out of 3 and even"—our escape seems awesome.[1] *[. . .]* That such consequences could follow from the choices and actions of national governments obliges students of government as well as participants in governance to think hard about these problems.

[. . .]

The principal purpose of this essay is to explore some of the fundamental assumptions and categories employed by analysts in thinking about problems of governmental behavior, especially in foreign and military affairs.

The general argument can be summarized in three propositions:

1. Analysts think about problems of foreign and military policy in terms of largely implicit conceptual models that have significant consequences for the content of their thought.

[. . .]

Conceptual models both fix the mesh of the nets that the analyst drags through the material in order to explain a particular action or decision and direct him to cast his net in select ponds, at certain depths, in order to catch the fish he is after.

2. Most analysts explain (and predict) the behavior of national governments in terms of various forms of one basic conceptual model, here entitled the Rational Policy Model (Model I).

Reprinted from *Conceptual Models of the Cuban Missile Crisis*, by Graham T. Allison, *The American Political Science Review*, Vol. 63(3), 1969, pp. 689-718. Copyright © 1969 by the American Political Science Association; reprinted by permission.

In terms of this conceptual model, analysts attempt to understand happenings as the more or less purposive acts of unified national governments. For these analysts, the point of an explanation is to show how the nation or government could have chosen the action in question, given the strategic problem that it faced. For example, in confronting the problem posed by the Soviet installation of missiles in Cuba, rational policy model analysts attempt to show how this was a reasonable act from the point of view of the Soviet Union, given Soviet strategic objectives.

3. Two "alternative" conceptual models, here labeled an Organizational Process Model (Model II) and a Bureaucratic Politics Model (Model III) provide a base for improved explanation and prediction.

Although the standard frame of reference has proved useful for many purposes, there is powerful evidence that it must be supplemented, if not supplanted, by frames of reference which focus upon the large organizations and political actors involved in the policy process. Model I's implication that important events have important causes, i.e., that monoliths perform large actions for big reasons, must be balanced by an appreciation of the facts (a) that monoliths are black boxes covering various gears and levers in a highly differentiated decision-making structure, and (b) that large acts are the consequences of innumerable and often conflicting smaller actions by individuals at various levels of bureaucratic organizations in the service of a variety of only partially compatible conceptions of national goals, organizational goals, and political objectives. Recent developments in the field of organization theory provide the foundation for the second model. According to this organizational process model, what Model I categorizes as "acts" and "choices" are instead outputs of large organizations functioning according to certain regular patterns of behavior. Faced with the problem of Soviet missiles in Cuba, a Model II analyst identifies the relevant organizations and displays the patterns of organizational behavior from which this action emerged. The third model focuses on the internal politics of a government. Happenings in foreign affairs are understood, according to the bureaucratic politics model, neither as choices nor as outputs. Instead, what happens is categorized as *outcomes* of various overlapping bargaining games among players arranged hierarchically in the national government. In confronting the problem posed by Soviet missiles in Cuba, a Model III analyst displays the perceptions, motivations, positions, power, and maneuvers of principal players from which the outcome emerged.

A central metaphor illuminates differences among these models. Foreign policy has often been compared to moves, sequences of moves, and games of chess. If one were limited to observations on a screen upon which moves in the chess game were projected without information as to how the pieces came to be moved, he would assume—as Model I does—that an individual chess player was moving the pieces with reference to plans and maneuvers toward the goal of winning the game. But a pattern of moves can be imagined that would lead the serious observer, after watching several games, to consider the hypothesis that the chess player was not a single individual but rather a loose alliance of semi-independent organizations, each of which moved its set of pieces according to standard operating procedures. For example, movement of separate sets of pieces might proceed in turn, each according to a routine, the king's rook, bishop, and their pawns repeatedly attacking the opponent according to a fixed plan. Furthermore, it is conceivable that the pattern of play would suggest to an observer that a number of distinct players, with distinct objectives but shared power over the pieces, were determining the moves as the resultant of collegial bargaining. For example, the black rook's move might contribute to the loss of a black knight with no comparable gain for the black team, but with the black rook becoming the principal guardian of the "palace" on that side of the board.

The space available does not permit full development and support of such a general argument. Rather, the sections that follow simply sketch each conceptual model, articulate it as an analytic paradigm, and apply it to produce an explanation. But each model is applied to the same event: the U.S. blockade of Cuba during the missile crisis. These "alternative explanations" of the same happening illustrate differences among the models—*at work.* A crisis decision, by a small group of men in the context of ultimate threat, this is a case of the rational policy model *par excellence.* The dimensions and factors that Models II and III uncover in this case are therefore particularly suggestive. The concluding section of this paper suggests how the three models may be related and how they can be extended to generate predictions.

MODEL I: RATIONAL POLICY

Rational Policy Model Illustrated

[. . .] In former President *[Lyndon B.]* Johnson's words, "the paradox is that this [Soviet deployment of an antiballistic missile system] should be happening at a time when there is abundant evidence that our mutual antagonism is beginning to ease." *[. . .]* With reference to what objective could the Soviet government have rationally chosen the simultaneous pursuit of these two courses of actions? This question arises only when the analyst attempts to structure events as purposive choices of consistent actors.

How do analysts attempt to explain the Soviet emplacement of missiles in Cuba? The most widely cited explanation of this occurrence has been produced by two RAND Sovietologists, Arnold Horelick and Myron Rush.[2] They conclude that "the introduction of strategic missiles into Cuba was motivated chiefly by the Soviet leaders' desire to overcome . . . the existing large margin of U.S. strategic superiority."[3] *[. . .]* In Sherlock Holmes style, they seize several salient characteristics of this action and use these features as criteria against which to test alternative hypotheses about Soviet objectives. For example, the size of the Soviet deployment, and the simultaneous emplacement of more expensive, more visible intermediate range missiles as well as medium range missiles, it is argued, exclude an explanation of the action in terms of Cuban defense—since that objective could have been secured with a much smaller number of medium range missiles alone. Their explanation presents an argument for one objective that permits interpretation of the details of Soviet behavior as a value-maximizing choice.

[. . .]

Most contemporary analysts (as well as laymen) proceed predominantly—albeit most often implicitly—in terms of this model when attempting to explain happenings in foreign affairs. Indeed, that occurrences in foreign affairs are the *acts* of *nations* seems so fundamental to thinking about such problems that this underlying model has rarely been recognized: to explain an occurrence in foreign policy simply means to show how the government could have rationally chosen that action.

[. . .]

Rational Policy Paradigm

I. Basic Unit of Analysis:
Policy as National Choice

Happenings in foreign affairs are conceived as actions chosen by the nation or national government. Governments select the action that will maximize strategic goals and objectives. These "solutions" to strategic problems are the fundamental categories in terms of which the analyst perceives what is to be explained.

II. Organizing Concepts

A. *National Actor.* The nation or government, conceived as a rational, unitary decision-maker, is the agent. This actor has one set of specified goals *[. . .]*, one set of perceived options, and a single estimate of the consequences that follow from each alternative.

B. *The Problem.* Action is chosen in response to the strategic problem which the nation faces. Threats and opportunities arising in the "international strategic market place" move the nation to act.

C. *Static Selection.* The sum of activity of representatives of the government relevant to a problem constitutes what the nation has chosen as its "solution." Thus the action is conceived as a steady-state choice among alternative outcomes (rather than, for example, a large number of partial choices in a dynamic stream).

D. *Action as Rational Choice.* The components include:

1. *Goals and Objectives*. National security and national interests are the principal categories in which strategic goals are conceived. Nations seek security and a range of further objectives. *[. . .]*

2. *Options*. Various courses of action relevant to a strategic problem provide the spectrum of options.

3. *Consequences*. Enactment of each alternative course of action will produce a series of consequences. The relevant consequences constitute benefits and costs in terms of strategic goals and objectives.

4. *Choice*. Rational choice is value-maximizing. The rational agent selects the alternative whose consequences rank highest in terms of his goals and objectives.

III. Dominant Inference Pattern

This paradigm leads analysts to rely on the following pattern of inference: if a nation performed a particular action, that nation must have had ends towards which the action constituted an optimal means. The rational policy model's explanatory power stems from this inference pattern. Puzzlement is relieved by revealing the purposive pattern within which the occurrence can be located as a value-maximizing means.

IV. General Propositions

[. . .] The basic assumption of value-maximizing behavior produces propositions central to most explanations. The general principle can be formulated as follows: the likelihood of any particular action results from a combination of the nation's (1) relevant values and objectives, (2) perceived alternative courses of action, (3) estimates of various sets of consequences (which will follow from each alternative), and (4) net valuation of each set of consequences. *[. . .]*

V. Specific Propositions

A. *Deterrence. [. . .]*
(1) A stable nuclear balance reduces the likelihood of nuclear attack *[. . .]* by increasing the likelihood

and the costs of one particular set of consequences which might follow from attack—namely, retaliation.
(2) A stable nuclear balance increases the probability of limited war. *[. . .]*

B. *Soviet Force Posture*. The Soviet Union chooses its force posture (i.e., its weapons and their deployment) as a value-maximizing means of implementing Soviet strategic objectives and military doctrine. A proposition of this sort underlies Secretary of Defense *[Melvin]* Laird's inference from the fact of 200 SS-9s (large intercontinental missiles) to the assertion that, "the Soviets are going for a first-strike capability, and there's no question about it."[4]

[. . .]

The U.S. Blockade of Cuba: A First Cut[5]

The U.S. response to the Soviet Union's emplacement of missiles in Cuba must be understood in strategic terms as simple value-maximizing escalation. American nuclear superiority could be counted on to paralyze Soviet nuclear power; Soviet transgression of the nuclear threshold in response to an American use of lower levels of violence would be wildly irrational since it would mean virtual destruction of the Soviet Communist system and Russian nation. American local superiority was overwhelming: it could be initiated at a low level while threatening with high credibility an ascending sequence of steps short of the nuclear threshold. All that was required was for the United States to bring to bear its strategic and local superiority in such a way that American determination to see the missiles removed would be demonstrated, while at the same time allowing Moscow time and room to retreat without humiliation. The naval blockade—euphemistically named a "quarantine" in order to circumvent the niceties of international law—did just that.

The U.S. government's selection of the blockade followed this logic. Apprised of the presence of Soviet missiles in Cuba, the President assembled an Executive Committee (ExCom) of the National Security Council and directed them to "set aside all other tasks to make a prompt and intense survey of the dangers and all possible courses of action."[6] *[. . .]* Six major categories of action were considered.

1. Do nothing. *[. . .]* Since the U.S. already lived under the gun of missiles based in Russia, a Soviet

capability to strike from Cuba too made little real difference. The real danger stemmed from the possibility of U.S. over-reaction. *[. . .]*

This argument fails on two counts. First, it grossly underestimates the military importance of the Soviet move. Not only would the Soviet Union's missile capability be doubled and the U.S. early warning system outflanked. The Soviet Union would have an opportunity to reverse the strategic balance by further installations, and indeed, in the longer run, to invest in cheaper, shorter-range rather than more expensive longer-range missiles. Second, the political importance of this move was undeniable. The Soviet Union's act challenged the American President's most solemn warning. *[. . .]*

2. Diplomatic pressures. Several forms were considered: an appeal to the U.N. or O.A.S. *[Organization of American States]* for an inspection team, a secret approach to *[Nikita]* Khrushchev, and a direct approach to Khrushchev, perhaps at a summit meeting. *[. . .]*

Each form of the diplomatic approach had its own drawbacks. To arraign the Soviet Union before the U.N. Security Council held little promise since the Russians could veto any proposed action. While the diplomats argued, the missiles would become operational. To send a secret emissary to Khrushchev demanding that the missiles be withdrawn would be to pose untenable alternatives. *[. . .]* This would tender an ultimatum that no great power could accept.

[. . .]

3. A secret approach to *[Fidel]* Castro. The crisis provided an opportunity to separate Cuba and Soviet Communism by offering Castro the alternatives, "split or fall." But Soviet troops transported, constructed, guarded, and controlled the missiles. Their removal would thus depend on a Soviet decision.

4. Invasion. The United States could take this occasion not only to remove the missiles but also to rid itself of Castro. A Navy exercise had long been scheduled in which Marines, ferried from Florida in naval vessels, would liberate the imaginary island of Vieques.[7] Why not simply shift the point of disembarkment? (The Pentagon's foresight in planning this operation would be an appropriate antidote to the CIA's Bay of Pigs!)

[. . .] American troops would be forced to confront 20,000 Soviets in the first Cold War case of direct contact between the troops of the super powers. Such brinksmanship courted nuclear disaster, practically guaranteeing an equivalent Soviet move against Berlin.

5. Surgical air strike. The missile sites should be removed by a clean, swift conventional attack. *[. . .]*

The initial attractiveness of this alternative was dulled by several difficulties. First, could the strike really be "surgical"? The Air Force could not guarantee destruction of all the missiles.[8] Some might be fired during the attack; some might not have been identified. In order to assure destruction of Soviet and Cuban means of retaliating, what was required was not a surgical but rather a massive attack—of at least 500 sorties. Second, a surprise air attack would of course kill Russians at the missile sites. Pressures on the Soviet Union to retaliate would be so strong that an attack on Berlin or Turkey was highly probable. Third, the key problem with this program was that of advance warning. Could the President of the United States, with his memory of Pearl Harbor and his vision of future U.S. responsibility, order a "Pearl Harbor in reverse"? For 175 years, unannounced Sunday morning attacks had been an anathema to our tradition.

6. Blockade. Indirect military action in the form of a blockade became more attractive as the ExCom dissected the other alternatives. An embargo on military shipments to Cuba enforced by a naval blockade was not without flaws, however. Could the U.S. blockade Cuba without inviting Soviet reprisal in Berlin? *[. . .]* If Soviet ships did not stop, the United States would be forced to fire the first shot, inviting retaliation. *[A]* blockade would deny the traditional freedom of the seas demanded by several of our close allies and might be held illegal, in violation of the U.N. Charter and international law, unless the United States could obtain a two-thirds vote in the O.A.S. *[. . .]*

In spite of these enormous difficulties the blockade had comparative advantages: (1) It was a middle course between inaction and attack, aggressive enough to communicate firmness of intention, but nevertheless not so precipitous as a strike. (2) It placed on Khrushchev the burden of choice concerning the next step. He could avoid a direct military clash by keeping his ships away. His was the last clear chance. (3) No possible military confrontation could be more acceptable to the U.S. than a naval engagement in the Caribbean. (4) This move permitted the U.S., by flexing its conventional muscle, to exploit the threat of subsequent non-nuclear steps in each of which the U.S. would have significant superiority.

Particular arguments about advantages and disadvantages were powerful. The explanation of the American choice of the blockade lies in a more general principle, however. As President Kennedy stated in drawing the moral of the crisis:

> Above all, while defending our own vital interests, nuclear powers must avert those confrontations which bring an adversary to a choice of either a humiliating retreat or a nuclear war. To adopt that kind of course in the nuclear age would be evidence only of the bankruptcy of our policy—of a collective death wish for the world.[9]

The blockade was the United States' only real option.

MODEL II: ORGANIZATIONAL PROCESS

For some purposes, governmental behavior can be usefully summarized as action chosen by a unitary, rational decisionmaker: centrally controlled, completely informed, and value maximizing. But this simplification must not be allowed to conceal the fact that a "government" consists of a conglomerate of semi-feudal, loosely allied organizations, each with a substantial life of its own. Government leaders do sit formally, and to some extent in fact, on top of this conglomerate. But governments perceive problems through organizational sensors. Governments define alternatives and estimate consequences as organizations process information. Governments act as these organizations enact routines. Government behavior can therefore be understood according to a second conceptual model, less as deliberate choices of leaders and more as outputs of large organizations functioning according to standard patterns of behavior.

To be responsive to a broad spectrum of problems, governments consist of large organizations among which primary responsibility for particular areas is divided. Each organization attends to a special set of problems and acts in quasi-independence on these problems. But few important problems fall exclusively within the domain of a single organization. Thus government behavior relevant to any important problem reflects the independent output of several organizations, partially coordinated by government leaders. Government leaders can substantially disturb, but not substantially control, the behavior of these organizations.

To perform complex routines, the behavior of large numbers of individuals must be coordinated. Coordination requires standard operating procedures: rules according to which things are done. Assured capability for reliable performance of action that depends upon the behavior of hundreds of persons requires established "programs." Indeed, if the eleven members of a football team are to perform adequately on any particular down, each player must not "do what he thinks needs to be done" or "do what the quarterback tells him to do." Rather, each player must perform the maneuvers specified by a previously established play which the quarterback has simply called in this situation.

At any given time, a government consists of *existing* organizations, each with a *fixed* set of standard operating procedures and programs. The behavior of these organizations—and consequently of the government—relevant to an issue in any particular instance is, therefore, determined primarily by routines established in these organizations prior to that instance. But organizations do change. Learning occurs gradually, over time. Dramatic organizational change occurs in response to major crises. Both learning and change are influenced by existing organizational capabilities.

[. . .]

Organizational Process Paradigm[10]

I. Basic Unit of Analysis: Policy as Organizational Output

The happenings of international politics are, in three critical senses, outputs of organizational processes. First, the actual occurrences are organizational outputs. *[. . .]* Government leaders' decisions trigger organizational routines. Government leaders can trim the edges of this output and exercise some choice in combining outputs. But the mass of behavior is determined by previously established procedures. Second, existing organizational routines for employing present physical capabilities constitute the effective options open to government leaders confronted with any problem. [. . .] The fact that fixed programs (equipment, men, and routines which exist at the particular time) exhaust the range of buttons that leaders can push is not always perceived by these leaders. But in every case it is critical for an understanding of what is actually done. Third, organizational outputs structure the situation within the narrow constraints of which leaders must contribute their "decision" concerning an issue. Outputs raise the problem, provide the information, and make the initial moves that color the face of the issue that is turned to the leaders. As Theodore Sorensen has observed: "Presidents rarely, if ever, make decisions—particularly in foreign affairs—in the sense of writing their conclusions on a clean slate. [. . .] The basic decisions, which confine their choices, have all too often been previously made."[11] If one understands the structure of the situation and the face of the issue—which are determined by the organizational outputs—the formal choice of the leaders is frequently anti-climactic.

II. Organizing Concepts

A. *Organizational Actors.* The actor is not a monolithic "nation" or "government" but rather a constellation of loosely allied organizations on top of which government leaders sit. This constellation acts only as component organizations perform routines.

B. *Factored Problems and Fractionated Power.* Surveillance of the multiple facets of foreign affairs requires that problems be cut up and parcelled out to various organizations. To avoid paralysis, primary power must accompany primary responsibility. But if organizations are permitted to do anything, a large part of what they do will be determined within the organization. Thus each organization perceives problems, processes

information, and performs a range of actions in quasi-independence (within broad guidelines of national policy). [. . .]

C. *Parochial Priorities, Perceptions, and Issues.* Primary responsibility for a narrow set of problems encourages organizational parochialism. These tendencies are enhanced by a number of additional factors: (1) selective information available to the organization, (2) recruitment of personnel into the organization, (3) tenure of individuals in the organization, (4) small group pressures within the organization, and (5) distribution of rewards by the organization. Clients (e.g., interest groups), government allies (e.g., Congressional committees), and extra-national counterparts (e.g., the British Ministry of Defense for the Department of Defense, ISA, or the British Foreign Office for the Department of State, EUR) galvanize this parochialism. Thus organizations develop relatively stable propensities concerning operational priorities, perceptions, and issues.

D. *Action as Organizational Output.* The preeminent feature of organizational activity is its programmed character: the extent to which behavior in any particular case is an enactment of preestablished routines.

[. . .]

Reliable performance of these tasks requires standard operating procedures (hereafter SOPs). Since procedures are "standard" they do not change quickly or easily. Without these standard procedures, it would not be possible to perform certain concerted tasks. But because of standard procedures, organizational behavior in particular instances often appears unduly formalized, sluggish, or inappropriate.

[. . .]

E. *Central Coordination and Control.* Action requires decentralization of responsibility and power. But problems lap over the jurisdictions of several organizations. Thus the necessity for decentralization runs headlong into the requirement for coordination. (Advocates of one horn or the other of this dilemma—responsive action entails decentralized power vs. coordinated action requires central control—account for a considerable part of the persistent demand for government reorganization.) *[. . .]*

Intervention by government leaders does sometimes change the activity of an organization in an intended direction. But instances are fewer than might be expected. As Franklin Roosevelt, the master manipulator of government organizations, remarked:

> The Treasury is so large and far-flung and ingrained in its practices that I find it is almost impossible to get the action and results I want.[. . .] But the Treasury is not to be compared with the State Department. You should go through the experience of trying to get any changes in the thinking, policy, and action of the career diplomats and then you'd know what a real problem was. But the Treasury and the State Department put together are nothing compared with the Na-a-vy. [. . .] To change anything in the Na-a-vy is like punching a feather bed. You punch it with your right and you punch it with your left until you are finally exhausted, and then you find the damn bed just as it was before you started punching.[12]

John Kennedy's experience seems to have been similar: "The State Department," he asserted, "is a bowl full of jelly."[13]

[. . .]

III. Dominant Inference Pattern

If a nation performs an action of this type today, its organizational components must yesterday have been performing (or have had established routines for performing) an action only marginally different from this action. *[. . .]* The characteristics of a government's action in any instance follows from those established routines, and from the choice of government leaders—on the basis of information and estimates provided by existing routines—among existing programs. The best explanation of an organization's behavior at *t* is *t* − *1*; the prediction of *t + 1* is *t*. Model II's explanatory power is achieved by uncovering the organizational routines and repertoires that produced the outputs that comprise the puzzling occurrence.

IV. General Propositions

A. *Organizational Action.* Activity according to SOPs and programs does not constitute far-sighted, flexible adaptation to "the issue" (as it is conceived by the analyst). *[. . .]*

1. SOPs constitute routines for dealing with *standard* situations. Routines allow large numbers of ordinary individuals to deal with numerous instances, day after day, without considerable thought, by responding to basic stimuli. *[. . .]* But specific instances, particularly critical instances that typically do not have "standard" characteristics, are often handled sluggishly or inappropriately.

2. A program, i.e., a complex action chosen from a short list of programs in a repertoire, is rarely tailored to the specific situation in which it is executed. Rather, the program is (at best) the most appropriate of the programs in a previously developed repertoire.

[. . .]

B. *Limited Flexibility and Incremental Change.* Major lines of organizational action are straight, i.e., behavior at one time is marginally different from that behavior at *t* − *1*. Simple-minded predictions work best: Behavior at *t + 1* will be marginally different from behavior at the present time.

1. Organizational budgets change incrementally—both with respect to totals and with respect to intra-organizational splits. Though organizations could divide the money available each year by carving up the pie anew (in the light of changes in objectives or environment), in practice, organizations take last year's budget as a base and adjust incrementally. *[. . .]*

2. Once undertaken, an organizational investment is not dropped at the point where "objective" costs outweigh benefits. Organizational stakes in adopted projects carry them quite beyond the loss point.

C. *Administrative Feasibility.* Adequate explanation, analysis, and prediction must include administrative feasibility as a major dimension. A considerable gap separates what leaders choose (or might rationally have chosen) and what organizations implement.

1. Organizations are blunt instruments. Projects that require several organizations to act with high degrees of precision and coordination are not likely to succeed.

2. Projects that demand that existing organizational units depart from their accustomed functions and perform previously unprogrammed tasks are rarely accomplished in their designed form.

3. Government leaders can expect that each organization will do its "part" in terms of what the organization knows how to do.

4. Government leaders can expect incomplete and distorted information from each organization concerning its part of the problem.

5. Where an assigned piece of a problem is contrary to the existing goals of an organization, resistance to implementation of that piece will be encountered.

V. Specific Propositions

1. *Deterrence.* The probability of nuclear attack is less sensitive to balance and imbalance, or stability and instability (as these concepts are employed by Model I strategists) than it is to a number of organizational factors. Except for the special case in which the Soviet Union acquires a credible capability to destroy the U.S. with a disarming blow, U.S. superiority or inferiority affects the probability of a nuclear attack less than do a number of organizational factors.

First, if a nuclear attack occurs, it will result from organizational activity: the firing of rockets by members of a missile group. The enemy's *control system*, i.e., physical mechanisms and standard procedures which determine who can launch rockets when, is critical. Second, the enemy's programs for bringing his strategic forces to *alert status* determine probabilities of accidental firing and momentum. [. . .]

2. *Soviet Force Posture.* Soviet force posture, i.e., the fact that certain weapons rather than others are procured and deployed, is determined by organizational factors such as the goals and procedures of existing military services and the goals and processes of research and design labs, within budgetary

constraints that emerge from the government leader's choices. The frailty of the Soviet Air Force within the Soviet military establishment seems to have been a crucial element in the Soviet failure to acquire a large bomber force in the 1950s (thereby faulting American intelligence predictions of a "bomber gap"). The fact that missiles were controlled until 1960 in the Soviet Union by the Soviet Ground Forces, whose goals and procedures reflected no interest in an intercontinental mission, was not irrelevant to the slow Soviet buildup of ICBMs *[intercontinental ballistic missiles]* (thereby faulting U.S. intelligence predictions of a "missile gap"). These organizational factors (Soviet Ground Forces' control of missiles and that service's fixation with European scenarios) make the Soviet deployment of so many MRBMs *[medium-range ballistic missiles]* that European targets could be destroyed three times over, more understandable. Recent weapon developments, e.g., the testing of a Fractional Orbital Bombardment System (FOBS) and multiple warheads for the SS-9, very likely reflect the activity and interests of a cluster of Soviet research and development organizations, rather than a decision by Soviet leaders to acquire a first strike weapon system. Careful attention to the organizational components of the Soviet military establishment (Strategic Rocket Forces, Navy, Air Force, Ground Forces, and National Air Defense), the missions and weapons systems to which each component is wedded (an independent weapon system assists survival as an independent service), and existing budgetary splits (which probably are relatively stable in the Soviet Union as they tend to be everywhere) offer potential improvements in medium and longer term predictions.

The U.S. Blockade of Cuba: A Second Cut

Organizational Intelligence. At 7:00 P.M. on October 22, 1962, President Kennedy disclosed the American discovery of the presence of Soviet strategic missiles in Cuba, declared a "strict quarantine on all offensive military equipment under shipment to Cuba," and demanded that "Chairman Khrushchev halt and eliminate this clandestine, reckless, and provocative threat to world peace."[14] This decision was reached at the pinnacle of the U.S. Government after a critical week of deliberation. What initiated that precious week were photographs of Soviet missile sites in Cuba taken on October 14. These pictures might not have been taken until a week later. In that case, the President speculated, "I don't think probably we would have chosen as prudently as we finally did."[15] U.S. leaders might have received this information three weeks earlier—if a U-2 had flown over San Cristobal in the last week of September.[16] What determined the context in which American leaders came to choose the blockade was the discovery of missiles on October 14.

There has been considerable debate over alleged American "intelligence failures" in the Cuban missile crisis.[17] But what both critics and defenders have neglected is the fact that the discovery took place on October 14, rather than three weeks earlier or a week later, as a consequence of the established routines and procedures of the organizations which constitute the U.S. intelligence community. *[. . .]*

The notorious "September estimate," approved by the United States Intelligence Board (USIB) on September 19, concluded that the Soviet Union would not introduce offensive missiles into Cuba.[18] No U-2 flight was directed over the western end of Cuba (after September 5) before October 4.[19] No U-2 flew over the western end of Cuba until the flight that discovered the Soviet missiles on October 14.[20] Can these "failures" be accounted for in organizational terms?

On September 19 when USIB met to consider the question of Cuba, the "system" contained the following information: (1) shipping intelligence had noted the arrival in Cuba of two large-hatch Soviet lumber ships, which were riding high in the water; (2) refugee reports of countless sightings of missiles, but also a report that Castro's private pilot, after a night of drinking in Havana, had boasted: "We will fight to the death and perhaps we can win because we have everything, including atomic weapons"; (3) a sighting by a CIA agent of the rear profile of a strategic missile; (4) U-2 photos produced by flights of August 29, September 5 and 17 showing the construction of a number of SAM *[surface-to-air missile]* sites and other defensive missiles.[21] Not all of this information was on the desk of the estimators, however. Shipping

intelligence experts noted the fact that large-hatch ships were riding high in the water and spelled out the inference: the ships must be carrying "space consuming" cargo.[22] These facts were carefully included in the catalogue of intelligence concerning shipping. For experts sensitive to the Soviets' shortage of ships, however, these facts carried no special signal. The refugee report of Castro's private pilot's remark had been received at Opa Locka, Florida, along with vast reams of inaccurate reports generated by the refugee community. This report and a thousand others had to be checked and compared before being sent to Washington. The two weeks required for initial processing could have been shortened by a large increase in resources, but the yield of this source was already quite marginal. The CIA agent's sighting of the rear profile of a strategic missile had occurred on September 12; transmission time from agent sighting to arrival in Washington typically took 9 to 12 days. Shortening this transmission time would impose severe cost in terms of danger to sub-agents, agents, and communication networks.

On the information available, the intelligence chiefs who predicted that the Soviet Union would not introduce offensive missiles into Cuba made a reasonable and defensible judgment.[23] Moreover, in the light of the fact that these organizations were gathering intelligence not only about Cuba but about potential occurrences in all parts of the world, the informational base available to the estimators involved nothing out of the ordinary. Nor, from an organizational perspective, is there anything startling about the gradual accumulation of evidence that led to the formulation of the hypothesis that the Soviets were installing missiles in Cuba and the decision on October 4 to direct a special flight over western Cuba.

The ten-day delay between that decision and the flight is another organizational story.[24] At the October 4 meeting, the Defense Department took the opportunity to raise an issue important to its concerns. Given the increased danger that a U-2 would be downed, it would be better if the pilot were an officer in uniform rather than a CIA agent. Thus the Air Force should assume responsibility for U-2 flights over Cuba. To the contrary, the CIA argued that this was an intelligence operation and thus within the CIA's jurisdiction. Moreover, CIA U-2's had been modified in certain ways which gave them advantages over Air Force U-2's in averting Soviet SAM's. Five days passed while the State Department pressed for less risky alternatives such as drones and the Air Force (in Department of Defense guise) and CIA engaged in territorial disputes. On October 9 a flight plan over San Cristobal was approved by COMOR *[Committee or Overhead Reconnaisance]*, but to the CIA's dismay, Air Force pilots rather than CIA agents would take charge of the mission. At this point details become sketchy, but several members of the intelligence community have speculated that an Air Force pilot in an Air Force U-2 attempted a high altitude overflight on October 9 that "flamed out," i.e., lost power, and thus had to descend in order to restart its engine. A second round between Air Force and CIA followed, as a result of which Air Force pilots were trained to fly CIA U-2's. A successful overflight took place on October 14.

This ten-day delay constitutes some form of "failure." In the face of well-founded suspicions concerning offensive Soviet missiles in Cuba that posed a critical threat to the United States' most vital interest, squabbling between organizations whose job it is to produce this information seems entirely inappropriate. But for each of these organizations, the question involved the issue: "*Whose* job was it to be?" Moreover, the issue was not simply, which organization would control U-2 flights over Cuba, but rather the broader issue of ownership of U-2 intelligence activities—a very long standing territorial dispute. Thus though this delay was in one sense a "failure," it was also a nearly inevitable consequence of two facts: many jobs do not fall neatly into precisely defined organizational jurisdictions; and vigorous organizations are imperialistic.

Organizational Options. Deliberations of leaders in ExCom meetings produced broad outlines of alternatives. Details of these alternatives and blueprints for their implementation had to be specified by the organizations that would perform these tasks. *[. . .]*

Discussion in the ExCom quickly narrowed the live options to two: an air strike and a blockade. The choice of the blockade instead of the air strike turned on two points: (1) the argument from morality

and tradition that the United States could not perpetrate a "Pearl Harbor in reverse"; (2) the belief that a "surgical" air strike was impossible.[25] *[. . .]* The majority of the members of the ExCom, including the President, initially preferred the air strike.[26] What effectively foreclosed this option, however, was the fact that the air strike they wanted could not be chosen with high confidence of success.[27]

[. . .]

Organizational Implementation. ExCom members separated several types of blockade: offensive weapons only, all armaments, and all strategic goods including POL (petroleum, oil, and lubricants). But the "*details*" of the operation were left to the Navy. Before the President announced the blockade on Monday evening, the first stage of the Navy's blueprint was in motion, and a problem loomed on the horizon.[28] The Navy had a detailed plan for the blockade. The President had several less precise but equally determined notions concerning what should be done, when, and how. For the Navy the issue was one of effective implementation of the Navy's blockade—without the meddling and interference of political leaders. For the President, the problem was to pace and manage events in such a way that the Soviet leaders would have time to see, think, and blink.

[. . .] Why not make the interception much closer to Cuba and thus give the Russian leader more time? *[. . .]* As Sorensen records, "in a sharp clash with the Navy, *[Kennedy]* made certain his will prevailed."[29] The Navy's plan for the blockade was thus changed by drawing the blockade much closer to Cuba.

[. . .]

What happened is not entirely clear. One can be certain, however, that Soviet ships passed through the line along which American destroyers had posted themselves before the official "first contact" with the Soviet ship. On October 26 a Soviet tanker arrived in Havana and was honored by a dockside rally for "running the blockade." Photographs of this vessel show the name *Vinnitsa* on the side of the vessel in Cyrillic letters.[30] But according to the official U.S. position, the first tanker to pass through the blockade was the *Bucharest*, which was hailed by the Navy on the morning of October 25. Again simple mathematical calculation excludes the possibility that the *Bucharest* and the *Vinnitsa* were the same ship. It seems probable that the Navy's resistance to the President's order that the blockade be drawn in closer to Cuba forced him to allow one or several Soviet ships to pass through the blockade after it was officially operative.[31]

This attempt to leash the Navy's blockade had a price. On Wednesday morning, October 24, what the President had been awaiting occurred. The 18 dry cargo ships heading towards the quarantine stopped dead in the water. This was the occasion of *[Secretary of State]* Dean Rusk's remark, "We are eyeball to eyeball and I think the other fellow just blinked."[32] But the Navy had another interpretation. The ships had simply stopped to pick up Soviet submarine escorts. The President became quite concerned lest the Navy—already riled because of Presidential meddling in its affairs—blunder into an incident. Sensing the President's fears, *[Secretary of Defense Robert]* McNamara became suspicious of the Navy's procedures and routines for making the first interception. Calling on the Chief of Naval Operations in the Navy's inner sanctum, the Navy Flag Plot, McNamara put his questions harshly.[33] Who would make the first interception? Were Russian-speaking officers on board? How would submarines be dealt with? At one point McNamara asked *[George W.]* Anderson what he would do if a Soviet ship's captain refused to answer questions about his cargo. Picking up the Manual of Navy Regulations the Navy man waved it in McNamara's face and shouted, "It's all in there." To which McNamara replied, "I don't give a damn what John Paul Jones would have done; I want to know what you are going to do, now."[34] The encounter ended on Anderson's remark: "Now, Mr. Secretary, if you and your Deputy will go back to your office the Navy will run the blockade."[35]

MODEL III: BUREAUCRATIC POLITICS

The leaders who sit on top of organizations are not a monolithic group. Rather, each is, in his own right, a player in a central, competitive game. The name of the game is bureaucratic politics: bargaining along regularized channels among players positioned hierarchically within the government. Government behavior can thus be understood according to a third conceptual model not as organizational outputs, but as outcomes of bargaining games. In contrast with Model I, the bureaucratic politics model sees no unitary actor but rather many actors as players, who focus not on a single strategic issue but on many diverse intra-national problems as well, in terms of no consistent set of strategic objectives but rather according to various conceptions of national, organizational, and personal goals, making government decisions not by rational choice but by the pulling and hauling that is politics.

The apparatus of each national government constitutes a complex arena for the intra-national game. Political leaders at the top of this apparatus plus the men who occupy positions on top of the critical organizations form the circle of central players. Ascendancy to this circle assures some independent standing. The necessary decentralization of decisions required for action on the broad range of foreign policy problems guarantees that each player has considerable discretion. Thus power is shared.

[. . .]

Men share power. Men differ concerning what must be done. The differences matter. This milieu necessitates that policy be resolved by politics. What the nation does is sometimes the result of the triumph of one group over others. More often, however, different groups pulling in different directions yield a resultant distinct from what anyone intended. What moves the chess pieces is not simply the reasons which support a course of action, nor the routines of organizations which enact an alternative, but the power and skill of proponents and opponents of the action in question.

This characterization captures the thrust of the bureaucratic politics orientation. If problems of foreign policy arose as discreet issues, and decisions were determined one game at a time, this account would suffice. But most "issues," e.g., Vietnam or the proliferation of nuclear weapons, emerge piecemeal, over time, one lump in one context, a second in another. Hundreds of issues compete for players' attention every day. Each player is forced to fix upon his issues for that day, fight them on their own terms, and rush on to the next. Thus the character of emerging issues and the pace at which the game is played converge to yield government "decisions" and "actions" as collages. Choices by one player, outcomes of minor games, outcomes of central games, and "foul-ups"—these pieces, when stuck to the same canvas, constitute government behavior relevant to an issue.

The concept of national security policy as political outcome contradicts both public imagery and academic orthodoxy. Issues vital to national security, it is said, are too important to be settled by political games. They must be "above" politics. To accuse someone of "playing politics with national security" is a most serious charge. What public conviction demands, the academic penchant for intellectual elegance reinforces. Internal politics is messy; moreover, according to prevailing doctrine, politicking lacks intellectual content. As such, it constitutes gossip for journalists rather than a subject for serious investigation. Occasional memoirs, anecdotes in historical accounts, and several detailed case studies to the contrary, most of the literature of foreign policy avoids bureaucratic politics. The gap between academic literature and the experience of participants in government is nowhere wider than at this point.

Bureaucratic Politics Paradigm[36]

I. Basic Unit Of Analysis:
Policy As Political Outcome

The decisions and actions of governments are essentially intra-national political outcomes: outcomes in the sense that what happens is not chosen as a solution to a problem but rather results from compromise, coalition, competition, and confusion among government officials who see different faces of an issue; political in the sense that the activity from which the outcomes emerge is best characterized as bargaining. *[. . .]*

II. Organizing Concepts

A. *Players in Positions.* The actor is neither a unitary nation, nor a conglomerate of organizations, but rather a number of individual players *[in a game].* Groups of these players constitute the agent

for particular government decisions and actions. Players are men in jobs.

Individuals become players in the national security policy game by occupying a critical position in an administration. For example, in the U.S. government the players include "Chiefs": the President, Secretaries of State, Defense, and Treasury, Director of the CIA, Joint Chiefs of Staff, and, since 1961, the Special Assistant for National Security Affairs; "Staffers": the immediate staff of each Chief; "Indians": the political appointees and permanent government officials within each of the departments and agencies; and "*Ad Hoc* Players": actors in the wider government game (especially "Congressional Influentials"), members of the press, spokesmen for important interest groups (especially the "bipartisan foreign policy establishment" in and out of Congress), and surrogates for each of these groups. Other members of the Congress, press, interest groups, and public form concentric circles around the central arena—circles which demarcate the permissive limits within which the game is played.

Positions define what players both may and must do. The advantages and handicaps with which each player can enter and play in various games stems from his position. So does a cluster of obligations for the performance of certain tasks. The two sides of this coin are illustrated by the position of the modern Secretary of State. First, he is the primary repository of political judgment on the political-military issues that are the stuff of contemporary foreign policy; consequently, he is a senior personal advisor to the President. Second, he is the colleague of the President's other senior advisers on the problems of foreign policy, the Secretaries of Defense and Treasury, and the Special Assistant for National Security Affairs. Third, he is the ranking U.S. diplomat for serious negotiation. *[. . .]* Finally, he is "Mr. State Department" or "Mr. Foreign Office," "leader of officials, spokesman for their causes, guardian of their interests, judge of their disputes, superintendent of their work, master of their careers."[37] But he is not first one, and then the other. All of these obligations are his simultaneously. *[. . .]* The necessity that he be close to the President restricts the extent to which, and the force with which, he can front for his department. When he defers to the Secretary of Defense rather than fighting for his department's position—as he often must—he strains the loyalty of his officialdom. The Secretary's resolution of these conflicts depends not only upon the position, but also upon the player who occupies the position.

For players are also people. *[. . .]* The core of the bureaucratic politics mix is personality. How each man manages to stand the heat in his kitchen, each player's basic operating style, and the complementarity or contradiction among personalities and styles in the inner circles are irreducible pieces of the policy blend. Moreover, each person comes to his position with baggage in tow, including sensitivities to certain issues, commitments to various programs, and personal standing and debts with groups in the society.

B. *Parochial Priorities, Perceptions and Issues.* Answers to the questions: "What is the issue?" and "What must be done?" are colored by the position from which the questions are considered. *[. . .]* To motivate members of his organization, a player must be sensitive to the organization's orientation. *[. . .]* Thus propensities of perception stemming from position permit reliable prediction about a player's stances in many cases. But these propensities are filtered through the baggage which players bring to positions. *[. . .]*

C. *Interests, Stakes, and Power.* Games are played to determine outcomes. But outcomes advance and impede each player's conception of the national interest, specific programs to which he is committed, the welfare of his friends, and his personal interests. These overlapping interests constitute the stakes for which games are played. Each player's ability to play successfully depends upon his power. Power, i.e., effective influence on policy outcomes, is an elusive blend of at least three elements: bargaining advantages (drawn from formal authority and obligations, institutional backing, constituents, expertise, and status), skill and will in using bargaining advantages, and other players' perceptions of the first two ingredients. Power wisely invested yields an enhanced reputation for effectiveness. Unsuccessful investment depletes both the stock of capital and the reputation. Thus each player must pick the issues on which he can play with a reasonable probability of success. But no player's power is sufficient to guarantee satisfactory outcomes.

[. . .]

F. *Action as Politics.* Government decisions are made and government actions emerge neither as the calculated choice of a unified group, nor as a formal summary of leaders' preferences. Rather the context of shared power but separate judgments concerning important choices, determines that politics is the mechanism of choice. Note the *environment* in which the game is played: inordinate uncertainty about what must be done, the necessity that something be done, and crucial consequences of whatever is done. These features force responsible men to become active players. The *pace of the game*—hundreds of issues, numerous games, and multiple channels—compels players to fight to "get other's attention," to make them "see the facts," to assure that they "take the time to think seriously about the broader issue." The *structure of the game*—power shared by individuals with separate responsibilities—validates each player's feeling that "others don't see my problem," and "others must be persuaded to look at the issue from a less parochial perspective." The *rules of the game*—he who hesitates loses his chance to play at that point, and he who is uncertain about his recommendation is overpowered by others who are sure—pressures players to come down on one side of a 51-49 issue and play. The *rewards of the game*—effectiveness, i.e., impact on outcomes, as the immediate measure of performance—encourages hard play. Thus, most players come to fight to "make the government do what is right." The strategies and tactics employed are quite similar to those formalized by theorists of international relations.

G. *Streams of Outcomes.* Important government decisions or actions emerge as collages composed of individual acts, outcomes of minor and major games, and foul-ups. Outcomes which could never have been chosen by an actor and would never have emerged from bargaining in a single game over the issue are fabricated piece by piece. Understanding of the outcome requires that it be disaggregated.

III. Dominant Inference Pattern

If a nation performed an action, that action was the *outcome* of bargaining among individuals and groups within the government. That outcome included *results* achieved by groups committed to a decision or action, *resultants* which emerged from bargaining among groups with quite different positions and *foul-ups*. Model III's explanatory power is achieved by revealing the pulling and hauling of various players, with different perceptions and priorities, focusing on separate problems, which yielded the outcomes that constitute the action in question.

IV. General Propositions

1. *Action and Intention.* Action does not presuppose intention. The sum of behavior of representatives of a government relevant to an issue was rarely intended by any individual or group. Rather separate individuals with different intentions contributed pieces which compose an outcome distinct from what anyone would have chosen.

2. *Where you stand depends on where you sit.* Horizontally, the diverse demands upon each player shape his priorities, perceptions, and issues. For large classes of issues, e.g., budgets and procurement decisions, the stance of a particular player can be predicted with high reliability from information concerning his seat. In the notorious B-36 controversy, no one was surprised by Admiral [Arthur] Radford's testimony that "the B-36 under any theory of war, is a bad gamble with national security," as opposed to Air Force Secretary Symington's claim that "a B-36 with an A-bomb can destroy distant objectives which might require ground armies years to take."[38]

[. . .]

Foreign policy Chiefs deal most often with the hottest issue *du jour*, though they can get the attention of the President and other members of the government for other issues which they judge important. What they cannot guarantee is that "the President will pay the price" or that "the others will get on board." They must build a coalition of the relevant powers that be. They must "give the President confidence" in the right course of action.

Most problems are framed, alternatives specified, and proposals pushed, however, by Indians. Indians fight with Indians of other departments; for example, struggles between International Security Affairs of the Department of Defense and Political-Military of the State Department are a microcosm of the action at higher levels. But the Indian's major problem is how to get the *attention* of Chiefs, how to get an issue decided, how to get the government "to do what is right."

In policy making then, the issue looking *down* is options: how to preserve my leeway until time clarifies uncertainties. The issue looking *sideways* is commitment: how to get others committed to my coalition. The issue looking *upwards* is confidence: how to give the boss confidence in doing what must be done. To paraphrase one of *[Richard]* Neustadt's assertions which can be applied down the length of the ladder, the essence of a responsible official's task is to induce others to see that what needs to be done is what their own appraisal of their own responsibilities requires them to do in their own interests.

V. Specific Propositions

1. *Deterrence.* The probability of nuclear attack depends primarily on the probability of attack emerging as an outcome of the bureaucratic politics of the attacking government. First, which players can decide to launch an attack? Whether the effective power over action is controlled by an individual, a minor game, or the central game is critical. Second, though Model I's confidence in nuclear deterrence stems from an assertion that, in the end, governments will not commit suicide, Model III recalls historical precedents. Admiral Yamamoto, who designed the Japanese attack on Pearl Harbor, estimated accurately: "In the first six months to a year of war against the U.S. and England I will run wild, and I will show you an uninterrupted succession of victories; I must also tell you that, should the war be prolonged for two or three years, I have no confidence in our ultimate victory."[39] But Japan attacked. [. . .] What patterns of bargaining could yield attack as an outcome? The major difference between a stable balance of terror and a questionable balance may simply be that in the first case

most members of the government appreciate fully the consequences of attack and are thus on guard against the emergence of this outcome. [. . .] If members of the U.S. government had been sensitive to the stream of decisions from which the Japanese attack on Pearl Harbor emerged, they would have been aware of a considerable probability of that attack. [. . .]

The U.S. Blockade of Cuba: A Third Cut

The Politics of Discovery. A series of overlapping bargaining games determined both the *date* of the discovery of the Soviet missiles and the *impact* of this discovery on the Administration. An explanation of the politics of the discovery is consequently a considerable piece of the explanation of the U.S. blockade.

Cuba was the Kennedy Administration's "political Achilles' heel."[40] The months preceding the crisis were also months before the Congressional elections, and the Republican Senatorial and Congressional Campaign Committee had announced that Cuba would be "the dominant issue of the 1962 campaign."[41] What the administration billed as a "more positive and indirect approach of isolating Castro from developing, democratic Latin America," Senators [Kenneth] Keating, [Barry] Goldwater, [Homer] Capehart, [Strom] Thurmond, and others attacked as a "do-nothing" policy.[42] In statements on the floor of the House and Senate, campaign speeches across the country, and interviews and articles carried by national news media, Cuba—particularly the Soviet program of increased arms aid—served as a stick for stirring the domestic political scene.[43]

These attacks drew blood. Prudence demanded a vigorous reaction. The President decided to meet the issue head-on. The Administration mounted a forceful campaign of denial designed to discredit critics' claims. The President himself manned the front line of this offensive, though almost all Administration officials participated. In his news conference on August 19, President Kennedy attacked as "irresponsible" calls for an invasion of Cuba, stressing rather "the totality of our obligations" and promising to "watch what happens in Cuba with the closest attention."[44] On September 4, he issued a strong

statement denying any provocative Soviet action in Cuba.[45] On September 13 he lashed out at "loose talk" calling for an invasion of Cuba.[46] The day before the flight of the U-2 which discovered the missiles, he campaigned in Capehart's Indiana against those "self-appointed generals and admirals who want to send someone else's sons to war."[47]

On Sunday, October 14, just as a U-2 was taking the first pictures of Soviet missiles, McGeorge Bundy was asserting:

> I *know* that there is no present evidence, and I think that there is no present likelihood that the Cuban government and the Soviet government would, in combination, attempt to install a major offensive capability.[48]

In this campaign to puncture the critics' charges, the Administration discovered that the public needed positive slogans. Thus, Kennedy fell into a tenuous semantic distinction between "offensive" and "defensive" weapons. This distinction originated in his September 4 statement that there was no evidence of "offensive ground to ground missiles" and warned "were it to be otherwise, the gravest issues would arise."[49] His September 13 statement turned on this distinction between "defensive" and "offensive" weapons and announced a firm commitment to action if the Soviet Union attempted to introduce the latter into Cuba.[50] Congressional committees elicited from administration officials testimony which read this distinction and the President's commitment into the *Congressional Record.*[51]

[. . .]

The Politics of Issues. The U-2 photographs presented incontrovertible evidence of Soviet offensive missiles in Cuba. This revelation fell upon politicized players in a complex context. As one high official recalled, Khrushchev had caught us "with our pants down." What each of the central participants saw, and what each did to cover both his own and the Administration's nakedness, created the spectrum of issues and answers.

At approximately 9:00 A.M., Tuesday morning, October 16, McGeorge Bundy went to the President's living quarters with the message: "Mr. President, there is now hard photographic evidence that the Russians have offensive missiles in Cuba."[52] Much has been made of Kennedy's "expression of surprise,"[53] but "surprise" fails to capture the character of his initial reaction. Rather, it was one of startled anger, most adequately conveyed by the exclamation: "He can't do that to me!"[54] In terms of the President's attention and priorities at that moment, Khrushchev had chosen the most unhelpful act of all. Kennedy had staked his full Presidential authority on the assertion that the Soviets would not place offensive weapons in Cuba. Moreover, Khrushchev had assured the President through the most direct and personal channels that he was aware of the President's domestic political problem and that nothing would be done to exacerbate this problem. The Chairman had *lied* to the President. Kennedy's initial reaction entailed action. The missiles must be removed.[55] The alternatives of "doing nothing" or "taking a diplomatic approach" could not have been less relevant to *his* problem.

These two tracks—doing nothing and taking a diplomatic approach   were the solutions advocated by two of his principal advisors. For Secretary of Defense McNamara, the missiles raised the spectre of nuclear war. He first framed the issue as a straightforward strategic problem. To understand the issue, one had to grasp two obvious but difficult points. First, the missiles represented an inevitable occurrence: narrowing of the missile gap. It simply happened sooner rather than later. Second, the United States could accept this occurrence since its consequences were minor: "seven-to-one missile 'superiority,' one-to-one missile 'equality,' one-to-seven missile 'inferiority'—the three postures are identical." McNamara's statement of this argument at the first meeting of the ExCom was summed up in the phrase, "a missile is a missile."[56] "It makes no great difference," he maintained, "whether you are killed by a missile from the Soviet Union or Cuba."[57] The implication was clear. The United States should not initiate a crisis with the Soviet Union, risking a significant probability of nuclear war over an occurrence which had such small strategic implications.

The perceptions of McGeorge Bundy, the President's Assistant for National Security Affairs, are the most difficult of all to reconstruct. There is no question that he initially argued for a diplomatic track.[58] But was Bundy laboring under his acknowledged burden of responsibility in Cuba I *[Bay of Pigs]*? Or was he playing the role of devil's advocate in order to make the President probe his own initial reaction and consider other options?

The President's brother, Robert Kennedy, saw most clearly the political wall against which Khrushchev had backed the President. But he, like McNamara, saw the prospect of nuclear doom. Was Khrushchev going to force the President to an insane act? At the first meeting of the ExCom, he scribbled a note, "Now I know how Tojo felt when he was planning Pearl Harbor."[59] From the outset he searched for an alternative that would prevent the air strike.

The initial reaction of Theodore Sorensen, the President's Special Counsel and "alter ego," fell somewhere between that of the President and his brother. Like the President, Sorensen felt the poignancy of betrayal. If the President had been the architect of the policy which the missiles punctured, Sorensen was the draftsman. Khrushchev's deceitful move demanded a strong counter-move. But like Robert Kennedy, Sorensen feared lest the shock and disgrace lead to disaster.

To the Joint Chiefs of Staff the issue was clear. Now was the time to do the job for which they had prepared contingency plans. Cuba I had been badly done; Cuba II would not be. The missiles provided the *occasion* to deal with the issue: cleansing the Western Hemisphere of Castro's Communism. As the President recalled on the day the crisis ended, "An invasion would have been a mistake—a wrong use of our power. But the military are mad. They wanted to do this. It's lucky for us that we have McNamara over there."[60]

[. . .]

The Politics of Choice. The process by which the blockade emerged is a story of the most subtle and intricate probing, pulling, and hauling; leading, guiding, and spurring. Reconstruction of this process can only be tentative. Initially the President and most of his advisers wanted the clean, surgical air strike. On the first day of the crisis, when informing *[U.N. Embassador Adlai]* Stevenson of the missiles, the President mentioned only two alternatives: "I suppose the alternatives are to go in by air and wipe them out, or to take other steps to render them inoperable."[61] At the end of the week a sizeable minority still favored an air strike. As Robert

Kennedy recalled: "The fourteen people involved were very significant. . . . If six of them had been President of the U.S., I think that the world might have been blown up."[62] What prevented the air strike was a fortuitous coincidence of a number of factors—the absence of any one of which might have permitted that option to prevail.

First, McNamara's vision of holocaust set him firmly against the air strike. His initial attempt to frame the issue in strategic terms struck Kennedy as particularly inappropriate. Once McNamara realized that the name of the game was a strong response, however, he and his deputy Gilpatric chose the blockade as a fallback. When the Secretary of Defense—whose department had the action, whose reputation in the Cabinet was unequaled, in whom the President demonstrated full confidence—marshalled the arguments for the blockade and refused to be moved, the blockade became a formidable alternative.

Second, Robert Kennedy—the President's closest confidant—was unwilling to see his brother become a "Tojo." His arguments against the air strike on moral grounds struck a chord in the President. Moreover, once his brother had stated these arguments so forcefully, the President could not have chosen his initially preferred course without, in effect, agreeing to become what RFK had condemned.

The President learned of the missiles on Tuesday morning. On Wednesday morning, in order to mask our discovery from the Russians, the President flew to Connecticut to keep a campaign commitment, leaving RFK as the unofficial chairman of the group. By the time the President returned on Wednesday evening, a critical third piece had been added to the picture. McNamara had presented his argument for the blockade. Robert Kennedy and Sorensen had joined McNamara. A powerful coalition of the advisers in whom the President had the greatest confidence, and with whom his style was most compatible, had emerged.

[. . .]

Thursday evening, the President convened the ExCom at the White House. He declared his tentative choice of the blockade and directed that preparations be made to put it into effect by Monday morning.[63]

NOTES

1. Theodore Sorensen, *Kennedy* (New York, 1965), p. 705.

2. Arnold Horelick and Myron Rush, *Strategic Power and Soviet Foreign Policy* (Chicago, 1965). Based on A. Horelick, "The Cuban Missile Crisis: An Analysis of Soviet Calculations and Behavior," *World Politics* (April, 1964).

3. Horelick and Rush, *Strategic Power and Soviet Foreign Policy*, p. 154.

4. *New York Times*, March 22, 1969.

5. As stated in the introduction, this "case snapshot" presents, without editorial commentary, a Model I analyst's explanation of the U.S. blockade. The purpose is to illustrate a strong, characteristic rational policy model account. This account is (roughly) consistent with prevailing explanations of these events.

6. Theodore Sorensen, *op. cit.*, p. 675.

7. Elie Abel, *The Missile Crisis* (New York, 1966), p. 102.

8. Sorensen, *op. cit.*, p. 684.

9. *New York Times*, June, 1963.

10. The formulation of this paradigm is indebted both to the orientation and insights of Herbert Simon and to the behavioral model of the firm stated by Richard Cyert and James March, *A Behavioral Theory of the Firm* (Englewood Cliffs, 1963). Here, however, one is forced to grapple with the less routine, less quantified functions of the less differentiated elements in government organizations.

11. Theodore Sorensen, "You Get to Walk to Work," *New York Times Magazine*, March 19, 1967.

12. Marriner Eccles, *Beckoning Frontiers* (New York, 1951), p. 336.

13. Arthur Schlesinger, *A Thousand Days* (Boston, 1965), p. 406.

14. U.S. Department of State, *Bulletin*, XLVII, pp. 715–720.

15. Schlesinger, *op. cit.*, p. 803.

16. Theodore Sorensen, *Kennedy*, p. 675.

17. See U.S. Congress, Senate, Committee on Armed Services, Preparedness Investigation Sub-committee, *Interim Report on Cuban Military Build-up*, 88th Congress, 1st Session, 1963, p. 2; Hanson Baldwin, "Growing Risks of Bureaucratic Intelligence," *The Reporter* (August 15, 1963), 48–50; Roberta Wohlstetter, "Cuba and Pearl Harbor," *Foreign Affairs* (July, 1965), 706.

18. R. Hilsman, *To Move a Nation* (New York, 1967), pp. 172–173.

19. U.S. Congess, House of Representatives, Committee on Appropriations, Subcommittee on Department of

Defense Appropriations, *Hearings*, 88th Congress, 1st Session, 1963, 67.

20. *Ibid.*, pp. 66–67.

21. For (1) Hilsman, *op. cit.*, p. 186; (2) Abel, *op. cit.*, p. 24; (3) Department of Defense Appropriations, *Hearings*, p. 64; Abel, *op. cit.*, p. 24; (4) Department of Defense Appropriations, *Hearings*, pp. 1–30.

22. The facts here are not entirely clear. This assertion is based on information from (1) "Department of Defense Briefing by the Honorable R. S. McNamara, Secretary of Defense, State Department Auditorium, 5:00 p.m., February 6, 1963." A verbatim transcript of a presentation actually made by General Carroll's assistant, John Hughes; and (2) Hilsman's statement, *op. cit.*, p. 186. But see R. Wohlstetter's interpretation, "Cuba and Pearl Harbor," 700.

23. See Hilsman, *op. cit.*, pp. 172–174.

24. Abel, *op. cit.*, pp. 26 ff; Weintal and Bartlett, *Facing the Brink* (New York, 1967), pp. 62 ff; *Cuban Military Build-up*; J. Daniel and J. Hubbell, *Strike in the West* (New York, 1963), pp. 15 ff.

25. Schlesinger, *op. cit.*, p. 804.

26. Sorensen, *Kennedy*, p. 684.

27. *Ibid.*, pp. 684 ff.

28. See Abel, *op. cit.*, pp. 97 ff.

29. Sorensen, *Kennedy*, p. 710.

30. *Facts on File*, Vol. XXII, 1962, p. 376, published by Facts on File, Inc., New York, yearly.

31. This hypothesis would account for the mystery surrounding Kennedy's explosion at the leak of the stopping of the *Bucharest*. See Hilsman, *op. cit.*, p. 45.

32. Abel, *op. cit.*, p. 153.

33. See *ibid.*, pp. 154 ff.

34. *Ibid.*, p. 156.

35. *Ibid.*

36. This paradigm relies upon the small group of analysts who have begun to fill the gap. My primary source is the model implicit in the work of Richard E. Neustadt, though his concentration on presidential action has been generalized to a concern with policy as the outcome of political bargaining among a number of independent players, the President amounting to no more than a "superpower" among many lesser but considerable powers. As Warner Schilling argues, the substantive problems are of such inordinate difficulty that uncertainties and differences with regard to goals, alternatives, and consequences are inevitable. This necessitates what Roger Hilsman describes as the process of conflict and consensus building. The techniques employed in this process often resemble those used in legislative assemblies, though Samuel Huntington's characterization of the process as "legislative" overemphasizes the equality of participants as opposed to the hierarchy which structures the game. *[. . .]*

37. Richard E. Neustadt, Testimony, United States Senate, Committee on Government Operations, Subcommittee on National Security Staffing, *Administration of National Security*, March 26, 1963, pp. 82–3.

38. Paul Y. Hammond, "Super Carriers and B-36 Bombers," in Harold Stein (ed.), *American Civil-Military Decisions* (Birmingham, 1963).

39. Roberta Wohlstetter, *Pearl Harbor* (Stanford, 1962), p. 350.

40. Sorensen, *Kennedy*, p. 670.

41. *Ibid.*

42. *Ibid.*, pp. 670 ff.

43. *New York Times*, August, September, 1962.

44. *New York Times*, August 20, 1962.

45. *New York Times*, September 5, 1962.

46. *New York Times*, September 14, 1962.

47. *New York Times*, October 14, 1962.

48. Cited by Abel, *op. cit.*, p. 13.

49. *New York Times*, September 5, 1962.

50. *New York Times*, September 14, 1962.

51. Senate Foreign Relations Committee; Senate Armed Services Committee; House Committee on Appropriation; House Select Committee on Export Control.

52. Abel, *op. cit.*, p. 44.

53. *Ibid.*, pp. 44 ff.

54. See Richard Neustadt, "Afterword," *Presidential Power* (New York, 1964).

55. Sorensen, *Kennedy*, p. 676; Schlesinger, *op. cit.*, p. 801.

56. Hilsman, *op. cit.*, p. 195.

57. *Ibid.*

58. Weintal and Bartlett, *op. cit.*, p. 67; Abel, *op. cit.*, p. 53.

59. Schlesinger, *op. cit.*, p. 803

60. *Ibid.*, p. 831.

61. Abel, *op. cit.*, p. 49.

62. Interview, quoted by Ronald Steel, *New York Review of Books*, March 13, 1969, p. 22.

63. Sorensen, *Kennedy*, p. 691.

PART VI

POWER INSIDE ORGANIZATIONS

The study of decision making naturally raises questions about who has the power to make organizational decisions and how that power is acquired and used. Any discussion of power requires a definition, but entire books written on the subject suggest it is not easy to offer one. A simple definition, derived from Weber, is that power is the ability to impose one's will on someone else despite his or her own preferences or resistance. This leaves thorny issues unresolved, such as how to distinguish power from influence, how to know if power rather than common agreement is at work in the absence of open dissent or resistance, and how to characterize situations in which some people have the ability to shape others' preferences so they seem to accept existing disparities of power, status, income, and living conditions even if they are disadvantaged as a result (Lukes 1974).

Within organizations, power has an obvious aspect; it is a characteristic of one's position in the chain of command and the official or formal rights attached to that position. In small or highly centralized organizations, one person or a small group might exercise complete control, but most organizations require some delegation of significant decision-making power to different positions, usually accompanied by monitoring from above and the power of superiors to reward or punish subordinates with raises, promotions, reprimands, or termination. There is also the power or influence that comes with having critical or important information, such as the professional's expert knowledge. Positional and professional power are distinct from charisma or force of personality, which are not considered here because they tend to be more idiosyncratic than structural, though there is a literature on leadership that considers this issue more systematically.

However, the most interesting work in the sociology of organizations examines power that is not specified by formal roles. Organizational rules and the design of work tasks may reflect the organization's power over its members in a more subtle way by setting ground rules and removing some of the need for personal supervision of subordinates, sometimes known as *unobtrusive control* (Gouldner 1954, pp. 158ff.; Perrow 1986, pp. 128ff.). Barker (1993) describes how the transition from traditional management to self-directed work teams in an electronics plant increased the level of management control because workers assumed supervisory functions as a team, felt greater personal responsibility for the product, and exerted intense peer pressure on one another to uphold the more stringent work norms that the team had developed, complete with tough sanctions for offenders. Given greater freedom, workers unconsciously came to accept management's standards as their own and to develop a greater commitment to them than when they were supervised personally.

In addition, superiors actively exercise power over subordinates in unexpected ways that extend beyond their official authority, including the shaping of subordinates' preferences. Individuals or departments that are seemingly equal manage to gain or exercise unequal power. Even official subordinates can exert informal power over those above them. Behind the formal structure, there is a shadow structure in which organizational politics plays out.

Previous readings give a number of examples of superiors extending their power through informal means. In Weber's classic view (Reading 1), organizational authority is attached to positions, not people, and has clearly defined boundaries, but Jackall (Reading 14) demonstrates that corporate managers can leverage their official power into a near-absolute personal loyalty and obedience. Managers who gain a role in making many appointments can create wide networks of loyalty and obligation. Braverman (Reading 3) argues that capitalist power is inscribed in the very structure of narrow, deskilled work tasks, Burawoy (Reading 15) argues that workers' remaining discretion functions to generate consent to the existing order, and Graham (Reading 12) shows how attempts to more deeply control workers' motivations in order to increase an organization's effort levels can generate resistance. Gideon Kunda also examines the use of ideological or cultural power in a study of managers and professional in a computer company (see Reading 27).

Examples of apparently equal individuals exercising unequal power include individuals who occupy central positions in formal and informal networks within the organization and who thus have access to more allies, information, and resources than otherwise similar individuals. Jackall noted that managers who succeed in making a wide circle of friends, joining strong cliques, and building informal alliances with peers inside their organization can also increase their influence through informal means such as intrigue and politics. Cliques with the most influence are sometimes called the *dominant coalition*.

Individuals in a position to control the flow of information also have power because they can control the knowledge available to others and guide others' decisions in ways that are favorable to their own point of view. If someone does not know the full range of options open to him or her and is dependent on others for this information, that individual not only is unable to argue for another course of action, but may even be unaware that an alternative is possible. Some individuals can effectively hoard information, knowledge, and expertise in order to create an artificial scarcity and ensure that others remain dependent on them.

Individuals can also gain power by connecting the organization with important external resources, often called *boundary spanners*. Boundary spanners can be in a unique position as gatekeepers for important information, outside resources, and external allies, customers, clients, and connections, which they can leverage into power and influence (Brass 1984).

Among departments, although line and staff have a certain formal equality on the organization chart, Dalton shows how line managers' importance to the organization's core mission allows them to ignore recommendations from research staff at will, despite the latter's expert knowledge (see Reading 14). Even among staff departments in American corporations, there is usually a clear hierarchy of informal power, with finance at the top and personnel or human resources at the bottom, reflecting their perceived relative value (Shaeffer and Janger 1982; see Reading 29).

The reason for this ranking of departments is not a mystery; those that are most directly involved in generating revenue for the organization make the greatest contribution to the organization's survival and can command the greatest deference, while others are perceived as overhead, more of a cost that needs to be justified and thus less essential. One staff manager summed up the distinction as one between "money using" and "money producing" departments (see Reading 35).

This general principle has been described by the "strategic contingencies" explanation of power differences, which argues that an important source of power is the possession of scarce skills that are critical to the organization's ongoing operation and that reduce operating uncertainties, because organizations value survival and most seek stability and routine (Hickson, Astley, Butler, and Wilson 1983). For example, Fligstein (1987) argued that power in large corporations shifted from owners and manufacturing executives in the early twentieth century to marketing executives in the 1930s to 1950s because single-product firms diversified into related product lines and depended more on marketing savvy in the introduction of new products. When legal changes in the 1950s redirected growth strategies toward mergers with firms in unrelated businesses (*conglomerate merger*), product and market knowledge became relatively less important than understanding investment and profit potential as a general skill, and finance executives were more likely to be selected as chief executives.

The classic statement of how relative equals become differentiated into those with and without power is Robert Michels' (1876–1936) study of European socialist trade unions and political parties in the early twentieth century, with whom he sympathized initially (Reading 17). In the beginning, these organizations were governed very democratically, with term limits on office holding, rotation of positions, popular participation in decision making, and active member oversight of administrative operations. However, as the size and complexity of the organizations increased, more decisions had to be delegated to officials, office holding became a more specialized and professional role, and opportunities for popular participation diminished. Selection to office relied more on scarce credentials, such as education, knowledge, and ability, rather than open elections. A salaried class of administrators gradually closed itself off from the membership it served and monopolized the benefits of office in its own interest. Democracy and participation became more ritualistic and the rank and file grew more passive. With the development of a more bureaucratic structure, the gap between the leaders and masses grew. Because the officials benefited from occupying positions within an organization, the maintenance and growth of the organization became ends in themselves, displacing the original goals. This elite became more middle class in background and outlook and more conservative. Its members sought cooperation with their supposed adversaries in government and business to safeguard their careers, spent more time negotiating and even socializing with these elites, and finally assimilated into that class. Grassroots participation was discouraged, and the organizations lost their vitality and potential for achieving fundamental social change.

Michels believed a similar process was the fate of all organizations. All democratic organizations eventually become de facto oligarchies because the mass of members do not have the specialized knowledge to govern directly, nor would it be practical in large organizations. Once leaders are given the power to conduct business efficiently, they use it to consolidate a position of privilege, and a functional division of labor is converted into enduring inequalities in income, power, and status. The reading reveals Michels to be simultaneously critical of this tendency and admiring of leaders' superior abilities compared to the masses, which prefigures Michels' own eventual abandonment of socialism for Mussolini's fascism.

Michels' insight applies to many democratically oriented organizations today, such as unions, political parties, and government, in which the membership often feels distant from the leadership they elect formally. Many Americans complain that their politicians are so removed from their own worlds they seem to form an elite that acts in its own collective interest, regardless of party affiliation, rather than representing the public or the voters who elected them (Halle 1984). Anyone who owns stock or is a member of a credit union knows that elections for the leadership of these organizations is almost always a formality rather than a genuine exercise in democracy. The role of elite power in ostensibly democratic organizations is also visible in the recent tendency of the executives of mutual insurance companies and community hospitals to convert these organizations to private ownership in ways that benefit themselves financially, often over the objections of members or other stakeholders traditionally involved in their governance (Goddeeris and Weisbrod 1998).

Still, many debate whether Michels' pessimistic "Iron Law of Oligarchy" is really a sociological law. Faith in democratic governance requires some assumption that poor performance and grossly self-serving behavior by the elite can ultimately be restrained by citizen involvement in politics and government. Part XIII, "Alternatives to Capitalist Bureaucracy," also discusses various forms of worker ownership and self-management in economic enterprises that strive to overcome tendencies toward oligarchy.

One contrast to Michels' view, perhaps easily exaggerated, is that subordinates can exercise power over their superiors. Certain subordinates, such as factory mechanics or computer technicians, have scarce skills and perform critical duties without which their organizations could not continue to function. Consequently, these employees receive considerable deference and attention despite their official subordinate status. Subordinates' general ability to withdraw informal cooperation from supervisors and even engage in sabotage can also limit the arbitrary exercise of power, at least in some circumstances, as the discussion of Gouldner's work illustrated (see Part IV). Managers and supervisors can find that potential employee resistance or sabotage make it not always worth the effort to impose their will. The sheer inertia of subordinates in large organizations accustomed to established routine can also frustrate managers' desires for change. Even if subordinates' resistance is not an issue, policies and communications can become distorted and even lost altogether as they are transmitted downward through multiple levels in a tall hierarchy (Kanter and Stein 1979, pp. 6ff.).

This has led Rosabeth Moss Kanter to argue that top executives in large organizations have much less genuine power than commonly believed, despite the considerable luxury and privilege accompanying their positions. She argues that top managers are insulated from the real action in lower levels of their organization, are often flattered by a closed inner circle, and have to contend with internal interest groups and the inertia of routine of those below them (Kanter and Stein 1979, pp.4ff.). Top executives can find that trying to alter established routines in a large organization is as difficult as trying to turn a large battleship around quickly.

Even if Kanter's view of the powerlessness of the powerful is exaggerated, she points to an important competing definition of power that is more functionalist than the traditional Weberian definition. For Kanter, power is the ability to accomplish things (Kanter 1977). It signifies the capacity to achieve goals, often in cooperation with others, rather than hierarchical control over others. This is sometimes known as "power to," or power as technique, as opposed to "power over," or domination (Hickson et al. 1983). In this view, those who have power in an organization are individuals who have the competence and ability to get things done by working effectively with others. The individual accumulates power by being able to demonstrate extraordinary performance in visible activities important for organization (Kanter 1977).

In this more functionalist view of power, the real problem occurs when individuals are made accountable for results but do not have sufficient power to achieve them. In reaction, they become irritable, petty, controlling toward subordinates and others, and excessively rules-minded, turf-conscious, and cautious as coping and defense mechanisms. This generates negative reactions and resistance from subordinates and others that only increase these individuals' sense of powerlessness and set in motion a new round of defensive behaviors by the person who feels pressured by unfair demands (Kanter 1977, pp. 186ff.)

Even apart these pathologies of powerlessness, Kanter recognizes that her relatively benign view of power as the ability to accomplish things has its dysfunctional aspects. Many ambitious managers launch visible and dramatic initiatives in order to show some kind of tangible achievement to further their careers, rather than because of the organization's genuine needs. This can include large projects or disruptive reorganizations that give managers the opportunity to create new debts of loyalty and fear and uncertainty among subordinates. "Each leader needs his or her monument, which can be a physical structure or a redesigned organizational chart" (Kanter 1977, p. 178; see also Badaracco and Webb 1995, p. 21). One detects March's nonrational decision making at work here, as well as Jackall's patrimonial bureaucracy.

It should be said that power is exercised in interorganizational as well as intraorganizational relations, as will be clear from the readings in Part VII on open systems organization theories. Power can also be exercised by organizations over the broader society, aspects of which will be considered in Part XI. The exercise of power *within* organizations is only one dimension of the relationship between power and organizations.

17

ORGANIZATIONS AND OLIGARCHY

ROBERT MICHELS

TECHNICAL AND ADMINISTRATIVE CAUSES OF LEADERSHIP

Introductory—The Need for Organization

Democracy is inconceivable without organization. A few words will suffice to demonstrate this proposition.

A class which unfurls in the face of society the banner of certain definite claims, and which aspires to the realization of a complex of ideal aims deriving from the economic functions which that class fulfils, needs an organization. Be the claims economic or be they political, organization appears the only means for the creation of a collective will. Organization, based as it is upon the principle of least effort, that is to say, upon the greatest possible economy of energy, is the weapon of the weak in their struggle with the strong.

The chances of success in any struggle will depend upon the degree to which this struggle is carried out upon a basis of solidarity between individuals whose interests are identical. In objecting, therefore, to the theories of the individualist anarchists that nothing could please the employers better than the dispersion and disaggregation of the forces of the workers, the socialists, the most fanatical of all the partisans of the idea of organization, enunciate an argument which harmonizes well with the results of scientific study of the nature of parties.

We live in a time in which the idea of cooperation has become so firmly established that even millionaires perceive the necessity of common action. It is easy to understand, then, that organization has become a vital principle of the working class, for in default of it their success is *a priori* impossible. The refusal of the worker to participate in the collective life of his class cannot fail to entail disastrous consequences. In respect of culture and of economic, physical, and physiological conditions, the proletarian is the weakest element of our

Reprinted and edited with the permission of The Free Press, a Division of Simon & Schuster, Inc., from *Political Parties: A Sociological Study of the Oligarchical Tendencies of Modern Democracy,* by Robert Michels, translated by Eden and Cedar Paul (1915/1962). Copyright © 1962 by the Crowell-Collier Publishing Co.

society. In fact, the isolated member of the working classes is defenseless in the hands of those who are economically stronger. It is only by combination to form a structural aggregate that the proletarians can acquire the faculty of political resistance and attain to a social dignity. The importance and the influence of the working class are directly proportional to its numerical strength. But for the representation of that numerical strength organization and coordination are indispensable. The principle of organization is an absolutely essential condition for the political struggle of the masses.

Yet this politically necessary principle of organization, while it overcomes that disorganization of forces which would be favorable to the adversary, brings other dangers in its train. We escape Scylla only to dash ourselves on Charybdis. Organization is, in fact, the source from which the conservative currents flow over the plain of democracy, occasioning there disastrous floods and rendering the plain unrecognizable.

Mechanical and Technical Impossibility of Direct Government by the Masses

[. . .] The practical ideal of democracy consists in the self-government of the masses in conformity with the decisions of popular assemblies. But while this system limits the extension of the principle of delegation, it fails to provide any guarantee against the formation of an oligarchical camerilla. Undoubtedly it deprives the natural leaders of their quality as functionaries, for this quality is transferred to the people themselves. The crowd, however, is always subject to suggestion, being readily influenced by the eloquence of great popular orators; moreover, direct government by the people, admitting of no serious discussions or thoughtful deliberations, greatly facilitates *coups de main* of all kinds by men who are exceptionally bold, energetic, and adroit.

[. . .]

The most formidable argument against the sovereignty of the masses is, however, derived from the mechanical and technical impossibility of its realization.

The sovereign masses are altogether incapable of undertaking the most necessary resolutions. The impotence of direct democracy, like the power of indirect democracy, is a direct outcome of the influence of number. In a polemic against Proudhon (1849), Louis Blanc asks whether it is possible for thirty-four millions of human beings (the population of France at that time) to carry on their affairs without accepting what the pettiest man of business finds necessary, the intermediation of representatives. He answers his own question by saying that one who declares direct action on this scale to be possible is a fool, and that one who denies its possibility need not be an absolute opponent of the idea of the state.[1] The same question and the same answer could be repeated today in respect of party organization. Above all in the great industrial centers, where the labor party sometimes numbers its adherents by tens of thousands, it is impossible to carry on the affairs of this gigantic body without a system of representation. [. . .]

It is obvious that such a gigantic number of persons belonging to a unitary organization cannot do any practical work upon a system of direct discussion. The regular holding of deliberative assemblies of a thousand members encounters the gravest difficulties in respect of room and distance; while from the topographical point of view such an assembly would become altogether impossible if the members numbered ten thousand. Even if we imagined the means of communication to become much better than those which now exist, how would it be possible to assemble such a multitude in a given place, at a stated time, and with the frequency demanded by the exigencies of party life? In addition must be considered the physiological impossibility even for the most powerful orator of making himself heard by a crowd of ten thousand persons.[2] There are, however, other persons of a technical and administrative character which render impossible the direct self- government of large groups. If Peter wrongs Paul, it is out of the question that all the other citizens should hasten to the spot to undertake a personal examination of the matter in dispute, and to take the part of Paul against Peter.[3] By parity of reasoning, in the modern democratic party, it is impossible for the collectivity to undertake the direct settlement of all the controversies that may arise.

Hence the need for delegation, for the system in which delegates represent the mass and carry out its will. Even in groups sincerely animated with the democratic spirit, current business, the preparation and the carrying out of the most important actions, is necessarily left in the hands of individuals. It is well known that the impossibility for the people to exercise a legislative power directly in popular assemblies led the democratic idealists of Spain to demand, as the least of evils, a system of popular representation and a parliamentary state.[4]

Originally the chief is merely the servant of the mass. The organization is based upon the absolute equality of all its members. [. . .] The democratic principle aims at guaranteeing to all an equal influence and an equal participation in the regulation of the common interests. All are electors, and all are eligible for office. The fundamental postulate of the *Déclaration des Droits de l'Homme* finds here its theoretical application. All the offices are filled by election. The officials, executive organs of the general will, play a merely subordinate part, are always dependent upon the collectivity, and can be deprived of their office at any moment. The mass of the party is omnipotent.

At the outset, the attempt is made to depart as little as possible from pure democracy by subordinating the delegates altogether to the will of the mass, by tieing them hand and foot. In the early days of the movement of the Italian agricultural workers, the chief of the league required a majority of four-fifths of the votes to secure election. When disputes arose with the employers about wages, the representative of the organization, before undertaking any negotiations, had to be furnished with a written authority, authorized by the signature of every member of the corporation. All the accounts of the body were open to the examination of the members, at any time. There were two reasons for this. First of all, the desire was to avoid the spread of mistrust through the mass, "this poison which gradually destroys even the strongest organism." In the second place, this usage allowed each one of the members to learn bookkeeping, and to acquire such a general knowledge of the working of the corporation as to enable him at any time to take over its leadership.[5] It is obvious that democracy in this sense is applicable only on a very small scale. In the infancy of the

English labor movement, in many of the trade unions, the delegates were either appointed in rotation from among all the members, or were chosen by lot.[6] Gradually, however, the delegates' duties became more complicated; some individual ability becomes essential, a certain oratorical gift, and a considerable amount of objective knowledge. It thus becomes impossible to trust to blind chance, to the fortune of alphabetical succession, or to the order of priority, in the choice of a delegation whose members must possess certain peculiar personal aptitudes if they are to discharge their mission to the general advantage.

Such were the methods which prevailed in the early days of the labor movement to enable the masses to participate in party and trade-union administration. Today they are falling into disuse, and in the development of the modern political aggregate there is a tendency to shorten and stereotype the process which transforms the led into a leader—a process which has hitherto developed by the natural course of events. Here and there voices make themselves heard demanding a sort of official consecration for the leaders, insisting that it is necessary to constitute a class of professional politicians, of approved and registered experts in political life. Ferdinand Tönnies advocates that the party should institute regular examinations for the nomination of socialist parliamentary candidates, and for the appointment of party secretaries.[7] Heinrich Herkner goes even farther. He contends that the great trade unions cannot long maintain their existence if they persist in entrusting the management of their affairs to persons drawn from the rank and file, who have risen to command stage by stage solely in consequence of practical aptitudes acquired in the service of the organization. He refers, in this connection, to the unions that are controlled by the employers, whose officials are for the most part university men. He foresees that in the near future all the labor organizations will be forced to abandon proletarian exclusiveness, and in the choice of their officials to give the preference to persons of an education that is superior alike in economic, legal, technical, and commercial respects.[8]

Even today, the candidates for the secretaryship of a trade union are subject to examination as to their knowledge of legal matters and their capacity as letter-writers. The socialist organizations engaged in political action also directly undertake the training of their own officials. Everywhere there are coming into existence "nurseries" for the rapid supply of officials possessing a certain amount of "scientific culture." Since 1906 there has existed in Berlin a Party-School in which courses of instruction are given for the training of those who wish to take office in the socialist party or in trade unions. The instructors are paid out of the funds of the socialist party, which was directly responsible for the foundation of the school. The other expenses of the undertaking, including the maintenance of the pupils, are furnished from a common fund supplied by the party and the various trade unions interested. In addition, the families of the pupils, in so far as the attendance of these at the school deprives the families of their breadwinners, receive an allowance from the provincial branch of the party or from the local branch of the union to which each pupil belongs. [. . .] As pupils, preference is given to comrades who already hold office in the party or in one of the labor unions.[9] Those who do not already belong to the labor bureaucracy make it their aim to enter that body, and cherish the secret hope that attendance at the school will smooth their path. Those who fail to attain this end are apt to exhibit a certain discontent with the party which, after having encouraged their studies, has sent them back to manual labor.

[. . .]

In England the trade unions and cooperative societies make use of Ruskin College, Oxford, sending thither those of their members who aspire to office in the labor organizations, and who have displayed special aptitudes for this career. In Austria it is proposed to found a party school upon the German model.

It is undeniable that all these educational institutions for the officials of the party and of the labor organizations tend, above all, towards the artificial creation of an *élite* of the working class, of a caste of cadets composed of persons who aspire to the command of the proletarian rank and file. Without wishing it, there is thus effected a continuous enlargement of the gulf which divides the leaders from the masses.

The technical specialization that inevitably results from all extensive organization renders necessary what is called expert leadership. Consequently the power of determination comes to be considered one of the specific attributes of leadership, and is gradually withdrawn from the masses to be concentrated in the hands of the leaders alone. Thus the leaders, who were at first no more than the executive organs of the collective will, soon emancipate themselves from the mass and become independent of its control.

Organization implies the tendency to oligarchy. In every organization, whether it be a political party, a professional union, or any other association of the kind, the aristocratic tendency manifests itself very clearly. The mechanism of the organization, while conferring a solidity of structure, induces serious changes in the organized mass, completely inverting the respective position of the leaders and the led. As a result of organization, every party or professional union becomes divided into a minority of directors and a majority of directed.

[. . .]

As organization develops, not only do the tasks of the administration become more difficult and more complicated, but, further, its duties become enlarged and specialized to such a degree that it is no longer possible to take them all in at a single glance. [. . .] In theory the leader is merely an employee bound by the instruction he receives. He has to carry out the orders of the mass, of which he is no more than the executive organ. But in actual fact, as the organization increases in size, this control becomes purely fictitious. The members have to give up the idea of themselves conducting or even supervising the whole administration, and are compelled to hand these tasks over to trustworthy persons specially nominated for the purpose, to salaried officials. The rank and file must content themselves with summary reports, and with the appointment of occasional special committees of inquiry. Yet this does not derive from any special change in the rules of the organization. It is by very necessity that a simple employee gradually becomes a "leader," acquiring a freedom of action which he ought not to possess. The chief then becomes accustomed to dispatch important business on his own responsibility, and to decide various questions relating to the life of the party without any attempt to consult the rank and file. It is obvious that democratic control thus undergoes a progressive diminution, and is ultimately reduced to an infinitesimal minimum. In all the socialist parties there is a continual increase in the number of functions withdrawn from the electoral assemblies and transferred to the executive committees. In this way there is constructed a powerful and complicated edifice. The principle of division of labor coming more and more into operation, executive authority undergoes division and subdivision. There is thus constituted a rigorously defined and hierarchical bureaucracy. In the catechism of party duties, the strict observance of hierarchical rules becomes the first article. The hierarchy comes into existence as the outcome of technical conditions, and its constitution is an essential postulate of the regular functioning of the party machine.

It is indisputable that the oligarchical and bureaucratic tendency of party organization is a matter of technical and practical necessity. It is the inevitable product of the very principle of organization. Not even the most radical wing of the various socialist parties raises any objection to this retrogressive evolution, the contention being that democracy is only a form of organization and that where it ceases to be possible to harmonize democracy with organization, it is better to abandon the former than the latter. Organization, since it is the only means of attaining the ends of socialism, is considered to comprise within itself the revolutionary content of the party, and this essential content must never be sacrificed for the sake of form.

[. . .]

For technical and administrative reasons, no less than for tactical reasons, a strong organization needs an equally strong leadership. As long as an organization is loosely constructed and vague in its outlines, no professional leadership can arise. The anarchists, who have a horror of all fixed organization, have no regular leaders. In the early days of German socialism, the *Vertrauensmann* (homme de confiance) continued to exercise his ordinary occupation. If he received any pay for his work for the party, the remuneration was on an extremely modest scale, and was no more than a temporary grant. His function could never be regarded by him as a regular source of income. The employee of the organization was still a simple workmate, sharing

the mode of life and the social condition of his fellows. Today he has been replaced for the most part by the professional politician, *Berzirksleiter* (U.S. ward-boss), etc. The more solid the structure of an organization becomes in the course of the evolution of the modern political party, the more marked becomes the tendency to replace the emergency leader by the professional leader. Every party organization which has attained to a considerable degree of complication demands that there should be a certain number of persons who devote all their activities to the work of the party. The mass provides these by delegations, and the delegates, regularly appointed, become permanent representatives of the mass for the direction of its affairs.

For democracy, however, the first appearance of professional leadership marks the beginning of the end, and this, above all, on account of the logical impossibility of the "representative" system, whether in parliamentary life or in party delegation. *[. . .]*

PSYCHOLOGICAL CAUSES OF LEADERSHIP

The Need for Leadership Felt by the Mass

[. . .] There is no exaggeration in the assertion that among the citizens who enjoy political rights the number of those who have a lively interest in public affairs is insignificant. In the majority of human beings the sense of an intimate relationship between the good of the individual and the good of the collectivity is but little developed. Most people are altogether devoid of understanding of the actions and reactions between that organism we call the state and their private interests, their prosperity, and their life. As de Tocqueville expresses it, they regard it as far more important to consider "whether it is worthwhile to put a road through their land,"[10] than to interest themselves in the general work of public administration. The majority is content, with Stirner, to call out to the state, "Get away from between me and the sun!" Stirner makes fun of all those who, in accordance with the views of Kant, preach it to humanity as a "sacred duty" to take an interest in public affairs. "Let those persons who have a personal interest in political changes concern themselves with these. Neither now nor at any future

time will 'sacred duty' lead people to trouble themselves about the state, just as little as it is by 'sacred duty' that they become men of science, artists, etc. Egoism alone can spur people to an interest in public affairs, and will spur them—when matters grow a good deal worse."[11]

In the life of modern democratic parties we may observe signs of similar indifference. It is only a minority which participates in party decisions, and sometimes that minority is ludicrously small. The most important resolutions taken by the most democratic of all parties, the socialist party, always emanate from a handful of the members. It is true that the renouncement of the exercise of democratic rights is voluntary; except in those cases, which are common enough, where the active participation of the organized mass in party life is prevented by geographical or topographical conditions.

[. . .] Even in countries like France, where collective political education is of older date, the majority renounces all active participation in tactical and administrative questions, leaving these to the little group which makes a practice of attending meetings. [. . .]

[. . .] The great majority of the members will not attend meetings unless some noted orator is to speak, or unless some extremely striking warcry is sounded for their attraction, such as, in France, "A bas la vie chère!", or, in Germany, "Down with personal government!" A good meeting can also be held when there is a cinema-show, or a popular scientific lecture illustrated by lantern-slides. In a word, the ordinary members have a weakness for everything which appeals to their eyes and for such spectacles as will always attract a gaping crowd.

It may be added that the regular attendants at public meetings and committees are by no means always proletarians—especially where the smaller centers are concerned. When his work is finished, the proletarian can think only of rest, and of getting to bed in good time. His place at meetings is taken by petty bourgeois, by those who come to sell newspapers and picture-postcards, by clerks, by young intellectuals who have not yet got a position in their own circle, people who are all glad to hear themselves spoken of as authentic proletarians and to be glorified as the class of the future.

The same thing happens in party life as happens in the state. In both, the demand for monetary supplies is upon a coercive foundation, but the electoral system has no established sanction. An electoral right exists, but no electoral duty. Until this duty is superimposed upon the right, it appears probable that a small minority only will continue to avail itself of the right which the majority voluntarily renounces, and that the minority will always dictate laws for the indifferent and apathetic mass. The consequence is that, in the political groupings of democracy, the participation in party life has an echeloned aspect. The extensive base consists of the great mass of electors; upon this is superposed the enormously smaller mass of enrolled members of the local branch of the party, numbering perhaps one-tenth or even as few as one-thirtieth of the electors; above this, again, comes the much smaller number of the members who regularly attend meetings; next comes the group of officials of the party; and highest of all, consisting in part of the same individuals as the last group, come the half-dozen or so members of the executive committee. Effective power is here in inverse ratio to the number of those who exercise it. Thus practical democracy is represented by the following diagram:—

Though it grumbles occasionally, the majority is really delighted to find persons who will take the trouble to look after its affairs. In the mass, and even in the organized mass of the labor parties, there is an immense need for direction and guidance. This need is accompanied by a genuine cult for the leaders, who are regarded as heroes. [. . .]

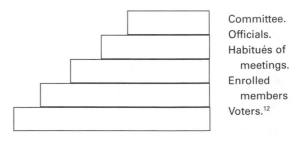

Committee.
Officials.
Habitués of
  meetings.
Enrolled
  members
Voters.[12]

Figure 21.1.

INTELLECTUAL FACTORS

Superiority of the Professional Leaders in Respect to Culture, and Their Indispensability; the Formal and Real Incompetence of the Mass

In the infancy of the socialist party, when the organization is still weak, when its membership is scanty, and when its principal aim is to diffuse a knowledge of the elementary principles of socialism, professional leaders are less numerous than are leaders whose work in this department is no more than an accessory occupation. But with the further progress of the organization, new needs continually arise, at once within the party and in respect of its relationships with the outer world. Thus the moment inevitably comes when neither the idealism and enthusiasm of the intellectuals, nor yet the goodwill with which the proletarians devote their free time on Sundays to the work of the party, suffice any longer to meet the requirements of the case. The provisional must then give place to the permanent, and dilettantism must yield to professionalism.

With the appearance of professional leadership, there ensues a great accentuation of the cultural differences between the leaders and the led. [. . .]

[. . .] The party mechanism, which, through the abundance of paid and honorary posts at its disposal, offers a career to the workers, and which consequently exercises a powerful attractive force, determines the transformation of a number of proletarians with considerable intellectual gifts into employees whose mode of life becomes that of the petty bourgeois. This change of condition at once creates the need and provides the opportunity for the acquisition, at the expense of the mass, of more elaborate instruction and a clearer view of existing social relationships. Whilst their occupation and the needs of daily life render it impossible for the masses to attain to a profound knowledge of the social machinery, and above all of the working of the political machine, the leader of working-class origin is enabled, thanks to his new situation, to make himself intimately familiar with all the technical details of public life, and thus to increase his superiority over the rank and file. In proportion as the profession of politician becomes a more complicated one, and in proportion as the rules of social legislation become more numerous, it is necessary for one who would understand politics to possess wider experience and more extensive knowledge. Thus the gulf between the leaders and the rest of the party becomes ever wider, until the moment arrives in which the leaders lose all true sense of solidarity with the class from which they have sprung, and there ensues a new class-division between exproletarian captains and proletarian common soldiers. When the workers choose leaders for themselves, they are with their own hands creating new masters whose principal means of dominion is found in their better instructed minds.

[. . .]

In parallelism with the corresponding phenomena in industrial and commercial life, it is evident that with the growth of working-class organization there must be an accompanying growth in the value, the importance, and the authority of the leaders. The principle of the division of labor creates specialism, and it is with good reason that the necessity for expert leadership has been compared with that which gives rise to specialism in the medical profession and in technical chemistry. Specialism, however, implies authority. Just as the patient obeys the doctor, because the doctor knows better than the patient, having made a special study of the human body in health and disease, so must the political patient submit to the guidance of his party leaders, who possess a political competence impossible of attainment by the rank and file.

Thus democracy ends by undergoing transformation into a form of government by the best, into an aristocracy. [. . .]

AUTOCRATIC TENDENCIES OF LEADERS

The Position of the Leaders in Relation to the Masses in Actual Practice

[. . .] Societies for cooperative production, on the other hand, and especially the smaller of these, offer in theory the best imaginable field for democratic collaboration. They consist of homogeneous elements belonging to the same stratum of the working class, of persons following the same trade, and accustomed to the same manner of life. In so far as the society needs a management, this management can readily be effected by all the members in common, since all possess the same professional competence, and all can lend a hand as advisers and coadjutors. In a political party it is impossible that every member should be engaged in important political work, and it is for this reason that in the political party there necessarily exists a great gulf between the leaders and the rank and file. But in a society for cooperative production, for bootmaking for example, all the members are equally competent in the making of boots, the use of tools, and knowledge of the quality of leather. There do not exist among them any essential differences in matters of technical knowledge. Yet despite the fact that the circumstances are thus exceptionally favorable for the constitution of a democratic organism, we cannot as a general rule regard productive cooperatives as models of democratic auto-administration. Rodbertus said on one occasion that when he imagined productive associations to have extended their activities to include all manufacture, commerce, and agriculture, when he conceived all social work to be effected by small cooperative societies in whose management every member had an equal voice, he was unable to avoid the conviction that the economic system would succumb to the cumbrousness of its own machinery.[13] The history of productive cooperation shows that all the societies have been faced with the following dilemma: either they succumb rapidly owing to discord and powerlessness resulting from the fact that too many individuals have the right to interfere in their administration; or else they end by submitting to the will of one or of a few persons, and thus lose their truly cooperative character. In almost all cases such enterprises owe their origin to the personal initiative of one or a few members. They are sometimes miniature monarchies, being under the dictatorship of the manager, who represents them in all internal and external relations, and upon whose will they depend so absolutely that if he dies or resigns his post they run the risk of perishing. This tendency on the part of the productive cooperative societies is further accentuated by their character as aggregates of individuals whose personal advantages decrease in proportion as the number of the members increases. Thus from their very nature they are subject to the same

immutable psychological laws which governed the evolution of the medieval guilds. As they become more prosperous, they become also more exclusive, and tend always to monopolize for the benefit of the existing members the advantages they have been able to secure. For example, by imposing a high entrance fee they put indirect obstacles in the way of the entry of new members. In some cases they simply refuse to accept new members, or pass a rule establishing a maximum membership. When they have need of more labor-power they supply this need by engaging ordinary wage-laborers. Thus we not infrequently find that a society for cooperative production becomes gradually transformed into a joint-stock company. It even happens occasionally that the cooperative society becomes the private enterprise of the manager. In both these cases Kautsky is right in saying that the social value of the working-class cooperative is then limited to the provision of means for certain proletarians which will enable them to climb out of their own class into a higher.

[. . .]

The Struggle Between the Leaders and the Masses

Those who defend the arbitrary acts committed by the democracy, point out that the masses have at their disposal means whereby they can react against the violation of their rights. These means consist in the right of controlling and dismissing their leaders. Unquestionably this defense possesses a certain theoretical value, and the authoritarian inclinations of the leaders are in some degree attenuated by these possibilities. In states with a democratic tendency and under a parliamentary regime, to obtain the fall of a detested minister it suffices, in theory, that the people should be weary of him. In the same way, once more in theory, the ill-humor and the opposition of a socialist group or of an election committee is enough to effect the recall of a deputy's mandate, and in the same way the hostility of the majority at the annual congress of trade unions should be enough to secure the dismissal of a secretary. In practice, however, the exercise of this theoretical right is interfered with by the working of the whole series of conservative tendencies to which allusion has previously been made, so that the supremacy of the autonomous and sovereign masses is rendered purely illusory. *[. . .]*

With the institution of leadership there simultaneously begins, owing to the long tenure of office, the transformation of the leaders into a closed caste.

Unless, as in France, extreme individualism and fanatical political dogmatism stand in the way, the old leaders present themselves to the masses as a compact phalanx—at any rate whenever the masses are so much aroused as to endanger the position of the leaders.

The election of the delegates to congresses, etc., is sometimes regulated by the leaders by means of special agreements, whereby the masses are in fact excluded from all decisive influence in the management of their affairs. These agreements often assume the aspect of a mutual insurance contract. In the German Socialist Party, a few years ago, there came into existence in not a few localities a regular system in accordance with which the leaders nominated one another in rotation as delegates to the various party congresses. In the meetings at which the delegates were appointed, one of the big guns would always propose to the comrades the choice as delegate of the leader whose "turn" it was. The comrades rarely revolt against such artifices, and often fail even to perceive them. Thus competition among the leaders is prevented, in this domain at least; and at the same time there is rendered impossible anything more than passive participation of the rank and file in the higher functions of the life of that party which they alone sustain with their subscription.[14] Notwithstanding the violence of the intestine struggles which divide the leaders, in all the democracies they manifest vis-à-vis the masses a vigorous solidarity. "They perceive quickly enough the necessity for agreeing among themselves so that the party cannot escape them by becoming divided."[15] This is true above all of the German social democracy, in which, in consequence of the exceptional solidity of structure which it possesses as compared with all the other socialist parties of the world, conservative tendencies have attained an extreme development.

When there is a struggle between the leaders and the masses, the former are always victorious if only they remain united. At least it rarely happens that the masses succeed in disembarrassing themselves of one of their leaders.

[. . .]

There is no indication whatever that the power possessed by the oligarchy in party life is likely to be overthrown within an appreciable time. The independence of the leaders increases concurrently with their indispensability. Nay more, the influence which they exercise and the financial security of their position become more and more fascinating to the masses, stimulating the ambition of all the more talented elements to enter the privileged bureaucracy of the labor movement. Thus the rank and file becomes continually more impotent to provide new and intelligent forces capable of leading the opposition which may be latent among the masses.[16] *[. . .]*

It cannot be denied that the masses revolt from time to time, but their revolts are always suppressed. It is only when the dominant classes, struck by sudden blindness, pursue a policy which strains social relationships to the breaking-point, that the party masses appear actively on the stage of history and overthrow the power of the oligarchies. Every autonomous movement of the masses signifies a profound discordance with the will of the leaders. Apart from such transient interruptions, the natural and normal development of thc organization will impress upon the most revolutionary of parties an indelible stamp of conservatism.

FINAL CONSIDERATIONS

Leadership is a necessary phenomenon in every form of social life. Consequently it is not the task of science to inquire whether this phenomenon is good or evil, or predominantly one or the other. But there is great scientific value in the demonstration that every system of leadership is incompatible with the most essential postulates of democracy. We are now aware that the law of the historic necessity of oligarchy is primarily based upon a series of facts of experience. Like all other scientific laws, sociological laws are derived from empirical observation. In order, however, to deprive our axiom of its purely descriptive character, and to confer upon it that status of analytical explanation which can alone transform a formula into a law, it does not suffice to contemplate from a unitary outlook those phenomena which may be empirically established; we must also study the determining causes of these phenomena. Such has been our task.

Now, if we leave out of consideration the tendency of the leaders to organize themselves and to consolidate their interests, and if we leave also out of considerations the gratitude of the led towards the leaders, and the general immobility and passivity of the masses, we are led to conclude that the principal cause of oligarchy in the democratic parties is to be found in the technical indispensability of leadership.

The process which has begun in consequence of the differentiation of functions in the party is completed by a complex of qualities which the leaders acquire through their detachment from the mass. At the outset, leaders arise *spontaneously*; their functions are *accessory* and *gratuitous*. Soon, however, they become *professional* leaders, and in this second stage of development they are *stable* and *irremovable*.

It follows that the explanation of the oligarchical phenomenon which thus results is partly *psychological*; oligarchy derives, that is to say, from the psychical transformations which the leading personalities in the parties undergo in the course of their lives. But also, and still more, oligarchy depends upon what we may term the *psychology of organization itself*, that is to say, upon the tactical and technical necessities which result from the consolidation of every disciplined political aggregate. Reduced to its most concise expression, the fundamental sociological law of political parties (the term "political" being here used in its most comprehensive significance) may be formulated in the following terms: "It is organization which gives birth to the dominion of the elected over the electors, of the mandataries over the mandators, of the delegates over the delegators. Who says organization, says oligarchy."

Every party organization represents an oligarchical power grounded upon a democratic basis. We find everywhere electors and elected. Also we find everywhere that the power of the elected leaders over the electing masses is almost unlimited. The oligarchical structure of the building suffocates the basic democratic principle. That which IS oppresses *that which ought to be*. For the masses, this essential difference between the reality and the ideal remains a mystery. Socialists often cherish a sincere belief that a new *élite* of politicians will keep faith better than did the old. The notion of the representation of popular interests, a notion to which the great majority of democrats, and in especial the working-class masses of the German-speaking lands, cleave with so much tenacity and confidence, is an illusion engendered by a false illumination, is an effect of mirage. [. . .] [T]he modern proletariat, enduringly influenced by glib-tongued persons intellectually superior to the mass, ends by believing that by flocking to the poll and entrusting its social and economic cause to a delegate, its direct participation in power will be assured.

The formation of oligarachies within the various forms of democracy is the outcome of organic necessity, and consequently affects every organization, be it socialist or even anarchist. Haller long ago noted that in every form of social life relationships of dominion and of dependence are created by Nature herself.[17] The supremacy of the leaders in the democratic and revolutionary parties has to be taken into account in every historic situation present and to come, even though only a few and exceptional minds will be fully conscious of its existence. The mass will never rule except *in abstracto*. Consequently the question we have to discuss is not whether ideal democracy is realizable, but rather to what point and in what degree democracy is desirable, possible, and realizable at a given moment. In the problem as thus stated we recognize the fundamental problem of politics as a science. Whoever fails to perceive this must, as Sombart says, either be so blind and fanatical as not to see that the democratic current daily makes undeniable advance, or else must be so inexperienced and devoid of critical faculty as to be unable to understand that all order and all civilization must exhibit aristocratic features.[18] The great error of socialists, an error committed in consequence of their lack of adequate psychological knowledge, is to be found in their combination of pessimism regarding the present, with rosy optimism and immeasurable confidence regarding the future. A realistic view of the mental condition of the masses shows beyond question that even if we admit the possibility of moral improvement in mankind, the human materials with whose use politicians and philosophers cannot dispense in their plans of social reconstruction are not of a character to justify excessive optimism. Within the limits of time for which human provision is possible, optimism will remain the exclusive privilege of utopian thinkers.

The socialist parties, like the trade unions are living forms of social life. As such they react with the utmost energy against any attempt to analyze their structure or their nature, as if it were a method of vivisection. When science attains to results which conflict with their apriorist ideology, they revolt with all their power. Yet their defense is extremely feeble. Those among the representatives of such organizations whose scientific earnestness and personal good faith make it impossible for them to deny outright the existence of oligarchical tendencies in every form of democracy, endeavor to explain these tendencies as the outcome of a kind of atavism in the mentality of the masses, characteristic of the youth of the movement. The masses, they assure us, are still infected by the oligarchic virus simply because they have been oppressed during long centuries of slavery, and have never yet enjoyed an autonomous existence. The socialist regime, however, will soon restore them to health, and will furnish them with all the capacity necessary for self-government. Nothing could be more antiscientific than the supposition that as soon as socialists have gained possession of governmental power it will suffice for the masses to exercise a little control over their leaders to secure that the interests of these leaders shall coincide perfectly with the interests of the led. [. . .]

The objective immaturity of the mass is not a mere transitory phenomenon which will disappear with the progress of democratization *au lendemain du socialisme*. On the contrary, it derives from the very nature of the mass as mass, for this, even when organized, suffers from an incurable incompetence for the solution of the diverse problems which present themselves for solution—because the mass *per se* is amorphous, and therefore needs division of labor, specialization, and guidance, "The human species wants to be governed; it will be. I am ashamed of my kind," wrote Proudhon from his prison in 1850.[19] Man as individual is by nature predestined to be guided, and to be guided all the more in proportion as the functions of life undergo division and subdivision. To an enormously greater degree is guidance necessary for the social group.

From this chain of reasoning and from these scientific convictions it would be erroneous to conclude that we should renounce all endeavors to ascertain the limits which may be imposed upon the powers exercised over the individual by oligarchies (state, dominant class, party, etc.). It would be an error to abandon the desperate enterprise of endeavoring to discover a social order which will render possible the complete realization of the idea of popular sovereignty. In the present work, as the writer said at the outset, it has not been his aim to indicate new paths. But it seemed necessary to lay considerable stress upon the pessimist aspect of democracy which is forced on us by historical study. We had to inquire whether, and within what limits, democracy must remain purely ideal, possessing no other value than that of a moral criterion which renders it possible to appreciate the varying degrees of that oligarchy which is immanent in every social regime. In other words, we have had to inquire if, and in what degree, democracy is an ideal which we can never hope to realize in practice. A further aim of this work was the demolition of some of the facile and superficial democratic illusions which trouble science and lead the masses astray. Finally, the author desired to throw light upon certain sociological tendencies which oppose the reign of democracy, and to a still greater extent oppose the reign of socialism.

The writer does not wish to deny that every revolutionary working-class movement, and every movement sincerely inspired by the democratic spirit, may have a certain value as contributing to the enfeeblement of oligarchic tendencies. The peasant in the fable, when on his death-bed, tells his sons that a treasure is buried in the field. After the old man's death the sons dig everywhere in order to discover the treasure. They do not find it. But their indefatigable labor improves the soil and secures for them a comparative well-being. The treasure in the fable may well symbolize democracy. Democracy is a treasure which no one will ever discover by deliberate search. But in continuing our search, in laboring indefatigably to discover the undiscoverable, we shall perform a work which will have fertile results in the democratic sense. We have seen, indeed, that within the bosom of the democratic working-class party are born the very tendencies to counteract which that party came into existence. Thanks to the diversity and to the unequal worth of the elements of the party, these tendencies often give rise to manifestations which border on tyranny. We have seen that the replacement of the traditional legitimism of the powers-that-be by the brutal plebiscitary rule of Bonapartist parvenus does not furnish these tendencies with any moral or aesthetic superiority. Historical evolution mocks all the prophylactic measures that have been adopted for the prevention of oligarchy. If laws are passed to control the dominion of the leaders, it is the laws which gradually weaken, and not the leaders. Sometimes, however, the democratic principle carries with it, if not a cure, at least a palliative, for the disease of oligarchy. *[. . .]* It is, in fact, a general characteristic of democracy, and hence also of the labor movement, to stimulate and to strengthen in the individual the intellectual aptitudes for criticism and control. We have seen how the progressive bureaucratization of the democratic organism tends to neutralize the beneficial effects of such criticism and such control. None the less it is true that the labor movement, in virtue of the theoretical postulates it proclaims, is apt to bring into existence (in opposition to the will of the leaders) a certain number of free spirits who, moved by principle, by instinct, or by both, desire to revise the base upon which authority is established. Urged on by conviction or by temperament, they are never weary of asking an eternal "Why?" about every human institution. Now this predisposition towards free inquiry, in which we cannot fail to recognize one of the most precious factors of civilization, will gradually increase in proportion as the economic status of the masses undergoes improvement and becomes more stable, and in proportion as they are admitted more effectively to the advantages of civilization. A wider education involves an increasing capacity for exercising control. Can we not observe every day that among the well-to-do the authority of the leaders over the led, extensive though it be, is never so unrestricted as in the case of the leaders of the poor? Taken in the mass, the poor are powerless and disarmed vis-à-vis their leaders. Their intellectual and cultural inferiority makes it impossible for them to see whither the leader is going, or to estimate in advance the significance of his actions. It is, consequently, the great task of social education to raise the intellectual level of the masses, so that they may

be enabled, within the limits of what is possible, to counteract the oligarchical tendencies of the working-class movement.

[. . .]

The democratic currents of history resemble successive waves. They break ever on the same shoal. They are ever renewed. This enduring spectacle is simultaneously encouraging and depressing. When democracies have gained a certain stage of development, they undergo a gradual transformation, adopting the aristocratic spirit, and in many cases also the aristocratic forms, against which at the outset they struggled so fiercely. Now new accusers arise to denounce the traitors: after an era of glorious combats and of inglorious power, they end by fusing with the old dominant class; whereupon once more they are in their turn attacked by fresh opponents who appeal to the name of democracy. It is probable that this cruel game will continue without end.

NOTES

1. Louis Blanc, "L'état dans une démocratie," *Questions d'aujourd'hui et de demain*, Dentu, Paris, 1880, vol. iii, p. 150.

2. Wilhelm Roscher, *Politik, Geschichtliche Naturlehre der Monarchie, Aristokratie und Demokratie*, Cotta, Stuttgart-Berlin, 1908, 3rd ed., p. 351.

3. Louis Blanc, op. cit., p. 144.

4. Cf. the letter of Antonio Quiroga to King Ferdinand VII, dated January 7, 1820 (Don Juan van Halen, *Mémoires*, Renouard, Paris, 1827, Part II, p. 382).

5. Egidio Bernaroli, *Manuale per la constituzione e il funzionamento delle leghe dei contadini*, Libreria Soc. Ital., Rome, 1902, pp. 20, 26, 27, 52.

6. Sidney and Beatrice Webb, *Industrial Democracy* (German edition), Stuttgart, 1898, vol. i, p. 6.

7. Ferdinant Tönnies, *Politik und Moral*, Neuer Frankf. Verl., Frankfort, 1901, p. 46.

8. Heinrich Herkner, *Die Arbeiterfrage*, Guttentag, Berlin, 1908, 5th ed., pp. 116, 117.

9. *Protokoll des Parteitags zu Leipzig*, 1909, "Vorwärts," Berlin, 1909, p. 48.

10. Trans. from Alexis de Tocqueville, *De La Democratie en Amerique*, Gosseliné, Pris, 1849, vol. p. 167.

11. Max Stirner (Kaspar Schmidt), *Der Einzige und sein Eigentum*, Reclam, Leipzig, 1892, p. 272.

12. This figure must not be regarded as intended to represent such relationships according to scale, for this would require an entire page. It is purely diagrammatic.

13. Karl Rodbertus, *Offener Brief an das Komitee des deutschen Arbeitervereins zu Leipzig*, in F. Lassalle's *Politische Reden und Schriften*, Hrsg. von E. Blum, Leipzig, K.F. Pfau [c.1895], vol. ii, p. 9.

14. Similar phenomena have been observed in party life in America (Astrogorsky, *La Démocratie, etc.*, ed, cit., vol. ii, p. 196).

15. Trans. from Antoine Elisée Cherbuliez, *Théorie des Garantis constitutionelles*, Ab. Cherbuliez, Paris, 1838, vol. ii, p. 253.

16. Thus Pareto writes: "If B [the new élite] took the place of A [the old élite] by slow infiltration, and if the social circulation is not interrupted, C [the masses] are deprived of the leaders who could incite them to revolt." (Trans. from Vilfredo Pareto, *Les Systèmes socialistes*, Giard and Brière, Paris, 1892, vol. i, p. 35).

17. Ludwig von Haller, *Restauration der Staatswissenschaften*, Winterhur, 1816, vol. i, pp. 304 et seq.

18. Werner Sombart, *Dennoch!*, et. cit., p. 90. Cf. also F. S. Merlino *Pro e contro il Socialismo*, ed. cit., pp. 262 et seq.

19. Charles Gide et Charles Rist, *Histoire des Doctrines économiques depuis les Physiocrates jusquà nos jours,* Larose et Tenin, Paris, 1909, p. 709.

PART VII

ORGANIZATIONS AS OPEN SYSTEMS: ORGANIZATIONS AND THEIR ENVIRONMENTS

A. Resource Dependency Theory

B. Institutional Theory

C. Organizational Ecology

In the mid- to late 1970s a remarkable flowering of organizational theory swept aside contingency theory and eclipsed a number of the other perspectives represented in previous sections. Almost all of the previous readings have examined the internal structure and functioning of organizations, considering the individual organization itself as if closed off from the outside world. The new perspectives were diverse, but all shared a view of organizations as open systems that are powerfully shaped by their organizational or broader societal environments. Some of the new open systems theories were more rationalistic in their orientation, and others treated the organization-environment dynamic in more social systems terms. They are among the most widely used theoretical perspectives in organization studies today.

The new focus represented an important insight that an organization's external environment may be a critical source of resources, constraints, ideas, standards, and opportunities that would be overlooked if one focused on the individual organization alone. Relevant features of an organization's environment can include the following:

- the labor force, suppliers, customers, and clients
- competitors
- other organizations with which an organization conducts transactions or has other relations
- professional associations or bodies, such as accreditation committees
- government
- communities in which the organization operates

- the existing stock of knowledge and technological resources
- the broader social and cultural environment.

The three open systems theories considered here are *resource dependency theory*, *institutional theory*, and *organizational ecology*, and all point to some or all of these environmental features as important.

A. RESOURCE DEPENDENCY THEORY

The readings in Part VI examined power within organizations. Resource dependency theory focuses on the consequences of power differences between organizations. Jeffrey Pfeffer and Gerald Salancik (Reading 18) began with the simple insight that all organizations need to draw resources from their environment, whether it is for their labor force, physical inputs, customers or clients, information, investment or funding, or the legal permission or normative legitimacy to operate. Most management writers examine the inside workings of an organization and tend to see activity as internally generated and reflecting the will of its leadership. However, Pfeffer and Salancik argue that an organization's behavior is mostly a response to environmental constraints or attempts to break free of them. Organizations are not autonomous, but often dependent on other organizations and seek ways to manage those dependencies.

Pfeffer and Salancik draw on Richard Emerson's (1962) theory of power-dependence relations to understand which organizations are more constrained by others. In this view, an individual or organization A has power over B to the extent that A has control over a resource that B needs badly, B does not have access to many alternative sources of supply, and B has no similar countervailing power over A.

For example, General Motors has power over its smaller suppliers to the extent that each of those suppliers individually accounts for a small fraction of a car's value and there are many competing firms offering the same part, whereas GM accounts for a large percentage of each supplier's sales and there are only a limited number of other buyers of the supplier's product. Clearly, the exchange is not equally important to both organizations; the relationship is asymmetrical. GM has the power to demand low prices and tight delivery schedules, whereas suppliers have fewer options and are highly dependent on GM's continued favor.

Organizations try to manage their environment to reduce dependence and uncertainty and to gain greater freedom of action and stability. Pfeffer and Salancik explain the drive for growth and the acquisition of suppliers and customer firms as mechanisms to reduce dependence on other actors and to secure tighter control of resources. Organizations also might try to win friends and gain access to information, bank loans, and other resources by offering positions on their board of directors to influential leaders of other organizations, members of the community, or those with political connections (Mizruchi 1996). Thus larger companies and those more subject to government regulation are more likely to have a higher percentage of outside directors as a way to co-opt otherwise unsympathetic or uninvolved actors. Hospitals that depend on outside fund-raising are more likely to select board members from the banking community. If these strategies fail, organizations can lobby the government directly for favorable tax and regulatory treatment (Pfeffer and Salancik 1978).

Some have criticized resource dependency theory for overemphasizing the political dimension of organizations while overlooking explanations of their actions based on internal management and efficiency considerations (Donaldson 1995). However, though resource dependency theory never developed into a theoretical school in the way that institutional theory and organizational ecology have done so, its insights into the nature and possible effects of interorganizational power relationships are part of the theoretical tool kit of almost everyone working in organizational studies today.

B. Institutional Theory

Institutional theory[1] also examines the impact of the environment on organizations from a natural or social systems perspective. Rational theories, such as mainstream economics or contingency theory, explain the structure and functioning of organizations on efficiency grounds. Paul J. DiMaggio and Walter W. Powell argue that this ignores the role of powerful external institutions such as the state, societal norms, traditions, and conventions, and imitation in shaping organizational practice (Reading 19). These forces exert pressure on organizations to conform to accepted standards independent of efficiency considerations. As institutionalists John W. Meyer and Brian Rowan write, the practices of "modern organization are enforced by public opinion, views of important constituents, social prestige, [and] laws" and represent "prefabricated formulae" that certify the organization as rational and modern (Meyer and Rowan 1977, pp. 343ff.). Bureaucracy has become a norm to which organizationsmust conform if they are to be recognized as legitimate by important actors in their environment. The members of an organization may not even be able to conceive of acting according to another model.

DiMaggio and Powell identify three processes that have channeled organizational practice into a similar, or isomorphic, direction independent of purely technical considerations.

Government exerts pressure through legal norms, such as recognition of the right to organize unions, government contracts and regulation, and affirmative action, which had powerful effects on company personnel practices (Baron, Dobbin, and Jennings 1986; Dobbin, Sutton, Meyer and Scott 1993). Powerful private organizations may also issue binding rules that bring subsidiaries or other dependent organizations into conformity. For example, participatory community organizations that interface with more hierarchical donors find themselves under pressure to become more bureaucratic to satisfy the grantors' demands for accountability and regularity. DiMaggio and Powell refer to this process as *coercive isomorphism.*

Organizations also imitate other, successful organizations, even if there is little understanding of the reasons for their success, due to bounded rationality. This creates enthusiasm for management fads and bandwagons that may or may not contribute to an organization's efficiency. DiMaggio and Powell refer to this as *mimetic isomorphism,* and suggest that some of the excitement over Japanese management techniques in the 1980s especially may have reflected this process. There is evidence that a company's external reputation is enhanced if it adopts teams and Total Quality Management (TQM) programs, such as found at Saturn or Isuzu, even when they have no measurable impact on financial performance measures (Staw and Epstein 2000). Interestingly, the reversal of U.S. and Japanese fortunes in the 1990s has created pressure among Japanese firms to emulate American organizational practices, such as eliminating job security for workers, based on what many would see as equally superficial evidence that such policies are the source of recent American success.

Organizational practice also reflects professional or societal conceptions of what is natural and appropriate, especially if championed by a particular group of advocates, which DiMaggio and Powell call *normative isomorphism*. Pamela Tolbert and Lynne Zucker (1983) found that municipal civil service reforms followed a two-phase pattern between the late nineteenth and early twentieth centuries. The first cities to adopt formal qualifications, examinations, and other merit-based hiring criteria were those with high immigrant populations, which were likely to use political loyalty and ethnic and personal favoritism in recruitment to government employment prior to civil service reform. However, cities that subsequently adopted the reforms did not have these characteristics. Tolbert and Zucker conclude that later adopters of civil service systems did so in order to appear modern, efficient, and rational, rather than in response to any practical need.

The first phase of diffusion may have reflected efficiency considerations, but the second phase reflected conformity pressures to adopt what was now taken for granted as appropriate and normative. To fail to adopt a civil service system would make a city's government appear backward and suspect. Adoption was also spurred by an advocacy group of middle-class professionals, the Progressives, who identified reform with progress and science. A contemporary example may be private corporations that have continued to use race-sensitive policies in the form of diversity management with the support of another group of professionals, human resource managers and consultants, even after affirmative action enforcement was relaxed (Kelly and Dobbin 1998).

In practice, DiMaggio and Powell's isomorphic processes are sensitizing concepts and are often present in combination. Thus, one finds that nonprofit groups adopt more formal structures and hire more paid staff to replace volunteers to gain government funds and because normative forces define one way of organizing as more professional than another. Likewise, when a public television station, hospital, or university adopts practices or an organizational structure similar to business, potential donors view it with greater legitimacy. In the current political climate, even government administration gains greater legitimacy when it adopts a business model. External legitimacy is so significant that organizations seek it even when the costs of such a strategy in a purely technical sense might exceed the benefits. For example, voluntary organizations might hire professionals to satisfy external constituencies even though this increases personnel costs and the distance between the organization and its members (Zucker 1983, pp. 18ff.).

However, the power of institutions does not always lead to deep changes. Sometimes, it prompts organizations to engage in various ceremonies or rituals to appease powerful constituencies or public attitudes (Meyer and Rowan 1977). Quality improvement programs may look good, but exist more on paper than in practice. Important-sounding but substantively empty "mission statements" may be announced with great fanfare, but have little effect on actual organizational functioning. Some practices may make strong claims to rationality. However, if no one actually reads, understands, or believes econometric analyses and forecasts, they may be used mostly to secure legitimacy in the eyes of investors, lenders, and others within the organization, as well as providing cover in case of failure, rather than because they are useful for efficiency reasons (Meyer and Rowan 1977; Galbraith and Merrill 1996).

Whereas Weber saw bureaucratization as part of an inevitable trend toward greater rationality and efficiency, institutional theory argues that similarities in organization structure and function are the result of pressures for conformity independent of technical efficiency. In this view, an organization's success depends as much on its external legitimacy in terms of the wider sociocultural environment as its internal operational efficiency.

Institutional theory, along with organizational ecology, is probably the most widely used intellectual perspective in organization studies today, but despite its usefulness in highlighting the nonrational and ceremonial nature of many purportedly rational practices, it has also attracted criticisms.

Institutional theory is a mixture of various explanations. It is unclear whether the argument is that organizations follow rules because they are a taken-for-granted part of the culture or because they are rewarded for or coerced into doing so, as resource dependency theory might also argue, though resource dependency theory is likely to explain the reasons why external organizations might exercise coercive pressure in far more rationalistic terms than institutional theory.

Power and conflict within organizations or contending social groups receive less attention in favor of explanations based on cognitive, normative, and legal variables. For example, institutional theory explains the recent spread of quality control techniques as a result of imitation and evolving norms rather than as a means to control labor, as Laurie Graham argues (see Reading 14). One wonders how institutional theory might explain the spread of Taylorism.

Others argue that often it is difficult to rule out competing, efficiency-based explanations (Donaldson 1995). Even Meyer and Rowan (1977) acknowledge that market-based organizations are likely to be more efficiency-driven than nonprofits like schools, hospitals, and government agencies, which were the focus of early institutionalist study. In government and nonprofit organizations, measuring organizational success is difficult because there is no simple profit criterion, competition between organizations that weeds out the less efficient is less developed, and the technical efficacy of the methods of operation is consequently less clear. This means that control is often achieved by measuring inputs, such as time at work, and ensuring conformity to professional and legal standards, rather than attempting to measure the quantity or quality of outputs, such as the number of students a teacher instructs or operations a surgeon performs (Scott 1998, p. 139).

Also, until recently, institutional theory has not accounted for organizational innovation and change in the face of external pressures to conform to norms and standards, coming close to an oversocialized view of organizational behavior. More recent developments in institutional theory identify factors contributing to deinstitutionalization such as changes in organizational membership, ownership, and control; new government regulations; and shifts in public opinion (Oliver 1992). However, one of the most important may be dramatic declines in performance, which points to the importance of traditional efficiency concerns, though responses to crises and even the definition of what constitutes a crisis may well be shaped by broader sociocultural forces.

Despite these issues, institutional theory remains the most important contemporary natural systems perspective dealing with nonrational aspects of organizations such as habit, imitation, fashion, ideology, norms, values, politics, and history.

C. ORGANIZATIONAL ECOLOGY

Organizational ecology, previously known as population ecology, is one of the most distinctive theories within organization studies. Not only does organizational ecology have virtually no interest in the internal workings of organizations, it is not concerned with individual organizations at all. Organizational ecology is a macro perspective that uses sophisticated mathematical models, often borrowed from population biology, to study the growth patterns of *populations* of organizations. This perspective has been used to study the growth of organizational populations as diverse as semiconductor manufacturing, breweries, day care centers, social service agencies, labor unions, political advocacy and protest organizations, newspapers, restaurants, and trade associations.

Organizational ecology begins with the assumption that organizations tend not to change internally once they are firmly established. The need to perform reliably leads most organizations to be set in their ways, which is efficient when the environment is stable. But resistance to internal change means that the evolution of the organizational landscape is mostly the result of organizational births and deaths, or foundings and disbandings, rather than change within existing organizations to adapt to altered circumstances. Consequently, environmental conditions, such as the intensity of competition for resources, rather than internal policies or decisions are the key to organizational success.

Glenn Carroll and Michael Hannan argue that the key environmental variable is the number of existing organizations (*population density*) of a given type (Reading 20). When examples of a new kind of organization first appear, the scarcity of similar organizations and their unfamiliarity mean that such organizations have low legitimacy and find it difficult to attract resources. Organizational birth rates are low, death rates are high, and the population grows slowly. However, additional births of such organizations increase their legitimacy. The mere growth of the organizational population breeds familiarity, enhances the legitimacy of existing cases, and encourages new foundings. Birth rates rise, death rates fall, and the organizational population grows rapidly. Eventually, the field becomes so crowded that organizations begin to compete for the same resources in a Darwinian process of natural selection. Organizational births fall and deaths rates rise again until the population stabilizes at the carrying capacity of the organizational environment, to use a concept from population biology. In short, as an organizational population grows, the birth rate of new organizations within it follows an inverted U-shaped pattern, while the death rate follows a U-shaped pattern. Rather than study particular organizations, organizational ecology studies the pattern of overall birth, death, and growth rates for particular organizational populations.

One can see the applicability of this framework to many cases. When the first insurance companies were formed, potential customers must have wondered whether they would honor the claims of policy holders. Workers may have wondered whether labor unions would genuinely be able to assist them with powerful employers. Customers of the first e-commerce businesses wondered whether it was safe to use their credit card online, and investors wondered whether any of the dot-com businesses were viable—both very real concerns even today. It is easy to see how new kinds of organizations face questions over their legitimacy until they become more common and accepted.

Issues of resource competition are also commonplace. The audience for 24-hour television news networks is not unlimited. Different political advocacy groups often draw from the same pool of liberal or conservative supporters, and those seeking to found a new one have to ask whether there is room or whether the resource space is full. Clearly, organizations compete with one another for resources, and a critical question is whether the resource niche for that kind of organization is crowded or not.

Organizational ecology has also investigated other aspects of organizational demography, such as whether organizations face special survival challenges when they are young (*liability of newness*) or at other ages, how the presence of other populations of similar or related organizations might either increase the legitimacy of or competitive threat to the particular population of interest, and whether specialist or generalist organizations are better adapted to certain kinds of resource niches.

Critics have also raised a number questions regarding organizational ecology. It is not always clear how to define the relevant population, because some kinds of organizations draw legitimacy from and compete for resources with neighboring forms of organizations: for example, ethnic newspapers are partly a self-contained population but also part of a wider population of general newspapers. Organizational inertia tends to be assumed in order to support an exclusive focus on environmental conditions, but is not really demonstrated empirically. The particular reasons for organizational failure are not examined, because the focus is on aggregate birth and death rates. The role of managerial discretion is relatively unexplored. Legitimacy processes are inferred from the statistical relationship between growing population and declining death rates, not examined directly. The faceless picture of aggregate birth and death rates also neglects the disproportionate power of large corporations and government agencies, which fail much less often, experience less selection pressure, and are more likely to control or construct their own environments in the service of their own interests (Perrow 1986).

Organizational ecology has responded to many of these criticisms, but has also faced internal problems when trying to elaborate its basic model. Efforts to demonstrate the special vulnerabilities of organizations according to the stage of their life cycle, such as youth or adolescence, or whether they are specialist organizations or generalists offering a wide range of products have produced inconclusive results.

Nevertheless, organizational ecology's insights regarding population processes and the effects of density on the prospects for organizational survival are part of the generally accepted wisdom within organizational studies.

NOTE

1. Institutional theory is also sometimes called *neo-institutional theory* to distinguish it from several previous schools using the same name.

18

THE EXTERNAL CONTROL OF ORGANIZATIONS

A Resource Dependence Perspective

JEFFREY PFEFFER

GERALD R. SALANCIK

[handwritten margin notes:]
Acquiring resource
① specify the certain resource?
② possession of resource
③ concentration of resource control
↛ The Resoure transaction and exchange with external org. dominate

ONE

AN EXTERNAL PERSPECTIVE ON ORGANIZATIONS

The central thesis of this book is that to understand the behavior of an organization you must understand the context of that behavior—that is, the ecology of the organization. This point of view is important for those who seek to understand organizations as well as for those who seek to manage and control them. Organizations are inescapably bound up with the conditions of their environment. Indeed, it has been said that all organizations engage in activities which have as their logical conclusion adjustment to the environment (Hawley, 1950:3).

At first glance, this position seems obvious. An open-systems perspective on organizations is not new (Katz and Kahn, 1966), and it is generally accepted that contexts, organizational environments, are important for understanding actions and structures. One of the purposes of this introductory chapter, besides elaborating the perspective we are going to be developing throughout the book, is to note that, in spite of the apparent obviousness of this position, much of the literature on organizations still does not recognize the importance of context; indeed, there are some reasons why such a neglect of contextual factors is likely to be maintained.

OVERVIEW

Most books about organizations describe how they operate, and the existence of the organizations is taken for granted. This book discusses how organizations manage to survive. Their existence is constantly in question, and their survival is viewed as problematic. How managers go about ensuring their organization's survival is what this book is about.

Our position is that organizations survive to the extent that they are effective. Their effectiveness derives from the management of demands, particularly the demands of interest groups upon which the organizations depend for resources and support. As we shall consider, there are a variety of ways of managing demands, including the obvious one of giving in to them.

The key to organizational survival is the ability to acquire and maintain resources. This problem would be simplified if organizations were in complete control of all the components necessary for their operation. However, no organization is completely self-contained. Organizations are embedded in an environment comprised of other organizations. They depend on those other organizations for the many resources they themselves require. Organizations are linked to environments by federations, associations, customer-supplier relationships, competitive relationships, and a social-legal apparatus defining and controlling the nature and limits of these relationships. Organizations must transact with other elements in their environment to acquire needed resources, and this is true whether we are talking about public organizations, private organizations, small or large organizations, or organizations which are bureaucratic or organic (Burns and Stalker, 1961).

Even seemingly self-contained organizations require some transactions with their environment for survival. The convents and abbeys which flourished during the Middle Ages were designed to be virtually self-sufficient. Needs were kept to a minimum; foods were grown within; and many required utensils, tools, and clothing were made by the abbey's available labor. An attempt was made, consciously, to isolate the organizations as much as possible from the secular world outside. But, abbeys were peopled by people, usually of one sex, and humans are mortal. This meant that new members had to be recruited from the outside, which required the organization to maintain relations with sources of recruits—prisons, wealthy families with illegitimate offspring, and so forth. Recruitment from the outside, therefore, imposed on the organization a need to devote some energy to elaborate socialization and indoctrination procedures. Moreover, these religious organizations had land, and to maintain their land, it was necessary to ensure a position of social legitimacy and political acceptance so that other groups would not attempt to seize the land for themselves.

The fact that organizations are dependent for survival and success on their environments does not, in itself, make their existence problematic. If stable supplies were assured from the sources of needed resources, there would be no problem. If the resources needed by the organization were continually available, even if outside their control, there would be no problem. Problems arise not merely because organizations are dependent on their environment, but because this environment is not dependable. Environments can change, new organizations enter and exit, and the supply of resources becomes more or less scarce. When environments change, organizations face the prospect either of not surviving or of changing their activities in response to these environmental factors.

Despite the importance of the environment for organizations, relatively little attention has been focused there. Rather than dealing with problems of acquiring resources, most writers have dealt with the problem of using resources. Theories of individual behavior in organizations, theories of motivation, leadership, interpersonal communication, theories of organizational design—each concerns the use of resources. The central goal of most theories is the maximization of output from given resources. Questions about how to motivate a worker to be productive are common. But questions about how resources come to be acquired are left unanswered or are completely neglected.

[. . .] A good deal of organizational behavior, the actions taken by organizations, can be understood only by knowing something about the organization's environment and the problems it creates for obtaining resources. What happens in an organization is not only a function of the organization, its structure, its leadership, its procedures, or its goals. What happens is also a consequence of the environment and the particular contingencies and constraints deriving from that environment.

Consider the following case, described by a student at the University of Illinois. The student had worked in a fast-food restaurant near the campus and was concerned about how the workers (himself) were treated. Involved in what he was studying the student read a great deal about self-actualizing, theories of motivation, and the management of human resources. He observed at the restaurant that workers would steal food, make obscene statements about the boss behind his back, and complain about the low pay. The student's analysis of the situation was a concise report summarizing the typical human relations palliatives: make the boring, greasy work more challenging and the indifferent management more democratic. The student was asked why he thought management was unresponsive to such suggestions. He considered the possibility that management was cruel and interested only in making a profit (and the operation was quite profitable). He was then asked why the employees permitted management to treat them in such a fashion—after all, they could always quit. The student responded that the workers needed the money and that jobs were hard to obtain.

This fact, that the workers were drawn from an almost limitless labor pool of students looking for any kind of part-time employment was nowhere to be found in the student's discussion of the operation of the restaurant. Yet, it was precisely this characteristic of the labor market which permitted the operation to disregard the feelings of the workers. Since there were many who wanted to work, the power of an individual worker was severely limited. More critical to the organization's success was its location and its ability both to keep competition to a minimum and to maintain a steady flow of supplies to serve a virtually captive market. If the workers were unsatisfied, it was not only because they did not like the organization's policies; in the absence of any base of power and with few alternative jobs, the workers had neither the option of voice nor exit (Hirschman, 1970).

More important to this organization's success than the motivation of its workers was its location on a block between the campus and dormitories, the path of thousands of students. Changes in policies and facilities for housing and transportation of students would have a far greater effect than some disgruntled employees. Our example illustrates, first, the importance of attending to contextual variables in understanding organizations, but also that organizational survival and success are not always achieved by making internal adjustments. Dealing with and managing the environment is just as important a component of organizational effectiveness.

A comparison of the phonograph record and the pharmaceutical industries (Hirsch, 1975) illustrates this point more directly. These two industries, Hirsch noted, are strikingly different in profitability. This difference in profits is more striking because the industries in many ways are otherwise similar: both sell their products through intermediaries, doctors in the case of pharmaceuticals, disc jockeys in the case of records; both introduce many new products; both protect their market positions through patent or copyright laws. What could account for the difference in profit? Hirsch argued that the pharmaceutical industry's greater profits came from its greater control of its environment; a more concentrated industry, firms could more effectively restrict entry and manage distribution channels. Profits resulted from a favorable institutional environment. Aware of the importance of the institutional environment for success, firms spent a lot of strategic effort maintaining that environment. They would engage in activities designed to modify patent laws to their advantage and in other efforts to protect their market positions.

[. . .]

THREE

SOCIAL CONTROL
OF ORGANIZATIONS

THE SOCIAL CONTROL
OF ORGANIZATIONAL CHOICE

[. . .] Three factors are critical in determining the dependence of one organization on another. First, there is the importance of the resource, the extent to which the organization requires it for continued operation and survival. The second is the extent to which the interest group has discretion over the resource

allocation and use. And, third, the extent to which there are few alternatives, or the extent of control over the resource by the interest group, is an important factor determining the dependence of the organization.

Resource Importance

An organization's vulnerability to extraorganizational influence is partly determined by the extent to which the organization has come to depend on certain types of exchanges for its operation. There are two dimensions to the importance of a resource exchange—the relative magnitude of the exchange and the criticality of the resource. These two dimensions are not completely independent.

The relative magnitude of an exchange as a determinant of the importance of the resource is measurable by assessing the proportion of total inputs or the proportion of total outputs accounted for by the exchange. An organization that creates only one product or service is more dependent on its customers than an organization that has a variety of outputs that are being disposed of in a variety of markets. Similarly, organizations which require one primary input for their operations will be more dependent on the sources of supply for that input than organizations that use multiple inputs, each in relatively small proportion. Single-material organizations—two examples are wood-product and petrochemical firms—are less common than single-output organizations. [. . .]

The second dimension of importance concerns the criticality of the input or output to the organization. The criticality of a resource in the functioning of an organization is more difficult to determine than the sheer magnitude of its use. Criticality measures the ability of the organization to continue functioning in the absence of the resource or in the absence of the market for the output. A resource may be critical to the organization even though it comprises only a small proportion of the total input. Few offices could function without electric power, even though the utility may be a relatively small component of the organization's expenditures.

The criticality of a resource for an organization may vary from time to time as conditions in the organization's environment change. A lawyer may be relatively unimportant until the organization is confronted with a major lawsuit that threatens its survival. In Crozier's (1964) example of the maintenance workers in a French factory, the workers were important only when and if the machinery broke down. As the environmental contingencies change, what is a critical resource may change also.

The fact that a resource is important to the organization's functioning is, in itself, not the source of the organization's problems. Problematic conditions of resources come from the environment. When the supply of a resource is stable and ample, there is no problem for the organization. Organizational vulnerability derives from the possibility of an environment's changing so that the resource is no longer assured.

[. . .]

Discretion Over Resource Allocation and Use

The second major determinant of dependence is the extent of discretion over the allocation and use of a resource possessed by another social actor. There are many forms of discretion over a resource, which is the capacity to determine the allocation or use of the resource. [. . .]

One basis for control over a resource is possession. Knowledge is one resource controlled in this fashion. An individual possesses his knowledge in a direct and absolute manner. He is the sole arbiter of its use by others. The basis for the power of such professionals as doctors, lawyers, and engineers, with respect to their clients, lies in the access to knowledge and information. Ownership or ownership rights are also a means of possessing a resource and therefore controlling it. However, unlike the case of knowledge and information, ownership is a form of indirect discretion in that it depends on a social-political conception and on enforceable social consensus. American and British oil firms that built and owned production facilities in other countries were only able to maintain their ownership while the legal and social foundations permitting their ownership existed. When their Middle East hosts passed a law giving themselves 51 percent ownership, the oil industry dramatically learned the tenuous nature of property rights. Thus, although ownership provides a basis for exerting control over a resource, it is not absolute and depends on the consent of others in the social system.

Another basis for control is access to a resource. It is possible to regulate access to a resource without owning it. Any process that affects the allocation of a resource provides some degree of control over it.

An executive secretary gains considerable power from the ability to determine who is permitted access to the boss. The agents of organizations who influence the allocation of the organization's contracts develop personal power from their positions, a point noted by Thompson (1962) in his discussion of organizations and output transactions. Thus, salesmen attempt to win the favor of purchasing agents because the purchasing agents influence the allocation of resources even though they do not own them. Lockheed's bribes to Japanese intermediaries were their means of gaining access to the government which purchased their planes.

making rules of possession, allocation

The final source of control derives from the ability to make rules or otherwise regulate the possession, allocation, and use of resources and to enforce the regulations. In addition to being a source of power, the ability to make regulations and rules can determine the very existence and concentration of power. Laws permitting, if not facilitating, the organization of workers into unions permit the concentration of power, while laws regulating interactions among competitors presumably limit the concentration of buyer and seller power. [. . .]

Rules also determine the extent to which dependence relations, developing from resource exchanges, can be used to accomplish the external control of behavior. In a series of cases brought under the antitrust laws, it has been determined that franchisors cannot compel their franchisees to buy machinery or other inputs from them. Other cases have held that sales territories cannot be restricted. In the absence of such prohibitions, the franchisors, with their greater power, would be able to control the activities of the franchisees much more tightly. Normative restraints also occasionally operate to limit the use and scope of interorganizational influence attempts.

Concentration of Resource Control *who owns it?*

That an interest group or organization controls a resource and that the resource is important, still does not assure that it will be able to create a dependency for another organization. The dependence of one organization on another also derives from the concentration of resource control, or the extent to which input or output transactions are made by a relatively few, or only one, significant organizations. The sheer number of suppliers or purchasers is not the critical variable. Rather, the important thing is whether the focal organization has access to the resource from additional sources. [. . .] Concentration of resource control, then, refers to the extent to which the focal organization can substitute sources for the same resource.

[. . .]

Concentration can arise in a multitude of ways. An organization can have a monopoly position legally protected or legally established, as in the case of electric and telephone utilities. Or, a group of firms can act together as one, constituting a cartel. For coordinated action to develop, it is not necessary for the organizations to communicate with one another. As Phillips (1960) has noted, when there are a small number of firms with similar goals and similar cost structures, implicit coordination is possible. Collective organizations and associations are another form of achieving concentration over some resource. Unions and, to a lesser extent, trade and professional associations are instances of these attempts to achieve coordinated action, or to have many organizations or individuals act as one.

[. . .]

Dependence *how much?*

Concentration of the control of discretion over resources and the importance of the resources to the organization together determine the focal organization's dependence on any given other group or organization. Dependence can then be defined as the product of the importance of a given input or output to the organization and the extent to which it is controlled by a relatively few organizations. A resource that is not important to the organization cannot create a situation of dependence, regardless of how concentrated control over the resource is. Also, regardless of how important the resource is, unless it is controlled by a relatively few organizations, the focal organization will not be particularly dependent on any of them. When there are many sources of supply or potential customers, the power of any single one is correspondingly reduced.

The dependence we are describing results from exchange processes and from the requirements of organizations to acquire resources and engage in exchange with their environments. Dependence, then, measures the potency of the external organizations or groups in the given organization's environment. It is a measure of how much these organizations must be taken into account and, also, how likely it is that they will be perceived as important and considered in the organization's decision making.

Countervailing Power and Asymmetric Dependence

Some writers have maintained that the concentration of resources is the basis of interorganizational influence (Mintz and Cohen, 1971). We disagree. The problems associated with concentrated power do not arise because the power is concentrated but because others are not able to muster equal power or equal concentration of opposition. The concentration of power itself is inevitable. It arises from a need to take organized action in cases where the interests of a number of parties are involved. And to the extent that the interests of one party cannot be achieved without other parties, concentration is necessary. The basis of organization is the concentration of effort, coordinating some set of activities to achieve some outcomes of interest to the participants. Perrow (1972) has seen this clearly and has consequently noted that the critical issue in organizations is not whether there will be a concentration of control but, rather, whose interests are being served by the organized, coordinated activities.

[. . .]

It is the case, however, that the concentration of force to accomplish something is more likely to cause those in opposition to concentrate and coordinate their actions also. Galbraith (1967) has spoken of this in terms of the notion of countervailing power—that the concentration of power or resources in one sphere tends to set up forces that result in a countervailing, concentrated opposition. There are many anecdotal instances of this occurring, though the phenomenon has not been subjected to systematic empirical testing. For instance, in the area of labor-management bargaining, it is known that if employers move to industry-wide bargaining, the union will also concentrate its bargaining efforts and work for industry-wide settlements. As companies have expanded abroad, developing production facilities for a product in many countries, unions have begun to explore the possibility of developing cross-national federations to engage in worldwide bargaining with a company or an industry, which would prevent a company facing a strike in one country from making up the production in its plants in other countries.

For the dependence between two organizations to provide one organization with power over the other, there must be asymmetry in the exchange relationship. If organization X sells to organization Y and is dependent on Y for absorbing its output, it is simultaneously true that Y purchases from X and is, therefore, dependent upon X for the provision of some required input. Asymmetry exists in the relationship when the exchange is not equally important to both organizations. This may occur because the organizations differ greatly in size, so that what is a large proportion of one's operations is a small proportion of the other's. For instance, General Motors purchases many components from a wide variety of relatively small suppliers. Many of these suppliers furnish virtually 100 percent of their output to General Motors, although each contributes only a small fraction to the total input of General Motors. Without asymmetry in the exchange relationship neither organization possesses a particular power advantage, reducing the likelihood that one organization will dominate interorganizational influences. [. . .]

When the net exchange between organizational entities is asymmetrical, some net power accrues to the less dependent organization. This power may be employed in attempting to influence or constrain the behavior of the other more dependent organization. To summarize the preceding discussion, the potential for one organization's influencing another derives from its discretionary control over resources needed by that other and the other's dependence on the resource and lack of countervailing resources or access to alternative sources. Perrow (1970) reports on a striking example of interorganizational influence deriving from asymmetrical exchanges. He reported that it was the practice of the large automobile-manufacturing firms to audit the records of their small suppliers, thereby ensuring that the small suppliers were not earning excessive profits on their transactions. In fact, it has been argued that the profitability of General Motors derives not so much from its production efficiencies but from its market position. It can take advantage of its suppliers' production efficiencies by using its influence to control the price at which it buys. General Motors absorbs much of the output of the small suppliers, while each supplier provides only a fraction of the input to General Motors. Further, while General Motors confronts a large number of firms competing for its business, the suppliers must sell to only three major automobile companies, with General Motors accounting for more than half the market. The small suppliers are quite dependent on General Motors, which, in controlling the market for cars, also controls the market for parts. Since General Motors can always decide the quantity to be purchased from each supplier, it can maintain the size and number of suppliers at a level sufficient to continue its position of relative power.

EMPIRICAL EXAMINATIONS OF INTERORGANIZATIONAL INFLUENCE

The concept of dependence is useful in understanding how organizational decision making is constrained by the environment. If organizations achieve their own ends by using their power to affect the behavior of other organizations, then it is possible to conceive of organizational behavior as the consequence of influences. While it is more common to view organizations as self-directed, making strategic decisions and vigorously pursuing courses of action, the concept of dependence suggests that organizations are partly directed by elements in their environment. Organizations formulate their own actions in response to the demands placed upon them by other organizations. The extent to which a given organization will respond to the demands of other organizations can be explained by the variables we have described previously, particularly focusing on the dependence of the organization on the various external organizations. Below, we describe two studies testing these ideas.

Israeli Managers

Aharoni (1971) interviewed the general managers of the 141 largest manufacturing plants in Israel and, as part of this study, asked them what they might do in a variety of hypothetical situations. These data were used in a study of the extent to which sales interdependence, foreign ownership, and financial problems could explain the managers' expressed willingness to comply with various governmental requests and policies (Pfeffer, 1972).

Each manager was presented with a hypothetical decision situation in which he was asked what level of profit he would be willing to accept on an investment in a development area. The Israeli government had designated certain areas for development and had encouraged firms to invest in these areas. Managers were asked to answer, along a seven-point scale, what rate of return they would be willing to forego to invest in the development area, assuming that, after government incentives and other considerations, they would earn 15 percent in the development area. An expressed willingness to accept lower returns was assumed to be a measure of the managers' commitment to accede to government demands.

Two sources of interdependence with the government were used to examine variation in the answers to this question. The government was both a purchaser of goods and a source of financing. We would expect that firms which sell a large proportion of their goods to the government would be more willing to comply with the government's request concerning plant location. And, we would also expect that firms which were in worse financial condition and were restricted in finding sources of financing would be more dependent on the government for financial assistance and would also be more willing to comply with the government's wishes.

To examine the hypothesis that dependence affects organizational decisions, the managers' responses regarding the size of the return they would be willing to give up to invest in the development area were correlated with the proportion of the firm's sales to the government. In Table 18.1, rank-order correlations are presented.

For total government sales combined, the correlation of .21 indicates that firms selling a larger proportion of their output to the government were willing to give up larger yields from investment elsewhere in order to comply with the government's request. The correlations in Table 18.1 also indicate that the proportion of sales to defense were the least related to willingness to comply, while sales to the Shekem, the Israeli equivalent of the American commissary or PX, were most related. This result is not surprising if we consider that a large number of firms can potentially supply the commissary, while there were only a few large firms selling to defense. Because the dependence was more asymmetrical in the case of firms selling to the commissary, those firms were more willing to comply as a function of their dependence on government sales.

Table 18.1. Correlations of Percentage Sales to Various Governmental Agencies and Willingness to Invest in Development Area

Government Agency	Correlation[a]	Level of Significance[a]
Defense	+.110	.04
Shekem	+.325	.001
Other government	+.160	.005
Total government	+.211	.001

a Kendall rank-order correlations

The firms' potential reliance on the government for financing was also related to their willingness to comply. The managers were asked, "Do you think your firm is limited in choosing its sources of funds?" and were given four responses, ranging from "No" to "Yes, always." This question was assumed to measure the firms' dependence on the government for assistance in financing. The correlation with the expressed willingness to invest in the development area was .11 ($p < .04$), consistent with our expectations but not a very strong relationship. Answers to another question asking about the influence the Ministry of Finance had on the firms' decisions correlated .17 ($p < .003$) with a question about access to alternative funding sources.

Although the strength of the relationships were not large, the results of the study of responses of Israeli managers (Pfeffer, 1972) were consistent with our argument that organizational actions are constrained by the environment to the extent the organization is dependent on the environment. The Israeli managers study has a number of limitations. Data were collected for other purposes; organizational behavior was assessed by asking about responses in hypothetical situations, even though the answers were provided by the same people who would make the actual decisions; and the data were collected by a respected professor of business who had been Dean of the Business School at Tel Aviv University. This last fact may have affected the responses given; for instance, the managers may have been reluctant to admit their willingness to forego higher profits or may have wanted to appear even more loyal to the interests of the country. Such factors would introduce randomness into the responses, attenuating the strength of the correlations.

Sales Interdependence and Affirmative Action

An attempt to gather more evidence on the effects of dependence (Salancik, 1976) was made shortly after the study of the Israeli managers. The context in this case was American firms and their responses to the government's requirement for affirmative action regarding the employment of women. In a series of presidential executive orders, first blacks and then women were included in the requirement that organizations doing business with the government not only cease discriminatory hiring practices but also engage in affirmative action to increase the proportion of such people in the work force.

To obtain some indication of the extent of response to these governmental demands, the top 100 defense contractors were examined. Letters were mailed to the executive vice-president inquiring about the firm's plans for hiring women MBA graduates in June. The letter, from a university department of business administration, implied the purpose in writing was to find out how to advise female graduates regarding job opportunities. The letter also asked for any information or brochures the firm might have. Careful records were kept of replies, including weighing the response and noting the time required to respond. Some firms did not reply, others sent short notes explaining they were not hiring, while others sent long letters from their affirmative action directors. Some firms sent brochures describing management opportunities for women in their organizations. From this information, each organization was rated according to how actively it appeared to be in pursuit of female management graduates. One measure of response was the length of time it took to obtain a reply. Another measure was the extent to which the response encouraged female management students to seek employment, with the most encouraging being those responses from the director of equal employment opportunity accompanied by brochures describing opportunities for women, while the least responsive was either no reply or a short note from a secretary indicating there were no positions. These two measures correlated highly ($r:.89$).

From the original sample of 100, some firms had to be dropped: some were only holding companies and did not direct hiring; some were engineering firms and did not hire people with only MBA degrees; for others sales information about them could not be publicly obtained. In all, 78 firms were examined. For each of these firms, 1970 information was collected on their total sales, sales to the government, and the proportion of the total procurement in the defense department each furnished. From these data, the following were computed: (1) the firm's percent of sales to the government, a measure of its dependence on the government; (2) the dollar amount of nongovernment sales, a measure of its potential visibility to the public; and (3) the firm's contribution to the total defense expenditures, a measure of the government's dependence on the firm. The one-third of the firms with the largest amount of dollar sales to nongovernment organizations were designated as large, visible organizations, while the remainder were considered to be less visible, smaller organizations. Within each category, the firms were further categorized according to their control of the market. A firm controlled the market to the extent it had a larger proportion of the total sales of that commodity. For instance, Colt Industries, in 1970, accounted for more than 50 percent of the small arms business with the government. Such concentration, we assumed, indicated greater government dependence on the firm for purchases.

As in the case of the decisions of the Israeli managers, our interest is in the way the organization's responsiveness to government demands varies with dependence on the government. One would expect firms to respond more to government pressures according to how dependent they were on the government for their business, which is measured by the proportion of their sales to the government. At the same time, one might expect that if the Department of Defense were dependent on a contractor because of the contractor's control of the production of a given item, the government would be less likely to pursue compliance vigorously. Some contractors, of course, because of pressures from other groups, might comply even if not under pressure from the Department of Defense. Large consumer goods firms, for instance, because of their public visibility, might be more inclined to comply even without government pressure. Thus, we would expect that the degree of responsiveness of contractors to affirmative action pressures as a consequence of their dependence on the government to itself vary with the visibility of the contractor and with his importance as a source of supply. For large, visible firms that are not major sources of defense supplies, the enforcement pressures should be greatest; for less visible contractors that are major suppliers of defense requirements, the enforcement should be least. From the point of view of the contractors confronted with pressures to comply, the decision should depend on how much they need the government as a purchaser of their output. Those firms very dependent on the government should be more responsive than those not so dependent. But we should also expect that, as the enforcement demands are less, the relationship between a firm's dependence and its compliance would also diminish.

The data testing this argument are presented in Table 18.2.

The four types of firms are ranked according to our assumptions about the amount of enforcement pressure they are likely to face, and the correlations represent the extent to which the firms of each type respond as a function of the proportion of their total sales to the government. As can be seen, when enforcement pressures are assumed to be greatest, responses evidencing concern for affirmative action are strongly related to the degree of the organization's dependence on the government ($r:.84$). This relationship diminishes as firms face less enforcement pressure. Indeed, for small firms that are important sources of supply, the relationship between the firm's dependence and the response to our inquiries about affirmative action is actually negative.

Summary

The concept of the social control of organizational choice is well illustrated by the data from the Israeli

Table 18.2. U.S. Defense Contractor's Responsiveness to Inquiry About Employment Opportunities for Women as a Function of Proportion of Sales to the Government, Firm Size, and Control of Production

Type of Firm	Correlation	Sample Size
Large, visible firm, not controlling production of items	.84[a]	13
Large, visible firm, with control of production of items	.46[b]	13
Small, less visible firm, not controlling production of items	.02	26
Small, less visible firm, with control of production of items	-.67[a]	26

a p <.01
b p <.05

managers and the American defense contractors. To the extent that the focal organization depended on the government, a greater influence on the decisions of the managers and the behavior of the contractors could be observed. Randall (1973), in a study of the responsiveness of state employment service officers to headquarter's requests for more training activity, found a similar result. It is exactly such influences on behavior, resulting from the organization's transactions or exchanges with external organizations, that are what is meant when we say that organizational behavior is constrained and shaped by the demands and pressures of organizations and groups in its environment.

Descriptively, it has been proposed that constraints on behavior result from situations of asymmetric interdependence, when there exists the discretion to control resources and enforce demands and when the focal organization's behavior is not already tightly constrained. In this setting, it is hypothesized that the organization will tend to be influenced more the greater the dependence on the external organization, or alternatively, the more important the external organization is to the functioning and survival of the organization. [...]

The effective organization, then, is the organization which satisfies the demands of those in its environment from whom it requires support for its continued existence. [...]

REFERENCES

Aharoni, Y. 1971. *The Israeli Manager*. Israeli Institute of Business Research, Tel Aviv University.

Burns, T., and G. M. Stalker. 1961. *The Management of Innovation*. London: Tavistock.

Crozier, M. 1964. *The Bureaucratic Phenomenon*. University of Chicago Press.

Galbraith, J. K. 1967. *The New Industrial State*. Boston: Houghton Mifflin.

Hawley, A. H. 1950. *Human Ecology*. New York: Ronald Press.

Hirsch, P.M. 1975. "Organizational effectiveness and the institutional environment." *Administrative Science Quarterly*, 20(3):327–344.

Hirschman, A.O. 1970. *Exit, Voice, and Loyalty*. Cambridge, Mass.: Harvard University Press.

Katz, D., and R. L. Kahn. 1966. *The Social Psychology of Organizations*. New York: John Wiley.

Mintz, M., and J. S. Cohen. 1971. *America, Inc.: Who Owns and Operates the United States*. New York: Dial Press.

Perrow, C. 1970. *Organizational Analysis: A Sociological View*. Belmont, Calif.: Wadsworth.

Perrow, C. 1972. *Complex Organizations: A Critical Essay*. Glenview, Ill.: Scott, Foresman.

Pfeffer, J. 1972. "Interorganizational influence and managerial attitudes." *Academy of Management Journal*, 15:317–330.

Phillips, A. 1960. "A Theory of interfirm organization." *Quarterly Journal of Economics*, 74:602–613.

Randall, R. 1973. "Influence of environmental support and policy space on organizational behavior." *Administrative Science Quarterly*, 18:236–247.

Salancik, G. R. 1976. "The role of interdependencies in organizational responsiveness to demands from the environment: the case of women versus power." Unpublished manuscript, University of Illinois.

Thompson, J. D. 1962. "Organizations and output transactions." *American Journal of Sociology*, 68:309–324.

19

The Iron Cage Revisited

Institutional Isomorphism and Collective Rationality in Organizational Fields

Paul J. DiMaggio

Walter W. Powell

In *The Protestant Ethic and the Spirit of Capitalism*, Max Weber warned that the rationalist spirit ushered in by asceticism had achieved a momentum of its own and that, under capitalism, the rationalist order had become an iron cage in which humanity was, save for the possibility of prophetic revival, imprisoned "perhaps until the last ton of fossilized coal is burnt" (Weber, 1952:181–82). In his essay on bureaucracy, Weber returned to this theme, contending that bureaucracy, the rational spirit's organizational manifestation, was so efficient and powerful a means of controlling men and women that, once established, the momentum of bureaucratization was irreversible (Weber, 1968).

The imagery of the iron cage has haunted students of society as the tempo of bureaucratization has quickened. But while bureaucracy has spread continuously in the eighty years since Weber wrote, we suggest that the engine of organizational rationalization has shifted. For Weber, bureaucratization resulted from three related causes: competition among capitalist firms in the marketplace; competition among states, increasing rulers' need to control their staff and citizenry; and bourgeois demands for equal protection under the law. Of these three, the most important was the competitive marketplace. "Today," Weber (1968:974) wrote:

it is primarily the capitalist market economy which demands that the official business of administration be discharged precisely, unambiguously, continuously, and with as much speed as possible. Normally, the very large, modern capitalist enterprises are themselves unequalled models of strict bureaucractic organization.

We argue that the causes of bureaucratization and rationalization have changed. The bureaucratization of the corporation and the state have been achieved. Organizations are still becoming more homogeneous, and bureaucracy remains the common organizational form. Today, however, structural change in organizations seems less and less driven by competition or by the need for efficiency. Instead, we will contend, bureaucratization and other forms of organizational change occur as the result of processes that make organizations more similar without necessarily making them more efficient. Bureaucratization and other forms of homogenization emerge, we argue, out of the structuration (Giddens, 1979) of organizational fields. This process, in turn, is effected largely by the state and the professions, which have become the great rationalizers of the second half of the twentieth century. For reasons that we will explain, highly structured organizational fields provide a context in which individual efforts to deal rationally with uncertainty and constraint often lead, in the aggregate, to homogeneity in structure, culture, and output.

ORGANIZATIONAL THEORY AND ORGANIZATIONAL DIVERSITY

Much of modern organizational theory posits a diverse and differentiated world of organization and seeks to explain variation among organizations in structure and behavior (e.g., Woodward, 1965; Child and Kieser, 1981). Hannan and Freeman begin a major theoretical paper (1977) with the question, "Why are there so many kinds of organizations?" Even our investigatory technologies (for example, those based on least-squares techniques) are geared towards explaining variation rather than its absence.

We ask, instead, why there is such startling homogeneity of organizational forms and practices; and we seek to explain homogeneity, not variation. In the initial stages of their life cycle, organizational fields display considerable diversity in approach and form. Once a field becomes well established, however, there is an inexorable push towards homogenization.

Coser, Kadushin, and Powell (1982) describe the evolution of American college textbook publishing from a period of initial diversity to the current hegemony of only two models, the large bureaucratic generalist and the small specialist. Rothman (1980) describes the winnowing of several competing models of legal education into two dominant approaches. Starr (1980) provides evidence of mimicry in the development of the hospital field; Tyack (1974) and Katz (1975) show a similar process in public schools; Barnouw (1966–68) describes the development of dominant forms in the radio industry; and DiMaggio (1981) depicts the emergence of dominant organizational models for the provision of high culture in the late nineteenth century.

What we see in each of these cases is the emergence and structuration of an organizational field as a result of the activities of a diverse set of organizations; and, second, the homogenization of these organizations, and of new entrants as well, once the field is established.

By organizational field, we mean those organizations that, in the aggregate, constitute a recognized area of institutional life: key suppliers, resource and product consumers, regulatory agencies, and other organizations that produce similar services or products.

[. . .]

Once disparate organizations in the same line of business are structured into an actual field (as we shall argue, by competition, the state, or the professions), powerful forces emerge that lead them to become more similar to one another. Organizations may change their goals or develop new practices, and new organizations enter the field. But, in the long run, organizational actors making rational decisions construct around themselves an environment that constrains their ability to change further in later years. Early adopters of organizational innovations are commonly driven by a desire to improve performance. But new practices can become, in Selznick's words (1957:17), "infused with value beyond the technical requirements of the task at hand." As an innovation spreads, a threshold is reached beyond which adoption provides legitimacy rather than improves performance (Meyer and Rowan, 1977). Strategies that are rational for individual organizations may not be rational if adopted by large numbers. Yet the very fact that they are normatively sanctioned increases the likelihood of their adoption. Thus organizations may try to change constantly; but, after a certain point in the structuration of an organizational field, the aggregate effect of individual change is to lessen the extent of diversity within the field. *[. . .]*

Zucker and Tolbert's (1981) work on the adoption of civil-service reform in the United States illustrates this process. Early adoption of civil-service reforms was related to internal governmental needs, and strongly predicted by such city characteristics as the size of immigrant population, political reform movements, socioeconomic composition, and city size. Later adoption, however, is not predicted by city characteristics, but is related to institutional definitions of the legitimate structural form for municipal administration.[1] *[. . .]* Freeman (1982:14) suggests that older, larger organizations reach a point where they can dominate their environments rather than adjust to them.

The concept that best captures the process of homogenization is *isomorphism*. In Hawley's (1968) description, isomorphism is a constraining process that forces one unit in a population to resemble other units that face the same set of environmental conditions. *[. . .]*

Following Meyer (1979) and Fennell (1980), we maintain that there are two types of isomorphism: competitive and institutional. Hannan and Freeman's classic paper (1977), and much of their recent work, deals with competitive isomorphism, assuming a system rationality that emphasizes market competition, niche change, and fitness measures. Such a view, we suggest, is most relevant for those fields in which free and open competition exists. It explains parts of the process of bureaucratization that Weber observed, and may apply to early adoption of innovation, but it does not present a fully adequate picture of the modern world of organizations. For this purpose it must be supplemented by an institutional view of isomorphism of the sort introduced by Kanter (1972:152–54) in her discussion of the forces pressing communes toward accommodation with the outside world. As Aldrich (1979:265) has argued, "the major factors that organizations must take into account are other organizations." Organizations compete not just for resources and customers, but for political power and institutional legitimacy, for social as well as economic fitness. The concept of institutional isomorphism is a useful tool for understanding the politics and ceremony that pervade much modern organizational life.

Three Mechanisms of Institutional Isomorphic Change

We identify three mechanisms through which institutional isomorphic change occurs, each with its own antecedents: 1) *coercive* isomorphism that stems from political influence and the problem of legitimacy; 2) *mimetic* isomorphism resulting from standard responses to uncertainty; and 3) *normative* isomorphism, associated with professionalization. This typology is an analytic one: the types are not always empirically distinct. For example, external actors may induce an organization to conform to its peers by requiring it to perform a particular task and specifying the profession responsible for its performance. Or mimetic change may reflect environmentally constructed uncertainties. Yet, while the three types intermingle in empirical setting, they tend to derive from different conditions and may lead to different outcomes.

Coercive Isomorphism. Coercive isomorphism results from both formal and informal pressures exerted on organizations by other organizations upon which they are dependent and by cultural expectations in the society within which organizations function. Such pressures may be felt as force, as persuasion, or as invitations to join in collusion. In some circumstances, organizational change is a direct response to government mandate: manufacturers adopt new pollution control technologies to conform to environmental regulations; nonprofits maintain accounts, and hire accountants, in order to meet tax law requirements; and organizations employ affirmative-action officers to fend off allegations of discrimination. Schools mainstream special students and hire special education teachers, cultivate PTAs and administrators who get along with them, and promulgate curricula that conform with state standards (Meyer et al., 1981). The fact that these changes may be largely ceremonial does not mean that they are inconsequential. As Ritti and Goldner (1979) have argued, staff become involved in advocacy for their functions that can alter power relations within organizations over the long run.

The existence of a common legal environment affects many aspects of an organization's behavior and structure. Weber pointed out the profound impact of a complex, rationalized system of contract law that requires the necessary organizational controls to honor legal commitments. Other legal and technical requirements of the state—the vicissitudes of the budget cycle, the ubiquity of certain fiscal years, annual reports, and financial reporting requirements that ensure eligibility for the receipt of federal contracts or funds—also shape organizations in similar ways. [. . .]

Meyer and Rowan (1977) have argued persuasively that as rationalized states and other large rational organizations expand their dominance over more arenas of social life, organizational structures increasingly come to reflect rules institutionalized and legitimated by and within the state (also see Meyer and Hannan, 1979). As a result, organizations are increasingly homogeneous within given domains and increasingly organized around rituals of conformity to wider institutions. At the same time, organizations are decreasingly structurally determined by the constraints posed by technical activities, and decreasingly held together by output controls. Under such circumstances, organizations employ ritualized controls of credentials and group solidarity.

Direct imposition of standard operating procedures and legitimated rules and structures also occurs outside the governmental arena. Michael Sedlak (1981) has documented the ways that United Charities in the 1930s altered and homogenized the structures, methods, and philosophies of the social service agencies that depended upon them for support. As conglomerate corporations increase in size and scope, standard performance criteria are not necessarily imposed on subsidiaries, but it is common for subsidiaries to be subject to standardized reporting mechanisms (Coser et al., 1982). Subsidiaries must adopt accounting practices, performance evaluations, and budgetary plans that are compatible with the policies of the parent corporation.

A variety of service infrastructures, often provided by monopolistic firms—for example, telecommunications and transportation—exert common pressures over the organizations that use them. Thus, the expansion of the central state, the centralization of capital, and the coordination of philanthropy all support the homogenization of organizational models through direct authority relationships.

We have so far referred only to the direct and explicit imposition of organizational models on dependent organizations. Coercive isomorphism, however, may be more subtle and less explicit than these examples suggest. Milofsky (1981) has described the ways in which neighborhood organizations in urban communities, many of which are committed to participatory democracy, are driven to developing organizational hierarchies in order to gain support from more hierarchically organized donor organizations. Similarly, Swidler (1979) describes the tensions created in the free schools she studied by the need to have a "principal" to negotiate with the district superintendent and to represent the school to outside agencies. In general, the need to lodge responsibility and managerial authority at least ceremonially in a formally defined role in order to interact with hierarchical organizations is a constant obstacle to the maintenance of egalitarian or collectivist organizational forms (Kanter, 1972; Rothschild-Whitt, 1979).

Mimetic Processes. Not all institutional isomorphism, however, derives from coercive authority. Uncertainty is also a powerful force that encourages imitation. When organizational technologies are poorly understood (March and Olsen, 1976), when goals are ambiguous, or when the environment creates symbolic uncertainty, organizations may model themselves on other organizations. The advantages of mimetic behavior in the economy of human action are considerable; when an organization faces a problem with ambiguous causes or unclear solutions, problemistic search may yield a viable solution with little expense (Cyert and March, 1963).

Modeling, as we use the term, is a response to uncertainty. The modeled organization may be unaware of the modeling or may have no desire to be copied; it merely serves as a convenient source of practices that the borrowing organization may use.

Models may be diffused unintentionally, indirectly through employee transfer or turnover, or explicitly by organizations such as consulting firms or industry trade associations. *[. . .]*

One of the most dramatic instances of modeling was the effort of Japan's modernizers in the late nineteenth century to model new governmental initiatives on apparently successful western prototypes. Thus, the imperial government sent its officers to study the courts, Army, and police in France, the Navy and postal system in Great Britain, and banking and art education in the United States (see Westney, forthcoming). American corporations are now returning the compliment by implementing (their perceptions of) Japanese models to cope with thorny productivity and personnel problems in their own firms. The rapid proliferation of quality circles and quality-of-work-life issues in American firms is, at least in part, an attempt to model Japanese and European successes. These developments also have a ritual aspect; companies adopt these "innovations" to enhance their legitimacy, to demonstrate they are at least trying to improve working conditions. More generally, the wider the population of personnel employed by, or customers served by, an organization, the stronger the pressure felt by the organization to provide the programs and services offered by other organizations. Thus, either a skilled labor force or a broad customer base may encourage mimetic isomorphism.

Much homogeneity in organizational structures stems from the fact that despite considerable search for diversity there is relatively little variation to be selected from. New organizations are modeled upon old ones throughout the economy, and managers actively seek models upon which to build (Kimberly, 1980). Thus, in the arts one can find textbooks on how to organize a community arts council or how to start a symphony women's guild. Large organizations choose from a relatively small set of major consulting firms, which, like Johnny Appleseeds, spread a few organizational models throughout the land. Such models are powerful because structural changes are observable, whereas changes in policy and strategy are less easily noticed. With the advice of a major consulting firm, a large metropolitan public television station switched from a functional design to a multidivisional structure. The stations' executives were skeptical that the new structure was more efficient; in fact, some services were now duplicated across divisions. But they were convinced that the new design would carry a powerful message to the for-profit firms with whom the station regularly dealt. These firms, whether in the role of corporate underwriters or as potential partners in joint ventures, would view the reorganization as a sign that "the sleepy nonprofit station was becoming more business-minded" (Powell, forthcoming). The history of management reform in American government agencies, which are noted for their goal ambiguity, is almost a textbook case of isomorphic modeling, from the PPPB of the McNamara era to the zero-based budgeting of the Carter administration.

Organizations tend to model themselves after similar organizations in their field that they perceive to be more legitimate or successful. The ubiquity of certain kinds of structural arrangements can more likely be credited to the universality of mimetic processes than to any concrete evidence that the adopted models enhance efficiency. John Meyer (1981) contends that it is easy to predict the organization of a newly emerging nation's administration without knowing anything about the nation itself, since "peripheral nations are far more isomorphic—in administrative form and economic pattern—than any theory of the world system of economic division of labor would lead one to expect."

Normative Pressures. A third source of isomorphic organizational change is normative and stems primarily from professionalization. Following Larson (1977) and Collins (1979), we interpret professionalization as the collective struggle of members of an occupation to define the conditions and methods of their work, to control "the production of producers" (Larson, 1977:49–52), and to establish a cognitive base and legitimation for their occupational autonomy. As Larson points out, the professional project is rarely achieved with complete success. Professionals must compromise with nonprofessional clients, bosses, or regulators. The major recent growth in the professions has been among organizational professionals, particularly managers and specialized staff of large organizations. The increased professionalization of workers whose futures are inextricably bound up with the fortunes of the organizations that employ them has rendered obsolescent (if not obsolete) the dichotomy between organizational commitment and professional allegiance that characterized traditional professionals in earlier organizations (Hall, 1968). Professions are subject to the same coercive and mimetic pressures as are organizations. Moreover, while various kinds of professionals within an organization may differ from one another, they exhibit much similarity to their professional counterparts in other organizations. In addition, in many cases, professional power is as much assigned by the state as it is created by the activities of the professions.

Two aspects of professionalization are important sources of isomorphism. One is the resting of formal education and of legitimation in a cognitive base produced by university specialists; the second is the growth and elaboration of professional networks that span organizations and across which new models diffuse rapidly. Universities and professional training institutions are important centers for the development of organizational norms among professional managers and their staff. Professional and trace associations are another vehicle for the definition and promulgation of normative rules about organizational and professional behavior. Such mechanisms create a pool of almost interchangeable individuals who occupy similar positions across a range of organizations and possess a similarity of orientation and disposition that may override variations in tradition and control that might otherwise shape organizational behavior (Perrow, 1974).

One important mechanism for encouraging normative isomorphism is the filtering of personnel. Within many organizational fields filtering occurs through the hiring of individuals from firms within the same industry; through the recruitment of fast-track staff from a narrow range of training institutions; through common promotion practices, such as always hiring top executives from financial or legal departments; and from skill-level requirements for particular jobs. Many professional career tracks are so closely guarded, both at the entry level and throughout the career progression, that individuals who make it to the top are virtually indistinguishable. [. . .] In addition, individuals in an organizational field undergo anticipatory socialization to

common expectations about their personal behavior, appropriate style of dress, organizational vocabularies (Cicourel, 1970; Williamson, 1975) and standard methods of speaking, joking, or addressing others (Ouchi, 1980). Particularly in industries with a service or financial orientation [. . .], the filtering of personnel approaches what Kanter (1977) refers to as the "homosexual reproduction of management." To the extent managers and key staff are drawn from the same universities and filtered on a common set of attributes, they will tend to view problems in a similar fashion, see the same policies, procedures and structures as normatively sanctioned and legitimated, and approach decisions in much the same way.

Entrants to professional career tracks who somehow escape the filtering process—for example, Jewish naval officers, woman stockbrokers, or Black insurance executives—are likely to be subjected to pervasive on-the-job socialization. [. . .]

[. . .] Professional and trade associations provide other arenas in which center organizations are recognized and their personnel given positions of substantive or ceremonial influence. Managers in highly visible organizations may in turn have their stature reinforced by representation on the boards of other organizations, participation in industry-wide or inter-industry councils, and consultation by agencies of government (Useem, 1979). In the nonprofit sector, where legal barriers to collusion do not exist, structuration may proceed even more rapidly. Thus executive producers or artistic directors of leading theatres head trade or professional association committees, sit on government and foundation grant-award panels, or consult as government- or foundation-financed management advisors to smaller theatres, or sit on smaller organizations' boards, even as their stature is reinforced and enlarged by the grants their theatres receive from government, corporate, and foundation funding sources (DiMaggio, 1982).

Such central organizations serve as both active and passive models; their policies and structures will be copied throughout their fields. Their centrality is reinforced as upwardly mobile managers and staff seek to secure positions in these central organizations in order to further their own careers. Aspiring managers may undergo anticipatory socialization into the norms and mores of the organizations they hope to join. Career paths may also involve movement from entry positions in the center organizations to middle-management positions in peripheral organizations. Personnel flows within an organizational field are further encouraged by structural homogenization, for example the existence of common career titles and paths (such as assistant, associate, and full professor) with meanings that are commonly understood.

It is important to note that each of the institutional isomorphic processes can be expected to proceed in the absence of evidence that they increase internal organizational efficiency. To the extent that organizational effectiveness is enhanced, the reason will often be that organizations are rewarded for being similar to other organizations in their fields. This similarity can make it easier for organizations to transact with other organizations, to attract career-minded staff, to be acknowledged as legitimate and reputable, and to fit into administrative categories that define eligibility for public and private grants and contracts. None of this, however, insures that conformist organizations do what they do more efficiently than do their more deviant peers.

Pressures for competitive efficiency are also mitigated in many fields because the number of organizations is limited and there are strong fiscal and legal barriers to entry and exit. Lee (1971:51) maintains this is why hospital administrators are less concerned with the efficient use of resources and more concerned with status competition and parity in prestige. Fennell (1980) notes that hospitals are a poor market system because patients lack the needed knowledge of potential exchange partners and prices. She argues that physicians and hospital administrators are the actual consumers. Competition among hospitals is based on "attracting physicians, who, in turn, bring their patients to the hospital." Fennell (p. 505) concludes that:

> Hospitals operate according to a norm of social legitimation that frequently conflicts with market considerations of efficiency and system rationality. Apparently, hospitals can increase their range of services not because there is an actual need for a particular service or facility within the patient population, but because they will be defined as fit only if they can offer everything other hospitals in the area offer.

These results suggest a more general pattern. Organizational fields that include a large professionally trained labor force will be driven primarily by status competition. Organizational prestige and resources are key elements in attracting professionals. This process encourages homogenization as organizations seek to ensure that they can provide the same benefits and services as their competitors.

PREDICTORS OF ISOMORPHIC CHANGE

It follows from our discussion of the mechanism by which isomorphic change occurs that we should be able to predict empirically which organizational fields will be most homogeneous in structure, process, and behavior. *[. . .]* The hypotheses are implicitly governed by *ceteris paribus* assumptions, particularly with regard to size, technology, and centralization of external resources.

A. *Organizational-level predictors*. There is variability in the extent to and rate at which organizations in a field change to become more like their peers. Some organizations respond to external pressures quickly; others change only after a long period of resistance. The first two hypotheses derive from our discussion of coercive isomorphism and constraint.

Hypothesis A-1: *The greater the dependence of an organization on another organization, the more similar it will become to that organization in structure, climate, and behavioral focus.* Following Thompson (1957) and Pfeffer and Salancik (1978), this proposition recognizes the greater ability of organizations to resist the demands of organizations on whom they are not dependent. A position of dependence leads to isomorphic change. Coercive pressures are built into exchange relationships. *[. . .]*

Hypothesis A-2: *The greater the centralization of organization A's resource supply, the greater the extent to which organization A will change isomorphically to resemble the organizations on which it depends for resources.* As Thompson (1967) notes, organizations that depend on the same sources for funding, personnel, and legitimacy will be more subject to the whims of resource suppliers than will organizations that can play one source of support off against another. In cases where alternative sources are either not readily available or require effort to locate, the stronger party to the transaction can coerce the weaker party to adopt its practices in order to accommodate the stronger party's needs (see Powell, 1983).

The third and fourth hypotheses derive from our discussion of mimetic isomorphism, modeling, and uncertainty.

Hypothesis A-3: *The more uncertain the relationship between means and ends the greater the extent to which an organization will model itself after organizations it perceives to be successful.* The mimetic thought process involved in the search for models is characteristic of change in organizations in which key technologies are only poorly understood (March and Cohen, 1974). [. . .]

Hypothesis A-4: *The more ambiguous the goals of an organization, the greater the extent to which the organization will model itself after organizations that it perceives to be successful.* There are two reasons for this. First, organizations with ambiguous or disputed goals are likely to be highly dependent upon appearances for legitimacy. Such organizations may find it to their advantage to meet the expectations of important constituencies about how they should be designed and run. [. . .] We contend that, in most situations, reliance on established, legitimated procedures enhances organizational legitimacy and survival characteristics. A second reason for modeling behavior is found in situations where conflict over organizational goals is repressed in the interest of harmony; thus participants find it easier to mimic other organizations than to make decisions on the basis of systematic analyses of goals since such analyses would prove painful or disruptive.

The fifth and sixth hypotheses are based on our discussion of normative processes found in professional organizations.

Hypothesis A-5: *The greater the reliance on academic credentials in choosing managerial and staff personnel, the greater the extent to which an organization will become like other organizations in its field.* Applicants with academic credentials have already undergone a socialization process in university programs, and are thus more likely than others to have internalized reigning norms and dominant organizational models.

Hypothesis A-5: *The greater the participation of organizational managers in trade and professional associations, the more likely the organization will be, or will become, like other organizations in its field.* [. . .]

B. *Field-level predictors.* The following six hypotheses describe the expected effects of several characteristics of organizational fields on the extent of isomorphism in a particular field. Since the effect of institutional isomorphism is homogenization, the best indicator of isomorphic change is a decrease in variation and diversity, which could be measured by lower standard deviations of the values of selected indicators in a set of organizations. [. . .]

Hypothesis B-1: *The greater the extent to which an organizational field is dependent upon a single (or several similar) source of support for vital resources, the higher the level of isomorphism.* The centralization of resources within a field both directly causes homogenization by placing organizations under similar pressures from resource suppliers, and interacts with uncertainty and goal ambiguity to increase their impact. [. . .]

Hypothesis B-2: *The greater the extent to which the organizations in a field transact with agencies of the state, the greater the extent of isomorphism in the field as a whole.* This follows not just from the previous hypothesis, but from two elements of state/private-sector transactions: their rule-boundedness and formal rationality, and the emphasis of government actors on institutional rules. Moreover, the federal government routinely designates industry standards for an entire field which require adoption by all competing firms. [. . .]

The third and fourth hypotheses follow from our discussion of isomorphic change resulting from uncertainty and modeling.

Hypothesis B-3: *The fewer the number of visible alternative organizational models in a field, the faster the rate of isomorphism in that field.* [. . .]

Hypothesis B-4: *The greater the extent to which technologies are uncertain or goals are ambiguous within a field, the greater the rate of isomorphic chan*ge. Somewhat counterintuitively, abrupt increases in uncertainty and ambiguity should, after brief periods of ideologically motivated experimentation, lead to rapid isomorphic change. As in the case of A-4, ambiguity and uncertainty may be a function of environmental definition, and, in any case, interact both with centralization of resources (A-1, A-2, B-1, B-2) and with professionalization and structuration (A-5, A-6, B-5, B-6). Moreover, in fields characterized by a high degree of uncertainty, new entrants, which could serve as sources of innovation and variation, will seek to overcome the liability of newness by imitating established practices within the field.

The two final hypotheses in this section follow from our discussion of professional filtering, socialization, and structuration.

Hypothesis B-5: The greater the extent of professionalization in a field, the greater the amount of institutional isomorphic change. Professionalization may be measured by the universality of credential requirements, the robustness of graduate training programs, or the vitality of professional and trade associations.

Hypothesis B-6: The greater the extent of structuration of a field, the greater the degree of isomorphics. Fields that have stable and broadly acknowledged centers, peripheries, and status orders will be more homogeneous both because the diffusion structure for new models and norms is more routine and because the level of interaction among organizations in the field is higher. While structuration may not lend itself to easy measurement, it might be tapped crudely with the use of such familiar measures as concentration ratios, reputational interview studies, or data on network characteristics.

[. . .]

We believe there is much to be gained by attending to similarity as well as to variation among organizations and, in particular, to change in the degree of homogeneity or variation over time. Our approach seeks to study incremental change as well as selection. We take seriously the observations of organizational theorists about the role of change, ambiguity, and constraint and point to the implications of these organizational characteristics for the social structure as a whole. The foci and motive forces of bureaucratization (and, more broadly, homogenization in general) have, as we argued, changed since Weber's time. But the importance of understanding the trends to which he called attention has never been more immediate.

NOTE

1. Knoke (1982), in a careful event-history analysis of the spread of municipal reform, refutes the conventional explanations of culture clash or hierarchal diffusion and finds but modest support for modernization theory. His major finding is that regional differences in municipal reform adoption arise not from social compositional differences, "but from some type of imitation or contagion effects as represented by the level of neighboring regional cities previously adopting reform government" (p. 1337).

REFERENCES

Aldrich, Howard. 1979. Organizations and Environments. Englewood Cliffs, NJ: Prentice-Hall.

Barnouw, Erik. 1966–68. A History of Broadcasting in the United States, 3 volumes. New York: Oxford University Press.

Child, John and Alfred Kieser. 1981. "Development of organizations over time." Pp. 28–64 in Paul C. Nystrom and William H. Starbuck (eds.), Handbook of Organizational Design. New York: Oxford University Press.

Cicourel, Aaron. 1970. "The acquisition of social structure: toward a developmental sociology of language." Pp. 136–68 in Jack D. Douglas (ed.), Understanding Everyday Life. Chicago: Aldine.

Collins, Randall. 1979. The Credential Society. New York: Academic Press.

Coser, Lewis, Charles Kadushin and Walter W. Powell. 1982. Books: The Culture and Commerce of Book Publishing. New York: Basic Books.

Cyert, Richard M. and James G. March. 1963. A Behavioral Theory of the Firm. Englewood Cliffs, NJ: Prentice-Hall.

DiMaggio, Paul. 1981. "Cultural entrepreneurship in nineteenth-century Boston. Part 1: The creation of an organizational base for high culture in America." Media, Culture and Society 4:33–50.

———. 1982. "The structure of organizational fields: an analytical approach and policy implications." Paper prepared for SUNY-Albany Conference on Organizational Theory and Public Policy. April 1 and 2.

Fennell, Mary L. 1980. "The effects of environmental characteristics on the structure of hospital clusters." Administrative Science Quarterly 25:484–510.

Freeman, John H. 1982. "Organizational life cycles and natural selection processes." Pp. 1–32 in Barry Staw and Larry Cummings (eds.), Research in Organizational Behavior. Vol. 4. Greenwich, CT: JAI Press.

Giddens, Anthony. 1979. Central Problems in Social Theory: Action, Structure, and Contradiction in Social Analysis. Berkeley: University of California Press.

Hall, Richard. 1968. "Professionalization and bureaucratization." American Sociological Review 33:92–104.

Hannan, Michael T. and John H. Freeman. 1977. "The population ecology of organizations." American Journal of Sociology 82:929–64.

Hawley, Amos. 1968. "Human ecology." Pp. 328–37 in David L. Sills (ed.), International Encyclopedia of the Social Sciences. New York: Macmillan.

Kanter, Rosabeth Moss. 1972. Commitment and Community. Cambridge, MA: Harvard University Press.

———. 1977. Men and Women of the Corporation. New York: Basic Books.

Katz, Michael B. 1975. Class, Bureaucracy, and Schools: The Illusion of Educational Change in America. New York: Praeger.

Kimberly, John. 1980. "Initiation, innovation and institutionalization in the creation process." Pp. 18–43 in John Kimberly and Robert B. Miles (eds.), The Organizational Life Cycle. San Francisco: Jossey-Bass.

Knoke, David. 1982. "The spread of municipal reform: temporal, spatial, and social dynamics." American Journal of Sociology 87:1314–39.

Larson, Magali Sarfatti. 1977. The Rise of Professionalism: A Sociological Analysis. Berkeley: University of California Press.

Lee, M. L. 1971. "A conspicuous production theory of hospital behavior." Southern Economic Journal 38:48–58.

March, James G. and Michael Cohen. 1974. Leadership and Ambiguity: The American College President. New York: McGraw-Hill.

March, James G. and Johan P. Olsen. 1976. Ambiguity and Choice in Organizations. Bergen, Norway: Universitetsforlaget.

Meyer, John W. 1979. "The impact of the centralization of educational funding and control on state and local organizational governance." Stanford, CA: Institute for Research on Educational Finance and Governance, Stanford University, Program Report No. 79–B20.

———. 1981. Remarks at ASA session on "The Present Crisis and the Decline in World Hegemony." Toronto, Canada.

Meyer, John W. and Michael Hannan. 1979. National Development and the World System: Educational, Economic, and Political Change. Chicago: University of Chicago Press.

Meyer, John W. and Brian Rowan. 1977. "Institutionalized organizations: formal structure as myth and ceremony." American Journal of Sociology 83:340–63.

Meyer, John W., W. Richard Scott and Terence C. Deal. 1981. "Institutional and technical sources of organizational structure explaining the structure of educational organizations." In Herman Stein (ed.), Organizations and the Human Services: Cross-Disciplinary Reflections. Philadelphia, PA: Temple University Press.

Milofsky, Carl. 1981. "Structure and process in community self-help organizations." New Haven: Yale Program on Non-Profit Organizations, Working Paper No. 17.

Ouchi, William G. 1980. "Markets, bureaucracies, and clans." Administrative Science Quarterly 25:129–41.

Perrow, Charles. 1974. "Is business really changing?" Organizational Dynamics Summer:31–44.

Pfeffer, Jeffrey and Gerald Salancik. 1978. The External Control of Organizations: A Resource Dependence Perspective. New York: Harper & Row.

Powell, Walter W. Forthcoming. "The Political Economy of Public Television." New Haven: Program on Non-Profit Organizations.

———. 1983. "New solutions to perennial problems of bookselling: whither the local bookstore?" Daedalus: Winter.

Ritti, R. R. and Fred H. Goldner. 1979. "Professional pluralism in an industrial organization." Management Science 16:233–46.

Rothman, Mitchell. 1980. "The evolution of forms of legal education." Unpublished manuscript. Department of Sociology, Yale University, New Haven, CT.

Rothschild-Whitt, Joyce. 1979. "The collectivist organization: an alternative to rational bureaucratic models." American Sociological Review 44:509–27.

Sedlak, Michael W. 1981. "Youth policy and young women, 1950–1972: the impact of private-sector programs for pregnant and wayward girls on public policy." Paper presented at National Institute for Education Youth Policy Research Conference, Washington, D.C.

Selznick, Philip. 1957. Leadership in Administration. New York: Harper & Row.

Starr, Paul. 1980. "Medical care and the boundaries of capitalist organization." Unpublished manuscript. Program on Non-Profit Organizations, Yale University, New Haven, CT.

Swidler, Ann. 1979. Organization Without Authority: Dilemmas of Social Control of Free Schools. Cambridge: Harvard University Press.

Thompson, James. 1967. Organizations in Action. New York: McGraw-Hill.

Tyack, David. 1974. The One Best System: A History of American Urban Education. Cambridge, MA: Harvard University Press.

Useem, Michael. 1979. "The social organization of the American business elite and participation of corporation directors in the governance of American institutions." American Sociological Review 44:553–72.

Weber, Max. 1952. The Protestant Ethic and the Spirit of Capitalism. New York: Scribner.

——. 1968. Economy and Society: An Outline of Interpretive Sociology. Three volumes. New York: Bedminster.

Westney, D. Eleanor. Forthcoming. Organizational Development and Social Change in Meiji, Japan.

Williamson, Oliver E. 1975. Markets and Hierarchies, Analysis and Antitrust Implications: A Study of the Economics of Internal Organization. New York: Free Press.

Woodward, John. 1965. Industrial Organization, Theory and Practice, London: Oxford University Press.

Zucker, Lynne G. and Pamela S. Tolbert. 1981. "Institutional sources of change in the formal structure of organizations: the diffusion of civil service reform, 1880–1935." Paper presented at American Sociological Association annual meeting, Toronto, Canada.

20

Density-Dependent Processes

Glenn R. Carroll

Michael T. Hannan

One of the major discoveries of human demographers concerns an empirical regularity known as "the demographic transition." Put simply, the demographic transition involves the changes associated with the movement of a society from a preindustrial to an industrial stage (Landry 1909; Landry 1934). In terms of vital rates, the demographic transition refers to a specific chronological sequencing of changes in vital rates from a point of roughly stable population size: first mortality rates decline, then fertility rates drop at some later time (Notestein 1945). As societies undergo the transition, the rate of population growth changes from low to high and then to low again. The details depend on the differences in the vital rates and the age distribution of the population (Kirk 1944; Davis 1945). Some societies pass through the transition rapidly. Other societies experience a significant lag between the decline in mortality rates and the decline in fertility rates, with the result that populations grow very large. However, as Chesnais (1992, 513) describes it, "the nature of demographic upheavals has evolved in almost identical manner from country to country." Comparative analysis of the demographic transition consists primarily of describing and explaining variations in the onset of declines in the vital rates and the magnitudes of change.

The demographic transition produces rapid population growth because of a particular pattern of historical *time dependence* in vital rates. In corporate demography, researchers have discovered that similar historic periods of rapid organizational population growth often arise because of a particular pattern of *density dependence* in vital rates. Such density dependence has been documented in scores of organizational populations in many different countries. The empirical regularities have also been

Table 20.1.   Estimates of Density Dependence in Vital Rates for Singapore Banks, 1840-1990

	Founding rate	*Failure rate*
Density	0.046*	-0.059*
Density squared/100	-0.026*	0.041*

* $p < .05$.
Source: Carroll and Teo (1998).

the subject of theoretical debate. The major outcome of these efforts has been the establishment of a general model of longterm organizational evolution: the density model of legitimation and competition (Hannan 1989; Hannan and Carroll 1992). This model assumes that change proceeds mainly through the selective replacement of different organizations, rather than through the adaptations of individual organizations. It posits two general forces as the drivers of selection: social legitimation and diffuse competition. Both forces are linked to the organizational density of a population (the number of organizations in the population).

[. . .]

CORPORATE DENSITY DEPENDENCE

An Empirical Illustration

As an illustration, Table 20.1 presents estimates of density-dependent effects in the vital rates of the banking population in Singapore.[1] As shown, the estimates all follow the nonmonotonic patterns typically found in corporate populations. Moreover, the relevant estimates are all statistically significant. Figures 20.1 and 20.2 show the predicted relationships between density and the vital rates, as given by these estimates. The figures illustrate clearly the common nonmonotonic relationships between density and organizational vital rates.

The parallel in turning points in Figures 20.1 and 20.2, which is characteristically seen in most populations, shows why nonmonotonic density dependence resembles (in some fashion) the demographic transition of human populations. When founding rates are at their maximum and mortality rates are simultaneously near their minimum, population growth will be exceedingly high. Indeed, the

population density trajectories for these and many other organizational populations often show an initial stage of slow growth, followed by one of rapid growth, and then proceeded by a stage of stabilization or decline. *[. . .]*

Despite the general similarity of estimated relationships between density and vital rates across many organizational populations, there is great diversity in the strength of the effects of density. Differences in these estimated effects imply high variation in the levels and speed at which the vital rates will turn with increases in density. As Chesnais (1992, 513) has noted for the demographic transition of human populations, the point is that: "similarity of trajectory does not preclude diversity of rates."

Comparative analysis of such variations in density-dependent rates across populations and contexts holds great promise for corporate demography, in our view. Hannan and Carroll (1992) made some initial efforts in this direction. They estimated and compared models of density dependence in five organizational populations in three countries. However, the widespread availability of measures of organizational density in a multitude of contexts means that the scope of comparative analysis could be much greater. *[. . .]*

THEORY OF DENSITY-DEPENDENT EVOLUTION

Good comparative social research uses a theoretical framework to guide investigation and facilitate interpretation. Research on corporate density dependence has from its inception been driven by a specific theory of organizational evolution. The theory of density-dependent organizational evolution holds that the general forces of social legitimation

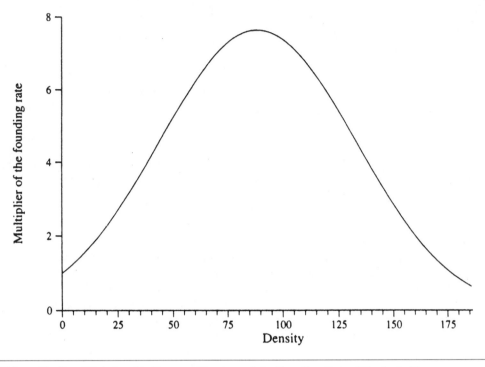

Figure 20.1.   Predicted Relationship Between Density and the Founding Rate of Banks in Singapore

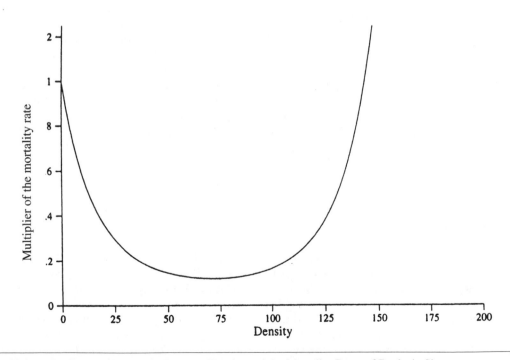

Figure 20.2.   Predicted Relationship Between Density and the Mortality Rates of Banks in Singapore

and competition drive changes in vital rates over time. It also contends that social legitimation and competition are themselves molded by organizational density.

The history of legitimation and competition for any organizational population arguably depends on idiosyncratic features of its form, the conditions under which it evolved, and the detailed texture of temporal and spatial variations in its environment. In other words, reconstructing the exact details of changing levels of legitimation and competition over the history of any one population demands attention to all of the unique features of that population's history. A key question in trying to understand organizational evolution concerns the importance of idiosyncrasy. Do special features of populations and their histories dominate, or do population histories work out minor variations on common patterns? The theory used in corporate demography takes a strong stance in favor of generality in terms of the overall forms of relationships.

Next we discuss the two main components of the theory. The first relates density to legitimation and competition, two concepts that researchers find difficult to measure directly over the full histories of organizational populations. The second links the vital rates to competition and legitimation.

Legitimation

What does it mean for an organizational form to be legitimated? One common answer holds that a form receives legitimation to the extent that its structure and routines follow the prevailing institutional rules. In this usage, legitimation means conformity with a set of rules, what DiMaggio and Powell (1983) termed coercive isomorphism. A second answer holds that an organizational form gains legitimation when it attains a socially taken-for-granted character (Meyer and Rowan 1977). A form acquires this second kind of legitimation, which we call *constitutive legitimation*, when relevant actors see it (perhaps implicitly) as the natural way to effect some kind of collective action.

These two conceptions of legitimation differ. What a society's laws endorse and prohibit might not correspond closely with what its members take for granted. It turns out that the conception of constitutive legitimation (taken-for-grantedness) has

been more productive for developing theory and research on organizational demography, because it has a clear-cut link with density. So, we restrict our attention to constitutive legitimation here. [. . .]

When a new organizational form appears, say automobile manufacturing in the late nineteenth century, it usually lacks constitutive legitimation.[2] This situation makes organizing difficult: capital sources are wary; suppliers and customers need to be educated; employees might be hard to identify and recruit; and in many instances hostile institutional rules must be changed. As the form is promulgated, legitimation increases. Initially, when there are few organizations in the population, the returns to legitimation of adding another organization are great. However, when the population contains many organizations, constitutive legitimation increases very little—perhaps not at all—as the density of the population rises. In other words, the constitutive legitimation of an organizational population increases with density at a decreasing rate and approaches a ceiling at high levels of density.

So, it seems clear that extreme rarity of a form poses serious problems of constitutive legitimation. If almost no instances of a form exist, it can hardly be taken as the natural way to achieve some collective end. On the other hand, once a form becomes common, it seems unlikely that increases in numbers will have a great effect on its institutional standing. In other words, legitimation responds to variations in density in the lower range, but the effect has a ceiling. [. . .]

The founding rates of populations surely must be affected by the constitutive legitimation of the organizational forms used. A taken-for-granted social form can be more readily visualized by potential organizers than one with dubious or unknown standing. Institutional rules endorsing particular organizational forms as the appropriate means for attaining collective goals also affect the ease of founding those types of organizations. The capacity to mobilize potential members and resources increases greatly when those who control resources take the organizational form for granted. Reducing the need for such justifications lowers the cost of organizing.

Constitutive legitimation also has a straightforward link with organizational mortality. Most institutional theories imply that legitimation enhances the life chances of organizations. Legitimation eases problem of maintaining flows of resources from the environment; it also enhances the ability of organizations to fend off challenges (Meyer and Rowan 1977).

Competition

Competition refers to some kind of negative effect of the presence of one or more actors on the life chances or growth rates of some focal actor. Some important kinds of competition are structured or directed, as when two actors engage in rivalry or so-called head-to-head competition. In other cases, the effects are indirect or diffuse, as when a set of actors are dependent upon a pool of limited resources. In such cases, the entry of additional actors into the arena lowers the life chances of a focal actor by increasing the demand on the resource base. Such diffuse competition does not require that the actors take account of each others' actions or even be aware of their existence. Both structured and diffuse competition are important to understanding the life chances of organizations.

The demographic theory of density dependence focuses on diffuse competition because of its clear relationship with density, viz., the intensity of diffuse competition within an organizational population rises as a function of the number of potential bilateral competitors. In a population of N organizations, as N increases linearly, the number of possible competitive relations increases geometrically (Hannan and Carroll 1992). This implies that diffuse competition rises with a population's density at an increasing rate. In other words, variations in the range of high density (relative to abundance of resources) have more impact on strength of competition than do variations in the lower range. When numbers are few, an increase of population size by a single organization increases the frequency and strength of competitive interactions slightly if at all. However, when density is high relative to the carrying capacity, addition of another organization greatly increases the competition. Viewed from the viewpoint of the actions of a single organization, the difficulty of fashioning a strategy that works against all (or most) competitors becomes extraordinarily difficult when very many pairwise interactions must be considered simultaneously.

[. . .]

Organizational analysts generally believe that intense competitive pressure within an organizational population depresses organizational founding rates. As the level of diffuse competition increases, more of the resources needed to build and sustain organizations have already been claimed by other organizations. Intense competition causes supplies of potential organizers, members, patrons, and resources to become exhausted. When diffuse competition is intense, fewer resources go unclaimed and markets get packed tightly.

Given a finite carrying capacity set by environmental conditions, as the number of potential competitors increases, the potential gains from founding an organization decline. Actors with the knowledge and skills to build organizations would be expected to defer attempts at building organizations in densely populated environments. This sort of process contributes to a negative relationship between competition and the founding rate. Capital markets and other macrostructures often reinforce this tendency. For example, rational investors typically avoid participating in new ventures in highly competitive markets. Likewise, professional associations and government agencies often try to restrict entry under intense competition. These arguments point in the same direction. The founding rate of an organizational population is inversely proportional to the intensity of competition within the population.

[. . .]

In the case of mortality, all relevant arguments imply that competition increases the hazard. Every organization must maintain a flow of resources from its environment to keep its structures intact. As competition intensifies, maintaining life-sustaining flows of resources becomes problematic for many, if not all, organizations in a population. Therefore, increasing diffuse competition lowers the life chances of organizations by complicating the task of maintaining a flow of essential resources. In other words, if competition is already intense, then further growth increases mortality rates, after controlling for the environmental conditions that affect carrying capacities.

INTERPRETING DENSITY DEPENDENCE

As might be expected given its fast popularity, the theory of density-dependent legitimation and competition has not escaped criticism. Virtually all of this commentary has been directed at the theory or at theoretical interpretations of the evidence. Little debate has centered on whether the widely observed empirical associations of nonmonotonic density dependence in vital rates are valid.[3]

Some Criticisms

Critiques of the theory and its interpretation convey three general themes. The first deals exclusively with the social legitimation process. Economists usually find this part of the theory intriguing; sociologists sometimes find it lacking. Why? What would cause sociologists to question the operation of a key sociological process? Some of the criticism is pure folly. However, the serious complaints usually call for either more direct measures of legitimation or for a broader conceptualization that includes legal or sociopolitical legitimacy. Nothing is wrong with either suggestion. Nonetheless, waiting for a breakthrough in measurement technology that allows one to assess directly and to compare across contexts the taken-for-granted nature of persons and other actors living decades and even centuries in the past might delay the research project for many years, perhaps forever. In the meantime, using a formal model to infer the operation of legitimation processes seems a sensible strategy.

In the view of most sociologists, legal or sociopolitical legitimacy is distinct from constitutive legitimation (Hannan and Carroll 1995). Little value would result from mixing the two into a single concept or measure, thus muddying up the waters. Taken alone, no one doubts that legal or sociopolitical legitimacy powerfully shapes organizational evolution. Consider, for instance, the organizational consequences of the Volstead Act, which prohibited the production and sale of alcohol products from 1920 to 1933. However, it is hard to build a predictive general theory around idiosyncratic, historically specific acts of legislation and the like. Instead, the better approach would seem to be to incorporate these developments as control variables based on an understanding of a population's history. Without such controls, tests of the density-dependent theory of legitimation and competition would be flawed. But this is clearly not the case, as examination of any major study of the theory shows that analysts have taken pains to control for such events.

The second general theme of critiques focuses on the density variable itself. According to these views, analysis of organizational density is an incomplete way to model evolution (Winter 1990; Haveman 1994). The opinion expressed recently by Nelson (1995, 69) typifies this position: "In assessing the relative importance of a particular routine in the industry mix, or analyzing whether it is expanding or contracting in relative use, it is not sufficient to 'count' the firms employing it. One must consider their size, or whether they are growing or contracting." Again, it is hard to disagree. Any theory or model is an abstraction and must involve simplifications. So, it is also not entirely clear what the critique implies for research on the density model.

One interpretation holds that tests of density dependence in organizational evolution need to control for organizational size, industry size, and temporal variation in both. No debate here. Although early tests often ignored these factors because of data unavailability, numerous recent tests all include such measures. These tests show unequivocally that density dependence is a unique and general phenomenon. Another interpretation of remarks by Nelson (1995) and others' remarks implies that other, possibly complementary, possibly competing general evolutionary theories of organizations based on characteristics such as size ought to be developed. Sure enough; the world of corporate demography is certainly big enough for multiple theories to coexist.

The third critical theme targets the diffuse-competition component of the model, whereby all organizations in the population potentially compete with each other. It argues that a better formulation for many contexts would be based on *direct* competition, using subsets of organizations that clearly draw from similar or overlapping resources. The operational consequences of this position entail either redrawing the boundaries for counting density so that only direct competitors are included or weighting density counts of population members based on proximity along some competitive dimension such as price or geography (McPherson 1983; Barnett and Carroll 1987; Baum and Mezias 1992; Baum and Singh 1994). As we discuss below, this approach might best be regarded as an extension or refinement of the basic density model (involving weighted density) applicable to particular contexts. Studies to date demonstrate high promise for its use in understanding and modeling interorganizational relationships. Nonetheless, questions remain about whether diffuse competition as modeled in the basic density model captures a distinct process or simply represents a good shorthand approximation to direct competition averaged across an entire population.

Qualitative Evidence

A complementary way of establishing the plausibility of theory involves examining the natural histories of organizational populations and looking for evidence of the large-scale operation of processes of constitutive legitimation and diffuse competition. Does a population's natural history conform to the general predictions of initial growth and development driven by legitimation and later, high-density evolution fueled primarily by competition? This approach is decidedly subjective, but it does lend plausibility to the theory when, for example, diverse histories portray similar longterm struggles for establishing constitutive legitimation or taken-for-grantedness, which has generally been the case in those histories reported. For instance, Hannan and Freeman (1989) describe how early labor unions faced hostile employers and laws that questioned their right to exist. Carroll (1984a) discusses Mott's (1962) and Schudson's (1978) accounts of battles of the legality of publishing as well as the difficulties of establishing a market for advertising. If constitutive legitimation had existed initially at the low-density points of these populations, then we believe that these histories would read differently.

Natural histories of organizational populations also suggest some intriguing possible embellishments of the theory. An interesting recurring observation of this kind concerns the level of and nature of social organization found early in the history of many industries or organizational populations. Simply put, actions in the origin periods of industries typically look and feel to sociologists like the actions of social movements. This is true for telephony (Barnett and Carroll 1993), newspapers (Olzak and West 1991), automobiles (Carroll and Hannan 1995b), labor unions (Hannan 1995), credit unions (Barron 1998), and health maintenance organizations (Strang 1995). Other industries have for the most part not been examined in this way.

What does this observation mean? A social movement is generally considered to be "the organized, sustained, self-conscious challenge to existing authorities" (Tilly 1984, 304). It is defined as

> a deliberate collective endeavor to promote change, in any direction and by any means possible . . . a movement's commitment to change and the raison d'être of its organization are founded upon the conscious volition, normative commitment to the movement's aims or beliefs, and active participation on the part of the followers or members. (Wilkinson 1971, 27)

So, to say that the origin periods of industries resemble social movements means that (1) they represent challenges to existing companies and industries and (2) they are populated with individuals and organizations devoted to causes, lifestyles, and visions of a better future for all (rather than with profit-maximizing entrepreneurs engaged in competitive battles based primarily on self-interest).

The theoretical implications of this observation have yet to be explored in any depth. They might be profound. *[. . .]*

NOTES

1. These models also include the estimated effects of other covariates—see Carroll and Teo (1998) for full specification.

2. In some cases, organizational forms might inherit legitimation from closely related existing forms. For instance, Boone et al. (2000) argue that the population of auditing firms inherited the legitimacy of the well-established population of accounting firms.

3. See, however, Petersen and Koput (1991), Hannan, Barron, and Carroll (1991), and Hannan and Carroll (1992, 132–138).

REFERENCES

Boone, Christophe, Vera Bröcheler and Glenn R. Carroll. 2000. "Custom Service: Application and Tests of Resource-Partitioning Theory Among Dutch Auditing Firms from 1880 to 1982." *Organization Studies*.

Carroll, Glenn R. and Albert C. Y. Teo. 1998. "How Regulation and Globalization Affected Organizational Legitimation and Competition Among Commercial Banks in Singapore, 1840–1994." Presented at the Annual Meetings of the Academy of Management.

Hannan, Michael T. and Glenn R. Carroll. 1992. *Dynamics of Organizational Populations: Density, Legitimation, and Competition.* New York: Oxford University Press.

Hannan, Michael T., David N. Barron, and Glenn R. Carroll. 1991. "On the Interpretation of Density Dependence in Rates of Organizational Mortality: A Reply to Petersen and Koput." *American Sociological Review,* 56:410–415.

Petersen, Trond and Kenneth W. Koput. 1991. "Density Dependence in Organizational Mortality: Legitimacy or Unobserved Heterogeneity?" *American Sociological Review,* 56:399–409.

PART VIII

ECONOMIC THEORIES OF ORGANIZATIONS

Traditionally, economics did not have a theory of organizations nor even think one necessary. Where there is market discipline, even a large, bureaucratic organization will behave no differently from a lone entrepreneur in all important respects if it is to maximize profits and survive, according to this view. Yet economics was confronted with the puzzle of why organizations exist at all and how to explain the distinctive issues that arise from these stable, long-term institutional arrangements.

In principle, all economic activity could be conducted through market transactions. All individuals at different stages of a production process could simply contract with one another on an *ad hoc* basis to acquire the inputs they needed and sell the outputs they produced. An assembly line could be organized as simply a collection of independent businessmen with each prior workstation buying components from the previous one and selling its semifinished products to the next. The concept is not completely fanciful, because different factories and companies in the same industries buy or make different proportions of their final output and there is not always an obvious reason why some plants take certain operations internal while others contract with outside suppliers for the same input. By the 1970s, the question of why administrative coordination within organizations exists at all and how it differs from simple markets were recognized as puzzles that needed explanation.

Economic accounts of organizations vary, but all begin with a strong assumption that individuals and organizations freely and rationally pursue their own self-interest. In general, economic theorists are reluctant to believe that actors engage in altruism, act irrationally, or follow norms, or that firms exercise power over either workers or other actors in the marketplace, though self-interest motivates them to seek monopoly advantage. There is a tendency to see existing institutional arrangements as efficient on the assumption that the discipline of market competition would have selected against them if they were not. In neoclassical economics, the market is a world of free and voluntary agreements among equals that promotes maximum welfare and, insofar as a society of organizations forces them to modify those assumptions, economists accept such qualifications reluctantly.

One of the most influential economic approaches to organizations is *agency theory* as developed by Michael Jensen and William Meckling (Reading 21). Though it is not always clear how to assign roles, in general, the party initiating a transaction or who has a broader interest in the relationship is considered the *principal* and the party that to whom tasks and some decision making are delegated is called the *agent*. Employers are usually considered principals and workers are their agents, and, in a large corporation, stockholders are principals and managers are their agents. The problem is that hired hands or agents cannot be assumed to share the interests of the principals who employ them; there is a high chance they maximize their own interest by seeking the greatest reward for the least effort possible. Because principals cannot monitor agents without incurring costs, due to bounded rationality, there are widespread *agency problems* in economic transactions that need to be addressed.

Jensen and Meckling examine the modern corporation from an agency theory perspective. Prior to the 1920s, owners ran virtually all business organizations. However, large corporations soon required greater financing than wealthy individuals or small groups of investors could provide, and stock was sold to the general public to raise funds. Soon stockholding became so dispersed that the official owners of the corporation were a very separate group of people from the actual managers running the organization, who tended to become more professionalized during this time. Stockholders became somewhat like Michels' passive rank and file, following the wishes of corporate management in annual votes for boards of directors and various policy resolutions.

Classical administrative theory since Gulick argued that organizations emerge to solve problems of complex cooperation, but this *separation of ownership from control*, as it was called, raised the problem that not everyone would cooperate as intended. Managers' operate with stockholders' money but exercise *de facto* rule and thus are free to give themselves high salaries and perks, large staffs, and easy performance standards—in short, to maximize their own interests rather than stockholder profits (*residual loss*).

Jensen and Meckling recommend various reforms in corporate governance to control possible management shirking. In principle, boards of directors should safeguard shareholder interests and discipline ineffective managers, but in practice board members are often drawn from top management or are allied with them. Jensen and Meckling advocate greater board independence and believe managers should be required to disclose more information to reduce investors' monitoring problems and bounded rationality. Stock-based compensation and other pay-for-performance schemes should be a greater fraction of managerial compensation because they align the incentives of principals and agents. Finally, if management continues to suboptimize, the stock market will provide the ultimate safeguard, as poor management will cause investors to sell and the corporate share prices to fall. Top management will face the threat of a takeover by management teams in other companies who see the stock as undervalued and who believe they can raise profits and the stock price once they gain a controlling share and install their own management. Ultimately, the market—in this case the market for corporate control—enforces discipline on self-seeking agents, though this process may work more or less swiftly.

Jensen and Meckling's recommendations for reforming corporate governance have had a large influence on actual practice. In the last twenty years, in response to what was perceived as excessive management autonomy and underperformance, stockholders have pressured companies to use more stock-based compensation for top executives, remove defensive barriers to takeover threats, disclose more information, allow greater stockholder oversight, and increase the independence of boards of directors (Useem 1993). There is some controversy over whether these changes have improved efficiency in socially desirable ways or placed such stress on managers to meet short-term profit goals that they sacrifice patient, long-term investment and the wages and jobs of workers in lagging business lines who are downsized to satisfy continual shareholder demands for high returns (Harrison and Bluestone 1988). In addition, top management had a strong incentive to exaggerate the performance of their companies by inflating quarterly earnings and stock prices to maintain the value of their stock options and salaries. Recent government investigations reveal that some of the largest and most respected corporations engaged in questionable or illegal accounting and business practices to give a better impression of corporate performance than was warranted; in some cases, such as Enron and WorldCom, the companies were on the verge of failure. Clearly, linking executive pay to performance does not always align the interests of managers and stockholders in the ways intended.

Oliver Williamson asks more basic questions (Reading 22). Why are there firms at all? Why not organize all economic activity using spot markets and one-time contracts among strangers? And, if firms are efficient, why are there many firms rather than just one giant organization for the entire economy? In fact, managers do choose whether to use markets or bureaucratic organizations, known as the make-or-buy decision, and the boundary that divides markets from bureaucratic hierarchies is drawn differently in different industries.

Though many argue that technology requires certain stages of the production process to be located in the same place, Williamson argues that there is no reason in principle why two individuals could not own two different stages even if they always only transact with one another and operate in complete cooperation. The real problem is the cost of market contracting, which Williamson calls *transaction costs*. Contracts are always costly to negotiate, monitor, and enforce, but sometimes they are so costly that it makes sense for the exchange to occur under the roof of a common organizational hierarchy rather than between two autonomous market actors. In this case, commands from a common superior rather than costly contract negotiations or litigation can resolve any disputes or potential problems between exchange partners more rapidly and completely.

When there are many buyers and sellers in a market and the goods and services offered are identical so that price is the only issue, then market contracting is not so costly and serves as an adequate governance device. If one exchange partner fails to honor an agreement to deliver goods at the agreed price, date, and quality, it is not expensive to switch partners.

But important goods and services are sometimes specialized to one particular use, which Williamson calls *asset specificity*. For instance, one kind of part may have only one supplier and only one buyer. If individual buyers and sellers continuously rely on one another to satisfy their needs, the partners are locked into a mutual relationship of dependency or *small numbers bargaining*. Put a different way, if the good or service cannot be bought from or sold to others on an open market, the discipline of market competition and possibility of exit are absent and there is a situation of *bilateral monopoly*.

If everyone operated in good faith or if it were easy to spot dishonesty, then one could still rely on market contracting without fear for one's own well-being.

But actors are *opportunistic*, and bounded rationality means that one cannot easily detect dishonesty until long after the fact, which becomes an even bigger problem when it is not easy to exit the relationship.

Williamson concludes that bureaucratic hierarchy replaces market transactions between independent actors when the transactions are frequent, the assets involved are specific to the particular buyer-seller relationship, and it is difficult to write contracts covering all contingencies and monitor compliance. In this case, the transaction costs of market contracting are so high that there must be a formal governance structure to protect sunk investments from the possibility that one or the other party might abuse their position. Discipline and monitoring within a common organization are more efficient than markets in detecting and eliminating opportunism because a superior has greater access to information on subunit efficiency and adjudication or disciplining power than two independent businesses that buy and sell from one another could exercise with respect to each other. Opportunism is also reduced because all subunits tend to work toward a common overall goal by virtue of belonging to the same organization, and the responsibilities of different subunits can be specified in an open-ended fashion rather than requiring a highly detailed contract.

Williamson uses his framework not just to explain why organizations in general replace markets, but also to account for their specific shape, particularly why organizations have come to progressively absorb their suppliers and sometimes their distributors over time, known as *vertical integration*, and why they provide long-term employment to their workers.

Williamson argues that single product firms integrated vertically when they found themselves so highly dependent on their regular suppliers that it made sense from a management perspective to integrate backward and internalize what had been market transactions to ensure a steady supply of inputs. Likewise, if a company produced a good requiring extensive demonstration and information before the sale and substantial servicing after the sale, the company may integrate forward into retail distribution. If commodities are perishable and carry the manufacturer's brand name, the manufacturer might integrate forward into wholesaling to safeguard the reputation of its products. Where there are no such hazards and dependencies, market transactions predominate. Thus, Williamson explains the rise of big business as an efficient adaptation to the problem of economizing on transaction costs.

In employment contracts, when workers develop firm-specific knowledge, both parties have a stake in ensuring continuity of the relationship, because the employer cannot easily find the specialized knowledge on the open labor market nor can workers easily find another employer willing to compensate them for it. The results are various institutions designed to promote long-term employment relations rather than short-term contracts, such as fixed pay scales rather than piecework, promotion ladders and pensions to encourage long-term attachment to the firm, and grievance procedures to resolve disputes.

Both agency theory and Williamson's transaction cost economics have been very influential in organization studies, but have also been criticized. They underscore the importance of rational calculation and individual self-interest in understanding organizational structure and practice, but give little attention to the possibility that outcomes may reflect the concentration of power among some actors such as corporate managers, rather than efficiency. Existing arrangements are assumed to be efficient otherwise they would have been eliminated through competitive selection, so the only task is to discover the positive function they serve. Also, unlike institutional theory, there is little awareness here that some practices, such as corporate organization or career ladders and long-term employment, may have spread because of imitation, cultural conceptions, and a perception that they were appropriate rather than carefully collected evidence of their superior efficiency.

Charles Perrow (Reading 23) notes that many of the problems of bounded rationality, opportunism, and small-numbers bargaining are replicated within firms. Mere common ownership is often not sufficient to solve monitoring problems. Different subunits may still engage in opportunism and overcharge their internal customers, especially when there is no market price comparison, the so-called *transfer pricing problem*. The real reason for the growth in organizational size in the late nineteenth and twentieth centuries, according to Perrow, is that firms seek security through growth. Mergers and vertical integration often reflect a drive for market power, rather than greater efficiency. The concept of transaction costs is sufficiently elastic to justify any arrangement, but there are many examples of corporate concentration or big business that do not seem to have superior efficiency properties.

In a different vein, Mark Granovetter (1985) argued that Williamson operated with an undersocialized view of the market and an oversocialized view of organizations. Williamson assumed that market activity was like Hobbes's state of nature, in which force and fraud were so common that a dictator in the form of the organizational command hierarchy was needed, while the stability and normative order it imposed were so complete that all opportunism disappeared. In truth, trust is often more important than a legalistic concern for contract language in interfirm relations. All economic relations require an overlay of social relations. Excessive legalism can itself generate ill will and performance to the letter of an agreement rather than its spirit. Granovetter argues that it is the quality of social relations between firms that is important and that vertical integration occurs when an effective network of personal relations is absent.

Though the study of organizations from an economics perspective has generated controversy in organization studies, it remains an important part of the conceptual tool kit used by researchers in the field.

21

THEORY OF THE FIRM

Managerial Behavior, Agency Costs and Ownership Structure

MICHAEL C. JENSEN

WILLIAM H. MECKLING

The directors of such [joint-stock] companies, however, being the managers rather of other people's money than of their own, it cannot well be expected, that they should watch over it with the same anxious vigilance with which the partners in a private copartnery frequently watch over their own. Like the stewards of a rich man, they are apt to consider attention to small matters as not for their master's honour, and very easily give themselves a dispensation from having it. Negligence and profusion, therefore, must always prevail, more or less, in the management of the affairs of such a company.

Adam Smith, *The Wealth of Nations*, 1776, Cannan Edition
(Modern Library, New York, 1937) p. 700.

Reprinted from the *Journal of Financial Economics*, Vol. 3, Michael C. Jensen and William H. Meckling, "Theory of the Firm: Managerial Behavior, Agency Costs and Ownership Structure," pp. 305–360. Copyright © 1976, reprinted with permission of Elsevier Science.

INTRODUCTION AND SUMMARY

1.1 Motivation of the Paper

In this paper we draw on recent progress in the theory of (1) property rights, (2) agency, and (3) finance to develop a theory of ownership structure for the firm. In addition to tying together elements of the theory of each of these three areas, our analysis casts new light on and has implications for a variety of issues in the professional and popular literature such as the definition of the firm, the "separation of ownership and control," the "social responsibility" of business, the definition of a "corporate objective function," the determination of an optimal capital structure, the specification of the content of credit agreements, the theory of organizations, and the supply side of the completeness of markets problem. [. . .]

1.2 Theory of the Firm: An Empty Box?

While the literature of economics is replete with references to the "theory of the firm" the material generally subsumed under that heading is not a theory of the firm but actually a theory of markets in which firms are important actors. The firm is a "black box" operated so as to meet the relevant marginal conditions with respect to inputs and outputs, thereby maximizing profits, or more accurately, present value. Except for a few recent and tentative steps, however, we have no theory which explains how the conflicting objectives of the individual participants are brought into equilibrium so as to yield this result. The limitations of this black box view of the firm have been cited by Adam Smith and Alfred Marshall, among others. More recently, popular and professional debates over the "social responsibility" of corporations, the separation of ownership and control, and the rash of reviews of the literature on the "theory of the firm" have evidenced continuing concern with these issues.[1]

A number of major attempts have been made during recent years to construct a theory of the firm by substituting other models for profit or value maximization; each attempt motivated by a conviction that the latter is inadequate to explain managerial behavior in large corporations.[2] Some of these reformulation attempts have rejected the fundamental principle of maximizing behavior as well as rejecting the more specific profit maximizing model. We retain the notion of maximizing behavior on the part of all individuals in the analysis to follow.

[. . .] We focus in this paper on behavioral implications of the property rights specified in the contracts between the owners and managers of the firm. [. . .]

1.4 Agency Costs

Many problems associated with the inadequacy of the current theory of the firm can also be viewed as special cases of the theory of agency relationships in which there is a growing literature.[3] [. . .]

We define an agency relationship as a contract under which one or more persons (the principal(s)) engage another person (the agent) to perform some service on their behalf which involves delegating some decision making authority to the agent. If both parties to the relationship are utility maximizers there is good reason to believe that the agent will not always act in the best interests of the principal. The *principal* can limit divergences from his interest by establishing appropriate incentives for the agent and by incurring monitoring costs designed to limit the aberrant activities of the agent. In addition in some situations it will pay the *agent* to expend resources (bonding costs) to guarantee that he will not take certain actions which would harm the principal or to ensure that the principal will be compensated if he does take such actions. However, it is generally impossible for the principal or the agent at zero cost to ensure that the agent will make optimal decisions from the principal's viewpoint. In most agency relationships the principal and the agent will incur positive monitoring and bonding costs (non-pecuniary as well as pecuniary), and in addition there will be some divergence between the agent's decisions[4] and those decisions which would maximize the welfare of the principal. The dollar equivalent of the reduction in welfare experienced by the principal due to this divergence is also a cost of the agency relationship, and we refer to this latter cost as the "residual loss." We define *agency costs* as the sum of:

(1) the monitoring expenditures by the principal,[5]

(2) the bonding expenditures by the agent,

(3) the residual loss.

Note also that agency costs arise in any situation involving cooperative effort (such as the co-authoring of this paper) by two or more people even though there is no clear cut principal-agent relationship. Viewed in this light it is clear that our definition of agency costs and their importance to the theory of the firm bears a close relationship to the problem of shirking and monitoring of team production which Alchian and Demsetz (1972) raise in their paper on the theory of the firm.

Since the relationship between the stockholders and manager of a corporation fit the definition of a pure agency relationship it should be no surprise to discover that the issues associated with the "separation of ownership and control" in the modern diffuse ownership corporation are intimately associated with the general problem of agency. We show below that an explanation of why and how the agency costs generated by the corporate form are born leads to a theory of the ownership (or capital) structure of the firm.

Before moving on, however, it is worthwhile to point out the generality of the agency problem. The problem of inducing an "agent" to behave as if he were maximizing the "principal's" welfare is quite general. It exists in all organizations and in all cooperative efforts—at every level of management in firms, in universities, in mutual companies, in cooperatives, in governmental authorities and bureaus, in unions, and in relationships normally classified as agency relationships such as are common in the performing arts and the market for real estate. The development of theories to explain the form which agency costs take in each of these situations (where the contractual relations differ significantly), and how and why they are born will lead to a rich theory of organizations which is now lacking in economics and the social sciences generally. We confine our attention in this paper to only a small part of this general problem—the analysis of agency costs generated by the contractual arrangements between the owners and top management of the corporation.

[. . .]

1.5. Some General Comments on the Definition of the Firm

Ronald Coase (1937) in his seminal paper on "The Nature of the Firm" pointed out that economics had no positive theory to determine the bounds of the firm. He characterized the bounds of the firm as that range of exchanges over which the market system was suppressed and resource allocation was accomplished instead by authority and direction. He focused on the cost of using markets to effect contracts and exchanges and argued that activities would be included within the firm whenever the costs of using markets were greater than the costs of using direct authority. Alchian and Demsetz (1972) object to the notion that activities within the firm are governed by authority, and correctly emphasize the role of contracts as a vehicle for voluntary exchange. They emphasize the role of monitoring in situations in which there is joint input or team production.[6] We sympathize with the importance they attach to monitoring, but we believe the emphasis which Alchian-Demsetz place on joint input production is too narrow and therefore misleading. Contractual relations are the essence of the firm, not only with employees but with suppliers, customers, creditors, etc. The problem of agency costs and monitoring exists for all of these contracts, independent of whether there is joint production in their sense; i.e., joint production can explain only a small fraction of the behavior of individuals associated with a firm. *[. . .]*

It is important to recognize that most organizations are simply *legal fictions*[7] *which serve as a nexus for a set of contracting relationships among individuals*. This includes firms, non-profit institutions such as universities, hospitals and foundations, mutual organizations such as mutual savings banks and insurance companies and co-operatives, some private clubs, and even governmental bodies such as cities, states and the Federal government, government enterprises such as TVA, the Post Office, transit systems, etc.

The private corporation or firm is simply one form of *legal fiction which serves as a nexus for contracting relationships and which is also characterized by the existence of divisible residual claims on the assets and cash flows of the organization which can generally be sold without permission of the other contracting individuals*. While this definition of the firm has little substantive content, emphasizing the essential contractual nature of firms and other organizations focuses attention on a crucial set of questions—why particular sets of contractual relations arise for various types of organizations, what the consequences of these contractual relations are, and how they are affected by changes exogenous to the organization. Viewed this way, it makes little or no sense to try to distinguish those things which are "inside" the firm (or any other organization) from those things that are "outside" of it. There is in a very real sense only a multitude of complex relationships (i.e., contracts) between the legal fiction (the firm) and the owners of labor, material and capital inputs and the consumers of output.

Viewing the firm as the nexus of a set of contracting relationships among individuals also serves to make it clear that the personalization of the firm implied by asking questions such as "what should be the objective function of the firm," or "does the firm have a social responsibility" is seriously misleading. *The firm is not an individual*. It is a legal fiction which serves as a focus for a complex process in which the conflicting objectives of individuals (some of whom may "represent" other organizations) are brought into equilibrium within a framework of contractual relations. In this sense the "behavior" of the firm is like the behavior of a market; i.e., the outcome of a complex equilibrium process. We seldom fall into the trap of characterizing the wheat or stock market as an individual, but we often make this error by thinking about organizations as if they were persons with motivations and intentions.

[. . .]

2. THE AGENCY COSTS OF OUTSIDE EQUITY

2.1 Overview

[. . .] If a wholly owned firm is managed by the owner, he will make operating decisions which maximize his utility. These decisions will involve not only the benefits he derives from pecuniary returns but also the utility generated by various non-pecuniary aspects of his entrepreneurial activities such as the physical appointments of the office, the attractiveness of the secretarial staff, the level of employee discipline, the kind and amount of charitable contributions, personal relations ("love," "respect," etc.) with employees, a larger than optimal computer to play with, purchase of production inputs from friends, etc. The optimum mix (in the absence of taxes) of the various pecuniary and non-pecuniary benefits is achieved when the marginal utility derived from an additional dollar of expenditure (measured net of any productive effects) is equal for each non-pecuniary item and equal to the marginal utility derived from an additional dollar of after tax purchasing power (wealth).

If the owner-manager sells equity *[stock]* claims on the corporation which are identical to his (i.e., share proportionately in the profits of the firm and have limited liability) agency costs will be generated by the divergence between his interest and those of the outside shareholders, since he will then bear only a fraction of the costs of any non-pecuniary benefits he takes out in maximizing his own utility. If the manager owns only 95 percent of the stock, he will expend resources to the point where the marginal utility derived from a dollar's expenditure of the firm's resources on such items equals the marginal utility of an additional 95 cents in general purchasing power (i.e., *his* share of the wealth reduction) and not one dollar. Such activities, on his part, can be limited (but probably not eliminated) by the expenditure of resources on monitoring activities by the outside stockholders. But as we show below, the owner will bear the entire wealth effects of these expected costs so long as the equity *[stock]* market anticipates these effects. Prospective minority shareholders will realize that the owner-manager's interests will diverge somewhat from theirs, hence the price which they will pay for shares will reflect the monitoring costs and the effect of the divergence between the manager's interest and theirs. *[. . .]*

As the owner-manager's fraction of the equity falls, his fractional claim on the outcomes falls and this will tend to encourage him to appropriate larger amounts of the corporate resources in the form of perquisites. This also makes it desirable for the minority shareholders to expend more resources in monitoring his behavior. Thus, the wealth costs to the owner of obtaining additional cash in the equity markets rise as his fractional ownership falls.

We shall continue to characterize the agency conflict between the owner-manager and outside shareholders as deriving from the manager's tendency to appropriate perquisites out of the firm's resources for his own consumption. However, we do not mean to leave the impression that this is the only or even the most important source of conflict. Indeed, it is likely that the most important conflict arises from the fact that as the manager's ownership claim falls, his incentive to devote significant effort to creative activities such as searching out new profitable ventures falls. He may in fact avoid such ventures simply because it requires too much trouble or effort on his part to manage or to learn about new technologies. Avoidance of these personal costs and the anxieties that go with them also represent a source of on the job utility to him and it can result in the value of the firm being substantially lower than it otherwise could be.

[. . .]

In practice, it is usually possible by expending resources to alter the opportunity the owner-manager has for capturing non-pecuniary benefits. These methods include auditing, formal control systems, budget restrictions, and the establishment of incentive compensation systems which serve to more closely identify the manager's interests with those of the outside equity holders, etc. *[. . .]*

[Total gross agency costs] are the costs of the "separation of ownership and control" which Adam Smith focused on in the passage quoted at the beginning of this paper and which Berle and Means (1932) popularized 157 years later. The solutions outlined above to our highly simplified problem imply that agency costs will be positive as long as monitoring costs are positive—which they certainly are.

The reduced value of the firm caused by the manager's consumption of perquisites outlined above is "non-optimal" or inefficient only in comparison to a world in which we could obtain compliance of the agent to the principal's wishes at zero cost or in comparison to a *hypothetical* world in which the agency costs were lower. But these costs (monitoring and bonding costs and "residual loss") are an unavoidable results of the agency relationship. Furthermore, since they are borne entirely by the decision maker (in this case the original owner) responsible for creating the relationship he has the incentives to see that they are minimized (because he captures the benefits from their reduction). Furthermore, these agency costs will be incurred only if the benefits to the owner-manager from their creation are great enough to outweigh them. In our current example these benefits arise from the

availability of profitable investments requiring capital investment in excess of the original owner's personal wealth.

In conclusion, finding that agency costs are non-zero (i.e., that there are costs associated with the separation of ownership and control in the corporation) and concluding therefrom that the agency relationship is non-optimal, wasteful or inefficient is equivalent in every sense to comparing a world in which iron ore is a scarce commodity (and therefore costly) to a world in which it is freely available at zero resource cost, and concluding that the first world is "non-optimal"—a perfect example of the fallacy criticized by Coase (1964) and what Demsetz (1969) characterizes as the "Nirvana" form of analysis.[8]

2.6. Factors Affecting the Size of the Divergence From Ideal Maximization

The magnitude of the agency costs discussed above will vary from firm to firm. It will depend on the tastes of managers, the ease with which they can exercise their own preferences as opposed to value maximization in decision making, and the costs of monitoring and bonding activities.[9] The agency costs will also depend upon the cost of measuring the manager's (agent's) performance and evaluating it, the cost of devising and applying an index for compensating the manager which correlates with the owner's (principal's) welfare, and the cost of devising and enforcing specific behavioral rules or policies. Where the manager has less than a controlling interest in the firm, it will also depend upon the market for managers. Competition from other potential managers limits the costs of obtaining managerial services (including the extent to which a given manager can diverge from the idealized solution which would obtain if all monitoring and bonding costs were zero). The size of the divergence (the agency costs) will be directly related to the cost of replacing the manager. If his responsibilities require very little knowledge specialized to the firm, if it is easy to evaluate his performance, and if replacement search costs are modest, the divergence from the ideal will be relatively small and vice versa.

The divergence will also be constrained by the market for the firm itself, i.e., by capital markets. Owners always have the option of selling their firm, either as a unit or piecemeal. Owners of manager-operated firms can and do sample the capital market from time to time. If they discover that the value of the future earnings stream to others is higher than the value of the firm to them given that it is to be manager-operated, they can exercise their right to sell. It is conceivable that other owners could be more efficient at monitoring or even that a single individual with appropriate managerial talents and with sufficiently large personal wealth would elect to buy the firm. In this latter case the purchase by such a single individual would completely eliminate the agency costs. If there were a number of such potential owner-manager purchasers (all with talents and tastes identical to the current manager) the owners would receive in the sale price of the firm the full value of the residual claimant rights including the capital value of the eliminated agency costs plus the value of the managerial rights.

[. . .]

7. CONCLUSIONS

The publicly held business corporation is an awesome social invention. Millions of individuals voluntarily entrust billions of dollars, francs, pesos, etc., of personal wealth to the care of managers on the basis of a complex set of contracting relationships which delineate the rights of the parties involved. The growth in the use of the corporate form as well as the growth in market value of established corporations suggests that at least, up to the present, creditors and investors have by and large not been disappointed with the results, despite the agency costs inherent in the corporate form.

Agency costs are as real as any other costs. The level of agency costs depends among other things on statutory and common law and human ingenuity in devising contracts. Both the law and the sophistication of contracts relevant to the modern corporation are the products of a historical process in which there were strong incentives for individuals to minimize agency costs. Moreover, there were alternative organizational forms available, and opportunities to invent new ones. Whatever its shortcomings, the corporation has thus far survived the market test against potential alternatives.

NOTES

1. Reviews of this literature are given by Peterson (1965), Alchian (1965, 1968), Machlup (1967), Shubik (1970), Cyert and Hedrick (1972), Branch (1973), Preston (1975).

2. See Williamson (1964, 1970, 1975), Marris (1964), Baumol (1959), Penrose (1958), and Cyert and March (1963). Thorough reviews of these and other contributions are given by *[. . .]* Alchian (1965).

Simon (1955) developed a model of human choice incorporating information (search) and computational costs which also has important implications for the behavior of managers. Unfortunately, Simon's work has often been misinterpreted as a denial of maximizing behavior, and misused, especially in the marketing and behavioral science literature. His later use of the term "satisfying" [Simon (1959)] has undoubtedly contributed to this confusion because it suggests rejection of maximizing behavior rather than maximization subject to costs of information and of decision making.

3. Cf. Berhold (1971), Ross (1973, 1974a), Wilson (1968, 1969), and Heckerman (1975).

4. Given the optimal monitoring and bonding activities by the principal and agent.

5. As it is used in this paper the term monitoring includes more than just measuring or observing the behavior of the agent. It includes efforts on the part of the principal to "control" the behavior of the agent through budget restrictions, compensation policies, operating rules etc.

6. They define the classical capitalist firm as a contractual organization of inputs in which there is "(a) joint input production, (b) several input owners, (c) one party who is common to all the contracts of the joint inputs, (d) who has rights to renegotiate any input's contract independently of contracts with other input owners, (e) who holds the residual claim, and (f) who has the right to sell his contractual residual status."

7. By legal fiction we mean the artificial construct under the law which allows certain organizations to be treated as individuals.

8. If we could establish the existence of a feasible set of alternative institutional arrangements which would yield net benefits from the reduction of these costs we could legitimately conclude the agency relationship engendered by the corporation was not Pareto optimal. However, we would then be left with the problem of explaining why these alternative institutional arrangements have not replaced the corporate form of organization.

9. The monitoring and bonding costs will differ from firm to firm depending on such things as the

inherent complexity and geographical dispersion of operations, the attractiveness of perquisites available in the firm (consider the mint), etc.

REFERENCES

Alchian, A. A., 1965, The basis of some recent advances in the theory of management of the firm, Journal of Industrial Economics, Nov., 30–44.

Alchian, A. A., 1968, Corporate management and property rights, in: Economic policy and the regulation of securities (American Enterprise Institute, Washington, DC).

Alchian, A. A., 1974, Some implications of recognition of property right transactions costs, unpublished paper presented at the First Interlaken Conference on Analysis and Ideology, June.

Alchian, A. A. and H. Demsetz, 1972, Production, information costs, and economic organization, American Economic Review LXII, no. 5, 777–795.

Baumol, W. J., 1959, Business behavior, value and growth (Macmillan, New York).

Berhold, M., 1971, A theory of linear profit sharing incentives, Quarterly Journal of Economics LXXXV, Aug., 460–482.

Berle, A. A., Jr. and G. C. Means, 1932, The modern corporation and private property (Macmillan, New York).

Branch, B., 1973, Corporate objectives and market performance, Financial Management, Summer, 24–29.

Coase, R. H., 1937, The nature of the firm, Economica, New Series, IV, 386–405. Reprinted in: Readings in price theory (Irwin, Homewood, IL) 331–351.

Coase, R. H., 1964, Discussion, American Economic Review LIV, no. 3, 194–197.

Cyert, R. M. and C. L. Hedrick, 1972, Theory of the firm: Past, present and future; An interpretation, Journal of Economic Literature X, June, 398–412.

Cyert, R. M. and J. G. March, 1963, A behavioral theory of the firm (Prentice Hall, Englewood Cliffs, NJ).

Demsetz, H., 1969, Information and efficiency: Another viewpoint, Journal of Law and Economics XII, April, 1–22.

Heckerman, D. G., 1975, Motivating managers to make investment decisions, Journal of Financial Economics 2, no. 3, 273–292.

Machlup, F., 1967, Theories of the firm: Marginalist, behavioral, managerial, American Economic Review, March, 1–33.

Marris, R., 1964, The economic theory of managerial capitalism (Free Press of Glencoe, Glencoe, IL).

Penrose, E., 1958, The theory of the growth of the firm (Wiley, New York).

Preston, L. E., 1975, Corporation and society: The search for a paradigm, Journal of Economic Literature XIII, June, 434–453.

Ross, S. A., 1973, The economic theory of agency: The principals problems, American Economic Review LXII, May, 134–139.

Ross, S. A., 1974a, The economic theory of agency and the principle of similarity, in: M. D. Balch et al., eds., Essays on economic behavior under uncertainty (North-Holland, Amsterdam).

Shubik, M., 1970, A curmudgeon's guide to microeconomics, Journal of Economic Literature VIII, June, 405–434.

Simon, H. A., 1955, A behavioral model of rational choice, Quarterly Journal of Economics 69, 99–118.

Simon, H. A., 1959, Theories of decision making in economics and behavioral science, American Economic Review, June, 253–283.

Smith, A., 1937, The wealth of nations, Cannan edition (Modern Library, New York).

Williamson, O. E., 1964, The economics of discretionary behavior: Managerial objectives in a theory of the firm (Prentice-Hall, Englewood Cliffs, NJ).

Williamson, O. E., 1970, Corporate control and business behavior (Prentice-Hall, Englewood Cliffs, NJ).

Williamson, O. E., 1975, Markets and hierarchies: Analysis and antitrust implications (The Free Press, New York).

Wilson, R., 1968, On the theory of syndicates, Econometrica 36, Jan., 119–132.

Wilson, R., 1969, La decision: Agregation et dynamique des orders de preference, Extrait (Editions du Centre National de la Recherche Scientifique, Paris) 288–307.

22

THE ECONOMICS OF ORGANIZATION

The Transaction Cost Approach

OLIVER E. WILLIAMSON

[. . .] The proposition that the firm is a production function to which a profit-maximization objective has been assigned has been less illuminating for organization theory purposes than for economics. Even within economics, however, there is a growing realization that the neoclassical theory of the firm is self-limiting. A variety of economic approaches to the study of organization have recently been proposed in which the importance of internal organization is acknowledged. The one described here emphasizes transaction costs and efforts to economize thereon. More than most economic approaches, it makes allowance for what Frank Knight (1965, p. 270) has felicitously referred to as "human nature as we know it."

Economic approaches to the study of organization, transaction cost analysis included, generally focus on efficiency. To be sure, not every interesting organizational issue can be usefully addressed, except perhaps in a minor way, in efficiency terms. A surprisingly large number can, however, especially if transaction cost aspects are emphasized. This is accomplished by making the transaction—rather than commodities—the basic unit of analysis and by assessing governance structures, of which firms and markets are the leading alternatives, in terms of their capacities to economize on transaction costs.

The transaction cost approach to the study of organizations has been applied at three levels of analysis. The first is the overall structure of the enterprise. This takes the scope of the enterprise as given and asks how the operating parts should be related one to another. Unitary, holding company, and multidivisional forms come under scrutiny when these issues are addressed. The second or middle level focuses on the operating parts and asks which activities should be performed within the

Reprinted from the *American Journal of Sociology, 87*(3), Oliver E. Williamson, "The Economics of Organization: The Transaction Cost Approach," pp. 548–577. Copyright © 1981 by the University of Chicago; reprinted by permission.

firm, which outside it, and why. This can be thought of as developing the criteria for and defining the "efficient boundaries" of an operating unit. The third level of analysis is concerned with the manner in which human assets are organized. The object here is to match internal governance structures with the attributes of work groups in a discriminating way.

Only issues of the two latter kinds are addressed in this paper. The study of both of these issues turns critically on the dimensionalizing of transactions. The antecedent literature from which the transaction cost approach derives is sketched in Section I. The rudiments of the approach, including the dimensionalizing of transactions, are then set out in Section II. Applications to the study of efficient boundaries are developed in Section III. Employment relation issues are addressed in Section IV. Comparisons with selected aspects of the organization theory literature and contrasts with "power" approaches to the study of organizations are made in Section V. Concluding remarks follow.

I. ANTECEDENTS

[. . .] Ronald Coase posed the problem [. . .] in his classic 1937 paper, "The Nature of the Firm." He, like others, observed that the production of final goods and services involved a succession of early stage processing and assembly activities. But whereas others took the boundary of the firm as a parameter and examined the efficacy with which markets mediated exchange in intermediate and final goods markets, Coase held that the boundary of the firm was a decision variable for which an economic assessment was needed. What is it that determines when a firm decides to integrate and when instead it relies on the market?

[. . .]

The legal literature to which I refer is concerned with contracting—especially the distinction between "hard and contracting" (or black-letter law) and "soft contracting" in which the contract serves mainly as framework. Karl Llewellyn's 1931 essay addressed these issues. He observed that transactions come in a variety of forms and that a highly legalistic approach can sometimes get in the way of the parties instead of contributing to their purposes. This is especially true where continuity of the exchange relation between the parties is highly valued.

Others who adopted and refined this theme include Steward Macaulay (1963), Lon Fuller (1964), Clyde Summers (1969), David Feller (1973), and Ian Macneil (1974). As Macneil puts it, the discrete transaction—"sharp in by clear agreement; sharp out by clear performance" (1974, p. 738)—is very rare in both law and economics, and we deceive ourselves by treating it otherwise. What he refers to as "relational" forms of contracting—which may involve arbitration, collective bargaining, and other types of obligational market exchange—are becoming more important and need to be recognized.

[. . .]

II. SOME RUDIMENTS

A transaction occurs when a good or service is transferred across a technologically separable interface. One stage of activity terminates and another begins. With a well-working interface, as with a well-working machine, these transfers occur smoothly. In mechanical systems we look for frictions: do the gears mesh, are the parts lubricated, is there needless slippage or other loss of energy? The economic counterpart of friction is transaction cost: do the parties to the exchange operate harmoniously, or are there frequent misunderstandings and conflicts that lead to delays, breakdowns, and other malfunctions? Transaction cost analysis supplants the usual preoccupation with technology and steady-state production (or distribution) expenses with an examination of the comparative costs of planning, adapting, and monitoring task completion under alternative governance structures.

Some transactions are simple and easy to mediate. Others are difficult and require a good deal more attention. Can we identify the factors that permit transactions to be classified as one kind or another? Can we identify the alternative governance structures within which transactions can be organized? And can we match governance structures with transactions in a discriminating (transaction-cost-economizing) way? These are the neglected issues with which organizational design needs to come to grips. These are the issues for which transaction cost analysis promises to offer new insights.

Behavioral Assumptions

It is widely recognized—by economists, lawyers, and others who have an interest in contracting—that complex contracts are costly to write and enforce. There is a tendency, however, to accept this fact as given rather than inquire into the reasons for it. As a result, some of the consequences of and remedies for costly contracting are less well understood than would otherwise be the case.

What is needed, I submit, is more self-conscious attention to "human nature as we know it." The two behavioral assumptions on which transaction cost analysis relies that both add realism and distinguish this approach from neoclassical economics are (1) the recognition that human agents are subject to bounded rationality and (2) the assumption that at least some agents are given to opportunism.

Bounded rationality needs to be distinguished from both hyperrationality and irrationality (Simon 1978). Unlike "economic man," to whom hyperrationality is often attributed, "organization man" is endowed with less powerful analytical and data-processing apparatus. Such limited competence does not, however, imply irrationality. Instead, although boundedly rational agents experience limits in formulating and solving complex problems and in processing (receiving, storing, retrieving, transmitting) information (Simon 1957), they otherwise remain "intendedly rational."

But for bounded rationality, all economic exchange could be efficiently organized by contract. *[. . .]* Given bounded rationality, however, it is impossible to deal with complexity in all contractually relevant respects. As a consequence, incomplete contracting is the best that can be achieved.

Ubiquitous, albeit incomplete, contracting would nevertheless be feasible if human agents were not given to opportunism. Thus, if agents, though boundedly rational, were fully trustworthy, comprehensive contracting would still be feasible (and presumably would be observed). Principals would simply extract promises from agents that they would behave in the manner of steward when unanticipated events occurred, while agents would reciprocally ask principals to behave in good faith. Such devices will not work, however, if some economic actors (either principals or agents) are dishonest (or, more generally, disguise attributes or preferences, distort data, obfuscate issues, and otherwise confuse transactions), and it is very costly to distinguish opportunistic from nonopportunistic types ex ante.

A different way of putting this is to say that while organizational man is computationally less competent than economic man, he is motivationally more complex. Thus, whereas economic man engages in simple self-interest seeking,[1] opportunism makes provision for self-interest seeking with guile. Problems of contracting are greatly complicated by economic agents who make "false or empty, that is, self-disbelieved threats or promises" (Goffman 1969, p. 105), cut corners for undisclosed personal advantage, cover up tracks, and the like.

That economic agents are simultaneously subject to bounded rationality and (at least some) are given to opportunism does not by itself, however, vitiate autonomous trading. On the contrary, when effective ex ante and ex post competition can both be presumed,[2] autonomous contracting will be efficacious. Of these two, effective ex ante competition is a much easier condition to satisfy: it merely requires that there be large numbers of qualified bidders at the outset. The subsequent transformation of an exchange relation involving large numbers to one involving small numbers during contract execution is what causes problems. Whether ex post competition is equally efficacious or breaks down as a result of contract execution depends on the characteristics of the transactions in question, which brings us to the matter of dimensionalizing.

Dimensionalizing

As set out elsewhere (Williamson 1979), the critical dimensions for describing transactions are (1) uncertainty, (2) the frequency with which transactions recur, and (3) the degree to which durable, transaction-specific investments are required to realize least cost supply. Only recurrent transactions are of interest for the purposes of this paper; hence attention will hereafter be focused on uncertainty and asset specificity, especially the latter.

Asset specificity is both the most important dimension for describing transactions and the most neglected attribute in prior studies of organization. The issue is less whether there are large fixed investments, though this is important, than whether such investments are specialized to a particular transaction. Items that are unspecialized among users pose few hazards, since buyers in these circumstances can easily turn to alternative sources and suppliers can sell output intended for one buyer to other buyers without difficulty. Nonmarketability problems arise when the specific identity of the parties has important cost-bearing consequences. Transactions of this kind may be referred to as idiosyncratic.

Asset specificity can arise in any of three ways: site specificity, as when successive stations are located in cheek-by-jowl relation to each other so as to economize on inventory and transportation expenses; physical asset specificity, as where specialized dies are required to produce a component; and human asset specificity that arises from learning by doing. The reason asset specificity is critical is that, once an investment has been made, buyer and seller are effectively operating in a bilateral (or at least quasi-bilateral) exchange relation for a considerable period thereafter. Inasmuch as the value of specific capital in other uses is, by definition, much smaller than the specialized use for which it has been intended, the supplier is effectively "locked into" the transaction to a significant degree. This is symmetrical, moreover, in that the buyer cannot turn to alternative sources of supply and obtain the item on favorable terms, since the cost of supply from unspecialized capital is presumably great. The buyer is thus committed to the transaction as well. Accordingly, where asset specificity is great, buyer and seller will make special efforts to design an exchange that has good continuity properties.

The site-specific assets referred to here appear to correspond with those Thompson describes as the "core technology" (1967, pp. 19–23). Indeed, the common ownership of site-specific stations is thought to be so "natural" that alternative governance structures are rarely considered. In fact, however, the joining of separable stations—for example, blast furnace and rolling mill, thereby to realize thermal economies—under common ownership is not technologically determined but instead reflects transaction-cost-economizing judgments. It will nevertheless be convenient, for the purposes of this paper, to assume that all site-specific stations

constitute a technological core the common ownership of which will be taken as given. Attention is thus focused on earlier stage, later stage, and lateral transactions. The efficient governance structure for these turns on physical asset and human asset specificity. Although these are often correlated, it will facilitate the argument to treat them sequentially. Thus, physical asset specificity is emphasized in Section III and human asset specificity is not introduced until Section IV.

III. Efficient Boundaries

The treatment of efficient boundaries in this section deals with only a part, albeit an interesting part, of the full set of organizational issues. Only two organizational alternatives are considered: either a firm makes a component itself or it buys it from an autonomous supplier. Thus mixed modes, such as franchising, joint ventures, etc., are disregarded. I also take the core technology as given and focus on a single line of commerce—say the activities of a particular manufacturing division within a larger industrial enterprise. The object is to describe how the economizing decisions which define the outer boundaries of this division are made.

Schematic Description

Suppose that there are three distinct production stages which, for site-specificity reasons, are all part of the same firm. This is the technological core. Suppose that raw materials are distinct and are naturally procured from the market. Suppose that two things occur at each production stage: there is a physical transformation, and components are joined to the "main frame." And suppose, finally, that the firm has a choice between own distribution and market distribution.

Let the core production stages be represented by $S1$, $S2$, $S3$ and draw these as rectangles. Let raw materials be represented by R and draw this as a circle. Let component supply be represented by $C1$-B, $C2$-B, $C3$-B if the firm buys its components and $C1$-O, $C2$-O, $C3$-O if it makes its own components. Draw these as triangles. Let distribution be given by D-B if the firm uses market distribution and D-O if the firm uses own distribution. Draw these as squares. Finally, let a solid line between units represent an actual transaction and a dashed line a potential transaction, and draw the boundary of the firm as a closed curve that includes those activities that the firm does for itself.

The closed curve that defines the efficient boundary of the firm in Figure 22.1 includes, in addition to the technical core, component *C2* and the distribution stage, *D*. Components *C1* and *C3* and raw materials are procured in the market. Obviously this is arbitrary and merely illustrative. It also oversimplifies greatly. It is relatively easy, however, to elaborate the schema to add to the core, to consider additional components, to include several raw material stages and consider backward integration into these, to break down distribution, etc. But the central points would remain unchanged, namely: (1) the common ownership of some stations—the core—is sufficiently obvious that a careful, comparative assessment is unneeded (site specificity will often characterize these transactions); (2) there is a second set of transactions in which own supply is manifestly uneconomic, hence market supply is indicated (many raw materials are of this kind); but (3) there is a third set of activities for which make-or-buy decisions can only be made after assessing the transformation and transaction cost consequences of alternative modes. The efficient boundary is the inclusive set of core plus additional stages for which own supply can be shown to be the efficient choice.

A Simple Model

The crucial issue is how the choice between firm and market governance structures for decisions related to point 3 above are made. Transaction cost reasoning is central to this analysis, but trade-offs between production cost economies (in which the market may be presumed to enjoy certain advantages) and governance cost economies (in which the advantages may shift to internal organization) need to be recognized.

[...]

The choice between firm and market organization arises in this last connection. If assets are nonspecific, markets enjoy advantages in both production cost and governance cost respects: static scale economies can be more fully exhausted by buying instead of making; markets can also aggregate

uncorrelated demands, thereby realizing risk-pooling benefits; and external procurement avoids many of the hazards to which internal procurement is subject.[3] As assets become more specific, however, the aggregation benefits of markets in the first two respects are reduced and exchange takes on a progressively stronger bilateral character. The governance costs of markets escalate as a result and internal procurement supplants external supply for this reason. Thus, the governance of recurrent transactions for which uncertainty is held constant (in intermediate degree) will vary as follows: classical market contracting will be efficacious whenever assets are nonspecific to the trading parties; bilateral or obligational market contracting will appear as assets become semispecific; and internal organization will displace markets as assets take on a highly specific character.

The advantages of firms over markets in harmonizing bilateral exchange are three. First, common ownership reduces the incentives to suboptimize. Second, and related, internal organization is able to invoke fiat to resolve differences, whereas costly adjudication is needed when an impasse develops between autonomous traders. Third, internal organization has easier and more complete access to the relevant information when dispute settling is needed. The incentive to shift bilateral transactions from markets to firms increases as uncertainty is greater, since the costs of harmonizing the interface vary directly with the need to adjust to changing circumstances.

[...]

Two Examples

The transaction cost arguments set out above are of a normative kind: what governance structure *should* be chosen. In contrast, the examples developed here describe what has been observed. The critical question is not whether the appropriate governance structure was selected at the outset but whether transaction cost factors, possibly manifested as difficulties that resulted from a maladapted structure, are responsible for the eventual configuration.

Automobile Body Manufacture. Klein et al. (1978, pp. 308–10) have examined the problems that arose

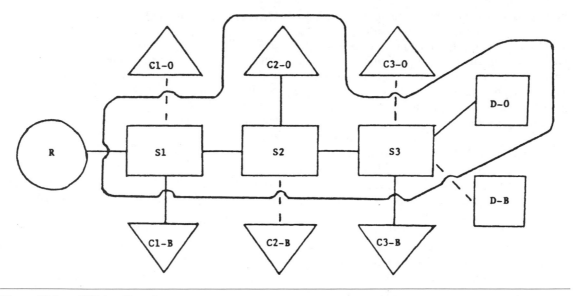

Figure 22.1.   Efficient Boundary

when a bilateral exchange relationship between Fisher Body and General Motors was attempted in the 1920s. The basic facts are these:

1. In 1919 General Motors entered a 10-year contractual agreement with Fisher Body whereby General Motors agreed to purchase substantially all its closed bodies from Fisher.

2. The price for delivery was set on a cost-plus basis and included provisions that General Motors would not be charged more than rival automobile manufacturers. Price disputes were to be settled by compulsory arbitration.

3. The demand for General Motors's production of closed body cars increased substantially above that which had been forecast. As a consequence, General Motors became dissatisfied with the terms under which prices were to be adjusted and urged Fisher to locate its body plants adjacent to GM assembly plants, thereby to realize transportation and inventory economies. Fisher Body resisted.

4. General Motors began acquiring Fisher stock in 1924 and completed a merger agreement in 1926.

Inasmuch as GM cars had distinctive body designs, the production of closed bodies required significant transaction-specific investments to be made. Site-specificity considerations reinforced this need. The transaction, moreover, was evidently beset by substantial demand and cost uncertainties. Since there was little to be gained from market procurement, while the governance costs of market procurement were predictably great, the transaction was one for which internal procurement was indicated. The strains that autonomous contracting experienced could thus have been anticipated, and the eventual reconfiguration from long-term contracting to common ownership is consistent with the basic transaction-cost-economizing argument.

Forward Integration. Chandler (1977) and Porter and Livesay (1971) report that extensive forward integration from manufacturing into distribution occurred in the last 30 years of the 19th century. The reasons for this are several, including the appearance of infrastructure (in the form of the railroad, telephone, and telegraph) and a variety of manufacturing developments. But the response to these developments was anything but uniform. Forward integration included retailing for some commodities (e.g., farm equipment and sewing machines), extended only to wholesaling for others (e.g., tobacco and certain branded items), and was negligible for still others (e.g., packaged groceries and dry goods). What were the determining factors?

[. . .] Integration into retailing occurred only for commodities that required considerable point-of-sale information, possibly to include demonstration, and follow-on service. Specialized human assets were evidently needed to provide such sales and service. Integration into wholesaling occurred for commodities that were perishable and branded. Forward integration occurred because contracts to turn over inventory and destroy older stocks were neither self-enforcing nor incentive-compatible, hence they placed the manufacturers' reputations at risk. Commodities that had none of these properties were sold through market distribution channels because no special hazards were posed. This progression of forward integration contingent on differential degrees of asset specificity and the differential hazards of opportunism is the principal implication of transaction cost reasoning and appears also to be the main factor explaining the selective degree of forward integration reported by Chandler.[4]

IV. MANAGING HUMAN ASSETS: THE EMPLOYMENT RELATION

The same general principles apply to the governance of human assets as apply to the efficient organization of transactions in general. Thus to use a complex structure for governing simple transactions is to incur unneeded costs, while to use a simple structure to govern a complex transaction invites strain. The questions are, How are human asset differences best described, what are the employment relation alternatives, and what is the appropriate correspondence between them?

The discussion is in two parts. The first addresses the organization of human assets at the staff level. The second deals with union organization, which applies primarily at the production level.

Governance, General

Recall that transactions are described in terms of three attributes: frequency, uncertainty, and asset specificity. The assets of interest here involve a continuing supply of services, whence frequency aspects will be suppressed and attention focused on the internal organizational aspects of uncertainty and asset specificity.

[. . .]

Note in this connection that skill acquisition is a necessary but not a sufficient condition for a human asset governance problem to arise. The nature of the skills also matters; the distinction between transaction-specific and nonspecific human assets is crucial. Thus, physicians, engineers, lawyers, etc., possess valued skills for which they expect to be compensated, but such skills do not by themselves pose a governance issue. Unless these skills are deepened and specialized to a particular employer, neither employer nor employee has a special interest in maintaining a continuing employment relation.[5] The employer can easily hire a substitute and the employee can move to alternative employment without loss of productive value.

Mere deepening of skills through job experience does not by itself pose a problem either. Thus, typing skills may be enhanced by practice, but if they are equally valued by current and potential employers there is no need to devise special protection for an ongoing employment relation. Knowledge of a particular firm's filing system, in contrast, may be highly specific (nontransferable). Continuity of the employment relation in the latter case is a source of added value.

Thus to the neoclassical proposition that the acquisition of valued skills leads to greater compensation, transaction cost reasoning adds the following proposition: skills acquired in a learning-by-doing fashion and imperfectly transferable across employers need to be embedded in a protective governance structure, lest productive values be sacrificed if the employment relation is unwittingly severed. The concern here is with what Knight has referred to as "the internal problems of the corporation, the protection . . . of members and adherents against each other's predatory propensities" (1965, p. 254). This poses a problem in the degree to which assets are firm-specific.

The internal organizational counterpart for uncertainty is the ease with which the productivity of human assets can be evaluated. This is essentially the metering problem to which Armen Alchian and Harold Demsetz refer in their treatment of the firm (1972). Their argument is that firms arise when tasks are technologically nonseparable, the standard example being manual freight loading. As they put it (1972, p. 779): "Two men jointly lift cargo into trucks. Solely by observing the total weight loaded per day, it is impossible to determine each person's marginal productivity. . . . The output is yielded by a team, by definition, and it is not a *sum* of separable outputs of each of its members."

When tasks are nonseparable in this sense, individual productivity cannot be assessed by measuring output—an assessment of inputs is needed. Sometimes productivity may be inferred by observing the intensity with which an individual works; this is the aspect emphasized by Alchian and Demsetz. Often, however, the assessment of inputs is much more subtle than effort accounting. Does the employee cooperate in helping to devise and implement complex responses to unanticipated circumstances, or does he attend to his own or local goals at the expense of others? Metering this, except over long observation intervals, can be inordinately difficult.

Human assets can thus be described in terms of (1) the degree to which they are firm-specific and (2) the ease with which productivity can be metered. The fact that Alchian and Demsetz consider only the latter explains the narrow construction of the employment relation in their assessment of economic organization. Both dimensions, however, are critical to an adequate assessment. Letting H_1 and H_2 represent low and high degrees of human asset specificity and M_1 and M_2 represent easy and difficult conditions of meterability, the following four-way classification of internal governance structures is tentatively proposed:

1. H_1, M_1: *Internal Spot Market.* Human assets that are nonspecific and for which metering is easy are essentially meeting market tests continuously for their jobs. Neither workers nor firms have an efficiency interest in maintaining the association. Workers can move between employers without loss

of productivity, and firms can secure replacements without incurring start-up costs. Hence no special governance structure is devised to sustain the relation. Instead, the employment relation is terminated when either party is sufficiently dissatisfied. An internal spot market labor relation may be said to exist. Examples include migrant farm workers and custodial employees. Professional employees whose skills are nonspecific (certain draftsmen and engineers) also fall into this category.

2. H_1, M_2: *Primitive Team.* Although the human assets here are non-specific, the work cannot be metered easily. This is the team organization to which Alchian and Demsetz refer (1972). Although the membership of such teams can be altered without loss of productivity, compensation cannot easily be determined on an individual basis.[6] The manual freight loading example would appear to qualify. This structure is referred to as a primitive team, to distinguish it from the relational team, described below.

3. H_2, M_1: *Obligational Market.* There is a considerable amount of firm-specific learning here, but tasks are easy to meter. Idiosyncratic technological experience (as described, for example, by Doeringer and Piore [1971, pp. 15–16]) and idiosyncratic organizational experience (accounting and data-processing conventions, internalization of other complex rules and procedures, and the like) both qualify. Both firm and workers have an interest in maintaining the continuity of such employment relations. Procedural safeguards will thus be devised to discourage arbitrary dismissal. And nonvested retirement and other benefits will accrue to such workers so as to discourage unwanted quitting (for a discussion, see Mortensen 1978).

4. H_2, M_2: *Relational Team.* The human assets here are specific to the firm and very difficult to meter. This appears to correspond with the "clan" form of organization to which William Ouchi (1980) has referred. The firm here will engage in considerable social conditioning, to help assure that employees understand and are dedicated to the purposes of the firm, and employees will be provided with considerable job security, which gives them assurance

against exploitation. Neither of these objectives can be realized independently of the other.

Relational teams are very difficult to develop, and it is uncertain how widespread or sustainable they are. It is argued that some of the Japanese corporations are organized in this way (for a discussion, see Lifson 1979), but the interpretation of this is subject to dispute. Certain utopian societies are organized as relational teams, but these have experienced severe continuity problems as the initial membership, which often was highly committed, retired or expired (see Kanter 1972; Manuel and Manuel 1979).

The above described match of internal governance structures with the internal transactional attributes just described is summarized in Figure 22.2. Admittedly, describing internal transactions in bivariate, binary terms simplifies considerably. The overall framework is nevertheless in place and refinements can be made as needed. (Thus, mixed internal governance structures will presumably arise to service transactions that take on intermediate, rather than extreme, M and H values.)

Some Remarks on Union Organization

The foregoing discussion of internal governance structures refers mainly to staff rather than production-level employees. Since it is among the latter that union organization appears, the question arises as to whether transaction cost reasoning has useful applications to the study of collective organization.

[. . .]

[T]he transaction cost approach to the study of unionization yields testable implications that do not derive from more familiar theories of unionization that rely on power or politics to drive the analysis (Freeman and Medoff 1979). The principal implications are: (1) the incentive to organize production workers within a collective governance structure increases with the degree of human asset specificity; and (2) the degree to which an internal governance structure is elaborated will vary directly with the degree of human asset specificity. Transaction cost analysis thus predicts that unions will arise early in such industries as railroads, where the skills are highly specific, and will arise late in such industries as migrant farm labor, where skills are nonspecific. It further predicts that the governance structure (job ladders, grievance procedures, pay scales) will

be more fully elaborated in industries with greater specificity than in those with less (steel vs. autos is an example). The preliminary data appear to support both propositions.[7]

The transaction cost hypothesis does not deny the possibility that unions will appear in settings where human asset specificity is slight. Where this occurs, however, the presumption is that these outcomes are driven more by power than by efficiency considerations. Employers in these circumstances will thus be more inclined to resist unionization; successful efforts to achieve unionization will often require the assistance of the political process; and, since power rather than efficiency is at stake, the resulting governance structure will be relatively primitive.

V. Relation to the Organizational Literature

Power

[. . .] The resource-dependency model sometimes makes reference to efficiency but more often relies on power in explaining organizational outcomes. Inasmuch as power is very poorly defined and hence can be used to explain virtually anything, the tautological objection to resource-dependency analysis is easily understood. Ready access to a power explanation has also had the unfortunate effect of removing efficiency analysis from center stage.

Thus consider Jeffrey Pfeffer's assertion that if "the chief executive in a corporation always comes from marketing . . . there is a clue about power in the organization" (1978, p. 23). Viewed from a power perspective, the argument evidently is that the marketing people in this corporation have "possession of control over critical resources" (1978, p. 17), have preferential access to information (1978, p. 18), and are strategically located to cope with "critical organizational uncertainty" (1978, p. 28). I do not disagree with any of this, but would make the more straightforward argument that the marketing function in this organization is especially critical to competitive viability.

As Ouchi and I have argued elsewhere (1981), those parts of the enterprise that are most critical to organizational viability will be *assigned* possession of control over critical resources, will *have* preferential

		HUMAN ASSETS	
		NONSPECIFIC (H$_1$)	HIGHLY SPECIFIC (H$_2$)
METERING	EASY(M$_1$)	SPOT MARKET	OBLIGATIONAL MARKET
	DIFFICULT(M$_2$)	PRIMITIVE TEAM	RELATIONAL TEAM

Figure 22.2.   The Governance of Internal Organization

access to information, and will be *dealing* with critical organizational uncertainties. In some organizations this may be marketing, in others it may be R & D, and in still others it may be production. Indeed, we argue that failure to assign control to that part of the enterprise on which viability turns would contradict the efficiency hypothesis but would presumably be explained as a power outcome.

Or consider the transformation of the merchant capitalist described by Glenn Porter and Harold Livesay. They report that during the first two centuries after the initial English settlement on the North American continent, "urban merchant capitalists . . . were the wealthiest, best informed, and most powerful segment of early American society" (1972, p. 6). These all-purpose merchants nevertheless gave way to specialized merchants early in the 19th century; such merchants then became "the most important men in the economy" (1972, p. 8). But specialized merchants in turn found their functions sharply cut back by the rise late in the 1800s of integrated manufacturers: "The long reign of the merchant had finally come to a close. In many industries the manufacturer of goods had also become their distributor. A new economy dominated

by the modern, integrated manufacturing enterprise had arisen" (1972, p. 12).

Power theory must confront two troublesome facts in explaining these changes. First, why would the all-purpose and later the specialized merchants ever permit economic activity to be organized in ways that would remove power from their control? Second, why did power leak out *selectively*—with the merchant role being appropriated extensively by some manufacturers but not by others? As discussed above and developed elsewhere (Williamson 1980), the transaction cost approach explains both in terms of efficiency. Perhaps power theory can sometimes add detail. However, until it has been much more carefully delimited—which, I submit, will entail dimensionalizing—power theory, as an overall approach to the study of organizational change, is a pied piper whose enticements are better resisted in favor of more mundane efficiency considerations.

VI. CONCLUDING REMARKS

Transaction cost analysis is an interdisciplinary approach to the study of organizations that joins economics, organization theory, and aspects of contract law. It provides a unified interpretation for a disparate set of organizational phenomena. Although applications additional to those set out here have been made, the limits of transaction cost analysis have yet to be reached. Indeed, there is reason to believe that the surface has merely been scratched.

Transaction cost reasoning probably has greater relevance for studying commercial than noncommercial enterprise, since natural selection forces operate with greater assurance in the former. Transaction cost economizing is nevertheless important to all forms of organization. Accordingly, the following proposition applies quite generally: governance structures that have better transaction cost economizing properties will eventually displace those that have worse, ceteris paribus. The *cetera*, however, are not always *paria*, whence the governance implications of transaction cost analysis will be incompletely realized in noncommercial enterprises in which transaction cost economizing entails the sacrifice of other valued objectives (of which power will often be one; the study of these trade-offs is an important topic on the future research agenda).

[. . .]

NOTES

1. As Peter Diamond has put it, standard "economic models . . . [treat] individuals as playing a game with fixed rules which they obey. They do not buy more than they can pay for, they do not embezzle funds, and they do not rob banks" (1971, p. 31). Only recently has this standard presumption come under scrutiny, often by making allowance for what insurance specialists refer to as "moral hazard," which is a particular form of opportunism.

2. Although large numbers of qualified bidders are frequently on a parity at the outset, winning a bid and executing a contract often introduces a disparity between the qualifications of winners and those of nonwinners, with the result that bidding competition involving large numbers is not equally effective at the contract renewal interval. For a discussion, see Williamson (1971; 1975, pp. 27–36; 1979); and Klein, Crawford, and Alchian (1978).

3. For a discussion of bureaucratic hazards, see Thompson (1967, pp. 152–54) and Williamson (1975, pp. 117–31).

4. Alfred Chandler advises me *[Oliver Williamson]* that he agrees broadly with this interpretation of his results.

5. This ignores transitional problems that may be associated with job relocation. All employees experience these, on which account protection against arbitrary dismissal is sought. But the further question is what *additional* safeguards are warranted. This matter turns on human asset specificity.

6. This assumes that output is a joint product and that input differences cannot be easily ascertained.

7. The arguments and the evidence are developed more fully in Scott R. Williamson (1980).

REFERENCES

Alchian, Armen A., and Harold Demsetz. 1972. "Production, Information Costs, and Economic Organization." *American Economic Review* 62 (December): 777–95.

Chandler, Alfred D., Jr. 1977. *The Visible Hand.* Cambridge, Mass.: Harvard University Press.

Coase, Ronald H. (1937) 1952. "The Nature of the Firm." Pp. 386–405 in *Readings in Price Theory*, edited by G. J. Stigler and K. E. Boulding. Homewood, Ill.: Irwin.

Diamond, Peter. 1971. "Political and Economic Evaluation of Social Effects and Externalities: Comment." Pp. 30–32 in *Frontiers of Quantitative Economics*, edited by M. Intrilligator. Amsterdam: North-Holland.

Doeringer, Peter, and Michael Piore. 1971. *Internal Labor Markets and Manpower Analysis.* Lexington, Mass.: Heath.

Feller, David E. 1973. "A General Theory of the Collective Bargaining Agreement." *California Law Review* 61 (May): 663–856.

Freeman, Richard B., and James L. Medoff. 1979. "The Two Faces of Unionism." *Public Interest* (Fall), pp. 69–93.

Fuller, Lon L. 1964. *The Morality of Law.* New Haven, Conn.: Yale University Press.

Goffman, Erving. 1969. *Strategic Interaction.* Philadelphia: University of Pennsylvania Press.

Kanter, Rosabeth Moss. 1972. *Community and Commitment.* Cambridge, Mass.: Harvard University Press.

Klein, Benjamin, Robert G. Crawford, and Armen A. Alchian. 1978. "Vertical Integration, Appropriable Quasi-Rents, and the Competitive Contracting Process." *Journal of Law and Economics* 21 (October): 297–326.

Knight, Frank H. 1965. *Risk, Uncertainty and Profit.* New York: Harper & Row.

Lifson, Thomas B. 1979. "An Emergent Administrative System: Interpersonal Networks in a Japanese

General Trading Firm." Working Paper 79-55, Harvard University, Graduate School of Business.

Llewellyn, Karl N. 1931. "What Price Contract?—an Essay in Perspective." *Yale Law Journal* 40 (May): 704–51.

Macaulay, Stewart. 1963. "Non-contractual Relations in Business." *American Sociological Review* 28:55–70.

Macneil, Ian R. 1974. "The Many Futures of Contract." *University of Southern California Law Review* 67 (May): 691–816.

Manuel, Frank E., and Fritzie P. Manuel. 1979. *Utopian Thought in the Western World.* Cambridge, Mass.: Harvard University Press.

Ouchi, William G. 1980. "Markets, Bureaucracies, and Clans." *Administrative Science Quarterly* 25 (March): 129–42.

Pfeffer, Jeffrey. 1978. *Organizational Design.* Northbrook, Ill.: AHM.

Porter, Glenn, and Harold C. Livesay. 1971. *Merchants and Manufacturers.* Baltimore: Johns Hopkins University Press.

Simon, Herbert A. 1957. *Models of Man.* New York: Wiley.

——. 1978. "Rationality as Process and as Product of Thought." *American Economic Review* 68 (May): 1–16.

Summers, Clyde. 1969. "Collective Agreements and the Law of Contracts." *Yale Law Journal* 78 (March): 525–75.

Thompson, James D. 1967. *Organizations in Action.* New York: McGraw-Hill.

Williamson, Oliver E. 1971. "The Vertical Integration of Production: Market Failure Considerations." *American Economic Review* 61 (May): 112–23.

——. 1975. *Markets and Hierarchies.* New York: Free Press.

——. 1979. "Transaction Cost Economics: The Governance of Contractual Relations." *Journal of Law and Economics* 22 (October): 233–61.

——. 1980. "Organizational Innovation: The Transaction Cost Approach." Discussion Paper no. 83, Center for the Study of Organizational Innovation, University of Pennsylvania, September.

Williamson, Oliver E., and William G. Ouchi. 1981. "The Markets and Hierarchies Program of Research: Origins, Implications, Prospects." In *Organizational Design*, edited by William Joyce and Andrew Van de Ven. New York: Wiley.

Williamson, Scott R. 1980. "A Selective History of the U.S. Labor Movement." B.A. thesis, Yale University.

23

MARKETS, HIERARCHIES, AND HEGEMONY

CHARLES PERROW

[. . .] Williamson's theory [(1975)] [. . .] is that hierarchies replaced markets because they were more efficient. Williamson focuses on transaction costs [. . .] as a neglected aspect of efficiency, and makes it the primary reason for organizing economic activity within one large organization rather than having several independent organizations that coordinate through buying and selling and lending. Williamson's theory is important for at least two reasons. First, it is one of the few instances of bringing concepts from the field of organizational behavior to bear upon problems formulated by economists. That I find the results unfortunate has nothing to do with the value of such attempts. Second, the theory deals with a basic problem of social structure, that of autonomy and control. Williamson sees the shift from a world of many producers coordinating their work through the market mechanism to a world of few producers who exercise control through the hierarchy of the large corporation as the result of a concern for efficiency in production and distribution.

I will emphasize the control of markets, the control of labor, and the social cost of undesirable sources of private profit. Any efficiencies that obtain through the reduction of the costs of transacting business [. . .] are, I argue, minor consequences. They neither motivate entrepreneurs nor make a substantial contribution to profits. Profits come from control of markets and competition, control of labor, and the ability to externalize many other costs that are largely social in nature, that is, to force communities and workers to bear them and not have them reflected in the price of the goods and services.

[. . .]

CONSISTENCY OF WILLIAMSON'S ARGUMENT

When I read through *Markets and Hierarchies* for the first time a few years ago I covered the first 116 pages with crabbed and crabby marginal notes to the effect that most of the transactional costs, first mover problems, opportunism, uncertainties, bounded rationality problems, and information impactedness are reproduced in the firm, and sometimes are even greater than those found in markets. Then I read Chapter 7 and found my comments unnecessary, because here Williamson himself notes the existence of these problems within the firm.

In doing so, he would appear to undercut his argument sorely and merely attest to the ubiquity of problems in organized activity, whether it is organized by markets or hierarchies. But he made no note of this, nor has he in his subsequent writings. (And to my surprise, his reviewers have not noted it either.) Chapters 8 and 9 go on to describe some ways of mitigating transaction costs in the firm, but quite inconclusively. There are no additional chapters that describe ways of mitigating the transaction costs of *markets*. Instead the remaining chapters go on to other matters as if the crucial Chapter 7, which was first published in 1973 but fortunately included in the 1975 volume, had not existed.

What do we find in Chapter 7? Virtually all the advantages of hierarchy for reducing transaction costs and opportunism are repealed. Within organizations fixed costs for internal procurement may be "easily" overstated; "fundamentally nonviable internal capability may be uncritically preserved"; managers are "notably reluctant to abolish their own jobs"; group subgoals "are easily given greater weight in relation to objective profitability considerations" (p. 119); cheating, or "exceptions from a system's rationality procurement standards," and logrolling are much easier than in market transactions, and system damaging reciprocities "are simply more extensive internally (I buy from your division, you support my project proposal or job promotion, and so forth) than in the market"—note that here we explicitly find that one of the key elements of transaction costs, group optimization and opportunism, is worse in the firm than in the market.

Fiat, acclaimed heretofore as the dispute settler par excellence, is "efficient for reconciling instrumental differences," that is, presumably telling workers where to get off. But, he continues, fiat "is poorly suited for mediating disputes that have internal power consequences." But presumably this would include all management disputes, and indeed all union-management disputes as well. Instead of fiat we get "compromise," which is close to a market mechanism for the crucial conflicts within the firm. Furthermore, "internal organization," that is, hierarchy, "specifically favors the extension of the compliance machinery," which of course is not a cost-free frictionless device at all, and "the firm might consciously resist the internalizing of incremental transactions for this reason as well." But we have been told, in the paper in this volume and in many others (and in the preceeding six chapters of the Williamson book), that it is the costs of compliance in market transactions that are so high, and here we find the costs may be higher within hierarchies.

This covers just two pages of this remarkable 14-page chapter. But let me go on. The next page reveals that the appearance of hierarchy is attended by sunk costs, information impactedness, unreasonable costs of distinguishing faulty from meritorious performance, partisan appeals from internal subgroups, and the lack of market discipline! On the next page we find that contracts within the firm lack tough-minded and calculative assessments, in contrast to contracts in the market. Furthermore, one of the inevitable developments of market relations that in turn leads people to turn to hierarchy, small numbers bargaining, appears within firms too. On the next page we find again that distortion and opportunism are particularly important in hierarchical relations (p. 123). And here Williamson comes close to saying that integrated firms are less adaptable to changing environments than specialized ones, which contradicts his general thesis. This reminds one of the curious dilemma that he makes for himself earlier, where he would forego the advantages of long-range planning provided by market contracts in favor of allowing events to simply unfold, a surprising virtue of the hierarchy (pp. 9, 25). Elsewhere it is hierarchy that allows long-term planning (e.g., p. 10). Long-term contracts bind the firm and raise transactions costs, he says, but he generally neglects the possibility that they actually allow long-term planning, rational investments, promote market stability, and so on.

Internal opportunism is elaborated on the next page, where we find: "Indeed, the typical internal transaction is really a small-numbers exchange relation writ large," which should make it considerably more serious than those faced in the market (p. 124). The next page tells us that performance assessment is only potentially better in the firm than in the market, and the potential is lost as the firm grows more complex, which it can only do by integrating functions and adding hierarchy. Complexity also limits its power to do internal auditing—and of course increases its need for it (p. 125).

Moving on, we learn that it is all even worse, for in contrast to the market, the costs of opportunism will not show up immediately, but will be delayed and lie hidden (p. 126).

A number of points are mentioned about the disadvantages of large size and complexity that are quite familiar to all of us—impersonality, narrow calculative commitment, lack of stockholder control, rip-off mentality, sabotage, alienation, and so on (pp. 127–129). There are even problems with the promotion ladder, a resource supposedly unavailable in market contracting (p. 129), and serious problems with wage distortions in large firms (p. 130). He says in a footnote that the discussion does not pretend to be exhaustive, but it is extensive enough to have undercut and in places even reversed all the previous arguments for the superior efficiency of hierarchy when we have recurring transactions, uncertainty, and specialized needs.

The next chapter attempts to argue that some of these problems would be mitigated in the M (multidivisional) form of firm. Perhaps, but his examples are not that persuasive to me. In one long example, he says the external capital market cannot get the information about choices of investment decisions that bosses of firms can get from their own divisions. Internally generated capital, though limited, can be placed where the promise is the greatest and doled out in increments with full disclosure of information from the part receiving it. It is trading breadth for depth (p. 148). But he is comparing the market's ability to assess a multidivisional firm, which is correctly seen as very limited, with

management's ability. Obviously management will know more than the market about its divisions. The true comparison is the market's ability to assess the capital needs of *several* nonintegrated firms versus management's ability to assess the needs of several of its own divisions. Here the superiority of the M form is quite unclear, because the market may be much more efficient in assessing several moderate-sized firms than in assessing two giant ones in which vertical integration has already taken place.

In fact, one of the criticisms of multidivisional firms is that their divisions are not subject to the so-called discipline of the marketplace, and they should be; management, while having internal information, may lack comparative information and tends to be too concerned with sunk costs, preoccupied with growth, and so on. Furthermore, the cost of information may be as high internally as in the market, where price signaling, profit statements, and prospectuses are efficient and cheap. This is the real implication of his example of Ford and the spark plugs: The market quickly told Ford what its own internal analysis could not determine (p. 93). Thus, contrary to Williamson's position, my position would be that when there are several firms competing in the capital market, investors can distribute their capital better and more efficiently than when they are confronted with two giant firms that have absorbed the several small ones. This is but one example of the way in which the material from Chapter 7 can be used to question the conclusions of the other chapters.

Another problem with the logic and consistency of the argument is the failure to define transaction costs. He says that this was Coase's problem—a lack of operational utility—and it made Coase's argument circular. But Williamson has a similar problem: Any competing analysis can be reinterpreted by saying that X or Y is really a transaction cost. He moves from quite plausible examples such as negotiating contracts, hiring lawyers, checking on delivery dates and quality, and other terms of specific contracts, to much more general and sweeping references such as the coordination and integration of the flow of goods and services. The latter examples might be seen as a transaction, in that goods move from one station to another, and every time they do a "transaction" has taken place if only to the extent that a worker has noticed it. But if we include such a wide variety of activities under the term "transactions," there is nothing distinctive about Williamson's assertions; everything has its costs, and if you wish to label a great many of these as transactions, then transaction costs will certainly predominate. For a theory that makes such a claim to distinctiveness, the failure to define the key term is both surprising and annoying.

[. . .]

So far I have dealt with the logic and consistency of the argument. I conclude that the elements of his market failures approach—principally transaction costs and opportunism—are at least as significant and sometimes more significant in hierarchical firms of modest or larger size as they are in markets composed of modest-sized firms. This may even be true of the less appropriate comparison of markets and firms, where the firms are very large and the markets thereby incapacitated. This conclusion is based upon assertions and citations provided by Williamson himself, and I could add generously to these assertions and citations to make the case even stronger. Finally, the lack of definition of the key concept, transactions, and its occasional tendency to embrace other aspects of organization that are normally treated separately, reduces the distinctiveness of the theory.

EMPIRICAL EVIDENCE—WILLIAMSON

But this is not my main criticism of the perspective. That there has been a shift from markets to hierarchies cannot be denied, and it is an extremely important development. My central criticism is that *[. . .]* Williamson offer*[s]* incorrect explanations for the shift. To illustrate though hardly demonstrate my point, I will discuss one contemporary and several historical examples. The contemporary illustration concerns changes in the popular music industry since the appearance of long-playing records and cheap radios, particularly FM. I have analyzed it in detail elsewhere (Perrow, 1979: 206–215), drawing extensively upon the work of Paul Hirsch, Richard Peterson, and David Berger, so I will be brief here. To summarize first, I argue that initially hierarchy and vertical integration were designed to obtain market control and oligopolistic advantages, rather

than the advantages of efficiency. Once you have these goodies, you can realize certain kinds of efficiencies, though others are foregone. Then hierarchy and vertical integration were rendered inefficient by technological changes, which disrupted market hegemony. A less hierarchical form was quickly adapted, because it had other efficiencies. Gradually, however, the dominant firms have moved back to a more oligopolistic position, because control, rather than efficiency, is the key issue. With growing control, they can afford to revert to vertical integration, and vertical integration limits entry and increases market control. Here is the case:

From Tin Pan Alley days until the 1950s the market was dominated by four giants who gradually gained control, on the basis of long-term contracts, of the artists (song writers, singers, bands), the key marketing vehicles (movie studios, record stores, radio programs), the producers, and the manufacturing process. Presumably large economies of scale were available and, by Williamson's reasoning, few transaction costs and little opportunism. The industry was profitable and growing at a respectable rate. What it did not recognize was a demand for more varied forms of music; this might have increased sales. The industry learned of this demand when four technological changes took place: the appearance of TV, which made radio stations very cheap, since it took away their advertising revenues; the appearance of FM, which increased the number of (cheap) stations; cheap transistor radios; and long-playing records. The majors, with their vertical integration and multidivisions, could not capitalize on the changes. They were bound by long-term employment contracts and sunk costs in production, manufacturing, and distribution. Entry costs were suddenly lowered. New firms appeared and experimented with new types of music that had always been performed in local areas but never recorded by the giants. Transaction costs for the small firms were apparently minimal; artists prepared their own productions and brought them to the small firms daily. Contracts were short-term and negotiated on the spot. Sunk costs were minimal as recording studios, stamping plants, and marketing groups sprang up, all ready to service a large number of record companies. A vast new market opened up, and a very variegated one. Hits no longer hung on for months but only for weeks, though they sold many more copies than had been true of the Doris Day, Frank Sinatra types marketed through Makebelieve Ballroom and movie musicals. The market dominance of the big four plummeted and disappeared, even though the expanded market meant that they too increased their sales and profits. The majors then dropped their vertical integration and copied the upstart firms by utilizing weekly contracts for producers and single-item contracts for artists, and by contracting out for studios and stamping plants and promotion. It was cheaper, more efficient and more profitable (though Williamson would presumably be aghast at the number of spot contracts negotiated). The risks were externalized to groups in the market rather than internalized and thus were spread around. But so were the opportunities. Sales, groups, hits, labels, and profits skyrocketed, as did the number of radio stations.

Why was not everyone happy with this profitable state of affairs? My guess is that it had nothing to do with the supposed inefficiencies of the market form of organizing economic activity, but a great deal to do with the insecurity that the new competition brought about and the sizeable profits that small and moderate sized firms were making. The giants feared they would lose their dominant positions, and thus their opportunity to participate at least proportionally in the rising volume of business and the rising rates of profits. In addition, they probably wanted to participate disproportionally—they coveted the profits of their small neighbors. Transaction costs would be trivial in the face of these matters.

In any event, here is what they did—though one of the majors ended up as a minor, and a small upstart firm emerged as a major. First, they increased their transaction costs by substituting expensive, risky, complicated long-term contracts with a few groups for the short, simple, low-risk spot contracts with many groups. To protect this investment they had to intervene in the market and forego the almost costless device of letting listeners decide which contracts made money and should be renewed, and for how long, and instead take the expensive and dangerous route of bribing the disc jockeys and others with money and then drugs to make sure that the few groups they had chosen received air time. Reportedly, they entered into sub

rosa contracts with organized crime to this effect. Their smaller competitors had to match this effort, further distorting the market and increasing the cost of entry. When this was not enough for the majors, they had to go to the cost of buying up whole radio stations. While stations are profitable, they are not nearly as profitable as the production and sale of records. Then the majors moved into buying up retail outlets, again restricting the selection of records. In all this, they were attempting to restore the hegemony that existed prior to 1955. I think all these expensive, "inefficient" efforts might fairly be billed as transaction costs, because the service received was selective exposure of their product.

The consequences for the industry are worth noting. While too much has changed for the industry to return to the happy pre-1955 days of 80 percent four-firm concentration ratios, the concentration ratio is approaching that level; cost of entry has increased; the price of records has increased beyond the raw materials price, I suspect; sales rate of growth has declined: and the variety being offered the consumer is being restricted. I expect that innovations such as digital recording are now more difficult because of the large sunk costs to be protected; I also expect that linkage with organized crime will grow. Offhand, it is hard to see the superiority of hierarchy over markets in this case, unless market control and concentration of profits is the criterion.

But is the case merely an exception? Williamson would probably say that it is. In Chapters 11 and 12 of his book he discusses undesirable distortions due to oligopoly, but he plainly considers them to be few in number; oligopoly itself is seen as an efficient and desirable form of organization, as is the conglomerate firm, though there might be some abuses. In contrast, I would consider the socially unredeeming aspects of oligopoly to be extensive and the motives assigned in the music case to be the typical ones. The only way in which this case might be considered an exception is that we rarely find examples of rapid and significant environmental changes that dislodge oligopolistic control; furthermore, after these environmental changes we are able to see oligopoly slowly and deliberately being reestablished.

[. . .]

NORMATIVE PRESUPPOSITION

This brings me to my last point. Recall that I have challenged the consistency of Williamson's argument, saying that the costs of bounded rationality and opportunism are present within as well as between firms; thus his argument is not distinctive and does not explain the appearance of hierarchy. I challenged the empirical evidence for his [. . .] position [. . .]. I suggested that the reasons for hierarchy and integration may have much less to do with efficiency than with the quite different matter of profits and economic power in an increasingly disabled market. Let me insert that I follow Polanyi (1957) in believing that markets are not natural to human society, that so-called free markets have never really existed, that there have been historically better ways of organizing economic activity, and that markets were largely rigged in the nineteenth century. So I would not necessarily favor market transactions; it is just that they appear to be better for people than hierarchical transactions.

There are at least three ways of organizing economic activity—through communal efforts with norms of other-regarding behavior; through markets, where there is more concern with opportunism; and through hierarchies, which are predicated upon the fear of autonomy. Markets substitute bargaining and negotiations for cooperative effort, survey the outputs, and adjust the next contract accordingly. But hierarchies substitute commands, surveillance of behavior, multiple control devices, and authority for bargaining and negotiation. Obey, don't bargain, they say. For Williamson [. . .] it is quite obvious that settling disputes through fiat is better than through negotiations and bargaining. If I am the one to be commanded, controlled, or "fiated," I would prefer bargaining and negotiations, written guarantees, legal statements of rights and obligations, and in general the ability to act as an autonomous agent, no matter what the transaction costs. I doubt that I am alone in this preference. Since hierarchy necessarily gives power to the few, I think the many would agree.

The novelist E. M. Forster gave only two cheers for democracy, a special case of the market we might say. He reserved three for love, the beloved republic, the closest to a community. I agree, and while I have no cheers for chaos, I have but one for hierarchies.

REFERENCES

Perrow, C. (1979). *Complex Organizations: A Critical Essay*, 2nd ed., Glenview, IL: Scott, Foresman.

Polanyi, K. (1957). *The Great Transformation*, Boston: Beacon Press.

Williamson, O. (1975). *Markets and Hierarchies*, New York: The Free Press.

PART IX

THE EVOLUTION OF BUSINESS ORGANIZATION
From Big Business to Post-Fordism?

A. Alfred Chandler's Account of the Rise of Big Business

B. Post-Bureaucratic Alternatives to Big Business

Although there are many kinds of organizations, business is now the one most widely researched in organization studies, and theories of the development of American business organization have changed in interesting ways. Broadly speaking, the history of the American economy is in many ways one of large organizations replacing decentralized markets from the late nineteenth through late twentieth centuries, followed by a reaction against the institutional order that emerged from this process that began in the 1970s and whose character is still much debated. It is a story of the movement from markets to hierarchies to either markets again, completely new forms of organization, or merely reorganized hierarchies, depending on the theory.

In the early nineteenth century, most businesses had few employees, had low output and productivity, and were run by their owners. Between 1850 and 1930, large sections of the economy came to be dominated by big business, beginning with the railroads. Though organizations varied widely, the following characteristics are variously associated with big business (Schmitz 1993):

- large size measured in terms of assets, employees, and number of branch plants and offices;
- the association of competitors into various kinds of federations and agreements (cartels, trusts, interlocking directorates) in the late nineteenth century and then their direct ownership and unified management by one or a few corporations as a result of mergers and acquisitions (*horizontal integration*);
- concentration of economic power and domination of markets by few producers (*oligopoly*);
- ownership of different stages of the production process, such as raw materials production, semifinished goods, and distribution, by a single organization (*vertical integration*);

- diversification into multiple product lines, initially related to one another, but after the 1950s often in unrelated businesses (*conglomerates*);
- capital requirements beyond the abilities of an owner-entrepreneur or small partnership, leading to a reliance on outside finance, usually bank loans or the stock market;
- diffusion of stock ownership that results in the substitution of owner-managers by a new class of salaried executives and managers (*separation of ownership and control*);
- pricing and allocation of raw materials and semifinished goods performed by the *"visible hand"* of administrative coordination, rather than the invisible hand of the market, as market transactions are internalized within the organization.

These developments have been called the *managerial revolution*, or the shift from proprietary or competitive capitalism to managerial capitalism.

Business historian Alfred Chandler gives one of the most influential explanations for the rise of managerial capitalism (Reading 24). Modern communications and transportation systems, such as steamships, railroads, and the telegraph, integrated local and regional markets into national markets. Mechanized mass production technology rather than craft technology was now feasible and well suited to supply this market cheaply. In some industries, the minimum efficient scale of production was so great that a few firms could meet the market demand. If there were too many producers, excess capacity could result in gluts, low prices, and business failures. Oligopoly was the natural outcome of such situations.

The advantage of mass production rested on *economies of scale*, which are cost savings that result from producing large quantities of a standard good. Whereas labor and raw materials costs increase with the number of items produced, the cost of buildings and equipment remains fixed and adds less to the final price of a product as the volume of production increases, because the costs can be spread across more units. In capital-intensive industries, the cost savings associated with high volume production due to economies of scale are substantial and encourage large production facilities.

But the high level of capital investment meant that equipment needed to be employed continuously to ensure the fixed costs per unit remained low. This meant that firms using new technologies not only were able to produce in mass quantities, but also were compelled to do so if they were to produce cheaply and remain in business. The need for a continuous, regular flow of large quantities of materials through all phases of supplier procurement, production, and distribution required conscious administrative coordination and unified management under common corporate ownership. To keep production and sales at high and predictable levels, firms acquired their suppliers and also created their own wholesale sales forces, dealers and franchisees, retail outlets, brand names, and advertising to win customer loyalty and preserve their company's reputation. A managerial hierarchy coordinated and supervised these functions within relatively autonomous divisions, while a corporate central office set strategy, allocated capital among divisions, and evaluated divisional financial performance.

The size and complexity of the managerial task required a corps of specialists and professionals rather than untrained amateurs trying to handle everything themselves. Salaried managers, chosen on the basis of competence, replaced personal or family control. By the 1920s, ownership became separated from control in many corporations. Stockholders increasingly became passive investors rather than active participants in the management of the enterprise, and boards of directors increasingly reflected the interests of top management rather than the stockholders they were supposed to represent. The number of business schools and professional associations grew, and modern management techniques, including Taylor's scientific management, increasingly replaced intuition, experiential knowledge, and gut instinct as guides to action. In short, the firm became increasingly rationalized and bureaucratic, with an elaborate hierarchy of offices, a division of labor among technically trained specialists, and the use of formal knowledge and impersonal rules and procedures to guide action. Chandler's view of the managerial revolution shares much with Weber's ideas about bureaucracy and its expansion.

Chandler's explanation of the emergence of big business is also similar to Williamson's account of the substitution of hierarchies for markets in that both see the purpose as reducing the uncertainties of market transactions (Reading 22). They differ insofar as Chandler sees this as mainly a technical problem of coordinating materials flows in a mass production environment, whereas Williamson believes it is a contracting problem that requires the restraint of other actors' opportunism and self-interest. Pfeffer and Salancik's resource dependency explanation of mergers also bears a family resemblance to these accounts (see Reading 18).

Chandler argues that the same factors led to the rise of big business in Germany, Japan, and elsewhere. Nations that continued to rely on smaller, individual- or family-owned firms, such as the United Kingdom, fell behind economically. In Chandler's view, efficiency accounts for the rise of big business and the managerial revolution, and those firms or nations that relied on small business were destined to fall behind economically.

Critics argue that this explanation is too functionalist and underestimates the importance of power motives. Corporations often grew and integrated horizontally to monopolize markets. Chandler ignores the history of antitrust legislation that developed in reaction to the concentration of corporation power in the form of cartels and monopolies. Likewise, vertical integration can restrain competition by excluding rivals from access to natural resources or the economies of scale associated with supplier operations owned by large customers. Chandler also ignores any principal-agency problems associated with the new corporate elite that made autonomous decisions on its own salaries, perks, and staff size. He also emphasizes the role of managerial efficiency in explaining big business success while ignoring the role of scientific management in cheapening labor requirements, which Taylor advocated and Braverman criticized (see Readings 2 and 3).

The criticism of Chandler's efficiency explanation only grew as the golden age of American growth and prosperity during the postwar period, which seemed to be the crowning achievement of the big business system whose development Chandler described, gave way to the stagnation and crisis of the 1970s. American companies faced not only deep recessions and general economic stagnation in the 1970s through mid-1980s, but also a flood of imports, especially from Japan. The recessions and slow growth severely reduced profits, but superior Japanese goods suggested the problem was deeper than the business downturn alone. Over roughly fifteen years, Japanese firms challenged significantly and often overwhelmed

American companies in markets such as transistor radios, cameras, color televisions, videocassette recorders, audio equipment, microwave ovens, computer hardware, photocopiers, steel, and automobiles. In most cases, Japanese quality, as well as price, was considered superior to American products. The onslaught left American industry reeling as it struggled to respond, and a wave of plant closures swept the industrial midwest in the early 1980s. Just as Chandler was formulating his explanation for the triumph of American corporate capitalism, it entered a deep crisis. American firms sought to imitate Japanese practice in various ways, such as by introducing quality control techniques like those in the factory Laurie Graham studied (Reading 11); by creating a more cooperative relationship with labor, as at Saturn (Reading 12); and by trying to build greater employee commitment through strong organizational cultures (Reading 27).

At the same time, dynamic elements seemed to emerge from this bleak picture. While large, traditional, so-called blue chip corporations stumbled, new, smaller startups in high technology fields such as computer software and hardware and biotechnology thrived.

The lethargy and competitive difficulties of large enterprises, such as U.S. Steel, General Motors, and virtually all conglomerates since the 1970s, suggested to many that managers had pursued growth for its own sake rather than to maximize efficiency, often because managerial compensation was tied to organizational size and size seemed to provide security and to buffer firms from market fluctuations. The competitiveness crisis in U.S. industry between 1975 and 1990 suggested that big business was not efficient and that other motives accounted for its emergence and growth. While Chandler (1990) continued to insist that big business was as efficient and important as always, most believe that the period since 1975 represents a new phase in American business organization, though they disagree on its nature.

There are three perspectives on the apparent eclipse of traditional big business in the past twenty-five years. The first argues that smaller, more entrepreneurial firms are replacing the large, oligopolistic corporation. Some argue that small business creates almost all new employment (Birch 1981). This view sees recent changes as a simple rollback of the managerial revolution, as small business and competitive capitalism reassert themselves (Birch 1981; Malone and Rockart 1991). Consistent with this view is the conservative shift toward free market government economic policies since Ronald Reagan's presidency, including measures such as deregulation, free-trade policies, lower minimum wages, and deunionization. Bureaucracy or hierarchies of all sorts, whether in business, labor, or government, are yielding to old-fashioned, almost nineteenth-century, free markets in this view.

The second perspective sees recent developments as potentially the beginning of a more novel form of business and economic organization rather than a return to nineteenth-century laissez-faire. Michael Piore and Charles Sabel (1984) argued that business began to operate in a less stable environment. The new conditions included wider swings in the business cycle, more intense international and domestic competition, growing importance of product quality relative to price, faster development of technology, and more rapidly changing consumer tastes, including a preference for more customization. This put pressure on mass production systems, which required large and stable markets for standardized goods to reap economies of scale and competed mainly on the basis of low price. The greater instability and fragmentation of consumer markets required a more innovative and, above all, flexible corporation. Economies of scale are now less important than *economies of scope*, the cost savings that result from using the same materials and equipment to produce many small batches of a variety of products, rather than large batches of a standard product. New computer-controlled production technology supports this move to greater variety and customization because it dramatically reduces the cost and time required for retooling, which had prevented the flexible use of industrial technology in the past. The new production strategy has been called flexible specialization, or *post-Fordism*, in contrast to the mass production or Fordist model.

Since Burns and Stalker, "innovative" and "flexible" have meant organic rather than traditional bureaucratic forms of organization, and the post-Fordist model is no exception. Faster-changing markets, consumer demand for quality, variety, and customization, shorter product life cycles, and foreign competition require flexible job definitions, cooperation between hierarchical levels and departments, greater worker decision making and skill, and fewer bureaucratic layers of approval to achieve faster response times. Computers and other information technology have the flexibility to achieve economies of scope and require greater mental work from the workers who use them. Piore and Sabel argue that smaller firms with less hierarchy, less rigid division of labor, and more skilled front-line workers are replacing the traditional bureaucratic corporation Chandler celebrated and the Taylorist manufacturing philosophy that often accompanied it. These firms give workers more skill, discretion, and decision-making power along the lines described by Richard Walton (Reading 10), as cooperation between management and labor replaces adversarial relations. Insofar as greater automation contributes to the increased use of skilled workers, Piore and Sabel's work is also consistent with Woodward's predictions.

The new firm also involves greater cooperation among managers and professionals in different departments within the firm who traditionally had limited contact with one another. Design engineers, manufacturing engineers, and sales and marketing professionals work together in interdepartmental teams to make sure that the products that are designed can be manufactured easily and sold to customers. This kind of communication and cooperation, which the Japanese called *concurrent engineering*, would seem like common sense, but was actually rare in American companies. Tall bureaucratic walls in American corporations separated departments, and design engineers were allowed to create product designs without feedback from the manufacturing and marketing departments regarding their feasibility or desirability. The resulting higher defect rates and lower customer satisfaction were some of the reasons Japanese products usually surpassed their American competitors.

Finally, close cooperation between firms in joint ventures, business alliances, and networks allows them to gain the advantages of vertical and horizontal integration without the bureaucratic costs. Competitors can simulate the advantages of horizontal integration by sharing large contracts and the costs of large investments or new ventures. This allows companies to meet large orders, pool capital, and spread risks without assuming high fixed costs. Firms and their suppliers also cooperate through concurrent engineering and the sharing of knowledge, expertise, and sometimes personnel. They gain the advantages of vertical integration in a looser organizational arrangement, such as that found in Japanese business groups or the interfirm networks in Silicon Valley, which comprise a cooperating community of small producers or *industrial district* (Saxenian 1994).

In the limiting case, organizations as stable entities almost disappear completely. A *virtual organization* might consist of a group of free agents in a professional community who come together for the purposes of a single project and then disband to work on their next projects, without any enduring coordinating central office or actor—almost the logical extension of Henry Mintzberg's adhocracy (1981; Kanter 1991). Michael Storper describes the evolution of filmmaking from mass production to flexible specialization in similar terms (1997). Alternatively, a firm might consist of a very small, stable core that contracts with others to perform most of the functions necessary for the business, such as Nike, which designs and sells athletic shoes but contracts for almost all manufacturing functions with outside factories and makes very little of what it sells itself (Harrison 1994). Computer technology is believed to facilitate this kind of decentralization by reducing the need for some kinds of middle-management record keeping and report generating and improving communication between organizations involved in business relationships (Malone and Rockart 1991l; Sproull and Kiesler 1991).

As Walter Powell argues, this is not simply a shift from hierarchies back to markets, in Williamson's terms, because the level of cooperation between firms in such a network goes far beyond a simple market contract (Reading 25). Powell's essay represents an interesting turn in his thinking, because his earlier work with DiMaggio argued that different kinds of organizations throughout society were becoming more bureaucratic, albeit for nonrational reasons, whereas this work argues that debureaucratization is the dominant trend. Although Powell does not explain how entrenched bureaucratic norms became deinstitutionalized, he does argue that the post-Fordist view is one of increasing economic and organizational decentralization without a return to the free-market capitalism of the past. The new model is neither bureaucratic nor entrepreneurial in the traditional sense.

Not everyone is convinced that the emerging form of business organization represents such a fundamental break with the past, and this represents a third view of the recent transition from a stable big business regime, distinct from both the neo-entrepreneurial and post-Fordist views. Bennett Harrison and Barry Bluestone (1988) argued that the profits crisis beginning in the 1970s led businesses to mount an offensive against labor and government regulation in order to cut costs and regain their competitive position. Business lobbied for lower taxes, government spending cuts, privatization of government functions, relaxed consumer and environmental regulation, lower minimum wages, and fewer protections for unions.

The new pressures also led businesses to restructure their internal operations. Firms increasingly used part-time and temporary contract employees to reduce the fixed costs associated with their permanent, full-time workforce, such as fringe benefits or severance pay obligations. The remaining permanent employees were subject to wage freezes, benefit cuts, and greater effort demands in the form of continuous improvement programs or just-in-time production, such as Laurie Graham described (Reading 12). Firms also downsized their own operations and subcontracted work to smaller, low-wage, nonunion domestic firms and to producers in low wage regions of the United States, Mexico, and Asia, which often operate under sweatshop conditions. In this view, "flexibility" meant a greater willingness to cut jobs, as well as reduce bureaucratic rules and structure.

There is also a change in operating philosophy as a free market rhetoric permeates organizational life and any assumption of permanence or security is discouraged as bureaucratic thinking (Smith 1990). Companies tell their employees they cannot expect a career within the organization and must think and act like independent contractors whose relationship with the organization is subject to continual reevaluation. Departments that used to provide goods or services to other departments internally now must compete for the business of "internal customers" on the same terms as external vendors.

As Harrison's reading in this section argues, he does not believe these developments represent a fundamental change in the underlying principles of business operation, just a harsher or more intense application of them (Reading 26). Harrison argues there is little genuine decentralization of business power or a return to an economy of small businesses, because most employment is still created directly or indirectly by large corporations producing directly or managing a web of subcontractors. Large firms are not offering more creative, fulfilling, or secure jobs, and most small firms are technologically backward, have lower profits and innovative capacity, and offer even lower wages and less job security than large firms. Concentrated economic power and the subordination of labor are not disappearing, they are just changing their character in what has come to be called the *neo-Fordist* theory of recent developments in business organization.

Some argue that the film industry provides effective evidence in favor of Harrison's ideas and against Storper's post-Fordist view as it has reconcentrated into a small number of media conglomerates. Corporations, such as Rupert Murdoch's News Corporation and AOL Time Warner, promote generic commercial films in multiple media outlets—such as television, newspapers, movie theaters, and video stores—depending on the company, and they program and control much of what Storper presents as a neo-craft form of production. The change in business organization is more modest in extent and less desirable in character than either the free market or the post-Fordist models of debureaucratization suggest, in the neo-Fordist view.

Empirical studies of trends in organizational structure, the impact of market turbulence on organizational structure, and the effects of structure on organizational performance and human resource practices also raise serious questions as to whether there is a real trend toward post-Fordist organization and whether the causes and consequences of such an organizational form are consistent with post-Fordist theory (Handel 2000; Handel 2002).

24

THE EMERGENCE OF MANAGERIAL CAPITALISM

ALFRED D. CHANDLER, JR.

INTRODUCTION

This case reviews the emergence of a new type of capitalism in the late 19th and early 20th centuries. What differentiated this new managerial capitalism from traditional personal capitalism was that basic decisions concerning the production and distribution of goods and services were made by teams, or hierarchies, of salaried managers who had little or no equity ownership in the enterprises they operated. Today the major sectors of market economies where the means of production are still privately, rather than state, owned, are operated through such managerial hierarchies. This has not always been the case.

Indeed such managerial hierarchies are entirely modern. As late as the 1840s, with very few exceptions owners managed and managers owned. There were salaried managers before the 19th century, primarily on plantations and estates, but they worked directly with owners. There were no hierarchies of managers comparable to that depicted on Figure 24.1. By the 1840s personally managed enterprises—those that carried out the processes of production and distribution in market economies—had become specialized, usually handling a single function and a single product. They operated a factory, mine, bank, or trading office. Where the volume of activity was not yet large enough to bring such specialization,

This case was prepared by Alfred Chandler, Jr., as the basis for class discussion rather than to illustrate either effective or ineffective handling of an administrative situation.

merchants often remained involved in manufacturing and banking as they had in the early years of capitalism. Some had partnerships in distant lands. But even the largest and most powerful of early capitalist enterprises were tiny by modern standards.

For example, the Medici Bank of the 15th century and that of the Fuggers in the 16th were far more powerful financial institutions in their day than any of today's giant non-state banks in America, Europe, and Japan are in ours. Yet the Medici Bank in 1470 operated only seven branches. The total number of individuals working in the branches and the home office in Florence was 57. Of these a dozen were considered managers. They, however, were not salaried employees. They were partners, albeit junior ones, who shared in the profits and who had "joint and unlimited liability" for losses.[1] Today's middling-size state banks have as many as 200 branches, 5,000 employees, 300 salaried managers (who have no liability at all); and such banks handle over a million transactions a day. That is, they process more transactions in a week than the Medici Bank processed in the century of its existence. Today, too, small industrial enterprises handle a far greater volume of transactions than did those giants of an earlier capitalism—the Hudson's Bay, the Royal African, or even the East India Company.

What made the difference was, of course, the technological revolution of modern times—an even more profound discontinuity in the history of civilized man than the urban revolution of the 11th to 13th centuries that created the first modern market economies and with them modern capitalism. The enormous increase in the volume of output and transactions was not so much the result of the First Industrial Revolution that began in Britain at the end of the 18th century; that is, it was not the result of the initial application of the new sources of energy—fossil fuel, coal—to the processes of production. It resulted much more from the coming of modern transportation and communication. The railroad, telegraph, steamship, and cable made possible modern mass production and distribution that were the hallmarks of the Second Industrial Revolution of the late 19th and early 20th centuries. These new high-volume technologies could not be effectively exploited unless the massive flows of materials were guided through the process of both production and distribution by teams of salaried managers.

Thus the first such managerial hierarchies appeared during the 1850s and 1860s to coordinate the movements of trains and flow of goods over the new railroad networks and messages over the new telegraph system.[2] They, then, quickly came into use to manage the new mass retailing establishments—the department stores, mail order houses, and chains or multiple shops—whose existence the railroad and the telegraph made possible. For example, by 1905, such an organization permitted Sears, Roebuck in Chicago to fill 100,000 mail orders in a single day—more than the average earlier American merchant filled in a lifetime. These administrative hierarchies grew to still much greater size in industrial enterprises that, again on the basis of modern transportation and communication, integrated mass production and mass distribution within a single business enterprise.

One way to review the emergence of managerial capitalism is, then, to focus on the evolution of this largest and most complex of managerial institutions—the integrated industrial enterprise. These integrated enterprises have had much in common whether they were American, European, or Japanese. They appeared at almost exactly the same moment in history in the United States and Europe and a little later in Japan, only because Japan was later to industrialize. They clustered in much the same types of industries; and finally, they grew in much the same manner. In nearly all cases they became large, first, by integrating forward, that is, investing in marketing and distribution facilities and personnel, by moving backwards into purchasing and control of raw and semi-finished materials, then, though much less often, by investing in research and development. In this way they created the multifunctional organization that is depicted in Figure 24.1. They soon became multinational by investing abroad, first in marketing and then in production. Finally they continued to expand their activities by investing in product lines related to their existing businesses, thus creating the organization depicted in Figure 24.2.

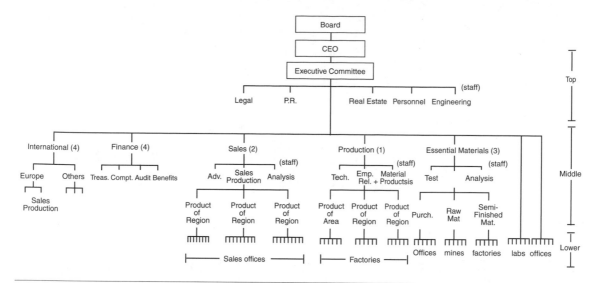

Figure 24.1. Multiunit, Multifunctional Enterprise

THE SIMILARITIES

Let us briefly examine these similarities in the location, timing, and processes of growth of this institution. The similarities in the location *[. . .]* are particularly striking. Table 24.1 indicates the location by country and by industries of all industrial corporations in the world which in 1973 employed more than 20,000 workers. (The industries are those defined as 2-digit industrial groups by the U.S. Census Standard Industrial Classification [SIC].) In 1973, 263 (65 percent) of the 401 companies were clustered in food, chemicals, oil, machinery, and primary metals. Just under 30 percent more were in 3-digit categories of other 2-digit groups—subcategories which had the same industrial characteristics as those in which the 65 percent clustered, such as cigarettes in tobacco; tires in rubber; newsprint in paper; plate glass in stone, glass, and clay; cans and razor blades in fabricated metals; and mass-produced cameras in instruments. Only 21 companies (5.2 percent) were in remaining 2-digit categories: apparel, lumber, furniture, leather, publishing and printing, instruments, and miscellaneous.

A second point that Table 24.1 makes—one that is central to an understanding of the evolution of this institution—is the predominance of American firms among the world's largest industrial corporations. Of the total of 401 companies employing more than 20,000 persons, over a half (212 or 52.6 percent) were American. The United Kingdom followed with 50 (12.5 percent), Germany with 29 (7.29 percent), Japan with 28 and France with 24. Only in chemicals, metals, and electrical machinery were there as many as four or five more firms outside of the United States than there were within it.

Table 24.2 shows that large industrial corporations have clustered throughout the 20th century in the United States in the same industries in which they were concentrated in 1973. The pattern *[. . .]* is much the same for Britain, Germany, and Japan. Other data document what is indicated here, that the American firms were larger, as well as more numerous, than those in other countries. For example, in 1948, only 50 to 55 of the British firms had assets comparable to those of the top 200 in the United States. In 1930, the number was about the same. For Germany and Japan it was smaller. Well before World War II, the United States had many more and many larger managerial hierarchies than did other nations—underlining the fact that managerial capitalism first emerged in that nation.

[. . .]

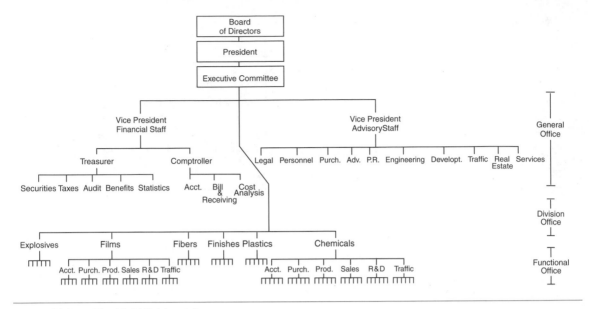

Figure 24.2. The Multidivisional Structure

EXPLANATION OF THE EVOLUTIONARY PROCESS

Why have these large integrated hierarchial enterprises appeared in some industries but rarely in others? And why did they appear at almost the same historical moment in the United States and Europe? Why did these industrial enterprises in advanced economies grow in the same manner, first, by integrating forward into volume distribution, then taking on other functions, and then becoming multinational and finally multiproduct?

Because these enterprises initially grew larger by integrating mass production with volume distribution, answers to these critical questions require a careful look at both these processes. Mass production is an attribute of specific technologies. In some industries the primary way to increase output was to add more workers and machines; in others it was by improving and rearranging the inputs, by improving the machinery, furnaces, stills and other equipment, by reorienting the process of production within the plant, by placing several intermediate processes of production required for a finished product within a single works, and by increasing the application of energy (particularly fossil fuel energy). The first set of industries remained "labor intensive"; the second set became "capital intensive." In this second set of industries, the technology of production permitted much larger economies of scale than were possible in the first. That is, it permitted much greater reduction in cost per unit of output as volume increased. So in these capital-intensive industries with large batch or continuous process technologies, large works operating at minimum efficient scale (scale of operation that brought the lowest unit costs) had a much greater cost advantage over small works than was true with labor-intensive technologies. Conversely, cost per unit rose much more rapidly when volume of production fell below minimum efficient scale (of, say, 80 to 90 percent of rated capacity), than was true in labor-intensive industries.

What is of basic importance for an understanding of the coming of the modern managerial industrial enterprise is that the cost advantage of the larger plants cannot be fully realized unless a constant flow of materials through the plant or factory is maintained to assure effective capacity utilization. The decisive figure in determining costs and profits is,

Table 24.1.   The Distribution of the Largest Manufacturing Enterprises with More than 20,000 Employees, by Industry and Nationality, 1973

S.I.C.		U.S.	Outside of the U.S.	U.K.	Germany	Japan	France	Others	Grand Total
20	Food	22	17	13	0	1	1	2	39
21	Tobacco	3	4	3	1	0	0	0	7
22	Textile	7	6	3	0	2	1	0	13
23	Apparel	6	0	0	0	0	0	0	6
24	Lumber	4	2	0	0	0	0	2	6
25	Furniture	0	0	0	0	0	0	0	0
26	Paper	7	3	3	0	0	0	0	10
27	Printing and Publishing	0	0	0	0	0	0	0	0
28	Chemical	24	28	4	5	3	6	10	52
29	Petroleum	14	12	2	0	0	2	8	26
30	Rubber	5	5	1	1	1	1	1	10
31	Leather	2	0	0	0	0	0	0	2
32	Stone, Clay, and Glass	7	8	3	0	0	3	2	15
33	Primary Metal	13	35	2	9	5	4	15	48
34	Fabricated Metal	8	6	5	1	0	0	0	14
35	Machinery	22	12	2	3	2	0	5	34
36	Electrical Machinery	20	25	4	5	7	2	7	45
37	Transportation Equipment	22	23	3	3	7	4	6	45
38	Measuring Instrument	4	1	0	0	0	0	0	5
39	Miscellaneous	2	0	0	0	0	0	0	2
	Diversified/Conglomerate	19	3	2	1	0	0	0	22
Total		211	190	50	29	28	24	59	401

NOTE: In 1970, the 100 largest industrial accounted for more than a third of a net manufacturing output in the United States and over 45 percent in the United Kingdom. In 1930, they accounted for about 25 percent of total net output in both countries.

SOURCE: *Fortune*, May 1974 and August 1974.

then, not rated capacity for a specified time period but rather throughput—that is amount actually processed in that time period. Throughput is thus the proper economic measure of capacity utilization. In the capital-intensive industries, the throughput needed to maintain minimum efficient scale requires not only careful coordination of flow through the processes of production but also the flows of inputs from the suppliers and the flow of outputs to the retailers and final consumers. Such coordination cannot happen automatically. It demands the constant attention of a managerial team, or hierarchy. Thus scale is only a technological characteristic. The economies of scale, measured by throughput, are organizational. Such economies depend on knowledge, skills, and

teamwork—on the human organization essential to exploit the potential of technological processes.

A well-known example illustrates these generalizations. In 1882, the Standard Oil "alliance" formed the Standard Oil Trust. The purpose was not to obtain control over the industry's output. That alliance, a loose federation of 40 companies each with its own legal and administrative identity but tied to John D. Rockefeller's Standard Oil Company through interchange of stock and other financial devices, already controlled close to 90 percent of the American output of kerosene. Instead, the Trust was formed to provide a legal instrument to rationalize the industry and to exploit more fully economies of scale. The Trust provided the essential legal means

Table 24.2.   The Distribution of the 200 Largest Manufacturing Firms in the United States by Industry*

S.I.C.		1917	1930	1948	1973
20	Food	39	32	26	22
21	Tobacco	6	5	5	3
22	Textiles	5	3	6	3
23	Apparel	3	0	0	0
24	Lumber	3	4	1	4
25	Furniture	0	1	1	0
26	Paper	5	7	6	9
27	Printing and Publishing	2	3	2	1
28	Chemical	20	18	24	27
29	Petroleum	22	26	24	22
30	Rubber	5	5	5	5
31	Leather	4	2	2	0
32	Stone, Clay, and Glass	5	9	5	7
33	Primary Metal	29	25	24	19
34	Fabricated Metal	8	10	7	5
35	Machinery	20	22	24	17
36	Electrical Machinery	5	5	8	13
37	Transportation Equipment	26	21	26	19
38	Instruments	1	2	3	4
39	Miscellaneous	1	1	1	1
	Diversified/Conglomerate	0	0	0	19
Total		200	200	200	200

* Ranked by assets.

to create a corporate or central office that could, first, reorganize the processes of production by shutting down some refineries, reshaping others, and building new ones and, second, coordinate the flow of materials, not only through the several refineries, but from the oil fields to the refineries and from the refineries to the consumers. The resulting rationalization made it possible to concentrate close to a quarter of the world's production of kerosene in three refineries, each with an average daily charging capacity of 6,500 barrels with two thirds of their product going to overseas markets. (At this time the refined petroleum products were by far the nation's largest nonagricultural export.) Imagine the diseconomies of scale—the great increase in unit costs—that would result from placing close to one fourth of the world's production of shoes, or textiles, or lumber into three factories or mills!

This reorganization of the Trust's refining facilities brought a sharp reduction in average cost of production of a gallon of kerosene. It dropped from 1.5 cents a gallon before reorganization to 0.54 cents in 1884 and 0.45 in 1885 (and profits rose from 0.53 cents a gallon to 1.003 cents), with costs at the giant refineries being still lower—costs far below those of any competitor. However, to maintain this cost advantage required that these large refineries have a continuing daily throughput of from 5,000 to 6,500 barrels or a three- to fourfold increase over earlier 1,500 to 2,000 barrels daily flow with concomitant increases in transactions handled and in the complexity of coordinating the flow of materials through the process of production and distribution.

The Standard Oil story was by no means unique. In the 1880s and 1890s, new mass production technologies—those of the Second Industrial Revolution—brought sharp reduction in costs as plants reached minimum efficient scale. In many industries the level of output was so high at that scale that a small number of plants were able to meet existing national and even global demand. The structure of these industries quickly became oligopolistic. Their few large enterprises competed worldwide. In many instances the first enterprises to build a plant with a high minimum efficient scale and to recruit the essential management team have remained until this day leaders in their industries. A brief review of the industries . . . in which the large enterprises have always clustered illustrates this close relationship between scale economies, the size of the enterprise, and industrial concentration.

In Groups 20 and 21—food, drink and tobacco—brand-new production processes in the refining of sugar and vegetable oils, in the milling of wheat and oats, and in the making of cigarettes brought rapid reductions in costs. In cigarettes for example, the invention of the Bonsack machine in the early 1880s permitted the first entrepreneurs to adopt the machine—James B. Duke in the United States and the Wills brothers in Britain—to reduce labor costs sharply—in Wills's case from 4 shillings per 1,000 to 0.3 pence per thousand.[3] Understandably Duke and Wills soon dominated and then divided the world market. In addition, most companies in Group 20, and also those producing consumer chemicals, such as soap, cosmetics, paints, and pills, pioneered in the use of new high-volume techniques for packing their products in small units that could be placed directly on retailers' shelves. The most important of these was the "automatic-line" canning process which, invented in the mid-1880s, permitted the filling of 4,000 cans an hour. The names of these pioneers—Campbell Soup, Heinz, Bordens, Carnation, Nestlé, Cadbury, Cross and Blackwell, Lever, Procter & Gamble, Colgate, and others—are still well known today.

In chemicals—Group 28—the new technologies brought even sharper cost reductions in industrial than in packaged consumer products. The mass production of synthetic dyes and synthetic alkalies began in the 1880s. It came a little later in synthetic nitrates, synthetic fibers, plastics, and film. The first three firms to produce the new synthetic blue dye—alizarine—dropped production costs from 200 marks per kilo in the 1870s to 9 marks by 1886; and those three firms—Bayer, BASF and Hochest—are still today, a century later, the three largest German chemical companies.[4]

Rubber production (Group 30), like oil, benefited from scale economies, even more in the production of tires than rubber footwear and clothing. Of the 10 rubber companies listed on the 1973 Table, nine built their first large factory between 1900 and 1908.[5] Since then, the Japanese company, Bridgestone, has been the only major new entrant into the global oligopoly.

In metals (Group 34), the scale economies made possible by maintaining a high volume throughput were also striking. Andrew Carnegie was able to reduce the cost of making steel rails by the new Bessemer steel process from close to $100 a ton in the early 1870s to $12 by the late 1890s.[6] In the refining of nonferrous metals, the electrolytic refining process invented in the 1880s brought even more impressive cost reductions, permitting the price of a kilo of aluminum to fall from 87.50 francs in 1888 to 47.50 francs in 1889, with the adoption of the new process, to 19 francs at the end of 1890 to 3.75 francs in 1895.[7]

In the machinery making industries (Groups 35–37), new technologies based on the fabricating and assembling of interchangeable metal parts were perfected in the 1880s. By 1886, for example, Singer Sewing Machine had two plants—one in New Jersey and the other in Glasgow, each producing 8,000 machines a week.[8] To maintain their output, which satisfied three fourths of the world demand, required an even more tightly scheduled coordination of flows of materials into, through, and out of the plant than did the mass production of packaged goods, chemicals, and metals. By the 1890s, a tiny number of enterprises using comparable plants supplied the world demand for typewriters, cash registers, adding machines, and other office equipment, for harvesters, reapers, and other agricultural machinery, and for the newly invented electrical and other volume-produced industrial machinery. The culmination of these processes came with the mass production of the automobile. By installing the moving assembly line in his Highland Park plant in 1913, Henry Ford reduced the labor time used in putting together a Model T chassis from 12 hours and 28 minutes man hours to one hour and 33 minutes.[9] This dramatic increase in throughput permitted Ford to drop the price of the touring car from over $600 in 1913 to $490 in 1914 and to $290 in the 1920s, to pay the highest wages, and to acquire one of the world's largest fortunes in an astonishingly short time.

On the other hand, in the SIC categories . . . where few large firms appear, that is in the older, technologically simple, labor-intensive industries such as apparel, textiles, leather, lumber, and publishing and printing, neither technological nor organizational innovation substantially increase minimum efficient scale. In these industries large plants do not offer significant cost advantages over small ones. In these industries the opportunities for cost reduction through material coordination of high-volume throughput by managerial teams remains limited.

The differentials in potential scale economies of different production technologies indicate not only why the large hierarchical firms appeared in some industries and not in others but also why they appeared suddenly in the last decades of the 19th century. Only with the completion of the modern transportation and communication networks—those of the railroad, telegraph, steamship, and cable—could materials flow into a factory or processing plant and the finished goods move out at a rate of speed and volume required to achieve substantial economies of throughput. Transportation that depended on the power of animals, wind, and current was too slow, too irregular, and too uncertain to maintain a level of throughput necessary to achieve modern economies of scale.

However, such scale and throughput economies do not in themselves explain why the new technologies made possible by the new transportation and communication systems caused the new mass producers to integrate forward into mass distribution. Coordination might have been achieved through contractual agreement with intermediaries—both buyers and sellers. Such an explanation requires a more precise understanding of the process of volume distribution, particularly why the wholesaler, retailer, or other commercial intermediaries lost their cost advantage vis-à-vis the volume producer.

The intermediaries' cost advantage lay in exploiting both the economies of scale and what has been termed "the economies of scope." Because they handled the products of many manufacturers, they achieved a greater volume and lower per unit cost (i.e., *scale*) than any one manufacturer in the marking and distribution of a *single* line of products. Moreover, they increased this advantage by the broader *scope* of their operation, that is by handling a number of *related* product lines through a single set of facilities. This was true of the new volume wholesalers in apparel, dry goods, groceries, hardware, and the like and even more true of the new mass retailers—the department store, the mail order house, and the chain or multiple shop enterprise.

The commercial intermediaries lost their cost advantages when manufacturers' output reached a comparable scale. As one economist has pointed out, "The intermediary will have a cost advantage over its customers and suppliers only as long as the volume of transactions in which he engages comes closer to that [minimum efficient] scale than do the transactions volumes of his customers or suppliers."[10] This rarely happened in retailing, except in heavily concentrated urban markets, but it often occurred in wholesaling. In addition, the advantages of scope were sharply reduced when marketing and distribution required specialized, costly product-specific facilities and skills that could not be used to handle other product lines. By investing in such product-specific personnel and facilities, the intermediary not only lost the advantages of scope but also became dependent on what were usually a small number of producers to provide those suppliers.

All these new volume-producing enterprises created their own sales organization to advertise and market their products nationally and often internationally. From the start they preferred to have a sales force of their own to advertise and market their goods. Salesmen of wholesalers and other intermediaries who sold the products of many manufacturers, including those of their competitors, could not be relied upon to concentrate on the single product of a single manufacturer with the intensity needed to attain and maintain market share necessary to keep throughput at minimum efficient scale.

Equally important, mass distribution of these products—many of them quite new—often required extensive investment in specialized product-specific facilities and personnel. Because the existing wholesalers and mass retailers made their profits from handling related products of many manufacturers, they had little incentive to make large investments in facilities and personnel that could only be useful for a handful of specialized products processed by a handful of producers on whom they would become dependent for the supplies essential to make this investment pay.

[. . .]

The mass marketing of new machines which were mass produced through the fabricating and assembling of interchangeable parts required a greater investment in personnel to provide the specialized marketing services than in product-specific plant and equipment.[11] The mass distribution of sewing machines for households and for the production of apparel, typewriters, cash registers, adding machines, mimeograph machines, and other office equipment, harvesters, reapers, and other agricultural machines, and, after 1900, automobiles and the more complex electrical appliances all called for demonstration, after-sales service, and consumer credit. As these machines had been only recently invented, few existing distributors had the necessary training and experience to provide the services or financial resources to provide extensive consumer credit.

On the other hand, the manufacturer had every incentive to do both. The provision of repair and service to help to assure that the product performed as advertised and control of the wholesale organization assured inventory as well as quality control. However, as a great many retailers were needed to cover the national and international markets, the manufacturers preferred to rely, as did the oil and tire companies, on franchised dealers. These retail dealers, who sold their products exclusively, were supported by a branch office network that assured the provision of services, credit, and supplies on schedule. Only the makers of sewing machines, typewriters, and cash registers went so far as to invest in retail stores. They did so primarily in concentrated urban areas where, before the coming of the automobile, only such stores were able to provide the necessary services and credit on a neighborhood basis.

[. . .]

In these ways and for these reasons, the large industrial firm that integrated mass production and mass distribution appeared in industries with two characteristics. The first and most essential was a technology of production in which the realization of potential scale economies and maintenance of quality

control demanded close and constant coordination and supervision of materials flows by trained managerial teams. The second was that volume marketing and distribution of their products required investment in specialized product-specific human and physical capital.

Where this was *not* the case, that is in industries where technology did *not* have a potentially high minimum efficient scale, where coordination was *not* technically complex, and where mass distribution did *not* require specialized skills and facilities, there was little incentive for the manufacturer to integrate forward into distribution. In such industries as publishing and printing, lumber, furniture, leather, and apparel and textiles, and specialized instruments and machines, the large integrated firm had few competitive advantages. In these industries, the small single-function firm continued to prosper and to compete vigorously.

Significantly, however, it was in just these industries that the new mass retailers—the department stores, the mail-order houses, and the chain or multiple stores—began to coordinate the flow of goods from the manufacturer to their consumer. In those industries where substantial scale economies did not exist in production, both the economies of scale and those of scope gave the mass retailers their economic advantage. In coordinating these flows, the mass retailers, like the mass producers, reduced unit costs of distribution by increasing the daily flow or throughput within the distribution network. Such efficiency, in turn, further reduced the economic need for the wholesaler as a middleman between the retailer and manufacturer.

In industries where this was the case, that is in those that had the two critical characteristics, the most important entrepreneurial act of the founders of an enterprise was the creation of an administrative organization. That is, it was, first, the recruitment of a team to supervise the process of production, then the building of a national and very often international sales network, and finally the setting up of a corporate office of middle and top managers to integrate and coordinate the two. Only then did the enterprise become multinational. Investment in production abroad followed, almost never preceded, the building of an overseas marketing network. So, too, in the technologically advanced industries, the investment in research and development followed the creation of a marketing network. In these firms, this linkage between trained sales engineers, production engineers, product designers, and the research laboratory became a major impetus to continuing innovation in the industries in which they operated. The result of such growth was an enterprise whose organization is depicted in *[Figures 24.1 and 24.2]*. The continuing growth of the firm rested on the ability of its managers to transfer resources in marketing, research and development, and production (usually those that were not fully utilized) into new and more profitable related product lines, a move that carried the organization shown on *[Figure 24.1]* to that illustrated by *[Figure 24.2]*. If the first step—that of integrating production and distribution—was not taken, the rest did not follow. The firms remained small, personally managed producing enterprises buying their materials and selling their products through intermediaries.

[. . .]

In the United States, the completion of the nation's basic railroad and telegraph network and the perfection of its operating methods in the 1870s and 1880s opened up the largest and fastest growing market in the world. Its population, which already enjoyed the highest per capita income in the world, was equal to that of Britain in 1850, twice that in 1900, and three times that in 1920.[12] American entrepreneurs quickly recruited the managerial teams in production necessary to exploit scale economies and made the investment in distribution necessary to market their volume-produced goods at home and abroad and did so in all the industries in which large industrial firms would cluster for the following century. Most of these firms quickly extended their marketing organizations overseas and then became multinational by investing in production facilities abroad, playing an influential role in a global oligopoly. (See Table 24.3.) Indeed, in some cases, particularly in mass-produced light machinery, the Americans enjoyed close to global monopoly well before the outbreak of World War I. By that time too, those in the more technologically advanced industries had begun to invest personnel and facilities in research and development.

These large manufacturing enterprises grew by direct investment in nonmanufacturing personnel

and facilities. They also expanded by merger and acquisition.[13] Here they began by making the standard response of manufacturers, both the European and American, to excess capacity to which, because of the high minimum efficient scale of their capital-intensive production processes, they were particularly sensitive. American manufacturers first attempted to control competition by forming trade associations to control output and prices and allocating marketing territories. However, because of the existing common law prohibition against combinations in restraint of trade, these associations were unable to enforce their rulings in courts of law. So manufacturers turned to the holding company device. Members of their association exchanged their stock for that of a holding company thus giving a central office legal power to determine output, prices, and marketing areas for the subsidiary firms.

For most American enterprises, the initial incorporation as a holding company took place to control competition. However, for some, like John D. Rockefeller, it became the first step for rationalizing the resources of an enterprise or even an industry in order to exploit fully the potential of scale economies. Even before the enforcement of the Sherman Antitrust Law in the early 20th century made contractual cooperation by means of a holding company legally suspect, a number of American enterprises had been transformed from holding companies to operating ones by consolidating the many factories of their subsidiaries into a single production department, unifying the several sales forces into a single sales department (including an international division) and then, though less often, investing in research and development. In a word, these enterprises were transformed from a loose federation of small operating concerns into a single centralized enterprise as depicted in Figure 24.1. These firms competed for market share and profits, rarely on price—the largest (and usually the oldest) remained the price leader—but on productive efficiency, on advertising, on the proficiency of their marketing and distribution services, and on product performance and product improvement.

In such large, complex organizations, decisions both as to current production and distribution and the allocation of resources for future production and distribution came to be made by full-time salaried

Table 24.3.   Multinational Companies in 1914 (American companies with two or more plants abroad or one plant and raw material-producing facilities)

Groups 20 & 21: Food and Tobacco	*Groups 35, 36 & 37: Machinery and Transportation Equipment*
American Chicle	American Bicycle
American Cotton Oil	American Gramophone
Armour	American Radiator
Coca-Cola	Crown Cork & Seal
H. J. Heinz	Chicago Pneumatic Tool
Quaker Oats	Ford
Swift	General Electric
American Tobacco	International Harvester
British American Tobacco	International Steam Pump (Worthington)
	Mergenthaler Linotype
Groups 28, 29, & 30: Chemicals &	National Cash Register
Pharmaceuticals, Oil, and Rubber	Norton
	Otis Elevator
Carborundum	Singer
Parke Davis (drug)	Torrington
Sherwin-Williams	United Shoe Machinery
Sterns & Co. (drug)	Western Electric
United Drug (drug)	Westinghouse Air Brake
Virginia-Carolina Chemical	Westinghouse Electric
Du Pont	
Standard Oil of N.J.	*Others*
U.S. Rubber	
	Alcoa (33)
	Gillette (34)
	Eastman Kodak (38)
	Diamond Match (39)

SOURCE: Mira Wilkins, *The Emergence of Multinational Enterprise* (Cambridge: Harvard University Press, 1970), pp. 212-123, 216.

managers. At the time of World War I, owners who still worked on a full-time basis with their hierarchies continued to have an influence on such decisions. By World War II, growth by diversification into new product lines not only greatly increased the size and complexity of the enterprise but still further scattered stock ownership. By then owners rarely participated in managerial decisions. At best they or their representatives were "outside" directors who met with the inside directors, that is the full-time salaried managers, at the most once a month and usually only four times a year. For these meetings the inside directors set the agenda, provided the information on which decisions were made, and of course were responsible for implementing the decisions. The outside directors still had the veto power, but they had neither the time, the information nor experience, and rarely even the motivation to propose alternate courses of action. By World War I, managerial capitalism had become firmly entrenched in the major sectors of the American economy.

[. . .]

NOTES

1. Raymond de Roover, *The Rise and Decline of the Medici Bank, 1397–1494* (Cambridge: Harvard University Press, 1963), pp. 87, 91. The earlier Peruzzi bank had branches managed by employees(*fattore*). "However, all

branches of major importance were managed by partners," p. 80.

2. Alfred D. Chandler, Jr., *The Visible Hand* (Cambridge: Harvard University Press, 1977), chaps. 3–6, for the coming of such hierarchies to manage railroad and telegraph systems and chap. 7 for their use in the management of mass distribution. Pages 231 and 232 describe the organization of Sears Roebuck.

3. B. W. E. Alford, *W. D. & H. O. Wills and the Development of the U. K. Tobacco Industry* (London: Methuen, 1973), pp. 143–49. Also Chandler, *Visible Hand*, pp. 249–58.

4. Sachio Kahu, "The Development and Structure of the German Coal-Tar Dyestuffs Firms," Akio Okochi and Hoshimi Uchida, eds., *Development and Diffusion of Technology* (Tokyo: University of Tokyo Press, 1979), p. 78.

5. This statement is based on a review of histories of and internal reports and pamphlets by the leading rubber companies.

6. Harold Livesay, *Andrew Carnegie and the Rise of Big Business* (Boston: Little, Brown, 1975), pp. 102–106,

155. When in 1873 Carnegie opened the first works directed entirely to producing rails by the Bessemer process, the cost dropped to $56.64 a ton. By 1859, with increase in sales, the cost fell to $25 a ton.

7. L. F. Haber, *The Chemical Industry During the Nineteenth Century* (Oxford: Oxford University Press, 1958), p. 92.

8. Chandler, *Visible Hand*, pp. 302–14.

9. Allan Nevins, *Ford: The Times, the Man, the Company* (New York: Charles Scribner's Sons, 1954), chaps. 18–20 (especially pages 473, 489, 511). Alfred D. Chandler, Jr., *Giant Enterprise: Ford, General Motors and the Automobile Industry* (New York: Arno Press, 1980), p. 26.

10. Scott J. Moss, *An Economic Theory of Business Strategy* (New York: Wiley, 1981), pp. 110–11.

11. Chandler, *Visible Hand*, pp. 402–11.

12. W. S. and E. S. Woytinsky, *World Population and Production* (New York: Twentieth Century Fund, 1953), pp. 383–85.

13. Chandler, *Visible Hand*, chap. 10.

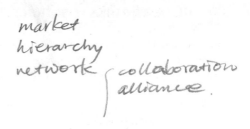

25

NEITHER MARKET NOR HIERARCHY

Network Forms of Organization

WALTER W. POWELL

I n recent years, there has been a considerable amount of research on organizational practices and arrangements that are network-like in form. This diverse literature shares a common focus on lateral or horizontal patterns of exchange, interdependent flows of resources, and reciprocal lines of communication.

[. . .]

MARKETS, HIERARCHIES, AND NETWORKS

I have a good deal of sympathy regarding the view that economic exchange is embedded in a particular social structural context. Yet it is also the case that certain forms of exchange are more social—that is, more dependent on relationships, mutual interests, and reputation—as well as less guided by a formal structure of authority. My aim is to identify a coherent set of factors that make it meaningful to talk about networks as a distinctive form of coordinating economic activity. We can then employ these ideas to generate arguments about the frequency, durability, and limitations of networks.

When the items exchanged between buyers and sellers possess qualities that are not easily measured, and the relations are so long-term and recurrent that it is difficult to speak of the parties as separate entities, can we still regard this as a market exchange? When the entangling of obligation and reputation reaches a point that the actions of the parties are interdependent, but there is no common ownership or legal framework, do we not need a new conceptual tool kit to describe and analyze this relationship? Surely this patterned exchange looks more like a marriage than a one-night stand, but there is no marriage license, no common household, no pooling of assets. In the language I employ below, such an arrangement is neither a market transaction nor a hierarchical governance structure, but a separate, different mode of exchange, one with its own logic, a network.

Many firms are no longer structured like medieval kingdoms, walled off and protected from hostile outside forces. Instead, we find companies involved in an intricate latticework of collaborative ventures with other firms, most of whom are ostensibly competitors. The dense ties that bind the auto and biotechnology industries, discussed below, cannot be easily explained by saying that these firms are engaged in market transactions for some factors of production, or by suggesting that the biotechnology business is embedded in the international community of science. At what point is it more accurate to characterize these alliances as networks rather than as joint ventures among hierarchical firms?

We need fresh insights into these kinds of arrangements. Whether they are new forms of exchange that have recently emerged of age-old practices that have gained new prominence [. . .], they are not satisfactorily explained by existing approaches. Markets, hierarchies, and networks are pieces of a larger puzzle that is the economy. The properties of the parts of this system are defined by the kinds of interaction that takes place among them. The behaviors and interests of individual actors are shaped by these patterns of interaction. Stylized models of markets, hierarchies, and networks are not perfectly descriptive of economic reality, but they enable us to make progress in understanding the extraordinary diversity of economic arrangements found in the industrial world today.

Table 25.1 represents a first cut at summarizing some of the key differences among markets, hierarchies, and networks. In market transactions the benefits to be exchanged are clearly specified, no trust is required, and agreements are bolstered by the power of legal sanction. Network forms of exchange, however, entail indefinite, sequential transactions within the context of a general pattern of interaction. Sanctions are typically normative rather than legal. The value of the goods to be exchanged in markets are much more important than the relationship itself; when relations do matter, they are frequently defined as if they were commodities. In hierarchies, communication occurs in the context of the employment contract. Relationships matter and previous interactions shape current ones, but the patterns and context of intraorganizational exchange are most strongly shaped by one's position within the formal hierarchical structure of authority.

The philosophy that undergirds exchange also contrasts sharply across forms. In markets the standard strategy is to drive the hardest possible bargain in the immediate exchange. In networks, the preferred option is often one of creating indebtedness and reliance over the long haul. Each approach thus devalues the other: prosperous market traders would be viewed as petty and untrustworthy shysters in networks, while successful participants in networks who carried those practices into competitive markets would be viewed as naive and foolish. Within hierarchies, communication and exchange is shaped by concerns with career mobility—in this sense, exchange is bound up with considerations of personal advancement. At the same time, intraorganizational communication takes place among parties who generally know one another, have a history of previous interactions, and possess a good deal of firm-specific knowledge, thus there is considerable interdependence among the parties. In a market context, it is clear to everyone concerned when a debt has been discharged, but such matters are not nearly as obvious in networks or hierarchies.

[. . .] One need not go as far as Polanyi (1957) did, when he argued that market transactions are characterized by an "attitude involving a distinctive antagonistic relationship between the partners," but it is clear that market exchanges typically entail limited personal involvement. "A contract connects two people only at the edges of their personalities" (Walzer, 1983, p. 83). The market is open to all comers, but while it brings people together, it does not establish strong bonds of altruistic attachments. The participants in a market transaction are free of any future commitments. The stereotypical competitive market is the paradigm of individually self-interested, noncooperative, unconstrained social interaction. [. . .]

Markets offer choice, flexibility, and opportunity. They are a remarkable device for fast, simple communication. No one need rely on someone else for direction, prices alone determine production and exchange. Because individual behavior is not

Table 25.1   Stylized Comparison of Forms of Economic Organization

Key Features	Market	Hierarchy	Network
	Forms		
Normative Basis	Contract— Property Rights	Employment Relationship	Complementary Strengths
Means of Communication	Prices	Routines	Relational
Methods of Conflict Resolution	Haggling— resort to courts for enforcement	Administrative fiat—Supervision	Norm of reciprocity Reputational concerns
Degree of Flexibility	High	Low	Medium
Amount of Commitment Among the Parties	Low	Medium to High	Medium to High
Tone or Climate	Precision and/or Suspicion	Formal, bureaucratic	Open-ended, mutual benefits
Actor Preferences or Choices	Independent	Dependent	Interdependent
Mixing of Forms	Repeat transactions (Geertz, 1978)	Informal organization (Dalton, 1957)	Status Hierarchies
	Contrast as hierarchical documents (Stinchcombe, 1985)	Market-like features: profit centers, transfer pricing (Eccles, 1985)	Multiple Partners
			Formal rules

dictated by a supervising agent, no organ of systemwide governance or control is necessary. Markets are a form of noncoercive organization, they have coordinating but not integrative effects. As Hayek (1945) suggested, market coordination is the result of human actions but not of human design.

Prices are a simplifying mechanism, consequently they are unsuccessful at capturing the intricacies of idiosyncratic, complex, and dynamic exchange. As a result, markets are a poor device for learning and the transfer of technological know-how. In a stylized perfect market, information is freely available, alternative buyers or sellers are easy to come by, and there are no carry-over effects from one transaction to another. But as exchanges become more frequent and complex, the costs of conducting and monitoring them increase, giving rise to the need for other methods of structuring exchange.

Organization, or hierarchy, arises when the boundaries of a firm expand to internalize transactions and resource flows that were previously conducted in the marketplace. The visible hand of management supplants the invisible hand of the market in coordinating supply and demand. Within a hierarchy, individual employees operate under a

regime of administrative procedures and work roles defined by higher level supervisors. Management divides up tasks and positions and establishes an authoritative system of order. Because tasks are often quite specialized, work activities are highly interdependent. The large vertically-integrated firm is thus an eminently social institution, with its own routines, expectations, and detailed knowledge.

A hierarchical structure—clear departmental boundaries, clean lines of authority, detailed reporting mechanisms, and formal decision making procedures—is particularly well-suited for mass production and distribution. The requirements of high volume, high speed operations demand the constant attention of a managerial team. The strength of hierarchical organization, then, is its reliability—its capacity for producing large numbers of goods or services of a given quality repeatedly—and its accountability—its ability to document how resources have been used (DiMaggio & Powell, 1983; Hannan & Freeman, 1984). But when hierarchical forms are confronted by sharp fluctuations in demand and unanticipated changes, their liabilities are exposed.

Networks are "lighter on their feet" than hierarchies. In network modes of resource allocation, transactions occur neither through discrete exchanges nor by administrative fiat, but through networks of individuals engaged in reciprocal, preferential, mutually supportive actions. Networks can be complex: they involve neither the explicit criteria of the market, nor the familiar paternalism of the hierarchy. [A] basic assumption of network relationships is that one party is dependent on resources controlled by another, and that there are gains to be had by the pooling of resources. In essence, the parties to a network agree to forego the right to pursue their own interests at the expense of others.

In network forms of resource allocation, individual units exist not by themselves, but in relation to other units. These relationships take considerable effort to establish and sustain, thus they constrain both partners ability to adapt to changing circumstances. As networks evolve, it becomes more economically sensible to exercise voice rather than exit. Benefits and burdens come to be shared. Expectations are not frozen, but change as circumstance dictate. A mutual orientation—knowledge which the parties assume each has about the other and upon which they draw in communication and problem solving—is established. In short, complementarity and accomodation are the cornerstones of successful production networks. As Macneil (1985) has suggested, the "entangling strings" of reputation, friendship, interdependence, and altruism become integral parts of the relationship.

Networks are particularly apt for circumstances in which there is a need for efficient, reliable information. The most useful information is rarely that which flows down the formal chain of command in an organization, or that which can be inferred from shifting price signals. Rather, it is that which is obtained from someone whom you have dealt with in the past and found to be reliable. You trust best information that comes from someone you know well. [. . .] Networks, then, are especially useful for the exchange of commodities whose value is not easily measured. Such qualitative matters as know-how, technological capability, a particular approach or style of production, a spirit of innovation or experimentation, or a philosophy of zero defects are very hard to place a price tag on. They are not easily traded in markets nor communicated through a corporate hierarchy. The open-ended, relational features of networks, with their relative absence of explicit quid pro quo behavior, greatly enhance the ability to transmit and learn new knowledge and skills.

Reciprocity is central to discussions of network forms of organization. Unfortunately it is a rather ambiguous concept, used in different ways by various social science disciplines. One key point of contention concerns whether reciprocity entails exchanges of roughly equivalent value in a strictly delimited sequence or whether it involves a much less precise definition of equivalence, one that emphasizes indebtedness and obligation. Game theoretic treatments of reciprocity by scholars in political science and economics tend to emphasize equivalence. [. . .] As a result, these scholars take a view of reciprocity that is entirely consistent with the pursuit of self-interest.

Sociological and anthropological analyses of reciprocity are commonly couched in the language of indebtedness. In this view, a measure of imbalance sustains the partnership, compelling another meeting (Sahlins, 1972). Obligation is a means through which parties remain connected to one another. Calling attention to the need for equivalence might well undermine and devalue the relationship. To be sure, sociologists have long emphasized that reciprocity implies conditional action (Gouldner, 1960). The question is whether there is a relatively immediate assessment or whether "the books are kept open," in the interests of continuing satisfactory results. This perspective also takes a different tack on the issue of self-interest. In his classic work *The Gift,* Marcel Mauss (1967 [1925]), attempted to show that the obligations to give, to receive, and to return were not to be understood simply with respect to rational calculations, but fundamentally in terms of underlying cultural tenets that provide objects with their meaning and significance, and provide a basis for understanding the implications of their passage from one person to another. Anthropological and sociological approaches, then, tend to focus more on the normative standards that sustain exchange; game theoretic treatments emphasize how individual interests are enhanced through cooperation.

Social scientists do agree, however, that reciprocity is enhanced by taking a long-term perspective. Security and stability encourage the search for new ways of accomplishing tasks, promote learning and the exchange of information, and engender trust. [. . .] Trust is, as Arrow (1974) has noted, a remarkably efficient lubricant to economic exchange. In trusting another party, one treats as certain those aspects of life which modernity rendered uncertain (Luhmann, 1979). Trust reduces complex realities far more quickly and economically than prediction, authority, or bargaining.

It is inaccurate, however, to characterize networks solely in terms of collaboration and concord. Each point of contact in a network can be a source of conflict as well as harmony. Recall that the term alliance comes from the literature of international relations where it describes relations among nation states in an anarchic world. Keohane (1986) has stressed that processes of reciprocity or cooperation in no way "insulate practitioners from considerations of power." Networks also commonly involve aspects of dependency and particularism. By establishing enduring patterns of repeat trading, networks restrict access. Opportunities are thus foreclosed to newcomers, either intentionally or more subtly through such barriers as unwritten rules or informal codes of conduct. In practice, subcontracting networks and research partnerships influence who competes with whom, thereby dictating the adoption of a particular technology and making it much harder for unaffiliated parties to join the fray. As a result of these inherent complications, most potential partners approach the idea of participating in a network with trepidation. In the various examples presented below, all of the parties to network forms of exchange have lost some of their ability to dictate their own future and are increasingly dependent on the activities of others.

ILLUSTRATIVE CASES OF NETWORK FORMS

[. . .]

Networks in Craft Industries

[. . .] Craft work tends to be project-based, while in bureaucratic organizations a product moves through a series of functional departments where different activities are performed. In craft work each product is relatively unique, search

procedures are non-routine, and the work process depends to a considerable degree on intuition and experimentation (Perrow, 1967). The examples presented below represent well-researched cases that highlight the many network features associated with craft production.

Construction. Robert Eccles (1981), in his research on the construction industry, found that in many countries the relations between a general contractor and his subcontractors are stable and continuous over long time periods, and only rarely established through competitive bidding. This type of quasi-integration results in what Eccles calls the "quasi-firm." Although most contracts are set under fixed price terms, no hierarchical organization arises, even though there are clear "incentive for shirking performance requirements." Instead, long-term and fairly exclusive association obviates the need for costly organizational monitoring. In an empirical study of residential construction in Massachusetts, Eccles found that it was unusual for a general contractor to employ more than two or three subcontractors in a given trade. This relationship obtained even when a large number of projects were done in the same year, and despite the fact that a number of alternative subcontractors werc available.

[. . .]

Film and Recording Industries. Sociologists who study popular culture have long known that the music and movie businesses were external economy industries in which there was heavy reliance on subcontracting and freelance talent. But recent research has shed new light on this particular method of matching investment capital and human capital. These industries thrive on short-term contracts, minimization of fixed overhead, mutual monitoring of buyers and sellers, and a constant weaving and interweaving of credits, relationships, and successes or failures. But the ostensibly open competition that one might expect to pervade these markets is minimal (Peterson & White, 1981). Instead, recurrent small-numbers contracting appears to be the norm.

Cultural industries are characterized by high variance and great unpredictability; conditions which breed high rates of social reconstruction or reproduction (Faulkner & Anderson, 1987). These "project markets" are complex, dynamic, and uncertain. The participants in the firm industry—producers, directors, cinematographers, actors, and musicians—appear at first glance to be highly mobile. They move from studio to studio, from one project to another, with few stable ties to any formal organization. But as Faulkner and Anderson (1987) show, in their analysis of participation in 2,430 films over a fifteen year period (1965–1980), considerable stability and recurrent contracting among the participants is the norm. It is the networks of participants, however, that are stable and enduring, not the film studios, where employees come and go and ownership changes frequently.

Not surprisingly, the key players in the film industry trust others with whom they have worked in the past and found to be reliable. What is striking about Faulkner's and Anderson's analysis is how dramatic the patterns of inclusion and exclusion are. Reproduction persists within film genres and between big money and small money films. They observe (p. 907) that "distinct networks crystallize out of a persistent pattern of contracting when particular buyers of expertise and talent (film producers), with given schedules of resources and alternatives, settle into self-reproducing business transactions with distinct (and small) sets of sellers (directors, cinematographers, and fashionable actors and actresses)." Commercial results feedback and then historically shape the next round of contracting.

These network patterns are interesting in their own right; but Peterson and White (1981) point out that even though they are powerful and long-lasting, they tend to be invisible to most observers. Instead of long-term rates of reproduction most participants observe individual acts of ranking, favors, and contacts.

These craft-based examples are not particularly unique. Network forms of social organization are found in many cultural industries, in research and knowledge production, and in various industrial districts—such as the diamond trade (Ben-Porath, 1980), the garment and fashion business in Milan and New York, the Lyonese silk industry (Piore & Sable, 1984), or the "Third Italy," discussed below. And many of the professions exhibit some network-like features. Architecture is a prime example; but so

apparently is engineering where, to judge from one recent study (Von Hippel, 1987), the informal trading of proprietary know-how among technical professionals in competing firms is extensive.[1] What these different activities share in common is a particular kind of skilled labor force, one with hands-on experience with production and the strategic ability to generate new products to keep pace with changing market demands. The people who perform the work have a kind of knowledge that is fungible, that is, not limited to an individual task but applicable to a wide range of activities. The organizations that complement these human capital inputs are highly porous—with boundaries that are ill-defined, where work roles are vague and responsibilities overlapping, and where work ties both across teams and to members of other organizations are strong.

Regional Economies and Industrial Districts

Recent economic changes have created, or perhaps recreated is a more apt description, new forms of collaboration among for-profit firms. In the previous century, a number of regions and industries were closely identified because both the social life and the economic health of such areas as Lyon and Sheffield were closely linked to the fate of the silk and cutlery trades, respectively (see Piore & Sabel, 1984; Sabel, 1989). This rediscovery or reinvigoration of the 19th century industrial districts points to the advantages of agglomeration, in which firms choose to locate in an area not because of the presence of an untapped market, but because of the existence of a dense, overlapping cluster of firms, skilled laborers, and an institutional infrastructure. [. . .]

German Textiles. Charles Sabel and his colleagues (1987) describe the German textile industry, centered in the prosperous state of Baden-Wurttemberg in southwestern Germany, as an "association of specialists, each with unmatched expertise and flexibility in a particular phase or type of production." This flourishing traditional craft industry employs a highly refined system of production that links small and medium-size firms with a wide range of institutional arrangements that further the well-being of the industry as a whole. These support services include industry research institutes, vocational training centers, consulting firms, and marketing agencies. Most textile producers are highly specialized; and, as Sabel et al. (1987) argue, the more distinctive each firm is, the more it depends on the success of the other firms' products that complement its own. This production system depends on an extensive subcontracting system in which key technologies are developed in a collaborative manner. The subcontractors are also connected to overlapping inter-industry supplier networks. These linkages allow textile makers to benefit from the subcontractors' experiences with customers in other industries, and the suppliers are, in turn, buffered from downturns in any one industry. All of these arrangements serve to strengthen the social structure in which textile firms are embedded and to encourage cooperative relations that attenuate the destructive aspects of competition.

The Emilian Model. Perhaps nowhere have socially integrated, decentralized production units had more of an impact than in Italy, where the economy has outgrown Britain's and is catching up to France's. Modena, the microcosm of Latin Europe's renaissance, is the center of Emilia-Romagna, in north central Italy, and it is here that Italy's economic performance has been most exceptional. Behind this success is both a set of unusual, to an American eye, political and social institutions, and a size distribution of firms that seem more suited to the nineteenth century than the late twentieth.[2]

Firms employing fewer than 50 employees engaged 49 percent of the Italian labor force, and the average manufacturing firm has only 9.19 employees (Lazerson, 1988, p. 330). The proportion of the labor force grouped in smaller units of employment is greater in Emilia than in Italy as a whole (Brusco, 1982). The success of these small enterprises rests on a different logic of production than found in a typical vertically-integrated firm.

These small firms are frequently grouped in specific zones according to their product, and give rise to industrial districts in which all firms have a very low degree of vertical integration (Brusco, 1982). Production is conducted through extensive, collaborative subcontracting agreements. Only a portion of the firms market final products, the others execute operations commissioned by the group of firms that initiate production. The owners of small firms typically prefer subcontracting to expansion or integration (Lazerson, 1988). The use of satellite firms allows them to remain small and preserve their legal and organizational structure as a small company. Often satellite firms outgrow the spawning firms. Though closely related and highly cooperative, the firms remain strictly independent entities.

These industrial districts embrace a wide range of consumer goods and engineering components and machines: knitwear in Modena, clothes and ceramic tiles in Modena and Reggio, cycles, motorcycles and shoes in Bologna, food processing machinery in Parma, and woodworking machine tools in Capri, to name but a few (see Brusco, 1982, pp. 169–170).

Why is production so widely decentralized and so spatially concentrated? The answer appears to be rather idiosyncratic to the Italian case. It is partly a response to labor union power in large firms, where union influence has proved to be a disincentive to job expansion. The small firms exhibit high wage dispersion, with highly skilled workers who have registered as artisans in order to make more than is standard in large-firm industrial relations agreements, and unskilled, temporary employees—students, the elderly, immigrants, who work off the books for much less than they would receive in a large factory, if they could find employment. The districts are also a response to changing tastes and technology, in particular the emerging popularity of custom rather than the standardized goods and the availability of high quality, flexible technologies that are compatible with the needs and budgets of small firms.

These decentralized organizational arrangements depend on a unique set of political and social institutions, most notably the fact that almost all local political authorities are controlled by the Communist party (Brusco, 1982; Lazerson, 1988). A combination of familiar, legislative, ideological, and historical factors buttress Emilia-Romagna's economic progress. The continued existence of the extended family provides for economic relations based on cooperation and trust, and facilitates the search for new employees through family and friendship networks (Lazerson, 1988). The CNA, a national organization with close ties to the Italian Communist party, represents some 300,000 artisanal firms and provides them with a rich array of administrative services. These artisanal associations prepare pay slips, keep the books, and pay the taxes, as well as establish consulting, marketing, and financial services (Brusco, 1982). By coordinating these various administrative activities, the associations establish on a cooperative basis the conditions for achieving economies of scale.

Brusco (1982) and Sabel (1989) make a persuasive case that the Emilian models fosters the skills and initiative of artisanal entrepreneurs. The number of entrepreneurs previously employed by large firms, particularly as foremen, is very high. By tapping both initiative and detailed production knowledge, the small firms are able to offer a vast array of new products. And these small firms, through their multitude of collaborative networks, are able to give shape to new ideas with a speed unimaginable in larger enterprises.

Extended Trading Groups. The kind of collaboration that obtains in the industrial districts of southwestern Germany or north central Italy is based in part on a set of local circumstances, but the principles of mutual organization on which the districts are based are more widely applicable. Interfirm cooperation is often found in economic activities based in a particular region, such as in Japan or Scandinavia, or in locales where firms from similar industries are spatially concentrated, such as Silicon Valley or Route 128 in the United States. The extended trading relationships that develop under these circumstances of physical proximity may vary considerably in their details, but their underlying logic is constant.

Ronald Dore (1983) argues that networks of preferential, stable trading relationships are a viable alternative to vertical integration. His work on the regionally concentrated Japanese textile industry, particularly its weaving segment, aptly illustrates this point. The industry was dominated in the 1950s by large mills, most of which were vertically integrated enterprises with cotton-importing, spinning and finishing operations. By 1980 the larger mills had closed and the integrated firms had divested and returned to

their original base in spinning. This "devolution" has led to a series of stable relationships among firms of different sizes. The key to this system is mutual assistance. Dore (1983) gives the example of a finisher who re-equips with a more efficient process, which gives him a cost advantage. This finisher, however, does not win much new business by offering a lower price. The more common consequence is that merchants go to their own finishers and say: "Look how X has got his price down. We hope you can do the same because we really would have to reconsider our position if the price difference goes on for months. If you need bank financing to get the new type of vat we can probably help by guaranteeing the loan." This type of relationship is, of course, not limited to the Japanese textile industry; similar patterns of reciprocal ties are found in many other sectors of the Japanese economy.

What are the performance consequences of these kinds of trading relationships? Dore suggests that the security of the relationship encourages investment by suppliers, as the spread of robotics among Japan's engineering subcontractors amply attests. Trust and mutual dependency result in a more rapid flow of information. In textiles, changes in consumer markets are passed quickly upstream to weavers, and technical changes in production also flow downstream rapidly. There is, Dore asserts, a general emphasis on quality. One would not terminate a relationship when a party cannot deliver the lowest price, but it is perfectly proper to terminate a relationship when someone is not maintaining quality standards.

More recently, Dore (1987) has maintained that Japanese economic relations in general do not have the properties (i.e., opportunism, short-term profit-maximization, and distrust) that we commonly associate with capitalist enterprise and on which we build our theories of economic organization (in particular, transaction cost economics). He contends that the costs of doing business in Japan are lower than in Britain or the United States because of concerns for reputation and goodwill and considerations of trust and obligation. Moreover, he argues, this embedding of business relations in moral and social concerns does not reduce economic vitality, it sustains it and provides Japan with a considerable edge.

But is Japan all that unique? Perhaps it is true, as Dore (1987) suggests, that as a nation, Japanese industry is organized more along the principles of an extended network (see also, Imai & Itami, 1984), but it does not appear to have a monopoly on these practices. Hagg and Johanson (1983), in an analysis of the industrial markets which comprise the core of the Swedish economy, describe a series of long term, stable relationships among industrial producers who share R&D resources and personnel. They suggest that the companies are actually investing in their connections with other companies, and in the process, losing their own identity to some extent. Instead of a competitive environment, there is a sharing of risks and resources and a pooling of information. Haag and Johanson argue that these arrangements eliminate costly safeguards and defensive measures and are better adapted to uncertainty. Competition in intermediate producer markets is not eliminated, rather coalitions of firms compete with other coalitions, not on the basis of price, but in terms of product development and knowledge accumulation.

[. . .]

It was not all that long ago that notions of industrial districts and spatially concentrated production were largely ignored—both intellectually and geographically. Now, every municipality seems busy at work trying to create their own Route 128 or Modena. The success of these forms of extended trading networks has several key ramifications:

1. One of the main consequences has been to blur the boundaries of the firm—boundaries are being expanded to encompass a larger community of actors and interests that would previously have either been fully separate entities or absorbed through merger;

2. A new constellation of forces is being recognized as crucial to economic success: whether in the Third Italy of Silicon Valley, spatially concentrated production involves the cooperation of local government, proximity to centers of higher education, a highly skilled labor pool, extensive ties to research institutes and trade associations, and cooperation among firms with specialized skills and overlapping interests;

3. The spread of technologically advanced, smaller units of enterprise—a growth that comes at the expense of larger companies and is not explained solely by the shift from manufacturing to services (Loveman, Piore & Sengenberger, 1987), and occurs without notable direct investment or significant employment increase, but rather as a result of expansion through various cooperative interorganizational relationships (Lorenzoni & Ornati, 1988).

Strategic Alliances and Partnerships

In many respects, partnerships and joint ventures are not new developments. They have been common among firms involved in oil extraction and petroleum refining as a means of spreading risks. Chemical and pharmaceutical firms have long conducted basic research jointly with university scientists. And some of the most complex partnerships have taken place in the commercial aircraft industry. Three major global players—Boeing, McDonnell Douglas, and Airbus Industrie—construct their planes via complex joint ventures among firms from many nations (Mowery, 1987). Boeing and Rolls Royce teamed up to produce the Boeing 757, and much of the construction of the Boeing 767 is done, through joint ventures, in Japan and Italy. Airbus Industrie is a four nation European aircraft consortium, supported in part through loans (or subsidies, if you take the competition's view) from European governments.

There is widespread evidence, however, that experimentation with various new kinds of interfirm agreements, collaborations, and partnerships have mushroomed in an unprecedented fashion (Friar & Hoewitch, 1985; Teece, 1986; Zagnoli, 1987; Hergert & Morris, 1988; Mowery, 1988). Firms are seeking to combine their strengths and overcome weaknesses in a collaboration that is much broader and deeper than the typical marketing joint ventures and technology licensing that were used previously. These new ventures may take the form of novel cooperative relationships with suppliers, or collaboration among several small firms to facilitate research and new product development. More generally, internally-generated-and-financed research is giving way to new forms of external R&D collaboration among previously unaffiliated enterprises. Indeed, in some industries, there appears to be a wholesale stampede into various alliance-type combinations that link large generalist firms and specialized entrepreneurial start-ups. Nor are these simply new means to pursue research and development; the new arrangements also extend to production, marketing, and distribution. And, in some circumstances, large firms are joining together to create "global strategic partnerships" (Perlmutter & Heenan, 1986) that shift the very basis of competition to a new level—from firm vs. firm to rival transnational groupings of collaborators.[3]

In the past, the most common way in which large companies gained expertise or products that they were unable to develop on their own was to acquire another company with the needed capability. Mergers and acquisitions in high technology fields have not disappeared, but their track record is generally poor (Doz, 1988). Partnerships are more frequent now because of growing awareness that other options have serious drawbacks. Recent efforts at various kinds of more limited involvement represent an important alternative to outright takeover. Equity arrangements—deals that combine direct project financing and varying degrees of ownership—are an example. A larger firm invests, rather than purchases, primarily for reasons of speed and creativity. The movement in large companies away from in-house development to partial ownership reflects an awareness that small firms are much faster at, and more capable of, innovation and product development. General Motors explained its 11 percent investment in Teknowledge, a maker of diagnostic systems that use a type of artificial intelligence, by noting that "if we purchased the company outright, we would kill the goose that laid the golden egg." Equity arrangements can be quite complex. Some small companies have several equity partners, and large companies find themselves in the novel position of negotiating product development contracts and licensing arrangements with companies that they partly own. Equity investments are typically "complemented by various agreements, such as research contracts from the larger firm to the smaller one, exclusive licensing agreements to the larger firm, and often loan and other financial agreements provided by the larger firm to the smaller one" (Doz, 1988, p. 32).

These developments, not surprisingly, are particularly common in technology-intensive industries (Mariti & Smiley, 1983; Zagnoli, 1987; Contractor & Lorange, 1988). Both the motivations for collaboration and the organizational forms that result are quite varied. Firms pursue cooperative agreements in order to gain fast access to new technologies or new markets, to benefit from economies of scale in joint research and/or production, to tap into sources of know-how located outside the boundaries of the firm, and to share the risks for activities that are beyond the scope or capability of a single organization. The ensuing organizational arrangements include joint ventures, strategic alliances, equity partnerships, collaborative research pacts of large scale research consortia, reciprocity deals, and satellite organizations. There is no clear cut relationship between the legal form of cooperative relationships and the purposes they are intended to achieve. The form of the agreement appears to be individually tailored to the needs of the respective parties, and to tax and regulatory considerations. The basic thrust, however, is quite obvious: to pursue new strategies of innovation through collaboration without abrogating the separate identity and personality of the cooperating partners.

In these process-oriented fields, knowing how to make a product and how to make it work is absolutely critical to success. In recent years, as product life cycles shorten and competition intensifies, timing considerations and access to know-how have become paramount concerns. Teece and Pisano (1987) suggest that, increasingly, the most qualified centers of excellence in the relevant know-how are located outside the boundaries of the large corporation. Fusfeld and Haklisch (1985) argue that corporations are becoming less self-sufficient in their ability to generate the science and technology necessary to fuel growth. [. . .]

Collaborative agreements involve a wide variety of organizations. While the joining together of small firms that possess entrepreneurial commitment and expertise in technology innovation with large scale corporate organizations that have marketing and distribution power represents the prototypical example, these arrangements are certainly not the only option. Many large firms are linking up with other large companies, particularly in international joint ventures.[4] These partnerships are unusual in that they involve the creation of dependencies and linkages among very large firms, such as Toyota and General Motors.

[. . .]

There are numerous factors both pushing and pulling U.S. multinationals into global alliances. On the push side are technological constraints. Much sophisticated technological knowledge is tacit in character (Nelson & Winter, 1982) and cannot easily be transferred by licensing. Indeed, it is the unwritten, intangible character of much firm-specific knowledge that has led U.S. firms, particularly the automakers, to form joint ventures with Japanese manufacturers in an effort to better understand their production processes. Similarly, Japanese companies have been attracted to joint projects with U.S. high tech firms because technological innovation cannot be simply purchased, it requires cumulative knowledge of the linkages among design, production, and sales.

On the pull side are financial concerns and the advantages of risk reduction. In joining a coalition with another firm, both partners may enjoy options that otherwise would not be available to them, ranging from better access to markets, pooling or exchanging technologies, and enjoying economies of scale and scope. Risk-sharing is very attractive in industries where each successive generation of products is expensive to develop, and product life cycles are short.

[. . .]

Cooperative arrangements are not necessarily easy to sustain, nor do they always entail success. They can create a host of management problems and they also raise serious questions about effective industrial policy. On the organizational front, Doz (1988) has cautioned that convergence of purpose is often difficult to achieve, consistency of effort can be undermined by parochial subunit goals, and middle managers and technical specialities may not share top management's enthusiasm for cooperation. Similarly, Borys and Jemison (1989) suggest that because partners have not previously worked together, they may misperceive one another's actions. They observe that collaborations often

begin with considerable resources, heavy obligations, and lofty expectations. Thus, the pressures to perform successfully may be considerable.

Collaboration can be fraught with other risks. Parties may bring hidden agendas to the venture. There is an ever-present threat that one party will capture the lion's share of the benefits, or defect with the other party's knowledge and expertise.[5] Some analysts worry that U.S. partners to global alliances may provide "mundane" services such as assembly, distribution, and marketing, which add little value to the product.[6] The key development work and the higher-paying, value-added jobs are taken overseas, and the U.S. firm merely completes the final stages. These issues are far from being resolved, but they point out the complex ways in which collaborative networks may or may not contribute to a country's stock of organizational talents.

Vertical Disaggregation

Evidence is accumulating that many firms are choosing to shrink their operations in response to the liabilities of large-scale organization. For example, Mariotti and Cainarca (1986) describe a "downsizing" pattern in the Italian textile industry, where there has been a decline in the number of vertically-integrated firms and growth in "intermediate governance structures." They attribute this development to three failures that plague vertically-integrated firms: an inability to respond quickly to competitive changes in international markets; resistance to process innovations that alter the relationship between different stages of the production process; and systematic resistance to the introduction of new products. Interestingly, in an earlier era, firms actively pursued a strategy of vertical integration in an effort to reap the benefits of administrative coordination, economies of scale, and risk reduction (Chandler, 1977). Today, these "strengths" have results in various weaknesses: structural inertia, slow response times, and decreased employee satisfaction.

Large organizations are designed to do certain things well over and over again. The more that behaviors are repeated, the more predictable they become; thus, the greater likelihood that these actions will become formalized. Child (1972) found that large organizations tend to be more rule-bound and to require greater documentation of their efforts. For certain kinds of activities, such practices are useful, but for others it can result in informational logjams and a serious mismatch between organizational outcomes and the demands of clients and customers in a changing environment. Thus, the very factors that make a large organization efficient and reliable at some tasks render it cumbersome and resistant to change when it comes to other actions (Nelson & Winter, 1982; Hannan & Freeman, 1984).

The information costs in large organizations are further compounded by motivational difficulties as well. One point that Alchian and Demsetz (1972) and Williamson (1975) implicitly demonstrate is that much of the internal structure of large organizations is designed to prevent collective action by employees. This basic attitude of suspicion may explain the finding by social psychologists that job satisfaction (as measured by turnover, absenteeism, and morale) declines with increases in organizational size and/or centralization (Porter & Lawler, 1965; Berger & Cummings, 1979). The design of organizations can affect the behavior of their members in a number of powerful ways.[7] In large hierarchical organizations, promotions up the career ladder are a key part of the reward structure. You have, then, little incentive to disagree with the operating decisions made by people above you in rank because they are the people who must decide on your promotion. Research suggests that hierarchical design dampens employee motivation because individuals are likely to be more committed when they have participated in a decision, and much less enthusiastic when they have been ordered by superiors to undertake a particular task (Hackman & Oldham, 1980).

When the pace of technological change was relatively slow, production processes were well understood and standardized, and production runs turned out large numbers of similar products, vertical integration was a highly successful strategy. But the disadvantages of large-scale vertical integration can become acute when the pace of technological change quickens, product life cycles shorten, and markets become more specialized. Firms are trying to cope with these new pressures in a variety of ways:

by explicitly limiting the size of work units, by contracting work out, or through more collaborative ventures with suppliers and distributors. One route leads firms to a rediscovery of the market, to the hostile world of arms-length relationships. Associated with a greater reliance on external contracts are strong efforts at cost-cutting, and greater managerial freedom in the deployment of resources and personnel. Another route leads firms to try to reorganize production, not so much through eliminating jobs, but by searching for new methods of collaboration among formerly antagonistic and/or competitive parties (Walton, 1985; Weitzman, 1984). Both responses entail some form of vertical disaggregation, or the shrinking of large corporate hierarchies.

The U.S. auto industry provides a good example of the crossroads many firms are at as they encounter the limits of vertical integration. The auto industry has undergone a profound shake-up, but the ultimate consequences of these changes have yet to be determined (see Dyer et al., 1987; Quinn, 1987). Prior to the mid-1970s, the big three automakers operated in a comfortable environment with little competitive pressure and scant customer demands for gas-efficient, high quality cars. The auto companies pursued a strategy of tight integration of production, which provided a means to guarantee supplies during periods of peak demand, as well as to protect the secrecy of annual styling changes. Vertical integration also kept down the prices of the independent parts suppliers with whom the companies traded. There was neither any give and take nor trust between the automakers and the subcontractors. Contracts were lost because a supplier bid .01 cents per item higher than a competitor (Porter, 1983). Automakers rigorously inspected supplier facilities, quality control procedures, stability of raw material sources, cost data, and management quality and depth (Porter, 1983, p. 278). They were reluctant to permit a supplier to manufacture a complete system. Instead, automakers preferred a competitive situation in which several firms supplied various components and the final assembly was done in-house.

Today this old system has crumbled in the face of international competition and fallen prey to the contradictions and short-term logic of the regime of competitive supplier relations. Heightened competition exposed a number of serious defects in this system. Abernathy (1978) has argued that vertical integration in the auto industry led to inflexibility. One consequence of tight technological interdependence is that change in any one part means the entire process must be altered. Pursuit of a cost-minimization strategy also reduced the automakers' ability to innovate. Susan Helper (1987), in an excellent analysis of supplier relations in the auto industry, observes that the old methods prevented suppliers from developing expertise, thereby reducing the skill requirements of their employees. This made it hard for them to develop any nonautomotive contracts and kept them dependent on the auto companies. It also had a chilling effect on innovation. There was neither any incentive nor capability for the suppliers to update equipment, suggest technological changes, or make long-range plans.

Because of their declining market share and lower profits, automakers are experimenting with an enormous variety of new approaches. A complex web of ties has developed among U.S. automakers, their Japanese rivals, American labor, and auto parts suppliers. These changes are transforming the way the U.S. auto industry operates, changing the nature of competition worldwide, and sharply blurring the distinction between domestic and imported cars. Joint venture activity is extensive: between Ford and Mazda, General Motors and Toyota, GM and Volvo, and Chrysler and Mitsubishi. Ownership is also held in tandem: Ford owns 25 percent of Mazda, GM 42 percent of Isuzu and 5 percent of Suzuki, Chrysler 12 percent of Mitsubishi Motors. These relationships involve close collaboration and joint production on some projects, and secrecy and exclusiveness on other models.

Equally extensive tinkering is underway with respect to subcontracting arrangements (Helper, 1987). The length of contracts have been expanded, from one year to three to five. More joint design work is being undertaken and sole-sourcing agreements are becoming more common. These new, more collaborative arrangements involve less monitoring and costly inspections, yet defect rates are much reduced. The automakers are becoming more dependent on the technological expertise of the suppliers, whose long-run health is now a factor in the automakers' profits.

At the same time, however, the automakers are pursuing a second strategy: outsourcing to low wage areas. They are simultaneously deciding which suppliers are worth investing in a long-term relationship with and determining which components can be obtained on the basis of price rather than quality. In these cases, there is little concern for collaboration or supplier design work; instead, the effort is aimed at finding third-world suppliers that can provide parts at the lowest possible price.

These disparate options graphically illustrate how practices such as subcontracting have a double edge to them: they may represent a move toward relational contracting (Macneil, 1978), with greater emphasis on security and quality; or they could be a return to earlier times, a part of a campaign to slash labor costs, reduce employment levels, and limit the power of unions even further. Hence, many of the current downsizing efforts seem, at the first glance, to be illogical. Some firms are seeking new collaborative alliances with parts suppliers while at the same time they are trying to stimulate competition among various corporate divisions and between corporate units and outside suppliers. Firms are proposing new cooperative relationships with labor unions and in the same motion reducing jobs and outsourcing them to foreign producers.

Are companies really as confused as it seems? Are these various actions merely the faulty experimentation of poor and indecisive managements? Not necessarily. Though many of the efforts at vertical disaggregation appear to work at cross purposes, there does appear to be an underlying theme. Strong competitive pressures within an industry reduce the number of levels of hierarchy within firms and push companies to redefine the boundaries of their organizations. Firms are externalizing the production of highly standardized components, and searching for new collaborative methods to produce components that require highly skilled, innovative efforts. These collaborations may entail new relationships with labor, close relationships with "outsiders" who are no longer viewed merely as providers of a component but rather as sources of technological creativity that large firms cannot duplicate internally, and new cooperative ventures with competitors to pool risks and to provide access to markets.

[. . .]

NOTES

1. In his study of the U.S. steel minimill industry, Von Hippel (1987) found the sharing of know-how to be based on professional networks, which develop among engineers with common research interests. When a request for technical assistance is made, the person being asked typically makes two calculations: (1) is the information being requested vital to the health of the firm or just useful, but not crucial? and (2) how likely is the requester to reciprocate at a later date? Even though no explicit accounting is made, assistance is commonly offered. Von Hippel argues that this "economically feasible and novel form of cooperative R&D" is probably found in many other industries as well.

2. While the organizational structure of Italian firms may not seem modern, they are decidedly successful and high-tech in their operations. Benetton, the fashionable clothing company, is an oftcited example. With some 2,000 employees, the company orchestrates relations backward with more than 350 subcontractors throughout western Europe and forward with some 100 selling agents and over 4,000 retail stores worldwide. The company's spectacular growth from small family business to far-flung empire has not been built on internalization or economies of scale, but on external relations for manufacturing, design, distribution and sales. These extended networks have both advantages in terms of speed and flexibility and liabilities with regard to maintaining quality standards. See Jarillo and Martinez (1987) and Belussi (1986) for detailed case studies of the company.

3. Competition over the marketing of tissue plasminogen activator (TPA), an enzyme may expect to be a major drug in treating heart attacks, is the most severe and complicated in biotechnology today. This competitive struggle illustrates how rival transnational alliances race for global market share. The U.S. firm Genentech is allied with Mitsubishi Chemical and Kyowa Hakko in Japan, while another American firm, Biogen, is collaborating with Fujisawa. Numerous other Japanese and European pharmaceutical alliances, ignoring Genentech's claims for patent priority for TPA, are busy with their own TPA research. This contest shows the intensity of transnational alliance competition, but at the same time that Genentech and Fujisawa are at odds over TPA, they are collaborating in the marketing of another biotech drug, tumor necrosis factor (TNF). Yoshikawa (1988) offers a good road map to the complex, crosscutting terrain of biotechnology strategic alliances.

4. The label "joint venture" implies the creation of a separate organization, but this need not be the case. Rather than form a new entity, partners can agree to a co-production arrangement. This is common in manufacturing, particularly aerospace, where each partner produces a section of the final product. Or firms may agree to a research partnership in which scientists and laboratories are shared. Similarly, exploration consortia in extractive industries need not create a new firm, but rather pool the costs and risks of existing activities.

5. Analysts have cautioned against alliances that involve a relative power imbalance, in which either one partner receives undue benefits or where one partner becomes so dependent on another that they may have no option other than to continue a relationship in which their share is increasingly inferior (see Teece, 1986). This fear, along with the worry that the partner will not perform according to expectations, explains why most potential partners approach an agreement with trepidation. These are typical and well-founded misgivings about any asymmetric exchange relationship.

6. Many commentators have voiced particular concerns about global partnerships, issues that are contested in the current "manufacturing matters" debate (see Cohen & Zysman, 1987). Reich and Mankin (1986) warn that friendly colleagues often revert to hostile competitors. In the Pentax-Honeywell and Canon-Bell & Howell alliances, Japanese partners took advantage of valuable U.S. technology and know-how only to later discard their American partners. *Business Week*, in its well-known March 3, 1986 issue, cautioned against the growth of "hollow corporations," that is, firms that have disaggregated so radically that they are left without any core expertise.

7. Top-down controls create distance between supervisors and subordinates, between powerful executives and less powerful employees. A vertical chain of command, and its accompanying layers of administration, undercuts management's ability to see its directives implemented and creates an environment in which employees see their work as but a tiny cog in a large impersonal machine. The diffuse control structure in large firms both dampens management's ability to move quickly and labor's sense of commitment to the enterprise.

REFERENCES

Abernathy, W. (1978). *The productivity dilemma.* Baltimore: Johns Hopkins University Press.

Alchian, A., & Demsetz, H. (1972). Production, information costs, and economic organization. *American Economic Review, 62,* 5, 777–795.

Arrow, K. (1974). *The limits of organization*. New York: Norton.

Belussi, F. (1986). New technologies in a traditional sector: The benetton case. Berkeley Roundtable on the International Economy working paper #19.

Ben-Porath, Y. (1980). The F-connection: Families, friends, and firms in the organization of exchange. *Population and Development Review, 6*, 1–30.

Berger, C., & Cummings, L. L. (1979). Organizational structure, attitudes and behavior." In Barry Staw (Ed.), *Research in Organizational Behavior* (Vol. 1, pp 169–208).

Borys, B., & Jemison, D. B. (1989). Hybrid organizations as strategic alliances: Theoretical issues in organizational combinations. *Academy of Management Review, 14*(2), 234–249.

Bradach, J. L., & Eccles, R. G. (1989). Markets versus hierarchies: From ideal types to plural forms. *Annual Review of Sociology, 15*, 97–118.

Braudel, F. (1982). *The wheels of commerce*. New York: Harper and Row

Brusco, S. (1982). The Emilian model: Productive decentralization and social integration. *Cambridge Journal of Economics, 6*, 167–184.

Chandler, A. D. (1977). *The visible hand*. Cambridge: Harvard University Press.

Child, J. (1972). Organizational structure and strategies of control: A replication of the Aston Study. *Administrative Science Quarterly, 18*, 168–185.

Cohen, S., & Zysman, J. (1987). *Manufacturing matters*. New York: Basic Books.

Contractor, F. J. & Lorange, P. (1988). *Cooperative strategies in international business*. Lexington, MA: Lexington Books.

Dalton, M. (1957). *Men who manage*. New York: Wiley.

DiMaggio, P., & Powell, W. W. (1983). The iron cage revisited: Institutional isomorphism and collective rationality in organizational fields. *American Sociological Review, 48*, 147–160.

Dore, R. (1983). Goodwill and the spirit of market capitalism." *British Journal of Sociology, 34*(4), 459–482.

Dore, R. (1987). *Taking Japan seriously*. Stanford, CA: Stanford University Press.

Doz, Y. (1988). Technology partnerships between larger and smaller firms: Some critical issues. *International Studies of Management and Organization, 17*(4), 31–57.

Dyer, Davis, M. S., & Webber, A. (1987). *Changing alliances*. Boston: Harvard Business School Press.

Eccles, R. (1981). The quasifirm in the construction industry. *Journal of Economic Behavior and Organization, 2*, 335–357.

Eccles, R. (1985). *The transfer pricing problem: A theory for practice*. Lexington, MA: Lexington Books.

Faulkner, R. R., & Anderson, A. (1987). Short-term projects and emergent careers: Evidence from Hollywood. *American Journal of Sociology, 92*(4), 879–909.

Friar, J., & Horwitch, M. 1985. "The emergence of technology strategy: A new dimension of strategic management." *Technology in Society 7*(2/3), pp. 143–178.

Fusfeld, H., & Haklisch, C. (1985). Cooperative R&D for competitors. *Harvard Business Review, 85*(6), 60–76.

Geertz, C. (1978). The bazaar economy: Information and search in peasant marketing. *American Economic Review, 68*(2), 28–32.

Gouldner, A. (1960). The norm of reciprocity: A preliminary statement. *American Sociological Review, 25*, pp. 161–178.

Hackman, R., & Oldham, G. (1980). *Work redesign*. Reading, MA: Addison-Wesley.

Hagg, I., & Johanson, J. (1983). *Firms in networks: A new view of competitive power*. Business and Social Research Institute, Stockholm.

Hannan, M., & Freeman, J. H. (1984). Structural inertia and organizational change. *American Sociological Review, 49*, 149–164.

Hayek, F. (1945). The use of knowledge in society. *American Economic Review, 35*, 519–530.

Helper, S. (1987). *Supplier relations and technical change*. Ph.D. dissertation, Dept. of Economics, Harvard University.

Hergert, M., & Morris, D. (1988). "Trends in international collaborative agreements." Pp. 99–109 in F. Contractor & P. Lorange (Eds.), *Cooperative strategies in international business*. Lexington, MA: Lexington Books.

Imai, K. & Itami, H. (1984). Interpenetration of organization and market. *International Journal of Industrial Organization, 2*, 285–310.

Jarillo, J.-C., & Martinez, J. I. (1987). Benetton S.p.A.: A case study. Working paper, IESE, Barcelona, Spain.

Keohane, R. (1986). Reciprocity in international relations. *International Oraganization, 40*(1), 1–27.

Lazerson, M. (1988). Organizational growth of small firms: An outcome of markets and hierarchies? *American Sociological Review, 53*(3), 330–342.

Lorenzoni, G., & Ornati, O. (1988). Constellations of firms and new ventures. *Journal of Business Venturing, 3*, 41–57.

Loveman, G., Piore, M., & Sengenberger, W. (1987). The evolving role of small business in industrial economies. Paper presented at conference on New Developments in Labor Market and Human Resource Policies, Sloan School, M.I.T.

Luhmann, N. 1979. *Trust and power*. New York: Wiley.

Macneil, I. (1978). Contracts: Adjustment of long-term economic relations under classical, neoclassical, and relational contract law. *Northwestern University Law Review, 72*(6), 854–905.

Macneil, I. (1985). Relational contract: What we do and do not know. *Wisconsin Law Review, 3*, 483–526.

Mariotti, S., & Cainarca, G. C. 1986. The evolution of transaction governance in the textile-clothing industry. *Journal of Economic Behavior and Organization, 7*, 351–374.

Mariti, P., & Smiley, R. H. (1983). Co-operative agreements and the organization of industry. *Journal of Industrial Economics, 31*(4), 437–451.

Mauss, M. (1967, 1925). *The gift*. New York: Norton.

Mowery, D. C. (1987). *Alliance politics and economics*. Cambridge, MA: Ballinger.

Mowery, D. C. (Ed.), (1988). *International collaborative ventures in U.S. manufacturing*. Cambridge, MA: Ballinger.

Nelson, R., & Winter, S. (1982). An *evolutionary theory of economic change*. Cambridge: Harvard University Press.

Perlmutter, H., & Heenan, D. (1986). Cooperate to compete globally. *Harvard Business Review, 86*(2), 136–152.

Perrow, C. (1967). A framework for the comparative analysis of organizations. *American Sociological Review, 32*, 194–208.

Peterson, R. A., & White, H. (1981). Elements of simplex structure. *Urgan Life, 10*(1), 3–24.

Piore, M. J., & Sabel, C. F. 1984. *The second industrial divide*. New York: Basic Books.

Polanyi, K. 1957. *The great transformation*. Boston: Beacon.

Porter, L., & Lawler, E. (1965). Properties of organization structure in relation to job attitudes and job behavior. *Psychological Bulletin, 64*(1), 23–51.

Porter, M. (1983). *Cases in competitive strategy*. New York: Free Press.

Quinn, D. P. (1987). Dynamic markets and mutating firms: The changing organization of production in automotive firms. Working paper presented at APSA meetings, Chicago.

Reich, R. B., & Mankin, E. (1986). "Joint ventures with Japan give away our future." *Harvard Business Review 86*, 2: 78–86.

Sabel, C. F. (1989). Flexible specialization and the re-emergence of regional economies. Pp. 17–70 in P. Hirst and J. Zeitlin (Eds.), *Reversing Industrial Decline*? Oxford, UK: Berg.

Sabel, C., G. Herrigel, R. Kazis, & Deeg, R. 1987. How to keep mature industries innovative. *Technology Review 90*(3), 26–35.

Sahlins, M. (1972). *Stone age economics*. Chicago: Aldine.

Stinchcombe, A. (1985). Contracts as hierarchical documents. Pp. 121–171 in A. Stinchcombe & C. Heimer, *Organization theory and project management*. Oslo: Norwegian University Press.

Teece, D. (1986). Profiting from technological innovation: Implications for integration, collaboration, licensing and public policy. *Research Policy, 15*(6), 785–305.

Teece, D., & Pisano, G. (1987). Collaborative arrangements and technology strategy. Paper presented at conference on New Technology and New Intermediaries, Center for European Studies, Stanford.

Von Hippel, E. (1987). Cooperation between rivals: Informal know-how trading. *Research Policy, 16*, 291–302.

Walton, R. (1985). From control to commitment in the workplace. *Harvard Business Review 85*, 2: 76–84.

Walzer, M. (1983). *Spheres of justice*. New York: Basic Books.

Weitzman, M. (1984). *The share economy*. Cambridge: Harvard University Press.

Williamson, O. E. (1975). *Markets and hierarchies: Analysis and antitrust implications*. New York: Free Press.

Yoshikawa, A. (1988). Japanese biotechnology: New drugs, industrial organization, innovation, and strategic alliances. BRIE Working Paper #33.

Zagnoli, P. (1987). Interfirm agreements as bilateral transactions? Paper presented at conference on New Technology and New Intermediaries, Center for European Studies, Stanford.

26

LEAN AND MEAN

The Changing Landscape of Corporate Power in the Age of Flexibility

BENNETT HARRISON

1

BIG FIRMS, SMALL FIRMS, NETWORK FIRMS

There are more than 1,200 booths arrayed across the football field-length floor of the David P. Lawrence Convention Center in Pittsburgh, Pennsylvania. The smells and tastes of cigarette smoke, coffee, and Coca-Cola fill the air. Everywhere, people (mostly men, but a surprising number of professional women, as well) are giving lectures, inspecting one another's wares, exchanging telephone numbers, and making deals.

We are attending a trade show of companies in the steel business. Companies from around the world are advertising their competence in a wide variety of activities. Some actually make steel bars, sheets, and related products. Others manufacture the machinery, parts, or computerized control systems. Still others offer the mill owners services ranging from design and plant maintenance to personnel management. And some specialize in disposing of the hazardous waste materials thrown off in the process of making steel.

As my friends and I pick up brochures and stop to chat with company representatives, we look for the presence of small, high-tech, independent entities. They are hard to find. Either the firms represented have themselves been created by consortia of companies from different countries, or they are branches, subsidiaries, or divisions of foreign multinationals whose parentage appears on the brochures and posters only in the small print (if at all). Sandwiched in between the row on row of cross-national companies, we occasionally encounter a certifiably independent, local small firm bearing the placard "Benton Harbor, Michigan," "Oakland, California," "Portland, Maine," or "Birmingham, Alabama."

But there is little doubt about who dominates these proceedings. It is the GEs, the IBMs, the Digitals, the Westinghouses, the 3Ms, the Hitachis, the Sumitomos, the Rockwell Internationals, the SKFs, the Bachmanns, the Ebners, the Herkules, the Siemens—alone, and together with their worldwide networks of large and small "partners." A similar convention of purveyors of construction or financial services—and of computer and semiconductor manufacturers, as well—would have an equally multinational character, dominated by the big firms.

To read the daily newspapers, this judgment must seem awfully surprising, to say the least. Headlines report on the crises of such giant corporations (and household names) as IBM, General Motors, and Sears Roebuck. We are bombarded with expert opinion about how these and other big firms have lost their competitive edge because of organizational rigidities and obsolete technological capabilities. The big firms, we are told, have become too inflexible, too rigid, and unable to adjust to the brave new world of heightened global competition, where only the fleet of foot—rather than the strong—survive.

At best, these observations tell only part of the story of how business is evolving in the closing years of the twentieth century. In the fields of computer hardware and software, IBM may again be in trouble—it has happened before—but those other standard-bearers in the industry, Intel (whose microprocessors drive most personal computers) and Microsoft (whose operating systems direct those Intel and other chips) go from victory to victory, and both are members in good standing of the Fortune 500 (to the extent that Intel's long-run command of the industrywide microprocessor standard *is* being challenged by other chip makers, the challenge is coming from such consortia as the Somerset group, created recently by IBM, Apple, and Motorola—all very big companies, indeed). The declining significance of the catalogue business of retailer Sears

Roebuck has been succeeded not by the emergence of a thousand small niche distributors but by even more successful mass retailers and distributors such as Lands End and Wal-Mart.

Other giant American companies have found ways to flourish in the new, more uncertain, more competitive environment. AT&T and Xerox are regularly cited by business analysts and executives as successful multinational corporations. And except for its problems with the same mammoth pension liabilities that are haunting companies in all of the mature industries, the Ford Motor Company has substantially transformed itself for the better—in only a decade.

We are constantly being told that technological change now systematically favors (or is mainly the product of) small companies. The idea is pervasive, but it simply is not correct. Take that quintessential high-tech activity: the design and manufacture of computers. It is no secret that in Japan, the computer industry has from the beginning been dominated by the NECs, the Toshibas, and the Fujitsus. But dominance by major firms is also true in America. In 1987 (the most recent year for which the appropriate data were published by the U.S. Bureau of the Census), 85 percent of all the individual enterprises in the computer industry in the United States did indeed employ fewer than 100 workers. Only about 5 percent of all computer makers had as many as 500 employees. Yet that comparative handful of firms—that 5 percent at the top—accounted for fully 91 percent of all employment and of all sales in the computer industry in that year.[1]

Meanwhile, in eastern Asia, the giant *keiretsu* of Japan and the *chaebol* of South Korea—huge industrial, service, and financial conglomerates—enter new domains of economic activity, from entertainment and health care to aerospace and medical technology, by adding more divisions to their already enormous holdings. If the Japanese economy is in some difficulty these days, the source lies mainly in the bursting of the speculative financial and real estate "bubble" of the 1980s; the rise of the exchange value of the yen, which has seriously dampened the exports on which that country's overall economic development strategy has long been based; and the global recessions which are just ending in the United States, if not yet in Europe.

Recent Japanese successes may indeed have been "miraculous," but no economy can grow without customers. Nevertheless, few knowledgeable students of Japan doubt the long-run technological and financial viability of Mitsubishi, Sumitomo, Fujitsu, or Toyota.

And even as Europe rides the next wave of consolidation of its Economic Community—now sure to extend some day to the Ural Mountains of Russia, albeit at a slower pace than was popularly expected when the Berlin Wall first fell—that continent is experiencing a veritable blizzard of mergers and acquisitions, and all manner of cross-border strategic alliances, involving both the public and the private sectors.

To see just how much the economic development action remains where it has been throughout the twentieth century—under the control of big corporations and their partners—one need only look at two commodities that are central to the daily lives of every North and South American (and Asian, and European) household: television sets and cars. The cost of developing the next generation of high-definition televisions is astronomical, and once the U.S. Federal Communications Commission (FCC) selects a standard, the winning design will immediately have a guaranteed mass market for TV sets oriented to that protocol. That is why some of the world's biggest high-tech corporations decided to form teams to develop the new standard system. Initially, one team included the French giant Thomson, the Dutch electronics conglomerate Philips, and NBC, probably the most famous American pioneer in recording technology. Other teams were led by General Instrument, working with M.I.T., and by Zenith, which joined forces with AT&T. But given the huge stakes, and with explicit shepherding by the FCC, the three teams announced in May 1993 a "grand alliance," under which they would share technical know-how and divide the eventual winnings.[2] This is not a story about the local Chamber of Commerce or the Elks Club. Rather, it is a story about big corporations and government industrial policy.

And what about cars? By the spring of 1993, it had become apparent that Toyota, Ford, and Honda were making great strides in developing truly global production systems. Parts manufactured in one location were being delivered to final assemblers based in another. Assembly lines located on every continent were turning out automobiles that were being shipped not only to local markets but across continents—even (in the case of Honda and Toyota) back to Japan, itself! The German car makers are moving in the same direction. Why? The answer: to hedge against unexpected currency fluctuations and to take even greater advantage of economies of large-scale production.[3] Again, this is hardly a story about industry growth driven by small business. If such direct foreign investments into *this* country have slowed down in recent years, blame it on the recession at home—*not* on the plans and deep pockets of the foreign giants.

Yet despite such examples, a multitude of writers continue to preach the virtues of small firms as the engines of contemporary economic growth. We are told that, as discretionary incomes increase and living standards reach historically unprecedented levels around the world, consumers increasingly seek more customized, fashion-oriented goods and services. Mass markets become saturated, the demand for such commodities as clothing and furniture becomes increasingly fragmented, and mass education and mass communications both facilitate and promote a growing heterogeneity in customers' tastes. In a fashion-conscious world, agility in identifying new wants and in getting new products to market becomes the key to winning the competitive wars.

These developments are said to conjoin to favor technically adroit, well-informed small enterprises—or at least give them a new fighting chance. Why? The answers we are offered are partly behavioral and partly technical. The bureaucratic organization of the big firms militates against agility. And the fragmentation of markets deprives the big firms of the opportunity to exploit various technical advantages that, over the course of the last century, were made possible by the drive toward standardization and mass production.

That's the theory. The facts show otherwise. With the usual few headline-capturing exceptions, small firms turn out to be systematically *backward* when it comes to technology. For example, on every continent, the big companies and establishments are far more likely than are the small ones to invest in, and to deepen their use of, computer-controlled factory automation.

And the argument that the proliferation of niche markets is inexorably driving a small firm renaissance reflects a misunderstanding of the nature of contemporary markets.

[. . .]

What the architects of the romance of small business are ignoring is that the big firms can produce for both mass *and* niche markets—a neat trick that few small firms can pull off. Thus, Toyota can deliver both its big-selling, inexpensive Corolla *and* the high-priced, world-class Lexus.

[. . .]

To be sure, small firms and individual business establishments do have a role to play in the evolving industrial structure of world capitalism. And managers most certainly care about "flexibility." But as I show later, the role that small firms are playing is typically that of follower, not leader. And while it may be enhancing the agility and profitability of individual firms, the search for flexibility—by the managers of both big and small companies—is also leading to practices that are undermining the employment security and incomes of a growing fraction of the population, exacerbating inequality and contributing to the underlying sense of futility that now characterizes politics worldwide.

CONCENTRATION WITHOUT CENTRALIZATION: HOW THE BIG FIRMS ARE REORGANIZING GLOBAL CAPITALISM

Announcements of the demise of concentrated economic power in the form of the large, resourceful, multidivisional, multiproduct, multiregional, often multinational corporation are premature. Yet the difficulties facing traditional big business are formidable. How then, *have* the survivors managed to cope? How do newly emergent large firms make it in a world that was thought to belong to the smallest of the small?

Rather than dwindling away, concentrated economic power is changing its shape, as the big firms create all manner of networks, alliances, short- and long-term financial and technology deals—with one another, with governments at all levels, and with legions of generally (although not invariably) smaller firms who act as their suppliers and subcontractors. True, production is increasingly being decentralized, as managers try to enhance their flexibility (that is, hedge their bets) in the face of mounting barriers to market entry and of chronic uncertainty about political conditions and customer demands in distant places. But decentralization of production does not imply the end of unequal economic *power* among firms—let alone among the different classes of workers who are employed in the different segments of these networks. In fact, the locus of ultimate power and control in what Robert B. Reich, the U.S. Secretary of Labor and a Harvard University lecturer, calls "global webs"[4] remains concentrated within the largest institutions: multinational corporations, key government agencies, big banks and fiduciaries, research hospitals, and the major universities with close ties to business. That is why I characterize the emerging paradigm of networked production as one of *concentration without centralization.*[5]

[. . .]

But the competitive success of the large corporations is not without its own contradictions. In particular, the restructuring experiments pursued by the big companies and their strategic partners since the 1970s are polarizing the population, contributing to the growing inequality among white-collar workers as well as between blue-collars and white-collars. The polarization is now evident and palpable. It manifests itself in terms of income, status, and economic security. [. . .]

It works this way: According to a central tenet of best-practice flexible production, managers first divide permanent ("core") from contingent ("peripheral") jobs. The size of the core is then cut to the bone—which, along with the minimization of inventory holding, is why "flexible" firms are often described as practicing "lean" production. These activities, and the employees who perform them, are then located as much as possible in different parts of the company or network, even in different geographic locations. A good example is the siting of the "back offices" of the big insurance companies, banks, and corporate headquarters. These facilities house masses of typically poorly paid, overwhelmingly female clerical workers, tucked away in suburban "office parks," far from the downtown corporate headquarters to which they are linked, where their companies' higher-level functions are performed.[6]

Although represented as state-of-the-art management, the practice of lean production (the principle applies as much to the service sector as to manufacturing) involves the explicit reinforcement or creation *de novo* of sectors of low-wage, "contingent" workers, frequently housed within small business suppliers and subcontractors.[7] The advent of these generally big firm-led core-ring production networks is almost surely adding to the national (and increasingly international) problem of "working poverty," in which people work for a living but do not earn a living wage. As a result, both within the big firms and their most trusted partners and suppliers, and ultimately over the economy as a whole, core employees become increasingly segregated from outside peripheral employees—a gap that is measurably reflected in the by now widely acknowledged phenomenon of growing earnings inequality among American (and, as we shall see, some overseas) workers.[8] I call this the dark side of flexible production.

To sum up the argument: I am suggesting that the emerging global economy remains dominated by concentrated, powerful business enterprises. Indeed, the more the economy is globalized, the more it is accessible only to companies with a global reach.

[. . .]

WHY SMALL FIRMS DO NOT DRIVE ECONOMIC GROWTH AND CREATE THE MOST NEW JOBS

My argument about the revitalization and transformation of the big firms and their production networks must sound even more surprising to a public that, for more than a decade, has been told repeatedly that *small* companies are now the engines of economic growth and development. According to the new conventional wisdom, the large corporation was in many respects becoming something of a dinosaur, increasingly unable to compete in a "postindustrial" world characterized by continually fluctuating consumer demands, heightened international competition, and

the need for more flexible forms of work and interfirm interaction.

As the big firms collapsed under their own weight, we were told, a panoply of small, flexible enterprises were rushing in to fill the ecological void. Small enterprises were said to be creating most of the new jobs in all of the world's highly industrialized countries. The world described by an earlier generation of scholars—Joseph Schumpeter, Raymond Vernon, John Kenneth Galbraith, and Alfred Chandler—was thought to be collapsing before our very eyes. Now it was the turn of the small, agile companies to drive technological progress.

But hard evidence shows that the importance of small businesses as job generators and as engines of technological dynamism has been greatly exaggerated. In the United States and Germany, after we factor out the ups and downs of the business cycle, the share of all jobs accounted for either by small companies or by individual workplaces with fewer than 100 employees (the official criterion for "small" that is used by the Paris-based Organization for Economic Cooperation and Development—the OECD—when making international comparisons) has hardly changed since the 1960s. Moreover, many de jure independent small companies turn out in varying degrees to be de facto dependent on the decisions made by managers in the big firms on which the smaller ones rely for markets, for financial aid, and for access to political circles. As we shall see later, there are also sound technical reasons why precisely the kinds of short period changes in the size distribution of firms that so appeal to the "small is beautiful" ideologies systematically exaggerate the relative importance of the tiniest companies, and overstate the fragility of the biggest corporations.

Still, on every continent, stories on the front pages and in the business sections of the leading newspapers and magazines feature seemingly endless anecdotes about an explosion in the number of small businesses. Thus, for the American economy as a whole, for mature as well as for high-tech industry, the consultant David Birch reckons that "very small firms [with fewer than 20 employees] have created about 88 percent of all net jobs in [1981–85]."[9] And *Business Week*, always an opinion setter on economic matters, announced in a lead story that "Small Is Beautiful Now in Manufacturing,"[10] while across the Atlantic, the London-based *Economist* editorialized:

> The biggest change coming over the world of business is that firms are getting smaller. The trend of a century is being reversed. . . . Now it is the big firms that are shrinking and small ones that are on the rise. The trend is unmistakable—and businessmen and policy makers will ignore it at their peril.[11]

Economists use the concept of economies of scale to describe the potential savings in unit production costs as facilities are operated at higher volumes. Scope economies are said to exist when the joint cost of making more than one product on the same basic equipment, or "platform," in the same facility is less than the cost of turning out the same set of products in separate facilities. Historically, these economies of scale and scope joined financial and supervising economies in reinforcing the tendency toward larger units of production and distribution.

Now, thanks to the advent of new, more flexible computer-based technologies, from electronic bar-code readers at the supermarket checkout counter to numerically controlled machine tools and flexible manufacturing systems for the factory floor or the laboratory workbench, these internal economies of scale and scope are said to be disappearing. In the words of the management consultant Tom Peters (of *In Search of Excellence* fame), "old ideas about economies of scale are being challenged. . . . Scale itself is being redefined. Smaller firms are gaining in almost every market."[12] The commentator George Gilder is only the most prominent popularizer of the even more extravagant claim that the smallest companies are now even *more* technologically sophisticated than the old giants.[13]

[. . .]

A rather more interesting variation on the small firm theme calls our attention to the survival from an earlier era (or in some places, the recent emergence) of networks of mostly small, loosely linked but spatially clustered firms. The businesses that make up these so-called industrial districts are described as typically utilizing a craft form of work organization. The alleged widespread adoption of small-scale

computerized automation helps to make these networks of what the M.I.T. economist Michael J. Piore and the M.I.T. sociologist and creator of the field of "industrial politics" Charles Sabel call "flexibly specialized" firms capable of rapidly reconfiguring themselves to meet the continually fluctuating demands of the world market.[14] In the modern era, the industrial districts were first discovered in north-central Italy in the 1970s, then elsewhere in Europe, and they have now become the object of both study and policy prescription in many different regions of Europe, North America, and eastern Asia.[15]

At a time when many Western and Third World political leaders continue to entertain the philosophy that further government involvement in the economy only erodes economic efficiency—probably the most long-lasting and pernicious legacy of the Reagan-Thatcher years—in Japan, North America, and Europe, local and regional governments have been actively supporting their industrial districts with a variety of infrastructural and business services. Tying it all together are (we are told) a sense among the locally oriented small firm owners and managers of shared long-run interest; of mutual *trust* deriving from repetitive mutual business contracting said to be *embedded* within deeply rooted local social relationships associated with political, familial, and (in some places) religious life; and the practice of *reciprocity* among all the actors in the community.[16] Giacomo Becattini, the prominent, elegant Florentine economist, calls this the "industrial atmosphere," borrowing an evocative language first coined by the British economist Alfred Marshall, who depicted the late-nineteenth-century steelmaking district around the town of Sheffield, and, more or less at the same time, by Alfred Weber, the German father of industrial location theory.[17]

More than anything else, it is the embedding that is thought to confer on these new growth poles of generally small enterprises the ability to capture simultaneously economies of scale and scope, but at the level of the district as a whole rather than within individual firms.[18] Therein lies their alleged competitive advantage over the large, vertically integrated, centralized, and concentrated monopolies that dominated economic life in the industrialized world for most of the twentieth century. In the elegantly argued and widely influential view of Piore and

Sabel, the world has come to a "second industrial divide," at which a resurgence of the nineteenth-century districts has been made possible by the growing complexities of a global economy, which make it ever more difficult for large, concentrated economic organizations to compete.[19]

WHY ARE WE SO READY TO ACCEPT THE SMALL FIRMS STORY?

[. . .] It is easy to see why both the entrepreneurial and the industrial district versions of the theory of small firm–led growth would become so popular in the 1980s, especially among policy makers. The 1970s constituted a historical moment when the managers of large corporations in many places seemed to have lost their strategic bearings. Moreover, by the end of that decade, and well into the 1980s, the very legitimacy of government was being challenged by newly reenergized conservative political movements that had succeeded in capturing political power and decisive influence on public opinion, especially in the United States and the United Kingdom but to some extent also in the Federal Republic of Germany, Austria, and eventually even Sweden, the country with the world's most highly developed welfare state. Both tendencies strengthened interest in and celebration of entrepreneurship, small business, free enterprise, deregulation, and decentralized ("free") markets.

This is the environment that has proved so hospitable to the questionable statistics of Birch and to the laissez-faire ideological tracts of Gilder, both of whom are outspoken advocates of economic development policies fashioned around the allegedly driving force of the dynamic small firm. It is the same environment that has given rise to such public policy conceptions as the enterprise zone, the industrial incubator, government deregulation, tax preferences for venture capital funds, and science parks—all in the interest of promoting and nurturing the growth of small businesses. This approach has acquired a special champion in the American media, in the influential magazine *Inc.*, and in Europe, in the London *Economist.*

Interestingly, the Left in many places has also become enchanted with many of the elements of such a program—although for different reasons. To many, the big firms seemed hopelessly inaccessible. Moreover, as socialist and social democratic parties and groups attained some degree of control over municipal, state, or provincial governments (and even the national government, as in France and Spain) during the depths of the recession of the late 1970s through early 1980s, it was both ideologically attractive and seemingly feasible politically to articulate a "progressive localism" that encouraged the development of cooperatives and other kinds of small firms. Nowhere was this inclination more apparent than in the United Kingdom. There, in the early 1980s, the small firm "renaissance"—and the Italian model in particular— caught the interest of several leaders of the Greater London Council and the Greater London Enterprise Board.[20]

In the United States, efforts to self-consciously construct (or preserve) industrial districts got under way in a number of states, including Massachusetts, Pennsylvania, and Michigan. The Washington-based Corporation for Enterprise Development became a prominent voice for the planned emulation of the Italian model. And in New York City, the architect C. Richard Hatch, who knows Italy intimately, advocated the transferability of the Italian model with the same fervor that, in the late 1960s, he brought to the argument that Third World import substitution strategies also made sense for the economic development of black urban ghettos in the United States.[21]

These initial efforts to create small firm–led American production networks on the Italian model have met with mixed results, at best. But the advocates have been working harder than ever to improve their performance and to gain political support from the White House and from a recently revitalized U.S. Small Business Administration. *[. . .]*

WHAT'S WRONG WITH THE SMALL FIRMS STORY?

[. . .] Take the job generation question. As a general proposition, across the industrial world, the biggest companies and plants unquestionably are downsizing, especially in manufacturing (on the other hand, at least in the United States the average individual facility in the *service* sector has actually

been getting *bigger*).[22] *Why* are manufacturers getting smaller? We know that managers are outsourcing work they used to perform inhouse.[23] They are also partnering with other existing firms, as a way of accessing new technical know-how, markets, territories, and capital without having to make new capacity-expanding investments themselves. In this regard, Bo Carlsson, a Case Western Reserve University industrial economist, reports that

> the share of multi-unit companies in U.S. manufacturing employment increased throughout the postwar period until the late 1970s. But after 1977, the share of multi-unit companies declined for the first time.... This suggests that subcontracting and outsourcing have become more important forms of disintegration in recent years.[24]

But then the increasing number of small firms turns out to be in part a function of the core-ring, lean production strategies of the *big* companies. It is the strategic downsizing of the big firms that is responsible for driving down the average size of business organizations in the current era, *not* some spectacular growth of the small firms sector, per se.[25] What we have witnessed over the last decade constitutes the lopping off of the tip of an iceberg more than it does a meltdown of the old prevailing structure.

In fact, in the United States, Germany, and Japan, once we account properly for the usual ups and downs of the business cycle, the shares of national employment in both small *establishments* (that is, in individual plants, stores, and offices) and small *enterprises* (entire companies) have hardly changed at all for several decades. The Japanese data for the most recent years actually record a slight *decline* in the small firm (and plant) shares of jobs. Only in the United Kingdom did the small firm (and establishment) shares grow steadily between the mid-1970s and the mid-1980s. But even there, this looks to be mainly the result of the sharp decline in the fortunes of the biggest corporations during the disastrous economic years of 1973 through 1983, these corporations' subsequent laying off of middle managers as well as shop floor workers, and the permanent shuttering of their older, most inefficient large factories—not some explosive growth of small business, per se.

Nor do countries with a high proportion of their overall manufacturing employment in small firms display systematically superior economic performance. Across the member nations of the OECD there is no correlation whatsoever between the relative importance to each country of small manufacturing firms and either the national unemployment rate or the rate of growth of overall national manufacturing employment.[26]

New attention to the *dynamics* of job creation and destruction over time does even more damage to a naive small firms story. For example, recent research from the United States and Germany points to a consistent tendency of the *largest* firms in any cohort to experience the fastest rates of growth over time, and the smallest chances of going out of business during any given interval of time.[27]

Still another kind of evidence has emerged that casts doubt on Birch's thesis that very small start-up businesses are the principal source of economic vitality in modern industrial economies. In 1989, after years of providing Birch with his data on company and establishment births and deaths in American industry, the Dun and Bradstreet Corporation (D&B) decided that it had had enough of being quoted so often as the source of the claims that small firms were creating most of the jobs in the United States.[28] So the company set its in-house economists to reassessing what their own numbers seemed to be saying.

What they found was startling. Among the 245,000 new companies that were started up in the United States in 1985—in the middle of the Reagan-era military- and real estate–driven economic boom—75 percent of the employment gains by 1988 occurred in those firms that, at birth, had *already* employed more than 100 workers when they were first launched. Moreover, this group of businesses constituted only *three-tenths of one percent* of the 1985 cohort.[29]

[. . .]

Finally, there is the matter of just how independent the small firms really are, especially in relation to the big firms for whom they act as suppliers and subcontractors. In their writing for the International Institute for Labour Studies (IILS) in Geneva, the Harvard Business School's Gary Loveman and IILS Director Werner Sengenberger conclude that "large enterprises often have very many legally independent subsidiaries. While the subsidiaries are *de jure* independent, they are *de facto* part of the large enterprise and should be accounted for, accordingly." For example, one German study found that "the 32 largest German manufacturing enterprises had in excess of 1,000 legally independent subsidiaries, and the number grew by almost 50 per cent from 1971 to 1983."[30] Once again, what we are seeing is evidence of how *production* may be decentralized, while power, finance, distribution, and control remain concentrated among the big firms.

For all the widespread interest in small firms as job generators, Birch and Gilder have failed to address a rather obvious companion question: How well do small companies do, vis-à-vis the largest firms, in providing their workers with a respectable standard of living? That is, how do wages, benefits, and such working conditions as occupational health and safety differ (if indeed they do) by the size of the organization? Certainly, for the purposes of evaluating the public policy implications of government subsidization of the small business sector, whether through grants, loans, tax incentives, or relaxation of environmental and other regulatory controls, these would seem to be important concerns.

[. . .]

For the United States, the definitive study of whether the big or the small firms offer better working conditions is to be found in a book published in 1990 by the economists Charles Brown, James Hamilton, and James Medoff.[31] *[. . .]* The authors found, first, that across American industry, "workers in large firms earn higher wages, and this fact cannot be explained completely by differences in labor quality, industry, working conditions, or union status." Second, employees of the big firms also enjoy "better benefits and greater job security than their counterparts in small firms." Third, in American political life, small firms are more likely than large ones to be granted exemptions from environmental or health and safety regulations, with the inevitable negative implications for their employees. Finally, workers in small firms are more likely to quit their jobs, and the fact that they express a greater desire to join unions (if they do not already belong to one) than do those working for big companies reinforces the strong impression that the workers themselves

perceive conditions as being better in the larger organizations.

I have been presenting evidence on how the distributions of jobs, wages, and benefits differ between big and small businesses. There are still other flaws in the small firms story. Earlier, I alluded to the belief that smaller companies and establishments are now actually *more* technologically innovative than the supposedly rigid and inflexible big firms. Some writers assert that computer-programmable machinery systematically favors smaller units of production.[32] Or, as Gilder argues, the dramatically shrinking scale (in other words, the miniaturization) of microelectronic components leads inexorably to a commensurate shrinking of the "optimal" scale of the firms that make them.[33]

Much new theory and empirical evidence adds up to a powerful challenge to this contention. There *is* no particular size of firm, nor any special scale of production, that any given technology invariably favors or requires—nor any one "best" design of jobs that employers everywhere will introduce in connection with some new round of automation. For example, the Carnegie Mellon University economist Wesley Cohen and his colleagues have shown that small firms do best as product rather than as process innovators, and then only under certain market conditions. In other settings, the large producers still have a measurable advantage, given their greater resources.[34] Carnegie Mellon's Kelley has conducted a number of econometric studies from which she concludes that big firms are far more likely to adopt and use both complex *and* small-scale factory automation than are smaller companies and factories. In fact, during the 1980s the technology gap between the smallest and the largest American manufacturers actually grew *wider*, according to private industry trade association data.[35]

Gilder's biggest error in reasoning is his disregard of the fact that even playing in the league where "microcosmic" technology is being created requires ever larger scale production and concentrated control over finance capital. Consider the remarks of Intel's board chairman, Gordon E. Moore, in announcing a corporate plan to turn Intel's Albuquerque, New Mexico, chip factory into the world's biggest facility of its kind: "This is our first billion-dollar factory, but it won't be our last. Chip factories are getting bigger and more expensive as our manufacturing technologies continue to become more complex. The entry fee to be a major player in the global semiconductor market of the '90s is $1 billion—payable in advance."[36]

[. . .]

TROUBLE IN PARADISE: HIERARCHY AND INEQUALITY IN THE INDUSTRIAL DISTRICTS

Small, independent firms are neither as bountiful nor as beautiful as the new conventional wisdom has led us to believe. But what about those *networks* of small firms, those locally oriented industrial districts in such regions as north-central Italy and California's Silicon Valley? Here, too, we can see signs of concentration without centralization—geographically and organizationally dispersed production, but with strategy, marketing, and finance ultimately controlled by (or, in the case of the Italian districts, coming increasingly under the control of) the big firms.[37]

As a growing number of Italian researchers and local government officials are themselves observing, as they pursue the economic development of their own areas, powerful "lead firms" from within and without the districts now threaten to alter the collaborative nature of interfirm relations inside the districts. Mergers and acquisitions are on the rise. Financial conglomerates are dictating production procedures to what used to be truly independent small firms.

I interpret neither the appearance (or reappearance) of hierarchy, nor unequal power and the remote control of key elements of a district's economy by outside corporations, as a sign of regional economic *failure*. Instead, such changes are more a sober reminder that, for all their intended local orientation, the districts are operating within much more extensive fields. In the context of a global system populated by big companies perpetually on the prowl for new profitable opportunities, the very success of a district can itself bring about changes that give rise to its opposite, and we observe the re-creation of hierarchical organization.

All of these concerns are relevant to constructing a richer, more balanced reassessment of the evolution of the Western Hemisphere's most dramatically successful high-tech region—Silicon Valley. Those who wish to characterize the Valley as an industrial district on the Italian model are not wrong. But they are offering only a partial perspective. Silicon Valley has many faces, each of which manifests a different aspect of the emerging post-1970s system of networked production that I have named concentration without centralization—including the dark side.

In the most romantic characterizations,[38] Silicon Valley's astonishing success as the home base for a myriad of companies that design, produce, and export computers, workstations, microchips, disk drives, and software is mainly a story about an adventuresome gang of creative, supremely—even belligerently—independent entrepreneurs, many of them refugees from other, less free-wheeling parts of the country and the world, practicing textbook-style free market economics.

Silicon Valley shows another face to other observers. As seen by AnnaLee Saxenian, a city planning professor at the University of California at Berkeley, Silicon Valley is a full fledged industrial district, a dense thicket of mostly small and medium-sized (but also some quite large) firms that alternately cooperate and compete with one another.[39] These networks of producers are said to be embedded in a local political economy that provides job training, finance capital, and an incessant flow of ideas and information about the latest design and production techniques. Well connected to the rest of the world, Silicon Valley's flexibly specialized firms nevertheless have a "Marshallian" orientation, in the sense that the district may trade with the rest of the world (and quite successfully, thank you), but *production* relationships remain (according to Saxenian) highly localized.

From yet a third perspective, Silicon Valley increasingly faces outward. According to a bevy of astute observers—including the management professor David Teece, the regional economist Ann Markusen, the technologists Kenneth Flamm and Martin Kenney, the management consultant Charles Ferguson, the political scientist Richard Gordon, and the urban planner Richard Florida—Silicon Valley as a production *system* was substantially created by major multinational corporations and remains profoundly dependent on them, and on the fiscal and regulatory support of the national government—especially as represented by the Department of Defense (as recently as the mid-1980s, Santa Clara County, the heart of Silicon Valley, remained one of the three top recipients of defense contracts in the United States).[40]

[...]

On every continent, the great majority of the good jobs within the districts themselves are held by men of the dominant color and ethnicity. Minorities, women, and immigrants are overwhelmingly treated as outsiders, consigned to jobs situated in the back rooms of these district's shops or outside these regions altogether, in the small factories and sweatshops that occupy the periphery of the geographically extensively production systems of which the districts, per se, constitute only the core. By drawing too narrow a box around the activity taking place solely *within* the districts, advocates are understating the degree of inequality among workers and between regions.

In Italy, a good example is Benetton, the maker of colorful clothing sold in spritely little franchise shops in seventy-nine countries—more than 300 shops in Japan, alone.[41] Most of the design and the high-end production work continue to be situated in or around Treviso, near Venice, where the firm was founded in the 1960s and where it is still headquartered. By contrast, nearly all of the labor-intensive assembly, pressing, and embroidery work is contracted out. A first tier of midsized firms perform R&D, design, or high-level manufacturing functions, collaborating closely with (but working for the most part on orders from) technicians and managers in the core corporation. In turn, these subcontractors are expected to manage successively lower order tiers of suppliers, situated within the Veneto region and farther away, in southern Italy, Turkey, and other low-wage areas.

These lower-tier suppliers are typically very small, highly specialized, and almost never unionized, and they are generally owned and run by small-town or rural men who employ a workforce consisting predominantly of women under the age of twenty-five. Labor costs in the lower-tier workshops are below the national average. Whether the national labor laws with respect to health and safety,

minimum wages, paid vacations, and the like are observed depends mainly on whether the local political parties, the owners' confederations, and the unions enforce them. As for skills, managers expect newly hired workers to be able to carry out assigned tasks within, at most, a year of coming on the job. The pace of production in the small contract shops can be extremely intense.

Finally, at the lowest level within this interregional and obviously hierarchical production system stands the *home worker*: lacking skills (or, at any rate, power), receiving the lowest wages, and having no legislated health and safety protection. Such home work appears to be more prevalent in the south of Italy than in the more urbanized north, but even on this question, the visitor gets contradictory stories.

The inequalities are not quite so stark in Silicon Valley, but there are important underlying similarities in the labor process and in its geography. As early as the 1970s, it was becoming apparent that the workforce employed inside the semiconductor companies at the heart of the Silicon Valley economy was highly stratified. As Saxenian documented in her earliest published research,[42] at the top of the hierarchy are the highly educated, well-paid managers, engineers, and other professionals. At the same time (and often within the same factories and laboratories), nearly half of all workers in the Valley's high-tech companies perform production and maintenance tasks, four-fifths of which are officially classified as semiskilled or unskilled. Wages in these jobs are dramatically lower, and benefits often nonexistent.[43]

During the 1960s and 1970s, immigration into Santa Clara County reflected this stratification. Well-educated engineers and scientists moved into the western foothills near Stanford University, to be closer to their offices and labs, as well as to the more expensive luxury homes and amenities. At the same time, the industry's demand for production workers stimulated an equally large in-migration of unskilled, predominantly Mexican, Chicano, and Asian workers. These workers were shunted off to new residential areas far from the heart of the Valley, especially in and around the explosively growing city of San Jose.

Now, as has been shown by the University of California political scientist Richard Gordon, the

San Jose urban planner Linda Kimball, and the UCLA professors Paul Ong, Allen Scott, and Michael Storper, there are whole neighborhoods of Los Angeles—hundreds of miles away from Santa Clara County—where both documented and undocumented workers perform unskilled and semiskilled assembly tasks, often at home, for contractors to the high-tech firms of Silicon Valley. In *those* neighborhoods, the quality of housing and public services is as far below that of the northern reaches of the Valley as one could possibly imagine.[44] These urban ghettos are as much a part of the famed "Silicon Valley production system" as are the engineering laboratories at Stanford, or the military R&D facilities within Lockheed's Missiles and Space Division in Santa Clara County.

WHY SHOULD WE CARE? RETHINKING NATIONAL AND REGIONAL ECONOMIC DEVELOPMENT IN A WORLD OF PRODUCTION NETWORKS

[. . .] If living in a world of lean and mean companies and their global networks of suppliers, strategic partners, and financiers is inescapable, then policy makers are sooner or later going to have to come to grips with the dark side of flexibility—if only to get themselves reelected. Because flexibility depends so fundamentally on the perpetuation of contingent work (that is, part-time, part-year, temporary, and contract work), the shift toward network forms of industrial organization promises to *strengthen*, not arrest, the politically volatile trend toward income polarization.

The class and associated wage structures that characterized nineteenth-century industrial capitalism could be depicted as a *pyramid* with a narrow top and a wide base. The rapid growth of a wage-earning middle class during the twentieth century (and especially in the years following World War II) effectively transformed that distribution into one with the shape of a *diamond*, featuring a small number of very rich individuals at the top, a declining fraction of very poor people at the bottom, and a burgeoning middle group.

But economists, sociologists, and journalists now almost universally (if reluctantly) agree that since

the 1970s the distribution of income has been changing its shape again, becoming an *hourglass* with an expanding upper end of well-paid professionals (including Reich's symbolic analysts), a growing mass of low-paid workers at the bottom, and a shrinking middle class made up of downwardly mobile former factory workers and middle managers made redundant by the philosophy of lean production. Moreover, it appears that this unsettling trend toward a polarization of earnings is occurring worldwide, albeit at varying rates. The consequences differ, also, since countries have such very different "safety nets" in place to prop up those who cannot make it in the labor market.[45]

Finding ways to maintain civilized labor and living standards in a world economy increasingly populated by forms of industrial organization that exacerbate such polarization will be no small feat. [. . .]

NOTES

1. Calculated from U.S. Bureau of the Census, *1987 Enterprise Statistics*, *Company Summary*, document ES87-3 (Washington, D.C.: U.S. Government Printing Office, 1991), table 3.

2. "How Every Team Could Win in the HDTV Derby," *Business Week*, March 29, 1993, p. 91; Diane Duston, "HDTV Competitors Agree to Work Together," *Boston Globe*, May 25, 1993, p. 37.

3. Jane Perlez, "Toyota and Honda Create Global Production System," *New York Times*, March 26, 1993, p. A1; Eike Schamp, "Towards a Spatial Reorganisation of the German Car Industry? The Implications of New Production Concepts," in *Industrial Change and Regional Development*: *The Transformation of New Industrial Spaces*, ed. Georges Benko and Mick Dunford (London: Belhaven Press/Pinter, 1991), pp. 159–70.

4. Robert B. Reich, *The Work of Nations*: *Preparing Ourselves for 21st Century Capitalism* (New York: Knopf, 1991).

5. Thus, I am adding the dimensions of power and inequality to the pioneering theorizing of Walter W. Powell, "Neither Market Nor Hierarchy: Network Forms of Organization," in *Research in Organizational Behavior*, ed. Barry M. Straw and Larry L. Cummings (Greenwich, Conn.: JAI Press, 1990), pp. 295–336. On the revitalization and reorganization of the big firms, see Rosabeth Moss Kanter, *When Giants Learn to Dance* (New York: Simon and Schuster, 1990).

6. Susan Christopherson, "Flexibility in the U.S. Service Economy and the Emerging Spatial Division of Labour," *Transactions of the Institute of British Geographers* 14 (1989): 131–43; and Katherine Nelson, "Labor Demand, Labor Supply, and the Suburbanization of Low-Wage Office Workers," in *Production, Work, Territory*, ed. Allen J. Scott and Michael Storper (Boston: Allen & Unwin, 1986), pp. 149–71.

7. Eileen Appelbaum, "Restructuring Work: Temporary, Part-Time, and At-home Employment," in *Computer Chips and Paper Clips: Technology and Women's Employment*, ed. Heidi Hartmann (Washington, D.C., National Academy Press, 1987), pp. 268–310; Virginia L. duRivage, ed., *New Policies for the Part-time and Contingent Workforce* (Armonk, N.Y.: Sharpe, for the Economic Policy Institute, 1992), containing papers by Appelbaum, Françoise Carre, Chris Tilly, and the editor; Beverly Lozano, *The Invisible Work Force: Transforming American Business with Outside and Home-Based Workers* (New York: Free Press, 1989); and James P. Womack, Daniel T. Jones, and Daniel Roos, *Machine That Changed the World* (New York: Rawson/MacMillan, 1990).

8. Bennett Harrison and Barry Bluestone, *The Great U-Turn: Corporate Restructuring and the Polarizing of America* (New York: Basic Books, 1988); Frank Levy and Richard Murnane, "U.S. Earnings Levels and Earnings Inequality: A Review of Recent Trends and Proposed Explanations," *Journal of Economic Literature* 30 (September 1992): 1333–81; Tim Smeeding, Michael O'Higgins, and Lee Rainwater, eds., *Poverty, Inequality, and Income Distribution in Comparative Perspective: The Luxembourg Income Study* (London: Harvester Wheatsheaf, 1990).

9. David L. Birch, *Job Creation in America: How Our Smallest Companies Put the Most People to Work* (New York: Free Press, 1987), p. 16.

10. "Small Is Beautiful Now in Manufacturing," *Business Week*, October 22, 1984, pp. 152–56.

11. "The Rise and Rise of America's Small Firms," *Economist*, January 21, 1989, pp. 73–74.

12. Tom Peters, "New Products, New Markets, New Competition, New Thinking," *Economist*, March 4, 1989, pp. 27–32.

13. George Gilder, *The Spirit of Enterprise* (New York: Basic Books, 1984) and *Microcosm: The Quantum Revolution in Economics and Technology* (New York: Simon & Schuster, 1989).

14. Michael J. Piore and Charles Sabel, *The Second Industrial Divide: Possibilities for Prosperity* (New York: Basic Books, 1984).

15. The key early Italian works are: Arnaldo Bagnasco, *Tre Italie: La Problematica Territoriale Dello Sviluppo Italiano* (Bologna: Il Mulino, 1977); Giacomo Becattini, "Sectors and/or Districts: Some Remarks on the Conceptual Foundations of Industrial Economics," in *Small Firms and Industrial Districts in Italy*, ed. Edward Goodman, Julia Bamford, and Peter Saynor (London: Routledge, 1989), pp. 123–35; Sabastiano Brusco, "Small Firms and Industrial Districts: The Experience of Italy," in *New Firms and Regional Development*, ed. David Keeble and Francis Weever (London: Croom Helm, 1986); and Brusco, "The Emilian Model: Productive Decentralization and Social Integration," *Cambridge Journal of Economics* 6 (June 1982): 167–84. The book that was most responsible for alerting a larger non-Italian public to the existence of the Italian industrial districts was by Piore and Sabel, *Second Industrial Divide*.

An entire United Nations conference in 1990 was devoted to comparing stories about industrial districts in different countries. See Frank Pyke and Werner Sengenberger, eds., *Industrial Districts and Local Economic Regeneration* (Geneva: International Institute for Labour Studies, International Labour Office, 1992).

16. Mark Granovetter, "Economic Action and Social Structure: The Problem of Embeddedness," *American Journal of Sociology* 91 (November 1985): 481–510; Edward Lorenz, "Neither Friends Nor Strangers: Informal Networks of Subcontracting in French Industry," in *Trust: Making and Breaking Cooperative Relations*, ed. Diego Gambetta (Oxford: Basil Blackwell, 1988), pp. 194–210; and Charles Sabel, "Studied Trust: Building New Forms of Cooperation in a Volatile Economy," in Pyke and Sengenberger, *Industrial Districts*.

17. Becattini, "Sectors and/or Districts"; Alfred Marshall, *Industry and Trade* (London: Macmillan, 1927, 3rd ed., originally published in 1919); Alfred Weber, *Theory of the Location of Industry*, trans. Carl Friedrich (Chicago: University of Chicago Press, 1929).

18. Allen J. Scott, *New Industrial Spaces* (London: Pion, 1988).

19. Piore and Sabel, *Second Industrial Divide*.

20. See Michael Best, "Sector Strategies and Industrial Policy: The Furniture Industry and the Greater London Enterprise Board," in *Reversing Industrial Decline?*, ed. Paul Hirst and Jonathan Zeitlin (Oxford: Berg, 1989); Best, *The New Competition* (Cambridge, Mass.: Harvard University Press, 1990); and Robin Murray, ed., *Technology Strategies and Local Economic Intervention* (Nottingham: Spokesmann 1989).

21. C. Richard Hatch, "Learning from Italy's Industrial Renaissance," *Entrepreneurial Economy* 6 (July/August 1987): 1–5.

22. Steven J. Davis, "Size Distribution Statistics from County Business Patterns Data" (Graduate School of Business, University of Chicago, September 1990, unpublished MS).

23. Bennett Harrison and Maryellen R. Kelley, "Outsourcing and the Search for 'Flexibility,'" *Work, Employment and Society* 7 (June 1993): 213–35; Kelley and Harrison, "The Subcontracting Behavior of Single vs. Multiplant Enterprises in U.S. Manufacturing: Implications for Economic Development," *World Development* 18 (September 1990): 1273–94.

24. Bo Carlsson and Erol Taymaz, "Flexible Technology and Industrial Structure in the U.S.," *Small Business Economics*, forthcoming.

25. For example, on the United States, see Jonathan Leonard, "On the Size Distribution of Employment and Establishments" (Haas School of Business, University of California at Berkeley, 1985, unpublished MS); and Leonard, "In the Wrong Place at the Wrong Time: The Extent of Frictional and Structural Employment," in *Unemployment and the Structure of Labor Markets*, ed. Kevin Lang and Jonathan Leonard (Oxford: Basil Blackwell, 1987). For similar evidence on Great Britain, see David Branchflower, N. Millward, and A. Oswald, "Unionism and Employment Behaviour," *Economic Journal* 101 (July 1991): 815–34.

26. David J. Storey and Steven G. Johnson, *Job Generation and Labour Market Change* (London: Macmillan, 1987), pp. 24–25.

27. In this country, such research has been most significantly advanced by Timothy Dunne, Mark Roberts, and Larry Samuelson; see "Patterns of Firm Entry and Exit in U.S. Manufacturing Industries," *Rand Journal of Economics* 19 (Winter 1988): 495–515; "Plant Turnover and Gross Employment Flows in the U.S. Manufacturing Sector," *Journal of Labor Economics* 7 (January 1989): 48–71; and "The Growth and Failure of U.S. Manufacturing Plants," *Quarterly Journal of Economics* 104 (November 1989): 671–98. See also Steven J. Davis and John Haltiwanger, "Gross Job Creation, Gross Job Destruction, and Employment Reallocation," *Quarterly Journal of Economics* 108 (August 1992): 819–63.

For similar analyses conducted in Germany, see Josef Bruderl and Rudolf Schussler, "Organizational Mortality: The Liabilities of Newness and Adolescence," *Administrative Science Quarterly* 35 (September 1990): 530–47.

28. David Wiesel and Buck Brown, "The Hyping of Small-Firm Job Growth," *Wall Street Journal*, November 8, 1988, p. B1.

29. "Small Businesses Tend to Stay Pint-Size," *Business Week*, July 31, 1989, p. 20. The full report is by Douglas P. Handler, "Business Demographics," Economic Analysis Department, Dun & Bradstreet Corporation, New York, unpublished MS, 1989. For a more theoretically sophisticated critique, see Stephen Fothergill's review of Birch's book in *Environment and Planning A* 21 (June 1989): 842–43.

30. Gary Loveman and Werner Sengenberger, "Introduction: Economic and Social Reorganization in the Small and Medium-Sized Enterprise Sector," in *The Re-Emergence of Small Enterprises: Industrial Restructuring in Industrialized Countries*, ed. Sengenberger, Loveman, and Michael J. Piore (Geneva: International Institute for Labour Studies, International Labour Office, 1990), p. 21.

31. Charles Brown, James Hamilton, and James Medoff, *Employers Large and Small* (Cambridge, Mass.: Harvard University Press, 1990).

32. The leading spokespersons for this view are two American economists, Zoltan Acs and David Audretsch. See *Innovation and Small Firms* (Cambridge, Mass.: M.I.T. Press, 1990); "Innovation, Market Structure, and Firm Size," *Review of Economics and Statistics* 69 (November 1987): 567–74; Acs, Audretsch, and Bo Carlsson, "Flexibility, Plant Size, and Industrial Restructuring," in *The Economics of Small Firms: A European Challenge*, ed. Acs and Audretsch (Boston: Kluwer, 1990). See also Carlsson, "The Evolution of Manufacturing Technology and Its Impact on Industrial Structure: An International Study," *Small Business Economics* 1 (Spring 1989): 21–37. This is also a central theme in Piore and Sabel, *Second Industrial Divide*.

33. Gilder, *Microcosm*.

34. Wesley M. Cohen and Richard C. Levin, "Empirical Studies of Innovation and Market Structure," in *Handbook of Industrial Organization*, vol. 2., ed. Richard Schmalense and Richard Willie (New York: North-Holland, 1989), pp. 1059–107; Cohen and Steven Klepper, "Firm Size versus Diversity in the Achievement of Technological Advance," *Small Business Economics*, forthcoming.

35. A close reading of statistics from McGraw-Hill's *American Machinist* magazine reveals that, between 1983 and 1989, the share of a plant's tool stock consisting of computer-controlled equipment—what engineers call programmable automation (PA)—grew sytematically larger, the *larger* the initial size of the plant. Moreover, in the course of the period, while the penetration rate rose in every plant size category, it rose proportionally more, the larger the plant. Thus, between 1983 and 1989, the PA penetration rate within the class of very small plants increased by 75 percent, but among plants with 500 or more employees, it rose by 142 percent (Bo Carlsson and Erol Taymaz, "Flexible Technology and Industrial Structure in the U.S.," *Small Business Economics*, forthcoming).

36. Quoted by Lawrence M. Fisher, "Intel Raising Capacity of Chip Factory," *New York Times*, April 2, 1993, p. C2.

37. Ash Amin and Kevin Robins, "The Re-Emergence of Regional Economies? The Mythical Geography of

Flexible Accumulation," *Environment and Planning D: Society and Space* 8 (March 1990): 7–34; Fiorenza Belussi, "Benetton Italy: Beyond Fordism and Flexible Specialization to the Evolution of the Network Firm Model," in *Information Technology and Women's Employment: The Case of the European Clothing Industry*, ed. S. Mitter (Berlin: Springer Verlag, 1989); Flavia Martinelli and Erica Schoenberger, "Oligopoly Is Alive and Well: Notes for a Broader Discussion of Flexible Accumulation," in *Industrial Change and Regional Development: The Transformation of New Industrial Spaces*, ed. Georges Benko and Mick Dunford (London: Belhaven Press/Pinter, 1991), chap. 6.

38. Gilder, *Microcosm*. See also Everett Rogers and Judith Larsen, *Silicon Valley Fever* (New York: Basic Books, 1984).

39. AnnaLee Saxenian, "Regional Networks and the Resurgence of Silicon Valley," *California Management Review* 33 (Fall 1990): 89–112.

40. Charles H. Ferguson, "From the People Who Brought You Voodoo Economics," *Harvard Business Review* 66 (May–June 1988): 55–62; Richard Florida and Martin Kenney, *The Breakthrough Illusion* (New York: Basic Books, 1990); Richard Gordon, "Innovation, Industrial Networks, and High Technology Regions," in *Innovation Networks: Spatial Perspectives*, ed. Roberto Camagni (London: Belhaven Press, 1991), pp. 174–95; Gordon, "State, Milieu, Network: Systems of Innovation in Silicon Valley," in *Systems of Innovation*, ed. Patrizio Bianchi and M. Quere (Paris: Groupe de Recherche Europeen sue les Milieux Innovateurs, forthcoming); Ann Markusen, Peter Hall, Scott Campbell, and Sabina Deitrick, *The Rise of the Gunbelt* (New York: Oxford University Press, 1990); David Teece, "Foreign Investment in Silicon Valley," *California Management Review* 34 (Winter 1992): 88–106.

41. This description is based on an exhaustive, multi-year case study of Benetton, conducted by Fiorenza Belussi, an Italian trade union researcher and a University of Sussex scholar in technology policy. See Belussi, "Benetton: Information Technology in Production and Distribution: A Case Study of the Innovative Potential of Traditional Sectors," Science Policy Research Unit, University of Sussex, Brighton, U.K., SPRU Occasional Paper No. 25, 1987; Belussi, "Benetton Italy"; Belussi, "La Flessibilita si fa Gerarchia: la Benetton," in *Nuovi Modelli D'Impresa Gerarchie Organizzative E Imprese Rete*, ed. Belussi (Milan: Franco Angeli, 1992), pp. 287–340; and Belussi and Massimo Festa, "L'Impresa Rete Del Modello Veneto: Dal Post-Fordismo Al Toyotismo? Alcune Note Illustrative Sulle Strutture

Organizzative Dell'Indotto Benetton," IRES-CGIL, Maestre, Veneto, November 1990, unpublished MS.

42. AnnaLee Saxenian, "The Urban Contradictions of Silicon Valley: Regional Growth and the Restructuring of the Semiconductor Industry," *in Sunbelt-Snowbelt: Urban Development and Regional Restructuring*, ed. Larry Sawers and William K. Tabb (New York: Oxford University Press, 1984), pp. 163–97.

43. Also see Florida and Kenney, *Breakthrough Illusion*, chap. 7; Lenny Siegel and Herb Borock, *Background Report on Silicon Valley: Report to the U.S. Civil Rights Commission* (Mountain View, Calif.: Pacific Studies Center, 1982); Siegel and John Markoff, *The High Cost of High Tech* (New York: Harper & Row, 1985).

44. Richard Gordon and Linda M. Kimball, "High Technology, Employment and the Challenges to Education," Silicon Valley Research Group, University of California at Santa Cruz, July 1985, unpublished MS; Paul M. Ong, "The Widening Divide: Income Inequality and Poverty in Los Angeles," Department of Urban Planning, School of Architecture and Urban Planning, University of California at Los Angeles, 1989, unpublished MS; Michael Storper and Allen Scott, "Work Organization and Local Labour Markets in an Era of Flexible Production," working paper no. 30, World Employment Programme Research, International Labour Office, Geneva, 1989.

45. Barry Bluestone and Bennett Harrison, *The Deindustrialization of America* (New York: Basic Books, 1982); U.S. Department of Commerce, Bureau of the Census, "Workers with Low Earnings: 1964 to 1990," *Current Population Reports: Consumer Income*, series P-60, no. 178 (Washington, D.C.: U.S. Government Printing Office, March 1992); Richard B. Freeman and Lawrence F. Katz, "Rising Wage Inequality: The United States vs. Other Advanced Countries," in *Working Under Different Rules*, ed. Richard B. Freeman (New York: Russell Sage, 1994), pp. 29–62; Harrison and Bluestone, *Great U-Turn*; Lynn A. Karoly, "The Trend in Inequality among Families, Individuals and Workers in the United States: A Twenty-five Year Prospective," in *Uneven Tides: Rising Inequality in America*, ed. Sheldon Danziger and Peter Gottschalk (New York: Russell Sage Foundation, 1993), pp. 19–97; Robert Kuttner, "The Declining Middle," *Atlantic Monthly*, July 1983, pp. 60–69; Levy and Murnane, "U.S. Earnings Levels and Earnings Inequality." A history of the often contentious debate during the 1980s over the trend toward polarizing incomes in the United States is offered by James Lardner, "The Declining Middle," *New Yorker*, May 3, 1993, pp. 108–14.

PART X

ORGANIZATIONAL CULTURE

Though there are many different definitions of culture, a society's culture is usually defined as its values, norms, beliefs, and attitudes, and the symbols and rituals used to express them. Institutional theory argues that the wider culture has a strong impact on organizational structure and functioning (see Reading 19). Another stream of research is interested in the culture *within* organizations, considered as social systems in their own right.

Organizational researchers have long recognized that different organizations have their own tone or "feel." Even when they are in the same industry or are performing the same function, different organizations may be more authoritarian or democratic, rule-bound or informal, innovative or resistant to change, accepting of or hostile toward diversity, or may have generally friendly or unfriendly atmospheres.

However, the recent interest in organizational culture reflected the spectacular global success of Japanese business in the 1970s–1980s. American corporations during the 1920s used policies collectively known as *welfare capitalism* to encourage employees to identify with the company and avoid unions. These policies included employment security, fringe benefits such as health care, company-sponsored unions, grievance mechanisms, suggestion systems, picnics and company-sponsored athletics, even company songs and other techniques, but only a few plans such as IBM's policies survived the Depression (Edwards 1979; Jacoby 1997). Japanese enterprises, which developed and maintained such paternalist policies and "family" atmosphere to a much greater degree, seemed to have intensely loyal and dedicated employees. Employee commitment and conscientious work attitudes became widely viewed as one of the secrets of Japanese business success. The recent interest in organizational culture among managers and some organizational researchers reflected a desire to improve morale, organizational commitment, and, hopefully, productivity.

The potential advantages of the Japanese approach are illustrated by a typology of organizational control techniques developed by Amitai Etzioni (1964). Some organizations, such as prisons and involuntary mental institutions, use physical sanctions or *coercion* to control their members. Others, such as most business organizations, use material or *utilitarian incentives* to induce members to behave in the desired ways. Still other organizations, such as churches or political parties, use *normative controls*, such as higher ideals or group acceptance, to persuade members to identify with and internalize the organization's goals, accepting them as their own. Organizations using normative control strategies elicit greater commitment from members than those using utilitarian methods, and those using coercion elicit the least. More recently, William Ouchi (1980), working in Williamson's transaction cost perspective, concluded from the Japanese experience that it can be cheaper to control people through socialization and norms than material incentives or bureaucratic rules.

However, as Joanne Martin (1992) argues, both actors and researchers can have different interpretations of the meaning of culture. She describes three approaches to the study of organizational culture: *integration*, *differentiation*, and *fragmentation*. Martin believes all three are necessary for fully appreciating how culture operates in organizations.

According to the integration perspective, members of an organization share a common viewpoint and consent to the basic principles of their culture, which are internally consistent and imply clear expectations for behavior. The integration perspective appeals to managers because it gives them a potential role as leaders in creating or transforming their corporate culture and offers the possibility of a committed workforce dedicated to organizational goals such as productivity and competitiveness. Some organizational researchers also endorse the view that for a set of beliefs or attitudes to count as culture it must be shared by a group.

However, the differentiation perspective recognizes the existence of sub-cultural differences within organizations and varying interpretations of cultural precepts and events, often reflecting conflicting group interests. Workers and managers may view the organizational culture differently, as Laurie Graham argued in her study of a Japanese-owned auto plant in Indiana (Reading 12). Different departments, such as the staff and line studied by Melville Dalton (Reading 13), may clash. Top managers and their subordinates may differ over issues of fairness and responsibility, as Robert Jackall (Reading 14) and others argue (Smith 1990). Different gender and racial groups may disagree over the degree of opportunity and bias within the organization (see Readings 28 and 29).

The differentiation perspective argues that there is no organization-wide consensus, only consensus within subcultures, and this view tends to give greater weight to how lower-status groups view the organization compared to the inte-gration perspective. The differentiation perspective often studies conflicts and resistance that are not acknowledged in management rhetoric or organizational research that stresses teamwork, harmony, and cooperation. Like critiques of Human Relations and humanistic management, this perspective often interprets efforts to build a common culture as a way of manipulating workers to gain greater effort from them and is not likely to appeal to managers.

Many researchers with a differentiation perspective are suspicious of top man-agement efforts to engineer strong cultures. They note that another name for cultural integration and consensus is conformity. The aim of building a strong culture is to shape workers' inner thoughts and feelings as well as their external behavior for commercial purposes.

The dedication and quasi-religious commitment that the new manager seeks to instill into his employees sometimes sits a little oddly with the nature of the company goal: It may be inspiring to hear of sales staff risking their life in a snow storm to ensure . . . regular delivery, but when the reader learns that the product is a high-salt, high calorie junk food, doubts about whether some of this shining dedication is perhaps misplaced begin to arise. (Martin 1992, p. 102)

But, the differentiation perspective need not be used only to study indoctrination and resistance. There is significant literature arguing for the benefits of gender and racial and ethnic diversity in organizations. Different perspectives and subcultures can enhance organizational effectiveness by opening the organization to diverse points of view. Diversity is increasingly a fact of life within the labor force from which all organizations draw and among the consuming public; organizations that reflect this diversity within their own organizations may enjoy a competitive advantage. Outside of business enterprises, it has long been recognized that the effectiveness of urban police is compromised when an overwhelmingly white force has responsibility for patrolling minority neighborhoods because of the social distance, preconceptions, mistrust, misunderstandings, and communication problems between the two groups, among other reasons.

Other subcultural differences within organizations, such as those between human resource, finance, and engineering departments, may be important for understanding organizational life but reflect different operating styles, training, and functions of groups that are neither in conflict nor even in sustained interaction with one another (Martin 1992, p. 90).

Finally, the fragmentation perspective views cultural systems as more ambiguous, lacking clarity at either the collective or subgroup levels. Like James March's view of decision making, the world contains great confusion and disorder, and people are only partially successful in making sense of corporate policies as well- or ill-intentioned or favorable or unfavorable to their interests and well-being. If subordinates are allowed to confront managers with their concerns in meetings, but then no action is taken, it is not clear if the lack of follow-up is unintentional or if the meeting is a hollow ritual intended to pacify workers. If the human resources department fails to adopt an employee-friendly policy, it is not clear whether the company lacks genuine concern for its workers or whether the department simply lacks the power within the company to lobby effectively. Individuals also have multiple identities, as, say, both women and managers, that might interfere with the coalescence of distinct, homogeneous groups with either shared or conflicting views. The centrality of ambiguity and uncertainty in the fragmentation perspective makes it an uncomfortable model for many researchers, as well as managers.

Managers embraced the idea of consciously shaping their organizational cultures because they operated from an integration perspective, but for Martin the actual results inevitably include the resistance and ambiguity associated with the differentiation and fragmentation perspectives, as well.

Gideon Kunda's study of a computer maker, High Technologies Corporation, or Tech, illustrates many of these ideas (Reading 27). Tech's charismatic founder created a highly distinctive corporate culture that emphasized technical excellence, ethical conduct, enthusiasm, very long hours, total involvement in work, self-direction and self-reliance, creativity, professional autonomy, a no-layoff pledge, and an antibureaucratic spirit that work should be fun, hierarchy limited, and formal structure and rules minimized. Tech's loose structure and professional, high-commitment culture correspond to Burns and Stalker's organic system (Reading 4) and has elements of Mintzberg's adhocracy. A steady stream of literature, training, group activities, public meetings, rituals, and supervisory and peer reinforcement inculcated the company's values and messages. Kunda cites Etzioni's work in arguing that employees' resulting emotional attachment to their work and self-direction reduced the need for more formal monitoring and control mechanisms.

Tech's corporate culture offered employees many positive benefits, but it demanded a great deal in return, including a substantial part of their personal identity. Though most employees liked both their jobs and their employer, many tried to dissociate themselves from the corporate culture or remained ambivalent. As McGregor argued (Reading 9), borrowing from Maslow, most people want a satisfying job, and self-fulfillment at work has often appeared to be the ideal antidote to the alienating qualities of bureaucracy. But a workplace that tries to serve both economic goals and human needs blurs the boundaries between self and work and threatens to absorb one's personal identity into a work role. In addition, to propose an identity between personal self-actualization and a company's business objectives invariably raises the kinds of questions about motives that critics have posed since Human Relations. Because strong corporate cultures try to shape how people think and feel, Kunda suggests they encroach on employees' private selves even as they offer a uncommon sense of community and working conditions that are generally superior to those of conventional firms.

But Kunda's concerns with the harmful effects of corporate culture initiatives have been partly overtaken by recent events. Since the early 1990s, the Japanese threat has receded, and the managers of large corporations now want their employees to act more as if they were free agents in a marketplace rather than permanent employees of an organization or members of a single community, as Bennett Harrison argued (see Reading 26). After Kunda studied the company, Tech faced economic difficulties in the 1990s and had to resort to layoffs. As with welfare capitalism more than fifty years earlier, when promises of security in return for commitment become too costly, they must be discontinued. For Tech and most other American companies since the 1990s, "The rhetoric of organizational communities and cultures is being replaced swiftly by the rhetoric of markets and entrepreneurs. . . . Out of the ashes of discredited bureaucracy, stuck with metaphors of obesity and waste, familiar notions again appear, including laissez-faire capitalism and the survival of the fittest" (Kunda and van Maanen 1999, pp. 73ff.). Eventually Tech was acquired by a younger competitor and ceased to exist as an independent company.

27

ENGINEERING CULTURE

Control and Commitment in a High-Tech Corporation

GIDEON KUNDA

1

CULTURE AND ORGANIZATION

"Welcome to Technology Region—Working on America's Future," proclaim the signs along Route 61, the region's main artery. It is early, but the nervous, impatient energy of high-tech is already pulsating through the spectacular countryside. Porsches, souped-up Chevies, Saabs, indeterminate old family station wagons, motorcycles, company vans, lots of Toyotas—the transportational variety is endless—edge their way toward the exit ramps and the clusters of "corporate parks," engineering facilities, conference centers, and hotels that are the place of daily congregation for the region's

residents. As their cars jerk along, some drivers appear engrossed in thought, a few may be observed speaking into tape recorders or reading documents from the corner of their eyes. In "the region" the future is now; time is precious; and for many of the drivers work has already begun.

The parking lot in front of High Technologies' Lyndsville engineering facility is rapidly filling. High Technologies Corporation—"Tech" to most of its employees—is one of the larger, more successful, and better known of the Region's corporate residents, and reputed to be on the "leading edge" of the high-tech industry. The Lyndsville facility is home to a number of Tech's more prominent and promising engineering groups. It is a low, sprawling, ugly building squatting behind the spacious parking

---

From *Engineering Culure: Control and Commitment in a High-Tech Corporation*, by Gideon Kunda. Copyright © 1992 by Temple University. Reprinted by permission of Temple University Press and Gideon Kunda.

lot carved out of the countryside a few miles off the highway.

[. . .]

The many hundreds of people employed at Lyndsville whose day begins as the night shift ends are, on the face of it, a fairly homogeneous group. The age is predominantly late twenties to mid-thirties. Almost all are white and—except for secretaries—most are male. Many would characterize their social status as "upscale." Almost all have college degrees, mainly in fields of the technical sort, with a majority in electrical engineering and computer science. The range of compensation is wide, but the average, by most standards, is well above the comfort zone. The dress code is loose, if rather drab. Business attire seems almost theatrically out of place and suggests association with the outside world, usually with "business types." The general demeanor combines a studied informality, a seemingly self-assured sense of importance, and a clearly conveyed impression of hard, involving, and strangely enjoyable, even addictive, work. Many routinely refer to their work as "state of the art"—of considerable quality, innovativeness, and profitability, and thus intrinsically, unquestionably, and self-evidently worthwhile.

Over the course of the workday, the Lyndsville facility appears to assume the character of its inhabitants: a combination of effort and informality, freedom and discipline, work and play. After early coffees or breakfast in the open cafeteria, the labyrinth of cubicles that occupies much of the internal space becomes the stage for a seemingly chaotic variety of individual activities and complex networks of interaction that take place against a background of subdued but persistent squeaks and whirs from terminals, keyboards, and printers. At first glance, one would be hard pressed to identify differences in rank, status, or power. In many identical and modest-looking cubicles, people are tapping away at computer terminals. Meeting rooms on the periphery are occupied by small groups in apparently intense, occasionally volatile, and sometimes playful discussion. In the central lab space, people are wandering between tangled cables connecting rather unimpressive-looking pieces of equipment to each other and to the ceiling. The cafeteria is occupied throughout the day. Although it often appears that people come and go as they please, it is fairly well established that long hours are the norm. Those not present are assumed to be working elsewhere. Many will continue working through the evening, some on their company-provided home terminals. Others will do so in their minds and—a few would report—even their dreams.

The observer, comparing the glimpsed scenes of life at Lyndsville with traditional or commonsensical images of work life in profit-seeking corporations, might wonder what is going on here. Are things as chaotic and uncontrolled as they seem? How and by whom are the collective interests maintained? Why do people work so hard and claim to enjoy it? Is it the work itself that is intrinsically satisfying? Or is it something about the social context in which it takes place? More broadly: what is it like to work here? Is this the organization of the future? Or is it perhaps a futuristic revival of the past?

To insiders, the scene at Lyndsville is "typical Tech"—a way of life taken for granted, with nothing to puzzle over. If asked to address some of the observer's concerns, many would retort rather matter-of-factly that what one has observed are nothing more than manifestations of Tech's "strong culture." If this at first seems somewhat tautological, it soon becomes apparent that "the culture" is a popular explanatory concept, frequently used as a description of the company, a rationale for people's behavior, a guideline for action, a cause for praise and condemnation, pride and despair, a quality that is said to distinguish Tech from other industries and even from other high-tech companies. "It is," many would say, "what makes us what we are." What do they mean? One answer is to be found among those who consider the "strong culture" their domain.

TECH CULTURE: A MANAGERIAL PERSPECTIVE

On this randomly selected workday, the Lyndsville engineering facility is the stage upon which practical managerial concerns with "the culture" are acted out. A few miles away, in a fairly spacious but still modest office at Tech's corporate headquarters, Dave Carpenter is preparing a presentation to be given at Lyndsville later in the day. He is one of the more senior managers in the Engineering Division, and has been with the company a long time. *[. . .]* The group at Lyndsville has recently been made part of his organization—"his world"—in one of the frequent reorganizations that are a way of life for Tech managers, or, as he would say, "a part of the culture."

For Dave, as for many managers, cultural matters are an explicit concern. Dave considers himself an expert. One wall of his office is covered with a large bookcase holding many managerial texts. Japanese management, in particular, intrigues him, and books on the subject take up a whole shelf. ("They know something about putting people to work—and we better find out what it is.") Dave has a clear view of what the culture is all about and considers it his job not only to understand, but to influence and shape it for those whose performance he believes to be his responsibility.

A key aspect of Tech culture, Dave often points out, is that formal structure tells you nothing. Lyndsville is a case in point. "It's typical Tech. The guys up there are independent and ambitious. They are working on state-of-the-art stuff—really neat things. Everyone, including the president, has a finger in the pot. The group is potentially a revenue generator. That they are committed there is no doubt. But they are unmanageable." How then, he wonders, can he make them see the light? Work in the *company's* interest? Cooperate? Stop (or at least channel) the pissing contests? And not make him look bad? Dave knows that whether he controls it or not, he "owns" it—another aspect of the culture. And as he reads the company, his own future can be influenced by the degree to which he is credited with the group's success. And he is being watched, just as he watches others. His strategy is clear. "Power plays don't work. You can't *make 'em* do *any*thing. They have to *want* to. So you have to work through the culture. The idea is to educate people without them knowing it. Have the religion and not know how they ever got it!"

And there are ways to do this. Today Dave will make his first appearance at Lyndsville. He will give a presentation about the role of Lyndsville's various technical projects in Tech's long-term business strategy. "Presentations are important in this culture," he says. "You have to get around, give them the religion, get the message out. It's a mechanism for transmitting the culture." Sending and interpreting "messages" are a key to working the culture. Dave is clear about what he wants to accomplish: generate some enthusiasm, let them work off some steam, celebrate some of the successes, show them that they are not out on their own, make his presence felt. And maybe give them an example of the right "mindset." In "the trenches" (a favorite expression), he is sure, there must be considerable confusion caused by "the revolving door"—the frequent changes of management. Lyndsville reputedly has quite a few good and committed people. It is a creative group. But it is also considered a tough, competitive environment. Some say it reminds them of the early days of Tech, when commitment and burnout went hand in hand. Perhaps. The company has been changing. But some things stay the same. Dave remembers life in the trenches. He was "there" years ago, he has paid his dues—including a divorce—and he still feels an affinity for the residents of the trenches, some of whom he will meet today. And, as always, he is prepared. He reaches for the tools of the culture trade—the "road show" color slides used at yesterday's strategy presentation to the executive committee—and selects the ones for today.

Concern with the culture is not just the domain of senior managers; it has also spawned a small internal industry that translates global concerns, ideas, and messages into daily activities. Near the front lobby of the Lyndsville building, a large conference room is being prepared for more routine "cultural shaping." Alone in the room, Ellen Cohen is getting ready to run her "Culture Module" for the "Introduction to Tech" workshop for new hires, also known as "bootcamp." It will take two hours, and if everything runs smoothly, she will stay for Dave Carpenter's presentation. ("It's a must for Techwatchers. You can learn a lot from attending.") She is an engineer who is now "totally into culture." Over the last few years she has become the resident "culture expert." "I got burnt out on coding. You can only do so much. And I knew my limits. So I took a management job and I'm funded to do culture now. Some people didn't believe it had any value-added. But I went off and made it happen, and now my workshops are all oversubscribed! I'm a living example of the culture! Now I do a lot of work at home. Isn't this company super?"

She is preparing her material now, waiting for the participants to arrive. On one table she is sorting the handout packages. Each includes copies of her paper "A Culture Operating Manual—Version II"; some official company materials; a copy of the latest edition of *Tech Talk*, with an interview with the president and extensive quotations from his "We Are One" speech; a review of academic work on "corporate cultures" that includes a key to the various disguised accounts of Tech; a glossary of Tech terms; and a xeroxed paper with some "culture exercises" she has collected for her files over the years. "It covers it all. What is a Techie. Getting Ahead. Networking. Being a Self-Starter. Taking Charge. How to Identify Burnout. The Subcultures. Presentations. Managing Your Career. Managing Your Boss. Women. Over the years I've gathered dynamite material—some of it too sensitive to show anyone. One day I'll write a thesis on all of this. In the meanwhile I'm funded to document and preserve the culture of Engineering. It's what made this company great. 'Culture' is really a 'people issue'— a Personnel or OD [Organization Development] type of thing, but they have no credibility in Engineering, and I'd rather stay here, close to the action. It's a fascinating company. I could watch it forever. Today I'm doing culture with the new hires. I tell them about how to succeed here. You can't just do the old nine-to-five thing. You have to have the right mindset. It's a gut thing. You have to get the religion. You can push at the system, you drive yourself. But I also warn them: 'Win big and lose big. You can really get hurt here. This place can be dangerous. Burnout City.' And I tell them the first rule: 'Do What's Right.' It's the company slogan, almost a cliche, but it captures the whole idea. 'Do What's Right.' If they internalize that, I've done my job. My job? They come in in love with the technology; that's dangerous. My job is to marry them to the company."

What does "Tech's strong culture" mean to Dave Carpenter and Ellen Cohen? First, and most broadly speaking, it is the context of their work life, a set of rules that guides the relationship between the company and "its people." At one level, the culture offers a description of the social characteristics of the company that also embodies a specification of required work behavior: "informality," "initiative," "lack of structure," "inherent ambiguity," "hard work," "consensus seeking," "bottom-up decision making," "networking," "pushing against the system," "going off, taking risks, and making things happen." But, as the frequently heard metaphors of "family," "marriage," and "religion" suggest, the rules run deeper. The culture also includes articulated rules for thoughts and feelings, "mindsets" and "gut reactions": an obsession with technical accomplishment, a sense of ownership, a strong commitment to the company, identification with company goals, and, not least, "fun." Thus, "the culture" is a gloss for an extensive definition of membership in the corporate community that includes rules for behavior, thought, and feeling, all adding up to what appears to be a well-defined and widely shared "member role."

But there is more. For Dave Carpenter and Ellen Cohen, as well as many others, the culture has a dual nature: it is not just the context but also the object of their work lives. The culture means not only the implicit and explicit rules that guide and shape their own behavior and experience of work; it is also the vehicle through which they consciously try to influence the behavior and experience of others. The "culture," in this sense, is something to be engineered—researched, designed, developed, and maintained—in order to facilitate the accomplishment of company goals. Although the product—a member role consisting of behavior, thoughts, and feelings—is not concrete, there are specified ways of engineering it: making presentations, sending "messages," running "bootcamp," writing papers, giving speeches, formulating and publishing the "rules," even offering an "operating manual." All are work techniques designed to induce others to accept—indeed, to become—what the company would like them to be.

This duality reflects a central underlying theme in the way culture is construed by many Tech managers: the "culture" is a mechanism of control. Its essence is captured in Dave Carpenter's words: "You can't make 'em do anything; they have to want to." In this view, the ability to elicit, channel, and direct the creative energies and activities of employees in profitable directions—to make them want to contribute—is based on designing a member role that employees are expected to incorporate as an integral part of their sense of self. It is this desire and the policies that flow from it, many insiders feel, that makes Tech "something else."

The use of culture in the service of control in a modern corporation might seem at first strange, even unique, to those for whom culture is a concept more meaningfully applied to Bornean headhunters or to the urban literati. Tech managers, however, are not alone. A practical concern with culture and its consequences is widely shared among those for whom the corporate jungle is of more than passing interest.

CULTURE AND CONTROL

In recent years, the concept of "corporate culture" has captured the imagination of both students and practitioners of management.

[. . .]

Moreover, a large and profitable body of popular managerial literature has capitalized on these ideas, proclaiming a relationship between culture and the "bottom line." Terrence Deal and Allen Kennedy (1982: 15), for example, claim that with a strong culture, a "company can gain as much as one or two hours of productive work per employee per day."

[. . .]

The popular managerial press is even less restrained. For example, in their best-selling *In Search of Excellence*, Thomas Peters and Robert Waterman (1982) convey their ideas with almost evangelical fervor. Management, they claim, is the art of creating strong corporate cultures by "shaping norms," "instilling beliefs," "inculcating values," "generating emotions." "Strong cultures" are based on intense emotional attachment and the internalization of "clearly enunciated company values" that often replace formal structures. Moreover, individualism is preserved; for employees, the companies "provide the opportunity to stick out, yet combine it with a philosophy and system of beliefs. . .that provide the transcending meaning—a wonderful combination" (p. 81). The ideal employees are those

who have internalized the organization's goals and values—its culture—into their cognitive and affective make-up, and therefore no longer require strict and rigid external control. Instead, productive work is the result of a combination of self-direction, initiative, and emotional attachment, and ultimately combines the organizational interest in productivity with the employees' personal interest in growth and maturity.

Thus, in the view of proponents of strong cultures, work in such companies is not merely an economic transaction; rather, it is imbued with a deeper personal significance that causes people to behave in ways that the company finds rewarding, and that require less use of traditional controls. The company, in this view, harnesses the efforts and initiative of its employees in the service of high-quality collective performance and at the same time provides them with "the good life": a benign and supportive work environment that offers the opportunity for individual self-actualization. Broader implications are often drawn from this depiction of corporate life. The prescriptive literature goes so far as to propose that such corporate cultures are a solution to the problems created by an allegedly overbureaucratized and underperforming organizational society. To accomplish this, managers are offered (often for a price) a variety of methods and techniques: participative decision making, overt uses of rituals and ceremony, the management of symbols and meanings, explicit formulation of a "corporate philosophy," and so forth. All supposedly produce the kind of employee whose orientation to work, Deal and Kennedy (1982: 9) approvingly suggest, is captured in the following quotation: "I feel like putting a lot of time in. There is a real kind of loyalty here. We are all working this together—working a process together. I'm not a workaholic—it's just the place. I love the place."

The concern with culture detected at Lyndsville and the convergence of practical and theoretical notions of culture and its management in the academic and managerial literature reflect a widespread and growing managerial interest in finding innovative solutions to the foremost problem of management: the conflict of interest that lies at the heart of the relations between organizations and their members. Purposeful collective action, whatever its circumstances, requires the coordination of activities of a diverse and heterogeneous membership. There is, however, an inherent conflict between the demands organizations place on the time and efforts of their members and the desires and needs of members when left to their own devices. Thus the age-old managerial dilemma: how to cause members to behave in ways compatible with organizational goals. Bureaucratic work organizations, Amitai Etzioni (1961) suggests, have traditionally relied mainly on utilitarian forms of control: the use of economic power to elicit compliance with rules and regulations from a work force concerned mainly with maximizing material rewards. The rhetoric of culture, however, indicates a shift in managerial sensibilities to a different form, one that Etzioni refers to as *normative control.*

Normative control is the attempt to elicit and direct the required efforts of members by controlling the underlying experiences, thoughts, and feelings that guide their actions. Under normative control, members act in the best interest of the company not because they are physically coerced, nor purely from an instrumental concern with economic rewards and sanctions. It is not just their behaviors and activities that are specified, evaluated, and rewarded or punished. Rather, they are driven by internal commitment, strong identification with company goals, intrinsic satisfaction from work. These are elicited by a variety of managerial appeals, exhortations, and actions. Thus, under normative control, membership is founded not only on the behavioral or economic transaction traditionally associated with work organizations, but, more crucially, on an experiential transaction, one in which symbolic rewards are exchanged for a moral orientation to the organization. In this transaction a member role is fashioned and imposed that includes not only behavioral rules but articulated guidelines for experience. In short, under normative control it is the employee's *self*—that ineffable source of subjective experience—that is claimed in the name of the corporate interest.

Attempts to implement normative control in industrial settings might be considered "something else," but the ideas on which it is founded are not new. In his classic *Work and Authority in Industry,* Reinhard Bendix (1956) identified an inexorable trend in the evolution of managerial ideology from the early days of Frederick Taylor's "Scientific Management" to the formulation of the theory and practice of "Human Relations" by Elton Mayo and the numerous scholars and practitioners who followed him. For Bendix, the essence of the trend was a growing managerial interest in the psychological absorption of workers by organizations. This represented, in his view, a systematic encroachment on previously private or unregulated domains of work life—irrational sentiments and attitudes—a sort of creeping annexation of the workers' selves, an attempt to capture the norms of the workplace and embed control "inside" members.

[. . .]

In sum, the recent popularity of the idea of strong corporate culture may be seen as the culmination of a pronounced historical trend in managerial ideology and practice toward forms of normative control. In the most general terms, shaping the employees' selves in the corporate image is thought to be necessary in order to facilitate the management and increase the efficiency of large-scale bureaucratic enterprises faced with what the managerial literature refers to as "turbulent environments": rapid technological change, intense competition, and a demanding and unpredictable labor force.

However one views its causes, the evolution of organizational forms based on a managerial ideology of normative control leads to heavy claims against the self—the thoughts, feelings, and experiences of members of work organizations. More than ever, domains of the self once considered private come under corporate scrutiny and regulation. What one does, thinks, or feels—indeed, who one is—is not just a matter of private concern but the legitimate domain of bureaucratic control structures armed with increasingly sophisticated techniques of influence.

[. . .]

How then are we to evaluate the widespread managerial concern with "strong cultures"? On the face of it, as we have seen, the essence of the ideology of strong cultures is a restatement and a reaffirmation of the doctrine of normative control. This formulation, moreover, attempts to preempt the well-known criticisms. In the strong corporate culture, its proponents assert, normative control offers increased freedom and autonomy rather than tyranny, individualism rather than groupthink, creativity rather than conformity; and, for those concerned with the techniques of implementation, it is claimed to be technically feasible, as illustrated in numerous anecdotes (some using Tech as a model) in the self-help managerial literature. If anything, in the gospel of strong culture, what was once seen as the breeding ground for the diseases of bureaucracy is now heralded as its antidote. Normative control—or at least the rhetoric associated with its practice—once again rides high.

Are these claims justified? Does the strong corporate culture indeed foster a form of affiliation that generates personal and collective "highs"? Or is it a new guise for tyranny in the workplace—an unwarranted invasion of privacy driven by commercial interests? Or is it just another cycle of empty managerial rhetoric that obscures the real and unchanging nature of work organizations and the people they employ? [. . .]

Some answers may be found at Lyndsville among those for whom "Tech culture" and its demands are an everyday reality. Are the people whom we encounter there happy automatons? Brainwashed Yuppies? Self-actualizing human beings? Do they think of their experiences at work as authentic expressions of themselves or as stylized roles? Is the Lyndsville engineering facility a prison or a playground?

On this randomly selected morning, a number of different experiences of the strong culture are being played out in the large, open office space beyond the conference rooms where those who live the culture spend their day. In one corner of the building, Tom O'Brien is hunched over his terminal, his back to the opening of his cubicle. He is wearing earplugs to close off the rest of the world. Things are going well, he would acknowledge, almost too well. His promotion just came through. He is now a "consulting engineer"—a title coveted by many Tech engineers. His contribution to a number of key projects is apparently being recognized by the faceless mass that determines reputation in the "technical community," and he is getting more and more electronic mail from all over the company. In his group he is considered the resident expert on XYZ technology. This year he earned close to 60K, and for the first time he was given stock options—the secret sign of inclusion. His current role is rather vaguely defined, and he can get involved in almost anything. In fact he is expected to, and he is aware of the pressure to "make things happen" and how it works on him. "That's the culture—designed ambiguity. It sucks people in," he says. He has been invited to join a number of task forces, and is thinking of learning some of the business issues. Recollections of his burnout episode a few years back and a brief and unsuccessful stint at a crazy start-up company have lost their painful edge.

Right now Tom is trying to understand the intricacies of a failing project. Rick Smith, the project manager, was finally removed, and someone has to figure out what the hell was going on: the technical problems and also some of the people issues. ("A lot of egos involved!") Tom was the natural choice. It temporarily adds a few extra hours to the working day, but it's fun, it's a challenge, it's involving. Today he came in earlier than usual, and he will probably spend most of the weekend on it. "Boy, did they ever screw up," he says as he stares at the screen. Every now and then an audible beep announces the arrival of an electronic message. He fights the temptation to flip screens. "It'll take a while today just to go through the mail and stay current. Things sure pile up when you're riding the wave. That's the culture. You have to learn to work it. And to protect yourself. People can get swept away. It's great. Like the joke. You get to choose which 20 hours to work out of the day."

Many at Tech would consider Tom a standard success story, a living affirmation of "the culture" and the claims of its proponents. On the face of it, he appears to have successfully incorporated the member role. The company and his work seem to be central to his sense of self. He works hard and seems to enjoy it. He is emotionally committed. He considers himself, and is acknowledged to be, self-directed, capable of "making things happen," and in need of little explicit supervision. He sees the freedom as a source of creativity and opportunity, beneficial both to him and to the company. Income is important, not only in material terms, but also as a symbol of recognition and inclusion. Yet, as Tom's recollection of his burnout episode suggests, there is a darker side to life at Tech, and its signs are never too far from the surface. For Tom it has perhaps receded into the past, now no more than a war story and even a source of pride. Nevertheless, he appears at times wary and watchful, even cynical or ironic about the culture, the company, and himself. . . .

For others, the dark side of the culture looms large. In a similar cubicle not far away, Rick Smith—recently removed from his position—is slowly cleaning out his desk. He stops every now and then to light another cigarette. Mary, his secretary, is in the outer cubicle pretending to be occupied even though the phones have stopped ringing. Like many other familiar and less familiar acquaintances of Rick's, she is behaving as if nothing has happened. He is not sure if he should be grateful for this studied "business as usual" demeanor, but he plays along with it. However, the large, half-filled cartons on the table and the blank screen on his terminal—sure indications of a standstill—belie the signs of routine. Rick would acknowledge that he has burnt out. "I should never have taken this job. Can't quite figure out when things started to go wrong. Bastards just threw me into this damn project. No feedback, no guidance, no support, no warning. 'It's Tech culture,' they say. 'Do What's Right,' Some help! I was so busy with all the details, never had time to get deep enough into the technical stuff. Had to rely on the group members. And they wouldn't communicate. With each other. Or with me. And the schedules were unrealistic in the first place. Probably because of all the politics. When we started to slip, things just fell apart. Everyone was watching. Probably whispering. I found out later that my boss was checking who was logged on at night. They do that. This company's like an aquarium. And my problems at home didn't help. Drinking more and more. What comes first—sipping or slipping? It hit the fan when I told them I was taking two weeks to dry out again—right before the last schedule slip. Luckily the guys in process engineering up in Hanover were willing to take me. The EAP [Employee Assistance Program] advisor here helped—he's a company shrink. Contracted and sworn to secrecy. A real professional. They have a lot of experience with this type of thing. Finally found something for me. Had to do a lot of looking first. Maybe I should take it easy for a while. Or even reconsider this whole damn company! If I can

afford to—there should be a warning out front: High Technologies—It's Hazardous to Your Health."

Rick Smith is a casualty. For most who know the company, it is an inevitable part of work there—indeed, of engineering in general. Not everyone, it is conceded, can live in such an environment: some leave, or distance themselves in one way or another from the company's strong demands. Occasionally, like Rick, they succumb. He appears to feel used, betrayed, manipulated, even oppressed: living in an "aquarium," constantly watched, driven to drink. If one wished to make a case that the culture is a guise for a benign yet invasive tyranny, he would be a prime example. Yet even as he expresses the pain of his situation, he is concerned with finding another job at Tech, plans to stay, expresses a certain gratitude to the company for providing help and tolerating failure, and cannot refrain from making an ironic observation about the company—the hallmark of successful membership. Indeed, he has made his burnout and alcoholism quite public. His personal suffering is an indication—to himself and to others—of the lengths to which he is willing to go in his desire to succeed, to contribute to the company, to adopt the member role. Economic need may account in part for this, but here, too, an observer might find evidence of considerable ambivalence.

[. . .]

These glimpses into life at Tech suggest that there is more to "the culture" than unilateral normative control. Managerial ideology and managerial action designed to impose a role on individuals are but one side of the question of control—they are normative demands. As Erving Goffman (1961a) points out, members are never passive objects of control; they are free to react: if conceptions are imposed, they are also systematically dealt with. Members are active participants in the shaping of themselves and of others. They may—at various times—accept, deny, react, reshape, rethink, acquiesce, rebel, conform, and define and redefine the demands and their responses. In other words, they create themselves within the constraints imposed on them. What kinds of creations have we observed at Lyndsville?

None of the people whose privacy we temporarily invaded are easily categorized as accepting or rejecting an imposed role, as subjects of a tyranny or beneficiaries of a benign environment. What they do appear to share is a profound ambivalence about their involvement. They seem aware of the company's demands and their significance. Although they exhibit signs of acceptance, they also indicate considerable wariness and even a degree of cynicism about the company's expectations, even as they are investing their efforts, planning to get ahead, or contemplating the price of failure. *[. . .]*

3

IDEOLOGY: TECH CULTURE CODIFIED

Tom O'Brien has been around the company for a while; like many others, he has definite ideas about "Tech culture" and what it takes to get things done in Engineering. But, as he is constantly reminded, so does the company. When he arrives at work each morning, he encounters evidence of the company point of view at every turn. First are the bumperstickers adorning many of the cars in the Lyndsville parking lot. "*I love Tech!*" they declare, somewhat unoriginally, the words underscored by the ubiquitous little red heart designed into the company logo. "This shit is everywhere," he says. "I got it on my own car."

If the bumperstickers seem trivial, almost tongue-in-cheek, the short walk to his cubicle takes him past a plethora of more serious stylized references to his experience as a member of the organization. Inside the building, just beyond the security desk, a large television monitor is playing a videotape of a recent speech by [company president] Sam Miller. As he walks by, he hears the familiar voice discuss "our goals, our values, and the way we do things." "It's the 'We are One' speech," he notes as he walks by, "nothing new." He has read the speech in a company newsletter, and excerpts are posted everywhere. Turning a corner, he stops by a large bulletin board fixed to the wall next to the library. On one side is a permanent display including the well-known statement of the "Company Philosophy" ("It's the Bible—the Ten Commandments for the Techie: make a buck and do it right"), and a selection of personnel policies titled "Your Rights and Obligations." On the other, clippings and copies of recent references to Tech in local, national, and trade newspapers are prominently posted. He glances at the latest addition, "High Motivation in High-Tech: The New Work Force"; an anonymous hand has highlighted the company name in bright yellow. By the cafeteria, where he stops for coffee, a flipchart calls attention to Dave Carpenter's presentation ("High Technologies' Strategy for the Future—How You Fit In. The talk will be videotaped"), and to a workshop on "Career Management at Tech: How to Make the Most of Yourself." Close by, piles of brochures are stacked on a table in front of the personnel office. Tom takes one, headed, "If you are experiencing signs of stress, perhaps you should give us a call." Inside it offers some words of wisdom: "Everyone experiences stress at some time. . . . Stress isn't necessarily a bad thing. . . . You can do something about stress." He turns into the workspace labyrinth, picks up his mail, and enters his cubicle, where he plans to spend the morning.

Cultural commentary finds him also in the relative seclusion of his own space. As he sits down, he switches on his terminal in a practiced, smooth move, absentmindedly logs on, and turns to the screen. On his technet mail he notices among the many communications another announcement of the afternoon events; a memo titled, "How Others See Our Values," reviewing excerpts on Tech Culture from recent managerial bestsellers; a request to be interviewed by a consultant for a culture study; and the daily review of all references to Tech in the press. In his mail ("the hardcopy"), he finds *Tech-knowledge*, one of a large number of company newsletters. On the cover is a big picture of Sam Miller against the background of a giant slogan—"We Are One." He also finds an order form for company publications, including Ellen Cohen's "Culture Operating Manual." His bookshelf has mostly technical material, but also a copy of *In Search of Excellence*, distributed to all professional and managerial employees, and a business magazine with a cover story on Tech's corporate culture, titled "Working Hard, Having Fun." For good measure, an "*I love Tech*" bumpersticker is fixed to his filing cabinet. The day has hardly begun, yet Tom is already surrounded by "the culture," the ever-present signs of the company's explicit concern with its employees' state of mind (and heart).

Although their stance toward such commentary varies considerably—for some it is "a useful guide to survival," for others "Big Brother shit," and for others yet an elaborate game or simply "the facts of life"—most insiders (as Tom would say) "speak Tech culture fluently": they easily reconstruct and often make use of its style and substance. For members, then, the company perspective on the culture is familiar, systematic, comprehensive, thought-out, well-articulated, and associated with the company's interest. It is, in other words, a pervasive "organizational ideology."

[. . .]

TOP MANAGEMENT: THE VOICE OF LEADERSHIP

Senior managers at Tech espouse a distinct and systematic view of the company and its members in written documents that formulate and codify the abstract principles underlying the managerial perspective, and in recorded speeches and interviews that offer personal interpretations of the official point of view.

[. . .]

For example, in the "Engineering Guide," immediately following the company philosophy, one finds an explicit formulation of the essence of the "corporate culture": the company is characterized by "informality" and "trust," its employees by "maturity" and "self-direction."

Tech Culture

High Technologies is a people-oriented company. The employees receive courteous, fair and equitable treatment. . . . Management expects hard work and a high level of achievement. . . . great deal of trust is placed in employees to give their best efforts to a job. . . . Employees are expected to act in a mature manner at all times. . . . The matrix organization is goal-oriented and depends on trust, communications and team work. As a result, most employees function as independent consultants on every level, interacting across many areas necessary to accomplish the task.

Honesty, hard work, moral and ethical conduct, a high level of professionalism, and team work, are qualities that are an integral part of employment at High Technologies. These qualities are considered part of the Tech culture. Employees conduct themselves in an informal manner and are on a first-name basis with everyone at all levels. . . . The opportunity for self-direction and self-determination is always present.

[. . .]

Finally, a booklet titled "Bet on Yourself: You, Your Career and High Technologies" explains the company policy with regard to career development, emphasizing the official view of the relationship between the company and its employees. "Freedom to manage work" coupled with "individual responsibility" and "self-management" are the key.

[. . .]

Three themes are apparent: Tech's depiction as an organic entity whose goals, shared by all, reflect a moral stance vis-à-vis the world; the company's "people oriented" social organization, combining paternal care and trust with an informal atmosphere, freedom of action with responsibility; and an elaboration of members' desired attributes. Required behaviors are vaguely defined: creativity, taking initiative, hard work, meeting commitments, "doing it right," are thought to reflect internalized values, beliefs, and feelings; "self-generated discipline," "attitude and desire to succeed," "caring," and "loyalty" are considered evidence of personal "growth" and "maturity."

Such documents are generally regarded as "apple pie and motherhood statements": abstract and idealized, they reflect management's desires, even wishful thinking, in formulations removed from everyday reality. They are rarely, therefore, the focus of attention. However, the principles they embody are frequently restated and interpreted in the less organized but more concrete words of senior managers attempting to explain, exemplify, substantiate, and validate the main themes of the managerial perspective.

Senior Managers Speak

The recorded thoughts, observations, and ideas of senior managers are perhaps the most frequently encountered form of ideological expression. Here, the managerial perspective is presented in the name of real people, whose experience is often used as evidence for its applicability. The focus is mostly on mundane concerns of business and technology, but explicit references to cultural matters are often present.

Newsletters are the most widespread media for disseminating the personal views of senior managers through interviews, reprints of speeches, and occasional signed editorials. Their number varies, but the average in Engineering is around two hundred; of these, most are funded by company budgets. Some are limited to the ranks of management, others to occupational groups, and others still to particular organizations. They appear weekly or monthly in employee maildrops or homes; others wait around to be picked up or appear magically on the technet. All are kept in the library stacks, and clippings of key items are routinely posted.

Speeches, presentations, and interviews given by senior managers are routinely videotaped. Edited versions are found in the libraries and are used by training and public relations groups. Some tapes are used in workshops and seminars; others, like Sam Miller's "We Are One" speech, are screened in public during lunchtime sessions and shown throughout the day in strategic locations. . . .

Senior managers address the three main themes of the managerial perspective: the company's moral purpose, the nature of its social organization, and the attributes of the member role. Sam Miller is a key figure in this rhetoric. He is widely recognized as someone with a distinct point of view, referred to by insiders as a "vision," a "philosophy," or a "religion." Regarded by many as the originator of "the culture" and a key figure in its preservation and maintenance, he is frequently interviewed, and ideas associated with him are well known and widely circulated.[1] Other senior managers repeat and interpret similar ideas.

[. . .]

The morality of the company's mission also extends to its internal social organization—commonly described as "people-oriented." In a taped speech, Miller relates that orientation to ideas derived from early Human Relations theorists:

We almost have a moral obligation to society. We owe it to society to do it. . . . What is most important is where your heart is. When we started Tech, the business fad was McGregor and Theory X and Y. Some tried and said: "I *knew* it wouldn't work." We made it work! And for an American company, we do it well!

[. . .]

Aspects of the company's "people orientation" are frequently adumbrated. In a recorded speech, the vice-president of Human Resources discusses the company's "commitment to its people":

We have always tried to transmit the notion that people are our most important asset. In a time of crisis, our initial reaction is to protect our employees. . . . During the past years our values regarding job security have been severely tested as never before. And while we do not guarantee full employment, we have lived up to our commitment to manage the business in a way that reduces the likelihood of resorting to involuntary separation of our people. High Technologies is its employees.

Much is also made of the balance of freedom and discipline that is supposed to characterize working life in the company. Freedom is reflected in enhanced autonomy for members, otherwise known as "bottom-up management." The vice-president of Engineering says in an interview:

I believe you just can't manage a fast-growing, fast-moving organization in detail from the top. It limits the growth if you try to do it that way. So we've continuously tried to push decision making functions down inside the organizations to product lines, to engineers.

Autonomy, in this view, must be coupled with responsibility:

One of the concepts that hasn't changed from the beginning of the company is that people are responsible for the success of the projects they propose. "He who proposes does," and is judged on the results. That fundamental philosophy hasn't changed. I hope it never does. We have to keep working to make sure that engineers feel they can propose things and go out and do them—that they aren't powerless, that they can get decisions made.

[. . .]

A certain experience of membership is thought to follow from incorporating these values.

"Excitement" and "fun," in particular, are frequent glosses for the emotional outcomes of hard, autonomous work. In a typical statement, the VP of Engineering describes his view of the desired state: "We spend a lot of time trying to make it fun to work here, make it challenging and exciting, make you feel as though you can make important contributions."

[. . .]

We must keep this atmosphere which generates creativity, makes people work hard and makes them *enjoy* working hard, challenges them to learn, challenges them to do new things, challenges them to take chances, and challenges them to be careful in their approach to things so that we never gamble the whole company—and this, I think, is still the goal, still the secret of our success.

[. . .]

CONCLUSION: CULTURE DECODED

[. . .] These images provide a backdrop to everyday life in the organization, forming a dense matrix of meaning that is constantly, if peripherally, in a member's view. Relentless repetition is the rule. The material is circulated on the technet, posted in public places, distributed in the mail, encountered in workshops, and used as decoration. Consequently, ideological formulations—ready-made words of wisdom, platitudes posing as insight—become a constant background noise.

[. . .]

The metaphors used to characterize Tech as a social entity are based on the imagery of "family" or analogies with morally sound institutions: religion and science.

[. . .]

Traditional forms of control associated with bureaucracy are relegated to a supporting role. Instead, control is thought of as the internalization of discipline reflected in the attitudes, orientations, and emotions of committed members. The company is presented as informal and flexible, and its management as demanding yet trusting. The community is characterized as "bottom-up," loose, free, a "people company." In this view, members are not constrained by enforced or traditional structures and

the explicit behavioral rules associated with them. On the contrary, they are expected to engage in a form of creative chaos where decisions emerge through a political process of negotiation between innovative members. Discipline is not based on explicit supervision and reward, but rather on peer pressure and, more crucially, internalized standards for performance. There is little mention of the economic structure, and the importance of economic rewards is underplayed, even frowned upon. It is a fact of life, but not one to be emphasized; instead, rewards are seen as arising from the experience of communion, of belonging, of participation in the community as organizationally defined.[2]

Describing a "culture" in this fashion does away with the sharp differences between categories of people that were once the hallmark of organization and focuses instead on the similarities. Thus, the functional and hierarchical distinctions between categories of members are underplayed and vague. The image is of a collection of undifferentiated individuals fulfilling the general requirements of appropriate membership. Unity and similarity are emphasized, authority and power deemphasized. . . .

The central image for the member role is that of the self-starter, the entrepreneur. Behavioral rules are vague: be creative, take initiative, take risks, "push at the system," and, ultimately, "do what's right."

[. . .]

Central to this view of the member role is the blurring of boundaries between self and organization. The member role is "incorporated," based on "strong identification," an inextricable connection to the company, with little "demarcation." It involves "the whole person" and is based on powerful emotional ties expressed in "zeal" or at least "enthusiasm."

[. . .]

4

PRESENTATIONAL RITUALS: TALKING IDEOLOGY

"It's not just work—it's a celebration!" is a company slogan one often hears from members attempting to describe life at Tech. Less formally, many refer to Tech as "a song and dance company."

And, more privately, some agree that "you have to do a lot of bullshitting in groups." Like much of the self-descriptive conventional wisdom that permeates the company, these observations—whether offered straightforwardly or cynically—contain a valid observation: everyday life at Tech is replete with ritual.

Ritual, most generally speaking, is "a rule-governed activity of a symbolic character which draws the attention of participants to objects of thought and feeling which they hold to be of special significance." At Tech, as insiders well know, members regularly participate in a variety of such structured face-to-face gatherings: speeches, presentations, meetings, lectures, parties, training workshops, and so forth. Dave Carpenter's planned appearance at Lyndsville and Ellen Cohen's culture seminar are examples, along with more routinely occurring events such as Tom O'Brien's weekly team meeting with the members of the ABC project. Whatever else they are intended to accomplish, these events are also occasions where participants, speaking as agents for the corporate interest, use familiar symbols—presentational devices, stylized forms of expression, company slogans and artifacts—to articulate, illustrate, and exemplify what members in good standing are to think, feel, and do. In short, these gatherings, which I will refer to as presentational rituals, are where the organizational ideology—the managerial version of Tech culture and the member role it prescribes—is dramatized and brought to life.

[. . .]

From this perspective, then, ritual may be seen as a mechanism of normative control. . . . In this sense, rituals are "mechanisms through which certain organizational members influence how other members are to think and feel—what they want, what they fear, what they should regard as proper and possible, and, ultimately, perhaps, who they are."

It is precisely this quality of ritual that appeals to Tech managers. At Tech, concern with the shaping of members' thoughts and feelings is high. Conventional managerial wisdom has it that extensive and recurring participation in ritual gatherings where the organizational ideology is enacted causes members to "internalize" the culture and infuses

them with the right "mindset" and the appropriate "gut reactions." In short, those with an interest in engineering culture consider presentational rituals a mechanism for transforming the abstract formulations of Tech's organizational ideology into the lived experience of members. "They are," in the words of one manager, "where Techies are made."

[. . .]

BOOTCAMP: LEARNING THE CULTURE

The Orientation Workshop, titled "Intro to Tech" but often referred to as "bootcamp," is a two-day training event offered several times a year. Designed for engineers with a few months experience in the company, it is fairly popular and draws attendees from beyond the target population. Since the workshop is thought to transmit valuable knowledge about the company, participants occasionally sign up for more than one session. More experienced managers from Engineering and other functions occasionally participate too, believing that understanding the company and its engineers provides an edge over the less knowledgeable.

Like other in-house training events, the intro workshop must be marketed and sold in order to survive the internal entrepreneurial process. "Bootcamp" has made it in the marketplace. It is a flagship event and an important vehicle for "getting the word down" and "getting the message out." Each session is advertised across the technet, and enrollment averages about twenty.

The workshop has a carefully planned and well-defined structure. The history, business interests, products, and culture of Tech are covered in sequence. Each topic is treated in a discrete module: a two-hour session based on a presentation by a trainer or an invited guest speaker. Participants sit around a large table. Each is given a name tag and a package of materials: paper, pencils, markers, the "Engineering Guide," an employee handbook, copies of Tech newsletters, a booklet describing the history of Tech, a number of internally published research papers on Tech culture, and a mimeographed copy of "The Sayings of Chairman Sam"—a compilation of anecdotes about Tech attributed to its founder and president. The schedule is heavy, running from early morning coffee through lunchtime yawns to five o'clock fidgets on two consecutive days. There are short coffee breaks between presentations, and a one-hour lunch break.

The module on Tech culture comes first. Ellen Cohen is the invited speaker. Introductions are made. The twenty-five participants give brief descriptions of their organizational location and technology. Most are "new hires" three to six months out of school; some have transferred from other companies. One or two have vaguely defined jobs in Corporate, there is an older engineer from Manufacturing, a fairly senior finance manager from Engineering, and a technician from Field Service.

"Culture" is not a notion that engineers take to easily, and newcomers are often unfamiliar with the appropriate behavior in Tech training seminars; consequently, the module—designed as a series of interactive exercises—requires some goading. After passing out handouts summarizing the talk, Ellen writes the word "culture" on a large flipchart and says:

"The topic today is culture. We have a spectrum of people here from all over the company. Feel free to chime in. 'Culture' has become something of a fad. First, what is 'culture'? What do you think?"

A young engineer slouching in the corner answers: "Fungus. I had a culture for my senior science project. But my dog ate it." Some laugh. Ellen smiles too, but continues undaunted. "We're looking at behavior, at people. What is the characteristic of people at Tech?" She waits, marker in hand, with a warm, inviting-looking smile, nodding in anticipation, perhaps indicating the signs of affirmation she is looking for. Her question hangs. No answers. Some coffee sipping. "You feel like you've all been chosen, right?" she says, nodding her head more vigorously and still smiling. Still no replies. The stony silence highlights the incongruity of her demeanor, but she persists. "What else? What are people like at Tech?" Some volunteers speak up, drawn in by discomfort, if nothing else: "Friendly." "Amicable." She writes it all on the flipchart. The tempo picks up: "Individual- and teamwork." "I'm expected to be a good corporate citizen." "Strong customer orientation." "People tend to like Tech no

matter how confused," she says, and adds: "How do you feel?"

Some of the participants raise their hands. She calls on each in turn.

"I like it here. I hope for profit. I respect Sam Miller a lot. Where I worked before you'd hope they fail! Here the executives aren't as ruthless as in other companies; they are more humane."

"I haven't met anyone here I don't respect."

"I flash off on the technet and get to people without them wondering why; they are open and willing to share information."

"People understand. There is tolerance for new people."

"There's a supportive atmosphere."

As they speak, Ellen makes encouraging sounds and lists key phrases on the chart: "profit; not ruthless; humane; respect; open; share info; tolerance; supportive."

When the sheet is full, she pulls it off the flipchart, pastes it to the wall, and says: "This is what makes Tech a different kind of place. People are relaxed and informal. What else?" Someone says: "There is little difference between engineers and managers; it's hard to tell them apart." "Authority Not a Big Deal," she writes in bold letters on the flipchart. Then she adds: "In other places you're incompetent till proved otherwise; here it's the other way around, right?" Not waiting for an answer, she writes "Confidence in Competence," and says: "They know what they are doing, or believe it." "A little too much," the guy sitting next to me whispers to his neighbor.

Disagreement soon surfaces. Jim, a technician who has been around the company for a number of years, raises his hand. In the interchange with the instructor that ensues, she uses his objections to make additional cultural points:

Jim: "You may be right. But I've noticed subcultures. It depends on where you work. Technical writers are considered lower than the dust on the floor. They are there to serve the engineers. In Field Service we are considered above them but not equal to engineers."

Ellen: "Tech is a technical company founded by engineers. Engineers hold a special place in some people's eyes. There are status differences based on what you know. But if we don't work together—we don't sell."

[. . .]

Ellen turns to the flipchart, writes, "We Are A Family," and says:

> "This is the most important one. We have a no-layoff policy. It's the ultimate backup plan. It would break some people's hearts if we had to do it. We face it as a family: cutting costs, hiring freezes. Every member is asked to contribute."

A young woman from Corporate who has been silent so far bursts out in a concerned, almost angry tone:

> "I work in Corporate. A lot of the stuff is only a myth there. I see the very high up people fighting to the death. There is no clear person with the last word. They bounce responsibility around."

She starts to give an example from a well-known failed project, but Ellen interrupts her rather brusquely:

> "Tech isn't wonderful or glowing. It's not. It's human. But it's the best I've seen! I was a nomad before I came here. I'm sorry you haven't seen the rest of the companies so you can appreciate Tech. [Pause.] That is another thing about Tech. People are quick to point out faults, as if they didn't have any. Where I worked before there was rampant empire building. Tech is much better. We are a state-of-the-art pioneer. There is great love and great criticism of the company."

The challenger has been reprimanded and temporarily silenced, and her challenge reinterpreted to support rather than undermine the ritual frame.

For some participants the culture module appears to make sense, and they join the discussion as supporters, challengers, questioners, or learners. Others seem more skeptical. They smile to themselves, or to a neighbor, or pull out computer printout, clearly indicating their lack of interest. They prefer the "hard data" and the facts. They see explicit cultural analysis as "fluff," the engineer's

term for discourse identified with the social sciences or with "people-oriented" managers.

The emotional intensity of the module's conclusion, however, seems to captivate all the participants. Ellen flips off the viewgraph, puts down the marker, and gives a short talk that sounds off-the-record, very personal, almost motherly:

> "There is a down side to all of this! There can be a lot of pain in the system! Be careful; keep a balance; don't overdo it, don't live off vending machines for a year. [Laughter.] You'll burn out. I've been there; I lived underground for a year, doing code. Balance your life. Don't say: 'I'll work like crazy for four years, then I'll get married.' I heard this from a kid. But who will he marry? Don't let the company suck you dry; after nine or ten hours your work isn't worth much anyway."

The sudden switch to a subversive-sounding message creates an air of rapt attention. All eyes are on her as she walks slowly from the flipchart to the center of the room. After a brief pause, she adds the finishing touch: "What kind of company do you think allows me to be saying these things to you?" Nobody stirs for a few moments, and then a break is called.

[. . .]

5

SELF AND ORGANIZATION

MANAGING ROLE RESPONSES

Role embracement—expressing identification with aspects of the member role—is a widely shared and often-recurring feature of self-reports. Generally referred to as "being a Techie," role embracement is reportedly experienced as a general orientation to the company, a combination of beliefs and feelings glossed by the label "loyalty." A typical explication is offered by an engineering manager.

> "You know, I like Tech. I don't think of leaving. People might say that the culture swallowed me, but there really is a feeling of loyalty I have. We have a lot of that in the culture. We like working for Tech. It is a positive company. You get really involved. I get a real charge when Tech gets a good press. Or when people I knew from this other company were dumping on Tech, I was offended. I didn't like hearing it. They made

millions with us! Because of us they got rich! They get all this free knowledge from us and say it with impunity! My husband works for Tech and he feels the same way. We spend time with friends talking about work; we're worse than doctors. I guess you can call me a Techie."

[. . .]

Role embracement, then, means submitting to the company's definition of one's self. Such submission, however, is typically presented as a form of voluntary exchange with the company. A number of different attributes of the company are often cited as facilitating such an exchange. One is the image of the president, who has come to symbolize the "philosophy" and everything that is unique about Tech. A positive view of Sam Miller is frequently heard, particularly at middle and lower levels (more senior managers often tend to be critical; it is a sign of the insider to be close enough to know "the real story"). For example, a mid-level manager, speaking, as many do, in the first person plural, acknowledges his belief in the validity of the ideology, identified with the president. Emotional attachment is presented as a fair exchange:

> "Maybe I've swallowed slogans, the party line, the whole Sam Miller 'do what's right' thing. But I *do* believe that Tech 'does what's right.' We don't lay off, even though some people deserve to be laid off. So you feel loyalty back. Sam Miller believes in 'taking care of your people,' and he gets paid back with loyalty. They've never done wrong by me."

A similar exchange is apparent in an engineering supervisor's description of the impact of a speech by Sam Miller:

> "I trust the man. He means well. There is a lot of honesty at the top and the bottom of the company. I don't know about the middle. But he really means it when he says it's the company's duty to take care of employees and customers. I've never met him, but I've seen the videotapes. He can be very powerful. I got excited when I heard him say: 'It's our moral duty to give the customers what they want.' *Moral duty!*"

[. . .]

A second factor facilitating the exchange is the perception of the company's positive treatment of its employees (often in comparison with other companies). Thus, an engineer compares Tech's tradition of job security to its competitors' approach:

> "Tech is good because they grow to your weakness; other places, they milk your knowledge dry and then kill you. At Data they pay great, but they fire you as soon as the downturn comes. This company keeps people and retrains them. I just love this company. I would die for it! There is a tradition of job security here: you can have your neck chopped off and it'll grow back again. You take your risks and you're not hurt too bad. Take Henderson's group: they were responsible for Jupiter and now they're back again. 'Fail and you're history' is just hype."

[. . .]

Engineers often portray Tech as "a good environment for engineering," a "country club" or an "engineers' sandbox" where engineers who are supposedly addicted to their work and emotionally attached to their projects can "play." An engineer in Advanced Development explains:

> "Tech has the best engineers. I'm an engineer, and I want state-of-the-art technology. At Chiptech they develop what Marketing tells them. I'm happy as long as you keep me away from marketing types. Tech caters to engineers. Its reputation in the industry is a country club for engineers.

[. . .]

Finally, some depict Tech's business practices and moral stance as worthy of one's commitment. Tech's way of doing business is often contrasted with the less than honest approaches presumably found elsewhere. One project manager contrasts Tech with "sleazy defense contractors"—the companies that develop products for the Department of Defense:

> "I worked for a while for a company that was built on those contracts. I worked on the ABM radar. It's not so much that I mind what the products end up doing. No. But all the dishonesty—the excessive costs, the stupidity, the unnecessary work—it really got me down. The norm was: hide the basic specs, follow the letter of the law and produce garbage, then get another contract. Disgusting stuff. Like telling reliability engineers to cook figures. At Tech at least we give customers an honest product. They get what they pay for. Most of the time. I feel good about that."

In sum, role embracement is a recurring theme in members' description of their subjective experience. . . .

Unqualified role embracement, however, is felt by many to be undignified. This is evident in the self-conscious quality of the descriptions, and in the emphasis on a fair and, more crucially, on a controlled exchange with the company. Thus, members claim the right to control the extent and the degree to which role demands are embraced. This capacity for role distancing—one that we have seen enacted in the course of organizational rituals—is often made explicit and elaborated with regard to both the cognitive and the emotional dimensions of the member role.

Cognitive distancing—disputing popular ideological formulations—is manifested when one suggests that one is "wise" to what is "really" going on. Being "wise" implies that despite behaviors and expressions indicating identification, one is also fully cognizant of their underlying meaning, and thus free of control: autonomous enough to know what is going on and dignified enough to express that knowledge.

One frequently encountered mode of cognitive distancing is cynicism. This is usually expressed as a debunking assertion, cast as a personal insight, that reality is very different from ideological claims. For example, an engineer questions the meaning of Tech culture:

> "It's like a religion, a philosophy that the company expounds. Sam Miller says, 'Do what's right,' be on the up and up, satisfy the customer, do the right thing by them. He's a weird bird, pushes all this morality stuff. There is a whole Sam Miller subculture. His memos circulate on the technet. It's like a kind of morality thing. You can go into Sam's office if you're not happy about a supervisor. I've heard of someone who has done it. Of course, nothing might get done. In this group, 'do what's right' means 'make your manager visible.' [Laugh.] Aren't all organizations like that?"

A second mode of cognitive distancing is that of detached theoretical observation, often referred to as "Tech watching." Its essence is the ability to interpret Tech reality and view it with scientific detachment; observations are frequently cast in the language of various social scientific disciplines Tech watching not only expresses a point of view that is distinct from ideology; it also reverses roles: members who are

often the subjects of organizational research become knowledgeable students of organizations (and of organizational researchers). A senior manager who has since left the company says:

> "'Tech culture' is a way to control people, to rationalize a mess, to get them to work hard, and feel good about it; it is really an ideology. Like all other ideologies it is part truth and part lie."
>
> *[. . .]*

Tech watching often takes the form of cultural commentary. Says an engineer, possessor of an undergraduate degree in sociology and a fan of Erving Goffman:

> "The company may appear informal, loose. Open offices, first names. But there is a *very* distinct status system here. People always ask who you work with. They won't ask you your title or your rank, or look at the size of your office. Once they have you placed, they will treat you accordingly."
>
> *[. . .]*

Distancing also occurs with respect to the feelings prescribed by the member role or associated with the organizational self. . . . Denial is accomplished by presenting one's motives for membership as purely instrumental. The relationship with the company is construed as contractual and economically driven, and its emotional aspects denied. For an engineer, this means not only avoiding the "people and the politics," where "emotions" are likely to be found—a typical response—but also a denial that one "loves one's work." An engineer says:

> "I wanted the security of working for a big company—no excitement and less pay. I don't identify with any organization. Those things are circles within circles; they come and go, but the job remains. I get green dollars, I do my best, I know my worth. I work flexible hours but *never* more than eight. Technology is *not* my hobby. I have no terminal at home, and I keep my social life separate. I'm a private person. I don't go to the workshops or to the meetings. That's for those who want to make an impression, those who want to get ahead. They can have it. None of the 'addicted to your work,' 'ego-involvement' bullshit. I do my job. All the weird political aspects of the project don't bother me. They fight all the time. They are defensive and paranoid. There is an 'ain't it awful' attitude. Finger

pointing. Accusing each other of screwing up. But I stay away from all of that emotional stuff."

[. . .]

. . . [D]enial of emotional involvement in work is contrasted both with recognized ideological role demands and with a caricatured depiction of those who accept them.

[. . .]

In sum, cognitive and emotional distancing reflect the felt necessity of maintaining a controllable distance from the beliefs and feelings prescribed by the member role and displayed as part of the organizational self. A ludic metaphor underlies members' attempts to convey this experience: the construction of an organizational self is seen as drama or as a game. Notions of performing, playing a game, watching oneself, strategically designing roles, and, ultimately, assuming a calculative stance toward the management of one's own thoughts and feelings are deeply ingrained in experience and explicitly articulated by members.

[. . .]

We have come full circle. If the attempt to engineer culture and accomplish normative control is aimed at defining the members' selves for them, this very attempt undermines its own assumptions. The engineers of culture see the ideal member as driven by strong beliefs and intense emotions, authentic experiences of loyalty, commitment, and the pleasure of work. Yet they seem to produce members who have internalized ambiguity, who have made the metaphor of drama a centerpiece of their sense of self, who question the authenticity of all beliefs and emotions, and who find irony in its various forms the dominant mode of everyday existence.

NOTES

1. Miller's presence is strongly felt throughout the company. A handbook titled "The Sayings of Chairman Sam" has been broadly distributed in training workshops as a lighthearted but still respectful rendition of the founder's thoughts. A more straightforward version of Miller's ideas is found in one of the first sections of the "Engineering Guide," along with the corporate

philosophy. Many Tech watchers attribute the culture directly to Miller's innovative thinking and to his long-standing (some would say obstinate) insistence on the preservation of some of its manifestations. Such a perspective is supported—and perhaps influenced—by managerial theorists who emphasize the role of founders and leaders in the formation of a culture, occasionally going so far as to present the company as an extension of the founder's personality (Kets de Vries and Miller, 1984; Schein, 1985). Regardless of one's stance toward such causal arguments, it is beyond doubt that this particular founder is a central symbol in whatever cultural formation has been accomplished or has developed at Tech.

2. The similarities between the ideology of Tech culture and popular conceptions of Japanese management are striking. Rohlen (1974) studied a Japanese bank where employees are supposed to develop an emotional attachment and express it through pride, dedication, and enthusiastic participation. The general ideal is "that of a collectivity, constituted of emotionally satisfying personal relationships, working in the spirit of concord for the general interest." In this system, "considerable attention is paid to the individual … as a human being with an inherent urge for satisfaction and accomplishment... There is no need for a person to be independent of his institutional connections in order to achieve happiness. There is no contradiction, that is, between institutionalized work and personal aspiration.... Devotion to duty, perfected through greater self-discipline, in time leads to a reduction of the disturbance caused by conflicting demands. The result is an improved state of personal spiritual freedom and a sense of joy focused on fulfillment in one's work" (pp. 51–52). Rohlen sees in this ideology echoes of the Confucian heritage, a way of relating the organizational ideology to the larger social environment.

One would be tempted to explain similarities to Tech culture as a manifestation of the current interest in Japanese management techniques in popular managerial literature. The concept of culture in organizations is in fact closely related to an interest in Japanese management (Ouchi, 1981). In this view, Japanese organizations have found the solution to the problem of control, and Tech ideology is an American attempt to emulate Japanese management by developing a complex and all-encompassing relationship between the company and its employees, most notably in the practice of guaranteed employment in return for "loyalty."

This explanation, however, is not sufficient. The roots of Tech policies and associated practices are in the 1950s, and its current language and ideas appear to be derived largely from local traditions, from Emerson through the "company town" to the Human Relations approach to management. Current discourse is full of references to these sources, as in Sam Miller's reference to Douglas McGregor. When the groundwork for Tech's organizational ideology was laid, Japan was still reeling from its encounter with the products of Western rationality. Moreover, as Rohlen points out, Japanese managers seem equally obsessed with Western management and its perceived efficiency and rationality. This ironic reversal highlights the universal managerial quest for more control and the role of cultural arguments in this process. Others, it seems, are seen through the mediating lens of the perceived deficiencies of one's own way of life.

REFERENCES

Bendix, Reinhard. 1956. *Work and Authority in Industry: Ideologies of Management in the Course of Industrialization.* New York: Wiley.

Deal, Terrence and Allen Kennedy. 1982. *Corporate Cultures: The Rites and Rituals of Corporate Life.* Reading, MA: Addison-Wesley.

de Vries, Manfred F. R. Kets, and Danny Miller. 1984. *The Neurotic Organization.* San Francisco: Jossey-Bass.

Etzioni, Amitai. 1961. *A Comparative Analysis of Complex Organizations.* New York: Free Press/ Glencoe.

Goffman, Erving. 1961. *Asylums.* Garden City, NY: Anchor.

Ouchi, William G. 1981. *Theory Z: How American Business Can Meet the Japanese Challenge.* Reading, MA: Addison-Wesley.

Peters, Thomas and Robert Waterman. 1982. *In Search of Excellence: Lessons from America's Best-Run Companies.* New York: Harper and Row.

Rohlen, Thomas P. 1974. *For Harmony and Strength: Japanese White-Collar Organization in Anthropological Perspective.* Berkeley: University of California Press.

Schein, Edgar H. 1985. *Organizational Culture and Leadership.* San Francisco: Jossey-Bass.

PART XI

ORGANIZATIONS AND SOCIETY: GENDER, RACE, CLASS, AND POLITICS

O rganizations are important as objects of study not only in their own right, but also because they shape the broader society. As the readings in this section demonstrate, organizations may reinforce various forms of social inequality, ameliorate them, or play a central role in creating them. The topics covered—gender, race, class, and political power—are central to an understanding of the shape of modern society.

GENDER

Gender differences are pervasive in the labor market. Even today, women's pay is about 75% of that earned by men with comparable education, similar age, and identical hours worked per week. Women and men are often found in different occupations. Traditionally, women were concentrated in clerical jobs, "caring" work (e.g., nurses, teachers, social workers), service occupations, and light-assembly factory jobs, whereas men had jobs in management and the professions, blue-collar crafts, and heavy industry manual work. This gender segregation across occupations remained constant for most of the past century, except for a significant decline in the 1970s. Men and women are rarely paid differently when they work in the same job and for the same employer, but even in gender-integrated occupations, men and women tend to work for different companies or at different locations. Both men and women earn less if they work in a mostly female occupation. Some fields, such as the relatively lower-status personnel or human resource function, have absorbed so many female managers and professionals that they have "tipped" and are now often new, majority-female "ghettos." Overall, about 60% of men and women would have to change their occupations if all occupations were to be integrated by gender today (England 1992; Reskin 1993).

On average, women are more likely to work in part-time jobs, smaller and less profitable firms, labor intensive industries, nonunion workplaces, and nonprofit organizations, all of which are associated with lower pay. Women's jobs often have shorter promotion ladders and fewer supervisory responsibilities, and, when they do include supervisory duties, are unlikely to involve supervision of men (England 1992; Reskin 1993).

The reasons for women's continuing economic disadvantage despite several decades of progress in some respects are much debated. Broadly speaking, one school of thought, particularly within mainstream labor economics, argues that organizations play little active role in maintaining gender inequality. Women prefer certain jobs because they are compatible with their family responsibilities, such as part-time work or jobs permitting episodic employment. Women freely choose or are socialized into preferring jobs that are less competitive or physically demanding and that involve creativity, working with people, and helping others, as opposed to maximizing income, status, or position (England 1992; Fuchs 1988).

Alternatively, employers may play an active role in gender outcomes by favoring men for hiring and promotion because of personal values about gender roles, beliefs about sex differences in skills, devaluation of the skills involved in caring work and other gender-typed tasks, a desire to create artificial distinctions that inhibit occupational solidarity across gender lines, and a desire to avoid male-female tensions that might result from workplace gender integration. If women perceive preexisting constraints on their opportunities, their occupational "choices" may also reflect these limitations (England 1992).

It is also possible that male coworkers rather than employers are the main constraint to women's advancement within organizations. Men may harass women in traditionally male preserves, refuse to teach them skills on the job, or refuse to engage in other supportive behaviors because women pose a threat to their masculinity. Because organizations often select supervisors and managers from among male former colleagues of female employees, the distinction between coworker and employer discrimination might be more theoretical than real in some cases. Men might also fear that the influx of women will lower wages or pose a threat to their masculinity. Consequently, women may be more able to enter male jobs when the jobs are becoming deskilled or suffering relative wage declines (England 1992).

Regardless of the explanation, it is clear that women occupy few of the very highest positions in business organizations despite great growth in the percentage of managers who are female, a barrier often called the *glass ceiling*. Only four women were chief executive officers of the top 1,000 American companies in 1996, two through family connections, and only about 2% to 2.5% of top management at the 500 largest American corporations were women. Only 28% of female vice presidents had operational responsibilities for profit and loss, as opposed to less prestigious staff functions such as human resources or public relations. Government does not have an altogether better record; only 7% of all cabinet members from Eisenhower to Clinton were female, and currently about 10% of Senate and House members are female (Zweigenhaft and Domhoff 1998, pp. 46, 57, 59, 62, 75; Bertrand and Hallock 2000).

Women represented less than one percent of members of the board of directors of the 1,300 largest American companies in 1977 and rose to about 10% in 1996, nearly twenty years later, but most companies with women on their boards did not have more than one. Few female directors were appointed to boards following a career in top corporate management, the traditional male route, as opposed to careers in university or nonprofit administration or membership in a family owning a large share of the firm (Zweigenhaft and Domhoff 1998, pp. 44ff.). This raises the question of whether even these women are truly integrated into high positions or whether they are tokens used to present an image of corporate diversity in a workplace culture that is otherwise unfavorable to women.

Rosabeth Moss Kanter's work is the classic statement of the dilemmas faced by women seeking to enter the male-dominated ranks of management (Reading 28). Kanter argues that the small percentage of women or any minority in management causes members to be treated as *tokens,* or symbols of the group, rather than as individuals. Because they are so conspicuous, women are subject to continual scrutiny and suspicion, treated as showpieces of the organization's commitment to change, or seen as useful mainly for representing the "woman's point of view" in discussions. Women are often placed in the no-win situation of being expected to act like men at work and being judged by men as either inadequate to the task or violating the norms for their gender if they embrace the male managerial norm too strongly. Kanter's reading also explores how women try to resist the stereotypical roles that are imposed on them derived from women's status in the broader society while not further alienating male colleagues with whom they must work. Kanter concludes that women will achieve genuine acceptance only when their numbers are roughly equal to those of men, which requires some kind of compulsory policy such as affirmative action, because entrenched male attitudes and low female representation are processes that reinforce one another when left on their own. Kanter believes the same arguments apply more generally to any minority group within organizations.

A later group of feminist organizational researchers argue that at a more basic level the assumptions of most organizations reflect masculine values, devalue female strengths, and in some ways harm the overall society as a result. Organizational theory since Weber associates bureaucracy with characteristics often stereotyped as male, such as impersonality, abstract rationality, legalism, emotional restraint, tough-minded approach to problems, assertiveness, competitive achievement orientations, and subordination of family to work roles. Organizations less often value the contrasting characteristics often associated with women, such as empathy, compassion, social connection to others, collaborative and non-competitive work relationships, and balance between work and family lives (Acker 1990; Martin 2000).

Women have formed feminist alternatives to bureaucracy, such as health clinics, rape crisis centers, feminist bookstores, and political activist groups. These organizations seek not only to accomplish an instrumental mission, such as delivering health care, but also to do so in the context of a caring community based on principles of equality, participatory democracy, personal empowerment, mutual respect, and consensual decision making, similar to the cooperative alternatives to capitalist bureaucracy described by Rothschild-Whitt (Reading 34). They reject the authoritarianism, hierarchy, competitive individualism, and even the aggression and intimidation that can characterize traditional organizations, as Jackall's description of corporate life illustrated vividly (Reading 14). By their style of operation as well as their more overt goals, feminist organizations seek to transform the lives of their members and the broader society (Martin 1990). Feminists argue that the basic nature of organizations and the society in which they are embedded need to be changed and that focusing simply on the greater assimilation of women into traditionally run organizations is insufficient; most organizations by their very nature are based on principles at odds with women's orientations and social position (Martin 2000).

While many feminist organizations continue to thrive, others, like normatively oriented cooperatives generally, have found themselves bureaucratizing in response to demands from external funding agencies or similar resource suppliers, as resource dependency theory might predict (Reading 18), or as a result of the emergence of a centralizing elite within them, as Michels would predict (Reading 17). Others dissolved into factional disputes over these developments or perceptions that the organization was compromising or deviating from the purity of its original vision.

RACE

There is much less work on race in organizations than on gender and even less on groups other then African Americans. Understanding African Americans' status within American organizations requires an understanding of the history of American race relations.

Although African Americans were first brought to this country in the seventeenth century, prior to the early twentieth century about 90% lived in the former Confederate states, which were mostly agricultural and economically backward. The labor used in the first phases of American industrialization (1850–1910) consisted almost entirely of different groups of white European immigrants, each of which tended to enter the job structure at the bottom and gradually move up as another wave of immigrants entered. African Americans did not begin to work in the industrialized North and Midwest in large numbers until European immigration ended with the onset of World War I. African American migration north continued until the mid-1960s, especially during World War II and the 1950s after an extended pause during the Great Depression. In a certain sense, then, African Americans are among the latest immigrants to the advanced economic regions of the United States. Hispanic migration to the industrial regions of the United States also began in earnest in the 1950s. Since the 1970s, there has been some reverse migration of African Americans to Southern states as they have grown more rapidly than the older industrial North and Midwest and the general population has shifted south and west.

However, there are important differences between the experience of African Americans and previous white immigrants. Although all newcomer groups faced hostility and prejudice from both natives and previous immigrants, the intensity of racist sentiment against blacks was unprecedented and constituted a significant barrier to both equal political representation in local government and economic mobility. In addition, by the 1970s when African Americans might be expected to begin moving up the occupational hierarchy, American industry entered the crisis described in previous sections, limiting mobility opportunities compared to those of previous generations of white immigrants. African Americans' anger at police hostility, local government indifference, and continued low economic standing in an expanding economy led to a wave of urban riots in the 1960s, which led to pressures to integrate the workplace through affirmative action and to increase African American representation in local government and police forces in the 1970s.

The exact source of discrimination against minorities has been the subject of some debate. Mainstream economists argue that employers have no motive to discriminate in hiring because they are interested only in obtaining the highest output at the lowest wage. If, for some reason, the market wage for equally qualified African Americans were to be lower than for whites, employers would hire African Americans in greater numbers until their wages were bid up to parity with whites. An employer who continued to indulge his "taste" for discrimination against lower-wage African Americans would be at a competitive disadvantage. In this view, discrimination could continue only if it were a firm's customers or coworkers who discriminated by refusing to patronize integrated businesses or work in integrated workplaces, because profit-maximizing employers have no motive to discriminate.

But research indicates that the firm is not just a rational system; it is also a social system. Employers openly refuse to hire African American men in part because the social differences between white business owners and African American job applicants generate a lack of trust. Firms with African American owners, supervisors, or clientele are much more likely to hire African American workers. Affirmative action policies of varying effectiveness and scope have also helped redress this imbalance somewhat (Reskin, McBrier, and Kmec 1999).

However, African Americans still constitute a very small percentage of upper management. Various surveys indicate that less than 1% of top management and 3% to 4% of corporate board members of the top 1,000 companies were African American in the 1990s. As with women, many of the board members are outside directors who are appointed for the visibility they have achieved outside the organization rather than by climbing through the ranks of corporate management. Only eleven African Americans served in the Cabinet through the first half of the Bush administration, only two served in the U.S. Senate during the twentieth century, and currently about 8% of House members are black (Zweigenhaft and Domhoff 1998, pp. 89ff., 100, 104, 113).

Sharon Collins discusses the barriers that face African American managers as they try to work up the corporate ladder (Reading 29). In some ways her findings are similar to Kanter's regarding tokenism, including the tendency to consign African Americans to less prestigious staff positions. However, Kanter's solution for improving the position of minorities, namely numerical parity with the majority group, does not transfer so easily from gender to racial minorities, because African Americans represent only about 13% of the overall population. Clearly, overcoming racial barriers will require a strategy other than achieving equal numerical representation between racial and ethnic minorities on the one hand, and whites, on the other.

Social Class

Although sociologists long studied socioeconomic inequality without reference to organizational context, organizations play a key role in determining an individual's place in the social hierarchy and the structure of that hierarchy. Although early sociological studies of attainment assumed that individual qualities, such as education, determine socioeconomic standing, others argue that rewards are attached to organizational positions and different organizations offer different opportunities for rewards that are at least partly independent of the individuals they employ (Baron 1984). Labor markets are *segmented*, in part by organizational characteristics, and result in otherwise similarly educated workers having access to jobs that are differently rewarded, which in turn is responsible for social class differentiation. Some firms offer higher wages, better promotion opportunities, and more favorable working conditions to otherwise equally qualified workers because of the history of the industry and the company, size of the company, technology used, product market power (oligopoly vs. competitive market), presence of unions, and government policies regulating different kinds of businesses.

Writing before the crisis of the 1970s and 1980s generated new models of post-Fordism and neo-Fordism, Richard Edwards provides a critical perspective on the development of the Fordist employment system that dominated the American economy in its golden age between 1940 and 1975 using a *segmented labor markets* perspective (Reading 30). Edwards constructs a typology of organizations and labor markets that describes contemporary practices as legacies of different periods of the historical development of capitalism.

Prior to the late nineteenth century, almost all business was small, owner managed, and reliant on relatively primitive management techniques. The supervision of labor, which Edwards calls *simple control*, involved direct oversight of workers and was often arbitrary and personalistic rather than systematic and rule-bound. The rise of big business in the late nineteenth century concentrated large numbers of blue-collar workers in factory and other settings, but these firms initially paid the same low wages and managed their labor force in the same fashion as small businesses, despite higher profits and more complex technology. However, the concentration of workers generated an awareness of common discontents among workers that led to resistance and protest. Managers of large firms gained greater control over their workers with the kind of de-skilling strategies Taylor advocated and Braverman criticized, as well as by tying work more closely to the work pace of the machinery workers used, which Edwards calls *technical control*. Eventually, managers responded to continued protests, especially the militant unions of the 1930s, with higher wages, career ladders rather than dead-end jobs, and codified rules delimiting workers' responsibilities and protecting them from arbitrary treatment, which Edwards calls *bureaucratic control*. These compromises took the edge off discontents but also served as a less obtrusive control system that disguised continuing capitalist power behind a mask of impersonal rules, such as Gouldner described (see Introduction to Part IV), and divided the working class as a whole. Workers became more focused on individualistic concerns with career advancement within bureaucratically controlled factories, which replaced the previous solidarity among workers in a plant that resulted from their sharing equally oppressive conditions. In addition, only that segment of the working class employed by large and powerful corporations, often called the *core* or *monopoly sector*, had access to these relatively favorable conditions of employment, while many others continue to work for smaller and less powerful organizations, called the *periphery* or *competitive sector*, under conditions of simple control. The spread of bureaucratic control techniques in large and progressive firms immediately following World War II detached a segment of the working class from the rest, giving these workers greater workplace rights and a stake in the corporate system. During this golden age of American capitalism from the late 1940s to early 1970s, middle-class incomes and lifestyles were increasingly extended to one segment of the working class, separating it from the rest.

However, the remaining smaller firms and subcontractors in the periphery did not have the economic resources to make such compromises and continued to pay low wages, offer few opportunities for upward mobility, and manage their labor force using simple control techniques. The American working class became divided into an upper segment, usually white and male, employed in well-paying, often unionized settings, and a lower segment, often female and minority, employed in lower wage manufacturing and service jobs. The different economic outcomes for these different groups reflect the structure of the organizations and the labor pools from which they draw, rather than resulting mainly from differences in personal abilities.

The relatively privileged segment of the working class became more conservative and increasingly derived its identity by distinguishing itself from the lower segment and identifying with the middle class, leading to a more divided and conservative working class politics than in most European countries. The upper-working-class jobs were to decline with the crisis of the American economy in the mid-1970s and give way to neo-Fordist or post-Fordist strategies, depending on which research one believes. However, these divisions in the working class left an enduring legacy of a weakened labor movement and weakened political opposition to free-market policies that remains visible today.

Organizations shape the character of a society's upper classes, as well as its working and middle classes. A prominent theory of America's corporate elite rejects the notion that a managerial revolution has created a class of managers separate from owners. According to this view, wealthy and powerful individuals or families still effectively control many corporations and often play a direct role in running their companies. Even where top managers do control firms, executives' business decisions are indistinguishable from those of traditional capitalists. In fact, the two groups are integrated into a common elite by virtue of friendship and social network ties resulting from participation in other organizations, such as elite schools, social clubs, philanthropic groups, membership in business and other policy associations such as the Business Roundtable or Council on Foreign Relations, and common membership on the boards of directors of different companies. The result is a coherent elite whose solidarity, awareness of common interests, and sense of common identity help them maintain a common front to preserve their wealth and power, especially in shaping government policy (Useem 1980).

POLITICS

Government policies reflect the preferences of organizations as well as other segments of the public. Businesses and business associations, labor unions, and advocacy groups affect politics through campaign contributions, lobbying, and the mobilization of their constituencies, though the nature and extent of the influence acquired through these means are much debated. Some argue that business exercises a powerful influence quite apart from these methods of direct intervention. Politicians need an expanding economy to supply tax revenues for government operations and programs and to maintain employment, which keeps politicians popular among voters, so even left-of-center governments adopt pro-business policies to remain politically secure; direct contributions or lobbying is unnecessary (Block 1987).

Still, the direct exercise of political influence by different organizations attracts attention and often concern over who is shaping policy. Ideally, policy in a democracy reflects the will of the voters. But, as Michels' work made clear, most members of the public are relatively passive. Modern research into social movements makes clear that formal or informal organization is often necessary to affect political outcomes and a well-organized minority can exercise influence that is disproportionate to its numbers.

There are three main research traditions on political influence processes that come from political sociology. The *pluralist* model believes policy is the outcome of struggles among multiple groups with overlapping memberships and interests that each win and lose some policy battles without any one group achieving dominance. *Power elite* or *instrumentalist* theories of the state hold that a relatively unified business coalition dominates political decision making and usually succeeds in using government as its tool despite opposition from weaker, more public-oriented groups (Vogel 1989). A third tradition, *state-centered theory*, argues that government policy is generally set internally by officials and administrators who operate autonomously from most direct lobbying and make policy either with general business interests in mind (Block 1987) or according to their own intellectual and political agendas (Skocpol 1985).

The power elite model itself led to internal debates over whether businesses pursued some general business interest or narrower self-interests specific to their own particular industry or company. For instance, steel companies might have an interest in protection from imports to keep prices high, but auto companies would favor cheap steel imports and tariffs on auto imports, which many other industries might oppose, especially if they feared retaliatory tariffs from other nations against their products. Researchers debated whether companies unify around a common agenda or look after mainly their own individual interests.

David Vogel tries to bridge pluralist and power elite perspectives by arguing that the relative power of business and other groups, such as labor, consumer, environmental, and other public interest groups, fluctuates over time. Business had a dominant position before to the late 1960s but then experienced a real decline from 1968 to 1977, as government enacted new regulations in the areas of health, safety, and consumer protection and increased social welfare spending. Business then regrouped its forces in reaction to the increased government activity and regained its dominant position as part of a strategy to return to profitability during the economic crisis of the mid-1970s. Before the late 1960s, business could count on cooperative government officials and a sympathetic or passive public to generate favorable policy, but now business groups recovered by intensified lobbying in Washington. They replaced ad hoc, personal, and uncoordinated lobbying with permanent and professional corporate pressure groups, such as political action committees (PACS), which contribute money to political campaigns and parties and lobby public officials, leading to a political debate over the influence of money in politics that continues today. Companies also engaged in public relations efforts to burnish their image and funded pro-business research in think tanks and universities (Vogel 1989).

Though Vogel argues that the power of business and opposing groups fluctuates over time, he acknowledges that business interests have been dominant more often than not (1989, p. 7). Power elite theory, free-market economists, and public interest advocates agree that government regulatory agencies are continually subject to the influence of the industries they are supposed to regulate, sometimes known as *co-optation* or *capture*. As a result of frequent interaction, regulators develop a friendly relationship with those they regulate and come to rely on them for information, cooperation, advice on how regulations are written, and sometimes future employment. Regulation originally intended in the public interest is transformed in ways that restrain competition, manage prices, and stabilize markets to the benefit of existing firms in the market. If the political administration depends on the industry for contributions and support, the process may not be so unconscious (Scott 1998, pp. 208, 336ff.).

Nevertheless, the study of social movements within sociology shows that opposing groups can make a difference. Within political sociology, *resource mobilization theory* has shown that under certain conditions, reform or protest groups can affect government policy if they have a strong organization, in the form of a bureaucratic organization, a looser, grass-roots federation or association, or simply strong interpersonal networks and bonds of community, which differ from the meaning of formal organization used in this volume. These kinds of organizations provide resources in the form of money, expertise, and the commitment of large, cohesive groups of supporters. In fact, it is often not the most deprived or aggrieved groups that protest the most, but the best organized and well-organized groups can have an influence greatly disproportionate to their numbers (Morris 1981; Jenkins 1983; Gamson and Schmeidler 1984).

There are debates as to whether a centralized social movement organization with a paid, professional staff is more or less effective than a decentralized, grass-roots movement using committed volunteers. Piven and Cloward argued that mass protest and disruption by the lower class are necessary to gain concessions from government and other institutions. They follow Michels in arguing that movements lose their effectiveness once they have a more bureaucratic organization because protest energy is diverted to organization building and the career concerns of leaders allow it to be more easily incorporated into conventional politics and neutralized or co-opted (Piven and Cloward 1977).

Others argue that more formal organization and professional staff provide benefits, such as more centrally coordinated action, technical expertise, ability to compete with other powerful, bureaucratic interest groups, and maintenance of the movement under difficult conditions, such as when popular participation is low and the indifference or hostility of those with power is great. Indeed, since the late 1960s and early 1970s, the role of professional advocacy groups, often with no actual members, has grown, while more participatory political and social activist groups have receded. Sometimes, professionals in social movement organizations substitute for, conflict with, or discourage volunteer participation, but at other times their role is to recruit volunteers, and they may even encourage greater militancy among the rank and file. A moderately centralized federation of relatively autonomous chapters is one compromise between the competing pressures of bureaucratic organization and popular participation (Jenkins 1983; Gamson and Schmeidler 1984; Staggenborg 1988; Kleidman 1994).

Still, there are powerful barriers to the organization of advocacy and oppositional groups. If the existence of a grievance were sufficient to generate protest and organized action, there would be much more protest than is the case. In principle, everyone has an interest in a clean environment, but only a small fraction of the public is actively involved in national environmental issues, for example. Mancur Olson, an economist, explained lack of popular participation in social movements on the basis of individual self-interest. If the benefits of success, such as a clean environment or preservation of national park land, are a *collective good*, meaning they are available to those who did not work to achieve them as well as those who did, people will not participate because they can "free ride" on the work of others. Because everyone is assumed to be motivated by such calculations of individual costs and benefits, Olson's theory of collective action predicts no one will participate unless the organization also provides some kind of selective or private incentives for participants, as well as the prestige and career benefits to motivate leaders or movement entrepreneurs. This theory discounts the role of group identity, solidarity, and moral commitment, and has been criticized for unrealistically low predictions of the level of social activism (Jenkins 1983). Still, Olson's theory partly explains why most citizens of democracies are passive and why so many popular grievances are not rallying points for organizations or the subject of great political or governmental concern.

The reading by Dan Clawson, Alan Neustadtl, and Denise Scott (Reading 31) describes how corporate political action committees (PACS) exercise political influence in the context of a largely passive democracy. PACS lobby and give campaign contributions to politicians. They can represent both narrow and broader business interests and constituencies. Aside from the simple power of money, they are able to influence government policy through their superior organization relative to citizen's and labor groups and the greater access to politicians to argue their positions which their superior resources afford.

28

MEN AND WOMEN OF THE CORPORATION

ROSABETH MOSS KANTER

NUMBERS: MINORITIES AND MAJORITIES

Up the ranks in Industrial Supply Corporation, one of the most consequential conditions of work for women was also among the simplest to identify: there were so few of them. On the professional and managerial levels, Industrial Supply Corporation was nearly a single-sex organization. Women held less than 10 percent of the exempt (salaried) jobs starting at the bottom grades—a 50 percent rise from a few years earlier—and there were no women at the level reporting to officers. When Indsco was asked to participate in a meeting on women in business by bringing their women executives to a civic luncheon, the corporate personnel committee had no difficulty selecting them. There were only five sufficiently senior women in the organization.

The numerical distributions of men and women at the upper reaches created a strikingly different inter-action context for women than for men. At local and regional meetings, training programs, task forces, casual out-of-the office lunches with colleagues, and career review or planning sessions with managers, the men were overwhelmingly likely to find themselves with a predominance of people of their own type—other men. For men in units with no exempt women, there would be, at most, occasional events in which a handful of women would be present alongside many men. Quite apart from the content of particular jobs and their location in the hierarchy, the culture of corporate administration and the experiences of men in it were influenced by this fact of numerical dominance, by the fact that men were the *many*.

Women, on the other hand, often found themselves alone among male peers. The twenty women in a three hundred-person sales force were scattered over fourteen offices. Their peers, managers, and customers were nearly all men. Never more than two women at a time were found in twelve-person personnel training groups. There was a cluster of professional women on the floor at corporate headquarters housing employee administration and training, but all except three were part of different groups where they worked most closely with men.

The life of women in the corporation was influenced by the proportions in which they found themselves. Those women who were few in number among male peers and often had "only woman" status became tokens: symbols of how-women-can-do, stand-ins for all women. Sometimes they had the advantages of those who are "different" and thus were highly visible in a system where success is tied to becoming known. Sometimes they faced the loneliness of the outsider, of the stranger who intrudes upon an alien culture and may become self-estranged in the process of assimilation. In any case, their turnover and "failure rate" were known to be much higher than those of men in entry and early grade positions; in the sales function, women's turnover was twice that of men. What happened around Indsco women resembled other reports of the experiences of women in politics, law, medicine, or management who have been the few among many men.

At the same time, they also echoed the experiences of people of any kind who are rare and scarce: the lone black among whites, the lone man among women, the few foreigners among natives. Any situation where proportions of significant types of people are highly skewed can produce similar themes and processes. It was rarity and scarcity, rather than femaleness *per se*, that shaped the environment for women in the parts of Indsco mostly populated by men.

The situations of Industrial Supply Corporation men and women, then, point to the significance of numerical distributions for behavior in organizations: how many of one social type are found with how many of another. As proportions begin to shift, so do social experiences.

THE MANY AND THE FEW: THE SIGNIFICANCE OF PROPORTIONS FOR SOCIAL LIFE

[. . .] To understand the dramas of the many and the few in the organization requires a theory and a

vocabulary. Four group types can be identified on the basis of different proportional representations of kinds of people, as Figure 28.1 shows. *Uniform* groups have only one kind of person, one significant social type. The group may develop its own differentiations, of course, but groups called uniform can be considered homogeneous with respect to salient external master statuses such as sex, race, or ethnicity. Uniform groups have a typological ratio of 100:0. *Skewed* groups are those in which there is a large preponderance of one type over another, up to a ratio of perhaps 85:15. The numerically dominant types also control the group and its culture in enough ways to be labeled "dominants." The few of another type in a skewed group can appropriately be called "tokens," for, like the Indsco exempt women, they are often treated as representatives of their category, as symbols rather than individuals. If the absolute size of the skewed group is small, tokens can also be solos, the only one of their kind present; but even if there are two tokens in a skewed group, it is difficult for them to generate an alliance that can become powerful in the group, as we shall see later. Next, *tilted* groups begin to move toward less extreme distributions and less exaggerated effects. In this situation, with ratios of perhaps 65:35, dominants are just a "majority" and tokens become a "minority." Minority members have potential allies among each other, can form coalitions, and can affect the culture of the group. They begin to become individuals differentiated from each other as well as a type differentiated from the majority. Finally, at about 60:40 and down to 50:50, the group becomes *balanced*. Culture and interaction reflect this balance. Majority and minority turn into potential subgroups that may or may not generate actual type-based identifications. Outcomes for individuals in such a balanced peer group, regardless of type, will depend more on other structural and personal factors, including formation of subgroups or differentiated roles and abilities.

It is the characteristics of the second type, the skewed group, that underlay the behavior and treatment of professional and managerial women observed at Indsco. If the ratio of women to men in various parts of the organization begins to shift, as affirmative action and new hiring and promotion policies promised, forms of relationships and peer

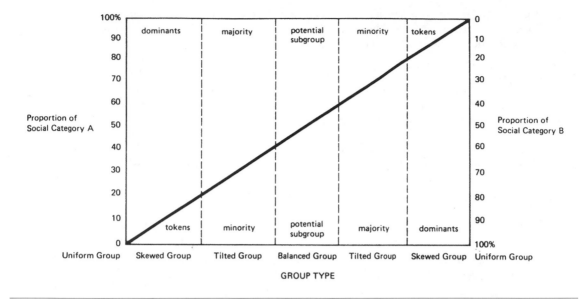

Figure 28.1. Group Types as Defined by Proportional Representation of Two Social Categories in the Membership

culture should also change. But as of the mid-1970s, the dynamics of tokenism predominated in Indsco's exempt ranks, and women and men were in the positions of token and dominant. Tokenism, like low opportunity and low power, set in motion self-perpetuating cycles that served to reinforce the low numbers of women and, in the absence of external intervention, to keep women in the position of token.

VIEWING THE FEW: WHY TOKENS FACE SPECIAL SITUATIONS

The proportional rarity of tokens is associated with three perceptual tendencies: visibility, contrast, and assimilation. These are all derived simply from the ways any set of objects are perceived. If one sees nine X's and one O:

X X X X X X O X X X

the O will stand out. The O may also be overlooked, but if it is seen at all, it will get more notice than any X. Further, the X's may seem more alike than different because of their contrast with the O. And it

will be easier to assimilate the O to generalizations about all O's than to do the same with the X's, which offer more examples and thus, perhaps, more variety and individuation. The same perceptual factors operate in social situations, and they generate special pressures for token women.

First, tokens get attention. One by one, they have higher visibility than dominants looked at alone; they capture a larger awareness share. A group member's awareness share, averaged over other individuals of the same social type, declines as the proportion of total membership occupied by the category increases, because each individual becomes less and less surprising, unique, or noteworthy. . . . But for tokens, there is a "law of increasing returns": as individuals of their type represent a *smaller* numerical proportion of the overall group, they each potentially capture a *larger* share of the awareness given to that group.

Contrast—or polarization and exaggeration of differences—is the second perceptual tendency. In uniform groups, members and observers may never become self-conscious about the common culture and type, which remain taken for granted and implicit. But the presence of a person or two bearing a different set of social characteristics increases the self-consciousness of the numerically dominant population and the consciousness of observers about what makes the dominants a class. They become more aware both of their commonalities and their difference from the token, and to preserve their commonality, they try to keep the token slightly outside, to offer a boundary for the dominants. There is a tendency to exaggerate the extent of the differences between tokens and dominants, because as we see next, tokens are, by definition, too few in numbers to defeat any attempts at generalization. It is thus easier for the commonalities of dominants to be defined in contrast to the token than in tilted or balanced groups. One person can be perceptually isolated and seen as cut off from the core of the group more than many, who begin to represent too great a share of what is called the group.

Assimilation, the third perceptual tendency, involves the use of stereotypes, or familiar generalizations about a person's social type. The characteristics of a token tend to be distorted to fit the generalization. Tokens are more easily stereotyped than people found in greater proportion. If there were enough people of the token's type to let discrepant examples occur, it is eventually possible that the generalization would change to accommodate the accumulated cases. But in skewed groups, it is easier to retain the generalization and distort the perception of the token. It is also easier for tokens to find an instant identity by conforming to the pre-existing stereotypes. So tokens are, ironically, both highly visible as people who are different and yet not permitted the individuality of their own unique, non-stereotypical characteristics.

[. . .]

Visibility, contrast, and assimilation are each associated with particular forces and dynamics that, in turn, generate typical token responses. These dynamics are, again, similar regardless of the category from which the tokens come, although the specific kinds of people and their history of relationships with dominants provide cultural content for specific communications. Visibility tends to create *performance pressures* on the token. Contrast leads to heightening of *dominant culture boundaries*, including isolation of the token. And assimilation results in the token's *role encapsulation*.

The experiences of exempt women at Industrial Supply Corporation took their shape from these processes.

PERFORMANCE PRESSURES: LIFE IN THE LIMELIGHT

Indsco's upper-level women, especially those in sales, were highly visible, much more so than their male peers. Even those who reported they felt ignored and overlooked were known in their immediate divisions and spotted when they did something unusual. *[. . .]*

In the sales force, where peer culture and informal relations were most strongly entrenched, everyone knew about the women. They were the subject of conversation, questioning, gossip, and careful scrutiny. Their placements were known and observed through the division, whereas those of most men typically were not. Their names came up at meetings, and they would easily be used as examples. Travelers to locations with women in it would bring back news of the latest about the women, along with other gossip. In other functions, too, the women developed well-known names, and their characteristics would often be broadcast through the system in anticipation of their arrival in another office to do a piece of work. A woman swore in an elevator in an Atlanta hotel while going to have drinks with colleagues, and it was known all over Chicago a few days later that she was a "radical." And some women were even told by their managers that they were watched more closely than the men. Sometimes the manager was intending to be helpful, to let the woman know that he would be right there behind her. But the net effect was the same as all of the visibility phenomena. Tokens typically performed their jobs under public and symbolic conditions different from those of dominants.

The Two-Edged Sword of Publicity

The upper-level women became public creatures. It was difficult for them to do anything in training programs, on their jobs, or even at informal social affairs that would not attract public notice. This provided the advantage of an attention-getting edge at the same time that it made privacy and anonymity impossible.

[. . .]

Many felt their freedom of action was restricted, and they would have preferred to be less noticeable, as these typical comments indicated: "If it seems good to be noticed, wait until you make your first major mistake." [. . .] "I don't have as much freedom of behavior as men do; I can't be as independent."

On some occasions, tokens were deliberately thrust into the limelight and displayed as showpieces, paraded before the corporation's public but in ways that sometimes violated the women's sense of personal dignity. One of Indsco's most senior women, a staff manager finally given two assistants (and thus managerial responsibilities) after twenty-six years with the company, was among the five women celebrated at the civic lunch for outstanding women in business. A series of calls from high-level officers indicated that the chairman of the board of the corporation wanted her to attend a lunch at a large hotel that day, although she was given no information about the nature of the event. When she threatened not to go unless she was given more information, she was reminded that the invitation had come down from the chairman himself, and of course she would go. On the day of the luncheon, a corsage arrived and, later, a vice-president to escort her. So she went, and found she was there to represent the corporation's "prize women," symbolizing the strides made by women in business. The program for the affair listed the women executives from participating companies, except in the case of Indsco, where the male vice-presidential escorts were listed instead. Pictures were taken for the employee newsletter and, a few days later, she received an inscribed paper-weight as a memento. She told the story a few weeks after the event with visible embarrassment about being "taken on a date. It was more like a senior prom than a business event." And she expressed resentment at being singled out in such a fashion, "just for being a woman at Indsco, not for any real achievement." Similar sentiments were expressed by a woman personnel manager who wanted a pay increase as a sign of the company's appreciation, not her picture in a newspaper, which "gave the company brownie points but cost nothing."

[. . .] Many of the tokens seemed to have developed a capacity often observed among marginal or subordinate peoples: to project a public persona that hid inner feelings. Although some junior management men at Indsco, including several fast trackers, were quite open about their lack of commitment to the company and dissatisfaction with aspects of its style, the women felt they could not afford to voice any negative sentiments. They played by a different set of rules, one that maintained the split between public persona and private self. One woman commented, "I know the company's a rumor factory. You must be careful how you conduct yourself and what you say to whom. I saw how one woman in the office was discussed endlessly, and I decided it would be better to keep my personal life and personal affairs separate." She refused to bring dates to office parties when she was single, and she did not tell anyone at work that she got married until several months later—this was an office where the involvement of wives was routine. [. . .]

Symbolic Consequences

The women were visible as category members, because of their social type. This loaded all of their acts with extra symbolic consequences and gave them the burden of representing their category, not just themselves. Some women were told outright that their performances could affect the prospects of other women in the company. In the men's informal conversations, women were often measured by two yardsticks: how *as women* they carried out the sales or management role; and how *as managers* they lived up to images of womanhood. In short, every act tended to be evaluated beyond its meaning for the organization and taken as a sign of "how women perform." This meant that there was a tendency for problematic situations to be blamed on the woman—on her category membership—rather than on the situation, a phenomenon noted in other reports of few women among many men in high-ranking corporate jobs. In one case of victim-blaming, a woman in sales went to her manager to discuss the handling of a customer who was behaving seductively. The manager jumped to the assumption that the woman had led him on. The result was an angry confrontation between woman and manager in which she thought he was incapable of seeing her apart from his stereotypes, and he said later he felt misunderstood.

Women were treated as symbols or representatives on those occasions when, regardless of their expertise or interest, they would be asked to provide the meeting with "the woman's point of view" or to explain to a manager why he was having certain problems with his women. They were often expected to be speaking for women, not just for themselves, and felt, even in my interviews, that they must preface personal statements with a disclaimer that they were speaking for themselves rather than for women generally. Such individuality was difficult to find when among dominants. But this was not always generated by dominants. Some women seized this chance to be a symbol as an opportunity to get included in particular gatherings or task forces, where they could come to represent all women at Indsco. "Even if you don't want *me* personally," they seemed to be saying to dominants, "you can want me as a symbol." Yet, if they did this, they would always be left with uncertainty about the grounds for their inclusion; they were failing to distinguish themselves as individuals.

[. . .]

The Tokenism Eclipse

The token's visibility stemmed from characteristics—attributes of a master status—that threatened to blot out other aspects of a token's performance. Although the token captured attention, it was often for her discrepant characteristics, for the auxiliary traits that gave her token status. The token does not have to work hard to have her presence noticed, but she does have to work hard to have her achievements noticed. In the sales force, the women found that their technical abilities were likely to be eclipsed by their physical appearances, and thus, an additional performance pressure was created. The women had to put in extra effort to make their technical skills known, and said they worked twice as hard to prove their competence.

[. . .]

Fear of Retaliation

The women were also aware of another performance pressure: not to make the dominants look bad. Tokenism sets up a dynamic that can make tokens afraid of being too outstanding in performance on group events and tasks. When a token does well enough to "show up" a dominant, it cannot be kept a secret, since all eyes are upon the token, and therefore, it is more difficult to avoid the public humiliation of a dominant. Thus, paradoxically, while the token women felt they had to do better than anyone else in order to be seen as competent and allowed to continue, they also felt, in some cases, that their successes would not be rewarded and should be kept to themselves. They needed to toe the fine line between doing just well enough and too well. One woman had trouble understanding this and complained of her treatment by managers. They had fired another woman for not being aggressive enough, she reported; yet she, who succeeded in doing all they asked and brought in the largest amount of new business during the past year, was criticized for being "too aggressive, too much of a hustler."

The fears had some grounding in reality. In a corporate bureaucracy like Indsco, where "peer acceptance" held part of the key to success in securing promotions and prized jobs, it was known how people were received by colleagues as well as by higher management. . . . Getting along well with peers was thus not just something that could make daily life in the company more pleasant; it was also fed into the formal review system.

At a meeting of ten middle managers, two women who differed in peer acceptance were contrasted. One was well liked by her peers even though she had an outstanding record because she did not flaunt her successes and modestly waited her turn to be promoted. She did not trade on her visibility. Her long previous experience in technical work served to certify her and elicit colleague respect, and her pleasant but plain appearance and quiet dress minimized disruptive sexual attributes. The other was seen very differently. The mention of her name as a "star performer" was accompanied by laughter and these comments: "She's infamous all over the country. Many dislike her who have never met her. Everyone's heard of her whether or not they know her, and they already have opinions. There seems to be no problem with direct peer acceptance from people who see her day-to-day, but the publicity she has received for her successes has created a negative climate around her." Some thought she was in need of a lesson for her cockiness and presumption. She was said to be aspiring too high, too soon, and refusing to play the promotion game by the same rules the men had to use: waiting for one's turn, the requisite years' experience and training. Some men at her level found her overrated and were concerned that their opinions be heard before she was automatically pushed ahead. A common prediction was that she would fail in her next assignment and be cut down to size. The managers, in general, agreed that there was backlash if women seemed to advance too fast.

And a number of men were concerned that women would jump ahead of them. They made their resentments known. One unwittingly revealed a central principle for the success of tokens in competition with dominants: to always stay one step behind, never exceed or excell. "It's okay for women to have these jobs," he said, "as long as they don't go zooming by *me*."

[. . .]

Tokens' Responses to Performance Pressures

A manager posed the issue for scarce women this way: "Can they survive the organizational scrutiny?" The choices for those in the token position were either to over-achieve and carefully construct a public performance that minimized organizational and peer concerns, to try to turn the notoriety of publicity to advantage, or to find ways to become socially invisible.

[. . .]

The token must often choose between trying to limit visibility—and being overlooked—or taking advantage of the publicity—and being labeled a "troublemaker."

BOUNDARY HEIGHTENING AND MEMBERSHIP COSTS: TOKENS IN DOMINANTS' GROUPS

Contrast, or exaggeration of the token's differences from dominants, sets a second set of dynamics in motion. The presence of a token or two makes dominants more aware of what they have in common at the same time that it threatens that commonality.

Indeed, it is often at those moments when a collectivity is threatened with change that its culture and bonds become exposed to itself; only when an obvious "outsider" appears do group members suddenly realize aspects of their common bond as insiders. *[. . .]*

Furthermore, as Everett Hughes pointed out, part of the hostility peer groups show to new kinds of people stems from uncertainty about their behavior when non-structured, non-routine events occur. Tokens cannot be assumed to share the same unspoken understandings that the rest of the members, share because of their common membership in a social category, one basis for closing ranks against those who are different. At best, then, members of the dominant category are likely to be uncomfortable and uncertain in the presence of a member of a different category. Other analysts have also shown that people with "incongruent statuses," like women in male jobs, strain group interaction by generating ambiguity and lack of social certitude.[1]

The token's contrast effect, then, can lead dominants to exaggerate both their commonality and the token's "difference." They move to heighten boundaries of which, previously, they might even have been aware. They erect new boundaries that at some times exclude the token or at others let her in only if she proves her loyalty.

Exaggeration of Dominants' Culture

Indsco men asserted group solidarity and reaffirmed shared in-group understandings in the presence of token women, first, by emphasizing and exaggerating those cultural elements they shared in contrast to the token. The token became both occasion and audience for the highlighting and dramatizing of those themes that differentiated her as the outsider. Ironically, tokens, unlike people of their type represented in greater proportion, are thus instruments for under*lining* rather than under*mining* majority culture. At Indsco, this phenomenon was most clearly in operation on occasions that brought together people from many parts of the organization who did not necessarily know each other well, as in training programs and at dinners and cocktail parties during meetings. Here the camaraderie of men, as in other work and social settings,[2] was based in part on tales of sexual adventures, ability with respect to "hunting" and capturing women, and off-color jokes. Other themes involved work prowess and sports, especially golf and fishing. The capacity for and enjoyment of drinking provided the context for displays of these themes. They were dramatized and acted out more fervently in the presence of token women than when only men were present.[3] When the men were alone, they introduced these themes in much milder form and were just as likely to share company gossip or talk of domestic matters such as a house being built. This was also in contrast to more equally mixed male-female groups in which there were a sufficient number of women to influence and change group culture and introduce a new hybrid of conversational themes based on shared male-female concerns.[4]

Around token women, then, men sometimes exaggerated displays of aggression and potency: instances of sexual innuendos, aggressive sexual teasing, and prowess-oriented "war stories." When a woman or two were present, the men's behavior involved "showing off," telling stories in which "masculine prowess" accounted for personal, sexual, or business success.

[. . .]

The women themselves reported other examples of "testing" to see how they would respond to the "male" culture. They said that many sexual innuendos or displays of locker-room humor were put on for their benefit, especially by the younger men. (The older men tended to parade their business successes.) One woman was a team leader at a workshop (and the only woman), when her team decided to use as its slogan, "The [obscenity] of the week," looking at her for a reaction. By raising the issue and forcing the woman to choose not to participate, the men in the group created an occasion for uniting against the outsider and asserting dominant group solidarity. Such events, it must be pointed out, were relatively rare and occurred only at those informal occasions outside of the business routine in which people were unwinding, letting themselves go, or, as in the training role plays, deliberately creating unreal situations. Most behavior at Indsco was more businesslike in tone. But the fact that such interaction ever occurred, even infrequently, around women served to isolate them and make them uncomfortable at those very moments

when, ironically, people were supposed to be relaxing and having fun.

[. . .]

Interruptions as Reminders of "Difference"

On more formal occasions, as in meetings, members of the numerically dominant category underscored and reinforced differences between tokens and dominants, ensuring that tokens recognized their outsider status, by making the token the occasion for "interruptions" in the flow of group events. Dominants prefaced acts with apologies or questions about appropriateness directed at the token; they then invariably went ahead with the act, having placed the token in the position of interrupter or interloper, of someone who took up the group's time. This happened often in the presence of the saleswomen. Men's questions or apologies represented a way of asking whether the old or expected cultural rules were still operative—the words and expressions permitted, the pleasures and forms of release indulged in. (Can we still swear? Toss a football? Use technical jargon? Go drinking? Tell "in" jokes?) Sometimes the questions seemed motivated by a sincere desire to put the women at ease and treat them appropriately, but the net effect was the same regardless of dominants' intentions. By posing these questions overtly, dominants made the culture clear to tokens, stated the terms under which tokens enter the relationship, and reminded them that they were special people. It is a dilemma of all cross-cultural interaction that the very act of attempting to learn what to do in the presence of the different kind of person so as to integrate him can reinforce differentiation.

[. . .] Most women did not want to make a fuss, especially about issues they considered trivial and irrelevant to their job status, like saying "goddamn" or how to open doors. Their interest in not being signaled out for special treatment made them quickly agree that things should proceed as they would if women were not present, and to feel embarrassment about stopping the flow of conversation. None wanted to be a "wet blanket"! As one said, "They make obscene suggestions for slogans when kidding around, looking to me for a reaction. Then they jump on me for not liking it."

Secondly, the tokens have been put on notice that interaction will not be "natural," that dominants will be "holding back," unless they agree to acknowledge and permit (and even encourage) majority cultural expressions in their presence. (It is important that this be stated, of course, for one never knows that another is holding back unless the other lets a piece of the suppressed material slip out.) At the same time, tokens have also been given the implicit message that majority members do *not* expect those forms of expression to be "natural" to the tokens' home culture; otherwise, majority members would not need to raise the question. Thus, the saleswomen were often in the odd position of reassuring peers and customers that they could go ahead and do something in the women's presence, like swearing, that the women themselves would not be permitted to do. They listened to dirty jokes, for example, but reported that they would not dare tell one themselves. In fact, whether or not to go drinking or tell jokes was a major question for women: "You can't tell dirty jokes. Clean jokes would go over like a lead balloon. So I sit there like a dummy and don't tell jokes."

Via difference-reminding interruptions, then, dominants both affirm their own shared understandings and draw the cultural boundary between themselves and tokens. The tokens learned that they caused interruptions in "normal" communication, and that their appropriate position was more like that of audience than that of full participant. But the women also found the audience position frustrating or wearying, as these statements indicated: "I felt like one of the guys for a while. Then I got tired of it. They had crude mouths and were very immature. I began to dread the next week because I was tired of their company. Finally, when we were all out drinking, I admitted to myself, this is not me; I don't want to play their game." And: "I was at a dinner where the men were telling dirty jokes. It was fun for a while; then it got to me. I moved and tried to have a real conversation with a guy at the other end of the table. The dinner started out as a comrade thing, but it loses its flavor, especially if you're the only woman. I didn't want them to stop on my account, but I wish I had had an alternative conversation."

Overt Inhibition: Informal Isolation

In some cases, dominants did not wish to have tokens around all the time; they had secrets to preserve or simply did not know how far they could trust the women, especially those who didn't seem to play by all the rules. They thus moved the locus of some activities and expressions from public settings to which tokens had access to more private settings from which they could be excluded. When information potentially embarrassing or damaging to dominants is being exchanged, an outsider-audience is not desirable, because dominants do not know how far they can trust the tokens. [. . .]

The result was sometimes "quarantine"—keeping tokens away from some occasions. Informal pre-meeting meetings were sometimes held. Some topics of discussion seemed rarely raised by men in the presence of many of their women peers, even though they discussed them among themselves: admissions of low commitment to the company or concerns about job performance, ways of getting around formal rules, political plotting for mutual advantage, strategies for impressing certain corporate executives. Many of the women did not tend to be included in the networks by which informal socialization occurred and politics behind the formal system were exposed, as researchers have found in other settings. One major project found that people with incongruent statuses, like the Indsco exempt women, were likely to become isolates in peer groups and to have less frequent interaction with the group than other members, outside of formally structured occasions.[5]

[. . .]

Loyalty Tests

At the same time that tokens may be kept on the periphery of colleague interaction, they may also be expected to demonstrate loyalty to their dominant peers. Failure to do so could result in further isolation; signs of loyalty, on the other hand, permitted the token to come closer to being included in more of the dominants' activities. Through loyalty tests, the group sought reassurance that the tokens would not turn against the dominants or use any of the information gained through their viewing of the dominants' world to do harm to the group. In the normal course of peer interactions, people learn all sorts of things about each other that could be turned against the other. Indeed, many colleague relationships are often solidified by the reciprocal knowledge of potentially damaging bits of information and the understanding that they both have an interest in preserving confidentiality. Tokens, however, pose a different problem and raise uncertainties, for their membership in a different social category could produce loyalties outside the peer cadre.

This was a quite rational concern on occasion. With government pressures and public interest mounting, Indsco women were often asked to speak to classes or women's groups or to testify before investigating committees. One woman was called in by her manager before her testimony at hearings on discrimination against women in business; he wanted to hear her testimony in advance and have censorship rights. She refused, but then made only very general and bland statements at the hearing anyway.

Dominants also want to know that tokens will not use their inside information to make the dominants look bad or turn them into figures of fun to members of the token's category outside with whom they must interact. The joking remarks men made when seeing women colleagues occasionally eating with the secretaries (e.g., "What do you 'girls' find so interesting to talk about?") revealed some of their concerns.

Assurance could be gained by asking tokens to join with or identify with the dominants against those who represented competing loyalties; in short, dominants pressured tokens to turn against members of their own category, just as occurred in other situations where women were dominants and men tokens.[6] If tokens colluded, they made themselves psychological hostages to the majority group. For token women, the price of being "one of the boys" was a willingness to occasionally turn against "the girls."

There were three ways token women at Indsco could demonstrate loyalty and qualify for a closer relationship with dominants. First, they could let slide (or even participate in) statements prejudicial to other members of their category. They could allow themselves to be viewed as "exceptions" to the "general rule" that others of their category have a variety of undesirable or unsuitable characteristics;

Hughes recognized this as one of the "deals" token blacks might make for membership in white groups.[7] Women who did well were sometimes told they were "exceptions" and exceptional, not like a "typical woman." It is an irony of the token situation that women could be treated as both representatives of their type and exceptions to it, sometimes by the same people.

At meetings and training sessions, women were occasionally the subjects of ridicule or joking remarks about their incompetence. Some of the women who were insulated by such innuendos found it easier to appear to agree than to start an argument. A few accepted the dominants' view fully. One of the first saleswomen denied in interviews having any special problems because she was a woman, calling herself "skilled at coping with a man's world," and said the company was right not to hire more women. Women, she said, were unreliable and likely to quit; furthermore, young women might marry men who would not allow them to work. (She herself quit a few years later.) In this case, a token woman was taking over "gatekeeping" functions for dominants, letting them appear free of prejudice while a woman acted to exclude other women.[8]

Tokens could also demonstrate loyalty by allowing themselves and their category to provide a source of humor for the group. Just as Hughes found that the initiation of blacks into white groups might involve accepting the role of comic inferior,[9] Indsco women faced constant pressures to allow jokes at the expense of women, to accept "kidding" from the men around them. When a woman objected, the men denied any hostility or unfriendly intention, instead accusing the woman, by inference, of "lacking a sense of humor." In order to cope, one woman reported, she "learned to laugh when they try to insult you with jokes, to let it roll off your back." Tokens could thus find themselves colluding with dominants through shared laughter.

Thirdly, tokens could demonstrate their gratitude for being included by not criticizing their situation or pressing for any more advantage. One major taboo area involved complaints about the job or requests for promotion. The women were supposed to be grateful for getting as far as they had (when other women clearly had *not*) and thus expected to bury dissatisfaction or aspirations.

Responses of Tokens to Boundary Heightening

The dilemma posed here for tokens was how to reconcile their awareness of difference generated by informal interaction with dominants with the need, in order to belong, to suppress dominants' concerns about the difference. As with performance pressures, peer group interaction around the tokens increased the effort required for a satisfactory public appearance, sometimes accompanied by distortions of private inclinations.

Of course, not all men participated in the dynamics noted. And some tokens managed to adapt very well. They used the same kind of language and expressed the same kinds of interests as many of the men. One woman loved fishing, she said, so when she came on as a manager and her office was concerned that that would end fishing trips, she could show them they had nothing to fear. Another had a boat on which she could take customers (along with her husband and their wives). A professional woman joined the men on "woman hunts," taking part in conversations in which the pro's and con's of particular targets were discussed. There were women known to be able to "drink the men under the table." It was never clear what the psychic toll of such accommodation was—whether, for example, such people would have made different choices in a balanced context—for they were also unlikely to talk about having any problems at all in their situation; they assumed they were full members.

Numerical skewing and polarized perceptions left tokens with little choice about accepting the culture of dominants. There were too few other people of the token's kind to generate a "counterculture" or to develop a shared intergroup culture. Tokens had to approach the group as single individuals. They thus had two general response possibilities. They could accept isolation, remaining only an audience for certain expressive acts of dominants. This strategy sometimes resulted in friendly but distant peer relations, with the risk of exclusion from occasions on which informal socialization and political activity took place. Or they could try to become insiders, proving their loyalty by defining themselves as exceptions and turning against their own social category.

[. . .]

To turn against others of one's kind (and thus risk latent self-hatred) can by a psychic cost of membership in a group dominated by another culture.

ROLE ENCAPSULATION

Tokens can never really be seen as they are, and they are always fighting stereotypes, because of a third tendency. The characteristics of tokens as individuals are often distorted to fit preexisting generalizations about their category as a group— what I call "assimilation." Such stereotypical assumptions about what tokens "must" be like, such mistaken attributions and biased judgments, tend to force tokens into playing limited and caricatured roles. This constrains the tokens but is useful for dominant group members. Whatever ambiguity there might be around a strange person is reduced by providing a stereotyped and thus familiar place for tokens in the group, allowing dominants to make use of already-learned expectations and modes of action, like the traditional ways men expect to treat women. Familiar roles and assumptions, further, can serve to keep tokens in a bounded place and out of the mainstream of interaction where the uncertainties they arouse might be more difficult to handle. In short, tokens become encapsulated in limited roles that give them the security of a "place" but constrain their areas of permissible or rewarded action.

Status Leveling

Tokens were often initially misperceived as a result of their numerical rarity. *[. . .]* Thus, women exempts at Indsco, like other tokens, encountered many instances of "mistaken identity"—first impressions that they were occupying a *usual female* position rather than their *unusual* (for a woman) job. In the office, they were often taken for secretaries; on sales trips on the road, especially when they traveled with a male colleague, they were often taken for wives or mistresses; with customers, they were first assumed to be temporarily substituting for a man who was the "real" salesperson; with a male peer at meetings, they were seen as the assistant; when entertaining customers, they were assumed to be the wife or date.

[. . .]

The Woman's Slot

There was also a tendency to encapsulate women and to maintain generalizations by defining special roles for women, even on the managerial and professional levels, that put them slightly apart as colleagues. Again, it was easy to do this with a small number and would have been much harder with many more women spilling over the bounds of such slots. A woman could ensure her membership by accepting a special place but then find herself confined by it. Once women began to occupy certain jobs, those jobs sometimes gradually came to be defined as "women's slots." One personnel woman at Indsco pointed this out. In her last career review, she had asked to be moved, feeling that, in another six months, she would have done and learned all she could in her present position and was ready to be upgraded. "They [the managers] told me to be patient; if I waited a year or two longer, they had just the right job for me, three grades up. I knew what they had in mind. Linda Martin [a senior woman] would be retiring by then from a benefits administration job, and they wanted to give it to me because it was considered a place to put a woman. But it had no *real* responsibilities despite its status; it was all routine work."

Affirmative action and equal employment opportunity jobs were also seen as "women's jobs." Many women, who would otherwise be interested in the growth and challenge they offered, said that they would not touch such a position: "The label makes it a dead end. It's a way of putting us out to pasture." There was no way to test the reality of such fears, given the short time the jobs had been in existence, but it could be observed that women who worked on women's personnel or training issues were finding it hard to move out into other areas. These women also found it hard to interest some other, secretly sympathetic managerial women in active advocacy of upward mobility for women because of the latter's own fears of getting too identified with a single issue. (Others, though, seized on it as a way to express their values or to get visibility.)

[. . .]

Stereotyped Informal Roles

Dominants can incorporate tokens and still preserve their generalizations by inducting tokens into stereotypical roles that preserve familiar forms of interaction between the kinds of people represented by the token and the dominants. In the case of token women in colleague groups at Indsco, four informal role traps were observed, all of which encapsulated the tokens in a category the men could respond to and understand. *[. . .]*

Mother. A token woman sometimes found that she became a "mother" to men in the group. One by one, they brought her their private troubles, and she was expected to comfort them. The assumption that women are sympathetic, good listeners and easy to talk to about one's problems was common, even though, ironically, men also said it was hard to level with women over task-related issues. One saleswoman was constantly approached by her all-male peers to listen to their problems with their families. In a variety of residential training groups, token women were observed acting out other parts of the traditional nurturant-maternal role: doing laundry, sewing on buttons for men.

[. . .]

As long as she is in the scarce position of token, however, it is unlikely that nurturance, support, and expressivity will be valued or that a mother can demonstrate and be rewarded for critical, independent, task-oriented behaviors.

Seductress. The role of seductress or sexual object is fraught with more tension than the maternal role, for it introduces an element of sexual competition and jealousy. The mother can have many sons; it is more difficult for the sexually attractive to have many swains. Should the woman cast as sex object (that is, seen as sexually desirable and potentially available—seductress is a perception, and the woman herself may not be consciously behaving seductively) share her attention widely, she risks the debasement of the whore. Yet, should she form a close alliance with any man in particular, she arouses resentment, particularly so because she represents a scarce resource; there are just not enough women to go around.

Ju Chinese culture also "iron"

In several situations I observed, a high status male allied himself with the seductress and acted as her "protector," partly because of his promise of rescue from sex-charged overtures of the rest of the men as well as because of his high status *per se*. The powerful male (staff member, manager, sponsor, etc.) could easily become the "protector" of the still "virgin" seductress, gaining through masking his own sexual interest what the other men could not gain by declaring theirs. However, this removal of the seductress from the sexual marketplace contained its own problems. The other men could resent the high-status male for winning the prize and resent the woman for her ability to get an "in" with the high-status male that they could not obtain as men. Although the seductress was rewarded for her femaleness and insured attention from the group, then, she was also the source of considerable tension; and needless to say, her perceived sexuality blotted out all other characteristics.

[. . .]

Pet. The "pet" was adopted by the male group as a cute, amusing little thing and symbolically taken along on group events as mascot—a cheerleader for shows of prowess. Humor was often a characteristic of the pet. She was expected to admire the male displays but not to enter into them; she cheered from the sidelines. Shows of competence on her part were treated as special and complimented just because they were unexpected (and the compliments themselves can be seen as reminders of the expected rarity of such behavior). One woman reported that when she was alone in a group of men and spoke at length on an issue, comments to her by men after the meeting often referred to her speech-making ability rather than the content of what she said (e.g., "You talk so fluently"), whereas comments the men made to one another were almost invariably content- or issue-oriented. Competent acts that are taken for granted when performed by males were often unduly "fussed over" when performed by exempt women, considered precocious or precious—a kind of look-what-she-did-and-she's-only-a-woman attitude. Such attitudes on the part of men encouraged self-effacing, girlish responses on the part of solitary women (who, after all, may be genuinely relieved to be included and petted) and prevented them from realizing or demonstrating their own power and competence.

Iron Maiden. The "iron maiden" is a contemporary variation of the stereotypical roles into which strong women are placed. Women who failed to fall into any of the first three roles and, in fact, resisted overtures that would trap them in a role (such as flirtation) might consequently be responded to as "tough" or dangerous. (One woman manager developed such a reputation in company branches throughout the country.) If a token insisted on full rights in the group, if she displayed competence in a forthright manner, or if she cut off sexual innuendos, she could be asked, "You're not one of those women's libbers, are you?" Regardless of the answer, she was henceforth regarded with suspicion, undue and exaggerated shows of politeness (by inserting references to women into conversations, by elaborate rituals of *not* opening doors), and with distance, for she was demanding treatment as an equal in a setting in which no person of her kind had previously been an equal. Women inducted into the "iron maiden" role were stereotyped as tougher than they are (hence the name) and trapped in a more militant stance than they might otherwise take. Whereas seductresses and pets, especially, incurred protective responses, iron maidens faced abandonment. They were left to flounder on their own and often could not find peers sympathetic to them when they had problems.

Responses of Tokens to Role Encapsulation

[. . .] It was also often easier to accept stereotyped roles than to fight them, even if their acceptance meant limiting the tokens' range of expressions or demonstrations of task competence, because they offered a comfortable and certain position. The personal consequence for tokens, of course, was a measure of self-distortion. . . . Submissiveness, frivolity, or other attributes may be feigned by people who feel they are prescribed by the dominant organizational culture.[10] *[. . .]*

The analysis also suggests another way in which tokenism can be self-perpetuating: acceptance of role encapsulation and attendant limitations on demonstration of competence may work to keep down the numbers of women in the upper ranks of the organization, thus continuing to put people in token positions. Role encapsulation confirms dominants' stereotypes and proves to them how right they were all along. On the other hand, some women try to stay away from the role traps by bending over backwards not to exhibit any characteristics that would reinforce stereotypes. This strategy, too, is an uneasy one, for it takes continual watchful effort, and it may involve unnatural self-distortion. Finally, token women must steer a course between protectiveness and abandonment. Either they allow other people to take over and fight their battles for them, staying out of the main action in stereotypical ways, or they stand much too alone. They may be unable by virtue of scarcity even to establish effective support systems of their own.

HOW MANY ARE ENOUGH?: THE TWO-TOKEN SITUATION

The examination of numerical effects leads to the additional question of tipping points: How many of a category are enough to change a person's status from token to full group member? When does a group move from skewed to tipped to balanced? What is the impact for a woman of the presence of another?

In the exempt ranks of Indsco, there were a number of instances of situations in which two rather than one woman were found among male peers, but still constituted less than 20 percent of the group. Despite Solomon Asch's classic laboratory finding that one potential ally can be enough to reduce the power of the majority of secure conformity,[11] in the two-token situation in organizations, dominants several times behaved in ways that defeated an alliance between the two women. This was done through setting up invidious comparisons. One woman was characteristically set up as superior, and the other as inferior—exaggerating traits in both cases. One was identified as the success, the other as the failure. The one given the success label felt relieved to be included and praised, recognizing that alliance with the identified failure would jeopardize her acceptance. The consequence, in one office, was that the identified success stayed away from the other woman and did not give her any help with her performance, withholding criticism she had heard that might have been useful, and the second woman soon left. In another case, a layer of the hierarchy

was inserted between two women who were at the same level: one was made the boss of the other, causing great strain between them. Dominants also could defeat alliances, paradoxically, by trying to promote them. Two women in a training group of twelve were treated as though they were an automatic pair, and other group members felt that they were relieved of responsibility for interacting with or supporting the women. The women reacted to this forced pairing by trying to create difference and distance between them and becoming extremely competitive. Thus, structural circumstances and pressures from the majority could further produce what appeared to be intrinsically prejudicial responses of women to each other. There were also instances in which two women developed a close alliance and refused to be turned against each other. Strong identification with the feminist cause or with other women was behind such alliances. Allied, two tokens could reduce some of the pressures and avoid some of the traps in their position. They could share the burden of representing womankind, and they could each be active on some pieces of "the woman's slot" while leaving time free to demonstrate other abilities and interests. Two women personnel trainers, for example, on a six-person staff, could share responsibility for programs on women without either of them becoming over-identified with it.

A mere shift in *absolute* numbers, then, as from one to two tokens, could potentially reduce stresses in a token's situation even while *relative* numbers of women remained low. But two were also few enough to be rather easily divided and kept apart. It would appear that larger numbers are necessary for supportive alliances to develop in the token context.

EFFECTS ON TOKENS AS INDIVIDUALS: STRESSES AND COSTS IN THE TOKEN SITUATION

The point is not that all of these things happen to token women, or that they happen only to people who are tokens. Some young men at Indsco complained that as new-hires they, too, felt performance pressures, uncertainties about their acceptance, and either over-protected or abandoned. But these issues were part of a transitional status out of which new-hires soon passed, and, in any event, men did not so routinely or dramatically encounter them. Similarly, age and experience helped women make a satisfactory accommodation, and over time, many women settled into comfortable and less token-like patterns. Some said that there was no problem they could not handle with time and that the manifestations of discrimination in their jobs were trivial. But still, the issues stemming from rarity and scarcity arose for women in every new situation, with new peers, and at career transitions. Even successful women who reported little or no discrimination said that they felt they had to "work twice as hard" and expend more energy than the average man to succeed. It is also clear that not all women in the token situation behave alike or engender the same responses in others. There was variety in the individual choices, and there were alternative strategies for managing the situation. But a system characteristic—the numerical proportion in women and men were found—set limits on behavioral possibilities and defined the context for peer interaction.

[. . .]

EXTENSIONS AND ORGANIZATIONAL IMPLICATIONS

[. . .] People's treatment, then, is not automatically fixed by inflexible characteristics but depends on their numbers in a particular situation. Change in the behavior and treatment of women in token positions is strongly tied to shifting proportions. But to argue for the importance of numbers smacks of advocacy of quotas, and many Americans object to quotas. Quantitative limits on expansion (which is how quotas are seen: not as more jobs for women, but fewer for men) have always seemed objectionable to some in the United States, especially when "individual rights" for the advantaged are involved, as shown in concerns over gasoline rationing or income ceilings. Yet, it seems clear that numbers, especially relative numbers, can strongly affect a person's fate in an organization. This is a *system* rather than an individual construct—located not in characteristics of the person but in how many people, like that person in significant ways, are also present. *System*

phenomena require *system-level intervention* to make change.

In the absence of external pressures for change, *tokenism is a self-perpetuating system.* Tokens of Type O who are successful in their professional roles face pressures and inducements to dissociate themselves from other O's, and thus they may fail to promote, or even actively block, the entry of more O's. At the same time, tokens who are less than successful and appear less than fully competent confirm the organization's decision not to recruit more O's, unless they are extraordinarily competent and not like most O's. And since just a few O's can make the X-majority people feel uncomfortable, X's will certainly not go out of their way to include more O's. In short, outside intervention is required to break the cycles created by the social composition of groups.

Most arguments made in favor of numerical guidelines in hiring and job placement limit their own effectiveness by making only part of the case. They say that *equality of opportunity* is the goal, but that this goal is hard to measure without *proof of outcome.* Therefore, numbers hired serve as a shorthand for, a measure of, non-discrimination in selection. However, there is also a strong case that can be made for number-balancing as a worthwhile goal in itself, because, inside the organization, relative numbers can play a large part in further outcomes—from work effectiveness and promotion prospects to psychic distress.

NOTES

1. The Hughes citation is to Everett Hughes, *Men and Their Work* (Glencoe, Illinois: Free Press, 1958), p. 109. See also Hughes, "Dilemmas and Contradictions of Status," *American Journal of Sociology*, 50 (March 1944): pp. 353–59. Judith Lorber came to some similar conclusions in "Trust, Loyalty, and the Place of Women in the Informal Organization of Work," presented at the 1975 Meetings of the American Sociological Association. On "status incongruence" as an explanatory variable in group member behavior, used in many of the same ways I use "tokenism" but without the explicit numerical connotations, see A. Zaleznik, C. R. Christensen, and F. J. Roethlisberger, *The Motivation, Productivity, and Satisfaction of Workers: A Prediction Study* (Boston: Harvard Business School Division of Research, 1958), especially pp. 56–68.

2. Jeane Kirkpatrick, *Political Woman* (New York: Basic Books, 1974), p. 113; Lionel Tiger, *Men in Groups* (New York: Random House, 1969).

3. Clearly I was limited in first-hand observations of how the men acted when alone, since, by definition, if I, as a female researcher, were present, they would not have been alone. For my data here I relied on tape recordings of several meetings in which the tape was kept running even during breaks, and on informants' reports immediately after informal social events and about meetings.

4. For supportive laboratory evidence, see Elizabeth Aries, *Interaction Patterns and Themes of Male, Female, and Mixed Groups*, Unpublished Doctoral Dissertation, Harvard University, 1973. Her work is discussed further in Appendix II.

5. Zaleznik et al., *Motivation, Productivity, and Satisfaction of Workers;* Hennig, *Career Development for Women Executives*; Epstein, *Woman's Place;* Brigid O'Farrell, "Affirmative Action and Skilled Craft Work," Unpublished Report, Cambridge, Mass., 1973 (available from Center for Research on Women, Wellesley College);
Carol Wolman and Hal Frank, "The Solo Woman in a Professional Peer Group," *American Journal of Orthopsychiatry*, 45 (January 1975): pp. 164–71.

6. Bernard E. Segal, "Male Nurses: A Study in Status Contradiction and Prestige Loss," *Social Forces*, 41 (October 1962): pp. 31–38. Personal interviews were used as a supplement.

7. Hughes, "Dilemmas and Contradictions of Status."

8. Laws, "Psychology of Tokenism."

9. Everett C. Hughes, "Race Relations in Industry," in *Industry and Society*, W. F. Whyte, ed. (New York: McGraw-Hill, 1946), p. 115.

10. John C. Athanassiades, "An Investigation of Some Communication Patterns of Female Subordinates in Hierarchical Organizations," *Human Relations*, 27 (1974): pp. 195–209.

11. Solomon E. Asch, "Effects of Group Pressure on the Modification and Distortion of Judgment," in *Group Dynamics*, second edition, D. Cartwright and A. Zander, eds. (Evanston, Illinois: Row Peterson, 1960), pp. 189–200.

29

BLACK MOBILITY IN WHITE CORPORATIONS

Up the Corporate Ladder But Out on a Limb

SHARON M. COLLINS

Spurred in part by threats of federal sanctions, white companies during the 1960s and 1970s incorporated a new echelon of college-educated blacks into previously closed managerial job and business-related professions (Farley 1984; Freeman 1981, 1976a, 1976b; Landry 1987). Indeed, the 1960s witnessed the reversal of a long-standing pattern of declining black-white income ratios with levels of education—and the ratio of black-to-white income rose most rapidly for managers. Employed black men, in particular, were in greater demand for prestigious occupations in the labor market. In 1960, only about 7 percent of non-white male college graduates were managers, compared with 18 percent of college-educated white men (Freeman 1976b). Between 1960 and 1970, the proportion of black male college graduates employed as managers increased almost twofold over the 1960 level (Freeman 1976b). And between 1970 and 1980, the number of black men holding executive, administrative, or managerial jobs increased each year at twice the rate of white men (Farley and Allen 1987).

Yet, even after more than 30 years of social and political pressure to diversify corporate manpower and management teams, the net result is more black managers but negligible gain for black men in the decision-making strongholds of white corporate America (Chicago Urban League 1977; Heidrick and Struggles 1979; Korn/Ferry 1986; 1990; Theodore and Taylor 1991). Despite gains in entry, African-Americans clearly stagnate in their climb up the managerial hierarchy, thereby failing to make inroads into key decision-making positions and in the racial redistribution of power.

Against a backdrop of sustained inequality in corporate job allocation, this paper asks whether constraints to blacks' corporate progress are manufactured in the work process. In the 1960s and 1970s, highly educated blacks experienced less discrimination in access to higher-paying corporate jobs, yet we know little about their careers. Nkomo and Cox (1990) examine macro- and micro-level variables related to job promotion; Kraiger and Ford (1985) focus on discrimination in performance evaluation; and others survey black managers' perceptions of corporate life (Jones 1986; Irons and Moore 1985). The responsibilities and assignments accorded black managers in the post-entry period are a crucial but neglected element for analysis.

This paper explores the problem of race and corporate mobility. It uses a unique data set: in-depth interviews with 76 of the most successful black executives employed in major Chicago-based white corporations in 1986. These black achievers in traditionally closed managerial occupations have had the greatest chance to enter into the higher echelons of organizations in functions tied to profitability. I explore the repercussions of a corporate division of labor on the career development of these managers.

Neoclassical economic theories and social structural explanations of race-based inequality in labor markets often are argued as oppositional insights. That is, human capital theory in economic literature and status attainment theory in sociology presume that economic progress among blacks is a color-blind function of supply-side characteristics such as education, ability, and individual preferences—not race conscious social forces and barriers. The lack of marketable skills, a dependent mentality, inferior education, and even relatively lower IQs are reasons for blacks' inability to gain parity with whites (Herrnstein and Murray 1994; Murray 1984; Smith and Welch 1983, 1986; Sowell 1983).

The opposing contention is that individuals' economic attainments are determined by structural aspects of the labor market. This alternate viewpoint attributes people's limited progress to the characteristics of their jobs (Doeringer and Piore 1971; Thurow 1975). Minorities and women, for example,

fill occupational niches that are in decline or that do not lead to advancement (Ghiloni 1987; Kanter 1977; Reskin and Roos 1990). Consequently, powerful and prestigious jobs with career growth opportunities—managerial jobs, in particular—are much more likely to be filled by white men. In contrast, insights from my study of black managers in the white private sector cast social structure and human capital as interactive, not as mutually exclusive explanatory schemes.

In this paper, I illustrate how a link between opportunity structure and human capital shaped subjects' abilities to achieve top jobs. In general, I view the managerial division of labor as mediating human capital. Therefore, these factors interactively influence blacks' progress in executive arenas. First, I argue that Chicago corporations deployed highly educated black labor out of mainstream positions and into "racialized" jobs. These are jobs created or reoriented during the 1960s and 1970s to carry out pro-black governmental policies and mediate black-related issues for white-owned companies. Affirmative action, urban affairs, community relations, and purchasing jobs are examples. Next, I show the impact of filling these jobs on executives' upward mobility. Initially, these jobs annointed black job holders with positive status in a company, thus attracting black talent. Over time, however, this structure of opportunity underdeveloped the human capital that corporations value. Consequently, racialized jobs marginalized the job holder's skills and, thus, the job holder. Ultimately, occupants' probability of moving into, competing for, and/or performing in, corporate areas that lead to decision-making positions (that is, general management, sales/marketing, production, finance/accounting, and human resources) was greatly diminished.

THE STUDY

I considered blacks to be "top executives" if: 1) they were employed in a banking institution and had a title of comptroller, trust officer, vice-president (excluding "assistant" vice president), president or chief officer; or 2) they were employed in a non-financial institution as department manager, director, vice president, or chief officer. In the mid-1980s, the respondents in this study held some of the more desirable and prestigious positions in Chicago's major corporations. About two-thirds (52) had the title of director or higher, including three chief officers, 30 vice presidents, and 19 unit directors. (The total includes three people with the title "manager" whose rank within the organization was equivalent to director.) The participants in this study were among the highest-ranking black executives in the country. Five of the executives interviewed were the highest-ranking blacks in corporations nation-wide. Almost half (32) were among the highest-ranking black in a company's nationwide management structure.

[. . .]

I distinguished two types of jobs held by blacks in white corporations: racialized and mainstream. A job was coded "racialized" when its description indicated an actual and/or symbolic connection to black communities, to black issues, or to civil rights agencies at any level of government. For example, one respondent was hired by the chief executive officer of a major retailer in 1968 specifically to eradicate discriminatory employment practices used in the personnel department. I coded this job "racialized" because it was designed to improve black opportunities in the company at a time when the federal government increasingly was requiring it.

In contrast, jobs in line and support areas that lack racial implications in a company were coded "mainstream." In this category, functions relate to total constituencies, and neither explicit nor implicit connections to blacks could be found in the job description. A vice president and regional sales manager for a *Fortune* 500 company in the manufacturing and retail food industry provides an illustration of a career consisting of mainstream jobs. A *Fortune* 15 East Coast oil company hired this manager as a market researcher in 1961; his job involved marketing only to the total (predominantly white) consumer market, not to "special" (predominantly black) markets. He was not assigned to black territories as a salesman nor as a sales manager although, he said, "Those kinds of things even happen now [and once] happened a lot." This manager was not responsible for a predominantly black sales force, nor for sales and marketing to the black community when he managed geographical areas.

In this paper, the "mainstream" is the pipeline of line and support jobs leading to senior executive positions that oversee the strategic planning, human resource/personnel development, or production components of a company. For example, the manager just cited moved up the mainstream sales hierarchy from salesman to sales manager, from zone manager to district manager, from area manager to division manager and, finally, to his current position as a firm officer. Granted, the pipeline narrows as it moves upward, yet the flow of occupants into these jobs fills the executive vice president, senior vice president, group vice president, functional vice president, and corporate specialist slots that comprise company officers. The typical track to top jobs in major corporations is through profit-oriented positions, such as sales, operations, and finance or, to a lesser degree through personnel or public relations (Korn/Ferry 1990).

A CORPORATE DIVISION OF LABOR

The corporate division of labor found among Chicago's top black executives is distinctly different than job patterns found among their white peers. In this study, African American executives with mainstream careers in the private sector stand out as the exception, not the rule. Only one-third (25) of the people I interviewed built careers that consisted entirely of mainstream jobs. On the other hand, 12 (16 percent) had one racialized job and about half (39) had two or more racialized jobs. One vice president and company director was a company ombudsman during the 1970s whose task was, he said, to "promote the visibility and good name" of the bank in the black community in Chicago. A second vice president built a career interspersed with black community relations jobs during the late 1960s and 1970s that, he said, "develop[ed] a good corporate citizenship image among blacks and . . . work[ed] with . . . local [black] agencies." A third vice president spent part of his tenure in an urban affairs job. He said:

> After the civil disorders, the riots . . . there was a tremendous movement . . . to have black [representation in the company]. Basically [my] job was to work with the [company] and come up with minority candidates.

To obtain a rough comparative illustration of black and white executive careers, I conducted an informal survey of top white executives by asking 20 CEOs of major Chicago private sector companies if they ever held affirmative action or urban affairs jobs. (I asked about these jobs specifically because they exemplify racialized jobs.) Only one had (or admitted having) a job in either of these areas. Some CEOs even seemed startled by the question. The CEO that had worked in urban affairs performed different tasks than those performed by my respondents. Although this man represented the company on several city-wide committees to improve race relations, his job, unlike the black executives I interviewed, was a part-time, temporary assignment, not a full-time, permanent position. The results of my informal survey suggest that—among the managerial elite in Chicago—blacks are likely to have held racialized jobs, but whites are not.

Disparate career patterns are not attributable to educational differences. Indeed, African American respondents' educational level closely parallel that of white male senior-level executives in 1986. Ninety-four percent of top executives in *Fortune 500* companies surveyed by Korn/Ferry (1986) had bachelors' degrees, and 42 percent had graduate degrees. Eighty-nine percent of respondents in my study had at least a bachelor's degree when they entered the private sector. Over one-third (38 percent) earned advanced degrees. Moreover, their level of education is well above the median level of about one year of college for salaried male managers in 1960 and in 1970 (U.S. Bureau of Census 1960, 1973). In addition, slightly more than one-half of the black graduates I interviewed received their college degrees from predominantly white institutions.

Career differences are not extensions of respondents' ports of entry into the private sector. Almost one-half of 45 people who filled affirmative action and urban affairs jobs started in the corporate mainstream with line positions. Therefore, black but not white managerial careers reflect a race conscious interaction with skill and education that tracked black managers into administrative jobs that emerged during the 1960s and 1970s.

The career of one man, who was succeeding in his company but then moved into an urban affairs position, exemplifies this interaction between race and career tracking. Between 1964 and 1967 this man rapidly ascended through a series of supervisory and store management slots to become an area supervisor, a middle management position. At 23, his annual salary was more than doubled by a performance-based bonus. Yet, in the midst of this mainstream success (i.e., succeeding in the route typically traveled by the company's top executives), this man was asked to create an urban affairs program. The circumstances that led to this request were relatively straightforward: Civil rights activists had confronted the company with specific demands backed by the threat of a nationwide boycott; and the company viewed blacks as a sizeable proportion of its customer base. The respondent said, "Basically [my] job was to work with the licensee department and [come] up with minority candidates around the country to become [store owners]." After completing a strenuous series of meetings with the company's top executives—which included the head of personnel, a senior vice president, the head of licensing, the corporate legal council, and finally, the company president—he was offered, and he accepted, the assignment.

Within this operations-driven corporation, a manager with demonstrated talent for business operations generally would be considered a serious contender for a top-level mainstream position. From this perspective, slotting this man in an urban affairs job appears to be a frivolous use of talent. But in 1968, no other blacks worked at the company's corporate offices (save for one black janitor) and the company was vulnerable to racial protest. Deploying a black middle-level manager, a known commodity, into corporate urban affairs was a rational business decision. Indeed, a white vice president of personnel who worked in a major Chicago firm during the 1960s and 1970s noted that top management often filled newly created affirmative action positions with their best workers. He explained that this strategy signalled to the rank and file workers the seriousness of a company's commitment. Senior corporate managers believed that transferring an experienced black line manager into affirmative action would increase the credibility of this collateral role and enhance its effectiveness.

Black social and political unrest infused black managerial capacities with race-related purposes

(Collins 1997). African Americans moved into urban affairs, affirmative action, and other racialized management jobs that required them to interact predominantly with black community organizations and/or to help white companies recruit black labor. A 53-year-old company director, who began his private sector managerial career in operations in a retail company, was deployed to set up the equal employment opportunity function for the company. He recalled that the perquisites accompanying the job were "very attractive [and] that was the place for us [blacks] to be."

Indeed, other occupants of affirmative action and urban affairs jobs who were recruited from mainstream line areas commented that black-oriented jobs appeared to be a route where talented blacks could advance rapidly. Senior-level white management, usually either senior vice presidents or chief executive officers, personally solicited 12 of the 22 recruits (55 percent) from the mainstream. Eleven (50 percent) were given salary increases, more prestigious job titles, and promises of future rewards. Nine people turned down the first attempt at recruitment because they evaluated the job to be a dead end, despite high pay and elevated titles, and were approached a second time by top management. A director of affirmative action and diversity took the job initially because, he said, "I remember the CEO saying, 'we want you to take this beautiful job. It's going to pay you all this money. It's going to make you a star.'"

RACIALIZED DIVISION OF LABOR AND MOBILITY

What impact did this allocative process have on upward mobility in white corporations? To compare the advancement associated with racialized and mainstream careers, I selected 64 respondents employed in the white private sector at least since 1972 to construct a career typology.[1] Three types of managerial careers—mainstream, mixed, and racialized—emerged, based on the jobs that these executives held. Respondents having no racialized jobs in their careers were coded as having mainstream careers (24 of 64). Respondents whose careers incorporated at least one, but not a majority, of racialized jobs were coded as having mixed careers (22 of 64), the careers of those with a majority of racialized jobs were coded as racialized (18 of 64).

LOWERED JOB CEILINGS

By the mid-1980s, racialized respondents had advanced less than respondents in mainstream careers. The top executives (i.e., chief officers and senior vice presidents) spent most of their careers in mainstream areas. There was little difference in the executive job titles associated with mixed and mainstream careers, possibly because the vast majority of mixed careers had only one or two racialized jobs in them.

In contrast, 80 percent of racialized careers terminated with director or manager titles. Only 38 percent of the mainstream careers, and 46 percent of mixed careers terminated with those titles. Not one manager in a racialized career progressed above vice president.

Those who stayed in racialized jobs were ambitious people who saw themselves as doing the best they could, given blacks' historically limited job possibilities in white companies. One equal employment opportunity manager had post-graduate work in physics and engineering. He had been with the company eight years when the employee relations director approached him to set up the company's first affirmative action program. This man accepted the offer because, he said, "I wanted to get into management. That was the first and only opportunity that I felt I was going to get." This executive weighed the job's perquisites against the void in managerial opportunities for blacks in white firms. Racialized managerial positions appeared to be a way to sidestep the career stagnation common among the handful of blacks who previously attained management roles but remained trapped in low-level positions. In the 1970s, such jobs seemed to offer faster mobility, greater freedom and authority, and higher visibility and access to white corporate power brokers than mainstream jobs.

I asked an affirmative action director for a major retail company in Chicago if he ever tried to move back into the mainstream after he took on equal employment opportunity functions. To my surprise he said that he turned down a buyer's job with his first employer. He said, "I was stubborn at that point. No, I didn't want that." Given that buyers were key people in that organization and that the job was a stepping stone to higher-paying positions, his refusal signals the attractiveness of racialized positions in companies in the early 1970s. He said,

Remember now, this [equal opportunity] stuff was exciting, and there's a trap that you get into. Those of us who are in this kind of area talk about it all the time. It's kind of a golden handcuffs trap. We used to go on the convention circuit around the country . . . the Urban League and the NAACP, promoting our individual corporations. We were visible. We were representing the company. We had big budgets. I mean, you know, you go to every convention. And [you can] get yourself two or three suites and entertain all the delegates. You could spend $15,000 or $20,000 at a convention. I never had that kind of money to spend, to sign a check, so it was very attractive.

The economic rewards and social status that accompanied racialized positions were unimaginable luxuries to blacks—in this or any employment sector—in the years preceding federal legislation. With the benefit of hindsight, the affirmative action director explained:

I believe that had I stayed in operations [I would have] continued to move up and that's where the clout is. But the opportunity just wasn't there [for blacks] when I first started with that company.

After a slight pause he added, somewhat ruefully, "things changed and it is now."

Only four of 18 managers with racialized careers (22 percent) were the highest ranking black executive in a company's Chicago location. In contrast, 31 of 46 managers who had a majority of mainstream functions in their careers (72 percent) were the highest-ranking black executive in a Chicago company. Acknowledging advancement limitations associated with racialized jobs, respondents alternately described them as "dead end jobs [that had] no power," "nigger jobs," and "money-using" versus "money producing" jobs. The affirmative action director quoted above said that creating and

administering the affirmative action function for his company was a misstep in his career.

If I had to go back and to it all over again, I would not stay in affirmative action. Them that brings in the dollars is where the most opportunity is. I advise my sons . . . stay out of the staff functions, although those functions are very necessary.

He went on to name people who took different routes, and who he viewed—somewhat wistfully—as "making it."

Not coincidentally, a manager's position in the corporate division of labor in 1986 coincided with his level of optimism about his future in a company (see Kanter 1977:135). About three-quarters of mainstream (19 of 26) but less than one-quarter of racialized respondents (4 of 20) believed in 1986 that their chances for a promotion or a lateral move leading to promotion in the company were "good" or "very good." Respondents in racialized careers in 1986 reported that they were at the end of their career ladders in white companies. Sixty-five percent (13 of 20) said there would be no additional moves for them in the company, neither lateral nor promotional. Moreover, their pessimism extended to their perceptions of their opportunities for upward mobility on the open job market. The director of affirmative action quoted above summarized this shared perception of future mobility: "ascension for me is over."

The white executive elite I interviewed informally shared the opinion that African-American managers in racialized jobs were "out of the mix," in other words, not in the running for top jobs in a company. The assessment of each group—black and white—is not surprising, because racialized jobs are predominantly support positions, although these jobs can be found in sales and operations areas.[2] White executives, in general, view support functions as one of the worst routes to top jobs in a company (Korn/Ferry 1990). Nkomo and Cox (1990) indicate line positions play a highly significant positive role in individuals' promotion success. Support jobs are less desirable than line jobs because they lack influence and have shorter and more limited chains of career opportunities (Kanter 1977). I suggest further that the chain of opportunity becomes even shorter when linked to a job with racial purposes. These jobs not only impose relatively lower career ceilings, they underdevelop the talents and skills that corporations value, and therefore marginalize the job holder.

LIMITED SKILL DEVELOPMENT

Pressures placed on companies by federal government legislation and by protests in urban black communities made racialized jobs valuable to companies. In placating blacks and buffering corporations from racial turmoil, racialized jobs were highly unstructured; employees handled new and unpredictable contingencies. More than 80 percent of first racialized jobs were created when the respondents filled them. Ultimately, however, this managerial division of labor undermined the development of black human capital. As job content evolved, racialized jobs became routine work centered on a narrow set of administrative tasks extracted from generalist personnel functions. One manager noted that his job in the 1970s involved recruiting blacks, but not whites, into a company. Another mentioned the job was essentially "[black] number counting." A third man said the company promoted him and increased his salary because he was serving a function. He admitted he was aware, even then, that his future in the company might be limited:

> You have a little stepladder . . . a logical progression [of personnel functions] you have to go through if you are to ever become a personnel director. I wasn't doing any of that. As far as I could see, the company wanted black folks to be my only responsibility.

The narrowness of the jobs' routines limited— not broadened—these people's development of knowledge and skills. An executive for a clothing manufacturer and retailer made this clear when he summarized his experience:

> [The company] sent me to Chicago for a week long workshop on affirmative action. In that one week I learned all I needed to know about affirmative action, and I haven't learned much since. It's the kind of field that nothing, well, a few laws might change, but the

concept doesn't. You don't branch out. There's nothing, oh, now how can I explain it? There's not a lot of specialties . . . in affirmative action. You deal with 6 or 7 basic laws, or regulations, and . . . once you know those there's not an awful lot more to learn. I'm serious about it. Since 1965 or 1972, I don't think I've learned very much more.

Racialized managers in the 1960s and 1970s initially were rewarded with mobility in their companies. Ultimately, however, they required little or no company investment for job preparation and training. This racialized structure of mobility, therefore, created and solidified career ceilings through a cumulative work experience. Although managers' status elevated when their departments, titles, and salaries grew, respondents weren't trained in other areas. When I asked managers for job descriptions associated with various promotions, one affirmative action manager in a segregated career dismissed the question, indicating that he was "essentially doing the same thing" in each affirmative action job, although the scope of each job and his title and grade-level changed. His report distinctly contrasts with those of respondents who were promoted in mainstream personnel. In the case of personnel executives, at least six distinct components of job experience were clearly delineated—including employee relations, employment, compensation and benefits, and labor relations.

In contrast, people who ascended racialized career ladders became more specialized and increasingly secluded from generalist management areas. One manager summarized the gulf between mainstream and racialized personnel in the following way:

> If you stay in affirmative action, when you go looking for a job you're going to be seen as the affirmative action person. And personnel jobs are bigger than that.

Narrowly defined racialized jobs rely on interpersonal skills and external relationships without building administrative skills and internal support networks important to advancement. For example, a manager in a manufacturing company described his urban affairs job as if he were an ambassador-at-large:

I just moved about. Traveled. Everything was coming out of the community and I was there. I'd make 10, sometimes 12, meetings [in the black community] a day.

An executive in the food industry described his affirmative action job in a strikingly similar way:

I spent most of my time in the [black] community trying to . . . let people know that there were jobs and positions available in this company. I did a lot of speaking with community groups.

An executive in a communications firm said, "Mostly I worked with local community agencies to get the word out that there were opportunities [in the company]."

A director of urban affairs linked his company with black civil rights and social service organizations and represented it in black-dominated settings. This college-educated man moved out of sales and became skilled at brokering the interest of his company, successfully "absorbing" the tensions between white companies and urban black constituencies. He said that in 1971:

[My role was to] make [the company] look good. I did what they needed done to look good in the community. They utilized me in that fashion. For eleven years I was just their spook who sat by the door, and I understood that. Certainly I was, and I charged them well for it.

MARGINALIZED JOB HOLDERS

The structure of upward mobility became restrictive so that success in segregated areas prolonged these managers' career segregation. Prolonged career segregation, in turn, further undermined these executives' value in mainstream corporate functions. . . . That is, racialized human capital became a factor in marginalizing respondents by limiting their value in mainstream corporate functions. People in segregated careers faced two alternatives for enhancing their chances for upward mobility: (1) to laterally move into an entirely different corporate area associated with mainstream planning, production, or human resources administration, or (2) to move laterally to the mainstream component of the racialized

area (e.g., from community relations to public relations). People who specialized in affirmative action, community relations, and other race-related jobs were stymied in both routes by real or perceived limits to their usefulness in mainstream fields.

When an affirmative action manager (and one-time comptroller) tried to re-enter the corporate mainstream, she found she was locked into her racialized niche at each turn. She said:

I tried to negotiate myself out [of affirmative action]. There didn't seem to be a lot of . . . future. I wanted to try to get back into merchandising at that point. Or go back into comptrolling or to go somewhere else in personnel. You know nothing ever came out of it. I even took a special class . . . to get accreditation in personnel, as a personnel generalist. Which I completed. [It] had absolutely no effect on me going anywhere. . . . It got to where the [job] level and the salary level to go and change fields is too high . . . to [be] able to sell me to someone else. The likelihood of me going outside of [affirmative action] at this point is pretty well zero.

The trade-off to rising in companies in racialized jobs that required specialized skills and external networks was that managers became cut off from the internal networks and skill-building that would enable them to move into, and then move up in, the corporation's job mainstream.

A community relations manager for a major electronics corporation—when noting that his company's commitment to urban affairs programs for blacks began to decrease noticeably in the 1980s—also illustrates this trade-off. Observing, as he put it, the "handwriting on the wall," he made multiple attempts to move out of his dissolving niche in the company and into a mainstream production area. He first attempted to get into production, and next into general administrative services. Describing these attempts he said:

I was just not able to make that break. I talked to [people] in various divisions that I was interested in, and I got the lip service that they would keep [me] in mind if something opened up. As it happened, that just did not develop. I can never remember being approached by anyone. Nothing [happened]—that I can really hang [onto] as an offer. People would ask, "have you ever run a profit and loss operation?"

Finally, he described himself as taking "hat in hand" and approaching senior management in 1982 to request duties he knew to be available in a general administrative area. He said:

Frankly, this was an attempt to seize an opportunity. This time I went and I asked for a [new assignment]. We had some retirement within the company and some reorganization. I saw an opportunity to help myself. The urban affairs was shrinking. A number of jobs we created [in urban affairs] were completely eliminated. It just happened that the opportunity [to pick up administrative services] was there. It had a significant dollar budget and profit and loss opportunity . . . it was concrete and useful. So I asked for it.

Yet he was only temporarily successful in his attempt to exchange urban affairs for a more stable assignment in administrative services. One year later he was invited to resign from the company because of poor performance.

The story told by a second urban affairs manager—who tried a move to warehouse distribution in a retail company—reveals similar constraints. This manager was a department director, a position that was targeted to be cut from the company. This manager also discovered that the trade-off for rising in a company in urban affairs was an inability to shift into any mainstream corporate function. Here is his assessment:

I was too old to do what you had to do to compete. . . . I was competing with 21 and 22 year olds to get into the system. They couldn't charge [my salary] to a store and have me doing the same thing the others [were] doing [for much less money]. You need the ground level experience. When I should have gotten it, I was busy running an affirmative action department.

Indeed, from a practical standpoint, retraining this individual would not likely reap a long-term benefit because of his age. Consequently, I asked this manager why he didn't move laterally into mainstream public relations, an area (apparently) he was more qualified to pursue. He responded:

I thought about it very seriously. I wondered where I was going with the system. It came up quite often. I talked about it when I first accepted this job. And at the end. They told me, "We don't know. We'll have to get back to you." They never did.

That his superiors never got back to him "at the end" may reflect the fact that the organization needed him precisely where he was placed. Or, it may result from the fact that he lacked a skill base and/or his superiors perceived that his skills differed from those managers who had moved up the ladder in generalized public relations. . . .

In short, because of limited skills and career "track records," people who were concentrated in racialized roles lacked the human capital to compete in mainstream company areas. The same skills that once made them valuable now constrained them.

Discussion

Rather than viewing human capital and structure as mutually exclusive explanatory variables, these interviews illustrate that the organization of managerial job assignments and job allocation create human capital deficits. Human capital and the structure of management occupations are not independent phenomena; they interact to mediate labor market outcomes. In the case of black managers, human capital explains the existence of a supply of black labor that companies could draw from when confronted with governmental anti-bias pressures in the 1960s and 1970s. Yet, although human capital was a necessary ingredient for entry and initial job attainments, it does not sufficiently explain who competes for and succeeds in attaining organization power. For black managers, the structure of opportunities associated with the managerial assignments looms large as an additional explanatory variable. The relationship between human capital is circular: A race-based system of job allocation creates a deficit in on-the-job training and experience, and this structurally imposed deficit, in turn, leads to human capital deficits that create barriers to black advancement.

[. . .]

Using a conflict perspective, career construction can be viewed as part of a process of social closure to defend the existing advantage of white managers (see Tomaskovic-Devey 1993). This idea is similar to Reskin and Roos's (1987) proposal that occupational sex segregation is best understood within the broader conceptual framework of status hierarchies. The corporate role in the allocation of jobs—and the assessment of their value—was not a function of objective or impersonal supply characteristics, but of a race-conscious employment discrimination. It is not clear that the subsequent deskilling of a black cohort depressed their wages, as Braverman (1974) suggested. Rather, this deskilling served a more pressing purpose. The problem for white corporate elites was how to incorporate protected groups of minorities while minimizing their impact on organizational culture and structure. The creation and allocation of racialized jobs was an efficient way to meet both goals. These jobs appeased governmental legislation and black demands for more economic resources, while reducing the threat of increased competition for managerial power in organizations along racial lines. Initially, racialized jobs had attractive characteristics that suggested they were important to a company—faster mobility, greater freedom, and high visibility to white power brokers, but over time, racialized functions became routinized and devalued. Ultimately, the peculiar evolution during the 1960s and 1970s of careers documented in this study diminished the black executive pool in Chicago corporations that could compete to manage mainstream units in the 1980s and beyond. Consequently, many respondents over the last three decades did not—and could not—blossom into black executives in powerful decision making roles.

NOTES

1. I selected the base year of 1972 because it takes about 15 to 20 years to reach upper management positions in the major companies in the non-financial sector of Chicago (Chicago Urban League 1977).

2. Sales functions involved helping white corporations orient products' positive images to black consumers. People in operations took on racialized functions when managing a predominantly black workforce and mediating black white relationships in racially volatile employment settings.

REFERENCES

Braverman, Harry. 1974. *Labor and Monopoly Capital: The Degradation of Work in the Twentieth Century.* Albany: State University of New York Press.

Chicago Urban League. 1977. *Blacks in Policy-Making Positions in Chicago.* Chicago: Chicago Urban League.

Collins, Sharon M. 1997. *Black Corporate Executives: The Making and Breaking of a Black Middle Class.* Philadelphia: Temple University Press.

Doeringer, Peter B., and Michael J. Piore. 1971. *Internal Labor Markets and Manpower Analysis.* Lexington, Mass.: D.C. Heath.

Farley, Reynolds. 1984. *Blacks and Whites: Narrowing the Gap?* Cambridge: Harvard University Press.

Farley, Reynolds, and Walter R. Allen. 1987. *The Color Line and the Quality of Life in America.* New York: Russell Sage.

Freeman, Richard. 1976a. *The Black Elite.* New York: McGraw-Hill.

——. 1976b. *The Over-Educated American.* New York: Academic Press.

——. 1981. "Black economic progress after 1964: Who has gained and why." In *Studies in Labor Markets*, ed. S. Rosen, 247–295. Chicago: University of Chicago Press.

Ghiloni, Beth W. 1987. "The velvet ghetto: Women, power, and the corporation." In *Power Elites and Organizations*, eds. G. William Domhoff and Thomas R. Dye, 21–36. Newbury Park, Calif.: Sage.

Heidrick and Struggles, Inc. 1979. *Chief Personnel Executives Look at Blacks in Business.* New York: Heidrick and Stuggles, Inc.

Herrnstein, Richard J., and Charles Murray. 1994. *The Bell Curve: Intelligence and Class Structure in American Life.* New York: Free Press.

Irons, Edward, and Gilbert W. Moore. 1985. *Black Managers in the Banking Industry.* New York: Praeger.

Jones, Edward W. 1986. "Black managers: The dream deferred." *Harvard Business Review* (May–June): 84–89.

Kanter, Rosabeth Moss. 1977. *Men and Women of the Corporation.* New York: Basic Books.

Korn/Ferry. 1985. *Korn/Ferry Internationals' Executive Profile: A Survey of Corporate Leaders in the Eighties.* New York: Korn/Ferry International.

——. 1990. *Korn/Ferry Internationals' Executive Profile: A Decade of Change in Corporate Leadership.* New York: Korn/Ferry International.

Kraiger, Kurt, and J. Kevin Ford. 1985. "A meta-analysis of ratee race effects in performance ratings." *Journal of Applied Psychology* 70:56–63.

Landry, Bart. 1987. *The New Black Middle Class.* Berkeley, Calif.: University of California Press.

Murray, Charles. 1984. *Losing Ground: American Social Policy 1950–1980.* New York: Basic Books.

Nkomo, Stella M., and Taylor Cox, Jr. 1990. "Factors affecting the upward mobility of black managers in private sector organizations." *The Review of Black Political Economy* 78:40–57.

Reskin, Barbara F., and Patricia Roos. 1990. *Job Queues, Gender Queues: Explaining Women's Inroads into Male Occupations.* Philadelphia: Temple University Press.

Reskin, Barbara F., and Patricia Roos. 1987. "Status hierarchies and sex segregation." In *Ingredients for Women's Employment Policy*, eds., Christine Bose and Glenna Spite, 71–81. Albany: State University of New York Press.

Smith, James P., and Finis R. Welch. 1983. "Longer trends in black/white economic status and recent effects of affirmative action." Paper prepared for Social Science Research Council conference at the National Opinion Research Center, Chicago.

———. National Opinion Research Center, Chicago. 1986. *Closing the Gap: Forty Years of Economic Progress for Blacks.* Santa Monica, Calif.: Rand Corporation.

Sowell, Thomas. 1983. "The Economics and Politics of Race." Transcript from "The Firing Line" program. Taped in New York City on November 1983 and telecast later by PBS.

Theodore, Nikolas C., and D. Garth Taylor. 1991. *The Geography of Opportunity: The Status of African Americans in the Chicago Area Economy.* Chicago: Chicago Urban League.

Thurow, Lester. 1975. *Generating Inequality.* New York: Basic Books.

Tomaskovic-Devey, Donald. 1993. *Gender and Racial Inequality at Work: The Sources and Consequences of Job Segregation.* Ithaca, N.Y.: ILR Press.

U.S. Bureau of Census. 1960. *Occupational Characteristics.* Series PC(2)-7A. Washington, D.C.: The Bureau of Census.

———. 1973. *Occupational Characteristics.* Series PC(2)-7A. Washington, D.C.: The Bureau of Census.

30

SEGMENTED LABOR MARKETS

RICHARD EDWARDS

1

THREE FACES FROM THE HIDDEN ABODE

Roughly one hundred million Americans must work for a living. About ninety-five million of them, when they can find jobs, work for someone else. Three of those workers, who reflect both the unity and the diversity of the American working class, are Maureen Agnati, Fred Doyal, and Stanley Miller. These three share a condition common to all workers, past and present: they must sell their labor time to support themselves. Yet they also lead very different work lives, and the differences contain in kernel form the evolving history of work in twentieth-century America. Indeed, the study of how their jobs came to be so different goes far toward explaining the present weakness and future potential of the American working class.

Maureen Agnati assembles coils at Digitex, Incorporated, a small Boston-area manufacturer of electronics components.[1] Digitex's founder established the firm in the 1930s and continues to manage it today. The company employs about 450 people, four-fifths of whom are production workers. The labor force is mainly female and Portuguese, with a sprinkling of other ethnic workers—Italian, Haitian, Greek, Polish, and Asian.

Maureen is a white, twenty-six-year-old mother of two girls. Her husband Tom works in a warehouse at a nearby sheet-metal company. Maureen has worked for Digitex off and on for a number of years; she started after her junior year in high school, quit at nineteen when her first child was born, returned for one month to get Christmas money quit again, and then returned again to work the spring months until the end of her older daughter's school term. Frequent job changes do not seem to be any problem at Digitex, and indeed, in some ways the company appears to encourage high turnover.

Maureen's work involves winding coil forms with copper wire. To do this, Maureen operates a machine that counts and controls the number of wraps put on each collar. She does the same task all day.

Nearly half of Digitex's workers are on the piece-rate system, which means that their wages partly depend on how fast they work. The company pays both a guaranteed base wage and a piece-rate bonus on top of the base. But the guaranteed wage is always low—roughly equal to the legal minimum wage—so the worker's attention turns to making the bonus. To be eligible for extra pay, a worker must exceed the particular job's "rate"; that is, the assigned minimum level of output needed to trigger the incentive system. The worker then earns a bonus depending on how many units she produces above the rate. The problem is that the rates are high and are often changed. For example, when Maureen returned to work this last time, she found that the rates were so "tight" that she frequently did not make any incentive pay at all. It seems to be common that when workers begin to make large premiums, the time-study man appears to "restudy" the job, and the rates cause a great deal of resentment.

The pay system causes resentment among the hourly workers too. The company keeps most of the information about wages secret; a worker cannot learn, for example, what her job's top pay is, how the job is classified, or even what the wage schedule is. Often two workers will discover that, while they are doing nearly the same work, their pay differs greatly.

As for the conditions of work, employees are watched constantly, like children in a classroom. The design of the machinery pretty much dictates what tasks have to be done at each work station, but in other ways the foreman actively directs the work. One way he does this is by assigning workers to particular stations. For example, Maureen was not hired specifically for "winding" and when she returned to work her foreman simply put her at the station. But he can change job assignments whenever he wishes, and he often moves people around. Since some jobs have easy rates and others have tight ones, the job he assigns Maureen to will determine both how much she makes and how hard she has to work.

The foreman and supervisors at Digitex have other ways of directing the work, too. They watch closely over the hours and pace of work, and they ring a bell to signal the beginning and end of work breaks. Workers must get permission to make phone calls or leave the work area. And despite the piece-rate system (which might seem to leave it up to the individual worker to determine how fast to work and hence how much pay she would receive), the bosses take a direct hand in speeding up production; workers who talk to nearby workers, who fail to make the rates, or who return late from breaks or lunch are likely to be targets for reprimands and threats. The various bosses (foremen, general foreman, and other officials) spend their days walking among the workers, noting and correcting any laggard performance.

The supervisors' immediate role in directing production gives them considerable power, of course, yet their full power springs from other sources as well. No real grievance process exists at Digitex, and supervisors can dismiss workers on the spot. Less drastically, foremen maintain a certain degree of control because they must approve any "benefits" the workers receive. They must approve in advance any requests for time off to attend a funeral, see a doctor, and so on. For hourly workers, the supervisors determine any pay raises; since the wage schedules are secret, supervisors can choose when and whom to reward, and in what amount. For piece-rate workers, who are not eligible for raises, the supervisors' decisions on rejects—what to count as faulty output and whether to penalize the workers for it—weigh heavily in bonus calculations. Foremen also choose favored workers for the opportunity to earn overtime pay. And when business falls off and the company needs to reduce its workforce, no seniority or other considerations intervene; the foremen decide which workers to lay off. Through these powers, supervisors effectively rule over all aspects of factory life. Getting on the foreman's good side means much; being on his bad side tends to make life miserable.

Maureen, like other production workers at Digitex, has few prospects for advancing beyond her current position. All people working under the piece-rate system, regardless of seniority, earn the same base pay. There are a few supervisory slots, but these jobs are necessarily limited in number and are currently filled. There simply is no place for them to grow. This fact perhaps accounts for the high turnover at Digitex: over half the employees have worked for the company for less than three years, and Maureen's pattern of frequently quitting her job does not seem to be unusual.

There has recently been a bitter struggle to build a union at Digitex. Maureen's attitude—"We could sure use one around here, I'll tell you that"—was perhaps typical, but the real issue was whether the company's powers of intimidation would prove stronger than the workers' desire for better conditions. Initially, the union won a federally monitored election to be the workers' bargaining agent. The company's hostility toward the union persisted, however; after signing an initial contract with the union it launched a vicious campaign to decertify the union. The second time around, the union lost. No union exists at Digitex today.

Fred Doyal works as process control inspector at General Electric's Ashland (Massachusetts) assembly plant. The plant used to be run by Telechron Clock Company, a small independent firm, but GE bought it out. Today, the plant's thousand or so workers manufacture small electrical motors, the kind used in clocks, kitchen timers, and other very small appliances. The plant is highly automated, and slightly over half of its workers are women.

Fred operates sound-testing machinery to check the motors' noise levels. He monitors two hundred or so motors a day. The procedure is routine—he picks up the motors from the assembly area, returns to the "silent room," mounts them on the decibel counter, and records the result—and he performs virtually the same sequence every day. GE pays Fred about $13,000 a year.

There is little need for the supervisor to direct the work pace; the machinery does that, and when "you come on the job, you learn that routine; unless there is some change in that routine, the foreman would not be coming to you and telling you what to do; he just expects you (and you do) to know your daily routine, when you do repetitious work." In fact, the foreman generally appears only when a special situation arises, such as defective materials or machine breakdown. Other than that, workers mainly have contact with their bosses on disciplinary problems.

Evaluation and discipline do bring in the supervisors, but the union's presence tends to restrict their power. In a sense, the company evaluates Fred's work daily: "Everything I do, I record, and I turn in daily reports." The reports provide information not only about the decibel level of the motors but also coincidentally about Fred's output. Yet he is very confident that if he does a reasonable amount of work, his job will be secure. If the company tried to fire him, it would have to demonstrate to an outside arbitrator that its action is justified. In fact, any time the company takes disciplinary action, the union contract says that arbitration is automatic. In arbitration, Fred notes, the union has found that "discharge on a long-service employee, unless there's a horrendous record on this person, or if it was for something like striking a supervisor or stealing, discharge would be considered too severe by an arbitrator. Usually, you know? Don't bet on it, but that's the usual case."

There are, of course, lesser penalties. The disciplinary procedure begins with the written warning, and when the worker gets three written warnings, he or she can be suspended. Fred himself has been suspended for two days for "refusing to do a certain type of work." Suspension means the loss of pay, and it is probably the most common discipline at Ashland. Fred has known people who were suspended for up to a week because of absenteeism, and for lesser periods because of tardiness and insubordination.

Fred is in his mid-fifties, and he has worked for GE for thirty years. He started as a stock handler in the Worcester (Massachusetts) plant, moved up to be a group leader in the packing department, then transferred to shipping. At one point he had several employees under him, but he was "knocked off that job in a cutback." When they consolidated the plants he moved to Ashland to work in quality control. Presently he does not supervise anyone.

While Fred was moving up, the company had no formal procedure for filling vacancies. Switching from one job to another depended on "merit and so forth . . . some of it was ass-kissing." Now, however, in a change that Fred traces directly to the coming of the union, a new system prevails. If any job opens up, it must be posted, and everyone can apply for it. Qualifications and seniority are supposed to be taken into account in determining who gets the job. The company usually wants to decide unilaterally who is qualified, but "the union fights the company on this all the way." In fact, in Fred's experience the union is usually successful: "The company, rather than get in a hassle, and if they have no particular bitch against this individual who has the most seniority, the company will give that person the job."

Men do a lot better at Ashland than women. The plant jobs seems quite rigidly stereotyped. Women fill most of the lower-paying positions on the clock-assembly conveyors, while the men tend to get the more skilled jobs elsewhere in the plant. Men's jobs are also more secure. In the event of a partial layoff, any worker in a higher-classified job can bump any other worker of equal or lesser seniority in a lower-classified job; but of course one cannot bump upwards. Women, since they tend to be in the lower classifications, have few others (mainly women) whom they can bump. Men have most of the women to bump.

Fred believes that General Electric has not overlooked the benefits of this system:

> Where that company has made all its money is on the conveyors; that's where they really build the clocks, see—a long assembly conveyor, thirty-five, forty women working on it. Those women are working every minute of the day; those women *really* make money for the company! The company didn't get rich on me, and the older I get, the less rich it's gonna get on me. But they got rich on those women. Those women are there every second, every second of their time is taken up. Now, they have on each of these conveyors what they call a group leader, and it's a woman, right? . . . These women are *highly* qualified, *highly* skilled, these group leaders. Way underpaid. There's a man that stock-handles the conveyor—man or a boy, whichever you want—he's just a "hunky," picks up boxes and puts them on the conveyor for the girls or moves heavy stuff. That man makes ten to fifteen dollars a week more than a woman who's a group leader.

In the supervisory staff, the sexual stereotyping is even more apparent. There are quite a few bosses, counting all the foremen, general foremen, and higher managers. Yet there are only two women. "There have always been two; not always the same two, but two."

Recently, the rigid sexual division seems to have lessened somewhat, and women have applied for jobs that formerly were off limits. According to Fred, the company is wary of turning them down, because it is worried about a government antidiscrimination suit. (GE subsequently settled the suit, agreeing to pay damages.) The union has made some attempt to change the ratio of women's to men's wages, but Fred acknowledges that it has been "unsuccessful."

[. . .]

Fred is a strong supporter of the union (the United Electrical Workers), and he has from time to time held various official positions in the local. He is completely disillusioned about the AFL-CIO ("They sold out a long time ago"). For him, just following the Democratic Party is not enough: "Any union movement that doesn't have a political philosophy in this country is doomed."

Stanley Harris works as a research chemist at the Polaroid Corporation. "Research chemist" may sound like a high-powered position, and indeed the pay is quite good: Stanley makes about $18,000. But in terms of the actual work involved, the position is more mundane. Stanley's bachelor degree equips him to do only relatively routine laboratory procedures. He cannot choose his own research, and he does not have a special area of expertise. He supervises no one, and instead his own work is done under supervision. Stanley is, in effect, a technical worker.

On first meeting Stanley, one is not surprised to learn of his middle-level occupation. He is white, roughly fifty years old, and seems well educated. Despite the fact that it is the middle of the workday, his proffered hand is clean (and soft). He wears no special work clothes, spurning both the heavy fabrics necessary in production jobs and the suit and tie affected by the managers. In the lab, of course, he wears a white protective smock, but beneath is an unstylish, small-collar Dacron sports shirt and chino pants.

Here and there, traces of a blue-collar background appear. Stanley has a few teeth missing. His speech retains a slight working-class accent, and occasionally his grammar betrays him. He mentions that he lives in Lynn (Massachusetts), an old working-class city outside of Boston.

Stanley's career tells much about the employment system at Polaroid. He joined the company nineteen years ago as a production worker, when he "ran out of money going through college." Having already completed the science curriculum, he went to night school to fulfill his liberal arts requirements while continuing to work at Polaroid. After obtaining his BS degree, he began applying for the research openings advertised on the company's bulletin boards, and since Polaroid's hiring policies give preference to those who are already employees, the company eventually promoted Stanley into one of the lab jobs. These jobs encompass many ranks, from assistant scientist all the way up to senior scientist. Stanley started at the bottom, and his current position, research scientist, appears in the middle of the hierarchy.

In most of the research jobs, the specific work to be done combines a particular product assignment with the general skills and work behavior expected of a research chemist. Stanley's supervisor assigns him a project within the "general sweep of problems, anything having to do with a company product." Stanley then methodically applies standard tests ("the state of the art"), one after the other, until he finds the answer or his supervisor redirects his efforts. Rather than having his workday closely supervised by his boss or directed by a machine, Stanley follows professional work patterns, habits that are, in fact, common to the eight hundred or so other research workers at Polaroid's Tech Square facility.

Stanley's supervisor formally evaluates his work performance in the annual review. Although the evaluation format seems to change frequently— "Right now it is very curt, either 'good,' 'bad,' or 'indifferent'; but in previous years it was something like four pages"—the purpose and importance of the review have not changed. Stanley believes that the evaluation is crucial to his chances for promotion. "It goes to someone who has to okay it, and if he doesn't know you and he sees on a piece of paper 'poor worker,' it hurts you."

The formal evaluations are especially important because, while Stanley's boss assigns him projects and evaluates his work, he has little say in Stanley's promotions or pay raises or discipline. Those decisions are made higher up, by applying the company's rules to the individual's case. As Stanley explains it, the company contributes the formula while the individual provides the numbers, and then somebody "upstairs" just has to do the calculation. The rules for advancement seem pretty clear.

An important illustration of Stanley's point is the company's layoff policy. When demand for Polaroid's cameras fell off during the 1974–1975 recession, the company laid off sixteen hundred workers, about 15 percent of its entire workforce. Such a deep cut could be expected to create lasting insecurity among Polaroid's workers, and it undoubtedly did among the younger workers. But not for Stanley; the company's seniority-based bumping system protects him. If Polaroid eliminates Stanley's current job, he can displace any worker with less seniority in any of the jobs that he has previously held. "I'm not worried because of the fact that I started at the bottom, and so in theory I could bump my way all the way back to the bottom." In Stanley's view, such an enormous economic disaster would be required before layoffs reached him that, "I figure we'll all be out of work."

Stanley summed up his attitude toward unions in one word: "antagonistic." But the reason for his hostility is, perhaps, surprising. "Like all the movements that are idealistic at the beginning, they [unions] have degenerated to where they benefit a select group. . . . I'm not saying the idea is bad, but they have been corrupted." Stanley sees no use for a union in his own job, since, "if I put out, I'll get the rewards; at least, that's what I've found."

Maureen Agnati, Fred Doyal, Stanley Miller. Three different workers, three different ways of organizing work. Today we observe their situations as simply different arrangements in production, but they are in fact endpoints in a long process of capitalist development that has transformed (and continues to transform) the American workplace. The change does not reflect inevitable consequences of modern technology or of industrial society, but rather the transformation occurred because continuing capital accumulation has propelled workers and their employers into virtually perpetual conflict. And while both technology and the requirements of modern social production play a part in the story to come, the roots of this conflict lie in the basic arrangements of capitalist production.

CONFLICT AND CONTROL IN THE WORKPLACE

[. . .] What the capitalist buys in the labor market is the right to a certain quantity of what Marx has called *labor power*, that is, the worker's capacity to do work. Labor power can be though of as being measured in time units (hours, days) and it may be improved or expanded by any skills, education, or other attributes that make it more productive than "simple" labor power. Thus, the capitalist, in hiring a carpenter for a day, buys one day's quantity of carpenter labor power.

But the capacity to do work is useful to the capitalist only if the work actually gets done. Work, or what Marx called *labor*, is the actual human effort in the process of production. If labor power remains merely a potentiality or capacity, no goods get produced and the capitalist has no products to sell for profit.

[. . .]

In a situation where workers do not control their own labor process and cannot make their work a creative experience, any exertion beyond the minimum needed to avert boredom will not be in the workers' interest. On the other side, for the capitalist it is true *without limit* that the more work he can wring out of the labor power he has purchased, the more goods will be produced; and they will be produced without any increased wage costs. It is this discrepancy between what the capitalist can buy in the market and what he needs for production that makes it imperative for him to control the labor process and the workers' activities. *[. . .]*

These basic relationships in production reveal both the basis for conflict and the problem of control at the workplace. Conflict exists because the interests of workers and those of employers collide, and what is good for one is frequently costly for the other. Control is rendered problematic because, unlike the other commodities involved in production, labor power is always embodied in people, who have their own interests and needs and who retain their power to resist being treated like a commodity. Indeed, today's most important employers, the large corporations, have so many employees that to keep them working diligently is itself a major task, employing a vast workforce of its own. From the capitalist's perspective, this is seen as the problem of management, and it is often analyzed simply in terms of the techniques of administration and business "leadership." But employment creates a two-sided

relationship, with workers contributing as much to its final form as managers or capitalists.

[. . .]

Typically, then, the task of extracting labor from workers who have no direct stake in profits remains to be carried out in the workplace itself. Conflict arises over how work shall be organized, what work pace shall be established, what conditions producers must labor under, what rights workers shall enjoy, and how the various employees of the enterprise shall relate to each other. The workplace becomes a battleground, as employers attempt to extract the maximum effort from workers and workers necessarily resist their bosses' impositions.

[. . .]

The labor process becomes an arena of class conflict, and the workplace becomes a contested terrain. Faced with chronic resistance to their effort to compel production, employers over the years have attempted to resolve the matter by reorganizing, indeed revolutionizing, the labor process itself. Their goal remains profits; their strategies aim at establishing structures of control at work. That is, capitalists have attempted to organize production in such a way as to minimize workers' opportunities for resistance and even alter workers' perceptions of the desirability of opposition. Work has been organized, then, to contain conflict. In this endeavor employers have sometimes been successful.

[. . .]

THE TYPES OF CONTROL

[. . .] In the nineteenth century, most businesses were small and were subject to the relatively tight discipline of substantial competition in product markets. The typical firm had few resources and little energy to invest in creating more sophisticated management structures. A single entrepreneur, usually flanked by a small coterie of foremen and managers, ruled the firm. These bosses exercised power personally, intervening in the labor process often to exhort workers, bully and threaten them, reward good performance, hire and fire on the spot, favor loyal workers, and generally act as despots, benevolent or

otherwise. They had a direct stake in translating labor power into labor, and they combined both incentives and sanctions in an idiosyncratic and unsystematic mix. There was little structure to the way power was exercised, and workers were often treated arbitrarily. Since workforces were small and the boss was both close and powerful, workers had limited success when they tried to oppose his rule. This system of "simple" control survives today in the small-business sector of the American economy, where it has necessarily been amended by the passage of time and by the borrowings of management practices from the more advanced corporate sector, but it retains its essential principles and mode of operation. It is the system of simple control that governs Maureen Agnati's job at Digitex.

Near the end of the nineteenth century, the tendencies toward concentration of economic resources undermined simple control; while firms' needs for control increased, the efficacy of simple control declined. The need for coordination appeared to increase not only with the complexity of the product but also with the scale of production. By bringing under one corporate roof what were formerly small independent groups linked through the market, the corporation more than proportionately raised the degree of coordination needed. Production assumed an increasingly social character, requiring greater "social" planning and implying an increased need for control. But as firms began to employ thousands of workers, the distance between capitalists and workers expanded, and the intervening space was filled by growing numbers of foremen, general foremen, supervisors, superintendents, and other minor officials. Whereas petty tyranny had been more or less successful when conducted by entrepreneurs (or foremen close to them), the system did not work well when staffed by hired bosses. The foremen came into increasingly severe conflict with both their bosses and their workers.

The workers themselves resisted speed-up and arbitrary rule more successfully, since they were now concentrated by the very growth of the enterprise.[2] From the Homestead and Pullman strikes to the great 1919–1920 steel strike, workers fought with their bosses over control of the actual process of production. The maturing labor movement and an emergent Socialist Party organized the first serious challenge to capitalist rule. Intensifying conflict in society at large and the specific contradictions of simple control in the workplace combined to produce an acute crisis of control on the shop floor.

The large corporations fashioned the most far-reaching response to this crisis. During the conflict, big employers joined small ones in supporting direct repression of their adversaries. But the large corporations also began to move in systematic ways to reorganize work. They confronted the most serious problems of control, but they also commanded the greatest resources with which to attack the problems. Their size and their substantial market power released them from the tight grip of short-run market discipline and made possible for the first time planning in the service of long-term profits. The initial steps taken by large companies—welfare capitalism, scientific management, and company unions—constituted experiments, trials with serious inherent errors, but useful learning experiences nonetheless. In retrospect, these efforts appear as beginnings in the corporations' larger project of establishing more secure control over the labor process.

Large firms developed methods of organization that are more formalized and more consciously contrived than simple control; they are "structural" forms of control. Two possibilities existed: more formal, consciously contrived controls could be embedded in either the physical structure of the labor process (producing "technical" control) or in its social structure (producing "bureaucratic" control). In time, employers used both, for they found that the new systems made control more institutional and hence less visible to workers, and they also provided a means for capitalists to control the "intermediate layers," those extended lines of supervision and power.

Technical control emerged from employers' experiences in attempting to control the production (or blue-collar) operations of the firm. The assembly line came to be the classic image, but the actual application of technical control was much broader. Machinery itself directed the labor process and set the pace. For a time, employers had the best of two worlds. Inside the firm, technical control turned the tide of conflict in their favor, reducing workers to attendants of prepaced machinery; externally, the system strengthened the employer's hands by expanding the number of potential substitute workers. But as factory workers in the late 1930s struck back with sit-downs, their action exposed the deep dangers to employers in thus linking all workers' labor together in one technical apparatus. The conflict at the workplace propelled labor into its "giant step," the CIO.

These forces have produced today a second type of work organization. Whereas simple control persists in the small firms of the industrial periphery, in large firms, especially those in the mass-production industries, work is subject to technical control. The system is mutually administered by management and (as a junior partner) unions. Jobs in the GE plant where Fred Doyal works fit this pattern.

There exists a third method for organizing work, and it too appeared in the large firms. This system, bureaucratic control, rests on the principle of embedding control in the social structure or the social relations of the workplace. The defining feature of bureaucratic control is the institutionalization of hierarchical power. "Rule of law"—the firm's law—replaces "rule by supervisor command" in the direction of work, the procedures for evaluating workers' performance, and the exercise of the firm's sanctions and rewards; supervisors and workers alike become subject to the dictates of "company policy." Work becomes highly stratified; each job is given its distinct title and description; and impersonal rules govern promotion. "Stick with the corporation," the worker is told, "and you can ascend up the ladder." The company promises the workers a *career*.

Bureaucratic control originated in employers' attempts to subject non-production workers to more strict control, but its success impelled firms to apply the system more broadly than just to the white-collar staff. Especially in the last three decades, bureaucratic control has appeared as the organizing principle in both production and nonproduction jobs in many large firms, and not the least of its attractions is that the system has proven especially effective in forestalling unionism. Stanley Miller's job at Polaroid is subject to bureaucratic control.

Continuing conflict in the workplace and employers' attempts to contain it have thus brought the modern American working class under the sway of three quite different systems for organizing and controlling their work: simple control, technical control (with union participation), and bureaucratic control. Of course, the specific labor processes vary greatly: Maureen Agnati's coil wrapper might have been a typewriter or a cash register, Fred Doyal's job might have been in a tire plant or a tractor factory, and Stanley Miller's work might have involved being a supervisor or skilled craftsman. Yet within this variety of concrete labors, the three patterns for organizing work prevail.

The typology of control embodies both the pattern of historical evolution and the array of contemporary methods of organizing work. On the one hand, each form of control corresponds to a definite stage in the development of the representative or most important firms; in this sense structural control succeeded simple control and bureaucratic control succeeded technical control, and the systems of control correspond to or characterize stages of capitalism. On the other hand, capitalist production has developed unevenly, with some sectors pushing far in advance of other sectors, and so each type of control represents an alternate method of organizing work; so long as uneven development produces disparate circumstances, alternate methods will coexist.

The following chapters explore the dynamic of class conflict within the labor process; but the impact of this dynamic extends far beyond the workplace. The redivision of labor splintered the working class; rather than creating new "classes," it has established enduring *fractions* of the same class, and, as the last chapter will suggest, by changing the constellation of class forces in society it has reconstituted the basis of American politics.

[. . .]

9

LABOR RE-DIVIDED, PART I: SEGMENTED LABOR MARKETS

Structural control has cast a longer shadow than is visible from within the firm itself. The new system of control has contributed to the redivision and segmentation of the American working class. Both exogenous divisions (especially racial and sexual ones) and new distinctions of capitalism's own making have become embedded in the economic structure of society. And the divisions within the working class have distorted and blunted the class opposition to capitalism, making for a weak socialist movement and a long period of relative stability within the regime of monopoly capitalism.

This marks a clear reversal of the tendency dominant in the nineteenth century. During American capitalism's first century it inherited and recruited a highly heterogeneous labor force, but it reshaped its wage laborers into an increasingly homogeneous class. In the twentieth century, the economic system has attracted groups as divergent as before, but capitalist development has tended to institutionalize, instead of abolish, the distinctions among them. In particular, the dichotemizing of the economy into core and periphery has introduced a new structural division in the conditions of employment. The rise of the large administrative staff, with its middle position between employers and manual workers, has further fractured the common class basis. Moreover, institutionalized racial and sexual discrimination has served to deepen the splits within the working class. In all these cases, capitalist development has not only splintered the working class, it has also institutionalized the divisions. It has created distinct and enduring "fractions."[3]

[. . .]

THE THREE LABOR MARKETS

The idea that labor markets treat groups differently needs little new justification.[4] Most people know, even if too few care, that the unemployment rate of blacks regularly runs at least double that of whites. At the other end of the spectrum, new Harvard Business School graduates can on average look forward to an annual income of $50,000 (or is it now $65,000?) within five years. Women's earnings, despite antidiscrimination legislation, have remained steady (within a few points) at 60 percent of male earnings throughout the postwar period. Between a third and a half of teenage black job-seekers normally cannot find work.

More novel is the notion that the various groups and the cross-cutting and overlapping divisions in the labor market can reasonably be arranged into a limited number of labor market segments.

[. . .]

The Secondary Market

One segment, the secondary market, is the preserve of casual labor—"casual," that is, not in the sweat required of the workers but rather in the lack of any worker rights or elaborate employer-imposed work structures. Here labor power comes closest to being treated simply as a commodity unfettered and unencumbered by any job structure, union, or other institutional constraints.

The secondary market includes many different types of jobs, and spans both production and non-production work. Low-skill jobs in small, nonunion manufacturing concerns constitute one part of this market. "Service" employment—the jobs of janitors, waiters and waitresses, hospital orderlies, delivery-men and messengers, attendants, guards, personal care workers, and other—represents a second major component. Another group consists of the lower-level positions in retail and wholesale trade: slots filled by sales clerks, order-takers, check-out clerks, inventory stockers, and so forth. The secondary market also includes increasing numbers of the lowest-level clerical jobs, those typing, filing, key-punching, and other positions that have become part of the large typing (or records-filing and retrieval or key-punching) pools. Finally, we must add migrant agricultural labor, seasonal employment required for the peak periods of planting and especially harvesting. Although other jobs such as part-time teaching or textile work in the South also fall into the secondary-market segment, the above categories contain the mass of secondary employment. Maureen Agnati's job, described in the first chapter, falls into the secondary market.

What marks these jobs as secondary is the casual nature of the employment. The work almost never requires previous training or education beyond basic literacy. Few skills are required and few can be learned. Such jobs offer low pay and virtually no job security. They are, in other words, typically dead-end jobs, with few prospects for advancement and little reward for seniority in the form of either higher pay or a better job. With little incentive to stay, workers may move frequently, and turnover in these jobs tends to be high. The only thing that a worker brings to a secondary job is labor power; the worker is treated and paid accordingly.

[. . .]

The Subordinate Primary Market

In contrast to the secondary jobs, primary jobs offer some job security, relatively stable employment, higher wages, and extensive linkages between successive jobs that the typical worker holds. While the particular mechanisms providing security and stability and the nature of the actual linkages differ between the two tiers of the primary market, all primary jobs share the characteristic of offering well-defined occupations, with established paths for advancement.

The subordinate and independent jobs diverge, however, because of other characteristics, and again no single dimension emerges from labor market behavior as the defining criterion. The subordinate primary market has within it both production and nonproduction jobs.[5] The biggest group includes the jobs of the traditional industrial working class—production jobs in the unionized mass-production industries: plant jobs in auto assembly, steelmaking, rubber and tire manufacturing, electrical products construction, farm implements production, machinery manufacture, metal fabrication, camera and other consumer products assembly, home appliance manufacture, and the like. The other large group of subordinate primary jobs includes the positions of unionized workers in lower-level sales, clerical, and administrative work, found mostly in the major retailing, utilities, and manufacturing corporations. Other subordinate primary jobs include the production-type positions in core firms in transportation (railroad engineers, interurban and transit system bus drivers, and airline maintenance personnel), in retailing and wholesaling (warehousemen) and in utilities and other sectors of the core economy.

These jobs are distinguished from the casual-labor jobs of the secondary market most fundamentally (though not invariably) by the presence of unions. The jobs are better-paying than secondary employment, and they generally involve long-term, stable work with prospects for advancement and some job guarantees. In the case of unionized workers, the steps for advancement and the employment guarantees are contained in union seniority clauses; for nonunionized workers, both the promotional paths and the guarantees are less

clear and are based only on employer practices, but they do exist. These are permanent, rather than temporary or casual, jobs.

On the other side, subordinate primary jobs are distinguished from independent primary jobs in that their work tasks are repetitive, routinized, and subject to machine pacing. The skills required are learned rather quickly (within a few days or weeks), and they are often acquired on the job. The jobs provide little opportunity for workers to have any control over their own jobs.

The job ladders that link one job with subsequent ones in the same occupation may derive either from the employing firm (as is generally the case with nonproduction jobs) of from industrial union rules (for production jobs), but in either case they tend to be firm-specific. That is, the path for advancement almost always depends on seniority within the firm, and indeed such seniority becomes, in this internal labor market, the necessary admission ticket to the better-paying positions higher on the job ladder. Workers have a big incentive to remain with one employer, and they show markedly lower turnover rates than secondary workers.

[. . .]

Unlike secondary workers, who are simply dismissed and cut adrift when business gets bad, subordinate primary workers usually continue some association with their union, perhaps receive union-negotiated supplemental unemployment benefits, and can be called back to work in order of seniority when business picks up. A worker laid off at the auto plants remains an (unemployed) auto worker, rather than simply joining the ranks of the anonymous unemployed.

The subordinate primary market, then, contains the jobs of the old industrial working class, reinforced by the lower-level jobs of unionized clerical employees. In these routinized, typically machine-operative positions, workers find that by staying on the job ladder they can progress to significantly higher wages and perhaps to better jobs. Schooling also pays off, especially, it appears, at the level of high school and the first few years of college. Cyclical unemployment is a not-uncommon feature in subordinate primary work, particularly in production or blue-collar positions; but even during spells of layoffs, subordinate primary positions display their distinctiveness from secondary work by the continuing connections between laid-off workers and their jobs.

The Independent Primary Market

Jobs in the independent primary market, like jobs in the subordinate primary market, offer stable employment with considerable job security, established patterns of career progression, and relatively high pay. But they differ from subordinate primary jobs in that they typically involve general, rather than firm-specific, skills; they may have career ladders that imply movements between firms; they are not centered on operating machinery; they typically require skills obtained in advanced or specialized schooling; they often demand educational credentials; they are likely to have occupational or professional standards for performance; and they are likely to require independent initiative or self-pacing.

Three groups of jobs dominate the independent primary market. The first fills the middle layers of the firm's employment structure and consists of jobs for long-term clerical, sales, and technical staff, foremen, bookkeepers, personal and specialized secretaries, supervisors, and so on. A second group of independent primary jobs grows out of craft work that employs electricians, carpenters, plumbers, steam-fitters, and machinists. A third large group of independent primary jobs includes the professional positions—accountants, research scientists, engineers, registered nurses and doctors, lawyers and tax specialists, and others. As the jobs in these three groups indicate, the independent primary market, like the other segments, spans both blue-collar and white-collar work.

Another characteristic of the independent primary market is the greater role played by the public sector. For professional and technical workers in particular, the state's share of employment has steadily advanced over the last three decades, to the point where the state now employs between 35 and 45 percent of all professional and technical workers. Teachers, social welfare workers, nurses, doctors, other health professionals, accountants, lawyers, engineers, and others have been hired in great numbers to carry out the state's permanent new functions in welfare, warfare, and regulation. Overall, the state sector appears to account for between a fifth and a third of all independent primary employment.

The average level of pay in independent primary jobs is, of course, significantly higher than in the other segments. [. . .]

Moreover, earnings in independent primary jobs show much greater increases in response to experience or age than in the other segments, confirming the existence of important promotional or career ladders linking prior employment with subsequent jobs. . . .

Similarly, formal education plays a much greater role in independent primary jobs. . . .

[. . .]

The jobs in this segment are skilled jobs, requiring relatively high levels of schooling or advanced training. As Michael Piore has noted, formal education (or craft union membership or licensing) is an essential requisite for employment; while educational requirements are often not taken seriously in the other segments and are more or less rigorously enforced depending on how tight the labor market is, in independent primary jobs the credentials become nearly absolute requirements for entry. Large returns accrue to both additional schooling and experience. Independent primary jobs, especially the professional and craft positions, have professional or occupational standards that govern performance, and so mobility and turnover tend to be both high and associated with advancement. Except for craft work, these jobs carry slight overall chances of lay-offs. Most strikingly, all independent primary jobs foster occupational consciousness; that is, they provide the basis for job-holders to define their own identities in terms of their particular occupation.

SYSTEMS OF CONTROL AND THE THREE LABOR MARKETS

If, as this research suggests, the labor market is segmented into three parts, what forces account for the division? [. . .]

Racial and sexual discrimination provide one set of forces leading to labor market segmentation. Blacks and women were pushed into particular race- or sex-stereotyped jobs, jobs that were consistent with the broader social evaluation of each group.

Blacks were hired into the dirtiest, most physically demanding, and lowest-skilled occupations, while women were pushed toward "helping" occupations, especially clerical work. Moreover, both groups, especially blacks, were intentionally recruited for particular occupations as a way for management to divide and thereby rule the firm's workforce. Blacks and women had little bargaining power and few alternate job possibilities, facts which ensured that their work would remain low-paying and with few job rights.

Intentional discrimination remains important, but increasingly it has been supplanted by institutional discrimination. And institutional discrimination, in addition to appearing in the form of segregated schooling and culturally biased tests, occurs through segmented labor markets. Thus, in probing the causes of segmented labor markets, we seek in part to understand how racial discrimination and sexual discrimination have become incorporated in the institutional processes of labor markets.

But the analysis of the preceding chapters provides yet another key to the origins of segmented labor markets; let me state it baldly before introducing the necessary qualifications. Labor markets are segmented because they express a historical segmentation of the labor process; specifically, a distinct system of control inside the firm underlies each of the three market segments. The secondary labor market is the market expression of workplaces organized according to simple control. The subordinate primary market contains those workplaces (workers and jobs) under the "mixed" system of technical control and unions. And the independent primary market reflects bureaucratically controlled labor processes. Thus, the fundamental basis for division into three segments is to be found in the workplace, not in the labor market; so to define the three market segments we now have a single criterion—the type of control system—rather than simply a cluster of market behavior characteristics.

It should be clear that the relationship between types of control and labor market segments is not perfect or exhaustive. Anomalies appear and, more importantly, development occurs such that any static typology can never adequately capture all the transitional and developmental situations. The accompanying chart asserts that most jobs are concentrated in

the diagonal cells (numbered I, II, and III) and that the off-diagonal cells are of minor importance. Yet certainly some jobs fall in the off-diagonal cells, and examples are listed in the chart. Nonetheless, the corresponding (diagonal) types of control and labor market segments appear to be poles of great magnetic force, attracting the majority of jobs.[6]

The system-of-control approach leads to a somewhat different understanding of the role of job skills, schooling, on-the-job training, experience, and other technical characteristics of labor. These characteristics are usually thought to create different types of labor (and so they do), and therefore to be the basis themselves of different treatment in the labor market. The relevance of these technical attributes, even their preeminence in certain cases, cannot be denied. However, the analysis presented here suggests that it is the system of control that creates the context within which experience, training, schooling, skills, and other attributes assume their importance. Rather than ignoring the technical relations of production, such an approach emphasizes that considerable choice surrounds the selection of any productive technique. In most industries, a range of techniques is already available. Even in those production processes where little choice exists, the decision whether to use high-skill or low-skill labor, for example, essentially depends on whether the firm finds it profitable to undertake the research and development necessary to convert high-skill production to low-skill production. Whether it is profitable depends in turn not only on the relative wage costs but also on the rate at which labor power is transformed into labor—that is, on the organization of the labor process itself. Thus, the reason experience and schooling are unimportant for explaining secondary workers' incomes but are crucial for explaining subordinate primary workers' incomes derives not so much from invariant differences in the nature of the products being produced and in the accompanying inherent skill requirements as from the consistently different ways of organizing the labor process. Secondary work is organized so as to minimize the need for experience and schooling, whereas subordinate primary work is organized so as to build upon these factors. The technical processes of production place certain limits on the range of organizational possibilities, of course, but

System of Control / Market Segment (Jobs)	Simple Control	Technical Control	Bureaucratic Control
Secondery	I. Small manufacturing jobs Service jobs Retail sales Temporary and typing-pool office work	Southern textile jobs	Part-time academic jobs
Subordinate Primary	Unionized garment workers	II. Jobs in auto and steel plants Assembly-line production work Machine-paced clerical work	Personal secretary jobs
Independent Primary	Jobs in small consulting firms	Technicians' jobs monitoring chemicals production	III. Jobs at IBM, Polaroid Craft work Nonproduction staff jobs

Figure 30.1. The Correspondence Between Systems of Control and Labor Market Segments for Sample Jobs

in practice these limits tend to provide considerable flexibility.[7]

[...]

Technical control at first seemed to require no alteration in the way the firm obtained its labor. Indeed, the early days of the Ford plants appeared to provide capitalists with that happy prospect of the unification of the potency of the reserve army outside the plant walls and the rigid internal discipline of technical control inside. Turnover was extremely high—certainly as high as in the secondary market today—and job security was nil.

Technical control united with secondary market-type casual labor lasted until the great CIO organizing drives of the 1930s. The success of the auto workers, steelworkers, electrical workers, rubberworkers, and others in building industrial unions doomed that combination and put in its place the configuration represented by cell II in the chart, technical control inside the firm matched with primary labor market-type job security, stability, and (through union seniority) promotional prospects. This configuration has

characterized the traditional mass-production industries throughout the postwar period.

In effect, the agreement that was worked out amounted to the establishment of an internal labor market. An internal market is simply a set of procedures contained wholly within the firm for performing the functions of the external market: the allocation and pricing of labor. Unions, as at U.S. Steel, for example, won for their members the rights to fill vacancies based on seniority and to have outside hiring done only at lower-paying, entry-level jobs. Union scales governed each job's pay.

Technical control, then, does not directly require primary market job rights, and the relation between them is not invariable. Certainly, the advantages of technical control and casual labor markets have motivated the corporations' investments in Brazil, South Korea, and other repressive countries where workers cannot establish unions or win job rights. Similarly, the attempt by core firms (most conspicuously GM) to move production facilities to the South indicates that at least some employers think that old-time benefits of technical control and secondary labor are possible even within the United States. GM may have thought it could horn in on the turf of J. P. Stevens and other textile manufacturers, who long ago discovered that technical control and nonunion labor were possible because of the South's peculiar blend of antiunion law and local custom.

Yet what was possible for an isolated textile industry does not appear possible generally. [. . .]

Technical control in the core firms brings unionization in its wake, and through unionization, the characteristics of primary-market employment.[8] Here seniority provisions and other union contract rules govern the allocation of workers to jobs, the wages to be paid, the relative vulnerability to layoff, and the protections and appeals from discipline and dismissal. The middle cell of the chart, then, must be understood as possessing the labor market characteristics that have emerged from a historic compromise—a bargain between core firms and industrial unions that leaves the management of the business in the employers' hands but guarantees to workers primary-market job rights.

Bureaucratic control also moved the firm out of secondary-market employment, not because of any compromise with workers but rather due to employers' efforts to avoid the need for such compromise. Bureaucratic control reversed the first-resort dependence on reserve-army discipline, and firms intentionally put in its place the greater job security, promotion prospects, and assumption of long-term employment that characterize primary-market jobs.

[. . .]

If technical control leads to subordinate primary employment and bureaucratic control to an independent primary market, simple control results in secondary-type jobs; in this case, both the labor process and the accompanying labor market are distinguished by the *lack* of elaborate structural or institutional features. The essence of simple control, in either its entrepreneurial or hierarchical form, is the arbitrary power of foremen and supervisors to direct work, to monitor performance, and to discipline or reward workers. Almost by definition, the workers in such a system can have little job security. More subtly, the absence of a structurally based control system provides little avenue or incentive for worker promotion, so secondary jobs turn into dead ends.

Secondary employers generally do not have the scale, the volume of profits, or the stability to make the long-term commitments necessary to establish primary-market employment. For example, guarantees of employment security and benefits and privileges rising with seniority typically require contractual obligations extending considerably into the future. Similarly, the administrative apparatus associated with formal periodic review of workers' performance, grievance appeals, and the like, requires a further long-term commitment of resources. The core firm, with its huge scale and extensive market power, plans for the long-term in all its operations, including the organization of its labor force; the periphery firm cannot.

The result of the great changes in work organization inside core firms, then, has been reflected in a corresponding change in labor markets. Systems of control in the core firms now differ from those in the firms of the competitive periphery, and in turn labor markets have become segmented. The different systems of control are not the only force pushing toward labor segmentation, but they surely are one of the most important.[9] This view of the aggregate job structure leads directly to an analysis of the labor force—that is, to the parts or fractions of the working class.

NOTES

1. This account is taken from Ann Bookman (1977); Bookman's work presents an exceptionally insightful description of supervision, control, and conflict at Digitex. Both the name of this firm and the names and personal details of all the workers have been changed to protect them.

2. Again we may quote Marx (1867, Vol. I, p. 331): "As the number of the cooperating laborers increases, so too does their resistance to the domination of capital, and with it, the necessity for capital to overcome this resistance by counter-pressure. The control exercised by the capitalist is not only a special function, due to the nature of the social labor-process, and peculiar to that process, but it is, at the same time, a function of the exploitation of a social labor-process, and is consequently rooted in the unavoidable antagonism between the exploiter and the living and laboring raw material he exploits."

3. In each period there have been pressures toward both homogenization and segmentation, as, for example, capitalists played upon ethnic divisions in the last century to break up working class solidarity, and they have integrated black auto workers into the mainstream white male

labor force in this century. But the dominant trend in the last century was homogenization, and, in this century, redivision.

4. Neoclassical economists, especially human capital theorists, remain committed to their ideal of the individual as economic agent. They have not been able to square this view with the facts, however, and sex and race continue to be important explanations in wage or income analysis; see, for example, Zvi Griliches and William Mason (1972).

5. Perhaps at one time "blue-collar" was an effective shorthand term for this market segment, but as many observers (David Gordon, 1972b; Paul Osterman, 1975; Harry Braverman, 1974) have noted, the blue- versus white-collar distinction has lost most of its persuasiveness. For one thing, many blue-collar jobs have achieved the pay, independence, mental labor components, and privileges formerly associated with white-collar status; more significantly, the machine-pacing, low pay, lack of privileges, and manual-labor job activities formerly thought to characterize only blue-collar employment have increasingly come to dominate at least the lower rungs of white-collar jobs. The old distinctions, which may well have been inaccurate for the past, become positively mystifying for the present, hence the need for new categories.

6. The secondary market includes periphery-sector manufacturing firms that have made increasing use of technical or mechanical methods of control, especially time and motion study and machine-pacing of individual jobs. These firms in general still retain simple control (arbitrary power of foremen and supervisors) as their basic organization of power reinforced by these mechanical means; most revealingly, the enforcement of machine paces is achieved through bullying and other personal tactics aimed at the worker. Nonetheless, the peripheral sector (containing all enterprises except core firms) displays great diversity, and so do its workplaces.

7. In the human capital version, only the technical characteristics matter, and they do not give rise to distinct markets but rather simply to different market outcomes because of people's different endowments of human capital; see Jacob Mincer (1974). In the dual labor market version, general versus specific skills, on-the-job learning versus lack of it, and so on become the causes of market segmentation; see Peter Doeringer and Michael Piore (1971). The statement here is equivalent to saying that within the range of possible techniques, there is sufficient choice to permit selection based on compatability with

different forms of work organization. The firm's choice cannot be described as "efficient," since this concept cannot be defined once we admit the distinction between labor and labor power but it certainly is the most profitable.

8. Note that the success of industrial unions in pushing mass-production core firms to subordinate primary-employment patterns does not in general derive from their ability to exclude other workers; instead, the unions' power derives from their ability to mobilize all those in the industry. In this sense segmentation results from the struggle over control of the labor process rather than through market exclusion.

9. Other sources are racism and sexism, the conscious efforts of employers to split the working class, and more diverse "cultural" factors involving family structure and schooling. See David Gordon, Richard Edwards, and Michael Reich (forthcoming).

REFERENCES

Bookman, Ann. 1977. *The Process of Political Socialization Among Women and Immigrant Workers: A Case Study of Unionization in the Electronics Industry.* Unpublished doctoral dissertation, Harvard University.

Braverman, Harry. 1974. *Labor and Monopoly Capital.* New York: Monthly Review Press,

Doeringer, Peter and Michael Piore. 1971. *Internal Labor Markets and Manpower Analysis.* Lexington, MA.: D.C. Heath, Lexington Books.

Gordon, David. 1972b. "From Steam Whistles to Coffee Breaks." *Dissent,* Winter 1972.

Gordon, David, Richard Edwards, and Michael Reich. Forthcoming. "Labor Market Segmentation in American Capitalism."

Griliches, Zvi and William Mason. 1972. "Education, Income, and Ability." *Journal of Political Economy,* May-June.

Marx, Karl. 1867 (Vol. I, p. 331). *Capital.* Volumes I, II, and III. New York: International Publishers, 1967. (Volume I first published in 1967.)

Mincer, Jacob. 1974. *Schooling, Experience, and Earnings.* New York: Columbia University Press.

Osterman, Paul. 1975. An Empirical Study of Labor Market Segmentation." *Journal of Industrial and Labor Relations.*

31

THE ACCESS PROCESS

Loopholes as a System

DAN CLAWSON

ALAN NEUSTADTL

DENISE SCOTT

The access process is key to most corporate government relations operations. Raising money, running the political action committee, and giving gifts are only means to an end, and the end is to gain "access" to members of Congress. This chapter challenges four myths or misconceptions about corporate political activity in the access process: that what matters is persuading members of Congress to vote a certain way on crucial laws; that corporations exert influence through an explicit exchange of PAC money for congressional votes; that Democrats and Republicans, or liberals and conservatives, differ fundamentally on the issue of special benefits for corporations and industries; and

that this process operates automatically with no significant effort by corporations and in any case has minimal consequences.

MYTH ONE: KEY VOTES ARE THE ISSUE

Many critics of PACs and campaign finance seem to feel that a corporate PAC officer walks into a member's office and says, "Senator, I want you to vote against the Clean Air Act. Here's $5,000 to do so." This view, in this crude form, is simply wrong. The (liberal) critics who hold this view seem to reason as follows: (1) we know that PAC money gives

From Chapter 4, *Money Talks: Corporate PACs and Political Influence*, by Dan Clawson, Alan Neustadtl, and Denise Scott. New York: Basic Books. Copyright © 1992; reprinted by permission.

corporations power in relation to Congress; (2) power is the ability to make someone do something against their will; (3) therefore campaign money must force members to switch their votes on key issues. We come to the same conclusion about the outcome—corporate power in relation to Congress—but differ from conventional critics on both the understanding of power and the nature of the process through which campaign money exercises its influence.

The debate over campaign finance is frequently posed as, "Did special interests buy the member's vote on a key issue?" Media accounts as well as most academic analyses in practice adopt this approach. With the question framed in this way, we have to agree with the corporate political action committee directors we interviewed, who answered, "No, they didn't." But they believed it followed that they have no power and maybe not even any influence, and we certainly don't agree with that. If power means the ability to *force* a member of Congress to vote a certain way on a major bill, corporate PACs rarely have power. However, corporations and their PACs have a great deal of power if power means the ability to exercise a field of influence that shapes the behavior of other social actors. [. . .] Members of Congress meet regularly with some people, share trust, discuss the issues honestly off the record, and become friends, while other people have a hard time getting in the door much less getting any help. Members don't have to be forced; most of them are eager to do favors for corporations and do so without the public's knowledge. [. . .]

High-Visibility Issues

Corporate PAC officers could stress two key facts: First, on important highly visible issues they cannot determine the way a member of Congress votes; second, even for low-visibility issues the entire process is loose and uncertain. The more visible an issue, the less likely that a member's vote will be determined by campaign contributions. If the whole world is watching, a member from an environmentally conscious district can't vote against the Clean Air Act because it is simply too popular.

[. . .]

Virtually all access-oriented PACs went out of their way at some point in the interview to make it clear that they do not and could not buy a member's vote on any significant issue. No corporate official felt otherwise; moreover, these opinions seemed genuine and not merely for public consumption. They pointed out that the maximum legal donation by a PAC is $5,000 per candidate per election. Given that in 1988 the cost of an average winning House campaign was $388,000 and for the Senate $3,745,000, no individual company can provide the financial margin of victory in any but the closest of races. A member of Congress would be a fool to trade 5 percent of the district's votes for the maximum donation an individual PAC can make ($5,000) or even for ten times that amount. Most PACs therefore feel they have little influence.

[. . .]

Low-Visibility Issues and Nonissues

This is true only if we limit our attention to highly visible, publicly contested issues. Most corporate PACs, and most government relations units, focus only a small fraction of their time, money, and energy on the final votes on such issues. So-called access-oriented PACs have a different purpose and style. Their aim is not to influence the member's public vote on the final piece of legislation, but rather to be sure that the bill's wording exempts their company from the bill's most costly or damaging provisions. If tax law is going to be changed, the aim of the company's government relations unit, and its associated PAC, is to be sure that the law has built-in loopholes that protect the company. The law may say that corporate tax rates are increased, and that's what the media and the public think, but section 739, subsection J, paragraph iii, contains a hard-to-decipher phrase. No ordinary mortal can figure out what it means or to whom it applies, but the consequence is that the company doesn't pay the taxes you'd think it would. For example, the 1986 Tax "Reform" Act contained a provision limited to a single company, identified as a "corporation incorporated on June 13, 1917, which has its principal place of business in Bartlesville, Oklahoma." With that provision in the bill, Philips Petroleum didn't mind at all if Congress wanted to "reform" the tax laws.

Two characteristics of such provisions structure the way they are produced. First, by their very nature such provisions, targeted at one (or at most a few) corporations or industries, are unlikely to mobilize widespread business support. Other businesses may not want to oppose these provisions, but neither are they likely to make them a priority, though the broader the scope the broader the support. Business as a whole is somewhat uneasy about very narrow provisions, although most corporations and industry trade associations feel they must fight for their own. Peak business associations such as the Business Roundtable generally prefer a "clean" bill with clear provisions favoring business in general rather than a "Christmas tree" with thousands of special-interest provisions. Most corporations play the game, however, and part of playing the game is not to object to or publicize what other corporations are doing. But they don't feel good about what they do, and if general-interest business associations took a stand they would probably speak against, rather than in favor of, these provisions.

Second, however, these are low-visibility issues; in fact, most of them are not "issues" at all in that they are never examined or contested. The corporation's field of power both makes the member willing to cooperate and gets the media and public to in practice accept these loopholes as noncontroversial. Members don't usually have to take a stand on these matters or be willing to face public scrutiny. If the proposal does become contested, the member probably can back off and drop the issue with few consequences, and the corporation probably can go down the hall and try again with another member.

[. . .]

The Bottom Line

When we asked corporate PAC officers to give us an example of what their office tries to do, about 90 percent described a tax loophole they had won. It reached the point where we started asking for an example of anything but taxes.

[. . .]

How much do these tax loopholes cost? Congress estimated the revenue loss through loopholes in the 1986 Tax "Reform" Act at $10.6 billion, but this number is taken seriously only by those who still believe in the tooth fairy. Consider Barlett and Steele's estimates for the losses incurred by just one loophole:

The cost of one break was originally placed by the Joint Committee at $300 million. After passage of the legislation, the figure was adjusted upward to $7 billion.

> That worked out to a 2,233 percent miscalculation, a mistake so large as to defy comprehension. It would be roughly akin to a family who bought a house expecting to pay $400 a month on its mortgage but who discovered, belatedly, the payments would actually be $9,332 a month.

Or consider the cost of the special tax provision to help the Long Island Power Authority buy and shut down the Shoreham nuclear power plant. This provision was buried in what Congress referred to as a deficit reduction measure. The Joint Committee on Taxation originally said the bailout would cost $1 million, then revised that just a tad to $241 million. The true cost is estimated at $3.5 to $4 billion.

This kind of special-interest provision is put into all kinds of bills, not just the Tax Code. In many ways the tax give-aways are the least of it. With them all we lose are tens of billions of dollars, a basic sense of fairness, and our trust in and respect for the political system. With clean air much more is at risk—all the same elements as the Tax Code, along with the cancer rate and the future of the earth. If a few million dollars are transferred to the Bechtel family (already on the *Forbes* list of the 400 richest Americans) as a subsidy for a luxury cruise ship, all we lose is money. But if industry is allowed to "save" a few hundred million by pumping poison into the air, we may never be able to clean it, and trying to do so will certainly cost a great deal more than the amount that the companies "saved" by picking our pockets. *[. . .]*

Business Hegemony

. . . One of the best indications of the power of business is that not only are corporations able to win themselves billions of dollars through tax loopholes, but they are able to do so without much public exposure or blame. *[. . .]*

On those rare occasions when the media do identify and focus on a provision, the company and member can and do defend themselves, providing a thousand reasons why this is good policy, why this provision isn't really a loophole at all, why this is a way of improving the bill, of preserving the spirit of the bill without creating unfortunate consequences that were never intended for this particular case. Benefitting a company in the member's district is always an adequate reason to support a provision. A member who helps a respectable business to increase its profits is almost never vulnerable.

[. . .]

MYTH TWO: MONEY IS EXPLICITLY EXCHANGED FOR VOTES

Getting Access and Shaping a Solution

The PAC plays its most crucial role in helping the corporation to gain access, but even here there is no one-to-one correspondence between money and outcome. Corporate PAC officials sometimes talked as if it were normal that anyone who wanted to see a member of Congress could do so—even if the person didn't live in the member's state or district. One executive saw this as a right, not a privilege: "You want to have access to the member so you or your experts can tell your story. That's what the Constitution guarantees." At other times gaining access was presented as a significant problem and the PAC as vital to this process. Fairly typical was a company whose plant in a specific area had come under attack for environmental pollution but whose PAC officer argued that "the entire economic framework of that whole section of the country" depends on the company's plant, which therefore put the company in a strong position. Some academics argue that this alone should guarantee the company success, but this executive didn't agree:

Interviewer: So does the PAC really change anything? Suppose you didn't have a PAC? You'd still have 2,000 employees and a $50 million payroll. . . .

PAC director: I wouldn't have the access, and it may sound like bullshit, but I'm telling you very sincerely, I wouldn't know Governor X to the degree that we know the governor and his staff; we wouldn't know Bob Y, the local congressman, as well as we know him; and we wouldn't know the junior senator as well.

Not everyone can get in to talk to every member, but when a lobbyist does get an appointment, it's necessary to be prepared with a carefully thought out proposal and supporting evidence or exhibits. The company lobbyist can't prepare this by him or herself; many other company officials must be actively involved.

When legislation appears on the horizon, we send a copy of the bill to one of our government relations people, and he has the ability to go around to our different business sector units and talk to people. If it's a tax bill, talk to our tax department. If it's a product liability bill, talk to the legal department and flesh out how that bill would affect our company. Based on that, we might have a couple of meetings with some of the people from our Washington office that covers that legislation and people from the business sector it would affect. They'll sit down and say, "Here's what the bill says. We think it's great," or "we think it's terrible. We can maybe amend it to say this instead of that. We can live with that." And that's how we come up with our positions on the issues.

[. . .] The more carefully a company's proposal is crafted and the more fully its arguments are supported, the more likely the member is to accept the proposal. Congressional staffs have expanded but are still minimal. If a small company correctly identifies a technical problem with the proposed wording of a bill but is unable to suggest a modification that fixes this problem without abandoning the entire bill, it is unlikely that the member's staff would have someone with the technical expertise needed to do so. The more effort required by the member, the less likely he or she is to work on the problem. This becomes a further structural factor favoring big business over most alternative groups, whether small business, the homeless, or environmental activists.

When corporate lobbyists meet with a member or key staffer, they feel they must have full and complete information, present it honestly, explain why their alternative proposal is reasonable, and make a case that it constitutes better policy. "It's all education. That's what lobbying really is. In fact, if you do it right, it's to supply the best information you can about your side, but the information you supply cannot be so biased that it's no good to them." [. . .] It is necessary to give the member the full picture, even facts that might hurt the company's case:

> You lose your reputation for honesty and integrity, and that's it. You are finished. So as much as you might say, "Well, I'll tilt this or scratch that," or "I'll take that column out of the chart," that doesn't pay in the long run. It really doesn't.

Once information has been presented fully and accurately, the lobbyist then makes the case for the company's proposed alternative. The alternative is not presented as naked self-interest: "screw the environment; we'll make an extra $50 million if we poison the river." Rather it should be put in practical and highminded terms: "No one cares more about the environment than we at the Loot-and-Pillage Corporation. We have been moving to upgrade our facilities as rapidly as is economically practical. However, our plant in Flaming River was built before this concern with the environment, and there is no rational way to fix it to meet these unreasonable standards. If this law were passed, we would have to close that plant; the issue here is not just the effect on our bottom line, but jobs for our loyal employees in Flaming River. The modification we propose would allow that plant to continue producing; the plant would improve its environmental record, and as soon as economically practicable it would meet the more rigorous standard. We have a study here showing that this would have a negligible effect on the environment and would save 1,247 jobs. If you are prepared to make this change, we'll be able to live with this bill. I realize that we don't always see eye-to-eye on all issues, but you've always been reasonable, our PAC has supported you in the past and hopes to do so in the future, we've worked together on other issues, and the change we are proposing here is totally reasonable."

In some cases the member simply accepts the proposed change for any of a variety of reasons: it really does seem totally reasonable; the plant is in his or her district and the potential job loss would be serious; the member has a long-standing friendship with the corporate lobbyist, always feels that

"what's good for business is good for America," or just wants campaign contributions and doesn't care that much about the environment. In many cases, however, the member has a set of tough questions and is not prepared to accept the company proposal until it is substantially modified. If the member asks, the lobbyist must give an honest and knowledgeable assessment of the likely political impact.

[. . .]

The nature of the friendly live-and-let-live relations between PACs and members of Congress means that if members can't accept the company's initial proposal they often ask the corporate lobbyist to help them fashion solutions:

> They say, "Here's what I think, here's what you think. Can you rework this out so I can give you a little piece of the pie and still not screw the other 93 percent of my district who want it the other way?" And we say, "Yes, if you can just do this. It doesn't change the bill, but at least it allows us to do this." It's the fun of the game.

[. . .]

. . . Sometimes the member of Congress is unwilling to help, and feels that the company's request is not reasonable, either because of the member's perception of good policy or because of the political realities. [. . .] The company has two choices: if the member is not vital to this issue (for example, does not chair the key committee or subcommittee), the company can just move down the hall and try other members. If the member is vital or if the concerns the member expressed seem likely to be widespread, the company can modify its proposal, which probably means another round of meetings with corporate managers, experts, and lawyers. The lobbyist needs to explain the member's concerns, and then the assembled company group needs to consider alternative solutions, and see whether some of them might be satisfactory to both the company and the member.

[. . .]

The PAC Is Only Part of the Process

Most PAC officers insist that money alone is not enough.

[. . .]

Corporate government relations specialists, members of Congress, and their staffs get to know each other and become friends. Most of these people, on both the corporate and congressional sides, are extremely likeable. The proportion of warm, friendly, outgoing, genuinely nice people is about as high as you will find anywhere. It's their job to be like that, but it's clear that it is much more than that, that the job attracts people with that kind of personality. The people who aren't like that probably don't succeed at the job and tend to leave it, but whatever the reason, these are people you can't help liking. Although we have a lot more in common with academics than with corporate lobbyists, we found the corporate lobbyists were often easier to talk with, and despite the differences in our viewpoints they were friendlier and pleasanter to be with. While this point is difficult to convey, it is crucial to understand how outgoing and nice lobbyists are, and that this was not a pose put on for professional purposes.

In addition to being likeable people who smooth over social situations and help put people at ease, corporate government relations personnel inhabit the same social world as members of Congress and their staffs. [. . .] Many corporate lobbyists formerly worked as congressional aides or political appointees in one or another government agency. People shift positions fairly frequently; the key person to contact may be someone you worked with not long before, or a fraternity brother, or a member of your club, or someone who serves with you on the board of a local charity. The men regularly play golf together. One PAC official interrupted our interview to take a phone call making arrangements for a golf foursome with Dan Rostenkowski (chair of the House Ways and Means Committee, the committee in charge of all tax legislation), discussing the need for a fourth with the right level of golf skills and the right personality who would make an enjoyable golf partner. Our man explained it was important that everyone have a good time, but that didn't mean you couldn't also talk a little business. [. . .]

Unplanned contacts come easily and regularly for people who live in the same neighborhoods, belong to the same clubs, share friends and contacts, and inhabit the same social world. One PAC officer had car problems when driving her babysitter home and was helped by a man she didn't know. He turned out to be a member of the House Ways and Means Committee, and she has continued to have dealings with him since. In fact, as one PAC officer noted, "It's hard to quantify what is social and what is business":

> I can go to lunch with people and take two minutes of their time talking about my issue, and then we can spend the rest of the time catching up on what's new. Some of those people are my best friends on the Hill. I see them personally, socially, and they're very good to me; they always help me with my issues. I don't think you have to spend two hours of somebody's time groaning and beating an issue into their heads.

[. . .]

Legally, campaign contributors may not explicitly exchange cash for influence. Unlike the explicit exchange of an outright purchase in the market, campaign contributions are gifts based on a basic trust the gift will be reciprocated if and when it is appropriate. . . . An explicit request for a quid pro quo would be not only illegal (and therefore risky to both parties), but gauche and inappropriate. An analogy can be made to a date: if a man takes a woman to an expensive restaurant and then to a major event, if he spares no expense to show that he cares about her and regards her as special, this increases the probability that she will agree to and want to have sex with him. However, were a man to propose an explicit exchange ("I'll buy you a steak if you'll spend the night with me"), the odds are high that the woman would be offended and the date a disaster.

[. . .]

This culture gives enormous advantages to long-term big players. Even if a corporation hasn't contributed to the member of Congress it most needs to see, other members and other corporate officials can provide introductions and testimonials. The member knows that the corporation is a major player, has been around for a long time, and has the resources to deliver. The corporation will be able to give a PAC contribution every election for as long as the member is in Congress and do so without straining corporate resources. [. . .] It is this sort of reputation that both individuals and corporations work for years to achieve. With such a reputation, very little needs to be made explicit. A wink and a nod communicate everything; even the wink and nod may be superfluous. [. . .]

MYTH THREE:
POLITICAL PARTY MATTERS

One popular conception labels the Democrats the party of the common people and the Republicans the party of big business. Another common perception is that conservatives support a level playing field and want government to avoid interfering with the free market. An example from each end of the political spectrum shows this is not the case. Steve Symms is an ultraconservative Republican from Idaho; his election was supported by virtually every conservative ideological PAC, and the *Almanac of American Politics* characterized him as "one of the closest things to a libertarian in Congress: he opposes practically every kind of government program." Nonetheless, in the 1986 Tax Reform Act he introduced a special provision to save Unocal $50 million. In the same bill at the other end of the (elected) political spectrum, Daniel Patrick Moynihan, Democrat of New York and rated by the *National Journal* as the most liberal senator on economic issues in 1982, sponsored special favors for a sports stadium in Buffalo, for a brokerage firm, and one that applied only to the royalties earned by five biomedical researchers in Rochester.

When we began these interviews, we knew that many Democrats and many well-known liberals were happy to do special-interest favors for corporations. Nonetheless, we assumed corporate PACs would have many enemies in Congress—people who were out to get them and that they in turn wanted to defeat. We regularly asked about this in interviews and were surprised to learn that corporations didn't really feel they had enemies in Congress. Yes, there were lots of members who opposed them on any given issue, but no, there weren't any members they considered unreasonable. Essentially *all* members of Congress are at least potentially willing to help them out, to give them access, to let them make their case. One PAC official told us, "You have guys that will hold rallies right outside this building here, hold news conferences and picket lines periodically, every year," attacking the company and its policies. However, "When they go to the Congress . . . they tend to ameliorate their anti-big business or proconsumer stance." Even the people who used to lead demonstrations against the company become more open to receiving information from and entering a dialogue with the company: "I don't want to say that they are the best friends we have in government, but you can go to them."

This doesn't mean that every corporation is happy with every member, only that almost no people were regularly mentioned as hostile to business.

[. . .]

The nonadversarial character of the member-lobbyist relationship depends on at least two factors— the legitimacy of U.S. business and the limited resources of public-interest movements. First, U.S. business is accorded great legitimacy and acceptance; the widespread notion that what's good for business is good for America is held in some fashion even by many of the critics of business. Except in rare instances where a highly visible disaster threatens lives or the environment, business is regarded as a pillar of the community—even when it argues that it should be able to pollute the atmosphere, threaten its workers' health and safety, and avoid its fair share of taxes. *[. . .]* Second, although the opponents of business became much more visible and effective in the late 1960s and have retained much of their political capacity, public-interest movements rarely have the resources to contest the *details* of congressional (or regulatory agency) actions. Environmental movements can and do put their issues on the agenda and manage to focus attention on a handful of the most visible corporate attempts to cripple the law by arguing for a "clean" bill without special exceptions. As such they are the main opposition corporate polluters need to worry about. But they have not been in a position to engage in hand- to-hand combat over each and every special exemption. Exposure by such movements is the main thing a member needs to fear, but there are tens of thousands of corporate special deals struck each year, and public-interest movements are lucky if they can focus major media attention on ten of these and minor attention on another hundred. Still less is the labor movement or any other organized representative of the bottom half of the income distribution able to contest corporate tax loopholes. Corporations are in a no-lose situation: no group pushes to impose extra burdens on corporations that try to win loopholes. If such groups existed and if members were frequently sympathetic to such claims, corporate lobbyists might modify their policy of honesty and full disclosure. This policy could be interpreted as an indication that members and corporations generally see themselves as basically on the same side, even if they differ on specifics—an interpretation that is further supported by the numerous occasions when members allow corporations to write the specific wording they want incorporated in a bill.

[. . .]

MYTH FOUR: BUSINESS WINS WITHOUT EFFORT

A different sort of misconception about the access or special-interest process is held by some people on the left of the political spectrum who feel that this process operates automatically, that business is guaranteed to win with no significant effort by corporations, and in any case that the consequences are minimal. Some people believe that Congress is unimportant and that all key decisions are made by the president and executive branch. The access process described in this chapter is what G. William Domhoff calls the special-interest process, and it is the simplest and least significant of his four processes of ruling-class domination. Structural Marxists such as Nicos Poulantzas or Fred Block argue that business does not need to be conscious of its interests or to mobilize to achieve its aims and that the nature of the system requires politicians and the state to do what business wants in order to maintain a healthy economy.

To some degree we agree with this reservation. The access process is not the sole basis for corporate power. The primary foundation of business power is the ability to make day-to-day business decisions unless and until the government intervenes. This, together with control over vast resources, makes it possible for a measly $1,000 to win the corporation not only access to the member but the member's support for a multimillion-dollar corporate benefit. However, access through a carefully placed PAC contribution is one component of corporate power and by no means a trivial one. *[. . .]*

Corporations find it cheap to gain access, but the process also demonstrates the limits to business power and the effort corporations must make to retain their privileged position. The access process is a limited response to legislation that business would prefer had never been proposed. Corporations seek special provisions to protect themselves only because they can't totally defeat the legislation. *[. . .]*

The limits to corporate power need to be recognized both theoretically and politically. A failure to do so leads to cynicism and despair—a sense that nothing can be done, that people can't make a difference. No question about it, the odds are stacked in favor of business, and the rest of us have to engage in massive struggles to win small victories—but victories are possible. We have won them in the past and will win them in the future. These are not only token victories either; they are real changes that bring substantial improvement. Unions have brought millions of workers higher living standards along with more dignity and respect. The environmental movement is responsible for some improvements, and some instances where we have been able to hold the line, in the struggle to preserve the earth. *[. . .]*

Even the special exceptions that corporations win for themselves require persistent effort. If members of Congress were always eager to do what corporations wanted, corporate PACs would not need to contribute to safe incumbents or establish personal connections through attending fundraisers. Corporate government relations departments wouldn't have to mount major campaigns to win their special exceptions. People can't be sure exactly how much difference the PAC makes, but there is a clear sense that it can provide a critical edge.

[. . .]

But in doing so PACs sometimes find themselves coerced to make contributions they resent. Part of this is just the endemic pressure by candidates discussed in the previous chapter. Another part, however, is PACs that would prefer to be ideological, to support conservatives without regard to access, sometimes find that they have to play the game and contribute to liberals who are anathema to them, in hopes of future access.

Language and Euphemism

[. . .] Many, although by no means all, of the PAC directors we spoke with are uncomfortable about the access process. They don't like what they do, feel it is slightly sleazy, and are embarrassed and defensive about it. Generally speaking they resent buying access and influence. The corporate government relations officials don't feel embarrassed about the policy changes they ask for and don't feel they are indefensible special-interest legislation. Their concern is that the members ought to be making better policy, and should not be giving their companies a hard time. PAC directors are uneasy that the corporation is supporting liberals that don't belong in public office. From the perspective of the people we interviewed, what troubles them is not their exercise of power—which they see as not really power at all but simply helping members to craft better public policy—but the limits to that power, the fact that they are drawn into cooperating with liberals rather than throwing the bums out. A few of the most pragmatic PAC directors didn't seem to mind this, primarily on the argument that these liberals are actually happy to cooperate and do favors for business. But many people we interviewed seemed uncomfortable contributing to what they see as antibusiness liberals. They wish they didn't have to do it but feel it is necessary to get the results they need from Washington. Corporate PAC directors often feel defensive about these donations, and most corporations respond by specifically reserving some of their money to support "probusiness" "free-market" candidates who are either running for open seats or challenging entrenched incumbents.

Policy Implications

[. . .] The access (or special-interest) process aids business control of society in at least two interrelated ways. First, the cumulative impact of these minor changes subverts the stated intent of the policy. When "minor" change is added to "minor" change, the ultimate bill does little to reform taxes or clean the air. . . . By the time the process is through the regulation is far from what it should have been; it fails to have much impact, but this is precisely the way it was designed and intended. . . .

Second, the access process serves and promotes business power because it is uniquely suited to frustrating the popular will. The process introduces endless delays and complications and moves issues out of the spotlight and into the backrooms where only "experts" and power brokers are allowed. The kinds of tax regulations we quoted earlier are designed to prevent the public from knowing what is happening. The process is successful in that it keeps people uninformed and their anger diffuse. A major investigation is necessary simply to know what the government is doing. The consequence is that people without lots of time and resources get discouraged and go away.

The access process thus becomes a major weapon used to frustrate and sidetrack social movements. People become cynical and discouraged, convinced that meaningful change is impossible, that the more things change the more they stay the same, that all politics is dirty, that "you can't fight city hall." This disillusionment can serve business's purpose, since an ineffective government leaves business in control of most decisions. *[. . .]*

PART XII

ORGANIZATIONAL DEVIANCE

Rational systems theories represent organizations as tools for achieving some goal, but sometimes members of the broader society view that goal or the means used to achieve it as illegitimate or as seriously mistaken, or individuals within the organization may make mistakes or use their position in ways that are illegitimate. Organizational deviance has been defined as anything occurring in an organization that departs from formal goals and/or normative standards or expectations and that results in an unanticipated and undesirable outcome. These are mistakes, misconduct, and disasters that violate organizational rules, government laws, and social expectations (Vaughan 1999).

Of course, groups may vary in their definition of what is deviant. Throughout most of the nineteenth and part of the twentieth centuries, depending on the activity, there were few effective laws against monopolies, predatory business practices, the use of dangerous drugs like morphine in over-the-counter patent medicines, sweatshop working conditions, strong-arm anti-union tactics, the manipulation of stock prices, deceptive advertising, and industrial pollution. Eventually, public pressure resulted in the outlawing of what some had considered merely sharp business practices.

Still, organizations of all sorts continue to act in ways considered illegitimate or illegal. The willful neglect of safety defects in the auto industry has remained a public concern in the thirty-five years since Ralph Nader wrote *Unsafe at Any Speed: The Designed-In Dangers of the American Automobile*. Tobacco companies continued to claim cigarettes posed no health risk long after their internal scientific research demonstrated otherwise. Government misconduct includes most famously the Watergate scandal, which began as a break-in at Democratic campaign headquarters by Nixon reelection campaign staff, eventually engulfing the entire administration in conspiracies and intrigue and revealing a long list of other illegal and unethical actions. Department of Defense procurement was a persistent source of scandal as weapons suppliers overcharged the government and top military officers regularly took jobs with defense contractors after retiring from the military. Charities have also been questioned about how they use the funds they raise, including the percentage spent on executive salaries, staff, and other overhead.

More recently, many stock market analysts made wildly optimistic estimates of the future value of new, Internet-related companies, and thus contributed to the overvaluation of stock prices that eventually harmed many investors when the bubble burst. Some charge that financial services firms allowed or encouraged their analysts to make such predictions to help their investment banking departments win business and commissions from appreciative dot-coms or merely as an irresponsible bid to gain attention in a blossoming stock market mania. These firms have tried to restore confidence in their objectivity by announcing that in the future they will disclose their investment banking relationships with the companies whose performance they analyze and require analysts to disclose their own stockholdings or prohibit them from buying shares in companies they follow, but it remains to be seen whether much changes ("Henry Blodget" 2001).

More seriously, decades of lax airport security following airline deregulation finally had catastrophic consequences when terrorists were able to commandeer four aircraft and use them to attack the Pentagon and destroy the World Trade Towers in New York City, killing an estimated 3,000 people in the deadliest attack on U.S. soil. The gaps in airline security reflected long-standing industry efforts to keep employee wages, including other security staff, as low as possible in what had become a highly competitive market and the willingness of government regulators to let the airlines have their way ("Federal Interest Varies" 2001).

Even when some within an organization attempt to stop problems before they get out of hand, mistakes and misconduct have a way of gathering their own momentum. In the late 1960s, B. F. Goodrich was so desperate to regain business from the defense contractor LTV that it made unrealistic promises about the quality and low price of a braking system it proposed to supply for LTV's new jets to be built for the U.S. Air Force (Vandivier 1979). The design engineer and management refused to heed warnings from a junior engineer and other lower-level personnel that the brake system was failing performance tests. Further investments of time and money led to an escalation of commitment. As the costs of admitting the mistake rose, Goodrich officials insisted that work on the system proceed as planned. Others aware of the problem inside the company continued to approve each new stage of the project to satisfy their superiors and pointed to other departments as more responsible for the overall project than they were. Everyone worried about the effects of blowing the whistle on their careers, as managers tend to blame the messengers who bring bad news, charge them with disloyalty to the organization, and deny the problem to save face.

Flight tests of the new plane by Air Force pilots resulted in near crashes due to brake failure. Goodrich consented to redesign the brake system along the lines recommended by the junior engineer who identified the problem originally. The FBI opened an investigation of Goodrich's actions as a conspiracy to commit fraud, and a Congressional committee also conducted an investigation. Goodrich officials vigorously denied any wrongdoing, and eventually the matter was dropped. Those within Goodrich who had objected to the project going forward were forced out, while those who went along with the project and were politically adept at shifting responsibility for the dirty work to others remained and were even promoted. Although no one individually may have been happy going along with the project, as members of a bureaucratic hierarchicy facing external economic pressures they agreed to decisions that endangered others' lives.

A study of recent graduates from the Harvard Business School found similar forces at work today. These recent MBAs reported their middle-manager bosses value performance above all, sometimes pressure them to engage in unethical actions, reward loyalty rather than an overinvestment in ethics, punish those who report bad news or blow the whistle on misconduct, and sometimes reward those who engage in unscrupulous action. Senior executives are either uninvolved at the operational level of detail at which the decisions are made or seek to dodge responsibility for them. Those surveyed believed that most who pressured them to act unethically were themselves under intense organizational pressure and feared for their careers, with some in jobs they could not fully handle. Those with more experience learn to accept these facts and choose carefully when to take a stand and when to compromise their ethics (Badaracco and Webb 1995; Vaughan 1999, p. 286).

More representative surveys also find that most who observe misconduct in their organizations do not report it to others inside or outside the organization, and those who do so usually face retaliation, such as closer monitoring by supervisors, negative performance evaluations, criticism or avoidance by coworkers, being forced from their jobs, and even industry blacklisting. Depression, feelings of powerlessness, financial difficulties, and health problems often follow. Whistle-blowing is often a traumatic experience for employees who take that path (Rothschild and Miethe 1999).

Nevertheless, the force of organizational circumstances and group complicity does not excuse individual responsibility. The most extreme examples of organizational deviance are from Nazi Germany, where governmental agencies and private corporations constructed and operated slave labor and extermination camps. These camps included inhumane medical experiments that used inmates like lab animals, injecting them with serious diseases or subjecting them to extreme heat, cold, or pain to study their physiological reactions. The camps involved some of the biggest names in German industry and German subsidiaries of American companies, which were then under German control, such as Bayer, Audi, Siemens, IBM, and Ford, as well as many ordinary Germans working for them and for the government directly.

Many individuals explained their actions to a shocked world by saying that they were only following orders from superiors and were just doing their job. Individuals could satisfy themselves they were blameless as long as they could claim limited authority and responsibility for the overall mission, deny knowledge of other department's actions, and claim to be merely cogs within a system over which they had no control. The hierarchy of command and division of labor in a Weberian bureaucracy diffused responsibility and became a refuge and excuse for uncritical service to an organization, no matter how corrupt and depraved its goals and methods.

But research on organizational deviance, mostly examining mistakes and disasters rather than misconduct, argues that many events are more the routine byproduct of normal system operation than deliberate calculations of the costs and benefits of engaging in questionable or unethical conduct. The reading by Charles Perrow explains his theory of normal accidents in complex technological systems, such as the Three Mile Island nuclear power plant accident, as a result of mishaps that become magnified when systems are composed of complexly interrelated parts and in which consequences of one part failing quickly stress or damage other parts of the system (Reading 32).

Diane Vaughan's explanation of the decision to launch the space shuttle *Challenger*, which exploded and killed all astronauts on board shortly after launch, illustrates some of Perrow's ideas, among others (Reading 33). Her reading indicates that disasters can result from an accumulation of rule violations and unacceptable events that are ignored or misinterpreted as unthreatening because of strong assumptions that the system is safe, thus neutralizing signs of danger. NASA's belief in the technical excellence of its operations, well-deserved given its past history, combined with new pressures to cut costs and subcontract more operations to outside manufacturers, led the agency to certify weak or defective components as an acceptable risk prior to the launch. Some of these problems may be remedied with greater oversight, but others reflect persistent problems within many organizations, such as bounded rationality, misperception and cognitive distortion, and the limits of interpretive abilities and sense making, as well as the organizational pressures to perform in an increasingly cost-conscious environment.

32

NORMAL ACCIDENTS
Living With High-Risk Technologies

CHARLES PERROW

INTRODUCTION

Welcome to the world of high-risk technologies. You may have noticed that they seem to be multiplying, and it is true. As our technology expands, as our wars multiply, and as we invade more and more of nature, we create systems—organizations, and the organization of organizations—that increase the risks for the operators, passengers, innocent bystanders, and for future generations. In this book we will review some of these systems—nuclear power plants, chemical plants, aircraft and air traffic control, ships, dams, nuclear weapons, space missions, and genetic engineering. Most of these risky enterprises have catastrophic potential, the ability to take the lives of hundreds of people in one blow, or to shorten or cripple the lives of thousands or millions more. Every year there are more such systems. That is the bad news.

The good news is that if we can understand the nature of risky enterprises better, we may be able to reduce or even remove these dangers. I have to present a lot of the bad news here in order to reach the good, but it is the possibility of managing high-risk technologies better than we are doing now that motivates this inquiry. There are many improvements we can make that I will not dwell on, because they are fairly obvious—such as better operator training, safer designs, more quality control, and more effective regulation. Experts are working on these solutions in both government and industry. I am not too sanguine about these efforts, since the risks seem to appear faster than the reduction of risks, but that is not the topic of this book.

Rather, I will dwell upon characteristics of high-risk technologies that suggest that no matter how effective conventional safety devices are, there is a form of accident that is inevitable. This is not good news for systems that have high catastrophic potential, such as nuclear power plants, nuclear weapons systems, recombinant DNA production, or even ships carrying highly toxic or explosive cargoes. It suggests, for example, that the probability of a nuclear plant meltdown with dispersion of radioactive materials to the atmosphere is not one chance in a million a year, but more like one chance in the next decade.

Most high-risk systems have some special characteristics, beyond their toxic or explosive or genetic dangers, that make accidents in them inevitable, even "normal." This has to do with the way failures can interact and the way the system is tied together. It is possible to analyze these special characteristics and in doing so gain a much better understanding of why accidents occur in these systems, and why they always will. If we know that, then we are in a better position to argue that certain technologies should be abandoned, and others, which we cannot abandon because we have built much of our society around them, should be modified. Risk will never be eliminated from high-risk systems, and we will never eliminate more than a few systems at best. At the very least, however, we might stop blaming the wrong people and the wrong factors, and stop trying to fix the systems in ways that only make them riskier.

The argument is basically very simple. We start with a plant, airplane, ship, biology laboratory, or other setting with a lot of components (parts, procedures, operators). Then we need two or more failures among components that interact in some unexpected way. No one dreamed that when X failed, Y would also be out of order and the two failures would interact so as to both start a fire and silence the fire alarm. Furthermore, no one can figure out the interaction at the time and thus know what to do. The problem is just something that never occurred to the designers. Next time they will put in an extra alarm system and a fire suppressor, but who knows, that might just allow three more unexpected interactions among inevitable failures. This interacting tendency is a characteristic of a system, not of a part or an operator, we will call it the "interactive complexity" of the system.

For some systems that have this kind of complexity, such as universities or research and development labs, the accident will not spread and be serious because there is a lot of slack available, and time to spare, and other ways to get things done. But suppose the system is also "tightly coupled," that is, processes happen very fast and can't be turned off, the failed parts cannot be isolated from other parts, or there is no other way to keep the production going safely. Then recovery from the initial disturbance is not possible; it will spread quickly and irretrievably for at least some time. Indeed, operator action or the safety systems may make it worse, since for a time it is not known what the problem really is.

Probably many production processes started out this way—complexly interactive and tightly coupled. But with experience, better designs, equipment, and procedures appeared, and the unsuspected interactions were avoided and the tight coupling reduced. This appears to have happened in the case of air traffic control, where interactive complexity and tight coupling have been reduced by better organization and "technological fixes." We will also see how the interconnection between dams and earthquakes is beginning to be understood. We now know that it involves a larger system than we originally thought when we just closed off a canyon and let it fill with water. But for most of the systems we shall consider in this book, neither better organization nor technological innovations appear to make them any less prone to system accidents. In fact, these systems require organizational structures that have large internal contradictions, and technological fixes that only increase interactive complexity and tighten the coupling; they become still more prone to certain kinds of accidents.

If interactive complexity and tight coupling—system characteristics—inevitably will produce an accident, I believe we are justified in calling it a *normal accident*, or a *system accident*. The odd term *normal accident* is meant to signal that, given the system characteristics, multiple and unexpected interactions of failures are inevitable. This is an expression of an integral characteristic of the system, not a statement of frequency. It is normal for us to die, but we only do it once. System accidents are uncommon, even rare; yet this is not all that reassuring, if they can produce catastrophes.

The best way to introduce the idea of a normal accident or a system accident is to give a hypothetical example from a homey, everyday experience. It should be familiar to all of us; it is one of those days when everything seems to go wrong.

A Day in the Life

You stay home from work or school because you have an important job interview downtown this morning that you have finally negotiated. Your friend or spouse has already left when you make breakfast, but unfortunately he or she has left the glass coffeepot on the stove with the light on. The coffee has boiled dry and the glass pot has cracked. Coffee is an addiction for you, so you rummage about in the closet until you find an old drip coffeemaker. Then you wait for the water to boil, watching the clock, and after a quick cup dash out the door. When you get to your car you find that in your haste you have left your car keys (and the apartment keys) in the apartment. That's okay, because there is a spare apartment key hidden in the hallway for just such emergencies. (This is a safety device, a *redundancy*, incidentally.) But then you remember that you gave a friend the key the other night because he had some books to pick up, and, planning ahead, you knew you would not be home when he came. (That finishes that *redundant pathway*, as engineers call it.)

Well, it is getting late, but there is always the neighbor's car. The neighbor is a nice old gent who drives his car about once a month and keeps it in good condition. You knock on the door, your tale ready. But he tells you that it just so happened that the generator went out last week and the man is coming this afternoon to pick it up and fix it. Another "backup" system has failed you, this time through no connection with your behavior at all (*uncoupled* or independent events, in this case, since the key and the generator are rarely connected). Well, there is always the bus. But not always. The nice old gent has been listening to the radio and tells you the threatened lock-out of the drivers by the bus company has indeed occurred. The drivers refuse to drive what they claim are unsafe buses, and incidentally want more money as well. (A safety system has foiled you, of all things.) You call a cab from your neighbor's apartment, but none can be had because of the bus strike. (These two events, the bus strike and the lack of cabs, are tightly connected, dependent events, or *tightly coupled* events, as we shall call them, since one triggers the other.)

You call the interviewer's secretary and say, "It's just too crazy to try to explain, but all sorts of things happened this morning and I can't make the interview with Mrs. Thompson. Can we reschedule it?" And you say to yourself, next week I am going to line up two cars and a cab and make the morning coffee myself. The secretary answers "Sure," but says to himself, "This person is obviously unreliable; now this after pushing for weeks for an interview with Thompson." He makes a note to that effect on the record and searches for the most inconvenient time imaginable for next week, one that Mrs. Thompson might have to cancel.

Now I would like you to answer a brief questionnaire about this event. Which was the primary cause of this "accident" or foul-up?

1. Human error (such as leaving the heat on under the coffee, or forgetting the keys in the rush)? Yes____ No____ Unsure____

2. Mechanical failure (the generator on the neighbor's car)? Yes____ No____ Unsure____

3. The environment (bus strike and taxi overload)? Yes____ No____ Unsure____

4. Design of the system (in which you can lock yourself out of the apartment rather than having to use a door key to set the lock; a lack of emergency capacity in the taxi fleet)? Yes____ No____ Unsure____

5. Procedures used (such as warming up coffee in a glass pot; allowing only normal time to get out on this morning)? Yes____ No____ Unsure____

If you answered "not sure" or "no" to all of the above, I am with you. If you answered "yes" to the first, human error, you are taking a stand on multiple failure accidents that resembles that of the President's Commission to Investigate the Accident at Three Mile Island. The Commission blamed everyone, but primarily the operators. The builders of the equipment, Babcock and Wilcox, blamed *only* the operators. If you answered "yes" to the second choice, mechanical error, you can join the Metropolitan Edison officials who run the Three Mile Island plant. They said the accident was caused by the faulty valve, and then sued the vendor,

Babcock and Wilcox. If you answered "yes" to the fourth, design of the system, you can join the experts of the Essex Corporation, who did a study for the Nuclear Regulatory Commission of the control room.

The best answer is not "all of the above" or any one of the choices, but rather "none of the above." (Of course I did not give you this as an option.) The cause of the accident is to be found in the complexity of the system. That is, each of the failures—design, equipment, operators, procedures, or environment—was trivial by itself. Such failures are expected to occur since nothing is perfect, and we normally take little notice of them. The bus strike would not affect you if you had your car key or the neighbor's car. The neighbor's generator failure would be of little consequence if taxis were available. If it were not an important appointment, the absence of cars, buses, and taxis would not matter. On any other morning the broken coffeepot would have been an annoyance (an *incident*, we will call it), but would not have added to your anxiety and caused you to dash out without your keys.

Though the failures were trivial in themselves, and each one had a backup system, or redundant path to tread if the main one were blocked, the failures became serious when they interacted. It is the *interaction* of the multiple failures that explains the accident. We expect bus strikes occasionally, we expect to forget our keys with that kind of apartment lock (why else hide a redundant key?), we occasionally loan the extra key to someone rather than disclose its hiding place. What we don't expect is for all of these events to come together at once. That is why we told the secretary that it was a crazy morning, too complex to explain, and invoked Murphy's law to ourselves (if anything can go wrong, it will).

That accident had its cause in the interactive nature of the world for us that morning and in its tight coupling—not in the discrete failures, which are to be expected and which are guarded against with backup systems. Most of the time we don't notice the inherent coupling in our world, because most of the time there are no failures, or the failures that occur do not interact. But all of a sudden, things that we did not realize could be linked (buses and generators, coffee and a loaned key) became linked. The system is suddenly more tightly coupled than

we had realized. When we have interactive systems that are also tightly coupled, it is "normal" for them to have this kind of an accident, even though it is infrequent. It is normal not in the sense of being frequent or being expected—indeed, neither is true, which is why we were so baffled by what went wrong. It is normal in the sense that it is an inherent property of the system to occasionally experience this interaction. Three Mile Island was such a normal or system accident, and so were countless others that we shall examine in this book. We have such accidents because we have built an industrial society that has some parts, like industrial plants or military adventures, that have highly interactive and tightly coupled units. Unfortunately, some of these have high potential for catastrophic accidents.

Our "day in the life" example introduced some useful terms. Accidents can be the result of *multiple failures*. Our example illustrated failures in five components: in design, equipment, procedures, operators, and environment. To apply this concept to accidents in general, we will need to add a sixth area—supplies and materials. All six will be abbreviated as the DEPOSE components (for design, equipment, procedures, operators, supplies and materials, and environment). The example showed how different parts of the system can be quite dependent upon one another, as when the bus strike created a shortage of taxis. This dependence is known as *tight coupling*. On the other hand, events in a system can occur independently as we noted with the failure of the generator and forgetting the keys. These are *loosely coupled* events, because although at this time they were both involved in the same production sequence, one was not caused by the other.

One final point which our example cannot illustrate. It isn't the best case of a normal accident or system accident, as we shall use these terms, because the interdependence of the events was comprehensible for the person or "operator." She or he could not do much about the events singly or in their interdependence, but she or he could understand the interactions. In complex industrial, space, and military systems, the normal accident generally (not always) means that the interactions are not only unexpected, but are *incomprehensible* for some critical period of time. In part this is because in these human-machine systems the interactions literally cannot be seen. In part it is because, even if they are seen, they are not believed. As we shall find out and as Robert Jervis and Karl Weick have noted, seeing is not necessarily believing; sometimes, we must believe before we can see.

Variations on the Theme

While basically simple, the idea that guides this book has some quite radical ramifications. For example, virtually every system we will examine places "operator error" high on its list of causal factors—generally about 60 to 80 percent of accidents are attributed to this factor. But if, as we shall see time and time again, the operator is confronted by unexpected and usually mysterious interactions among failures, saying that he or she should have zigged instead of zagged is possible only after the fact. Before the accident no one could know what was going on and what should have been done. Sometimes the errors are bizarre. We will encounter "noncollision course collisions," for example, where ships that were about to pass in the night suddenly turn and ram each other. But careful inquiry suggests that the mariners had quite reasonable explanations for their actions; it is just that the interaction of small failures led them to construct quite erroneous worlds in their minds, and in this case these conflicting images led to collision.

Another ramification is that great events have small beginnings. Running through the book are accidents that start with trivial kitchen mishaps; we will find them on aircraft and ships and in nuclear plants, having to do with making coffee or washing up. Small failures abound in big systems; accidents are not often caused by massive pipe breaks, wings coming off, or motors running amok. Patient accident reconstruction reveals the banality and triviality behind most catastrophes.

Small beginnings all too often cause great events when the system uses a "transformation" process rather than an additive or fabricating one. Where chemical reactions, high temperature and pressure, or air, vapor, or water turbulence is involved, we cannot see what is going on or even, at times, understand the principles. In many transformation systems we generally know what works, but sometimes do not know why. These systems are particularly vulnerable to small failures that "propagate" unexpectedly, because of complexity and tight coupling. We will examine other systems where there is less transformation and more fabrication or assembly, systems that process raw materials rather than change them. Here there is an opportunity to learn from accidents and greatly reduce complexity and coupling. These systems can still have accidents—all systems can. But they are more likely to stem from major failures whose dynamics are obvious, rather than the trivial ones that are hidden from understanding.

Another ramification is the role of organizations and management in preventing failures—or causing them. Organizations are at the center of our inquiry, even though we will often talk about hardware and pressure and temperature and the like. High-risk systems have a double penalty: because normal accidents stem from the mysterious interaction of failures, those closest to the system, the operators, have to be able to take independent and sometimes quite creative action. But because these systems are so tightly coupled, control of operators must be centralized because there is little time to check everything out and be aware of what another part of the system is doing. An operator can't just do her own thing; tight coupling means tightly prescribed steps and invariant sequences that cannot be changed. But systems cannot be both decentralized and centralized at the same time; they are organizational Pushmepullyous, straight out of Dr. Doolittle stories, trying to go in opposite directions at once. So we must add organizational contradictions to our list of problems.

Even aside from these inherent contradictions, the role of organizations is important in other respects for our story. Time and time again warnings are ignored, unnecessary risks taken, sloppy work done, deception and downright lying practiced. As an organizational theorist I am reasonably unshaken by this; it occurs in all organizations, and it is a part of the human condition. But when it comes to systems with radioactive, toxic, or explosive materials, or those operating in an unforgiving, hostile environment in the air, at sea, or under the ground, these routine sins of organizations have very nonroutine consequences. Our ability to organize does not match the inherent hazards of some of our organized activities. Better organization will always help any endeavor. But the best is not good enough for some that we have decided to pursue.

Nor can better technology always do the job. Besides being a book about organizations (but painlessly, without the jargon and the sacred texts), this is a book about technology. You will probably learn more than you ever wanted to about condensate polishers, buffet boundaries, reboilers, and slat retraction systems. But that is in passing (and even while passing you are allowed a considerable measure of incomprehension). What is not in passing but is essential here is an evaluation of technology and its "fixes." As the saying goes, man's reach has always exceeded his grasp (and of course that goes for women too). It should be so. But we might begin to learn that of all the glorious possibilities out there to reach for, some are going to be beyond our grasp in catastrophic ways. There is no technological imperative that says we *must* have power or weapons from nuclear fission or fusion, or that we *must* create and loose upon the earth organisms that will devour our oil spills. We could reach for, and grasp, solar power or safe coal-fired plants, and the safe ship designs and industry controls that would virtually eliminate oil spills. No catastrophic potential flows from these.

It is particularly important to evaluate technological fixes in the systems that we cannot or will not do without. Fixes, including safety devices, sometimes create new accidents, and quite often merely allow those in charge to run the system faster, or in worse weather, or with bigger explosives. Some technological fixes are error-reducing—the jet engine is simpler and safer than the piston engine; fathometers are better than lead lines; three engines are better than two on an airplane; computers are more reliable than pneumatic controls. But other technological fixes are excuses for poor organization or an attempt to compensate for poor system design. The attention of authorities in some of these

systems, unfortunately, is hard to get when safety is involved.

When we add complexity and coupling to catastrophe, we have something that is fairly new in the world. Catastrophes have always been with us. In the distant past, the natural ones easily exceeded the human-made ones. Human-made catastrophes appear to have increased with industrialization as we built devices that could crash, sink, burn, or explode. In the last fifty years, however, and particularly in the last twenty-five, to the usual cause of accidents— some component failure, which could be prevented in the future—was added a new cause: interactive complexity in the presence of tight coupling, producing a system accident. We have produced designs so complicated that we cannot anticipate all the possible interactions of the inevitable failures; we add safety devices that are deceived or avoided or defeated by hidden paths in the systems. The systems have become more complicated because either they are dealing with more deadly substances, or we demand they function in ever more hostile environments or with ever greater speed and volume. And still new systems keep appearing, such as gene splicing, and others grow ever more complex and tightly tied together. In the past, designers could learn from the collapse of a medieval cathedral under construction, or the explosion of boilers on steamboats, or the collision of railroad trains on a single track. But we seem to be unable to learn from chemical plant explosions or nuclear plant accidents. We may have reached a plateau where our learning curve is nearly flat. It is true that I should be wary of that supposition. Reviewing the wearisome Cassandras in history who prophesied that we had reached our limit with the reciprocating steam engine or the coal-fired railroad engine reminds us that predicting the course of technology in history is perilous. Some well-placed warnings will not harm us, however. *[. . .]*

33

RATIONAL CHOICE, SITUATED ACTION, AND THE SOCIAL CONTROL OF ORGANIZATIONS

The Challenger *Launch Decision*

DIANE VAUGHAN

anagement decisions in the business world that value competitive and economic success more highly than the well-being of workers, consumers, or the general public so often have come to public attention that today's most widely accepted model of corporate criminality portrays managers of profit-seeking organizations as "amoral calculators" whose illegal actions are motivated by rational calculation of costs and opportunities (Kagan & Scholz 1984). Driven by pressures from the competitive environment, managers will violate the law to attain desired organizational goals unless the anticipated legal penalties (the expected costs weighed against the probability of delaying or avoiding them) exceed additional benefits the firm could gain by violation. The amoral calculator model locates the cause of business misconduct in the calculations of individual decisionmakers. [. . .]

The amoral calculator model also has wide acceptance as an explanation for the misconduct of other types of organizations that violate laws, administrative rules, and regulations. Though not corporate profit seekers, to survive, all organizations

Rational Choice, Situated Action, and the Social Control of Organizations: The Challenger *Launch Decision,* by Diane Vaughan. *Law and Society Review,* Vol 32(1), 1998, pp. 23-61. Copyright © 1998 by the Law and Society Association; reprinted by permission. All rights reserved.

443

must compete for scarce resources (Pfeffer & Salancik 1978; Vaughan 1983:54–66). Competition for scarce resources encourages research institutions to falsify data in order to win grants and prestige; universities to violate NCAA recruiting regulations in order to guarantee winning athletic teams; police departments to violate the law to make arrests that bring recognition and funding; political parties and governments to commit illegalities to secure national and international power. [. . .]

Punishment is considered an important tool for the social control of organizations because of institutionalized beliefs that the ultimate cause of organizational offending is rational actors who will include the costs of punishment in their calculations and be deterred from violative behavior. [. . .] The priority given a legalistic deterrence approach has persisted under two ironic conditions. First, research has produced little data about how decisions to violate are made. It may be true that in many circumstances, decisions to violate fit the amoral calculator model. But absent a body of research examining these decisions, strategies for control will rest on untested assumptions. Second, research has produced abundant data affirming regulatory ineffectiveness in controlling organizational misconduct (Stone 1975; Coffee 1977, 1981; Ermann & Lundman 1978; Katz 1979; Anderson 1980; Diver 1980; Wheeler & Rothman 1982; Wheeler, Mann, & Sarat 1988; Shapiro 1984; Ewick 1985; J. W. Coleman 1987; Cullen, Maakestad, & Cavender 1987; Vaughan 1990; Weisburd et al. 1991). [. . .] Perhaps strategies other than punishment should be given greater consideration and priority.

In this article I take the position that to lay a foundation for strategies for control that are maximally effective, the sociolegal research agenda must include efforts to develop greater understanding about the causes of organizational misconduct. The amoral calculator model decontextualizes decisionmaking. However, the choices people make tend to be rational within situational contexts. Consequently, I argue for case studies that explore decisions to violate in naturalistic settings in order to investigate the link between social context and preference formation, the uncharted territory of rational choice theory (Cook & Levi 1990:1–16; Hechter & Kanazawa 1997).
[. . .]

RESEARCH CHALLENGES TO THE RATIONAL CHOICE/DETERRENCE MODEL

[. . .] Quantitative studies using organizations as the units of analysis (usually corporations) consistently have identified a correlation between competition, economic strain, and violative behavior (Sutherland 1949; Staw & Swajkowski 1975; Clinard & Yeager 1980; Simpson 1986). The impossibility of micro-analysis of choice in this research notwithstanding, the persistent relationship between economic strain and violative behavior has lent credibility to an amoral calculator model of decisionmaking that goes like this: When an organization experiences structural strain to achieve its goals, individuals acting in their organization roles weigh the costs and benefits of their actions, choosing to violate laws and rules to attain organization goals.

[. . .]

The amoral calculator model received early support from Geis's (1967) classic case study of the heavy electrical equipment antitrust case, widely cited and reproduced in anthologies. Presenting the first in-depth view of executives' thoughts and perceptions about their violations, Geis quoted CEOs who stated they were aware of the illegality and its harmful social consequences as they colluded about price fixing. Twenty years later another famous case affirmed the model. Documents surfaced in the Ford Pinto case showing, in writing, Ford executives' calculation of costs and benefits in a redesign decision that juxtaposed the cost of redesign against the quantified loss of human life in accidents if the redesign were not done. Lives had already been lost; nonetheless, production continued (Cullen et al. 1987). Research based on interviews with managers also lent support to the model (Clinard 1983; Jackall 1988; Kram, Yeager, & Reed 1989).

While suggestive and supportive, this evidence remains far from definitive.

[. . .]

In contrast to the amoral calculator model, some managers violate for reasons other than instrumental action directly tied to achieving competitive success: incompetence, misunderstanding of laws, or improper attention to regulatory requirements (Kagan & Scholz 1984). Also, how managers actually assess risks in the workplace is far from the systematic calculation the rational choice model implies: Decisionmakers do not weigh all possible outcomes but instead rely on a few key values; the magnitude of possible bad outcomes is more salient, so that there is less risk taking when greater stakes are involved; in practice, quantifying costs and benefits of a line of action is not easy (March & Shapira 1987). *[. . .]*

When the effect of the organization as a locus of choice is taken fully into account, social context becomes obvious as an influence in decisionmaking, shaping what an individual perceives to be rational at a given moment. Because of specialization and division of labor, employees may be unaware of their illegality because their action was part of a chain of actions by invisible others: Each individual act was legitimate, but together all the acts constituted a violation of which some individual participants were ignorant (Gross 1980; Finney & Lesieur 1982; Vaughan 1983). Also, an extensive body of research and theory on decisionmaking in organizations shows that the weighing of costs and benefits does occur, but individual choice is constrained by institutional and organizational forces: Decision practices and outcomes are products of external contingencies, political battles, unacknowledged cultural beliefs, and formal and informal internal pathologies that undercut both the determination of goals and their achievement (Dalton 1950; Allison 1971; Zucker 1977; Feldman & March 1981; Wildavsky 1987; Feldman 1989).

These constraints on choice are reinforced in organizations as executives set the premises for decisionmaking through organizational routines that reduce uncertainty. Decisionmaking is more an example of rule following than of calculation of costs and benefits. *[. . .]* Rather than a model of perfect rationality, decisionmaking in organizations is characterized by "bounded rationality"; performance is described as "satisficing" rather than optimizing (Simon 1957, 1976; March & Simon 1958). The notion of individual rationality has become so circumscribed and discredited that some organization theorists even have described the decision process by the "garbage can model" (March & Olsen 1979) and characterized managers as "muddling through" (Lindblom 1959)—a far cry from the imagery of cool, calculated managerial capability suggested by the ideology of rational choice theory. In fact, Weick (1979, 1995) argues that often the only rationality that might be credited to the process is imposed retrospectively by participants in order to justify a particular decision. Wilensky's (1967:vii) observation sums up the case against a decontextualized rational choice model from an organizational behavior perspective:

> Too many critics of the organizational and political sources of our troubles see diabolical plots where there is only drift, a taste for reckless adventure where there is only ignorance of risks, the machinations of a power elite where there is, in William James' phrase, only a "bloomin' buzzin' confusion."

[. . .]

SITUATED ACTION: THE STRUCTURE/ CULTURE/AGENCY NEXUS

A fundamental sociological understanding is that interaction takes place in socially organized settings. Rather than isolating action from its circumstances, the task of scholars is to uncover the relationship between the individual act and the social context.

[. . .]

Theorists are refining the link between an individual's position in a structure and interpretive practices, meaning, and action at the local level (Bourdieu 1977; Hall 1987; Smith 1987; Haraway 1988; P. Collins 1990, 1991; Emirbayer & Goodwin 1994; Hays 1994). *[. . .]* Although differing in important ways, each perspective draws attention to culture: the tacit understandings, habits, assumptions, routines, and practices that constitute a repository of unarticulated source material from which more self-conscious thought and action emerge. Also significant is the role of history: Both the macro-level historic moment, as its normative and legal standards affect individual tacit understandings, and micro-level individual history/experience are critical to individual interpretation and meaning (Elias 1993; Emirbayer & Mische 1998).

The important role of culture in situated interpretation, meaning, and action is reinforced by *[. . .]* the new institutionalism, which explains that organizational forms and behaviors take the form they do because of prevailing values and beliefs that have become institutionalized to varying degrees (Meyer & Rowan 1977; Zucker 1977; Powell & DiMaggio 1991). New institutionalists argue that cultural rules constitute actors (state, organizations, professions, and individuals), thus defining legitimate goals for them to pursue and therefore affecting action and meaning at the local level. Decisionmaking, from this perspective, is always rational; however, institutionalized categories of structure, thought, and action shape preferences, directing choice toward some options and not others (Douglas 1987; Wildavsky 1987; DiMaggio & Powell 1991:10–11). [. . .] Granovetter's (1985, 1992) work on the socially embedded character of economic action points to the relative autonomy and/or relative dependence between the forms of economic action and social organization and the institutionalized cultural belief systems within which they are located. In contrast to the new institutionalism, agency is at the heart of this analysis. Agents can be individuals or organizational forms, but the embeddedness perspective prohibits reduction to a decontextualized rational actor. Because agency is central, economic action can take a variety of forms, so in a common cultural system variations will exist that cannot be explained in cultural terms only.

[. . .]

This complex conceptual package illuminates many aspects of situated action. Decisionmaking, in this schema, cannot be disentangled from social context, which shapes preferences and thus what an individual perceives as rational. Moreover, the situated action paradigm acknowledges that purposive social action can regularly produce unexpected outcomes, thus challenging all rational actor accounts of social behavior. Finally, it draws attention to the need for research that examines the structure/culture/agency nexus. A full theoretical explanation of the action of any social actor needs to take into account, to the greatest extent possible, its situated character: Individual activity, choices, and action occur within a multilayered social context that affects interpretation and meaning at the local level.

[. . .]

The 1986 *Challenger* tragedy produced data that opened up the structure/culture/agency nexus,

generating the grounded situated action schema presented in the preceding section (Vaughan 1996). My data were personal interviews, government investigation reports and hearing transcripts, publications by historians, scientists, engineers, and journalists, plus more than 200,000 original National Aeronautics and Space Administration (NASA) and contractor documents, assembled by the Presidential Commission investigating the disaster and stored at the National Archives, Washington (Presidential Commission on the Space Shuttle *Challenger* Accident 1986). The latter archive included over 9,000 pages of legal deposition transcripts, documentation of NASA rules and procedures, engineering reports, risk assessments, correspondence and memos, safety panel reports, daily engineering activity sheets, pre-launch decisionmaking records, and computerized problem tracking system printouts. These resources allowed me to make a chronological reconstruction of the history of decisionmaking about the Solid Rocket Boosters, the technical cause of the accident, at NASA from 1977 through the *Challenger* launch. The result is a historical ethnography of decisionmaking in a naturalistic setting that situates decisions within the structures and processes that shaped interpretive work, preference formation, and choice. [. . .]

HOW DEVIANCE BECAME NORMAL: THE *CHALLENGER* CASE

In the aftermath of the tragedy, the historically accepted explanation of the controversial 1986 *Challenger* launch decision conformed to the amoral calculator model. Warned by contractor engineers that launching was risky in the unprecedented cold temperatures that were predicted at launch time, NASA managers nonetheless proceeded with the launch because the schedule had become all-important at the space agency. Underfunded by Congress, the Space Shuttle program depended on income from commercial satellite companies: the greater the number of flights per year, the greater the number of commercial payloads, the greater the income. Realizing the importance of schedule (the historically accepted explanation went), the managers who were immediately responsible for the decision responded to these pressures by disregarding the advice of their own engineers, knowingly violating rules about passing safety concerns up the hierarchy in the process. Seven astronauts, including Christa McAuliffe, Teacher-in-Space, lost their lives. The conjunction of competitive pressures, scarce resources, rule violations, and overriding of the objections of engineers suggested intent: managerial decisionmaking as violative behavior—a calculated, amoral, consequentialist, rational choice.

Production pressure played a critical role in the fatal decision, but the historically accepted explanation of why *Challenger* was launched was wrong. Many key assumptions supporting it were flawed. Most critical for establishing the intent implicit in an amoral calculator explanation, NASA documents describing rules and procedures showed that managerial actions identified as rule violations by the Presidential Commission were in fact actions that conformed to NASA rules. The data forced me to conclude that the disaster resulted from mistake, not misconduct. Because no rules were violated, the case does not conform to traditional understandings of organizational misconduct that have employees violating laws and rules in pursuit of organization goals, nor does it exhibit the intent to do wrong implied in the amoral calculator model of decisionmaking. However, the analysis resulted in a discovery of even greater significance for theories of organizational misconduct than anything I originally envisioned. My case study shows that in the years preceding the *Challenger* launch, engineers and managers together developed a definition of the situation that allowed them to carry on as if nothing were wrong when they continually faced evidence that something *was* wrong. This is the problem of the normalization of deviance.

The story begins, not on the eve of the *Challenger* launch, when managers and engineers argued about whether to go forward or not, but nearly 10 years earlier. The past—previous engineering analysis, conclusions, and launch decisions—was an all-important context for decisionmaking on the eve of the launch. Prior to the *Challenger* launch, the Solid Rocket Boosters (SRBs) were often damaged on shuttle missions. After each incident, the work group recommended

to their superiors to accept risk and fly. After the disaster, continuing to launch despite evidence of damage on many flights seemed not only deviant but an amoral, calculated choice to a public shocked by the death of the astronauts. Why didn't they stop launching until they had solved the problem? Because at the time decisions were being made, each technical anomaly was first defined as an escalated risk; then, after engineering analysis, decisionmakers redefined it as normal and acceptable. Each decision seemed logical, rational, and non-controversial as cumulatively they expanded the amount of technical deviation that was acceptable. Flying with frequent and increasingly serious anomalies became routine and officially condoned. Three factors, in combination, explain the normalization of technical deviation at NASA: the production of a cultural belief system in the work group, the culture of production, and structural secrecy.

The Production of Culture

Risk assessment was a bottom-up process at NASA. The managers and engineers assigned to do the technical work on Space Shuttle component parts assessed risk daily, using NASA guidelines and relying on engineering tests, post-flight analyses, and calculations. Then, in a formal pre-launch decision process known as Flight Readiness Review (FRR), these work groups presented their risk assessments and recommendations about launching to superiors in what was a multilayered, multiparticipant, adversarial review process. Because the shuttle design had no precedent, risk was always negotiated and often controversial. But in order to launch shuttles, work groups had to assay each technical component and find it an "Acceptable Risk," following prescribed NASA and engineering methods. Arriving at this official designation had them routinely converting technical uncertainty into certainty.

[. . .]

Initially, no technical deviations in booster performance were predicted by engineers. When anomalies began occurring, social context affected the SRB work group's interpretation of the damage. The immediate social context was one in which having technical problems was normal and expected because (1) the design was unprecedented and therefore untested in flight and (2) the shuttle was designed to be reusable. Consequently, having booster anomalies was not deviant because engineers and managers expected that all returning flights would have some damage that had to be fixed prior to the next launch. Patterns of information as boosters were inspected after each mission also affected the definition of the situation. Most launches had no booster anomalies. When they occurred, they seemed to be random. [. . .] Each time, engineers were able to identify the cause of the failure and fix it, assuring themselves by tests, calculations, and scientific methods that the problem was within the bounds of acceptable risk. Subsequent missions would have no anomalies. Then a new incident would occur.

The preexisting definition of the situation, and the scientific procedures and engineering analysis on which it was based, became the context against which the risk of each succeeding anomaly was measured. [. . .] The incremental character of damage also had a normalizing effect. Had all the changes occurred at once, had damage been occurring on every flight due to a common cause, or had there been a discernable pattern of damage, the work group would have had some strong, clear signals with the potential to challenge the cultural belief in risk acceptability. Instead, the damage occurred incrementally, each incident's significance muted by social context and a learning-by-doing approach that had engineers interpreting each episode as separate and local.

The immediate social context and patterns of information explain *how* the cultural belief in acceptable risk developed. But *why* did their official definition of the situation persist, in the face of evidence of continuing problems? This is the problem of cultural persistence. Macro-level factors—the culture of production and structural secrecy—contributed to and affirmed the work group's belief in acceptable risk prior to *Challenger*.

The Culture of Production

The culture of production reinforced and maintained the work group's belief in acceptable risk because their actions conformed to its mandates. Thus, they saw continuing to launch under the conditions they faced as normative and conforming, not deviant. By culture of production, I mean institutionalized cultural belief systems that shaped interpretation, meaning, and action at the local level (Van Maanen & Barley 1985; Zucker 1977). [. . .] In contrast to the historically accepted explanation that depicted a unidimensional NASA culture dominated by production concerns, the culture of production incorporated three cultural imperatives: the original technical culture of excellence created during the Apollo era (methodological rigor and quantitative science), political accountability (production and cost concerns), and bureaucratic accountability (attention to rules and procedures). Production pressure does not lose salience in this revisionist account but gains importance because of its seductive influence: Production pressures affected the choices of managers and engineers alike, by affecting decisionmaking at a prerational level.

[. . .] Of the cultural meaning systems that typify engineering as a profession, three were influential in work group decisionmaking. First, in the engineering of unprecedented large-scale technical systems, uncertainty, learning by experience, and developing ad hoc rules to guide technical decisions are taken-for-granted understandings about how work gets done (Wynne 1988). Second, "satisficing," not "optimizing," was normal and acceptable in the engineering profession (Simon 1957, 1976). The education of engineers prepares them to work in production systems where technology is product-oriented and cost/safety trade-offs are routine, so satisficing on design is common and nondeviant (Petroski 1985; Meiksins 1988; Kunda 1992). Third, technical assessments are grounded in "trust in numbers" and "trust in rules": Quantitative methods and scientific objectivity in risk assessment hold sway over intuitive sensibilities (Jasanoff 1986; Porter 1995); engineers are trained to work in hierarchical organizations where rule following is associated with safety (Meiksins 1988; Petroski 1985).

These institutionalized beliefs of the engineering profession materialized in the NASA organization in distinctive ways that contributed to the normalization of technical deviation on the SRBs. During the Apollo program of the 1960s, NASA's original technical culture was founded on a mandate for technical excellence (McCurdy 1993). The emphasis was on the "dirty hands" approach: Contractors were only used occasionally, and most work was done in house so that top administrators and technicians alike got their hands "dirty" by staying in close touch with the technology. This approach was joined by a near-obsessive emphasis on technical excellence, scientific positivism, and rigor in both method and data analysis. However, at the inception of the shuttle program in the 1970s, NASA's purist technical culture was joined by an additional cultural mandate: political accountability that called for attention to cost and schedule (Romzek & Dubnick 1987). As the Apollo program neared its end, consensus for the U.S. space program was undermined by the U.S. involvement in Vietnam. The war created a drain on the budget, raising questions about continued space explorations.

NASA administrators developed the Space Shuttle Program as the post-Apollo goal. Confronted by congressional recalcitrance and opposition, agency administrators proposed that the shuttle would not be a drain on the budget because it would be, to a great extent, self-funding. NASA officials pushed the vehicle as a reusable "space bus" that could fly many missions a year. Designed with a large payload bay, the shuttle would carry experiments from aerospace R&D firms and commercial satellites to be put in orbit, thus collecting money for each mission. When the proposal went to Congress, the projected number of missions assured a continued source of income from a space vehicle that administrators insisted would make space flight "routine and economical." The shuttle was endorsed on this basis. Reduced funding had converted the R&D space agency into one that operated like a business, complete with production cycles and concerns about cost and efficiency.

A second alteration in NASA culture that occurred was that bureaucratic accountability rose in importance (Romzek & Dubnick 1987). Bureaucratic accountability had always been esteemed: Rules were essential for coordinating work and for safety. However, in the 1980s, the agency became bureaupathological. Contracting out, formerly an occasional practice, became institutionalized. The consequence was that an immense new rule structure was necessary to coordinate NASA/ contractor relations. The dirty hands approach was compromised: Many NASA engineers and technicians now had contractor oversight responsibilities, so were burdened with procedural tasks and huge amounts of paperwork. Soon after shuttle missions began in 1981, still another layer of bureaucracy was added. The 1980s were notable for the decreased regulation of business and the increased regulation of government agencies, which imposed another system of accountability on the space agency. The result of these changes was that rule following and procedural conformity rivaled the original technical culture and political accountability. History and politics had not eliminated the original technical culture of the Apollo era, but added political accountability and bureaucratic accountability to it. The result was that engineers and managers assigned to the shuttle hardware were struggling to conform to the mandates of the original technical culture while also conforming to political accountability (cost and schedule) and bureaucratic accountability (procedural requirements).

The Macro-Micro Connection

The work group conformed to the culture of production, which had an impact on cognition (Zucker 1977). [. . .] Post-flight analyses of the Space Shuttle missions produced quantitative evidence (the original technical culture) convincing the work group that the booster design was officially an "Acceptable Risk." Although they understood that the boosters were working, they did not understand why they were working as they were. Growing doubt, uncertainty, and anxiety about the unknown notwithstanding, concern about cost and schedule (political accountability) inhibited the work group from halting missions for the lengthy period necessary for additional tests. Following the rules, which they unfailingly did (bureaucratic accountability), had a social-psychological effect. Conforming to every rule and procedure—going by the book—assured them that their official risk assessments were correct, sustaining the cultural belief that the design was an "Acceptable Risk." Repeatedly and officially, they recommended "Go." As the problem unfolded in the years prior to *Challenger*, each decision seemed logical, correct, and rational. The social context and patterns of information that affected the definition of the situation were reinforced by the institutionalized cultural frame within which the interpretive work was done.

Structural Secrecy

Because the process of deviance normalization went on from 1977 until the fatal *Challenger* launch, we must wonder why no one outside the work group noticed and acted. Structural secrecy was the third factor that contributed to the persistence of the work group's cultural belief in acceptable risk. The effect of structural secrecy was to inhibit people outside the work group from overturning the definition of the situation. Structural secrecy refers to the way that the structure of organizations and their regulatory relations impedes knowledge and understanding of activities in the workplace. In the aftermath of the *Challenger* tragedy, managers were wrongly accused of individual secrecy: intentionally violating rules to hide information about booster problems from others in the organization. No rule violations occurred. Instead, it was routine characteristics of inter- and intra-organizational relationships—conditions common to all organizations—that concealed the seriousness of the technical problem on the Solid Rocket Boosters from people outside the work group, preventing them from identifying the trend and intervening in some way that might have altered the decisionmaking pattern prior to the *Challenger* launch decision.

Secrecy is built into the very structure of organizations. As organizations grow large, actions that occur in one part of the organization are, for the most part, not observable in others. Division of labor between subunits, hierarchy, and geographic dispersion segregate knowledge about tasks and goals. Distance—both physical and social—interferes with the efforts of those at the top to "know" the behavior of others in the organization—and vice versa. Specialized knowledge further inhibits knowing. The language associated with a different task, even in the same organization, can conceal rather than reveal. Changing technology also interferes with knowing, for assessing information requires keeping pace with these changes—a difficult prospect when it takes time away from one's primary job responsibilities. Also—and ironically—rules created to communicate more information can result in knowing less. Rules that guarantee wide distribution of information can increase the paperwork on individual desks so that a lot is not read. Executive summaries, although effectively conveying major points, condense and omit information, selectively concealing and revealing.

Paradoxically, NASA had developed both a prelaunch decisionmaking procedure and a safety regulatory system designed to protect against structural secrecy. The formal, hierarchical, pre-launch decision chain known as Flight Readiness Review (FRR) was designed to maximize information exchange by pulling all parts of the organization together for risk assessments prior to a launch. All engineering risk assessments were distributed in advance and orally presented in FRR, where they were critiqued aggressively by people outside the work groups whose sole responsibility was to uncover flaws in the analyses. Moreover, NASA had both internal and external safety review panels designated as safety regulatory agencies with oversight responsibilities in every aspect of technical work. However, structural secrecy remained (Vaughan 1990). While structural secrecy had many unanticipated negative consequences for safety, here I will isolate only one: information dependencies and how they kept people outside the work group from identifying the pattern of normalizing technical deviation and intervening.

In NASA's bottom-up risk assessment system, it was the work groups' construction of risk—and the engineering evidence support of their assessments—that were the basis for all launch decisions. FRR and safety regulatory systems were designed to challenge and oversee existing risk assessments and the scientific procedures and technical knowledge that went into work group launch recommendations. But the shuttle was made up of 60 million component parts. FRR participants and regulators were inundated with information about each part. Instead of enlightening upper-level managers, the deluge of information obfuscated many problems (Feldman & March 1981). Hence, people with oversight responsibility relied on oral interpretation and briefings in FRR and other inquiries. Removed from the hands-on work and reliant on work groups for the engineering on which risk assessments were based, these others could only challenge what was presented to them. When the SRB work group repeatedly defended its position with quantitative data, as those assigned to the Solid Rocket Booster Project did in the years preceding the *Challenger* tragedy, top NASA administrators and safety officials became persuaded the design was an acceptable risk. The work group's construction of risk was affirmed up the hierarchy, becoming the official organizational construction of risk prior to each launch.

NASA's oversight structure functioned effectively as a review system, but information dependencies interfered with its ability to identify basic assumptions that were in error. The House Committee on Science and Technology, whose investigation followed that of the Presidential Commission, concluded that administrators and regulators only knew what work groups told them. [. . .]

Thus, the official definition of the boosters as an "Acceptable Risk" persisted through the end of 1985. *Challenger* was the first launch of 1986. The decision to launch *Challenger* was one decision in a stream of decisions about the boosters. The debate that night was situated in history and social organization: The interplay of the production of culture in the work group, the culture of production, and structural secrecy affected the interpretive work and action of all participants.

The Eve of the Launch

The *Challenger* launch had been approved in FRR two weeks before the 27 January eve-of-launch discussion. But this was an emergency meeting, called because the temperature forecast resulted in a revised assessment of risk acceptability for the boosters before launch the next morning. So the 34 participants, located at agency and contractor facilities in Utah, Alabama, and Florida, held the discussion on a teleconference. It was unprecedented in several ways: the predicted cold temperature, the no-launch recommendation that the contractor engineers made, and the geographic locations of the participants. [. . .]

NASA's cultural mandate for political accountability undermined the proceedings at the outset. Contractor engineers in Utah, aware of deadlines and cost concerns, immediately set a deadline for their preparations so the teleconference might begin and a decision reached before midnight, when time-consuming and expensive pre-launch procedures

would begin at the launch site at Cape Kennedy, Florida. Rushing to meet their own deadline, contractor engineers divided up responsibility for the charts of engineering analysis, faxing them to other places without collectively assessing them. The result? NASA managers identified errors in the charts that contradicted the argument contractor engineers were making, so the analysis did not live up to the rigorous quantitative standards of NASA's original technical culture. Political accountability showed itself a second time when NASA managers, surprised that a flawed engineering analysis would be the basis for a no-launch decision when schedule was so important, gave their usual adversarial challenges in unusually harsh ways, intimidating contractor engineers and managers.

Throughout the discussion, structural secrecy blocked understanding. Engineering launch recommendations were always face to face in FRR. However, this night the participants were in three facilities of the NASA/contractor structure, an unreflexive choice that went unquestioned because teleconferences had become a normal way of doing business between contractors and NASA. In separate locations, with no video hook-up, words and inflections had to convey everything. Body language, facial expression, who was present or absent—additional information that adds to interpretive abilities and conveying meaning—were unavailable. At a critical moment, the effect of structural secrecy was increased when the contractor representatives went off the teleconference line for a caucus. During that period, contractor administrators reversed their own engineers' recommendation. They returned to the teleconference with a recommendation to accept risk and fly. Separated by distance and a mute button, no one at the other two locations knew that the contractor engineers still objected. Further, the contractor engineers were unaware that people in the other two locations were expecting the launch to be stopped.

The cultural mandate of bureaucratic accountability had people going by the book, which also had a deleterious affect on the discussion. First, conformity to normative expectations about specialized knowledge and hierarchical relations affected talk: Some people were silent who had information that might have altered the outcome. Some deferred to authority; others, concluding that they had not worked on the booster problems recently enough or were insufficiently informed for other reasons, kept their insights to themselves, deferring to the few engineers presenting the analysis. Second, in unprecedented conditions, all participants followed all the usual NASA rules and procedures about how launch decisions were to be made. As in the past, conforming to rules had the latent social-psychological effect of affirming the correctness of the decision: All contractor engineers but one left the teleconference believing that the boosters would incur addition damage, not expecting a catastrophe. The one person who did fear the worst said nothing on the teleconference, abiding by NASA's bureaucratic norms about who legitimately could speak during an engineering decision and under what circumstances.

But conformity had a still greater consequence. Immediately following the disaster, many of the participating engineers admitted their analysis was flawed, stating that "we didn't have the data to convince NASA," so the preexisting engineering analysis that supported acceptable risk stood. However, retrospection and the luxury of hindsight show that they *did* have the data. After the disaster, two investigators (nonengineers) working for the Presidential Commission did a trend analysis of all launches, examining the relationship between temperature and booster damage. The quantitative data conclusively proved the correlation between cold temperature and damage (Vaughan 1996:382–83). But the work group did not create that chart, which would have conformed to the positivistic mandates of the original technical culture, thereby stopping the launch. Customarily, in conditions of uncertainty, people fall back on habits and routines (Mileti, Sorenson, & Bogard 1985). In unprecedented circumstances, with time to think things through, the engineers and managers in the work group followed all the mandates of the culture of production. No one had the idea to proceed in a different way.

Consider this. Whereas a rigorous, quantitative engineering analysis may assure safety in a pro-launch decision, in a no-launch decision under unprecedented, uncertain launch conditions, accepting qualitative observations and intuitive insight from technical experts closest to the technology would have been appropriate. Whereas hierarchical, adversarial FRR discussion style is suitable for pro-launch recommendations, a democratic sleeves-rolled-up let's-all-put-our-heads-together-to-see-what-we-can-make-of-these-data strategy would have been a logical response. Again, we have the luxury of hindsight. The situation looked very different to them at the time. The work group conformed to the triumvirate of cultural imperatives, resulting in an official decision that incorporated yet another anomalous condition, thus extending the bounds of acceptable risk a final time.

On the Social Control of Organizations

[. . .] Rational choice theorists are the first to admit that the power and scope of rational choice theory is limited because insufficient progress has been made toward a theory of preference formation (Friedman & Hechter 1988:214; Hechter & Kanazawa 1997:208). Such a theory must rest on understanding not just the preferences actors hold when choices are made but how those preferences come about. This case generated the grounded theory of situated action, showing how social context can shape preference formation; moreover, it suggests how social context can decouple rational choice from outcomes. It demonstrates that individual choice cannot be understood by isolating it from its organizational context, and neither can the organization be isolated from the external environment. The work group's production of a cultural belief about booster risk, the culture of production, and structural secrecy were seductive shapers of preferences and interests during the teleconference and the years preceding it. And so was history. Decisionmaking was greatly influenced by precedent, in contrast to most macroscopic sociological rational choice theories, which assume that actors are forward-looking maximizers (Hechter & Kanazawa 1997:209).

In the years preceding the *Challenger* launch, the intersection of institutionalized cultural beliefs, organization structure, and culture affected cognition: The work group created a frame of reference through which booster performance was assessed. It became institutionalized, shaping interpretive practices so that decisionmakers viewed their actions as conforming, not deviant, as outsiders—and the decisionmakers themselves—viewed these same actions after the disaster. They imagined benefits, not costs, as a result of their decisions. The eve-of-launch teleconference was called because conditions changed: Many engineers felt that launching would bring only costs. But in the process of assessing risk, the interpretation, meaning, and actions of participants were shaped by the same social factors that affected previous decisions. The preexisting definition of booster risk remained the work group's official position. Each and every launch recommendation was a rational choice, made rational by the situated character of social action, which narrowed the options and influenced the choices decisionmakers saw as rational at the time. Preference formation looms large in this schema. In contrast, the amoral calculator model brackets individual choice from social location, history, and preexisting definitions of the situation, emphasizing the calculation of future consequences at the expense of the preconditions of choice.

NASA made a decision that caused extensive social harm, but absent was any evidence of intent to do that harm, or the calculated, knowing violation of rules or ethical or normative standards essential to the amoral calculator model of organizational misconduct. This was true not only for the SRB work group but also for political elites inside and outside the space agency: top NASA officials, Congress, and the Administration. These powerful elites set up the tragedy in the years preceding *Challenger* by making political bargains that (1) made routine and economic space flight a priority, interjecting production pressures into the culture; (2) institutionalized contracting out, altering organization structure and adding layers of bureaucratic accountability, interjecting another dimension to the culture; (3) allowed civilians to fly on the shuttle to promote the agency and its goals. Yet missing from the original media-generated, historically accepted explanation of amorally calculating managers were the invisible workings of power and politics that contributed to the outcome. At the time they were made, these elite decisions, too, were absent intent to do harm or violate laws, defined as normal and acceptable by the top officials who made them.

What happened at NASA was not organizational misconduct, as scholars typically have understood it. No rules were violated in launch decisionmaking

about the Solid Rocket Boosters; no one intended any harm. Yet the case reveals a dimension of organizational life that seems singularly important for understanding organizations that do violate laws and rules to attain goals. Although it was technical anomalies that were normalized at NASA, the normalization of deviance stands as a fundamental process that may play a role in facilitating rule violations and misconduct when they do occur in other organizations. *[. . .]*

The basis for research connecting culture with the normalization of deviance was laid by Sutherland (1949), who theorized that crime is learned in interaction in primary groups and will occur when individuals develop "definitions favorable to violation" that exceed "definitions unfavorable to violation." The first to tap into culture empirically was Quinney (1963), who compared occupational norms of pharmacists, finding that those who were oriented toward business norms were more likely to violate than those who were oriented toward professional norms (see also Green 1997). *[. . .]* The Ford Pinto case study, often cited to support amoral calculation, also suggests that an internal normative environment developed where deviance became normalized within the organization.[1] Three important books, originating in other disciplines, argue that individuals committing heinous crimes against individuals and humanity defined their own actions by the cultural standards of organizations—political parties, nation-states, the military; thus, they saw their actions as conforming, not deviant: Arendt's *Eichmann in Jerusalem* (1963); Kelman and Hamilton's *Crimes of Obedience* (1989), and most recently, Goldhagen's controversial and hotly disputed *Hitler's Willing Executioners* (1996). All three show how power, politics, and elites created cultures that normalized deviant actions. When discovered, a horrified world defined these actions deviant, yet they were normative within the culture of the work and occupations of the participants who acted in conformity with organizational mandates.

The lesson suggested by the *Challenger* case and these others is that the legal and regulatory apparatus might better investigate and elevate the importance of additional strategies of social control. The potential deterrent impact of sanctions cannot figure into individual calculations when history, culture, and structure congeal in a worldview under which behavior that is objectively deviant to outsiders is normal and legitimate within a particular social context. When deviance becomes normalized, individuals see their actions as conforming, not deviant; consequently, they see their actions as accruing benefits, not costs. [. . .] Punishment is appropriate; people must be held responsible for action resulting in social harm. It may be used against offending organizations and/or their employees to accomplish other than deterrence: to make people publicly accountable for their actions, to assure restitution or retribution, for example (Schlegel 1990). However, as a strategy of social control, punishment does not go far enough. It decontextualizes decisions to violate, neglecting the social context that leads people to make the choices that they do. The organization may be fined; the responsible individuals may be incarcerated, fined, fired, transferred, or offered early retirement, but if the social context of decisionmaking is not altered, the next position incumbent's decisionmaking will be subject to the same organizational contingencies. Without attention to these other factors, the legal and administrative apparatus—and the public—are wrongly persuaded that once the responsible person is punished, the problem is solved. But the more difficult to diagnose goals, policies, cultures, and structures that create definitions favorable to harmful social acts remain unchanged, perpetuating the possibility of recurrence. . . .

NOTE

1. An internal memo documenting the calculations of costs and benefits surfaced in the investigation of the Ford Motor Company's decision to manufacture a flawed Pinto design. It showed Ford officials calculated the cost of redesigning the Pinto to eliminate the flaw and the cost of retooling to manufacture a new, safe design. Then they calculated the probability of accidents and loss of life, estimating the value of a human life at $200,000. The cost of redesign far outweighed the cost of accidents. Production went forward. But Frank Cullen, author of the authoritative research on the case noted. "It may be that they did so because they were conforming to norms of the organization culture and the competitive auto industry, so it was not a deviant act, in their opinion, but simply good business" (personal communication, November 1994). See Cullen et al. 1987.

REFERENCES

Allison, Graham T. (1971) *The Essence of Decision: Explaining the Cuban Missile Crisis*. Boston: Little, Brown.

Anderson, Douglas D. (1980) "Who Owns the Regulators?" 4 *Wharton Mag.* 14–21.

Arendt, Hannah (1963) *Eichmann in Jerusalem*. New York: Viking.

Bourdieu, Pierre (1977) *Outline of a Theory of Practice*. Cambridge: Cambridge Univ. Press.

Clinard, Marshall B. (1983) *Corporate Ethics and Crime*. Beverly Hills, CA: Sage Publications.

Clinard, Marshall B., & Peter C. Yeager (1980) *Corporate Crime*. New York: Free Press.

Coffee, John C. (1977) "Beyond the Shut-Eyed Sentry: Toward a Theoretical View of Corporate Misconduct and Effective Legal Response," 63 *Virginia Law Rev.* 1099–1278.

———— (1981) "No Soul to Damn, No Body to Kick: An Unscandalized Inquiry into the Problem of Corporate Punishment," 79 *Michigan Law Rev.* 386–459.

Coleman, James W. (1987) "Toward an Integrated Theory of White-Collar Crime," 93 *American Sociological Rev.* 406–39.

Collins, Patricia Hill (1990) *Black Feminist Thought*. London: Harper Collins.

——— (1991) "Learning from the Outsider within," in M. M. Fonow & J. Cook, eds., *Beyond Methodology: Feminist Scholarship as Lived Research*. Bloomington: Indiana Univ. Press.

Cook, Karen Schweers, & Margaret Levi, eds. (1990) *The Limits of Rationality*. Chicago: Univ. of Chicago Press.

Cullen, Frank T., William J. Maakestad, & Gray Cavender (1987) *Corporate Crime under Attack: The Ford Pinto Case and Beyond*. Cincinnati: Anderson.

Dalton, Melville (1950) *Men Who Manage*. New York: Wiley.

DiMaggio, Paul J., & Walter W. Powell (1991) "Introduction," in Powell & DiMaggio, eds. 1991.

Diver, Colin (1980) "A Theory of Regulatory Enforcement," 28 *Public Policy* 257–99.

Douglas, Mary (1987) *How Institutions Think*. London: Routledge & Kegan Paul.

Elias, Norbert (1993) *Time: An Essay*. Oxford: Blackwell.

Emirbayer, Mustafa, & Jeff Goodwin (1994) "Network Analysis, Culture, and the Problem of Agency," 99 *American J. of Sociology* 1411–54.

Emirbayer, Mustafa, & Ann Mische (1998) "What Is Agency?" 103 *American J. of Sociology* 962–1023.

Ermann, M. David, & Richard J. Lundman (1978) "Deviant Acts by Complex Organizations: Deviance and Social Control at the Organizational Level of Analysis," 19 *Sociological Q.* 55–67.

Ewick, Patricia (1985) "Redundant Regulation: Sanctioning Broker-Dealers," 7 *Law & Policy* 421–45.

Feldman, Martha S. (1989) *Order without Design.* Stanford, CA: Stanford Univ. Press.

Feldman, Martha S., & James G. March (1981) "Information in Organizations as Sign and Symbol," 26 *Administrative Science Q.* 171–84.

Fine, Gary Alan (1992) "Agency, Structure, and Comparative Contexts: Toward A Synthetic Interactionism," 15 *Symbolic Interaction* 87–107.

Finney, Henry, & H. R. Lesieur (1982) "A Contingency Theory of Organizational Crime," in S. B. Bacharach, ed., *The Social Psychological Process* (Research in the Sociology of Organizations). Greenwich, CT: JAI Press.

Friedman, Debra, & Michael Hechter (1988) "The Contribution of Rational Choice Theory to Macrosociological Research," 6 *Sociological Theory* 201–18.

Geis, Gilbert (1967) "The Heavy Electrical Equipment Antitrust Cases of 1961," in M. B. Clinard & R. Quinney, *Criminal Behavior Systems.* New York: Holt, Rinehart, & Winston.

Goldhagen, Daniel Joshua (1996) *Hitler's Willing Executioners.* New York: Alfred A. Knopf.

Granovetter, Mark (1985) "Economic Action and Social Structure: The Problem of Embeddedness," 91 *American J. of Sociology* 481–510.

_____ (1992) "Economic Institutions as Social Constructions: A Framework for Analysis," 35 *Acta Sociologica* 3–12.

Green, Gary (1997) *Occupational Crime.* Chicago: Nelson-Hall.

Gross, Edward (1980) "Organization Structure and Organizational Crime," in G. Geis & E. Stotland, eds., *White-Collar Crime: Theory and Research.* Newbury Park, CA: Sage Publications.

Hall, Peter M. (1987) "Interactionism and the Study of Social Organization," 28 *Sociological Q.* 1–22.

Haraway, Donna (1988) "Situated Knowledges: The Science Question in Feminism as a Site of Discourse on the Privilege of Partial Perspective," 14 *Feminist Studies* 575–99.

Hawkins, Keith O., & J. M. Thomas, eds. (1984) *Enforcing Regulation.* Boston: Kluwer-Nijhoff.

Hays, Sharon (1994) "Structure and Agency and the Sticky Problem of Culture," 12 *Sociological Theory* 57–72.

Hechter, Michael (1987) *Principles of Group Solidarity.* Berkeley: Univ. of California Press.

Hechter, Michael, & Satoshi Kanazawa (1997) "Sociological Rational Choice Theory," 23 *Annual Rev. of Sociology* 191–214.

Jackall, Robert (1988) *Moral Mazes: The World of Corporate Managers.* New York: Oxford Univ. Press.

Jasanoff, Sheila (1986) *Risk Management and Political Culture.* New York: Russell Sage Foundation.

Kagan, Robert A., & John T. Scholz (1984) "The 'Criminology of the Corporation' and Regulatory Enforcement Strategies," in Hawkins & Thomas, eds. 1984.

Katz, Jack (1979) "Legality and Equality: Plea Bargaining in the Prosecution of White-Collar and Common Crime," 13 *Law & Society Rev.* 431–59.

Kelman, Herbert C., & V. Lee Hamilton (1989) *Crimes of Obedience* New Haven, CT: Yale Univ. Press.

Kram, Kathy E., Peter C. Yeager, & Gary Reed (1989) "Decisions and Dilemmas: The Ethical Dimension in the Corporate Context," in J. E. Post, ed., 11 *Research in Corporate Social Performance and Policy* 21–54.

Kunda, Gideon (1992) *Engineering Culture: Control and Commitment in a High-Tech Corporation.* Philadelphia: Temple Univ. Press.

Lindblom, Charles (1959) "The Science of Muddling Through," *19 Public Administration Rev.* 79–88.

March, James G., & Johan P. Olsen (1979) *Ambiguity and Choice in Organizations.* Bergen: Universitctsforlaget.

March, James G., & Zur Shapira (1987) "Management Perspectives on Risk and Risk Taking," 33 *Management Science* 1404–18.

March, James G., & Herbert A. Simon (1958) *Organizations.* New York: Wiley.

McCurdy, Howard (1993) *Inside NASA: High Technology and Organizational Change in the U.S. Space Program.* Baltimore: Johns Hopkins Univ. Press.

Meiksins, Peter (1988) "The Revolt of the Engineers Reconsidered," 29 *Technology & Culture* 219–46.

Meyer, John, & Brian Rowan (1977) "Institutionalized Organizations: Formal Structure as Myth and Ceremony," 83 *American J. of Sociology* 340–63.

Mileti, Dennis, John Sorenson, & William Bogard (1985) *Evacuation Decision-Making: Process and Uncertainty.* Oak Ridge, Tenn.: Oak Ridge National Laboratory.

Petroski, Henri (1985) *To Engineer Is Human: The Role of Failure in Successful Design.* New York: St. Martin's.

Pfeffer, Jeffrey, & Gerald Salancik (1978) *The External Control of Organizations.* New York: Harper & Row.

Porter, Theodore M. (1995) *Trust in Numbers*. Princeton, NJ: Princeton Univ. Press.

Powell, Walter W., & Paul J. DiMaggio, eds. (1991) *The New Institutionalism in Organizational Analysis*. Chicago: Univ. of Chicago Press.

Presidential Commission on the Space Shuttle *Challenger* Accident (1986) *Report to the President by the Presidential Commission on the Space Shuttle Challenger Accident*. 5 vols. Washington, DC: GPO.

Quinney, Richard (1963) "Occupational Structure and Criminal Behavior: Prescription Violation by Retail Pharmacists," 11 *Social Problems* 179–85.

Romzek, Barbara S., & Melvin J. Dubnick (1987) "Accountability in the Public Sector: Lessons from the *Challenger* Tragedy," 47 *Public Administration Rev.* 227–38.

Schlegel, Kip (1990) *Just Deserts for Corporate Criminals*. Boston: Northeastern Univ. Press.

Schlegel, Kip, & David Weisburd, eds. (1992) *White-Collar Crime Reconsidered*. Boston: Northeastern Univ. Press.

Shapiro, Susan (1984) *Wayward Capitalists*. New Haven, CT: Yale Univ. Press.

Simpson, Sally S. (1986) "The Decomposition of Antitrust: Testing a Multi-level Longitudinal Model of Profit Squeeze," 51 *American Sociological Rev.* 859–79.

Simon, Herbert A. (1957) *Models of Man: Social and Rational*. New York: Wiley.

_____ (1976) *Administrative Behavior: A Study of Decision-Making Processes in Administrative Organizations*. 3d ed. New York: Free Press.

Smith, Dorothy (1987) *The Everyday World as Problematic*. Boston: Northeastern Univ. Press.

Staw, Barry M., & Eugene Swajkowski (1975) "The Scarcity Munificence Component of Organizational Environments and the Commission of Illegal Acts," 20 *Administrative Science Q.* 345–54.

Stone, Christopher D. (1975) *Where the Law Ends*. New York: Harper & Row.

Sutherland, Edwin H. (1949) *White-Collar Crime*. New York: Dryden Press.

Van Maanen, John, & Steve Barley (1985) "Cultural Organization: Fragments of a Theory," in P. J. Frost et al., eds, *Organizational Culture*. Beverly Hills, CA: Sage Publications.

Vaughan, Diane (1983) *Controlling Unlawful Organizational Behavior*. Chicago: Univ. of Chicago Press.

_____ (1990) "Autonomy, Interdependence, and Social Control: NASA and the Space Shuttle *Challenger*," 35 *Administrative Science Q.* 225–57.

_____ (1996) *The Challenger Launch Decision: Risky Technology, Culture, and Deviance at NASA*. Chicago: Univ. of Chicago Press.

Weick, Karl F., (1979) *The Social Psychology of Organizing*. Reading, MA: Addison-Wesley.

_____ (1995) *Sensemaking in Organizations*. Thousand Oaks, CA: Sage Publications.

Weisburd, David, Stanton Wheeler, Elin Waring, & Nancy Bode (1991) *Crimes of the Middle Classes*. New Haven, CT: Yale Univ. Press.

Wheeler, Stanton, Kenneth Mann, & Austin Sarat (1988) *Sitting in Judgment: The Sentencing of White-Collar Offenders*. New Haven, CT: Yale Univ. Press.

Wheeler, Stanton, & Mitchell Rothman (1982) "The Organization as Weapon in White-Collar Crime," 80 *Michigan Law Rev.* 1403–27.

Wildavsky, Aaron (1987) "Choosing Preferences by Constructing Institutions: A Cultural Theory of Preference Formation." 81 *American Political Science Rev.* 3–21.

Wilensky, Harold (1967) *Organizational Intelligence: Knowledge and Policy in Government and Industry*. New York: Basic Books.

Wynne, Brian (1988) "Unruly Technology: Practical Rules, Impractical Discourses, and Public Understanding," 18 *Social Studies of Science* 147–67.

Zucker, Lynn (1977) "The Role of Institutionalization in Cultural Persistence," 42 *American Sociological Rev.* 726–43.

PART XIII

DEMOCRATIC ALTERNATIVES TO CAPITALIST BUREAUCRACY
Worker Ownership and Self-Management

Reforming bureaucracy by reducing hierarchy and increasing worker control are persistent themes in organization studies from Burns and Stalker's organic system to Walton's high performance work teams (see Readings 4 and 10). More critical researchers, such as Richard Edwards, advocate full worker ownership and self-management of economic enterprises. Indeed, worker-run cooperatives first emerged as an alternative to the large capitalist enterprise when big business first began displacing small business and craft production in the late nineteenth century, though many did not survive long. More recently, a wave of cooperatives emerged during the late 1960s and 1970s out of the spirit of the 1960s and in reaction to conventional, bureaucratic, and corporate organizations, though many of these also faded away in time. Responding to the wave of plant closures in American manufacturing during the economic crisis of the late 1970s and 1980s, production workers sometimes used their own savings, wage concessions, and pension funds to buy the plants from their employers, another alternative to the traditionally owned business called *employee stock ownership plans* (ESOPs).

As this suggests, worker-owned enterprises can have mainly economic or utilitarian motivations, such as saving jobs in a conventionally owned plant threatened with closure, or they can be cooperatives with a more self-conscious normative or ideological orientation, usually some kind of commitment to workplace democracy, participation, equality, community, self-actualization, and social responsibility. Cooperatives are not merely seeking to save or create jobs; they are building an alternative way of life to the bureaucratic and profit-driven norms of the wider society. Employee-owned enterprises with more purely economic motivations generally operate more like traditional businesses, though pressures for more democratic participation arise inevitably in all employee-owned enterprises.

Employee-owned businesses can differ from more traditional organizations in at least three areas: the division of labor among workers, division of labor between management and workers, and governance of the enterprise.

Some worker-owned enterprises, including many ESOPs, are run no differently from traditional businesses. Workers own a majority of the stock, but their governance rights may entitle them to elect only a minority of members to the board of directors because banks and management demand a majority of seats as a condition for their providing additional necessary capital and expertise (Russell 1988). Workers may have little voice in managing the company, and tasks may be organized according to traditional scientific management principles. In this case, worker ownership means little more than holding stock in one's employer, even if it is collectively a majority share.

In some ESOPs, workers became so dissatisfied with management high-handedness that they decided to strike. The media enjoyed reporting the irony of workers striking against the company they owned, but the stories often failed to mention that workers felt aggrieved because they made wage concession, supplied capital, and were led to think of themselves as owners, but were given no meaningful input into how the business was run. Accustomed to a separation of ownership from control, top management may have operated under the assumption that stockholders passively ratify their decisions or simply sell their shares when dissatisfied. They seemed not to realize that things would be different when the stockholders also were employees who constituted a real, spatially concentrated, functioning social group complete with dense personal ties, rather than a geographically dispersed, abstract class of persons who had little but stock ownership in common. Because of their dual role as both employees and investors, employee shareholders have a special stake in how their company is run and become disillusioned when they realize that talk of their becoming owners is mostly management rhetoric. Worker protest is not surprising under these circumstances, and many of these firms involved either failed or eventually reverted to more traditional private or investor ownership.

Many of these conflicts between worker-owners and managers occurred in the late 1970s through the mid-1980s. In an early essay on the subject, William Foote Whyte and Joseph Blasi (1982) lament that in subsequent examples of conversions to worker ownership, the parties seemed unaware of the lessons of previous experience, and the lessons often remain unlearned today. United Airlines, which has been owned by its pilots, machinists, and some nonunion salaried workers since 1994, is the largest employee-owned company in the United States, with about 100,000 employees in 2001. Though the buyout saved thousands of jobs that would have been cut, middle management always opposed worker participation in decision making, and the CEO made major business decisions, such as committing $4.3 billion to purchase US Airways, without consulting the employee-owners despite earlier union wage concessions. Discontented employees engaged in significant work slowdowns and threatened to strike, eroding the company's earnings and further illustrating the problem of employee ownership without any meaningful employee voice ("Divided, an Airline Stumbles" 2001).

In other cases, such as the plywood manufacturing cooperatives in the northwest United States, the normatively oriented cooperatives described by Joyce Rothschild-Whitt (Reading 34), and foreign cooperative movements, such as Mondragón in Spain's Basque region or the Israeli *kibbutzim*, workers have actual control over the management of the enterprise. They may choose to have all workers rotate through all positions, including management, and pay everyone an equal wage, or they may hire a manager and others for a few positions requiring specialized knowledge and have a more differentiated pay scale. Indeed, a complex operation may require a worker-owned enterprise to hire people with special qualifications and match the salaries of conventional firms as an economic incentive to attract the necessary expertise. However, the intrusion of bureaucratic principles such as hierarchy, inequality, and the division of labor is a continual threat to the democratic and cooperative character of these organizations.

Michels (Reading 17) argued that oligarchy inevitably displaces democracy in all large and complex organizations, which may be one reason why most worker cooperatives are relatively small. Hierarchical decision making can be faster than participatory democracy, especially in larger organizations; this is not surprising, because a boss giving orders and directions works faster than group decision making in which common agreement must be reached. Also, professional specialists and technical experts are sometimes required, rather than amateurs or less trained part-timers. Even when job rotation inhibits development of an inner group of managers and professionals, informal leaders emerge based on personal effectiveness, charisma, or willingness to contribute extra effort. As the readings in this section show, democratic organizations must struggle to prevent greater power from accruing to those with superior position, knowledge, and influence.

However, though democracy may entail long group meetings rather than decisions handed down from above, one of the presumed rewards is greater commitment of those involved in the process. Because all agree to the decisions, there is no division between principal and agent, less alienation, greater self-motivation and peer pressure, and lower supervision costs, consistent with Etzioni's model of normative control.

Normatively oriented employee-owned enterprises face other dilemmas. They may become so successful that they become attractive for conversion to traditional profit-driven firms by a member willing to buy the others out or by an outside buyer. Or, as the organization expands, it may seek to keep its benefits exclusive by hiring labor and creating a two-class system of elite owner-workers and outsider-subordinates that may begin to look more like a traditional capitalist partnership—albeit one with an unusually large number of partners—than a cooperative, a development sometimes called "enterprise egoism" or "collective selfishness" (Gunn 2000).

Alternatively, the idealism and emotional involvement generated by these organizations may encourage not only commitment but also factions accusing others of compromising and endangering the original goals of the group. For example, when a volunteer, cooperative, alternative radio station (WORT) in Madison, Wisconsin, seemed to be establishing itself on a firmer financial footing, professionalizing its staff, and introducing more hierarchical management, one radio program host complained:

> I quit doing the "Breakfast Special" not because I was tired of doing the show, but because I had come to feel I was fronting for an organization so enamored of its own financial success that it had forgotten where that success started. What I hear on the air and what I have observed behind the scenes convinces me that WORT has become little more than another hip capitalist enterprise with a closed system of governance and a lust for legitimacy.

Ironically, this member, who protested that the station was selling out, later moved up to a successful career at National Public Radio himself—far more conventional and remunerative work than ever contemplated at the independent station.

Cooperatives have always faced the dilemma of how far to adapt to the more hard-headed and hard-hearted norms of the wider capitalist economy, and these problems have only grown as the world has turned more toward a free-market, for-profit philosophy. Cooperatives such as the Israeli *kibbutzim* and Spain's Mondragón have adopted more traditional business principles, such as increased managerial authority, increased pay inequality, greater use of hired labor in the case of Mondragón, and greater individual property rights in the case of the *kibbutzim* (Gunn 2000; Mort and Brenner 2000; cf. Rosner 2000).

A frequent question is why the cooperative form is not more common if it overcomes the alienation and powerlessness that are the lot of most in traditional work organizations. Rothschild-Whitt cites a number of reasons, such as most people's inexperience with participatory democracy, the lack of a supportive external organizations that can provide technical, financial, and other assistance, and the unsympathetic attitudes of the broader society. But these obstacles are less prominent in the cases of Mondragón and the Israeli *kibbutzim*. Perhaps the fact that the Mondragón system never spread beyond Spain's tightly knit Basque region or that the *kibbutzim* never accounted for more than 6% of Jews of European ancestry, despite widespread popular regard and support from Israel's socialist governments, indicates that the real problem is that few people really want an alternative to capitalist hierarchy (Nozick 1978). Many people seem to prefer subordinate status in an authority relationship even when a long-standing egalitarian alternative is available, perhaps because it is more remunerative (Alchian and Demsetz 1972). This has been called a neo-Hobbesian theory of the business firm, because it argues that people willingly subordinate themselves to an authoritarian ruler for their own benefit, which the seventeenth-century English philosopher Thomas Hobbes argued was the explanation for monarchy (Bowles 1985).

Nevertheless, the impulse toward workplace democracy persists. The reading by Joyce Rothschild-Whitt describes the cooperatives that emerged in the United States from the movements of the 1960s (Reading 34). In a significant revision of the original Whyte and Blasi (1982) article written especially for this volume, Whyte, Blasi, and Kruse describe the failed early ESOPs and their more limited, successful descendants in the United States and the successes and challenges facing the American plywood cooperatives, Mondragón, and the Israeli *kibbutzim* (Reading 35).

34

THE COLLECTIVIST ORGANIZATION

An Alternative to Rational-Bureaucratic Models

JOYCE ROTHSCHILD-WHITT

This article represents a first approach to a model of collectivist organization, a model that is premised on the logic of substantive rationality rather than formal rationality. To date, theories of organizational action have assumed, explicitly or implicitly, that norms of formal rationality prevail (Thompson, 1967). Indeed, in a modern society they almost always do. This decade, however, has given rise to a wide array of work organizations that self-consciously reject the norms of rational-bureaucracy and identify themselves as "alternative institutions." The emergence of these contrabureaucratic organizations calls for a new model of organization that can encompass their alternative practices and aspirations.

Max Weber delineated four types of social action: traditional, affectual, instrumentally rational, and value rational. The first three forms of social action correspond respectively to traditional, charismatic, and legal-rational bases of authority, with each type of authority implying a particular type of organization to implement its aims. But the last type of social action, value-rationality, has no counterpart in his typology of authority and organization. Some recent scholars have begun to look to Weber's missing type, value-rational authority, to understand certain kinds of professional and church organizations (Satow, 1975; Wood, 1978).

A value-rational orientation to social action is marked by a "belief in the value for its own sake . . . independent of its prospects of success" (Weber, 1968:24). It is evidenced by actions that put into practice people's convictions.

[. . .]

From Joyce Rothschild-Whitt, "The Collectivist Organization: An Alternative to Rational-Bureaucratic Models," *American Sociological Review,* Vol. 44(August), pp. 509-527. Copyright © 1979; reprinted by permission of the American Sociological Association.

This paper aims to develop an ideal-type model of collectivist-democratic organization. It is an attempt to delineate the form of authority and the corresponding mode of organization that follows from value-rational premises. As such it is grounded in observations of counter-bureaucratic organizations which aspire to being "collectives," or in Weberian terms, which have explicitly rejected instrumentally-rational social action in favor of value-rational behavior. [. . .]

RESEARCH SETTINGS AND METHODS

During the 1970s the United States has witnessed an impressive proliferation of what have popularly come to be termed *alternative institutions*. Alternative institutions may be defined in terms of their members' resolve to build organizations which are parallel to, but outside of, established institutions and which fulfill social needs (for education, food, medical aid, etc.) without recourse to bureaucratic authority.

Parallel, oppositional organizations have been created in many service domains—e.g., free medical clinics, free schools, legal collectives, alternative media collectives, food cooperatives, research collectives, communes. Grassroots cooperative businesses are proliferating as well, especially in fields with relatively low capitalization needs such as restaurants, bookstores, clothing manufacture and retail, auto repair, housing construction, alternative energy installation, newspapers, and so forth. They are burgeoning at a remarkable rate. For instance, in 1967 there were about 30 free schools in the United States. By 1973 there were over 800 documented free schools (New Schools Exchange Directory, 1967; 1973). A 1976 directory locates some 5,000 alternative organizations nationwide, and does not even claim to be exhaustive (Gardner, 1976). These collectively owned and managed work enterprises represent one of the enduring legacies of the anti-authority movements of the 1960s.[1]

Little social scientific research has been devoted to this social development. Some research studies describe one or another of these alternative work organizations, but few point to commonalities which link them. This paper identifies some of the structural commonalities and attempts to develop a general organizational framework of collectivist-democracy in which specific cases may be understood.

[. . .]

I selected for study five collectivist work organizations that were as varied as possible: a free medical clinic, a legal collective, a food cooperative, a free school, and an alternative newspaper.[2] All are located in a medium-sized city in California. Although they differ greatly as to the type of product or service they provide, organizational size, funding sources, technology utilized, and so forth, they are unified by the primacy each gives to developing a collectivist-democratic form of organization.

Participant observation was conducted in each of the research settings ranging in duration from six months to two years per organization. Observational material was amplified by structured interviews with selected members of each of the organizations, with a mean interview time of 2¼ hours. This was followed by questionnaire surveys to the membership of three of the organizations under study.

Each theoretical point in the paper is grounded in numerous instances from the empirical material. I have tried to select those few that seem most characteristic of the data. Of course, no number of illustrations can ever constitute a "proof." The theoretical formulations in this work should be assessed for their logical consistency, clarity, integration, and especially for the extent to which they are found to be generic properties of collectivist organizations.

The Collectivist Organization: Characteristics

Collectivist-democratic organizations can be distinguished from bureaucratic organizations along at least eight dimensions. Each of these characteristics will be taken up in turn, and a summarizing chart will follow.

Authority

When we're talking about collectives, we're talking about an embryonic creation of a new society. . . . Collectives are growing at a phenomenal rate all over this country. The new structures have outgrown the science of analyzing them. Sociology has to catch up with reality. . . . Collectivism is an attempt to supplant old structures of society with new and better structures. And what makes our's superior is that the basis of authority is radically different. (Staff member, Alternative Paper).

The words of this activist get right to the heart of the matter: authority. Perhaps more than anything else, it is the basis of authority that distinguishes the collectivist organization from any variant of bureaucracy. The collectivist-democratic organization rejects rational-bureaucratic justifications for authority. Here authority resides not in the individual, whether on the basis of incumbency in office *or* expertise, but in the collectivity as a whole.

This notion stems from the ancient anarchist ideal of "no authority." It is premised on the belief that social order can be achieved without recourse to authority relations (Guerin, 1970). Thus it presupposes the capacity of individuals for self-disciplined, cooperative behavior. Indeed, collectivist organizations routinely emphasize these aspects of human beings. Like the anarchists, their aim is not the transference of power from one official to another, but the abolition of the pyramid in toto: organization without hierarchy.

[. . .]

It does not take formal motions and amendments, it does not usually take votes, majorities do not rule, and there is no two-party system. Instead there is a "consensus process" in which all members participate in the *collective* formulation of problems and *negotiation of decisions*.[3] All major policy issues, such as hiring, firing, salaries, the division of labor, the distribution of surplus, and the shape of the final product or service, are decided by the collective as a whole. Only decisions which appear to carry the consensus of the group behind them, carry the weight of moral authority. Only these decisions, changing as they might with the ebb and flow of sentiments in the group, are taken as binding and legitimate. These organizations are collectively-controlled by their members or workers: hence the name *collectivist* or *collectivist-democratic* organization.

[. . .] Individuals, of course, may be delegated carefully circumscribed areas of authority, but authority is delegated and defined by the collectivity and subject to recall by the collectivity.

Rules. Collectivist organizations also challenge the bureaucratic conception that organizations should be bound by a formally established, written system of rules and regulations. Instead, they seek to minimize rule use. But, just as the most bureaucratic of organizations cannot anticipate, and therefore cannot circumscribe, *every* potential behavior in the organization, so the alternative organization cannot reach the theoretical limit of *zero* rules. Collectivist organizations, however, drastically can reduce the number of spheres of organizational activity that are subject to explicit rule governance.

In the most simple of the collectivist organizations in this study, the free high school, only one explicit organizational rule was formulated: no dope in school. This rule was agreed upon by a plenary meeting of the school's students and staff primarily because its violation was perceived to threaten the continued existence of the school. Other possible rules also were discussed at the Free School, rules that might seem self-evident in ordinary schools such as "each student should take X number of classes" or "students are required to attend the courses for which they are registered," but these did not receive the consensual backing of the school's members.

In place of the fixed and universalistic rule use which is the trademark of bureaucracy, operations and decisions in alternative organizations tend to be conducted in an ad hoc manner. Decisions generally are settled as the case arises, and are suited to the peculiarities of the individual case. No written manual of rules and procedures exists in most collectives, though norms of participation clearly obtain. While there is little attempt to account for decisions in terms of literal rules, concerted efforts are made to account for decisions in terms of substantive ethics. *[. . .]*

One of the chief virtues of extensive rule use in bureaucracy is that it permits predictability and appeal of decisions. The lack of universalistic standards in prebureaucratic modes of organization invited arbitrary and capricious rule. In bureaucracy decisions could be calculated and appealed on the basis of their correspondence to the written law. In collectivist organizations, however, decisions are not necessarily arbitrary. They are based on substantive values (e.g., equality) applied consistently, if not universally. This permits at least some calculability on the basis of knowing the substantive ethic that will be invoked in a particular situation.

Social Control. From a Weberian point of view, organizations are tools. They are instruments of power for those who head them. But what means does the bureaucracy have of ensuring that lower-level personnel, people who are quite distant from the centers of power, effectively will understand and implement the aims of those at the top? This issue of social control is critical in any bureaucracy. Perrow (1976) examines three types of social control mechanisms in bureaucracies: direct supervision, standardized rules, and selection for homogeneity. The first type of control, direct supervision, is the most obvious. The second is far less obtrusive, but no less effective: standardized rules, procedures, and sanctions. Gouldner (1954) showed that rules can substitute for direct supervision. This allows the organization considerable decentralization of everyday decision making, and even the appearance of participation, for the *premises* of those decisions have been carefully controlled from the top. Decentralized decision making, when decisional premises are set from the top via standardized rules, may be functionally equivalent to centralized authority (cf. Blau, 1970; Bates, 1970; Perrow, 1976).

Collectivist organizations generally refuse to legitimate the use of centralized authority *or* standardized rules to achieve social control. Instead, they rely upon personalistic and moralistic appeals to provide the primary means of control, as Swidler (1979) demonstrates in her examination of free schools. In Etzioni's (1961) terms, compliance here is chiefly normative. One person appeals to another, "do X *for me*," "do X in the interest of equality," and so forth.

The more homogeneous the group, the more such appeals can hold sway. Thus, where personal and moral appeals are the chief means of social control, it is important, perhaps necessary, that the group select members who share their basic values and world view. All five of the alternative organizations in this study tried to do that. At the Law Collective, for instance, I asked how they decide whether to take in a new member:

They have to have a certain amount of past experience in political work . . . [,] something really good and significant that checks out. . . . Secondly, they have to share the same basic assumptions as far as politics goes and they have to be willing to accept the collective way of doing things. . . .

Such recruitment criteria are not at all uncommon or hidden in alternative work organizations.

In Perrow's (1976) terms alternative organizations eschew first- and second-level controls, but accept third-level controls. Third-level controls are the most subtle and indirect of all: selection of personnel for homogeneity. On this level social control may be achieved by selecting for top managerial positions only people who "fit in"—people who read the right magazines, go to the right clubs, have the right style of life and world view. This is also true in collectivist organizations. Where people are expected to participate in major decisions (and this means *everyone* in a collective and high-level managers in a bureaucracy) consensus is crucial, and people who are likely to challenge basic assumptions are avoided. A person who reads the *Wall Street Journal* would be as suspect in applying for a position at the Law Collective, as a person who reads the *New Left Review* would be at ITT. Both kinds of organizations utilize selection for homogeneity as a mechanism for social control.

Social relations. Impersonality is a key feature of the bureaucratic model. Personal emotions are to be prevented from distorting rational judgements. Relationships between people are to be role-based, segmental, and instrumental. Collectivist organizations, on the other hand, strive toward the ideal of community. Relationships are to be wholistic, affective, and of value in themselves. The search for community may even become an instance of goal displacement, as when, for example, a free school comes to value community so highly that it loses its identity as a school and becomes a commune (see, e.g., Kaye, 1972).

Recruitment and Advancement. Bureaucratic criteria for recruitment and advancement are resisted in the collectivist organization. Here employment is not based on specialized training or certification, nor on any universalistic standard of competence. Instead, staff are generally recruited and selected by collectives on the basis of friendship and social-political values. Personality attributes that are seen as congruent with the collectivist mode of organization, such as self-direction and collaborative styles, also may be consciously sought in new staff (see, e.g., Torbert, 1973).

Employment does not constitute the beginning of a career in collectivist organizations in the usual sense, for the collective does not provide a life-long ladder to ever-higher positions. Work may be volunteer or paid, and it may be part-time or full-time or even 60 hours per week, but it is not conceptualized as a career. Bureaucratic career advancement (based on seniority and/or achievement) is not a meaningful concept in collective work organizations, for there is no hierarchy of offices. Therefore, there can be no individual *advancement* in positional rank (though there may be much change in positions).

[...]

Incentive Structure. Organizations use different kinds of incentives to motivate participation. Most bureaucratic workplaces emphasize remunerative incentives and few employees could be expected to donate their services if their paychecks were to stop. Collectivist organizations on the other hand, rely primarily on purposive incentives (value fulfillment), secondarily on solidary incentives such as friendship, and only tertiarily on material incentives (Clark and Wilson, 1961). According to Etzioni (1961), this kind of normative compliance system tends to generate a high level of moral commitment to organization. [...] Because collectivist work organizations require a high level of commitment, they tend to utilize some of these mechanisms as well as value-purposive incentives to generate it. Indeed, work in collectives is construed as a labor of love, and members may pay themselves very low salaries and may expect each other to continue to work during months when the organization is too poor to afford their salaries.

[...] At the Free Clinic, for instance, a member describes motivation:

> Our volunteers are do-gooders. . . . They get satisfaction from giving direct and immediate help to people in need. This is why they work here.

While at the Alternative Newspaper, the following is more illustrative:

> Our motives were almost entirely political. We were moving away from a weathermen type position, toward the realization that the revolution will be a very gradual thing. . . . We wanted to create a base for a mass left. To activate liberals and open them up to left positions. To tell you the truth, the paper was conceived as a political organ.

At the Food Co-op it is the value of community that is most stressed, and the Co-op actively helps to create other community-owned and controlled institutions in its locale.

However, we should guard against an overly idealistic interpretation of participation in alternative organizations. In these organizations, as much as any, there exists an important *coalescence of material and ideal interests.* Even volunteers in these organizations, whose motives on the face of it would appear to be wholly idealistic, also have material incentives for their participation.

For example, staff members at the Free Clinic suspect that some volunteers donate their time to the clinic "only to look good on their applications to medical school." Likewise, some of the college students who volunteered to teach at the Free School believed that in a tight market, this would improve their chances of getting a paid teaching job. And, for all the talk of community at the Food Co-op, many members undoubtedly joined simply because the food was cheaper. Because material gain is not part of the acceptable vocabulary of motives in these organizations, public discussion of such motives is suppressed.

Nonetheless, for staff members as well as for volunteers, material incentives coalesce with moral incentives. At the Law Collective, for instance, legal workers often used their experience there to pursue the bar, since California law allows eligibility for the bar through the alternative means of apprenticing under an attorney for three years. At the Alternative Newspaper, a few staff members confided that they had entered the paper to gain journalistic experience.

Yet members of alternative institutions often deny the existence of material considerations and accept only the idealistic motivations. In the opinion of one long-time staffer at the Alternative Paper:

> I don't think anyone came for purely journalistic purposes, unless they're masochists. I mean it doesn't pay, the hours are lousy, and the people are weird. If you want professional journalistic experience you go to a straight paper.

In many ways, she is right: Alternative institutions generally provide woefully inadequate levels of remuneration by the standards of our society. But, it does not impugn the motives of participants to recognize that these organizations must provide some material base for their members if they are to be alternative places of employment at all.

At the Free Clinic full-time staff were all paid $500 per month during 1974–1975, at the Law Collective they were paid a base of $250 per month plus a substantial supplement for dependents, and at the Alternative Paper they received between $150 and $300 per month, in accordance with individual "needs." These pay levels were negotiated in open discussion of the collectives as a whole, as were decisions regarding the entire labor process. If these wage levels appear exploitative, it is a case of self-exploitation. It is the subsistence wage levels which permit the young organization to accumulate capital and to reinvest this surplus in the organization rather than paying it out in wages. This facilitates the growth of the organization and hastens the day when it may be able to pay higher salaries.

Many collectives have found ways to help compensate for the meager salaries they pay their members. The Law Collective stocked food so that members could eat at least a meal or two per day at the office for free. The collective also maintained a number of cars that its members could share, thereby eliminating the need for private automobile ownership. Free Clinic staff decided to allow themselves certain fringe benefits to compensate for what they regarded as underpaid work: two weeks of paid vacation time each year, plus two additional weeks of unpaid vacation (if desired); one day off every other week; and the revised expectation that staff would regularly work a 28–30 rather than 40-hour week. But these are compensations or supplements for a generally poor income, and like income, they

do not motivate people to work in alternative organizations, they only make work there possible.

First and foremost, people come to work in an alternative organization because it offers them substantial control over their work. Collective control means that members can structure both the product of their work and the work process in congruence with their ideals. Hence, the work is purposeful to them. It is not infrequently contrasted with alienating jobs that they have had, or imagine, in bureaucracies:

> A straight paper would have spent a third of a million dollars getting to where we are now and still wouldn't be breaking even. We've gotten where we are on the sweat of our workers. They've taken next to no money when they could have had 8,000 to 15,000 in straight papers doing this sort of job. . . . They do it so they can be their own boss. So they can own and control the organization they work in. So they can make the paper what *they* want it to be. . . . (interview, member of Alternative Newspaper)

Social Stratification. In the ideal-type bureaucracy, the dimensions of social stratification are consistent with one another. Specifically, social prestige and material privilege are to be commensurate with one's positional rank, and the latter is the basis of authority in the organization. Thus, a hierarchical arrangement of offices implies an isomorphic distribution of privilege and prestige. In this way, hierarchy institutionalizes (and justifies) inequality.

In contrast, egalitarianism is a central feature of the collectivist-democratic organization. Large differences in social prestige or privilege, even where they are commensurate with level of skill or authority in bureaucracy, would violate this sense of equity. At the Free Clinic, for instance, all full-time staff members were paid equally, no matter what skills or experience they brought to the clinic. At the Law Collective and Alternative Newspaper pay levels were set "to each according to his need." Here salaries took account of dependents and other special circumstances contributing to need, but explicitly excluded considerations of the worth of the individual to the organization. In no case I observed was the ratio between the highest pay and the lowest pay greater than two to one.

In larger, more complex, democratic organizations wages are still set, and wage differentials strictly limited, by the collectivity. For example, in the 65 production cooperatives that constitute the Mondragón system in Spain pay differentials are limited to a ratio of three to one in each firm (Johnson and Whyte, 1977). In the worker-owned and managed refuse collection firms in San Francisco, the differential is only two to one, or less (Russell, 1979; Perry, 1978). Schumacher (1973:276) reports a seven to one ratio between the highest and the lowest paid at Scott Bader, a collectively-owned firm in England. The cooperatively-owned plywood mills in the Pacific Northwest pay their members an equal wage (Bernstein, 1976:20–1). By comparison, the wage differential tolerated today in Chinese work organizations is 4:1; in the United States it is about 100:1.

Prestige, of course, is not as easily equalized as is pay. Nonetheless, collectivist organizations try in a variety of ways to indicate that they are a fraternity of peers. Through dress, informal relations, task sharing, job rotation, the physical structure of the workplace, equal pay, and the collective decision-making process itself—collectives convey an equality of status. [. . .]

Differentiation. A complex network of specialized, segmental roles marks any bureaucracy. Where the rules of scientific management hold sway, the division of labor is maximized: jobs are subdivided as far as possible. Specialized jobs require technical expertise. Thus, bureaucracy ushers in the ideal of the specialist-expert and defeats the cultivated, renaissance man of an earlier era (Weber, 1946:240–4).

In contrast, differentiation is minimized in the collectivist organization. Work roles are purposefully kept as general and wholistic as possible. They aim to eliminate the division of labor that separates intellectual workers from manual workers, administrative tasks from performance tasks. Three means are commonly utilized toward this end: role rotation, teamwork or task sharing, and the diffusion or demystification of specialized knowledge through internal education.

[. . .] In the completely democratized organization, everyone manages and everyone works. This may be the most fundamental way in which the collectivist mode of organization alters the social relations of production.

This alteration in the division of labor is perhaps best illustrated by the Free School, an organization in which administrative functions were quite simple, and undifferentiated. The Free School had no separate set of managers to administer the school. Whenever administrative tasks were recognized, "coordination meetings" were called to attend to them; these were open to all interested teachers and students. Coordinators were those who were willing to take responsibility for a particular administrative task (e.g., planning curriculum, writing a press release, organizing a fund-raiser). A coordinator for one activity was not necessarily a coordinator for another project. Further, the taking on of administrative tasks was assumed to be a part-time commitment which could be done along side of one's other responsibilities. Coordinators, then, were *self-selected, rotated, and part-time.* No one was allowed to do administration exclusively. By simplifying administration and opening it up to the membership-at-large, the basis and pretense of special expertise was eliminated.

The school even attempted to break down the basic differentiation between students and staff, regarding students not as clients but as members with decision-making rights and responsibilities. The Free Clinic also tried to integrate its clients into the organization. For instance, it created spaces on its board of directors for consumers of medical care and recruited many of its volunteers from the ranks of its patients.

Most alternative organizations are more complex than the Free School. They cannot assume that everyone in the organization knows how (or would want to know how) to do everything. Thus, they must develop explicit procedures to achieve universal competence. Such procedures, in effect, attack the conventional wisdom of specialized division of labor and seek to create more integrated, multi-faceted work roles.

The Alternative Newspaper, for example, utilizes task sharing (or team work), apprenticeships, and job rotations toward this end. Instead of assigning one full-time person to a task requiring one person, they would be more likely to assign a couple of people to the task part-time. Individuals' allocations of work often combine diverse tasks, such as 15 hours writing, 15 hours photography, and 10 hours production. In this way, the distribution of labor combines satisfying tasks with more tedious tasks and manual work with intellectual work. People do not enter the paper knowing how to do all of these jobs, but the emphasis on task sharing allows the less experienced to learn from the more experienced. [. . .] Thus, while the Alternative Paper must perform the same tasks as any newspaper, it attempts to do so without permitting the usual division of labor into specialties or its concomitant monopolization of expertise.

Minimizing differentiation is difficult and time consuming. The Alternative Paper, for instance, spent a total of fifteen hours and forty minutes of formal meeting time and many hours of informal discussion in planning one systematic job rotation. Attendance at the planning meetings was 100%. The time and priority typically devoted to internal education in collectivist organizations makes sense only if it is understood as part of a struggle against the division of labor. The creation of an equitable distribution of labor and wholistic work roles is an essential feature of the collectivist organization.

Table 34.1 summarizes the ideal-type differences between the collectivist mode of organization and the bureaucratic. Democratic control is the foremost characteristic of collectivist organization, just as hierarchal control is the defining characteristic of the smoothly-running bureaucracy. Thus, collectivist-democratic organization would transform the social relations to production. Bureaucracy maximizes formal rationality precisely by centralizing the locus of control at the top of the organization; collectives decentralize control such that it may be organized around the alternative logic of substantive rationality.

IMPERFECT DEMOCRACY: CONSTRAINTS AND SOCIAL COSTS

Various constraints limit the actual attainment of democracy, and even to the extent that the collectivist-democratic ideal is achieved, it may produce social costs that were unanticipated.

[. . .]

Time. Democracy takes time. This is one of its major social costs. Two-way communication structures may produce higher morale, the consideration of more innovative ideas, and more adaptive solutions to complex problems, but they are undeniably slow (Leavitt, 1964:141–50). Quite simply, a boss can hand down a bureaucratic order in a fraction of the time it would take a group to decide the issue democratically.

The time absorbed by meetings can be extreme in democratic groups. During the early stages of the Alternative Newspaper, for instance, three days out of a week were taken up with meetings. Between business meetings, political meetings, and "people" meetings, very little time remained to do the tasks of the organization. Members quickly learn that this is unworkable. Meetings are streamlined. Tasks are given a higher priority. Even so, constructing an arrangement that both saves time and ensures effective collective control may prove difficult: Exactly which meetings are dispensable? What sorts of decisions can be safely delegated? How can individuals still be held accountable to the collectivity as a whole? These sorts of questions come with the realization that there are only 24 hours in a day.

There is a limit, however, to how streamlined collectivist meetings can get. In the end, commitment to decisions and their implementation can only be assured in collectives through the use of the democratic method. Unilateral decisions, albeit quicker, would not be seen as binding or legitimate. With practice, planning and self-discipline, groups can learn to accomplish more during their meeting time. But once experience is gained in how to conduct meetings, time given to meetings appears to be directly correlated with level of democratic control. The Free Clinic, for instance, could keep its weekly staff meetings down to an average of one hour and fifteen minutes only by permitting individual decision making outside-the-meeting to a degree that would have been unacceptable to members of the Alternative Paper, where a mean of four hours was given over to the weekly staff meeting.

Homogeneity. Consensus, an essential component of collectivist decision making, may require from the outset substantial homogeneity. To people who would prefer diversity, this is a considerable social cost.

Table 34.1. Comparisons of Two Ideal Types of Organization

Dimensions	*Bureaucratic Organization*	*Collectivist-Democratic Organization*
1. Authority	1. Authority resides in individuals by virtue of incumbency in office and/or expertise; hierarchal organization of offices. Compliance is to universal fixed rules as these are implemented by office incumbents.	1. Authority resides in the collectivity as a whole; delegated, if at all, only temporarily and subject to recall. Compliance is to the consensus of the collective which is always fluid and open to negotiation.
2. Rules	2. Formalization of fixed and universalistic rules; calculability and appeal of decisions on the basis of correspondence to the formal, written law.	2. Minimal stipulated rules; primacy of ad hoc, individuated decisions; some calculability possible on the basis of knowing the substantive ethics involved in the situation.
3. Social Control	3. Organizational behavior is subject to social control, primarily through direct supervision or standardized rules and sanctions, tertiarily through the selection of homogeneous personnel especially at top levels.	3. Social controls are primarily based on personalistic or moralistic appeals and the selection of homogeneous personnel.
4. Social Relations	4. Ideal of impersonality. Relations are to be role-based, segmental and instrumental.	4 Ideal of community. Relations are to be wholistic, personal, of value in themselves.
5. Recruitment and Advancement	5a. Employment based on specialized training and formal certification.	5a. Employment based on friends, social-political values, personality attributes, and informally assessed knowledge and skills.
	5b. Employment constitutes a career; advancement based on seniority or achievement.	5b. Concept of career advancement not meaningful; no hierarchy of positions.
6. Incentive Structure	6. Remunerative incentives are primary.	6. Normative and solidarity incentives are primary; material incentives are secondary.
7. Social Stratification	7. Isomorphic distribution of prestige, privilege, and power; i.e., differential rewards by office; hierarchy justifies inequality.	7. Egalitarian; reward differentials, if any, are strictly limited by the collecivity.
8. Differentiation	8a. Maximal division of labor: dichotomy between intellectual work and manual work and between administrative task and performance tasks.	8a. Minimal division of labor: administration is combined with performance tasks; division between intellectual and manual work is reduced.
	8b. Maximal specialization of jobs and functions; segmental roles. Technical expertise is exclusively held; ideal of the specialist-expert.	8b. Generalization of jobs and functions; wholistic roles Demystification of expertise: ideal of the amateur factotum.

Bureaucracy may not require much homogeneity, partly because it does not need the moral commitment of its employees. Since it depends chiefly on remunerative incentives to motivate work and since in the end it can command obedience to authority, it is able to unite the energies of diverse people toward organizational goals. But, in collectives where the primary incentives for participation are value-purposive and the subordinate-superordinate relation has been delegitimated, moral commitment becomes necessary. Unified action is possible only if individuals substantially agree with the goals and processes of the collective. This implies a level of homogeneity (in terms of values) unaccustomed and unnecessary in bureaucracy.

Consequently, collectivist organizations also tend to attract a homogeneous population in terms of social origins. [. . .] In addition to being of financially privileged origins, people in alternative organizations tend to come from well-educated families. [. . .] Thus, the need for substantial agreement on the values, goals and processes of the collective, in effect, has limited their social base. This is an important constraint to members who would like to broaden the base of their social movement.

[. . .]

Emotional Intensity. The familial, face-to-face relationships in collectivist organizations may be more satisfying than the impersonal relations of bureaucracy, but they are also more emotionally threatening. The latter may be experienced as a social cost of participatory organization.

Interpersonal tension is probably endemic in the directly democratic situation, and members certainly perceive their workplaces to be emotionally intense. At the Law Collective a member warns that "plants die here from the heavy vibes." At the Alternative Newspaper I observed headaches and other signs of tension before meetings in which devisive issues would be raised. A study of the New England town meeting found citizens reporting headaches, trembling, and even fear for one's heart as a result of the meetings. Altogether, a quarter of the people in a random sample of the town spontaneously suggested that the conflictual character of the meetings disturbed them (Mansbridge, 1979; 1973).

[. . .]

To allay these fears of conflict, townspeople utilize a variety of protective devices: criticism is concealed or at least softened with praise, differences of opinion are minimized in the formulation of a consensus, private jokes and intimate communications are used to give personal support during the meetings. Such avoidance patterns have the unintended consequence of excluding the not fully-integrated member, withholding information from the group, and violating the norms of open participation. Further, these same fears of conflict and avoidance patterns are in evidence even in groups which are highly sensitive to these issues and in which many members have been trained in group process (Mansbridge, 1979).

Structural tensions inherent in collectivist organization render conflict difficult to absorb. First, the norm of consensual decision making in collectives makes the possibility of conflict all the more threatening because unanimity is required (where a majoritarian system can institutionalize and absorb conflicting opinions). Second, the intimacy of face-to-face decision making personalizes the ideas that people espouse and thereby makes the rejection of those ideas harder to bear (while a more formal bureaucratic system, to the extent that it disassociates an idea from its proponent, makes the criticism of ideas less interpersonally risky).

Nondemocratic Individuals. Due to prior experiences, many people are not very well-suited for participatory-democracy. This is an important constraint on its development.

The major institutions of our society, such as educational institutions, combine to reinforce ways of thinking, feeling, and acting that are congruent with capitalist-bureaucratic life and incompatible with collectivist orientations. [. . .]

In the face of these behavior-shaping institutions, it is very difficult to sustain collectivist personalities. It is asking, in effect, that people in collectivist organizations constantly shift gears, that they learn to act one way inside their collectives and another way outside. In this sense, the difficulty of creating and sustaining collectivist attributes and behavior patterns results from a cultural disjuncture. It derives from the fact that alternative work organizations are as yet isolated examples of collectivism in an otherwise capitalist-bureaucratic context. Where they are not isolated, that is, where they are part of an interlocking network of cooperative organizations, such as the Mondragón system in Spain (Johnson and Whyte, 1977) this problem is mitigated.

[. . .]

Nevertheless, a number of recent case studies of democratic workplaces, one of the worker-owned refuse collection companies (Russell et al., 1979; Perry, 1978) and one of a women's health collective (Bart, 1979), reveal that the experience of democratic participation can alter peoples' values, the quality of their work, and ultimately, their identities.

[. . .]

In this vein, Pateman has amassed a considerable body of evidence from research on political socialization in support of the classical arguments of Rousseau, Mill, and Cole. She concludes:

> We do learn to participate by participating and . . . feelings of political efficacy are more likely to be developed in a participatory environment. . . . The experience of a participatory authority structure might also be effective in diminishing tendencies toward non-democratic attitudes in the individual. (1970:105)

[. . .]

Environmental Constraints. Alternative organizations, like all organizations, are subject to external pressures. Because they often occupy an adversary position vis-à-vis mainstream institutions, such pressures may be more intense. Extra-organizational constraints on the development of collectivist organizations may come from legal, economic, political, and cultural realms.

It is generally agreed among free schoolers, for instance, that building and fire codes are most strictly enforced for them (Kozol, 1972; Graubard, 1972). This is usually only a minor irritant, but in extreme cases, it may involve a major disruption of the organization, requiring them to move or close down. One small, collectively-run, solar power firm was forced to move its headquarters several times through this sort of legal harassment. At one site, the local authorities charged over a hundred building "violations" (Etzkowitz, 1978). An even more far-reaching legal obstacle is the lack of a suitable statute for incorporating employee-owned and controlled firms. The Alternative Newspaper, for example, had to ask an attorney to put together corporate law in novel ways in order to ensure collective control over the paper.[4]

The law can be changed but the more ubiquitous forces against collectivism are social, cultural, and economic. In fact, alternative organizations often find that bureaucratic practices are thrust on them by established institutions. The Free School, for example, began with an emphatic policy of absolutely no evaluative records of students. In time, however, it found that in order to help its students transfer back into the public schools or gain entrance into college, it had to begin keeping or inventing records. The preoccupation of other organizations with records and documents may thus force record keeping on a reluctant free school. In another free school, the presence of a steady stream of government communications and inspectors (health, building, etc.) pushed the organization into creating a special job to handle correspondence and personal visits of officials (Lindenfeld, 1979).

Alternative organizations often strive to be economically self-sustaining, but without a federated network of other cooperative organizations to support them, they cannot. Often they must rely on established organizations for financial support. This acts as a constraint on the achievement of their collectivist principles. For instance, in order to provide free services, the Free Clinic needed and received financial backing from private foundations as well as from county revenue-sharing funds. This forced them to keep detailed records on expenditures and patient visits and to justify their activities in terms of outsiders' criteria of cost-effectiveness.

In less fortunate cases, fledgling democratic enterprises may not even get off the ground for failure to raise sufficient capital. Two recent attempts by employee groups to purchase and collectively manage their firms reveal the reluctance of banks to loan money to collectivist enterprises, even where these loans would be guaranteed by the government. From the point of view of private investors, collective ownership and management may appear, at best, an unproven method of organizing production, and at worst, a dangerous method.

For a consistent source of capital, collectivist enterprises may need to develop cooperative credit unions as the Mondragón system has done (Johnson and Whyte, 1977) or an alternative investment fund. *[. . .]*

Individual Differences. All organizations, democratic ones notwithstanding, contain persons with very different talents, skills, knowledge, and personality attributes. Bureaucracies try to capitalize on these individual differences, so that ideally people with a particular expertise or personality type will be given a job, rewards, and authority comensurate with it. In collectives such individual differences may constrain the organization's ability to realize its egalitarian ideals.

Inequalities in influence persist in the most egalitarian of organizations. In bureaucracies the existence of inequality is taken for granted, and in fact, the exercise of power is built into the opportunity structure of positions themselves (Kanter, 1977). However, in collectivist organizations, this may be less true. Here, precisely because authority resides in the collectivity as a unit, the exercise of influence depends less on positional opportunities and more on the personal attributes of the individual. Not surprisingly, members who are more articulate, responsible, energetic, glamorous, fair, or committed carry more weight in the group. . . .

Some individual differences are accepted in the collectivist organization, but not all, particularly not differences in knowledge. In bureaucracy differences of skill and knowledge are honored. Specialized jobs accompany expertise. People are expected to protect their expertise. Indeed, this is a sign of professionalism, and it is well-known that the monopolization of knowledge is an effective instrument of power in organizations (Weber, 1968; Crozier, 1964). For this very reason, collectivist organizations make every attempt to eliminate differentials in knowledge. Expertise is considered not the sacred property of the individual, but an organizational resource. In collectives, individually-held skills and knowledge are demystified and redistributed through internal education, job rotation, task sharing, apprenticeships, or any plan they can devise toward this end.

The diffusion or demystification of knowledge, while essential to help equalize patterns of influence,

involves certain trade-offs. Allowing a new person to learn to do task X by rotating her/him to that job may be good for the development of that person, but it may displace an experienced person who had received a sense of satisfaction and accomplishment in job X. Further, encouraging novices to learn by doing may be an effective form of pedagogy, but it may detract from the quality of goods or services that the organization provides, at least (theoretically) until universal competence in the tasks of the organization is reached.

Even in the collectivist organization that might achieve universal competence, other sources of unequal influence would persist (e.g., commitment level, verbal fluency, social skills). The most a democratic organization can do is to remove the bureaucratic bases of authority: positional rank and expertise. *[. . .]*

CONCLUSION

The organizations in this study are admittedly rare and extreme cases. To the extent that they reject received forms of organization, they present an anomaly. For precisely this reason they are of great theoretical significance. By approaching the polar opposites of bureaucracy, they allow us to establish the limits of organizational reality.

[. . .]

Fundamentally, bureaucracy and collectivism are oriented to qualitatively different principles. Where bureaucracy is organized around the calculus of formal rationality, collectivist-democracy turns on the logic of substantive rationality.

NOTES

1. The nineteenth century and the first third of the twentieth century saw at least 700 cases of producers' cooperatives (Aldrich and Stern, 1978). These were in many ways the forerunners of the contemporary wave of collectives and cooperatives discussed in this paper. Historically, cooperatives have come in distinct waves—the 1840s, the 1860s, the 1880s and the 1920s–1930s. Their longevity has varied widely between industries (Aldrich and Stern, 1978). Those of the nineteenth century had a median duration of less than ten years, while more than half of the worker cooperatives of the 1920s and

1930s (particularly in the plywood industry and in the refuse collection industry) are still in operation today (Jones, 1979). Since the current wave of collectives is largely a post-1970 phenomenon and is still on the rise, it is too early to say how long it will last.

2. All persons and organizations have been given fictitious names in this paper. For a more detailed account of the research sites and methods see Rothschild-Whitt (1976; 1978).

3. As organizations grow beyond a certain size they are likely to find purely consensual processes of decision making inadequate, and may turn to direct voting systems. Other complex, but nevertheless democratic, work organizations may sustain direct democracy at the shop floor level, while relying upon elected representative systems at higher levels of the organization (cf. Edelstein and Warner, 1976).

4. The result of this effort was a two-tiered structure: the paper was incorporated as a general corporation and a trust, which owns all the stock in the paper. Each six months of full-time work is worth one voting share in the trust. This grants ultimate control of the paper to the staff, past and present. Immediate control is exercised by the board of directors of the corporation, which consists of the currently working staff. As a member of the paper said, "the structure is neither graceful nor simple, but it . . . guarantees that the working staff will maintain editorial control, and makes it nearly impossible ever to sell the paper."

REFERENCES

Aldrich, Howard and Robert Stern. 1978. "Social structure and the creation of producers' cooperatives." Presented at the Ninth World Congress of Sociology, Uppsala.

Bart, Pauline and Melinda Bart. 1979. "Collective work and self-identity: the effect of working in a feminist abortion collective." In F. Lindenfeld and J. Rothschild-Whitt (eds.), *Workplace Democracy and Social Change*. Boston: Porter Sargent.

Bates, F. L. 1970. "Power behavior and decentralization." Pp. 175–6 in M. Zald (ed.), *Power and Organizations*. Nashville: Vanderbilt University Press.

Bernstein, Paul. 1976. *Workplace Democratization: Its Internal Dynamics*. Kent: Kent State University Press.

Blau, Peter. 1970. "Decentralization in bureaucracies." Pp. 150–74 in M. Zald (ed.), *Power and Organizations*. Nashville: Vanderbilt University Press.

Clark, Peter B. and James Q. Wilson. 1961. "Incentives systems: a theory of organizations." *Administrative Science Quarterly* 6:129–66.

Crozier, Michael. 1964. *The Bureaucratic Phenomenon*. Chicago: University of Chicago Press.

Edelstein, J. David and Malcolm Warner. 1976. *Comparative Union Democracy: Organization and Opposition in British and American Unions*. New York: Wiley.

Etzioni, Amitai. 1961. *A Comparative Analysis of Complex Organizations*. Glencoe: Free Press.

Etzkowitz, Henry. 1978. "The liberation of technology." *WIN Magazine* 14.

Gardner, Richard. 1976. *Alternative America*. Privately published.

Gouldner, Alvin. 1954. *Patterns of Industrial Bureaucracy*. Glencoe: Free Press.

Graubard, Allen. 1972. *Free the Children*. New York: Pantheon Books.

Guerin, Daniel. 1970. *Anarchism: From Theory to Practice*. New York: Monthly Review Press.

Johnson, Ana Gutierrez and William Foote Whyte. 1977. "The Mondragón system of worker production cooperatives." *Industrial and Labor Relations Review* 31:18–30.

Jones, Derek. 1979. "Producer cooperatives in the U.S.: An examination and analysis of socio economic performance." Unpublished paper. Department of Economics, Hamilton College.

Kanter, Rosabeth Moss. 1977. *Men and Women of the Corporation*. New York: Basic Books.

Kaye, Michael. 1972. *The Teacher Was the Sea: The Story of Pacific High School*. New York: Links Books.

Kozol, Jonathon. 1972. *Free Schools*. Boston: Houghton-Mifflin.

Leavitt, H. J. 1964. *Managerial Psychology*. Chicago: University of Chicago Press.

Lindenfeld, Frank. 1979. "Problems of power in a free school." In F. Lindenfeld and J. Rothschild-Whitt (eds.), *Workplace Democracy and Social Change*. Boston: Porter Sargent. In press.

Mansbridge, Jane. 1973. "Town meeting democracy." *Working Papers for a New Society* 1:5–15.

———. 1979. "Fears of conflict in face-to-face democracies." In F. Lindenfeld and J. Rothschild-Whitt (eds.), *Workplace Democracy and Social Change*. Boston: Porter Sargent. In press.

Pateman, Carole. 1970. *Participation and Democratic Theory*. Cambridge, Eng.: Cambridge University Press.

Perrow, Charles. 1976. "Control in organizations: the centralized-decentralized bureaucracy." Presented at annual meeting of American Sociological Association, New York.

Perry, Stewart. 1978. *Dirty Work, Clean Jobs, Proud Men.* Berkeley: University of California Press.

Rothschild-Whitt, Joyce. 1976. "Conditions facilitating participatory-democratic organizations." *Sociological Inquiry* 46:75–86.

———. 1978. *Organizations Without Hierarchy: A Comparative Study of Collectivist-Democratic Alternatives to Bureaucracy.* Ph.D. dissertation, Department of Sociology, University of California, Santa Barbara.

Russell, Raymond. 1979. "Rewards of participation on the worker-owned firm." In F. Lindenfeld and J. Rothschild-Whitt (eds.), *Workplace Democracy and Social Change.* Boston: Porter Sargent. In press.

Satow, Roberta Lynn. 1975. "Value-rational authority and professional organizations: Weber's missing type." *Administrative Science Quarterly* 20:526–31.

Schumacher, E. F. 1973. *Small Is Beautiful: Economics as if People Mattered.* New York: Harper and Row.

Swidler, Ann. 1979. *Organization Without Authority: Dilemmas of Social Control in Free Schools.* Cambridge, Ma.: Harvard University Press.

Thompson, James D. 1967. *Organizations in Action,* New York: McGraw-Hill.

Torbert, William. 1973. "An experimental selection process for a collaborative organization." *Journal of Applied Behavioral Science* 9:331–50.

Weber, Max. 1946. From *Max Weber: Essays in Sociology.* Trans. and ed. by Hans Gerth and C. Wright Mills. New York: Oxford University Press.

———. 1968. *Economy and Society.* Ed. by Guenther Roth and Claus Wittich. New York: Bedminster Press.

Wood, James R. 1978. *Legitimate Leadership in Voluntary Organizations: The Controversy Over Social Action in Protestant Churches.* Unpublished monograph. Department of Sociology, University of Indiana, Bloomington.

35

WORKER OWNERSHIP, PARTICIPATION AND CONTROL

Toward a Theoretical Model

WILLIAM FOOTE WHYTE

JOSEPH R. BLASI

DOUGLAS LYNN KRUSE

W hat happens when labor governs itself? We see both problems and potentialities. If the potentialities are to become realities, we need to review the variety of experiences people have had in employee ownership and labor management relations to arrive at a theoretical framework. Such a framework is essential for guiding us toward the public policy implications of our research.

In the employee-owned firm or worker cooperative production organization, the administration of that firm must provide for two interrelated but conceptually separable functions: organizational governance and the management of work. At the minimum, these must be accomplished without reducing efficiency beyond what they firm would have had without employee ownership.

Regarding what the organization *is* and what it *ought* to be, we see members' thinking being shaped by four organizational models: *authoritarian, bargaining, town meeting* or *community democracy,* and *entrepreneurial capitalism.* We are not assuming that members have a theoretical model explicitly in mind as they design an organization, live and work in it, and react to it. We do claim that people have implicit models in mind, however vague those visualizations may be, and that they do tend to judge current experience and future plans in terms of such models. Each of the four models has certain strengths and weaknesses. These need to be recognized and assessed so that we can move forward to build a new theoretical model, which may combine some of the features of the three existing models.

1. Authoritarian Model

The authoritarian model comes down to us particularly through the work of F. W. Taylor and his disciples in the scientific management movement (Taylor 1911). Few executives today would acknowledge that they are followers of Taylor, but they fail to recognize to what extent their present policies and practices in fact follow the basic assumptions of Taylorism. In this model, ultimate control is outside of the work force, in the hands of key investors, government (if a public organization), or, if within the company, in the hands of the management group.

This model has advantages at least insofar as it makes clear what is to be expected in the management of work. The model sets up a formally structured organization and administration, dividing various functions from each other and linking them together in a hierarchical pattern. It provides for the division of labor, which is necessary for any organization where a variety of tasks is performed, especially when the organization grows beyond what can be handled by a small group. The model also makes clear how discipline is to be handled, because it allocates all of the power to the hands of management.

The disadvantages of this model are now well known, but it may be useful to sketch them briefly as a background against which we can examine the other models.

Though the doctrine indicates that supervisors and executives have the legitimate right to control work activities because of their expertise, in fact the basis of control becomes *power* rather than *expertise*. Especially in large organizations, those making decisions affecting workers and work activity tend to be so far removed from the scene of action that

they can have little idea of the work-a-day effects of their decisions.

The model makes no allowance for differences in interests separating workers from management. It is assumed that what is good for management and the investors is good for labor, and the model provides no means whereby labor can challenge this assumption.

Especially as such organizations grow, they tend to become rigid, losing the flexibility required for coping with technological, social and economic changes.

Although some division of labor is necessary for all but the simplest and smallest organizations, the Taylorism model tends to push such division to impractical extremes. The dominant assumption has been that efficiency is best achieved when the work performed by labor is subdivided into small elements so that workers perform repeatedly the same simple operation. Individual worker and union reactions to the extreme de-skilling of jobs that can take place have become painfully apparent in recent years, especially when technological advancement is used as the pretext to empty jobs of meaning. Some researchers have offered startling pictures of this reality and the alternatives (Zuboff 1988).

The model assumes that thinking will be done by management and that workers serve the organization best when they simply do what they are told. In other words, the model utilizes the muscles and physical skills of workers, but makes no mental demands beyond those required to understand the instructions of management. Social researchers who compared Japanese with U.S. management when Japan overtook various American manufacturing sectors during the seventies and eighties came to the conclusion that the ability of a nation exceedingly poor in material resources to overtake resource-rich America was apparently based to a considerable extent on the much fuller utilization of the total human resources of the firm, including the brains of blue-collar workers (Cole 1979; for an update on the Japanese system of participation, see Kato 2000, and on its evolution see Moriguchi 2000).

2. Bargaining Model

In the bargaining model, the company is divided into two segments, management and workers, with a union representing workers.

This model has certain clear advantages. It provides for some degree of democratization in the governance of the organization. It recognizes explicitly the interests of labor and provides for representatives of the workers to bargain with management on a wide range of issues.

The model provides some protection against the arbitrary exercise of authority, giving workers a channel of appeal against unfair decisions. Furthermore, in many cases, when local union and management cannot agree on a given grievance, that grievance may be referred to an impartial arbitrator, so that the final decision is taken out of the hands of management.

The model also offers the possibility of establishing collective responsibility among workers, which can be useful to management as well as to workers. That is, some management people find it advantageous to work out production and discipline problems in consultation with local union officers rather than having to deal individually with a large number of workers.

On the disadvantage side, it is often argued that the bargaining model undermines managerial authority. Although it does indeed place some limits on the exercise of that authority, in a well-established union-management relationship, we generally find contract provisions and unwritten understandings that tend to protect the authority necessary to administer an organization. In the simplest form, such provisions do not allow the worker the right to disobey the orders of his supervisor (except in extreme situations) but do protect the worker's right to challenge the legitimacy of an order through lodging a grievance. The standard rule is that you obey, so that the work can go on, but then you follow a judicial process in challenging the order.

We have encountered many bargaining situations in which the two parties seem to be engaged in a zero-sum game. Workers assume that whatever they gain must be at the expense of management, and management people make a similar assumption. The bargaining model often tends to produce rigidities that may be so extreme as to threaten the existence of the organization. In the course of the power struggle, with neither party trusting the other, the union pushes for detailed and explicit statements of work rules and work loads. Management may find the accumulation of such rules a severe barrier to the maintenance of a competitive position in the industry. In that situation, management often approaches union leaders in an effort to get their agreement to renegotiate the work rules so as to provide the company with the flexibility necessary to meet changing conditions. Management may even argue that the union's refusal to make these adjustments will make it necessary to close the plant. Because union leaders may have heard the same threats before, they tend to assume that management is bluffing once again. If they are persuaded of the economic necessity of renegotiating the work rules, the union leaders may nevertheless hesitate to embark on this path for fear that the rank and file members will accuse them of selling out to management. Thus, the parties may bargain themselves into a self-destructive impasse.

These disadvantages are by no means inevitable. The model can be so adapted as to promote union-management cooperation in improving productivity and the quality of working life. Recently, a 1994 national survey of workers has shown that most American workers desire cooperative decision-making and conflict-resolution aspects of the trade union system (Freeman and Rogers 1999). We will explore these possibilities later.

3. TOWN MEETING OR COMMUNITY DEMOCRACY MODEL

In the town meeting model, the members of the organization have the power to make decisions. When it comes to voting, the principle followed is one member, one vote.

In the society where civil government is based upon one citizen, one vote, this model for a work organization has an obvious appeal. It fits in with democratic values and with our norms of equal rights for all (Mansbridge 1973).

The disadvantages of the model are found largely in the major area that it does not encompass: the management of work. In the town meeting, all citizens can indeed participate and have equal voting rights, but the town meeting usually assembles only once a year, except for occasional special meetings. The town meeting does decide certain policy questions and elects the board of selectmen, but the members of the community do not do the official work of that community. Getting the work done is the responsibility of a few elected officials. Thus, the town meeting model provides no guidance on the division of labor, on the allocation of authority and responsibility, on the need for specialization either because of skill or leadership competence, on the imposition of disciplinary measures, and so on. Therefore, those who implicitly guide their organizational thinking in terms of this model are left to imagine how a democratic organization would manage work activities. This gap between the theoretical model and the needs of a work organization leads to major confusions, frustrations, and conflicts.

4. ENTREPRENEURIAL CAPITALISM MODEL

In the entrepreneurial capitalism model, the members of the organization are guided by the results of the organization in a market economy. They restructure power, prestige, and resource allocation in the organization to maximize adaptation to market technological innovation and market success. This model germinated principally in service and electronic industries after WWII and was accelerated by the rise of the semiconductor, computer, software, Internet, and bio-technology industries from 1980 to 2000. This model does not recognize the traditional advantages of Taylorism or bargaining. Each worker is seen as possessing important knowledge that is central to the success of the organization. Because the product of the organization is based principally on knowledge, innovation, and discretionary individual problem solving in a highly competitive market, traditional management authority has been significantly short-circuited. Managers typically "rule" by argumentation and team problem solving. The traditional status hierarchy of the Taylorist work organization is flattened in these organizations. Status and prestige result from successful problem solving. Organizations tend to be structured around teams that are coordinated rather than operated from a central authority. Resources tend to be shared based on performance rather than the rankings of the traditional hierarchy. Profit sharing, the extensive use of stock options beyond the executive leadership, and tight labor markets that give knowledge

workers special power tend to characterize these organizations. The entrepreneurial capitalist model has evolved slowly since WWII with the Hewlett-Packard Company as a flagship (Packard 1995). More recently, both Intel and Microsoft have been widely recognized as examples of this type of organization (Jackson 1997; Cusumano 1998).

WHAT HAPPENS UNDER WORKER OWNERSHIP?

Here, we will focus our attention on the United States but will draw upon cases from abroad in posing and seeking to answer theoretical and practical questions. In the first place, because we find distinctively different sets of problems shaped by the way the worker-owned organization came into being, we need to separate our analysis for two major types of organizations: those grass-roots organizations, created anew where no production or service organization existed before, and those in which worker ownership arises out of the efforts of organizational members and community people to save jobs in a privately owned plant threatened with shut down.

Grass-Roots Cooperatives

Gross-roots worker cooperatives first emerged in the 1700s in the United States. Between the 1700s and the 1900s, these cooperatives typically emerged as a result of idealistic or religious founders, disaffected striking workers, or attempts by worker movements like the Knights of Labor to develop a cooperative commonwealth (Commons 1917–1935). A few cooperatives were documented in a study of employee ownership at the end of the 1920s (National Industrial Conference Board 1928). During the New Deal, the Roosevelt Administration tried to promote producer cooperative farms for workers (Banfield 1951). The late 1960s and the 1970s witnessed a burgeoning of small grass-roots production or service cooperatives (Rothschild-Whitt 1979). There was no common register for such firms at the time of Rothschild-Whitt's comprehensive study in the seventies; they are created and sometimes disappear in a short time. Thus, researchers were not able to say how many existed in the United States, but the number was estimated to be well over 5,000 in 1979. They tended generally to serve local markets and to arise in types of enterprises requiring small amounts of capital per worker. Characteristically, the members of the organization are young people in their twenties and thirties, either single, divorced, or separated, and therefore without heavy family responsibilities. The members are predominantly of middle-class origins. For them, membership in a worker-owned printing company or restaurant is inspired in part by a revolt against the authority that is represented by "the establishment," which they tend to see in terms of large, bureaucratic organizations. In rejecting the individualism of U.S. culture, they also reject the example of their elders who have secure economic positions.

Members of such grass-roots collectives are in effect struggling with the problem of filling the work organization gap in the town meeting or community democracy model.

The norm of equality among the members is a key principle in structuring the organization, but what it means in practice poses a number of difficult questions. Do equal rights have to be translated into equal participation by members in making decisions? Must all members receive the same pay, without regard to skill or length of service? Or should those who have greater than average family responsibilities receive more money? Should jobs be rotated among the members so that everyone has a chance to perform every job—in spite of differences in levels of skill?

We often find members expressing guilt feelings because they have deviated from the norms of equality to deal with practical problems. For example, as a small worker-owned television repair firm reached the point in which it was becoming increasingly inefficient to have the skilled craftsmen doing their own paper work, they brought in a young woman to do their bookkeeping. They decided indeed to pay her less than the skilled repairmen, but the leader of the organization was concerned with what he assumed to be a violation of democratic principles.

Grass-roots collectives tend to have characteristic problems in the handling of authority. Because the organization comes into being out of a rejection of systems of authority in traditional organizations, members naturally tend to be suspicious of anyone who appears to be giving orders.

The ideal is that all decisions shall be collective decisions. Furthermore, the members correctly recognize that a frequent use of voting in resolving disagreements can undermine group solidarity, and therefore they aim at decision making through consensus. Especially as conditions change and the organization grows, collective decision making can absorb enormous amounts of time and lead to the frustration of the members. The problem becomes especially serious when the organization grows beyond the limits of a small face-to-face group. In the small, informal group, even when the members all adhere to the rhetoric that they are all equal and that they have no leader, informal leadership inevitably does arise, so it may be possible to maintain efficiency with group consensus decision making, but the growth of the organization separates people in functions and in space and multiplies the problems of coordination. It is at this point that many previously successful grass-roots collectives tend to break down. The implicit organizational model provides no guidance in the handling of these more complex problems, and they fail to evolve a satisfactory model of their own.

We estimate that the number of grass-roots cooperatives today is much smaller than when Rothschild-Whitt wrote. A 1991 listing by the ICA Group of Boston, which has helped set-up worker cooperatives, catalogued 304 firms owned by a total of 102,343 workers with annual sales of nearly $10 billion (ICA 1991). Some examples have been mentioned in the press quite recently. In 2001, unemployed Internet workers set up a cooperative called 78 Squareset in Wisconsin (Gertzen 2001), and a cooperative healthcare group in the Bronx has received some press attention (Roel 1994). Additional worker cooperatives in the nineties include Chroma Technology, Common Wealth Printing, Cooperative Home Care Associates, Big Timberworks, Childspace, Workers Owned Sewing Company Community, Builders Cooperative South Mountain Company, Inc., and Las Flores Metalarte in Puerto Rico (ICA 1991; Adams, Gordon and Shirey 1993; Adams and Shirey 1993).

Some Early Firms Converted to Worker Ownership

The 1970s were marked by the sudden emergence all over the United States of cases in which employers or employees and community people saved jobs in an impending plant shut down through buying the plant and establishing a new employee-owned or employee-community-owned company. This was a reaction to profound changes taking place in the economy as conglomerates shed units and international competition mounted. Contrary to commonly held views that the plants being abandoned are inevitably "lemons," we found that some of the plants being shut down had actually been consistent profit makers but had not yielded a high enough level of profits to satisfy the top management of the conglomerate (Whyte 1978). In such cases, workers and sometimes also local managers would be satisfied to save the jobs, even if the firm was not making spectacular profits. The problem in such cases is one of transferring ownership so that those who have the major financial stake in the continuation of the firm can become owners. The new firm can then survive even without major technological or local management changes.

In other cases, we have found that the losses of the local plant can be clearly attributed to mismanagement by remote control by conglomerate top executives who have been imposing decisions on situations they do not understand.

In the cases studied by Cornell University's New Systems of Work and Participation Program during this period, we found universally an atmosphere of euphoria at the time of the transformation of ownership and in the early months of employee or employee-community ownership. Over the next months, characteristically we found growing dissatisfaction, sometimes accompanied by severe conflict. The disillusionment of workers and the resulting conflicts arise out of a failure of management to recognize that an employee-owned firm cannot be managed effectively by following the authoritarian model.

Mohawk Valley Community Corporation

In 1976, the Mohawk Valley Community Corporation arose out of a divestiture by Sperry-Rand Corporation (Stern, Wood and Hammer, 1979; Hammer and Stern 1980). The plant and jobs were saved by an extraordinarily effective areawide campaign led by the director of the Mohawk Valley

Economic Development District and local management people, with the active participation of union leaders. To secure a $2 million loan from banks and $2 million in credit from the Economic Development Administration, the organizers of the campaign first had to sell nearly $2 million worth of stock—and this in a depressed area where unemployment was running over 11%. The organizers of the campaign based their strategy on selling the stock in small amounts to large numbers of people. Thirty-five hundred people bought stock, and only about 240 of those were then employed in the Herkimer plant. Management and workers together purchased about 34% of the stock, with community people holding the other two thirds.

A month after the dramatic success of this job-saving campaign, four key people from the Herkimer case spoke to a seminar at Cornell University. A spirit of brotherly love then prevailed between union leaders and management, both parties sharing the pride in their great achievement. When asked whether his management had made any plans for involving worker participation in decision making, President Robert May shook his head, replying, "We haven't got around to that yet." After a pause he added, "Maybe we should install a suggestion box."

Fifteen months later, when the same cast of characters spoke at a seminar, Whyte met privately with the presidents of the blue- and white-collar workers' unions before the session to ask how things were going. The president of the white-collar union replied, "You ask any worker what it means to work in that plant now. They'll tell you, 'I've got a job.' That's all. Nothing else has changed. This place doesn't run any different now than it did when Sperry-Rand owned it."

The president of the blue-collar workers union confirmed this general interpretation, and added that his union at that time had five grievances ready to go to arbitration—an extraordinary number for a small plant.

In later contacts with workers and union leaders over a period of months, we found them experiencing increasing dissatisfaction in their relations with management. They also pointed out to us again and again gross inefficiencies in the production operations that they could correct if management were interested in discussing these problems with them.

After an initial successful year financially, Mohawk Valley Community Corporation ran into serious reverses, which led to a cutting of expenses and reduction of the workforce to the point where it fell close to 100. This decline could not be blamed exclusively upon the lack of any effective utilization of the brains of the workers. Still, the workers were convinced that the company would be in better shape if they had some input into decision making.

At the time, the company was clearly on the road back to traditional private ownership. Then, four members of management purchased enough newly issued shares to give themselves 50% of the voting stock and therefore absolute control. In the end, worker ownership proved to be only a transitional strategy for this firm.

South Bend Lathe

In the South Bend Lathe (SBL) case, our information comes simply from correspondence and an early interview with President Richard Boulis and from media accounts, but SBL so clearly fits the pattern we are describing as to justify generalizing on the basis of fragmentary information.

In 1975, SBL was one of the most publicized cases of employee ownership yet to appear, and it initially had extraordinary success financially. In this conglomerate divestiture case, 100% of the stock was coming to be owned by employees through an ESOP (Employee Stock Ownership Plan). As he appointed the trustees who vote the stock, Boulis was firmly in control initially; the full voting rights were expected to pass to the workforce within a few years of implementing the ESOP.

Our first contact with SBL was through a letter Whyte wrote to President Boulis, expressing interest in the case. In his answer, Boulis closed with a sentence that has become one of our favorite quotations: "We tell our people that they have all the advantages of ownership without any of the headaches of management." We wondered then how long it would be before the workers would begin agitating for a share in those "headaches."

When the Steelworkers' local union went out on strike in September 1980, Boulis was still running the company as if he had personally owned all of it.

He had even declined to let his fellow shareholders know what salary he was paying himself.

Boulis blamed the strike on the union, particularly because its higher officers had never forgiven him and the local for trading the pension plan in on an ESOP and had sued in court to rescind that decision. According to newspaper and magazine reports, the union leaders had an entirely different interpretation that fits far better with what we have seen in similar cases elsewhere.

Warren Brown, writing in the *Washington Post* (1980), quotes the following words of a young machinist, Randy Reynolds, who had played an important role in persuading workers to accept the ESOP:

> What we have had there for the last five years is ownership without control. . . . We've bent over backwards since 1975 to make a good product and keep it selling. . . . We've kept our mouths shut—covered up our differences with management to avoid publicity. . . .
>
> But all we got was the same treatment we had before the ESOP, maybe even worse. We made no decisions. We have no voice. We're owners in name only.

According to Boulis,

> Employee ownership does not mean employee management. Somebody has to give the orders to make things happen. You can't run a business by committee.

Did SBL workers want to run the company? The *Washington Post* reporter could not find anyone who expressed himself in that way. He gave this interpretation of the prevailing sentiments:

> None said he wanted to manage the firm, per se. But they all said that they expected ownership conferred on them a kind of collegial equality with management in which their opinions would be listened to, their views sought.

The *Post* reporter closes his article with Boulis reporting on what he has learned. He says that, when the strike ends, he is going to try

> to improve internal communications. When we bought this company, I didn't have time for human relations.

I didn't have time to go around patting people on their butts. . . . I didn't think about anything except keeping this business going and making money. But now, maybe I'll find some time for human relations. I guess I'll have to.

Anyone who thinks he can provide effective leadership for an employee-owned company by going around "patting people on their butts" is unlikely ever to learn what it takes to build an effective system of cooperative problem solving. However, several months after the strike, Boulis worked out with the union a program called "share circles" (apparently an adaptation of the Japanese Quality Control Circles), and this opening to worker participation might have led to a successful melding of elements of the three organizational models. Nevertheless, when the ESOP is designed exclusively by management (as in this case), it is possible to structure the trust agreement in such ways as to keep legal control in the hands of management indefinitely, in which case opportunities for workers' participation will depend upon what management concedes voluntarily or under union pressure. SBL struggled to exist throughout the eighties under the twin weight of poor-labor management relations and the harsh pressure of cheaper imports. The company filed for bankruptcy in 1992 and was sold to a private owner.

Is there a way that a firm converted to employee ownership can avoid such frustration and conflicts? That is possible only if the leaders recognize the need to develop a new organizational model, which incorporates features from all three models described above. This seemed to be going on in the case of the Rath Packing Company headquartered in Waterloo, Iowa.

The Rath Packing Company

Rath was once a well-established, high-quality meat packing firm that at the time of its financial crisis employed close to 3,000 employees. The Rath case differed from the three sketched above in important respects. Whereas in those cases key members of management had led the drive to save the plant, in the Rath case the leaders of Local 46 of the United Food and Commercial Workers Union led the campaign. Furthermore, the union leaders were determined not only to save the jobs, but also to keep ultimate control in the hands of the workers.

The leaders in the case worked out a complex arrangement in which the union would forego certain previously bargained benefits for its members, putting those funds into an escrow account to be plowed back into the capital structure of the company when it became majority employee-owned. They also agreed to a $20 a week payroll deduction over a period of more than two years to enable members to buy newly issued stock that would constitute 60% of the total stock then outstanding. They further arranged to enlarge the board of directors so as to provide a majority of those selected by union leaders.

This led finally to an arrangement in which workers would put their stock in an Employee Stock Ownership Trust, whose trustees are elected by the workers on a one worker, one vote basis—this being, in effect, an adaptation of one of the main elements of the town meeting or community democracy model. The trustees thus gained majority control over the board of directors.

This was a case where a simple change in ownership would not be sufficient to secure the continuance of the firm. The workers were gaining majority ownership of a firm that was in effect bankrupt. The infusion of new capital from the U.S. Department of Housing and Urban Development and from the escrow fund set aside by workers, plus their $20 a week payroll deduction to buy stock, provided the investment capital necessary to carry out an ambitious modernization program, bringing in more efficient machines, but the company remained in a precarious financial situation. Major improvements in productivity were required to assure the survival of Rath.

After preliminary discussions (by Christopher Meek of Cornell University and Warner Woodworth of Brigham Young University with union leaders Lyle Taylor and Charles Mueller), Whyte met with Meek and Woodworth, the union leaders, and key management executives to explore the possibility of developing at the Rath Company the kind of joint union-management problem-solving program (Whyte and McCall, 1980) that had been highly successful in private companies through the Jamestown (New York) Area Labor-Management Committee. This led to agreement on a comprehensive program starting at the top with the establishment of a joint steering committee and extending into each of the major departments, which set up joint "action-research teams" to conduct detailed and systematic work on productivity improvements in their departments.

This is not simply a matter of arriving at "good communication" between union and management, as is too often assumed by those who hope to see more cooperative relations develop. Research and experience at Jamestown and elsewhere have led to the development of a systematic methodology through which the two parties, starting from their traditional adversarial positions, negotiate agreements, first at the company steering committee level to establish the scope and limits of the cooperative program, and agree upon the procedures to be carried out as that program is extended into the operating departments.

In each department, the action-research team goes through a common series of stages. Members begin with a brainstorming meeting to bring out all of the problems of productivity and quality of working life they face. They then move on in subsequent meetings to establish priorities and to assign responsibilities for the development of information and ideas. Finally, they present for management implementation a proposed solution of the problem studied.

In the early stages of the Jamestown Area Labor-Management Committee, we discovered one major cause for the breakdown of these in-plant cooperative projects. The pattern was that monthly meetings of the plant labor-management committee would be devoted to discussions within which labor members were pointing out problems, making criticisms and suggestions, and management people were trying to respond by saying that they would study the problems and propose actions by the next meeting. In other words, the initiative in pointing out problems and calling for action was in the hands of labor, and the burden in additional work activities and possibly additional expenditures fell entirely upon management. In this situation, management people found themselves overburdened with these new demands. The general result was that they would make some effort to respond to labor's initiatives, but would not have sufficient time to do systematic work on all of

the problems raised and therefore would constantly be in a position of reporting back less progress than labor had expected. After this process had gone on for some months, seeing little in the way of concrete results, labor members would begin complaining that the meetings were "just talk and no action" and come to the conclusion that the committee was just another management device to manipulate workers. As management people recognized this growing labor dissatisfaction and came to resent the additional work burden imposed by the process, management would increasingly find occasion to postpone or cancel meetings until the time came when the labor-management committee existed only on paper.

The Jamestown model as it evolved and the model then followed at Rath avoided this pitfall by assuring that worker members of the action research teams participate actively in the study and proposed resolution of problems. Furthermore, at Rath, workers were subsequently involved in an extraordinary range of problems, including the major investment decisions for the purchase of new machines, the redesign of the work flow, and so on. In the Rath case, we observed a melding of the community democracy model with the collective bargaining model, where the parties bridge the gap in the community democracy model by filling in policies and procedures for organizing and carrying out the work. This is not to say that the melding process was easy. Where a high degree of mistrust has existed between workers and management in the past, there are many occasions when the joint problem-solving process breaks down, and the workers and management people revert to the traditional adversarial role. One of the key functions of the third party providing technical assistance in such cases is to recognize the importance of the negative feelings being expressed by both sides, and then help the parties to move back to focus on concrete problems whose resolution will benefit both parties.

Rath also represented an attempted integration of the authoritarian model with the collective bargaining and community democracy models. Here, again, the process was not easy. Because a major shift in power had taken place at the top of the organization, there were some occasions when workers flatly refused to follow the orders of their foremen and middle-management people. A few managers could not tolerate the change and left the company. Others assumed that to hold their positions they must just do what the union leaders tell them to do or what has been explicitly agreed upon by the union and management. Union and management leaders dealt with the problems by insisting that workers still were obligated to carry out the foremen's orders.

Unfortunately, Rath ran into a spate of bad luck. Two CEOs who went through a selection process died before they began work. Economic problems related to the pork industry and cut-throat competition created losses. Under these conditions, the union and management had trouble agreeing on further cuts. The former union head became the CEO of Rath, but these problems continued to weaken his ability to succeed. Finally, Rath declared bankruptcy in November 1983. A large outside food processing company, IBP, subsequently renovated and took over the Waterloo, Iowa plant (Hammer and Stern 1986).

Weirton Steel Corporation

In 1982, one of the most publicized employee buyouts in the world took place at Weirton Steel Corporation in Weirton, West Virginia (see Blasi 1987). The employees exchanged wage and benefit adjustments for an ESOP that controlled the company and had a substantial role in corporate governance at the board level. Under CEO Charles Loughhead, Weirton developed extensive employee participation in problem solving along with a determined program to communicate with its thousands of employees. Strong union-management cooperation resulted. But Weirton, like the others, ran into a management team that opposed a culture of participation. Employee involvement gradually declined until management even refused to recognize Weirton's special role as an employee-owned company. Competition from foreign steel and the refusal of the Clinton Administration carefully to apply the law about illegal foreign dumping and extensive subsidies to foreign steel manufacturers weakened the firm until it was de-listed from the New York Stock Exchange and in a very weak position by the end of 2001. Versions of the Weirton story happened to a variety of other steel mills, notably, Northwestern Steel, which went bankrupt in 2000.

Employee ownership was also tried at a number of airlines.

Obviously, most of these failures involve firms that were going through transitions and had unions; in fact, most had a history of poor union-management relations. Employee buyouts of such firms continued throughout the seventies and eighties (for a review, see Blasi and Kruse 1991: 62–68, 97–107; NCEO 1989). Although there is no question that the firms that received the most publicity did not survive, no research exists that quantifies the ultimate result of all the employee buyouts of failing firms in this period. As we shall see below, research in the nineties would yield a less idealistic, albeit a more favorable accounting of the worker ownership phenomenon.

Of course, the melding of the four models discussed above does not leave the main features of the authoritarian model intact. Managers and supervisors must recognize that if they are to function effectively in this new situation, they must exercise their authority in a more participatory fashion than has been customary in the past. Some progress was made in some of the cases, but it was complicated by past history and a poor economic environment. Such organizational changes require major learning processes on the part of management as well as on the part of union leaders and workers. Some firms began to master these learning processes, but were overcome by the powerful economic adjustments overtaking the U.S. economy in the last quarter of the 20th century.

EXAMINATION OF SOME WELL-ESTABLISHED CASES

Up to this point, we have been examining the difficulties experienced by a particular kind of organization in the United States as it searches for a viable model that will support the successful development of worker cooperatives or employee-owned firms. Before drawing general conclusions from those cases, let us examine four examples within which firms structured on the basic principles of the community democracy model (one member, one vote) have successfully maintained themselves over the years.

The U.S. Plywood Cooperatives

The outstanding examples in the United States are found among the cooperative plywood manufacturing firms in the Pacific Northwest. The first such firm was established in the 1920s, and by the 1960s there were as many as 21 cooperative plywood companies (Bernstein 1976). Most of these were started by workers pooling their resources (generally $1,000 per member) to start a new firm, but in about one third of the cases, the worker cooperative arose out of taking over a plant being shut down by a private firm. The firms are characterized not only by equal voting rights, but also by equal pay. Everyone gets the same pay for hours worked except for the manager, who is hired by the worker-directors and serves the firm on a contract they negotiate with him. Some studies have shown that the plywood cooperatives, over a period of years, have outperformed private plywood firms substantially in productivity and also in the financial rewards of the worker members. A large proportion of this difference may be accounted for by the smaller number of management and supervisory personnel in the plywood cooperatives. For example, when a private company bought out one of the plywood cooperatives, the first move of the new management was to employ *seven additional foremen* (Greenberg, 1981). In the traditional private firm, operating under the authoritarian model, much of the foreman's job involves policing the workforce, checking on when workers are goofing off, doing careless work, and otherwise reducing efficiency. If workers take over these organization and disciplinary responsibilities themselves, they can save enormous sums of money for their company.

Although the plywood cooperatives have been extraordinarily successful financially during much of this period, many of them have reverted to private ownership. In the mid-1970s, Paul Bernstein reported that the number of firms was down from 21 to 16, and in 1981, he records the number "close to a dozen" (Bernstein 1981). Here, we have a dramatic demonstration of the catch-22 situation that worker cooperatives find themselves involved in when ownership is based upon stock. When such a stock ownership plan is adopted (subject to one qualification to be introduced later), the cooperative firm can go out of business either because it fails or because it is highly successful and is unable to transfer stock from one generation of workers to another.

In the plywood cases, the workers have avoided one obvious trap involved in stock ownership plans where there is no limit on the number of shares and therefore control tends to gravitate toward higher levels of the company. In all cases, plywood cooperative stock has been limited to one share per worker. However, this has not been a major barrier to the loss of worker ownership in the most successful companies. In the first place, as the firm expands and new workers come in, collective selfishness tends to dominate personnel policies. The original worker-owners recognize that their stock and their stock dividends will increase in value if they decline to dilute their equity by making stock available to the new workers. In this case, the workforce tends to divide into two segments, worker-owners and hired labor, with the predictable consequences in the weakening of labor solidarity.

When a worker-owner retires, he would of course be glad to sell his share of stock to a non-owner-worker, but, by that time in a successful company, the value of the stock will be far beyond the means of the worker. For example, Bernstein reports two cases in which employees sold stock originally purchased for $1,000 for close to $100,000 per share. Because it is only individual private investors or private companies that pay such a price, there is an inevitable tendency for the most successful firms to revert to private ownership. Paradoxically, it is only in the marginally successful firms with such a structure of ownership that the worker-owners have a real possibility of maintaining worker-ownership as the firm passes on from one generation of workers to another.

Both the number of firms and the percentage of the plywood market they control has gone down over the nineties. Some observers believe that a support network plays a crucial part in the ability of a cooperative sector to grow and sustain itself. Mondragón in Spain is an excellent example of this point.

The Mondragón Cooperative Sector of Spain (Basque Region)

What has become the most dynamic element in Spain's industrial economy had its origin in the small industrial city of Mondragón in the Basque country in 1956 when five men, with support from friends and members of the community, founded the industrial cooperative, ULGOR. By 1980, the small beginning had expanded into a system of 87 industrial production cooperatives with close to 18,000 worker-members. Mondragón has become Spain's leading manufacturer of stoves and refrigerators and of one type of steel. The cooperatives have also been able to compete effectively in international markets, including winning bids against multinational corporations to build turn-key plants in developing nations (Johnson and Whyte 1977; for a more recent overview see Whyte and Whyte 1988; for a critical view, see Kasmir 1996).

The cooperative production firms have been supported and linked together by the *Caja Laboral Popular*, a cooperative banking organization that had over 300,000 individual members by 1980. The Caja has provided approximately 50% of the capital necessary for the growth of the system and has also provided technical assistance in the creation and development of cooperatives. The cooperatives are also linked together with a cooperative educational system, begun in 1943 under the leadership of Father José María Arizmendi. What began as a two-year institution to provide training in industrial skills to young working class boys has since expanded to serve thousands of students all the way to college degrees in engineering or business administration. Also linked with the system are consumer cooperatives, housing cooperatives, cooperative construction firms, and schools.

At the outset, the production firms were structured in terms of two different organizational models—community democracy and authoritarian—and it was not until almost two decades later that the leaders of the system recognized the inherent contradictions between those two models. The governance of the firm is provided by the application of the fundamental rule of community democracy: one member, one vote. Equality in voting rights is accompanied by an extraordinarily narrow range of pay differentials, in comparison with those prevailing in private firms. The way this system works out is that the workers at the low end of the pay scale receive somewhat more than workers at the same level in private industry, whereas the top executive receives

substantially less. There are no standard provisions for rotation of jobs, but, as the firms have expanded, there have been increasing opportunities for members to move to higher-paying jobs.

The linkage between the firm and the educational system remains throughout workers' careers. When demand for company products slackens, instead of being laid off, workers may retain their pay while studying, thus encouraging worker self-improvement and also worker commitment to the firm.

When the first firms were established, the leaders of the system believed that to compete with private industry, they had to organize work in terms of what they took to be the principles of modern industrial management. In effect, they adopted the Taylor authoritarian model with its hierarchy of supervision and control and with assembly lines and other methods of detailed division of labor and job simplification.

In a small organization in which all of the members could readily get together informally to discuss their problems, these frequent face-to-face contacts between the chief executive of the firm and rank-and-file workers opened the way for the kind of informal adjustments that made it possible to harmonize the community democracy model with the authoritarian model. In large organizations, this kind of informal adjustment was not possible. Although the members held ultimate control through electing the Board of Directors, an annual meeting for that purpose was not sufficient to resolve the contradictions between community democracy and the authoritarian model. It seems significant that the only strike yet to occur in Mondragón production firms took place in the oldest and largest firm, ULGOR. The 1974 strike involved only some 400 members out of a total workforce of 3,400, and it lasted only 48 hours. Nevertheless, the outbreak of this conflict shocked the leaders of the system and precipitated a reassessment of the system's design, leading to two major changes.

Now, the leaders of the system reached out to learn of experiences elsewhere in the world in democratizing the work place itself. This led to rapid changes in some of the firms in the direction of abandoning assembly lines in favor of groups working around a table, moving toward autonomous or self-managing work groups, increasing responsibilities for quality and for the organization of the work for the workers themselves, and so on. In effect, they were reshaping the authoritarian model through introducing elements of democratic governance in the workplace.

The ULGOR crisis also precipitated a move in the direction of the collective bargaining mode. From the beginning, workers had elected a Social Council to advise management on matters of personnel policy and social benefits. In contrast to the election of the Board of Directors, for which members voted altogether for a given slate of nominees, the representatives on the Social Council were chosen so as to represent particular work groups or departments. The idea was to have one representative on the Social Council for every ten workers but to limit the size of the council to a maximum of 60 members—which meant that in ULGOR each councilor represented 50 members.

Prior to the ULGOR strike, the Social Council tended to be considered ineffective by many workers, and, in fact, the strike arose out of the refusal of a group of dissident members to take their grievance to the Social Council. The ULGOR crisis led to a thorough-going reexamination of the role of the Social Council and to serious efforts to strengthen its influence in the larger firms through giving it power to conduct studies of policies and procedures, with staff assistance, so as to strengthen its recommendations to management. However, though the scope of the concerns of the Social Council approximate those of a union in a collective bargaining situation, the leadership of the system firmly opposed giving the Social Council any power of decision making. A critical debate on the structure of the Social Council involved the question of who should be its chairperson. From the outset, the chief executive of the firm had also chaired the Social Council, the theory being that this would give the Council members direct access to the top executive. Those urging change argued that this arrangement deprived the Social Council of its independence and therefore undermined its usefulness, but their views did not prevail. On the other hand, this reevaluation seemed to lead to a greater tendency of management to consult with the Social Council on all major questions. Furthermore, of course, when a recommendation of the Social Council is rejected by management, the council can call for a special meeting of the general assembly of all worker-members, which then has the power, if it so votes, to overrule management.

Under the Franco regime, unions not ultimately controlled by the state were outlawed, and there was no overt union activity within the cooperatives. With the general democratic transformation of Spain following the death of the dictator, unions have arisen in several of the cooperatives. It remains to be seen whether the growth of unionization will signal a strengthening of the collective bargaining model within the overall system; if so, the unions may eventually displace the Social Council as representing worker concerns on economic and social questions.

In the eighties, the group was radically restructured in preparation for the European Single Market and new competition. The changes concentrate power in the hands of managers. The group was reported to be considering listing stakes in its industrial cooperatives on the stock market in order to help finance expansion plans ("Mondragón" 2001). As one journalist wrote, "Increased salary differentials, advertising campaigns in *Fortune* and alliances with companies like Hotpoint have had many co-op workers wondering whether in the new Mondragón Cooperative Corporation some members are more equal than others." As one member put it, "Unless we can make management more accountable to the co-operatives' social councils decision-making will get further and further from rank and file co-op members" (*The Guardian*, 1993).

The Kibbutz Cooperative Sector in Israel

In Israel, by the mid-seventies, 100,000 people were organized into small towns or communities called kibbutzim that comprise approximately 3.5% of the general population. A kibbutz is basically organized as a community of families governed by a general assembly based on the democratic principle of one member, one vote, exercised through a weekly town meeting. Today, the Kibbutzim constitute 2.5% of Israel population, yet their contribution to the national economy amounts to 40% in agriculture, 7% in industrial output, 9% in industrial export and 10% in tourism. Industry today constitutes about 70% of the total Kibbutz production, the result of gradual transition from agriculture to advanced industry. Being science-oriented and more capital intensive, Kibbutz industries require highly qualified and trained workers today (see the Kibbutz Industry Association Web site at http://www.kia.co.il/odot/kibbutz.htm).

The type of worker-ownership originally used by the kibbutz was unique (Blasi 1980, 1986). It was not based on shares of stock and there was no membership fee. New kibbutz "neighborhoods" are started with loans and technical assistance from various Jewish agencies and the Federation of Kibbutz Communities after prospective members engage in a substantial period of planning, work in other kibbutzim, and evolution of a socially cohesive group. A kibbutz is owned by its members, but, according to legal charter, a kibbutz cannot be sold and the assets cannot be divided by the members. This is to prevent the "collective selfishness"—about which some critics have observed regarding the plywood cooperatives discussed above—from destroying the structure of worker ownership.

The fact that new membership was historically principally a social and not an economic decision also means that the kibbutz was substantially more open to a wide variety of individuals who are judged to be responsible, good workers interested in cooperative ideals. If individual members leave, they have very explicit severance pay provisions based on a number of factors. Should the majority of members of a kibbutz decide to dissolve it, short of provisions made for severance and transitional expenses, the assets would return to an overall kibbutz holding company for use in continuing the development of the worker-owned sector. The kibbutz, therefore, initially overcame a number of the problems of worker ownership by carefully developing an organization based on membership rights and ownership rights, but restricting the legal ability of owners to do away with worker control and ownership itself. This is really an extension of the community democracy model to a model constitution for economic democracy.

As a cooperative small town, a kibbutz was an amalgam of industries, agricultural branches, membership services branches, and educational institutions. Every member has an equal right to housing, medical care, education for children, food and meals (available in a common dining area or in members' homes), higher education and occupational training, access to a community car pool and (in most communities) unlimited public transportation coupons within the country, occasional overseas vacations, and a paid vacation based on years of membership. Members receive no wages, but participate in a series of yearly meetings and in committees that plan how the community's profits will be spent for both industrial and agricultural development and the maintenance of the many services for members. Members do receive annual cash allotments for personal expenses. The community has a commitment to provide employment for all members and, like Mondragón, depends on committees within the cooperative itself and within the federation and affiliated industrial research arms and vocational training arms to develop new industrial or agricultural branches and plan for the transition from one form of enterprise to another. Like Mondragón, which operates its own system of social security, the kibbutzim provide complete social security for their members throughout old age, support for sick or disabled members or those in job transition, and complete medical insurance. Thus, both the kibbutz and Mondragón can be conceived of as systems of labor governance that reduce both the size of government and dependency on government services.

The kibbutzim began in 1910 with the establishment of a successful agricultural worker cooperative in Israel, Degania Aleph. In recent years, while agriculture continues to be pursued, industrial operations have become increasingly important. From the very beginning, individual kibbutzim linked themselves together to form kibbutz federations, which function similarly to Mondragón's *Caja Laboral Popular* in guiding the development of educational and cultural programs, providing technical assistance, operating management and vocational training colleges, providing capital through mutual banks, and acting as liaison with governmental public bodies.

Unlike Mondragón, the workplace and the neighborhood are integrated in the kibbutz. People who work together meet together to discuss community affairs, serve on educational committees that oversee their children's schools, participate in community cultural events, and together elect community

Table 35.1   Labor Governance in the Kibbutz

Topic	Plant committees	Plant management board	Workers' assembly	Kibbutz committees	Kibbutz general assembly
Production	–	Suggestion	Decision	Discussion	Confirmation
Investment and development plans	–	Suggestion	Decision	Discussion	Confirmation
Work arrangements	–	Suggestion	Decision	–	–
Technical and professional problems	Discussion	Decision	Information	–	–
Choice of candidates for training	Decision	Suggestion	Decision	Discussion	Confirmation
Election of management team	–	Discussion	Discussion	Suggestion	Decision
Election of other offices	Suggestion	–	Decision	–	–

economic and social officials, and decide community policy. Income is not determined by type of work or by position in an organization, but by membership and the egalitarian ethic.

It is often thought that kibbutzim are characterized by a shared political or religious ideology or a high degree of ethnic homogeneity. Only a small number of the communities are religious (orthodox), the others being secular communities that view Judaism more as a cultural heritage. It is true that 95 % of the neighborhoods are affiliated through their Federations with the Israeli Labor Party. Most communities include members from 10 to 30 countries, although Sephardic Jews are clearly underrepresented.

Table 35.1 illustrates the facets of labor governance in the kibbutz (Leviatan and Rosner, 1980).

The kibbutz has attempted to maximize participation while clearly delineating the degrees of authority and the areas of expertise most appropriate for the different participatory institutions. Though all plant officials were elected by the plant's worker assembly, the one exception was the plant manager. This person was nominated by the kibbutz-wide nomination committee, discussed by the plant's workers, and then appointed by the kibbutz. The individual might not necessarily come from among plant workers and the individual has been viewed as having a responsibility not only to the workers of the plant but to the community as a whole.

Traditionally, within the kibbutz as a whole and in industrial plants and other branches, all coordinating and managerial positions are rotated in order to prevent the creation of a managerial class. These coordinators or officers do not receive any special economic rewards. This rotation is possible and practical for several reasons. First, the kibbutz plan ahead of time for such leadership positions and uses its aggressive system of higher education and vocational training to prepare such coordinators so that a steady pool of expertise exists. Second, research has found that kibbutz plants that abide by the principle of rotation can devote less time to supervision, and have better communication channels between managers and workers, more opportunity for advancement, more knowledge of its members about the plant, and a trend toward greater economic effectiveness (Leviatan and Rosner 1980).

Because of pressure put on kibbutz movements to absorb new immigrants and opportunities for increased financial success and expansion, some kibbutzim have brought in outsiders (generally Arabs or new immigrant Jewish labor, often Sephardic) as hired labor. Leviatan and Rosner again have found that the federations without much hired labor have just as successfully organized factories and performed efficiently in a wide range of industries, whereas those with hired labor have had less formal participation, more supervisory personnel, less trust between workers and management, less rotation, and less involvement of kibbutz members in the life of their community. Notably, this increase in hierarchy occurred among both kibbutz members and hired workers. Since 1975, there has been steadily declining use of hired labor in kibbutz industries, and an increasing emphasis upon capital investment. This policy has enabled most kibbutz firms to remain small and highly participatory while achieving higher productivity per worker than the average Israeli firm and growing rapidly in sales and exports.

The kibbutz industries have had similar experiences to Mondragón in plant organization. Initially, they, too, imported assembly line technology in toto, but they are becoming increasingly sensitive to autonomous work and the importance of a detailed community-wide planning of a new industry.

Since the 1950–1975 period, when most of the original studies and research on which our views of the traditional kibbutz are based were carried out, the kibbutz has undergone radical changes. (Ben Rafael 1997; Gavron 2000) In the mid-eighties, the kibbutz movement confronted a massive financial crisis. They had been considered safe credit risks, and this led to accumulated debt. The rise of more right-wing centrist governments reduced sympathy for the Labor-leaning kibbutz movement. When Israel's government decided to use high interest rates in the eighties to tame hyperinflation, heavily indebted kibbutzim found themselves in serious trouble. At the same time, the traditional social and economic patterns of the kibbutz have undergone some alteration. Some kibbutzim turned over large factories to boards run by outside business people. Some stopped communal dining. Kibbutzim began to discuss whether it made sense to pay individuals extra for extra work or value to the community, although only a small number made this radical move initially. The kibbutz has been becoming more of a cooperative town and less of a commune.

The Modern U.S. Employee Equity Sector

Between the seventies and 2001, yet another established model has appeared. Significant numbers of U.S. workers and corporations have been involved in a large employee equity sector. The ESOP allows corporations to contribute stock or cash to buy stock in the company where a worker is employed to a company-controlled trust that holds stock for the workers until he or she retires. Typically, the employee ownership gradually accumulates over time as companies buy stock for workers. Broad-based stock option plans refer to traditional stock option plans that include more than 50% of nonexecutives. Stock purchase plans allow employees to use their savings to buy company stock. Finally, 401(k) plans are a major vehicle for employee ownership even though they do not have employee ownership in their name. They have been the fastest growing form of retirement plan in the United States over the last two decades, and they are the second fastest growing form of employee ownership assets in the United States after broad-based stock option plans. Basically, a 401k plan is a tax-sheltered retirement plan in which an employee can save money on a pretax basis.

The National Center for Employee Ownership (www.nceo.org) estimates that 8.5 million Americans participate in ESOPs and stock bonus plans, 8–10 million participate in broad stock option plans, and 15.7 million participate in stock purchase plans. Polling data suggest that about 25% of U.S. private sector workers have some form of employee equity.

Table 35.2 provides data on the percentage of employee ownership in firms among these different formats of employee ownership. It shows that employee equity is mainly not majority employee ownership except among private companies where we estimate 2000–3000 majority employee-owned firms have emerged as a result of tax incentives that allow retiring small business owners to sell to the employees and pay no capital gains tax (see http://www.the-esop-emplowner.org/ for information).

The broad-based employee equity sector has emerged largely as a result of a coincidence of factors. Federal enabling legislation and tax incentives provided the basis. Corporate interest in tying compensation to company performance instead of focusing on fixed wages offered a motive, while worker interest in having more equity in a time of flat inflation-adjusted fixed wages offered the demand.

Studies of both publicly traded and privately-held employee ownership firms have proved that worker participation remains a challenge. (Blasi 1987; Blasi and Kruse 1991) However, Blair, Kruse, and Blasi (2000) and Blasi and Kruse (2001) have demonstrated

Table 35.2   Percent of Employee Ownership by Type of Firm

Category	0–10%	11–30%	31–50%	51–100%
Private co. ESOPs	20%	35%	25%	20%
Public co. ESOPs	62%	34%	3%	1%
401(k) plans	85%	10%	5%	0%
Stock options	45%	53%	2%	0%
Stock purchase plans	100%	0%	0%	0%

NOTE: Rows sum to 100.
SOURCE: National Center for Employee Ownership, Oakland, California. Note: A detailed discussion of the basis for these estimates is available at http://www.nceo.org/library/co-stat.html. The data for employee stock purchase plans is based on a random sample of 100 companies on the New York Stock Exchange in 2001 collected by Joseph Blasi and Douglas Kruse that is unpublished. We estimate that figures are higher for smaller NASDAQ companies. Stock option figures are estimates of the percentage of total outstanding company stock that the options represent. Percentages are higher in smaller companies and high-technology companies. We do not have an estimate for employee stock purchase plans. The number of private company ESOPs with 51% to 100% ownership increases to 30% when the question is what percentage of stock the plan will own in five years. Also appears in Blasi, Kruse, Sesil, and Kroumova (2002).

that employee ownership firms have higher rates of survival than other firms. Recently, Blasi and Kruse (1997) reviewed a quarter century of empirical research on employee ownership. The conclusion from this and other research (Rosen, Klein and Young 1985) is that employee ownership companies often have better performance than nonemployee ownership companies, particularly when employee ownership is combined with worker participation in management.

LESSONS FROM ESTABLISHED CASES

Let us now draw upon these established cases to see to what extent they provide answers to problems we have seen emerging in the U.S grass-roots collectives and in firms with varying amounts and approaches to employee ownership. After a quarter century of developments, case studies, and empirical research, some generalities can be suggested. We draw the following conclusions:

1. In each of the cases, overcoming the authoritarian model of management has been a challenge for the workers and managers involved. Mondragón's growth and new market orientation has created tensions over governance. Nevertheless, research has shown that the firms that have both worker participation and worker ownership are the

most likely to improve their performance. In this sense, the idealism of the early experiments has proven most relevant to the market realities of the 21st century;

2. The bargaining model of employee ownership has had a rocky history. The failure of well-publicized cases of employee buyouts in older unionized settings is well documented. Unfortunately, the wrong conclusion is often drawn from these cases. In most of these cases, employee ownership was introduced into firms that had a history of extremely poor labor-management relations and often poor economic performance. Without choosing managers who approved of a more participatory culture and without investment in training both workers and managers in participatory management, it is easy to understand how matters became unraveled. In cases like Rath Packing, sincere efforts at participation were made, but they were not able to overcome the poor technological state of that factory, the stark competitive forces of that industry, and decades of mistrust between labor and management. Despite this well-researched negative history on early worker buyouts, there is no systematic evidence that employee ownership and unions are incompatible. Indeed, there is now a lot of impressionistic evidence of many small businesses with unions that have sponsored employee ownership plans where workers buy out a retiring owner.

Though these have not been systematically studied, it appears that the history of more friendly union-management relations in these smaller family-oriented settings has set the stage for more cooperation than in the well-publicized union buyouts of the seventies.

3. There is no doubt that the many observers and participants in the early of employee ownership experiments in the seventies developed a strong set of expectations that smoothly functioning worker commonwealths would be the result of eliminating the ownership division between workers and managers. Worker ownership did not eliminate Taylorism, but clearly exacerbated frustration with Taylorism where the two had to share the same company culture. Although the kibbutz originally went far down the road in implementing a more town meeting model, there has always been variation among kibbutz factories in how participatory they really were. Market problems have pushed the kibbutzim to function more and more like worker-owned firms in cooperative towns rather than like utopian commonwealths. Even Mondragón has had trouble maintaining high levels of worker participation.

In the United States, attempts to create worker commonwealths from worker buyouts largely failed, and widespread employee ownership never succeeded in uniformly adopting worker participation.

In the eighties and nineties a far-reaching employee ownership sector finally emerged in the United States. This indicates that—whether desirable or not—extensive worker ownership can exist without extensive worker control. Early observers feared that this would empty employee ownership of all of its meaning (Blasi 1987; Blasi and Kruse 1991). For a while, that was the case. Ultimately, however, the practical realization inside companies and the consistent research finding that combining ownership and participation could improve firm performance and ultimately benefit managers, workers, and nonworker shareholders has made this apparently nonideological sector, a strong source of a participation ideology. The expectation of participation and the language of participation have now become the national norm. The cases that are recommended for imitation to managers by managers themselves are the cases that draw on a town meeting or community democracy model. There is no question that

wider demands in U.S. culture for less hierarchy in the workplace have also influenced what is happening in the employee ownership sector.

4. Job rotation may have advantages in some cases in broadening the experience of workers and strengthening the commitment to an egalitarian ideology, but job rotation clearly is not indispensable for the functioning of an efficient worker ownership firm. Any standard pattern of job rotation will prove to be impractical in cases where the firm includes jobs of a wide range of skills and knowledge up to those which can be performed only by individuals having special skills and educational background. In fact, in the kibbutzim, though rotation was practiced for general managerial jobs, positions in engineering, chemistry, and other technical specialties are generally not subject to rotation.

5. Although more equal pay may be practical in some cases—such as in small cohesive firms where teamwork is valued and majority employee ownership is the reality—this is not an indispensable principle for a financially successful worker ownership firm. However, the pay scale must seem equitable to the members of the organization. This will mean that the range between the top and bottom pay in such a firm will be less than that prevailing where a company is owned by management or private investors. However, this smaller differential may be mainly a result of the employee equity itself, which will provide workers in these firms with greater overall income than workers receiving only fixed wages (on the evidence of whether U.S. employee ownership firms provide more overall wealth to workers, see Blasi, Kruse, Sesil, and Kroumova, forthcoming).

6. Both the kibbutz and the Mondragón systems show that the survival of worker ownership broadly depends on a strong supportive infrastructure of enterprise associations and financial institutions with a healthy dose of local culture. The U.S. employee ownership sector has a few nonprofit associations that are trying to create a sector identity through local networks and regional and national conferences. One can argue that their infrastructural institutions are what have allowed both Mondragón and the kibbutz movement to try to overcome serious

threats to their survival from the hyper-competitive market environment in which they both now find themselves. On the other hand, preliminary research in 2001 indicates that the track record of survival for U.S. worker ownership firms is not bad for companies that had more than 20% employee ownership in the 1970s or converted to partial employee ownership during this period. The survival record of a few conflict-ridden union firms should not be taken as the measure of this question. However, to date there is no systematic study of the survival rate of majority employee owned firms in the United States in the 20th century.

7. In the seventies, it was an open question whether worker ownership in the United States would develop in the direction of ESOP benefit plans in companies or worker cooperatives. At the time, the stability of both Mondragón and the kibbutz and the gradual decline in numbers of the plywood cooperatives suggested that for the worker ownership firm is to survive, control must be based upon labor membership as in cooperatives rather than upon ownership through employee benefit plans. In Israel, the factory is owned by the kibbutz community, but, except for certain broad questions of the relation of the firm to the community, the factory itself is generally governed by the kibbutz members who work in it. The financial base of the Mondragón system is built upon debt rather than equity. That is, upon entering the firm, the member pays a fee to the cooperative, and this fee is treated as if it were a loan, drawing interest and growing through annual profit sharing. Therefore, short of the financial collapse of the whole Mondragón system, there is no way in which the firms can revert to private ownership. A quarter century later, though worker cooperatives exist in the United States, other noncooperative formats of employee ownership are clearly dominant. The most recent is the emergence of entrepreneurial employee ownership among high technology firms that provide a high percentage of their total shares outstanding to workers in the form of stock options. It is still too early to tell whether the fundamental survival of an employee ownership sector in the United States requires a strict observance of the cooperative format. Perhaps, the current U.S. sector will have

serial employee ownership; that is, employee ownership will be stable in firms as long as they survive but there will be no infrastructure to guide the employee ownership identity from generation to generation as in the kibbutz and Mondragón. With the benefit of 25 years of hindsight, however, it is now clear that even the kibbutz and Mondragón are not immune to market forces.

8. The newest development in the United States is the emergence of an entrepreneurial employee ownership sector in high technology industries. These firms focus on employee equity rather than direct employee ownership. Although decidedly nonunion, many espouse an anti-hierarchical company ideology that grows out of a theory of what patterns of distributing power, prestige, and resources are required for knowledge workers to produce consistent innovation and wealth. Again, ironically, though this newest worker ownership arena is heavily market-oriented and ostensibly has little apparent connection to worker cooperatives or ESOPs, the culture of participation initially appears to be more at its center than it was in the ESOP movement of the seventies.

9. An organizational infrastructure to help financing and to provide technical assistance is essential for development and maintenance of a system of cooperative firms. In Israel, an overall Kibbutz Federation and several smaller associations provide important financial and technical assistance. In Mondragón, the *Caja Laboral Popular* has been the key organization in financing and guiding growth and in keeping the firms linked together. In the case of the plywood cooperatives, each firm existed as a more or less isolated unit in a sea of private enterprise. To be sure, there is an association of cooperative plywood firms, but the association is relatively weak and not equipped to play the major role of the building and supporting structure we have noted in Israel and in Spain. This means that those in the United States interested in promoting the development of cooperative firms should recognize the need to build an organizational infrastructure, with assistance from universities and government, to provide educational and technical assistance and financing.

10. In the Israeli and Spanish examples, we find that the cooperatives are built upon a foundation of shared values. This does not mean that all worker-members must share these values; rather it means that the organizational leaders must develop and articulate an ideology that both justifies the form of the organization and guides its development. They must develop the organization mission beyond simply producing goods or services and providing jobs for its members. Furthermore, they must be concerned with linking these values to concrete policies and practices and to the periodic reassessment of the relationship between theory and practice so as to assure themselves that they are not trying to implement values that are impossible of realization or, on the other hand, engaging unthinkingly in policies and practices incompatible with their values.

One of the weaknesses of the plywood cooperatives has been the lack of any guiding ideology. To be sure, they did arise out of a culture of immigrants or children of immigrants from Scandinavia, where cooperative values are prominent, but the driving force behind the formation and development of the plywood cooperatives seems to have been much more pragmatic: to create jobs and earn income for worker-members. In the grass-roots collectives in the United States, we often find a common ideology within the leadership group setting up the firm, but all too often this ideology points the organization toward policies and practices that prove to be unworkable. In many of the early firms that become employee-owned out of conglomerate divestitures, we found a complete lack of any guiding ideology adjusted to the new situation.

There is some evidence that a value system of participation and governance is slowly developing among nonprofit organizations that support ESOPs and entrepreneurial employee ownership and in many individual firms themselves. It remains to be seen how durable this value system can be without stronger infrastructural institutions.

What can be done in situations where a guiding ideology is lacking? Clearly, it will not be helpful to suggest, "Go out and get yourself an ideology." Benchmarking with other firms that have a workable culture of participation is a useful first step.

11. If we assume that workers and management people always have some kind of organizational model at least vaguely in mind, and if we assume that these implicit conceptions tend to shape the behavior of those who hold them, then it is important for the people involved to make the implicit conceptions explicit and to begin discussion of how to build a model that will be congruent with their values and, at the same time, workable. The four organizational models we have posed at the start of this chapter may be a useful starting point for such a discussion. The new social system emerging out of a worker-management discussion and analysis process may then contain selected elements of these four models, combined with new elements growing out of the experience and ideas of those who are going to live and work under the principles and policies they establish.

REFERENCES

Adams, Frank, Gordon, Fred, and Shirey, Richard (1993). *Workers' Owned Sewing Company: Making the Eagle Fly Friday.* Boston, Mass.: The ICA Group.

Adams and Shirey (1993). "Workers' Owned Sewing Company: Making the Eagle Fly Friday." Boston, Mass.: The ICA Group.

Banfield, Edward. (1951). *Government Project.* Glencoe, Illinois: Free Press.

Ben Rafael, Eliezer. (1997). *Crisis and Transformation: The Kibbutz at Century's End.* Albany, NY: SUNY Press, Suny Series in Israeli Studies.

Bernstein, Paul. (1976). *Workplace Democratization: Its Internal Dynamics.* Kent: Kent State University Press.

Bernstein, Paul. (1981). "Worker Ownership and Community Redevelopment," *The Corporate Examiner,* March. (National Council of Churches of Christ in the USA).

Blair, Margaret, Kruse, Douglas, and Blasi, Joseph. (2000). "Is Employee Ownership an Unstable Form? Or a Stabilizing Force?" in *The New Relationship: Human Capital in the American Corporation.* T. Kochan and M. Blair (Editors). Washington, D.C.: The Brookings Institution.

Blasi, Joseph. (1980). *The Communal Future: The Kibbutz and the Utopian Dilemma.* Philadelphia: Norwood Editions.

Blasi, Joseph. (1986). *The Communal Experience of the Kibbutz.* New Brunswick, NJ: Transaction Books.

Blasi, Joseph and Kruse, Douglas L. (1991). *The New Owners: The Mass Emergence of Employee Ownership in Public Companies and What It Means to American Business.* NY; HarperCollins, 1991. (Text available on the Internet at: www.rci.rutgers. edu/~blasi.)

Blasi, Joseph, Kruse, Douglas, Sesil, James, and Kroumova, Maya. (2002). "An Assessment of Employee Ownership in the United States With Implications for the EU.," *International Journal of Human Resource Management*, forthcoming.

Brown, Warren. (1980, September 30). "Workers at Employee-Owned Firm Find the Going Rough." *Washington Post,* p. A4.

Cole, Robert E. (1979). *Work, Mobility and Participation: A Comparative Study of American and Japanese Industry.* Berkeley and Los Angeles: University of California Press.

Commons, John R. (1918–1935). *History of Labour in the United States.* New York: The Macmillan Company, 1918–35. (Multiple volumes.)

Freeman, Richard and Rogers, Joel. (1999). *What Workers Want?* Ithaca, NY: Cornell University Press.

Gavron, Daniel. (2000). *The Kibbutz: Awakening From Utopia.* London: Rowman & Littlefield.

The Guardian. (1993, January 2).

Gertzen, Jason. (2001). "Laid-Off Workers Start High-Tech Co-Op; Former Sonic Foundry Employees Wanted to Have a Say in Decisions," *Milwaukee Journal Sentinel,* July 8.

Greenberg, Edward. (1981). "Industrial Self-Management and Political Attitudes," *American Political Science Review* 75:1 March.

Hammer, Tove and Stern, Robert. (1980). "Employee Ownership: Implications for the Organizational Distribution of Power," *Academy of Management Journal* 23:78–100.

Hammer, Tove and Stern, Robert. (1986). "A Yo-Yo Model of Cooperation: Union Participation in Management at the Rath Packing Company," *Industrial and Labor Relations Review* 39 (April):334–49.

ICA Group. (1991) *The Directory of Workers' Enterprises in North America.* Boston, Ma.: The ICA Group.

Jackson, Tim. (1997). *Inside Intel: Andy Grove and the Rise of the World's Most Powerful Chip Company.* NY: Penguin/Dutton.

Johnson, Ana Gutierrez and Whyte, W. F. (1977). "The Mondragón System of Worker Production Cooperatives," *Industrial and Labor Relations Review,* October 31:18–30.

Kasmir, Sharryn. (1996). *The Myth of Mondragón: Cooperatives, Politics, and Working-Class Life in a Basque Town.* Albany, NY: State University of New York Press.

Kato, Takeo. (2000). *The Recent Transformation of Participatory Employment Practices in Japan.*

Cambridge, Ma.: National Bureau of Economic Research, NBER Working Paper No. w7965.

Kruse, Douglas and Blasi, Joseph. (1997). "Employee Ownership, Employee Attitudes, and Firm Performance: A Review of the Evidence," in *The Human Resource Management Handbook, Part I.* D. Lewin, D. J. B. Mitchell, and M. Zaidi (Editors). Greenwich, Conn.: JAI Press, pps. 113–152. (Also available as a NBER Working Paper at www.nber.org.)

Kruse, Douglas and Blasi, Joseph. (2001). *Press Release: Study on the Population of Privately-Held U.S. Firms With ESOPs.* New Brunswick, N.J.: Rutgers University School of Management and Labor Relations. (For a summary of the study, see http://www.nceo.org/library/esop_perf.html, and for the data tables, see http://www.nceo.org/library/ esop_perf_tables.html)

Leviatan, Uri and Rosner, Menachem. (1980). *Work and Organization in Kibbutz Industry.* Philadelphia: Norwood Editions.

Mansbridge, Jane. (1973). "Town Meeting Democracy," *Working Papers for a New Society,* 1:5–15.

"Mondragón." (2001). *El Pais,* September 16, page 9.

Moriguchi, Chiaki. (2000). *The Evolution of Employment Relations in U.S. and Japanese Manufacturing Firms, 1900–1960: A Comparative Historical and Institutional Analysis,* NBER Working Paper No. w7939.

NCEO (National Center for Employee Ownership). (1989). *The Employee Ownership Union Handbook.* Oakland, Ca.: National Center for Employee Ownership. (This organization is on the Internet at www.nceo.org.)

National Industrial Conference Board. (1928). *Employee Stock Purchase Plans in the United States.* New York: National Industrial Conference Board.

Packard, David. (1995). *The HP Way: How Bill Hewlett and I Built Our Company.* New York: HarperBusiness.

Roel, Ronald E. (1994). "On the Job: Developing Career in Home Health Care," *Newsday,* April 17.

Rosen, Corey, Klein, Katherine, and Young, Karen. (1985). *Employee Ownership in America: The Equity Solution.* NY: Free Press.

Rothschild-Whitt, Joyce. (1979). "The Collectivist Organization: An Alternative to Rational-Bureaucratic Models," *American Sociological Review,* 44:509–527.

Stern, Robert N., Wood, Hayden, and Hammer, Tove. (1979). *Employee Ownership in Plant Shutdown: Prospects for Employment Stability.* Kalamazoo, MI: The Upjohn Institute for Employment Research.

Taylor, F. W. (1911). *The Principles of Scientific Management.* New York: Harper & Bros.

Whyte, W. F. (1978). "In Support of Voluntary Employee Ownership," *Society*, 15:6, September–October, 73–82.

Whyte, William F. and McCall, Donald. (1980). "Self Help Economics," *Society*, 17:4.

Whyte, William Foote, and Whyte, Kathleen. (1988). *Making Mondragón: The Growth and Dynamics of a Worker Cooperative Complex*. Ithaca, NY: Cornell University Press.

Zuboff, Shoshana. (1988) *In the Age of the Smart Machine: The Future of Work and Power*. NY: Basic Books.

PART XIV

GOVERNMENT, NONPROFIT AGENCIES, AND VOLUNTARY ASSOCIATIONS

Although most organizational research in the last twenty to thirty years has studied for-profit businesses, organizational sociology initally focused more on government agencies, schools, hospitals, charities, and other nonprofit institutions. Recent research has added studies on voluntary associations and activist or social movement organizations. These organizations, though diverse, can be expected to differ from private, for-profit business in terms of their goals, structures, and operations.

GOVERNMENT

Part XI, "Organizations and Society," introduced three main traditions from political sociology that relate to the study of how government works. The power elite or instrumentalist theory of the state argues that government policy usually benefits influential, privileged groups, particularly big business, which plays an active role in shaping the political process. Pluralist theory, popular mostly in the 1950s and 1960s, argued that the free interplay of contending groups determined policy, without any particular group exercising dominance.

Different varieties of state-centered theory argue that government organs have relative autonomy from specific organized groups and make policies on their own initiative. A more critical variant argues that government serves the general interest of business while remaining above the fray of particular corporate and industry lobbyists because the economy might weaken in the absence of a favorable business climate, and the public's continued support for the political system is based on the expectation that the state will insure general economic well-being (Block 1987).

Piven and Cloward (1971) argued that government aid to the poor is also designed in ways that are functional for the capitalist order. Benefit levels are usually designed to be lower than the lowest wages in the labor market to compel workers to accept whatever paid work is available. Aid to the poor may expand during periods of crisis and protest, such as during the Great Depression and the 1960s, but the goal is more to grant enough concessions to quiet discontent than to genuinely reform society.

Less critical state-centered theory explains government policies, including the growth of the welfare state, as reflecting the particular intellectual and political agendas of officials able to influence policy making and the institutional structure of the state, such as degree of government centralization, bureaucratic structure, division of power among branches of government, legal system, and structure of party competition (Skocpol 1985).

Another school of thought, derived from economics, explains both the political behavior of interest groups and politicians as motivated by rational self-interest and relatively unconstrained by norms or rules (See Part VIII, "Economic Theories of Organizations"). *Public choice theory* argues that most government intervention in the economy is not public-spirited, but reflects the efforts of diverse interest groups, business and nonbusiness, to use government for their own private gain. According to this view, price supports, tariffs, tax breaks, minimum wages, labor laws, social security, public schools, government agencies such as the Labor, Agriculture, and Commerce Departments and Small Business Administration, and almost all other government programs satisfy particular constituencies who use political means to force the public to pay for special benefits they could not gain on their own in the free market. Because the benefits of any individual program are concentrated on an organized group and the costs for individual taxpayers are small when spread over an unorganized public, programs have a focused group of supporters while potential opponents who bear the costs are a disorganized, passive mass. Consequently, established programs are rarely discontinued even if most people do not benefit from them. Politicians collaborate in this process or even seek out groups they can reward with government favors because of the political loyalties they gain. Public choice theory concludes that a laissez-faire economic policy in which the government does as little as possible to alter market processes is best for taxpayers who would otherwise subsidize all manner of special interests that were effective in lobbying for their particular program.

Finally, in the study of government there is the narrower, empirical study of bureaucratic politics and practices that is less closely linked to these or other theoretical traditions, but often folds them and mainstream organization theory into their accounts. This view is represented in the readings by Graham Allison (Reading 16) and Michael Lipsky (Reading 36) among others.

Many conclude that government is often less efficient than for-profit business because of weaker incentives, such as civil service employment systems and lack of competition, and they call for the greater use of market mechanisms, as public choice theory argues. But studies also show that part of the reason for lesser efficiency in the traditional sense is that the public expects government to operate differently than private business. The public expects government be fair and accountable, and this is directly responsible for many of the elaborate rules, procedures, and safeguards that require compliance and the numerous bureaucrats charged with monitoring and executing them, all of which are sometimes perceived as red tape. Civil service systems and the protections they provide incumbents were implemented to prevent political favoritism in the hiring and operation of government administration. More vividly, police might be more efficient in the narrow sense of apprehending suspects and deterring crime if they did not need warrants or have to follow rules on the use of force, but most people in a democracy are unwilling to forego the protections afforded by such rules that regulate the conduct of government organizations.

Rules also multiply when the public attaches social objectives to procurement and service delivery, such as ensuring greater opportunities for small business, women, minorities, and the disabled, paying prevailing wages, and protecting the environment (Wilson 1989). The public also expects government services, such as Social Security, the post office, and the public school system, to provide universal coverage, whereas a private provider would seek to limit coverage of harder to serve and more costly segments of the population in order to save money.

People expect government to be responsive to demands other than narrow efficiency considerations. A private, for-profit command hierarchy might be faster and cheaper, but this kind of system operates without democratic accountability or public purposes.

But less rational explanations account for some of the problems with government operations. Many agencies do not control their own activities, which are often mandated by the legislature, where compromises between political opponents can result in inefficiency or ineffective performance by design. Onerous internal planning studies, cumbersome procedures and deliberations, monitoring and reporting requirements, and provisions for legislative intervention and judicial review may contribute little to organizational effectiveness, but this may be part of the reason they were mandated. Legislative opponents of some government agency activities may seek to hobble them through excessive bureaucratic requirements if they cannot be defeated outright (Moe 1990, pp. 133ff.).

This is not to deny that part of the responsibility for rigidity and inefficiency lies with the agencies themselves. Because they do not face a profit constraint, measures of performance are not always straightforward or strictly applied. Robert Merton noted that rules can remain in force even when their original purpose is no longer served, bureaucrats are rewarded for conforming to rules rather than granting exceptions, and government services are often monopolies shielded from the discipline of competition. Bureaucrats can block necessary change desired by political reformers. Heads of large agencies are political appointees who will only occupy their offices for a few years, which makes them somewhat dependent on an agency's permanent staff that has accumulated specific technical and administrative expertise and that is difficult to replace. Career civil servants are often indifferent to typically short-lived bursts of reform energy, often with justification, and can often convert superiors to their own view of how the department should function (Warwick 1975, pp. 170ff.).

NONPROFITS AND VOLUNTARY ASSOCIATIONS

Nonprofit agencies would seem to provide one way to avoid some of the problems of both government and for-profit provision of social services. Nonprofits are defined by U.S. tax law as organizations that are prohibited from distributing their net income as dividends to owners or investors or from paying above-market salaries to management, and that must serve some broader, public or collective purpose in return for exemption from paying taxes and tax deductibility of donations for contributors (DiMaggio and Anheier 1990). Nearly one million nonprofits constitute 10% of the economy today (Weisbrod 1998, p. 2).

Nonprofits are diverse in their goals and structure; they include religious groups, certain recreational groups, charities, some hospitals and social service organizations, philanthropic foundations, organized advocacy groups, and educational, research, and cultural institutions, such as universities and art museums, among others. In principle they avoid both the red tape that comes with government's accountability to the public and private enterprise's calculus of self-interest and profit. Because they do not have to satisfy private investors or owners whose goal is profit maximization, they are often trusted to work more for the public good. They harness the dedication and normative commitment of volunteers, professional employees, and donors to serve needs not met by either government or business.

However, nonprofits are not always unambiguously altruistic. Many rely on user fees. They may use salaried staff who see their work simply as paid employment, though they usually receive lower pay than comparable jobs in the for-profit sector. Even volunteers may pursue individual goals and social and psychological benefits from participation that conflict with organizational or charitable goals, such as a desire for status, prestige, recognition, friendship, or its opposite, a tendency toward factionalism. Because volunteers donate their time and because participation is based on commitment rather than economic need, leaders have limited power to issue commands or control workers through threats of sanctions, unlike in a traditional bureaucratic hierarchy. Volunteers may disagree with paid staff over whether the latter's role is to support and assist members, direct them, or replace them in carrying out operational activities (Harris 1998).

At the management level, those controlling nonprofits sometimes work to make their organizations large, wealthy, prestigious, and powerful, which often results in greater bureaucratization, as well as enhancing the wealth and power of the leadership (Weisbrod 1998). Public service may take a back seat to organization building and the business of charity or culture. Even nonprofits that do not have such ambitions often find themselves bureaucratizing over time, particularly when they seek government funding.

Just as the size of nonprofits can reflect the desire for material gain and personal power on the part of their leaders, it may also reflect societal choices to assign some of the business of solving social problems to charitable organizations rather than to taxpayers. Though government often contracts out public services to private agencies for efficiency reasons, there has also been a tendency in the last twenty years to rationalize cutbacks in social programs with the claim that the voluntary sector will make up the difference. This is part of a general retreat from government involvement in the economy resulting from reactions to more liberal government policies in the 1960s and the economic slowdown beginning in the 1970s that produced a conservative backlash and a greater pro-business tilt in public policy. At the same time, the increased prestige of free-market models has meant that some nonprofit institutions, especially hospitals and health insurance, are increasingly converted to or displaced by organizations run on a commercial basis (Goddeeris and Weisbrod 1998). Other nonprofits, such as university research institutes, seek funding and partners in the for-profit sector, and risk compromising their original educational and research missions when they conflicts with the commercial purposes of their financial backers (Weisbrod 1998).

Still, nonprofits generally have a less "bottom-line" or profit-maximizing mentality than for-profit businesses, and they have been found to charge lower prices and provide greater access to persons regardless of ability to pay in health care, where the two forms of organization compete (Weisbrod 1998).

On the level of interaction, human service organizations, such as health care, the police, or welfare offices, differ from more familiar organizations because people are their raw materials that must be processed, changed, or transformed. This is more than a technical operation because the decision to allocate scarce resources to particular recipients also symbolizes an evaluation of clients' social worth, and clients' reactions to that process play an important role in determining the character and relative success of the service-delivery process. Though social services are viewed as symbols of the caring society, the relationship between client and provider is inevitably a power relationship. Service delivery may involve favoritism and institutional and personal judgments of who is deserving or most easily or least expensively served, known as "creaming" of the client population. Staff may be indifferent and rigid in applying rules, as well as frustrated with their limited resources and their inability to do more for clients. Clients may react to agency unresponsiveness with hostility or by adopting the role of supplicant in the hopes of receiving consideration (Hasenfeld 1992a; Hasenfeld 1992b).

Michael Lipsky's reading in this section illustrates many of these themes (Reading 36). Lipsky studied street-level government bureaucracies, which play a central role in the relationships between citizens and their government. He shows how the behavior of those with a social service mission is powerfully shaped by their low levels of funding, which confronts providers with the dilemma of deciding how to ration services but also gives them power to control client behavior, an account that is in many ways consistent with Piven and Cloward's view of government's role in a laissez-faire market economy.

Government workers often enter these jobs with some kind of commitment to public service and doing good, but become disillusioned by the practical realities of trying to meet great social needs with the very limited resources the system makes available to them.

36

STREET-LEVEL BUREAUCRACY

Dilemmas of the Individual in Public Services

MICHAEL LIPSKY

DILEMMAS OF THE INDIVIDUAL IN PUBLIC SERVICES

This book is in part a search for the place of the individual in those public services I call street-level bureaucracies. These are the schools, police and welfare departments, lower courts, legal services offices, and other agencies whose workers interact with and have wide discretion over the dispensation of benefits or the allocation of public sanctions.

[. . .]

I argue that the decisions of street-level bureaucrats, the routines they establish, and the devices they invent to cope with uncertainties and work pressures, effectively *become* the public policies they carry out. I argue that public policy is not best understood as made in legislatures or top-floor suites of high-ranking administrators, because in important ways it is actually made in the crowded offices and daily encounters of street-level workers. I point out that policy conflict is not only expressed as the contention of interest groups but is also located in the struggles between individual workers and citizens who challenge or submit to client-processing.

One aspect of the way workers, clients, and citizens-at-large experience street-level bureaucracies is the conflicts that they encounter in wanting their organizational life to be more consistent with their own preferences and commitments. For example, people often enter public employment, particularly street-level bureaucracies, with at least some commitment to service. Teachers, social workers, public interest lawyers, and police officers in part seek out these occupations because of their potential as socially useful roles. Yet the very nature of this work prevents them from coming even close to the ideal conception of their jobs. Large classes or huge caseloads and inadequate resources combine with the uncertainties of method and the unpredictability of clients to defeat their aspirations as service workers.

Ideally, and by training, street-level bureaucrats respond to the individual needs or characteristics of the people they serve or confront. In practice, they must deal with clients on a mass basis, since work requirements prohibit individualized service. Teachers should respond to the needs of the individual child; in practice, they must develop techniques to respond to children as a class. Police officers should respond to the implications of the presenting case; in reality, they must develop techniques to recognize and respond to types of confrontations, and to process categories of cases accordingly. At best, street-level bureaucrats invent benign modes of mass processing that more or less permit them to deal with the public fairly, appropriately, and successfully. At worst, they give in to favoritism, stereotyping, and routinizing—all of which serve private or agency purposes.

Some street-level bureaucrats drop out or burn out relatively early in their careers. Those who stay on, to be sure, often grow in the jobs and perfect techniques, but not without adjusting their work habits and attitudes to reflect lower expectations for themselves, their clients, and the potential of public policy. Ultimately, these adjustments permit acceptance of the view that clients receive the best that can be provided under prevailing circumstances.

Compromises in work habits and attitudes are rationalized as reflecting workers' greater maturity, their appreciation of practical and political realities, or their more realistic assessment of the nature of the problem. But these rationalizations only summarize the prevailing structural constraints on human service bureaucracies. They are not "true" in an absolute sense. The teacher who psychologically abandons his or her aspirations to help children to read may succumb to a private assessment of the status quo in education. But this compromise says nothing about the potential of individual children to learn, or the capacity of the teacher to instruct. This potential remains intact. It is the *system* of schooling, the organization of the schooling bureaucracy,

that teaches that children are dull or unmotivated, and that teachers must abandon their public commitments to educate.

In the same way, the judicial system "teaches" that police officers must be impersonal and highly reactive to hints of disobedience among youth, and that judges are unable to make informed determinations or consign defendants to institutions that will help the offender or deter future offenses. Although the potential for thoughtful and useful determinations and interventions is not contradicted in any individual instance, the system teaches the intractability of the juvenile crime problem.

Should teachers, police officers, or welfare workers look for other work rather than perpetuate unfair, ineffective, or destructive public practices? This would leave clients to others who have even less concern and interest in service ideals. It would mean giving up the narrow areas in which workers have tried to make a difference or in which some progress is foreseen.

Should they stay on, contributing to discredited and sometimes brutalizing public agencies? If current patterns repeat themselves this would mean fighting the losing battle against cynicism and the realities of the work situation, and watching as service ideals are transformed into struggles for personal benefits.

Should they struggle from within to change the conditions under which citizens are processed by their agencies? This path seems the hardest to maintain and is subject to the danger that illusions of difference will be taken for the reality of significant reform.

The structure of street-level bureaucracy confronts clients with dilemmas bearing on action. Consumers of public services, once they have decided on or been consigned to a place of residence, with rare exceptions cannot choose the public services to which they will be subject. They must accept the schools, courts, and police forces of their communities. If they are poor they must also accept the community's arrangements for health care, welfare, public housing, and other benefit programs. In approaching these institutions they must strike a balance between asserting their rights as citizens and accepting the obligations public agencies seek to place upon them as clients. As citizens they should seek their full entitlement; as bureaucratic subjects they feel themselves obliged to temper their demands in recognition of perceived resource limitations and the agencies' organizational needs. Although it is apparent that exceptions are often made and additional resources often found, clients also recognize the potential costs of unsuccessfully asserting their rights.

[. . .] Should I wait my turn and submit to the procedures of the agency, despite reservations? I risk being unable to gain attention to my particular needs and concerns. Should I speak out forcefully and demand my rights? I risk the antagonism of the workers by disrupting office procedures.

Clients experience similar uncertainties in attempting to obtain proper services through collective action. The parent who organizes others to protest school actions, or the welfare recipient who challenges welfare policy, even if he or she perceives the possibilities of collective responses, risks receiving a reputation as an unreliable troublemaker toward whom favorable treatment should not be extended.

A final set of dilemmas confronts citizens who are continuously, if implicitly, asked to evaluate public services. Indeed, recent legislative initiatives to limit state and local spending have largely been understood as attacks on governmental performance and the ineffectiveness of social services.

What are the policy alternatives? When all the "fat" has been trimmed from agency budget and all the "waste" eliminated, the basic choices remain: to further automate, systematize, and regulate the interactions between government employees and citizens seeking help; to drift with the current turmoil that favors reduced services and more standardization in the name of cost effectiveness and budgetary controls; or to secure or restore the importance of human interactions in services that require discretionary intervention or involvement.

But how much can human intervention be eliminated from teaching, nursing, policing, and judging? The fact is that we *must* have people making decisions and treating other citizens in the public services. We are not prepared as a society to abandon decisions about people and discretionary intervention to machines and programmed formats. Yet how can one advocate greater attention to the intervening

and discretionary roles of street-level bureaucrats in the face of the enormous and often well-deserved popular discontent with the effectiveness and quality of their work?

[. . .]

1

THE CRITICAL ROLE OF STREET-LEVEL BUREAUCRATS

Public service workers currently occupy a critical position in American society. Although they are normally regarded as low-level employees, the actions of most public service workers actually constitute the services "delivered" by government. Moreover, when taken together the individual decisions of these workers become, or add up to, agency policy. Whether government policy is to deliver "goods"—such as welfare or public housing—or to confer status—such as "criminal" or "mentally ill"—the discretionary actions of public employees are the benefits and sanctions of government programs or determine access to government rights and benefits.

Most citizens encounter government (if they encounter it at all) not through letters to congressmen or by attendance at school board meetings but through their teachers and their children's teachers and through the policeman on the corner or in the patrol car. Each encounter of this kind represents an instance of policy delivery.

Public service workers who interact directly with citizens in the course of their jobs, and who have substantial discretion in the execution of their work are called *street-level bureaucrats* in this study. Public service agencies that employ a significant number of street-level bureaucrats in proportion to their work force are called *street-level bureaucracies.* Typical street-level bureaucrats are teachers, police officers and other law enforcement personnel, social workers, judges, public lawyers and other court officers, health workers, and many other public employees who grant access to government programs and provide services within them. People who work in these jobs tend to have much in common because they experience analytically similar work conditions.

[. . .] As providers of public benefits and keepers of public order, street-level bureaucrats are the focus of political controversy. They are constantly torn by the demands of service recipients to improve effectiveness and responsiveness and by the demands of citizen groups to improve the efficacy and efficiency of government services. Since the salaries of street-level bureaucrats comprise a significant proportion of nondefense governmental expenditures, any doubts about the size of government budgets quickly translate into concerns for the scope and content of these public services.

[. . .]

CONFLICT OVER INTERACTIONS WITH CITIZENS

A second reason street-level bureaucrats tend to be the focus of public controversy is the immediacy of their interactions with citizens and their impact on peoples' lives. The policy delivered by street-level bureaucrats is most often immediate and personal. They usually make decisions on the spot (although sometimes they try not to) and their determinations are focused entirely on the individual. *[. . .]*

The decisions of street-level bureaucrats tend to be redistributive as well as allocative. By determining eligibility for benefits they enhance the claims of some citizens to governmental goods and services at the expense of general taxpayers and those whose claims are denied. By increasing or decreasing benefits availability to low-income recipient populations they implicitly regulate the degree of redistribution that will be paid for by more affluent sectors.

In another sense, in delivering policy street-level bureaucrats make decisions about people that affect their life chances. To designate or treat someone as a welfare recipient, a juvenile delinquent, or a high achiever affects the relationships of others to that person and also affects the person's self-evaluation. Thus begins (or continues) the social process that we infer accounts for so many self-fulfilling prophecies. The child judged to be a juvenile delinquent develops such a self-image and is grouped with other "delinquents," increasing the chances that he or she will adopt the behavior thought to have been incipient in the first place. Children thought by their

teacher to be richly endowed in learning ability learn more than peers of equal intelligence who were not thought to be superior.[1] Welfare recipients find or accept housing inferior to those with equal disposable incomes who are not recipients.[2]

[. . .]

Finally, street-level bureaucrats play a critical role in regulating the degree of contemporary conflict by virtue of their role as agents of social control. Citizens who receive public benefits interact with public agents who require certain behaviors of them. They must anticipate the requirements of these public agents and claimants must tailor their actions and develop "suitable" attitudes both toward the services they receive and toward the street-level bureaucrats themselves. Teachers convey and enforce expectations of proper attitudes toward schooling, self, and efficacy in other interactions. Policemen convey expectations about public behavior and authority. Social workers convey expectations about public benefits and the status of recipients.

[. . .]

2

STREET-LEVEL BUREAUCRATS AS POLICY MAKERS

Street-level bureaucrats make policy in two related respects. They exercise wide discretion in decisions about citizens with whom they interact. Then, when taken in concert, their individual actions add up to agency behavior. *[. . .]*

DISCRETION

Unlike lower-level workers in most organizations, street-level bureaucrats have considerable discretion in determining the nature, amount, and quality of benefits and sanctions provided by their agencies.[3] Policemen decide who to arrest and whose behavior to overlook. Judges decide who shall receive a suspended sentence and who shall receive maximum punishment. Teachers decide who will be suspended and who will remain in school, and they make subtle determinations of who is teachable. Perhaps the most highly refined example of street-level bureaucratic discretion comes from the field of corrections. Prison guards conventionally file injurious reports on inmates whom they judge to be guilty of "silent insolence." Clearly what does or does not constitute a dirty look is a matter of some subjectivity.[4]

This is not to say that street-level workers are unrestrained by rules, regulations, and directives from above, or by the norms and practices of their occupational group. On the contrary, the major dimensions of public policy—levels of benefits, categories of eligibility, nature of rules, regulations and services—are shaped by policy elites and political and administrative officials. Administrators and occupational and community norms also structure policy choices of street-level bureaucrats. These influences establish the major dimensions of street-level policy and account for the degree of standardization that exists in public programs from place to place as well as in local programs.

To the extent that street-level bureaucrats are professionals, the assertion that they exercise considerable discretion is fairly obvious. Professionals are expected to exercise discretionary judgment in their field. They are regularly deferred to in their specialized areas of work and are relatively free from supervision by superiors or scrutiny by clients. Yet even public employees who do not have claims to professional status exercise considerable discretion. Clerks in welfare and public housing agencies, for example, may exercise discretion in determining client access to benefits, even though their discretion is formally circumscribed by rules and relatively close supervision.

Rules may actually be an impediment to supervision. They may be so voluminous and contradictory that they can only be enforced or invoked selectively. In most public welfare departments, regulations are encyclopedic, yet at the same time, they are constantly being changed. With such rules adherence to anything but the most basic and fundamental precepts of eligibility cannot be expected. Police behavior is so highly specified by statutes and regulations that policemen are expected to invoke the law selectively. They could not possibly make arrests for all the infractions they observe during their working day. (Like doctors and clergymen in many jurisdictions, they are required to be on-duty and ready to intervene even during their off-duty hours.) Similarly, federal civil-rights compliance officers have so many mandated responsibilities in comparison to their resources that they have been free to determine their own priorities.[5] It would seem that the proliferation of rules and responsibilities is only problematically related to the degree of discretion street-level bureaucrats enjoy.[6]

[. . .]

Since many of the problems discussed here would theoretically disappear if workers' discretion were eliminated, one may wonder why discretion remains characteristic of their jobs. The answer is that certain characteristics of the jobs of street-level bureaucrats make it difficult, if not impossible, to severely reduce discretion. They involve complex tasks for which elaboration of rules, guidelines, or instructions cannot circumscribe the alternatives. This may be the case for one of at least two reasons.

First, street-level bureaucrats often work in situations too complicated to reduce to programmatic formats. Policemen cannot carry around instructions on how to intervene with citizens, particularly in potentially hostile encounters. Indeed, they would probably not go out on the street if such instructions were promulgated, or they would refuse to intervene in potentially dangerous situations. Similarly, contemporary views of education mitigate against detailed instructions to teachers on how and what to teach, since the philosophy prevails that to a point every child requires a response appropriate to the specific learning context.

Second, street-level bureaucrats work in situations that often require responses to the human dimensions of situations. They have discretion because the accepted definitions of their tasks call for sensitive observation and judgment, which are not reducible to programmed formats. It may be that uniform sentencing would reduce inequities in the criminal justice system. But we also want the law to be responsive to the unique circumstances of individual transgressions. We want teachers to perceive the unique potential of children. In short, to a degree the society seeks not only impartiality from its public agencies but also compassion for special circumstances and flexibility in dealing with them.

A third reason discretion is not likely to be eliminated bears more on the function of lower-level workers who interact with citizens than with the nature of the tasks. Street-level discretion promotes workers' self-regard and encourages clients to believe that workers hold the key to their well-being. For both workers and clients, maintenance of discretion contributes to the legitimacy of the welfare-service state, although street-level bureaucrats by no means establish the boundaries of state intervention.

[. . .] To the extent that tasks remain complex and human intervention is considered necessary for effective service, discretion will remain characteristic of many public service jobs.

[. . .]

DIFFERENCES BETWEEN STREET-LEVEL BUREAUCRATS AND MANAGERS

The maintenance and enhancement of discretion is so important that some detailed illustrations may be useful.

Lower-court judges have recently encouraged the development of a great many alternatives to incarceration, in essence turning the courts into social work referral services. In Massachusetts and elsewhere lower-court judges can refer presumptive offenders to many social programs, the successful completion of which will result in obviating their sentences. These include programs to provide first offenders with counseling, job training, and placement assistance, and alcoholics, reckless drivers, and drug offenders with appropriate counseling. In addition, judges have the services of psychiatrists, social workers, probation officers, and others who might be able to provide treatment as an alternative to imprisonment. These developments have been conceived by humanitarian reformers who believe, along with many judges, that prisons create more criminals than they deter by exposing people to experienced crooks, and by pragmatists, who recognize that the courts have become revolving doors of repeat appearances without deterrent effect.

It is conspicuous to court observers that these programs take a heavy burden off the judge. The judge is now able to make what appears to be a constructive decision rather than simply to choose between the unattractive alternatives of sending a person to jail or releasing the putative offender without penalty. Indirect evidence that these programs fill critical institutional needs is suggested by the Boston pretrial diversion programs. These programs were utilized beyond their capacity by judges, sometimes without regard for the extremely important initial interview or the relatively stringent eligibility requirements the programs sought to impose in order to maximize effectiveness. Dependent upon judges for referrals and, indeed, for their programs' existence, administrators found it difficult to refuse judges who referred too many clients, or inappropriate clients, to them.[7]

The Veterans Administration hospital system is a fascinating bureaucracy because it employs doctors, the preeminent professionals, in highly rule-bound organizations. The country's system of socialized medicine for the indigent veteran has developed an extremely complex series of rules because of simultaneous congressional concern to provide veterans with hospital services, maintain strict cost accounting, and (particularly in the past) not compete with private medical practice. In large part because the VA system was to provide hospital care, leaving to private physicians the business of office consultations, the VA hospitals were prohibited from treating patients on an outpatient basis.

However, there was an allowable exception to the rule limiting services to hospitalized veterans. Under the "Pre-Bedcare" category (PBC) veterans who required health services prior to their anticipated admission (for example, blood tests prior to surgery) could be treated. Despite various requirements intended to limit PBC treatment to those whose admission was clearly expected, actual admission to the hospitals from PBC lists was traditionally very low. It seems that doctors, chafing under the restriction that they could not treat patients according to their best estimate of need, were treating patients as outpatients under the fiction that they were expected to be admitted. [. . .] [I]t seems that doctors were able to utilize existing bureaucratic structures to impose their views of proper treatment on the organization, despite organizational efforts to circumscribe their discretion.

Street-level bureaucrats will also use existing regulations and administrative provision to circumvent reforms which limit their discretion. In December 1968, in response to pressure from the Department of Housing and Urban Development, the Boston Housing Authority (BHA) adopted new tenant-selection guidelines designed to insure housing project racial integration. The plan utilized what was known as the "1-2-3 rule." To eliminate personnel discretion in assignments the 1-2-3 rule provided that prospective tenants would be offered places only in the housing projects with the three highest vacancy ratios. If these offers were refused, the application would be returned to the bottom of the waiting list.

The BHA integration plan did not work. Many housing authority employees objected to assigning people to projects in which they did not want to live. They were particularly concerned for their traditionally favored clientele, the elderly, poor whites who populated the "better" BHA projects. Among the reasons the reform did not work were that housing authority personnel were so inundated with work that proper administrative controls were not feasible, and in the chaos of processing applications, those who wished to favor some prospective tenants over others were able to do so. Housing officials took advantage of provisions for exceptions to the 1-2-3 rule, interpreting reasonable provisions for flexibility in extremely liberal ways when they wanted to. They volunteered information to favored prospective tenants concerning how to have their applications treated as emergencies or other high-priority categories, while routinely processing the applications of others. Applications were frequently lost or misplaced so that workers could favor tenants simply by locating their files and acting on them, while other files remained unavailable for processing. Meanwhile, public housing managers contributed to the sustained biases of the agency by failing to report vacancies to the central office when they occurred, not informing prospective tenants when units were available, or showing tenants they wished to discourage only unattractive or unsafe units, although others in the project were available. Thus the press of work combined with workers' desires to continue to serve particular clients restored the discretionary powers the new rules were designed to eliminate.[8]

[. . .]

7

RATIONING SERVICES: LIMITATION OF ACCESS AND DEMAND

Theoretically there is no limit to the demand for free public goods. Agencies that provide public goods must and will devise ways to ration them.

[. . .]

The rationing of the level of services starts when clients present themselves to the worker or agency or an encounter is commanded. Like factory workers confronted with production quotas, street-level bureaucrats attempt to organize their work to facilitate work tasks or liberate as much time as possible for their own purposes. This is evident even in those services areas in which workers have little control over work flow. For example, police often cannot control work flow because most police assignments are in response to citizen initiated calls. Dispatchers, however, make every effort to permit officers to finish one call before beginning another. Officers often take advantage of this practice by postponing reporting the completion of a call until after they have finished accumulated paperwork. In this way police officers regularize the work flow despite substantial irregularity in requests for assistance.

[. . .]

[Official efforts to influence the flow of work] range from the mild advisory of the post office providing patrons with information concerning the times when delays are likely to be longest, to the extreme measures taken by a New York City welfare office that closed its doors at noon rather than admit a greater number of Medicaid applicants than could be processed by available personnel in an eight-hour day.[9]

[. . .]

THE COSTS OF SERVICE

[. . .] Confronted with more clients than can readily be accommodated street-level bureaucrats often choose (or skim off the top) those who seem most likely to succeed in terms of bureaucratic success

criteria. This will happen despite formal requirements to provide clients with equal chances for service, and even in the face of policies designed to favor clients with relatively poor probabilities of success. Employment counselors, for example, may send to jobs people who have the greatest chance to gain employment anyway, to the neglect of people who are more difficult to place. The Upward Bound program, dedicated to enriching the educational backgrounds of disadvantaged high school students, constantly had to guard against projects taking students whose chances of getting into college were already fairly high.

Why does creaming take place, particularly in the face of official opposition to the practice? In every case of creaming the agency's incentives reward successes with clients, but they provide no substantial rewards for the risks taken. . . . If all clients are equally worthy but all cannot be served, increasing the rate of personal or agency success becomes primary.

[. . .]

Differentiation among clients may take place because of workers' preferences for some clients over others.

First, some clients simply evoke workers' sympathy or hostility. Like the Israeli customs officials, workers may be inclined to "give the underdog a break"[10] or may favor clients with similar ethnic backgrounds, as when racial or ethnic favoritism prevails in discriminatory decision making. The Boston Housing Authority workers who tended to favor white elderly applicants probably were responding to both ethnic and sympathy appeals when they selectively provided them with critical information.

It would be as much of a mistake to infer that ethnic or racial appeals always prevail in affecting discretionary judgments as that they never prevail. Bureaucratic norms operate to restrict the range of determinations made in this way. Thus, black police officers may make particular efforts to act in role-prescribed ways when confronting black citizens. Displaying the complementary tendency, white bureaucrats may be more lenient or tolerant with black clients out of fear of being accused of racial biases. The report from San Francisco that black school children tended to receive good grades and were told that they were doing well in school, but in fact were not learning at an acceptable rate, is a vicious example of what can happen when street-level bureaucrats over-react to the potential for biased behavior.

[. . .]

A second circumstance of biased behavior is evident when street-level bureaucrats respond to general orientations toward clients' worthiness or unworthiness that permeate the society and to whose proliferation they regularly contribute. This is one of the most well-grounded generalizations that can be made concerning client processing. Juvenile court judges determine sentencing severity on the basis of the apparent worthiness of the defendant.[11] Policemen make decisions concerning citizens on the basis of whether or not they display respect. Trauma-team personnel tend to work harder to save the lives of the young than the old, the high-status citizen rather than the low.[12] Other emergency room personnel make moral evaluations of clients and treat them accordingly.[13]

[. . .]

[T]here is every reason to think that the general evaluations of social worth that inform the society will also inform the decisions of street-level bureaucrats in the absence of strong incentives to the contrary.

[. . .]

9

CONTROLLING CLIENTS AND THE WORK SITUATION

[. . .] In the previous chapters I discussed ways in which patterns of street-level practice function to ration services. A second general function of street-level practice is not so much to limit services or choose among clients, but to obtain client cooperation with client-processing procedures. The work that clients are expected to cooperate with may or may not be consistent with agencies' policy declarations. It will, however, be consistent with street-level bureaucrats' conceptions of how to process work with minimal risk of disruption to routine practice.

[...] Here I consider selected aspects of practice that commonly contribute to routine control of clients.

1. Street-level bureaucrats interact with clients in settings that symbolize, reinforce, and limit their relationship. It is practically a cliche to observe that the severe appointments of a courtroom, dominated by a bench behind which a black-robed judge looks down at other courtroom participants, convey the power of the system of laws over the individual. Separate entrances for judges, commands to stand whenever the judge arrives or departs, and the unintelligibility of the court clerk further contribute to the mysteries of the courtroom.

Each service setting functions somewhat differently, but in their different ways each contributes to client compliance. Many offices in which people seek service are structured to separate clearly the workers from the clients by means of an imposing information desk. Clients, when interviewed, are led to "offices" that, lacking partitions, violate privacy by permitting everyone to view (and listen in on) everyone else's work. Fixed rows of desks in schools, all facing the teacher, physically represent the demand for order that teachers and schools require. Like uniforms, settings facilitate the functioning of the bureaucracies by drawing attention to the location of power and cuing the expectations of clients.

These messages are not accidental. They are fostered by the agencies and generally consented to by the society.

[...] Are clients important and valued as people? Provide them with comfortable chairs and sofas on which to sit while they wait, ask them if they are comfortable, and reassure them if they must wait that they have not been forgotten. Are clients of little account? Neglect these considerations and have a small, cramped waiting room with little attention available. It would be mistaken to think of service settings as accidental. It is often a matter of policy that public services are able, or consider themselves unable, to plan for client comfort.

2. Clients are isolated from one another. Public service bureaucracies are organized so that clients have little knowledge of others in the same position. Most client processing is shielded from the scrutiny of other clients. Isolated clients are more likely to think of themselves as responsible for their situations.

They are unlikely to see their condition as a reflection of social structure and their treatment as unacceptable.

When client processing is done in public, the impression is accurately conveyed that clients are competing with one another for the attention or favor of street-level bureaucrats. As suggested earlier, in the brutal realities of triage, clients perceive that they gain special treatment or the attention of workers only at the expense of other clients. The bureaucratic defense against special treatment is also germane here: "If I give it to you I would have to give it to everyone." In street-level settings in which clients do know each other—in schools, mental hospitals, prisons—client control is fostered by the competitive systems of rewards, fostering among clients individual orientations rather than collective solutions to problem solving.

Street-level bureaucracies tend to resist organization by clients when it occurs. They tend to regard client organizations as unnecessary, frivolous, likely to be irresponsible, or not representative of clients' true interests. There are no objective measures of the validity of such assertions. From some perspectives any or all might be true. However, these assertions are most usefully regarded as defenses against client organization, intended to diminish their influence among potential recruits or third parties whose support is sought, or to lay the groundwork for an intransigent official response. In the past decade prison inmates, black high-school students, and welfare recipients all have been regularly subject to such official responses when they have attempted to organize.

Public officials often prefer to suppress or disorient client organizations because they can never be sure at what point they will peak or major concessions will be required. *[...]*

3. The services and procedures of street-level bureaucrats are presented as benign. Actions affecting clients are always taken in their best interest. Clients are expected to be grateful for benefits they receive. Where street-level bureaucracies constrain clients who are not regarded as guilty—as in schools, hospitals, and noncriminal arrests by the police (e.g., apprehension of alcoholics)—the ideology of benign intervention is particularly necessary to justify practices of questionable value to both client and worker groups. When combined with

clients' deference to the more extensive education, training, and expertise of street-level bureaucrats, the ideology that street-level bureaucrats' intervention is in the interest of clients appears to be a particularly important instrument of control.

[. . .]

Street-level bureaucrats develop sanctions to punish disrespect to routines of order. These sanctions are often particularly significant because they are invoked to affect compliance with bureaucratic order rather than to affect behavior relevant to service. For example, teachers, like policemen, have mechanisms that function to provide clues to potential troublemakers and to exclude from society (in the case of teachers, the society of the school) those whose offenses threaten the working fabric of the institution. Children who are suspended for not having a pass, arriving late to class, being absent excessively, or smoking in the bathrooms are guilty not of educational sins but may find interviews terminated in the rare cases when they are not willing to conform to the (reasonable) procedures demanded of them by attorneys.[14] At another point in the legal process judges tend to sanction defendants on the basis of the seriousness of rule violations, and also on the basis of their lack of respect for agents of the law.[15]

Some insight into the significance for street-level bureaucrats of procedures fostering control over clients can be gained by examining the implications of threatening to deny workers these procedural coping devices. The intensity of the resistance of police officers to citizen review boards can be associated with the fear that people who do not appreciate the pressures and risks of police work will sit in judgment on officers who do what they have to do in order to protect themselves. Teachers in traditional schools similarly fear the removal of the sanctions that, rightly or wrongly, they believe to be effective deterrents to student misconduct.

[. . .]

MANAGING THE CONSEQUENCES OF ROUTINE PRACTICE

Street-level practices ration service, organize clients' passage through the bureaucracy, and conserve scarce organizational and personal resources. For various reasons these practices sometimes prove inadequate, or they evoke client reactions that cannot be handled through routine procedures. Cases that deviate from routine processing are not exempt from routinization, however. Instead street-level bureaucracies call on additional practices to manage the first-round costs of processing people in routine ways. These practices function to absorb dissatisfaction with common procedures, thereby permitting agencies to continue to process the majority of cases routinely.

[. . .]

Street-level bureaucrats regularly refer difficult or problem cases to other people employed in their organization. Often this is uncomplicated, as when novices ask supervisors or more experienced workers to handle clients who present difficulties. The referral of difficult cases to more experienced workers hardly requires comment. From the point of view of service quality, the problem arises when referrals are made not because cases defy workers' abilities, but because they interfere with routine procedures. They must be treated as special by a bureaucracy which cannot afford to hear complaints or vigorous dissent from decisions at the same time that other clients *with similar claims but less inclination to speak out* are also being processed. The problem is kicked upstairs, not to seek expertise but to manage dissent or noncompliance. Thus street-level bureaucracies introduce the "pressure specialist"[16] to hear and decide on clients who pursue their cases vigorously.

The pressure specialist serves in several ways. Dissenting clients are siphoned off, permitting routine procedures to be imposed for the vast majority. Pressure specialists also perform onerous tasks that would otherwise taint the entire staff. For example, severe punishments in schools are usually meted out by an administrator or designated disciplinarian, protecting teachers from having to punish severely students whom they are simultaneously asked to instruct.

The availability of a pressure specialist in some respects protects the worker from the clients' strong negative feelings by providing an alternative to decision making. Rather than listen to clients complain, or worry that a decision may evoke client hostility, the worker can process the case through a pressure referral. Thus the worker's legitimacy is partially protected by the availability of a channel that places responsibility for difficult decisions in the hands of others.

Workers can use the availability of pressure specialists to enhance the prospects of favored clients. For example, welfare workers often take pleasure in artfully presenting cases to supervisors in such a way that they are likely to endorse the worker's judgment. Or street-level bureaucrats can scuttle clients' prospects without clients' knowledge by giving the appearance of bureaucratic neutrality but privately providing damaging information to supervisors.

The possibility that decisions can be appealed also enhances the legitimacy of the bureaucracy to the client. For this to work on a sustained basis, however, two conditions must be met. First, and quite obviously, it must look like channels for appeal are open. Second, and less obviously, these channels must be costly to use, rarely successful, and, if successful, certainly not well publicized. The reason for this is simply that if appeals channels were inexpensive to use or likely to be successful they soon *would be* used by clients seeking increased benefits or a favorable disposition. The channels of appeal would soon be clogged, and the manifest unfairness that some clients receive more than others because they sought more would undermine the system.

Thus appeals ordinarily require long delays, the services of advocates, complicated administrative procedures associated with filing, and general hostility from the challenged agency.[17] Recent innovations responsive to client pressure often require public agencies to publish the requirements for appealing and inform clients of their rights to appeal, provide responses within a specified time period, and offer counsel to clients seeking appeals. These innovations still require considerable determination and energy from individual clients.

Public agencies also seek to insure that appeals cannot be sought collectively. The appeals process can function so long as a single client cannot gain redress for a class of clients. So long as individual clients cannot win benefits for groups, public agencies can ration the claims of large numbers of clients in many ways, and thus gain protection from an inundation of client demands.

These observations are generally supported by examining the volume of appeals in public agencies. For example, through the early 1960s there was almost a total lack of appeals from welfare decisions, although federal law required each state to establish an appeals procedure. In New York City, where a relatively liberal welfare environment prevailed compared to the rest of the country, only 15 appeals were taken in 1964, although half a million people were on welfare at the time.[18]

Appeals can also be discouraged by the high probability that they will not succeed. Allegations of police brutality are rarely made through official channels because of the conviction that they will not receive a sympathetic hearing from the officers who sit on the hearing boards. In Rochester, for example, where 102 complaints alleging "unnecessary force" were registered in the five- to seven-year period after 1965, only two were upheld by the police internal inspection office; of the 368 alleging unnecessary force and other improper behavior, forty-six were sustained.[19]

[. . .]

A typical response of many public agencies to the claims generated by minority and women's rights movements has been to establish special units to hear citizen complaints and to take responsibility for institutional change in these areas. Police departments have established internal review boards (sometimes with outside citizen participation) and community relations units to present a sympathetic face to the black community. Public school systems have hired community relations specialists and affirmative action officers to take responsibility for the complaints of minorities and women and to articulate agency perspectives consistent with the interests of these groups. These steps have contributed to increased minority and female employment in the bureaucracies, symbolic rewards to these constituencies, perhaps genuine changes in the attitudes of some agency personnel, and possibly greater responsiveness to clients in some circumstances.

However, these innovations also function to protect the bureaucracies from pressures for change, and they insulate street-level bureaucrats from the need to confront certain client populations. Police departments channel what they label minority cases to human relations units when questions about racial attitudes are raised, freeing ordinary officers from having to resolve them. The affirmative action office takes responsibility for recruiting women to the work force, absolving the people who normally do the hiring from having to change their attitudes about female employees. Moreover, the ordinary worker recognizes the essentially symbolic and non-integral nature of the new unit and may display toward it the same antipathy extended toward the group it is supposed to represent. Thus community relations officers are correctly made to feel that they are not respected by patrol officers.[20] Equal opportunity officers responsible for integrating work forces have to struggle to obtain respect from within the institutions that hire them.

[. . .]

12

THE BROADER CONTEXT OF BUREAUCRATIC RELATIONS

In considering the potential for change in street-level bureaucracies it would be a mistake to restrict analysis to the coping dilemmas and adaptations of service workers, or the patterns of practice that develop among them. The resolution of contradictory tendencies in street-level bureaucracies cannot be understood without examining the role of these public agencies in the society and the ways in which the society impinges on the character of bureaucratic relations.

[. . .]

In what ways do street-level bureaucracies reflect and perpetuate the values of the larger society? There are at least two respects in which the structure of relationships between workers and clients appears to be derived from the particular character of American society.

First, street-level bureaucracies are affected by the prevailing orientations toward the poor in the United States. These orientations include the deep conviction that poor people at some level are responsible for the conditions in which they find themselves, and that receiving benefits labeled "for the poor" is shameful. These convictions are epitomized in the observation that public programs for poor people are almost always treated in the press as costs to society, not benefits.

These attitudes toward social services for the poor amount to a general stigmatization of poor people. Stigma leads to a general reluctance to join the deviant group in the society on the one hand, and on the other hand provides subtle justification for patterns of practice that result in inadequate service provision. Prevailing attitudes toward the poor permit rationalization of patterns that result in client neglect, which would be more difficult to rationalize if clients were middle class and generally respected. The same may be observed in agencies of training and control. Some lower courts and public schools, for example, develop community reputations for dealing mostly with low-income clients, and they develop patterns of practice that process people less respectfully than similar institutions with middle-class clienteles.

Intersecting with attitudes toward the stigmatized poor are attitudes prevalent in the larger society regarding clients' racial or ethnic backgrounds. Racism also affects the extent to which public employees regard clients as worthy, and it affects the extent to which patterns of practice evolve that distinguish among clients in terms of their racial backgrounds.

Second, the politics of the larger society affect street-level bureaucracies and their clients in the dynamic relationship between the requirements of providing services and their perceived costs. Governmental initiatives for programs of social service and control expand or contract, grow more quickly or more slowly, in part depending upon the relative degree of concern over crisis or control. In periods of social turmoil or widely perceived crisis (the depression of the 1930s, the ghetto revolts of the 1960s, the "Sputnik" crisis in education in the 1950s) service benefits and/or funds for training and control functions increase. In periods of relative quiescence pressures are exerted to return the balance to a ratio of benefits to costs more favorable to costs. Social analysts may disagree on the precise dynamics of the dialectics of expansion and contraction of governmental social service and control policies. But there should be little doubt that public bureaucracies that normally process clients vacillate in their generosity toward client treatment. Street-level bureaucracies are alternately able to treat clients with greater degrees of latitude and forced to restrict options and more narrowly designate benefits.[21]

In the current period street-level bureaucrats are under pressure to develop more restrictive patterns of practice. They are under pressure to increase case loads and to be more formally accountable, and they are generally asked to expand or maintain coverage in the face of static or declining budgets. [...]

It seems apparent that American street-level bureaucracies must be understood as organizational embodiments of contradictory tendencies in American society as a whole. The welfare state calls for and requires social programs to ameliorate the neglect and insecurity of the economic system, to prepare people for roles in the economy, or to manage their deviation from expectations of appropriate behavior.[22] In the ideology of the welfare state humanitarian impulses are coincident with the requirements of system maintenance.

This, of course, begins to explain how people with humanitarian impulses can work for impersonal, paternalistic, or repressive public service agencies. Most people never question that the requirements of the state are congruent with the needs and interests of large numbers of people. Thus, teachers with compassion for children work in brutalizing schools and picture themselves as victimized by the same system that victimizes their pupils. Social workers with compassion for poor people participate in assigning inadequate benefit levels to welfare recipients and wish they could do more.[23]

The legitimacy of the political and economic system depends on the appearance of providing for those who cannot provide for themselves and responding openly and fairly to citizens' claims. Public service workers actively translate this requirement into programs. But government policy is not likely in fact to respond fully to the needs of citizens for at least two reasons relevant to this discussion.

First, there is no agreement as to what those needs are. What it means to "respond fully to citizen needs" is a socially determined concept albeit defined by a process that gives more weight to policy elites than clients. As continuing controversies in such areas as health care, welfare, and legal services reveal, the demands of citizens are open-ended while

program costs must be kept within certain bounds. Indeed, the definition of those boundaries is the basic issue in social welfare policy making.

Second, there is a powerful imperative to maintain private responsibility for social needs and to make dependency punishable by welfare, public hospitals, and inner-city schools. Granted that street-level bureaucracies exist outside of the welfare context, and that limitations on program expenditures must be encountered *at some point*. Yet it is not at all clear that the United States inevitably had to develop relatively low social service and benefit levels compared to other advanced industrial countries.[24] In an assessment of income and service provision an independent role should be assigned to a perceived need among policy-making elites to limit benefit and service provisions, allegedly to enhance individual and family self-reliance and to stigmatize the status of worklessness and poverty.

In short, this is a political system that, whatever its current levels of social welfare expenditures, must also symbolically project images of adequate and reasonably comprehensive social welfare programming to taxpayers and middle-class consumers, while in fact it limits support and assistance. Such a system develops mechanisms to maintain legitimacy and deflect criticism that the society does not provide adequately for its citizens. Street-level bureaucrats mediate between citizens and the state in that clients' inability to obtain benefits or services and inequities of distribution may be understood by clients as personal malfeasance of street-level bureaucrats or administrative agency disarray.

[...]

Street-level bureaucrats' needs to control their work situations force them to defend themselves and the current arrangements. Agency expectations and occupational norms preclude the excuse that working conditions prevent effective efforts on clients' behalf, despite private recognition that this is the case. This defensiveness separates street-level bureaucrats from their potential allies in improving working conditions for mutual benefit.

[...]

Teachers, social workers, legal aid lawyers, and police officers all enter the work force at least in part with a desire to make a contribution to individuals or to the community. In some fields public agencies have a monopoly on jobs available to people in certain professions. Social workers may be able to seek employment in private as well as public agencies, but young adults aspiring to become police officers or teachers largely have to seek public employment if they want to work in these areas.

Once attracted to these occupations, however, the dynamics of street-level bureaucracies combine to persuade workers that they are destined to be ineffective in their chosen fields, that clients may not substantially benefit from their efforts, or that conditions of successful intervention are not likely to be available. These conclusions are all the more persuasive because they appear to be substantially true, at least in the short run. It is difficult to aid clients in ways consistent with idealized conceptions of assistance within street-level bureaucracies as they are currently structured, particularly when the least experienced workers are thrown into the most difficult work environments.

Thus, generations of thoughtful and potentially self-sacrificing people are disarmed in their social purpose. They come to believe that it is impossible to find conditions conducive to good practice, and that public agencies cannot be otherwise structured. Their choices appear to be to leave public employment for other work or to resign themselves to routine processing of clients while instructing the next generation of idealists that there is little sense in hoping for change or in rendering human services.

Similarly, the practice of street-level bureaucrats leads to the self-fulfilling prophecy that relations with clients cannot change. The actions of street-level bureaucrats confirm for clients that they will continue to be treated as they have always been treated. This perpetuates the cycle of the irrelevance of professional help and reinforces tendencies toward despair and inaction. This is the most painful part of the estrangement of workers from their original purpose. These orientations reinforce the tendencies originating in the culture toward enhancement of private interests and the abandonment of social purpose.

[. . .]

CONTRADICTORY TENDENCIES IN STREET-LEVEL BUREAUCRATIC RELATIONS

Of the attributes that support change in street-level bureaucracies at least five should be noted. First, public programs of entitlement and control provide at least the potential for mobilizing clients and sympathetic publics toward greater accountability in implementation and administration.

[. . .]

This consideration is likely to be important in proportion to the population covered by service. One possibility is that public agencies will simply differentiate among high- and low-status clients. But another is that service will improve for all if high-status clients are included in the population mix. As public-health care delivery becomes more and more generalized and less the concern of low-income populations, it is more likely that clients will be able to have an impact on service quality. Likewise, parents of children in an integrated school can have a greater impact on the quality of service than can parents of a segregated school whose needs can be more easily isolated.

[. . .]

Second, professional norms of behavior toward clients provide a measure of resistance to bureaucratization. Street-level bureaucrats' claims of professional status imply a commitment that clients' interests will guide them in providing service. The implicit bargain between the professions and society is that in exchange for self-regulation they will act in clients' interest without regard for personal gain and without compromising their advocacy.

This is not to say that street-level bureaucrats do not also confront organizational demands. On the contrary, the essence of their dilemma is that they are partly professional and partly bureaucratic. However, the potential for appealing to the professional dimension of these work roles means that there is an irreducible minimum consideration of the importance of respecting clients' individuality and acting accordingly.

[. . .]

Third, street-level bureaucrats by definition interact constantly with clients. This provides the salutary condition that workers must continually attend to the people they are supposed to serve and their problems. However elaborate the defense mechanisms developed to shield themselves from the enormity of clients' needs, street-level bureaucrats at some level retain a sense that the people with whom they come in contact are not sufficiently served by the agencies designated to do so. Thus, one might speculate that street-level bureaucrats more than other organizational workers are able to retain a concept of the notion of need in relation to what is actually being provided. This residual awareness may provide a resource that can be tapped.

Fourth, lower-level workers maintain a degree of control over their work environment. Individually street-level bureaucrats exercise discretion to control the work situation. Collectively many street-level bureaucrats are able to have a significant say in the rules under which they are employed. Particularly at the individual level this discretion is not likely to be significantly eroded so long as street-level bureaucrats' jobs require them to make discretionary judgments that cannot be entirely programmed.

Finally, there is a distinct but neglected precedent for organized public employees championing the needs of clients. Teachers have included limitations on classroom size as an objective to be sought through collective bargaining. They have sought this objective not only to improve working conditions but also to create the environment in which they could function optimally as teachers. Likewise, social workers have struck on behalf of improved benefit levels for clients.[25]

The cynic may wish to point out the strategic advantage to public workers of couching bargaining objectives in altruistic terms (although managers are equally guilty, insisting that they act on behalf of taxpayers and the economic well-being of the community). Still, cynical or not, such alliances, the stuff of politics, may be exploited by client groups, particularly when, in collective bargaining in the fiscal crisis, wage gains are subordinated to improvements in working conditions.

The impulse to provide fully, openly, and responsively for citizens' service needs exists alongside the need to restrict, control, and rationalize service inadequacies or limitations. This is the central contradiction of social services. It is more than simply a tension between costs and benefits. It is critical to reassure mass publics that their elemental needs will be taken care of if they are not met privately and to rationalize service inadequacies by deflecting responsibility away from government.

Through street-level bureaucracies the society organizes the control, restriction, and maintenance of relatively powerless groups. Antagonism is directed toward the agents of social services and control and away from the political forces that ultimately account for the distribution of social and material values. Thus the American system of service delivery and control is shaped by the aspirations of the population and by the requirements of the larger political and social system. In this sense the United States, no less than other political systems, lends public bureaucracy its particular character.

NOTES

1. The seminal work here is Robert Rosenthal and Lenore Jacobson, *Pygmalion in the Classroom* (New York: Holt, Rinehart and Winston, 1968).

2. Martin Rein, "Welfare and Housing," Joint Center Working Papers Series, no. 4 (Cambridge, Mass.: Joint Center for Urban Studies, Spring, 1971, rev. Feb. 1972).

3. See Chris Argyris, *Integrating the Individual and the Organization* (New York: John Wiley, 1964), pp. 35–41.

4. Frank L. Morris, Sr., "The Advantages and Disadvantages of Black Political Group Activity in Two Northern Maximum Security State Prisons" (Ph.D. diss., Massachusetts Institute of Technology, 1976), p. 40.

5. For example, the Office of Civil Rights of the Department of Health, Education, and Welfare has responsibility to monitor potential violations as follows: racial discrimination under Title VI of the Civil Rights Act of 1964 in 16,000 public school districts, 2,800 institutions of higher education, and 30,000 institutions of health and social services; in the same areas, discrimination against handicapped people under Section 504 of the Vocational Rehabilitation Act of 1973; sex discrimination under Section 799A of the Public Health Service Act in 1,500 health education institutions, and under Section 745, sex discrimination in nursing schools; sex discrimination under Title IX, Education Amendments of 1972, in 16,000 public school districts; discrimination by federal contractors under Executive Order 11246, innumerable contractors at 863 higher-education campuses, and more than 3,500 additional locations. Virginia Balderama, "The Office of Civil Rights as a Street-Level Bureaucracy," unpublished seminar paper, University of Washington, March, 1976.

6. David Perry and Paula Sornoff report that welfare workers' behavior with clients in California is ruled by 115 pounds of regulations; that the average police officer is obliged to enforce approximately 30,000 federal, state, and local laws. Perry and Sornoff, "Street Level Administration and the Law: The Problem of Police Community Relations," *Criminal Law Bulletin*, vol. 8, no. 1 (January–February, 1972), p. 46.

7. This paragraph is based upon personal observations, conversations with court personnel, and sustained discussions with workers in the Boston Court Resources Project.

8. See Jon Pynoos, "Breaking the Rules: The Failure to Select and Assign Public Housing Tenants Equitably," (Ph.D. diss., Harvard University, 1974).

9. The latter case is cited by Barry Schwartz, *Queuing and Waiting* (Chicago: University of Chicago Press, 1975), p. 24. This excellent volume provides many insights into issues of priorities in client treatment and the costs of seeking service.

10. Brenda Danet, "'Giving the Underdog a Break': Latent Particularism among Customs Officials," in Elihu Katz and Brenda Danet, eds., *Bureaucracy and the Public* (New York: Basic Books, 1973), pp. 329–337.

11. Robert Emerson, *Judging Delinquents* (New York: Aldine, 1969).

12. Barney Glaser and Anselm Strauss, "The Social Loss of Dying Patients," *American Journal of Nursing*, vol. 64 (June, 1964), pp. 119–121.

13. Julius Roth, "Some Contingencies of the Moral Evaluation and Control of Clientele: The Case of the Hospital Emergency Room," in Yeheskel Hasenfeld and Richard English, eds., *Human Service Organizations*, (Ann Arbor, Mich.: University of Michigan Press, 1974), pp. 499–516.

14. Hosticka, "Legal Services Lawyers Encounter Clients: A Study in Street-Level Bureaucracy." Unpublished Ph.D. dissertation.

15. Maureen Mileski, "Courtroom Encounters," *Law and Society Review*, vol. 5, no. 5 (May, 1971), p. 503.

16. Rikva Bar-Yosef and E. O. Schild, "Pressures and Defenses in Bureaucratic Roles," in Elihu Katz and Brenda Danet, eds., *Bureaucracy and the Public* (New York: Basic Books, 1973), p. 295.

17. On the difficulty of filing complaints against the police see Walter Gellhorn, *When Americans Complain* (Cambridge, Mass.: Harvard University Press, 1966), pp. 186ff.

18. Frances F. Piven and Richard A. Cloward, *Regulating the Poor: The Functions of Public Welfare* (New York: Pantheon, 1971), p. 173. Piven and Cloward attribute the low number of appeals to the control of the welfare system over clients, resulting in their acquiescence to the system of welfare on its terms, a thesis consistent with earlier arguments in this book.

19. David C. Perry and Paula Sornoff, "Politics at the Street Level; The Select Case of Police Administration and the Community" (rev. version of a paper presented to the Annual Meeting of the American Political Science Association, Washington, D.C., 1972), pp. 62–63.

20. See, for example, David C. Perry and Paula Sornoff, "Street Level Administration and the Law: The Problem of Police-Community Relations," *Criminal Law Bulletin*, vol. 8, no. 1 (January–February, 1972), p. 54.

21. The dynamics of the dialectic of expansion and contraction in public service benefits are treated in Frances F. Piven and Richard Cloward, *Regulating the Poor* (New York: Pantheon, 1971). See also Michael Lipsky, *Protest in City Politics* (Chicago: Rand McNally, 1970), chap. 2; Murray Edelman, *Political Language* (New York: Academic Press, 1977), chap. 3.

22. For illuminating discussions of the role of social welfare programs, broadly conceived, in contemporary American society, see James O'Connor, *The Fiscal Crisis of the State* (New York: St. Martin's, 1973); Piven and Cloward, *Regulating the Poor*; Ira Katznelson, "The Crisis of the Capitalist City: Urban Politics and Social Control," in Willis Hawley and Michael Lipsky, eds., *Theoretical Perspectives on Urban Politics* (Englewood Cliffs, N.J.: Prentice-Hall, 1976), pp. 214–229.

23. See Jeffry Galper, *The Politics of Social Services* (Englewood Cliffs, N.J.: Prentice-Hall, 1975).

24. On national variations in welfare benefit levels and administrative organization see Harold Wilensky, *The Welfare State and Equality: Structural and Ideological Roots of Public Expenditures* (Berkeley, Calif.: University of California Press, 1975).

25. For one example of public employees seeking improved services for citizens see the efforts of the Service Employees International Union to obtain better patient care and treatment facilities at Boston City Hospital. *Boston Herald-American*, May 25, 1978, p. 7.

REFERENCES

Acker, Joan. 1990 (June). "Hierarchies, Jobs, Bodies: A Theory of Gendered Organizations." *Gender and Society*. 4(2):139-158.

Adler, Paul S. 1993. "Time-and-Motion Regained." Pp. 255–275 in *The Learning Imperative*, Robert Howard, ed. Cambridge, Ma.: Harvard Business Review Book.

Adler, Paul S. and Robert E. Cole. 1993. "Designed for Learning: A Tale of Two Auto Plants." *Sloan Management Review*. Spring:85–94.

Akerlof, George A. 1982. "Labor Contracts as Partial Gift Exchange." *Quarterly Journal of Economics*. 97:543–69.

Albrow, Martin. 1970. *Bureaucracy*. London: Macmillan.

Alchian, Armen A. and Harold Demsetz. 1972. "Production, Information Costs, and Economic Organization." *American Economic Review*. 62:777–795.

Appelabum, Eileen and Rosemary Batt. 1994. *The New American Workplace: Transforming Work Systems in the United States*. Ithaca, N.Y.: ILR Press.

Argyris, Chris. 1984 [1960]. "The Impact of the Formal Organization Upon the Individual." Pp. 261–278 in *Organization Theory*, Derek S. Pugh, ed. New York: Penguin.

Attewell, Paul. 1987. "The Deskilling Controversy." *Work and Occupations*. 14:323–346.

Badaracco, Joseph L. Jr. and Allen P. Webb. 1995. "Business Ethics: A View From the Trenches." *California Management Review*. 37:8–28 (Winter).

Barker, James R. 1993. "Tightening the Iron Cage: Concertive Control in Self-Managing Teams." *Administrative Science Quarterly*. 38:408–437.

Barley, Stephen R. and Gideon Kunda. 1992. "Design and Devotion: Surges of Rational and Normative Ideologies of Control in Managerial Discourse." *Administrative Science Quarterly*. 37:363–399.

Baron, James N. 1984. "Organizational Perspectives on Stratification." *Annual Review of Sociology*. 10:37–69.

Baron, James N., Frank R. Dobbin, and P. Devereaux Jennings. 1986. "War and Peace: The Evolution of Modern Personnel Administration in U.S. Industry." *American Journal of Sociology*. 92:350–383.

Baron, James N., Michael T. Hannan, and M. Diane Burton. 1999. "Building the Iron Cage: Determinants of Managerial Intensity in the Early Years of Organizations." *American Sociological Review*. 64:527–547.

Berggren, Christian. 1994. "NUMMI vs. Uddevalla." *Sloan Management Review*. Winter:37–49.

Bertrand, Marianne and Kenneth Hallock. 2000. "The Gender Gap in Top Corporate Jobs." Working Paper 7931. Cambridge, Ma.: National Bureau of Economic Research.

Birch, David L. 1981. "Who Creates Jobs?" *The Public Interest*. 65:3–14.

Blau, Peter M., Cecilia McHugh Falbe, William McKinley, and Phelps K. Tracy. 1976. "Technology and Organization in Manufacturing." *Administrative Science Quarterly*. 21:20–40.

Blau, Peter M. and Marshall W. Meyer. 1987. *Bureaucracy in Modern Society*. (3rd ed.). New York: Random House.

Blauner, Robert. 1964. *Alienation and Freedom*. Chicago: University of Chicago Press.

Block, Fred L. 1987. *Revising State Theory: Essays in Politics and Postindustrialism*. Philadelphia: Temple University Press.

Bowles, Samuel. 1985. "The Production Process in a Competitive Economy: Walrasian, Marxian, and Neo-Hobbesian Models." *American Economic Review*. 76:16–36.

Brass, Daniel J. 1984. "Being in the Right Place: A Structural Analysis of Individual Influence in an Organization." *Administrative Science Quarterly*. 29:518–539.

Braverman, Harry. 1974. *Labor and Monopoly Capital*. New York: Monthly Review.

Burawoy Michael. 1979. *Manufacturing Consent: Changes in the Labor Process Under Monopoly Capitalism*. Chicago: University of Chicago Press.

Burns, Tom. 1984 [1963]. "Mechanistic and Organismic Structures." Pp. 43–55 in *Organization Theory*, Derek Pugh, ed. New York: Penguin.

Butler, Richard. 1990. "Decision-making Research: Its Uses and Misuses." *Organization Studies*. 11:11–16.

Chandler, Alfred D. 1990. "The Enduring Logic of Industrial Success." *Harvard Business Review*. March–April:131–140.

Child, John. 1997. "Strategic Choice in the Analysis of Action, Structure, Organizations, and Environment: Retrospect and Prospect." *Organization Studies*. 18:43–76.

Dawson, Sandra and Dorothy Wedderburn. 1980. "Joan Woodward and the Development of Organization Theory." Pp. xiii–xl in *Industrial Organization: Theory and Practice*, Joan Woodward, ed., second edition. Oxford: Oxford University Press.

DiMaggio, Paul J. and Helmut K. Anheier. 1990. "The Sociology of Nonprofit Organizations and Sectors." *Annual Review of Sociology*. 16:137–159.

"Divided, an Airline Stumbles." 2001. *New York Times*. March 14 (Part 13).

Dobbin, Frank, John R. Sutton, John W. Meyer, W. Richard Scott. 1993. "Equal Opportunity Law and the Construction of Internal Labor Markets." *American Journal of Sociology*. 99:396–427.

Donaldson, Lex. 1995. *American Anti-Management Theories of Organization*. New York: Cambridge University Press.

Edwards, Richard. 1979. *Contested Terrain: The Transformation of the Workplace in the Twentieth Century*. New York: Basic Books.

Emerson, Richard M. 1962. "Power-Dependence Relations." *American Sociological Review*. 27:31–40.

England, Paula. 1992. *Comparable Worth: Theories and Evidence*. New York: Aldine de Gruyter.

Etzioni, Amitai. 1964. *Modern Organizations*. Englewood Cliffs, N.J.: Prentice-Hall.

Fayol, Henri. 1916/1949. "General Principles of Management" in *General and Industrial Management* by Henri Fayol. London: Sir Isaac Pitman and Sons.

Fayol, Henri. 1937. "The Administrative Theory in the State." Pp. 99–115 in *Papers on the Science of Administration*, Luther Gulick and L. Urwick, eds. Fairfield, N.J.: Augustus M. Kelley.

"Federal Interest Varies, but Cost-Cutting Is Constant for Security Firms." 2001. *New York Times*. November 15 (Part 12).

Fischer, Frank and Carmen Sirianni. 1984. "Organization Theory and Bureaucracy: A Critical Introduction." Pp. 3–23 in *Critical Studies in Organization Theory and Bureaucracy*, Frank Fischer and Carmen Sirianni, eds. Philadelphia: Temple University Press.

Fligstein, Neil. 1987. "The Intraorganizational Power Struggle: Rise of Finance Personnel to Top Leadership in Large Corporations, 1919–1979." *American Sociological Review*. 52:44–58.

Fuchs, Victor R. 1988. *Women's Quest for Economic Equality*. Cambridge, Ma.: Harvard University Press.

Galbraith, Craig S. and Gregory B. Merrill. 1996. "The Politics of Forecasting: Managing the Truth." *California Management Review*. 38:29–43 (Winter).

Gallie, Duncan. 1978. *In Search of the New Working Class: Automation and Social Integration Within the Capitalist Enterprise*. Cambridge: Cambridge University Press.

Gamson, William A. and Emilie Shmeidler. 1984. "Organizing the Poor." *Theory and Society*. 13:567–585.

Garson, Barbara. 1988. *The Electronic Sweatshop: How Computers are Transforming the Office of the Future into the Factory of the Past.* New York: Simon and Schuster.

Gilbreth, Lillian. 1955. *Management in the Home: Happier Living Through Saving Time and Energy.*

Goddeeris, John H. and Burton A. Weisbrod. 1998. "Conversion from Nonprofit to For-Profit Legal Status: Why Does it Happen and Should Anyone Care?" Pp. 129–148 in *To Profit or Not To Profit: The Commercial Transformation of the Nonprofit Sector*, Burton A. Weisbrod, ed. Cambridge: Cambridge University Press.

Gouldner, Alvin W. 1954. *Patterns of Industrial Bureaucracy*. New York: Free Press.

Granovetter, Mark. 1985. "Economic Action and Social Structure: The Problem of Embeddedness." *American Journal of Sociology*. 91:481–510.

Guillen, Mauro F. 1994. "The Age of Eclecticism: Current Organizational Trends and the Evolution of Managerial Models." *Sloan Management Review*. Fall:75–86.

Gulick, Luther and L. Urwick, eds. 1977 [1937]. *Papers on the Science of Administration*. Fairfield, N.J.: Augustus M. Kelley.

Gunn, Christopher. 2000. "Markets Against Economic Democracy." *Review of Radical Political Economics*. 32:448–460.

Halle, David. 1984. *America's Working Man*. Chicago: University of Chicago Press.

Handel, Michael J. 2000. "Is There a Trend Toward Post-Fordist Organization?" unpub. ms.

Handel, Michael J. 2002. "The Post-Fordist Theory of Organization: An Empirical Examination." unpub. ms.

Harris, Margaret. 1998. "Doing It Their Way: Organizational Challenges for Voluntary Associations." *Nonprofit and Voluntary Sector Quarterly*. 27:144–158.

Harrison, Bennnett. 1994. *Lean and Mean: The Changing Landscape of Corporate Power in the Age of Flexibility*. New York: Basic Books.

Harrison, Bennnett and Barry Bluestone. 1988. *The Great U-Turn: Corporate Restructuring and the Polarizing of America*. New York: Basic Books.

Hasenfeld, Yeheskel. 1992a. "The Nature of Human Service Organizations." Pp. 3–23 in *Human Services as Complex Organizations*, Yeheskel Hasenfeld, ed. Newbury Park, Ca.: Sage.

Hasenfeld, Yeheskel. 1992b. "Theoretical approaches to Human Service Organizations." Pp. 24–44 in *Human Services as Complex Organizations*, Yeheskel Hasenfeld, ed. Newbury park, Ca.: Sage.

Heckscher, Charles and Anne Donellon, eds. 1994. *The Post-Bureaucratic Organization: New Perspectives on Organizational Change*. Thousand Oaks, Ca.: Sage.

"Henry Blodget to Leave Merrill Lynch." 2001. *New York Times*. November 15 (Part 12).

Hickson, David J., Graham Astley, Richard J. Butler, and David C. Wilson. (1983). *Research in Organizational Behavior*, Volume 3. New York: JAI Press/Elsevier Science.

Hirschhorn, Larry. 1984. *Beyond Mechanization*. Cambridge, Ma.: MIT Press.

Jacoby, Sanford M. 1997. *Modern Manors: Welfare Capitalism Since the New Deal*. Princeton: Princeton University Press.

Jenkins, J. Craig. 1983. "Resource Mobilization Theory and the Study of Social Movements." *Annual Review of Sociology*. 9:527–553.

Kanter, Rosabeth Moss. 1977. *Men and Women of the Corporation*. New York: Basic Books.

Kanter, Rosabeth Moss. 1991. "The Future of Bureaucracy and Hierarchy in Organizational Theory: A Report from the Field." Pp. 63–87 in *Social Theory For a Changing Society*, Pierre Bourdieu and James S. Coleman, eds. Boulder, Co.: Westview Press.

Kanter, Rosabeth Moss and Derick Brinkerhoff. 1981. "Organizational Performance: Recent Developments in Measurement." *Annual Review of Sociology*. 7:321–349.

Kanter, Rosabeth Moss and Barry A. Stein. 1979. *Life in Organizations: Workplaces as People Experience Them*. New York: Basic Books.

Kelly, Erin and Frank Dobbin. 1998. "How Affirmative Action Became Diversity Management: Employer Response to Antidiscrimination Law, 1961 to 1996." *American Behavioral Scientist*. 41:960–984.

Kleidman, Robert. 1994. "Volunteer Activism and Professionalism in Social Movement Organizations." *Social Problems*. 41:257–276.

Kochan, Thomas A., Harry C. Katz, and Robert B. McKersie. 1989. *The Transformation of American Industrial Relations*. New York: Basic Books.

Kunda, Gideon and John Van Maanen. 1999. "Changing Scripts at Work: Managers and Professionals." *Annals of the American Academy of Political and Social Science*. January:64–80.

Lawrence, Paul and Jay Lorsch. 1967. *Organization and Environment: Managing Differentiation and Integration*. Boston: Graduate School of Business Administration, Harvard University.

Leidner, Robin. 2001. "*Manufacturing Consent* Reexamined." *Contemporary Sociology*. 30:439–442.

Lindblom, Charles E. 1959. "The Science of Muddling Through." *Public Administration Review*. 19:79–88.

Lukes, Steven. 1974. *Power: A Radical View*. London: Macmillan.

Malone, Thomas W. and John F. Rockart. 1991. "Computers, Networks, and the Corporation." *Scientific American*. September:128–135.

March, James G. and Herbert A. Simon. 1958. *Organizations*. New York: Wiley.

March, James G. and Johan P. Olsen. 1981. "Organizational Choice under Ambiguity." Pp. 248–262 in *The Sociology of Organizations: Basic Studies*, Oscar Grusky and George A. Miller, eds. New York: Free Press.

March, James G. and Zur Shapira. 1992. "Behavioral Decision Theory and Organizational Decision Theory." Pp. 273–303 in *Decision Making: Alternatives to Rational Choice Models*, Mary Zey, ed. Newbury Park, Ca.: Sage.

Marsden, Peter V., Cynthia R. Cook, and Arne L. Kalleberg. 1996. "Bureaucratic Structures for Coordination and Control." Pp. 59–86 in *Organizations in America: Analyzing Their Structures and Human Resource Practices*, Arne L. Kalleberg, David Knoke, Peter V. Marsden, and Joe L. Spaeth, eds. Thousand Oaks, Ca.: Sage.

Martin, Joanne. 1992. *Cultures in Organizations: Three Perspectives*. New York: Oxford University Press.

Martin, Joanne. 2000. "Hidden Gendered Assumptions in Mainstream Organizational Theory and Research." *Journal of Management Inquiry*. 9(2):207-216.

Martin, Patricia Yancey. 1990 (June). "Rethinking Feminist Organizations." *Gender and Society*, 4(2):82-206.

Merton, Robert K. (1957/1985). *Social Theory and Social Structure*. New York: The Free Press.

Maslow, Abraham H. 1992 [1943]. "A Theory of Human Motivation." Pp. 159–169 in *Classics of Organization Theory*, Jay M. Shafritz and J. Steven Ott, eds. Pacific Grove, Ca: Brooks/Cole Publishing.

Meyer, John W. and Brian Rowan. 1977. "Institutionalized Organizations: Formal Structure as Myth and Ceremony." *American Journal of Sociology*. 83:340–363.

Mintzberg, Henry. (1981, January-February). "Organization Design: Fashion or Fit." *Harvard Business Review*, 103-116.

Mintzberg, Henry. 1985. "The Manager's Job: Folklore and Fact." Pp. 417–440 in *Organization Theory*, Derek S. Pugh, ed. Middlesex: Penguin.

Mintzberg, Henry and Jim Waters. 1990. "Does Decision Get in the Way?" *Organization Studies*. 11:1–6.

Mizruchi, Mark S. 1996. "What Do Interlocks Do? An Analysis, Critique, and Assessment of Research on Interlocking Directorates." *Annual Review of Sociology*. 22–271–298.

Moe, Terry. 1990. "The Politics of Structural Choice: Toward a Theory of Public Bureaucracy." Pp. 116–153 in *Organization Theory*, Oliver E. Williamson, ed. New York: Oxford University Press.

Morgan, Gareth. 1997. *Images of Organization*. Thousand Oaks, CA: Sage.

Morrill, Calvin. 1995. *The Executive Way: Conflict Management in Corporations*. Chicago: University of Chicago Press.

Morris, Aldon. 1981. "Black Southern Student Sit-In Movement: An Analysis of Internal Organization." *American Sociological Review*. 46:744–767.

Mort, Jo-Ann and Gary Brenner. 2000. "Kibbutzim: Will They Survive the New Israel?" *Dissent*. Summer:64–70.

Nelson, Daniel. 1995. "Industrial Engineering and the Industrial Enterprise." Pp. 35–50 in *Coordination and Information: Historical Perspectives on the Organization of Enterprise*, Naomi R. Lamoreaux and Daniel M.G. Raff, eds. Chicago: University of Chicago Press.

Nozick, Robert. 1978. "Who Would Choose Socialism?" *Reason*. May:22–23.

Oliver, Christine. 1992. "The Antecedents of Deinstitutionalization." *Organization Studies*. 13:563–588.

Ouchi, William. 1980. "Markets, Bureaucracies, and Clans." *Administrative Science Quarterly*. 25:129–141.

Pennings, Johannes. 1973. "Measures of Organizational Structure: A Methodological Note." *American Journal of Sociology*. 79:686–704.

Perrow, Charles. 1986. *Complex Organizations: A Critical Essay*. New York: Random House.

Pfeffer, Jeffrey and Gerald R. Salancik. 1978. *The External Control of Organizations*. New York: Harper and Row.

Piore, Michael J. and Charles Sabel. 1984. *The Second Industrial Divide*. New York: Basic Books.

Piven, Frances Fox and Richard A. Cloward. 1971. *Regulating the Poor*. New York: Pantheon.

Piven, Frances Fox and Richard A. Cloward. 1977. *Poor People's Movements: Why They Succeed, How They Fail*. New York: Pantheon.

Powell, Walter W, Kenneth W. Koput, Laurel Smith-Doerr. 1996. "Interorganizational Collaboration and the Locus of Innovation: Networks of Learning in Biotechnology." *Administrative Science Quarterly*. 41:116–145.

Pugh, Derek S. and David J. Hickson. 1989. *Writers on Organizations*. Newbury Park, Ca: Sage.

Reskin, Barbara. 1993. "Sex Segregation in the Workplace." *Annual Review of Sociology*. 19:241–270.

Reskin, Barbara F., Debra B. McBrier, and Julie A. Kmec. 1999. "The Determinants and Consequences of Workplace Sex and Race Composition." *Annual Review of Sociology*. 25:335–361.

Rosner, Menachem. 2000. "A 'Third Way' to Save the Kibbutz?" *Dissent*. Fall:89–92.

Rothschild, Joyce and Terance D. Miethe. 1999. "Whistle-Blower Disclosures and Management Retaliation: The Battle to Control Information About Organization Corruption." *Work and Occupations*. 26:107–128.

Russel, Raymond. 1988. "Forms and Extent of Employee Participation in the Contemporary United States." *Work and Occupations*. 15:374–395.

Saxenian, Analee. 1994. *Regional Advantage: Culture and Competition in Silicon Valley and Route 128*. Cambridge, Ma.: Harvard University Press.

Schmitz, Christopher J. 1993. *The Growth of Big Business in the United States and Western Europe, 1850–1939*. London: Macmillan.

Scott, W. Richard. 1975. "Organizational Structure." *Annual Review of Sociology*. 1:1–20.

Scott, W. Richard. 1998. *Organizations: Rational, Natural, and Open Systems*. Upper Saddle River, N.J.: Prentice Hall.

Shaeffer, Ruth G. and Allen R. Janger. 1982. "Who Is Top Management?" New York: The Conference Board.

Shorter, Edward and Charles Tilly. 1974. *Strikes in France, 1830–1968*. New York: Cambridge University Press.

Skocpol, Theda. 1985. "Bringing the State Back In: Strategies of Analysis in Current Research." Pp. 3–37 in *Bringing the State Back In*, Peter B. Evans, Dietrich Rueschemeyer, Theda Skocpol, eds. New York: Cambridge University Press.

Sloan, Alfred P. 1963. *My Years With General Motors*. New York: Doubleday.

Smith, Leonard V. 1994. *Between Mutiny and Obedience: The Case of the French Fifth Infantry Division During World War I*. Princeton, N.J.: Princeton University Press.

Smith, Vicki. 1990. *Managing in the Corporate Interest: Control and Resistance in an American Bank*. Berkeley and Los Angeles: University of California Press.

Sproull, Lee and Sara Kiesler. 1991. "Computers, Networks, and Work." *Scientific American*. September:116–123.

Staggenborg, Suzanne. 1988. "The Consequences of Professionalization and Formalization in the Pro-Choice Movement." *American Sociological Review*. 53:585–606.

Starbuck, William. 1981. "A Trip to View the Elephants and Rattlesnakes in the Garden of Aston." Pp. 167–198 in *Perspectives in Organizational Design and Behavior*, Andrew H. van de Ven and William F. Joyce, eds. New York: Wiley.

Staw, Barry M. and Lisa D. Epstein. 2000. "What Bandwagons Bring: Effects of Popular Management Techniques on Corporate Performance, Reputation, and CEO Pay." *Administrative Science Quarterly*. 45:523–556.

Staw, Barry M. and Jerry Ross. 1989. "Understanding Behavior in Escalation Situations." *Science*. 246:216–220 (October).

Storper, Michael. (1997). *The Regional World: Territorial Development in a Global Economy*. New York: Guilford.

Tolbert, Pamela S. and Lynne G. Zucker 1983. "Institutional Sources of Change in the Formal Structure of Organizations: The Diffusion of Civil Service Reform, 1880–1935," *Administrative Science Quarterly*. 30:22–39.

United States, Department of Health, Education, and Welfare. 1973. *Work in America: Report of a Special Task Force to the Secretary of Health, Education, and Welfare*. Cambridge, Ma., MIT Press.

Useem, Michael. 1980. "Corporations and the Corporate Elite." *Annual Review of Sociology*. 6:41-77.

Useem, Michael. 1993. *Executive Defense: Shareholder Power and Corporate Reorganization*. Cambridge, Ma.: Harvard University Press.

Vandivier, Kermit. 1979. "Why Should My Conscience Bother Me?" Pp. 160–1175 in *Life in Organizations: Workplaces as People Experience Them*. Rosabeth Moss Kanter and Barry A. Stein, eds. New York: Basic Books.

Vaughan, Diane. 1999. "The Dark Side of Organizations: Mistake, Misconduct, and Disaster." *Annual Review of Sociology*. 25:271–305.

Vogel, David. 1989. *Fluctuating Fortunes: The Political Power of Business in America*. New York: Basic Books.

Warwick, Donald P. 1975. *A Theory of Public Bureaucracy: Politics, Personality, and Organization in the State Department*. Cambridge, Ma.: Harvard University Press.

Weber, Max. 1978 [1921]. *Economy and Society*, Guenther Roth and Claus Wittich eds. Berkeley: University of California Press.

Weisbrod, Burton A. 1998. "The Nonprofit Mission and Its Financing: Growing Links Between Nonprofits and the Rest of the Economy." Pp. 1–22 in *To Profit or Not To Profit: The Commercial Transformation of the Nonprofit Sector*, Burton A. Weisbrod, ed. Cambridge: Cambridge University Press.

Whyte, William Foote and Joseph R. Blasi. 1982. "Worker Ownership, Participation, and Control: Toward a Theoretical Model." *Policy Sciences*. 14:137–163.

Wilson, James Q. 1989. *Bureaucracy: What Government Agencies Do and Why They Do It*. New York: Basic Books.

Womack, James, Daniel Jones, and Daniel Roos. 1990. *The Machine That Changed the World*. New York: Rawson Associates.

Wren, Daniel A. 1987. *The Evolution of Management Thought*. New York: John Wiley.

Zuboff, Shoshana. 1988. *In the Age of the Smart Machine: The Future of Work and Power*. New York: Basic Books.

Zucker, Lynne G. 1983. "Organizations as Institutions." Pp. 1–47 in *Research in the Sociology of Organizations*, Samuel B. Bachrach, ed. Greenwich, Ct.: JAI Press.

Zweigenhaft, Richard L. and G. William Domhoff. 1998. *Diversity in the Power Elite: Have Women and Minorities Reached the Top?* New Haven: Yale University Press.

Index

ABOUT THE EDITOR

Michael J. Handel, PhD, is Assistant Professor of Sociology at the University of Wisconsin—Madison and a research associate at the Levy Economics Institute. He researches changes in organizational structure and functioning, such as the presumed trend toward post-bureaucratic forms and more participative work practices, and their effects on employee well-being. He also studies the effects of information technology on organizations and the nature of work, skills, and wages. He holds a master's degree in anthropology from the University of Pennsylvania and a doctorate in sociology from Harvard University.